The Musical Theater
of Stephen Schwartz

The Musical Theater
of Stephen Schwartz

From Godspell *to* Wicked *and Beyond*

Paul R. Laird

ROWMAN & LITTLEFIELD
Lanham • Boulder • New York • Toronto • Plymouth, UK

Published by Rowman & Littlefield
4501 Forbes Boulevard, Suite 200, Lanham, Maryland 20706
www.rowman.com

10 Thornbury Road, Plymouth PL6 7PP, United Kingdom

British Library Cataloguing in Publication Information Available

Library of Congress Cataloging-in-Publication Data

Laird, Paul R., author.
  The musical theater of Stephen Schwartz : from Godspell to Wicked and beyond /
Paul R. Laird.
    pages cm
  Includes bibliographical references and index.
  ISBN 978-0-8108-9191-3 (cloth : alk. paper) — ISBN 978-0-8108-9192-0 (ebook)
  1. Schwartz, Stephen—Criticism and interpretation. 2. Musicals—New York (State)—
New York—History and criticism. I. Title.
  ML410.S42L36 2014
  782.1'4092—dc23   2013046660

∞™ The paper used in this publication meets the minimum requirements of
American National Standard for Information Sciences—Permanence of Paper
for Printed Library Materials, ANSI/NISO Z39.48-1992. Printed in the
United States of America

Contents

~

Acknowledgments

Writing a book is like embarking on a long trip without an itinerary. You never know what will happen next as you proceed from point to point, and it is difficult to know when the journey might end. I conceived this project in 2006 and 2007, beginning in earnest during my sabbatical from the University of Kansas in spring semester 2008. The greatest challenge to completing this book came in 2009 when I was working on *Wicked* and discovered enough primary material for a separate book. The result was *"Wicked": A Musical Biography*, published by Scarecrow Press in 2011. That became a two-year process, and when I returned to this study there was still much to write.

Clearly my acknowledgments for this study must begin with the subject of the book. I met Stephen Schwartz at a conference in May 2004, and he has since been generous in granting live and telephone interviews, answering questions via e-mail, and previewing quotations derived from these encounters. Schwartz has been extremely productive in the last nine years. A habitual creator of new works and tireless reviser of songs and scores from the past, Schwartz had plenty to do besides assisting a musicologist with his research. I have been humbled and flattered by his help.

My thanks also go to Schwartz's assistant Michael Cole, who answered many queries and facilitated my contact with Schwartz. I appreciate greatly Cole's many acts of kindness, sometimes executed within minutes over e-mail. This book would simply not have been possible without the materials that Schwartz and Cole made available.

Among the first things that they sent me were e-mail addresses for people with whom Schwartz has worked. This led to interviews and contacting other potential subjects. For kindly answering my questions, mostly in telephone interviews, I thank Herbert Braha, William David Brohn, John Caird, Jeff Church, Nina Faso, Peggy Gordon, Gordon Greenberg, Kim Josephson, Leon Katz, Robin Lamont, Edgar Lansbury, Sonia Manzano, Stephen Nathan, Stephen Oremus, Hila Plitmann, Stephen Reinhardt, Andrew Rohrer, Valéry Ryvkin, Scott Schwartz, Joseph Stein, Jamie Stevens, Charles Strouse, Susan Tsu, and Ernie Zulia. A number of these people also read material derived from these interviews; space did not allow results from each of these interviews to appear. John Caird graciously opened his personal archive of materials concerning *Children of Eden* at his home in London for several days in July 2008. Jeff Church allowed me to observe the workshop and rehearsals for *Geppetto and Son* at the Coterie Theatre in Kansas City in 2006. Peggy Gordon put me in touch with those associated with the original versions of *Godspell*. Joseph Stein graciously lent me a number of scripts that helped clarify the history of *Rags*. Charity Wicks willingly made her doctoral dissertation on *Séance on a Wet Afternoon* available to me electronically. Elaine Gorzelski, president of Harmonie Park Press, allowed me to republish a revised version of an article that I wrote on Stephen Schwartz's work on Leonard Bernstein's *Mass*, a piece that first appeared in the Festschrift *On Bunker's Hill: Essays in Honor of J. Bunker Clark*.[1] I also thank Shari Wied of Hal Leonard Publishing Company, Arminda Trevino of Carlin America, John White of Boosey & Hawkes, Brian Mellblom of Alfred Music, and Charmaine Ferenczi of Schreck Rose Dapello & Adams LLP for their assistance in arranging copyright permissions for quoting lyrics. For these and other kindnesses that have helped make this study possible, I thank these generous people.

My research has been assisted by a number of members of library staffs and fellow scholars. I am grateful to the wonderful people at the New York Public Library for the Performing Arts at Lincoln Center for their timely and expert help on numerous visits, and also to those who have assisted me at the Museum of the City of New York Theater Archive, the British Library, and at the Victoria and Albert Museum Theater Archive at the Blythe House in London. My visit to the Blythe House and John Caird's personal archive was made possible by the University of Kansas General Research Fund. Staffs at the Opera Santa Barbara and Kansas City Repertory Theater answered queries and kindly supplied photographs. Carol de Giere, author of the first book on Stephen Schwartz's life and work, was always friendly and helpful and suggested worthwhile paths of inquiry. She serves as webmaster for www

.stephenschwartz.com, and in that capacity has also been very helpful. I have had the valuable opportunity to present fruits of my research at meetings of the Society for American Music, Sound, Stage, and Screen conferences sponsored by the journal *Studies in Musical Theatre*, and at the Association for Theater in Higher Education, receiving worthwhile feedback and counsel from various colleagues, including William A. Everett, John Graziano, John Koegel, James Leve, Thomas Riis, John Staniunas, and Jessica Sternfeld. I also thank William A. Everett for inviting me to present lectures on Schwartz for his classes on Broadway musicals at the University of Missouri at Kansas City, and John and Roberta Graziano for inviting me to stay at their home during some of my research trips to New York City. My thanks to Stu Lewis for making recordings available to me and providing useful insights. My colleagues at the University of Kansas—Roberta Freund Schwartz, Charles Freeman, Alicia Levin, and Ketty Wong, along with our musicology graduate students and students in my class on Broadway musicals—listened to presentations of some of this material and provided feedback. Many thanks to Melissa Cummins, Amelia Davidson, Jessica Freyermuth, Ashley Hirt, Caitlin Laird, Joy Laird, Christy Miller, and Elizabeth Sallinger for their assistance with the index. My profound apologies if I have left anyone off of this list.

Writing a book is a satisfying but lonely profession, and my family has been unfailingly understanding and helpful. My wife, Joy Laird, has been my delightful and loving companion for over thirty years, and I am forever grateful for her patient comprehension of the various large projects that I have published throughout our lives together. My daughter, Caitlin, now a voice major at the University of Kansas School of Music, also shows her enthusiasm and interest in my work. It is to these two wonderful presences in my life that I dedicate this book, along with my father, Robert K. Laird (1923–2007), who shared with me his love for musicals and his fine collection of LPs. As much as anyone, he set me on the path that led to writing books on Broadway. Thanks, Dad.

~

Introduction

Stephen Schwartz has been a leading composer and lyricist for the American musical theater for more than four decades. Carol de Giere made an important contribution to our understanding of his life and work with her biography published in 2008.[1] Writing for a wide audience, de Giere includes emphases on Schwartz's life, his role in each of his major projects, his collaborations, and what one might learn about the creative act from Schwartz's example. Although we cover some of the same ground, our books are different in intention. This is not a biography; my primary emphases are Schwartz's projects and his music. Biographical issues inevitably surface but are less important in my book than his work as a composer, lyricist, director, and theatrical creator. I have tried to build upon de Giere's *Defying Gravity* by adding to our understanding of the history of each project with fresh information gleaned from interviews and primary sources such as draft scripts, scores, and correspondence. My access to such sources has been uneven, but they were especially available in relation to *Pippin, Rags, Children of Eden, Séance on a Wet Afternoon, Mit eventyr (My Fairytale)*, and *My Antonia*. Access to a large number of primary documents made possible my book on *Wicked*,[2] and for this study of all of Schwartz's output similar detail would have been possible on *Children of Eden* and *Séance on a Wet Afternoon*. Such extensive consideration of these two shows would have gone beyond the possible scope of this study, but the reader will note that there is more detail on those works than any other. Another feature of my book is consideration of Schwartz's shows in the United Kingdom, made possible by research in the Victoria and Albert Museum Theatre Collection.

The other major goal of this book is analysis of Schwartz's work as a composer and lyricist. Carol de Giere describes some of his songs, dealing primarily with lyrics and general aspects of the music. One of my major interests is what musical traits in a theatrical song contribute to its effectiveness. A secondary emphasis is the many musical styles that Schwartz accesses in his music. My analyses were assisted by material gleaned from interviews with Schwartz. Instead of including musical examples, there are references to track numbers and time indices in commercial recordings of Schwartz's major shows, an effective illustration for all types of readers. Boosey & Hawkes has placed the orchestral score of *Séance on a Wet Afternoon* on its website. With no recording yet available of the opera, I have referred readers to passages in this score. What emerges from musical consideration of all of Schwartz's scores is a portrait of a composer with extensive knowledge of both popular and classical music who adeptly applies varied musical styles where each will help the audience to understand a character's motivation and current dramatic situation. Schwartz began his professional career writing in the styles of popular Motown hits and such singer/songwriters as Laura Nyro and James Taylor. As his career progressed, Schwartz incorporated new stylistic tendencies in his music, such as shifting and unusual meters (from the strong influence of Leonard Bernstein); more chromaticism and added tones in his harmonies; and bitonality. When called to write music that describes the supernatural or another abnormal situation, especially in *Wicked* and *Séance on a Wet Afternoon*, Schwartz favors augmented triads with added tones. He has also provided musico-dramatic unity to his later scores with repeated motives in the tradition of operatic composition, especially in *Children of Eden*, *Wicked*, and *Séance*. Coverage of Schwartz's lyrics appears in reference to most of his projects, especially for those where he has only provided words. Schwartz does not cultivate a strong style as a wordsmith—one, for example, does not encounter from him many of the virtuosic rhymes like those of Stephen Sondheim or Lorenz Hart—but his lyrics focus on emotional states and effective images, contributing to the popularity of his songs.

Chapters progress more or less in chronological order with the exception of grouping Schwartz's Hollywood work together in Chapter 10 and several of his less famous works in Chapter 14. Chapter 1 is a consideration of his musical training and years as a theater directing major at Carnegie Mellon University, where his role in creating original student musicals provided invaluable experience. The conception of *Godspell* and analysis of Schwartz's music for the show appears in Chapter 2, which benefited from interviews with actors and others who helped create the show. Schwartz's work with Bernstein on *Mass* in 1971 is the subject of Chapter 3, an association that influenced Schwartz's future compositions. Chapter 4 concerns *Pippin*, one of Schwartz's most popular scores, but also the show where he learned how difficult it could be to work with a Broadway legend like Bob Fosse. *The Magic Show*, another hit and built around Doug Henning's impressive illusions, is the topic of Chapter 5. The next chapter involves *The Baker's Wife*, the first show in Schwartz's career that he worked on for years with his collaborators. *Working*, considered in Chapter 7, was a project where Schwartz worked on the book, directed, wrote music, and invited other songwriters to contribute numbers. He only wrote lyrics for *Rags*, the subject of Chapter 8, another show that the creators labored on for years. Chapter 9 includes an account of Schwartz's long collaboration with John Caird on *Children of Eden*. Chapter 10 summarizes Schwartz's Hollywood work, primarily as a lyricist, but he wrote words and music for *The Prince of Egypt*. My research on *My Son Pinocchio: Geppetto's Musical Tale*, the subject of Chapter 11, included the opportunity to observe the show's development in a workshop at the Coterie Theatre in Kansas City. Chapter 12, on *Wicked*, is a brief summary of my book on that show. The years spent writing this book encompassed Schwartz's entire time of working on *Séance on a Wet Afternoon*, meaning that Chapter 13 traces the opera's conception from composition to performances in Santa Barbara and New York. The less famous pieces described in Chapter 14 complete the picture of Schwartz as he brought his abilities to works conceived far from Broadway and Hollywood. The epilogue is a brief look at his distinctive place in today's theatrical and musical culture.

~

Permissions

If It Wasn't For You
A Little Taste Of Heaven
Meadowlark
Merci, Madame
Proud Lady
Serenade
Where Is The Warmth?
from THE BAKER'S WIFE
Music and Lyrics by Stephen Schwartz
Copyright (c) 1977 (Renewed) and 1990 Grey Dog Music (ASCAP)
Publishing and allied rights Administered by Williamson Music, a Division
of Rodgers & Hammerstein: an Imagem Company
International Copyright Secured   All Rights Reserved
www.stephenschwartz.com
Reprinted by Permission of Hal Leonard Corporation

If I Have To Live Alone
from THE BAKER'S WIFE
Music and Lyrics by Stephen Schwartz
Copyright (c) 1976 Grey Dog Music
Copyright Renewed
Publishing and allied rights Administered by Williamson Music, a Division
of Rodgers & Hammerstein: an Imagem Company
International Copyright Secured   All Rights Reserved
www.stephenschwartz.com
Reprinted by Permission of Hal Leonard Corporation

Blame It On The Summer Night
Brand New World
Children Of The Wind
Greenhorns
Rags
Uptown
What's Wrong With That?
from RAGS
Lyric by Stephen Schwartz
Music by Charles Strouse Copyright (c) 1986, 1987, 1989 Charles Strouse
and Grey Dog Music (ASCAP)
Publication and allied rights owned by Charles Strouse Publishing and Grey
Dog Music (Administered by Williamson Music, a Division of Rodgers &
Hammerstein: an Imagem Company)

Childhood's End
Close To Home
The Expulsion
Father's Day
The Flood
The Gathering Storm
Generations
Grateful Children
The Hardest Part Of Love
The Hour Of Darkness
In Pursuit Of Excellence
In The Beginning
In Whatever Time We Have
Let There Be
Lost In The Wilderness
The Naming
Perfect
A Piece of Eight
Precious Children
A Ring Of Stones
Sailor Of The Skies
The Spark Of Creation
The Spark Of Creation Reprise 2
Stranger To The Rain
The Tree of Knowledge
The Wasteland
A World Without You
from CHILDREN OF EDEN
Music and Lyrics by Stephen Schwartz

All The Livelong Day
It's An Art
Neat To Be A Newsboy
Something To Point To
from WORKING
Music and Lyrics by Stephen Schwartz
Copyright (c) 1978 Grey Dog Music (ASCAP)
Publishing and allied rights Administered by Williamson Music, a Division
of Rodgers & Hammerstein: an Imagem Company
International Copyright Secured All Rights Reserved
www.stephenschwartz.com
Reprinted by Permission of Hal Leonard Corporation

Finale
The Wizard And I
from the Broadway Musical WICKED
Music and Lyrics by Stephen Schwartz
Copyright (c) 2003 Grey Dog Music
All Rights Reserved　Used by Permission
Reprinted by Permission of Hal Leonard Corporation

Alas For You
Learn Your Lessons Well
Light Of The World
Tower Of Babble
Turn Back, O Man
from The Musical GODSPELL
Words and Music by Stephen Schwartz
Copyright (c) 1971 by Range Road Music Inc., Quartet Music, Inc. and S &
J Legacy Productions LLC Copyright Renewed
International Copyright Secured　All Rights Reserved
Used by Permission
Reprinted by Permission of Hal Leonard Corporation

By My Side
from the Musical GODSPELL
Words and Music by Jay Hamburger and Peggy Gordon
Copyright (c) 1971 by Range Road Music Inc., Bug Music-Quartet Music
and S & J Legacy Productions LLC
Copyright Renewed

If I Never Knew You (Love Theme from POCAHONTAS)
Just Around The Riverbend
Listen With Your Heart
Mine, Mine, Mine
Colors Of The Wind
Savages (Part 1)
The Virginia Company
from Walt Disney's POCAHONTAS
Music by Alan Menken
Lyrics by Stephen Schwartz
(c) 1995 Wonderland Music Company, Inc. and Walt Disney Music Company

The Bells Of Notre Dame
The Court Of Miracles
Heaven's Light
Hellfire
Out There
from Walt Disney's THE HUNCHBACK OF NOTRE DAME
Music by Alan Menken
Lyrics by Stephen Schwartz
(c) 1996 Wonderland Music Company, Inc. and Walt Disney Music Company

When You Believe
from THE PRINCE OF EGYPT
Words and Music by Stephen Schwartz
Copyright (c) 1997 DWA Songs (ASCAP)

SIMPLE JOYS (from "Pippin")

Words and Music by STEPHEN SCHWARTZ
Copyright © 1972 (Renewed) STEPHEN SCHWARTZ
All Rights Administered by JOBETE MUSIC CO., INC. and EMI MILLS MUSIC, INC.
Print Rights on behalf of EMI MILLS MUSIC, INC. Administered Worldwide by ALFRED MUSIC

MAGIC TO DO (from "Pippin")

Music and Lyrics by STEPHEN SCHWARTZ
Copyright © 1972 (Renewed) STEPHEN SCHWARTZ
All Rights Administered by EMI BMPC CORP. (ASCAP) and JOBETE MUSIC CO., INC.
All Rights for JOBETE MUSIC CO., INC. Controlled and Administered by EMI APRIL MUSIC INC. (ASCAP)
Print Rights for EMI BMPC CORP. Controlled and Administered by AL-FRED MUSIC

WITH YOU (from "Pippin")

Music and Lyrics by STEPHEN SCHWARTZ
Copyright © 1972 (Renewed) STEPHEN SCHWARTZ
All Rights Administered by EMI BMPC CORP. (ASCAP) and JOBETE MUSIC CO., INC.
All Rights for JOBETE MUSIC CO., INC. Controlled and Administered by EMI APRIL MUSIC INC. (ASCAP)
Print Rights for EMI BMPC CORP. Controlled and Administered by AL-FRED MUSIC

SPREAD A LITTLE SUNSHINE (from "Pippin")

Music and Lyrics by STEPHEN SCHWARTZ
Copyright © 1972 (Renewed) STEPHEN SCHWARTZ
All Rights Administered by EMI BMPC CORP. (ASCAP) and JOBETE MUSIC CO., INC.

KIND OF WOMAN (from "Pippin")
Music and Lyrics by STEPHEN SCHWARTZ

EXTRAORDINARY (from "Pippin")
Music and Lyrics by STEPHEN SCHWARTZ

LOVE SONG (from "Pippin")
Music and Lyrics by STEPHEN SCHWARTZ

SWEET, SWEET, SWEET
Music and Lyrics by STEPHEN SCHWARTZ

◜◞

CHAPTER ONE

An Introduction
to Stephen Schwartz

His Output and Tenacity

A significant figure in the American musical theater for over four decades, Stephen Schwartz served as composer/lyricist for four highly successful shows in their initial runs: Godspell (1971), Pippin (1972), The Magic Show (1974), and Wicked (2003). Although careers of musical theater creators are often long, it is rare for a writer to have nearly three decades between hits. Those years were not empty in Schwartz's career, and they illustrate a fascinating aspect of his work. When a musical fails artistically or commercially, or falls short in both areas, Schwartz continues to work with his collaborators— sometimes for decades—striving until the show is in an acceptable form for licensed performances. For The Baker's Wife (1976) this process took twenty-nine years between the long, out-of-town tour that closed before reaching Broadway and a successful, finished version at the Paper Mill Playhouse in Milburn, New Jersey, in 2005. Working (1978), adapted by Schwartz and Nina Faso from Studs Terkel's book by the same name, had a short Broadway run, but revisions soon thereafter resulted in a successful version that has been performed often, and Schwartz has participated in updates of the show. Rags (1983), for which Schwartz wrote the lyrics, ran in New York for only four performances, and work continued at varying intensities with composer Charles Strouse and book writer Joseph Stein nearly until Stein's death in 2010, but they did not finish the show to their satisfaction. Schwartz's next musical, for which he wrote music and lyrics, was Children of Eden, a project

Stephen Schwartz. *Photo by Ralf Rühmeier*

that occupied more than a decade of work from the mid-1980s until its completion in 1997, again with a successful production at the Paper Mill, resulting in Schwartz's favorite show in his output and another popular property.

The core of Schwartz's work has been his most famous musicals, but he has been involved in a number of other significant projects. Soon after Schwartz worked on *Godspell*, Leonard Bernstein asked him to write the English lyrics for *Mass* (1971), for which Schwartz also helped develop a plot. Between stage and films he has worked on a number of properties intended first for families, most famously three animated films: *Pocahontas* (1995, lyrics), *The Hunchback of Notre Dame* (1996, lyrics), and *The Prince of Egypt* (1998, music and lyrics). *The Hunchback of Notre Dame* has appeared on stage in Germany as *Der Glöckner von Notre Dame* (1999). Other films with appeal for children have included music and lyrics for *Geppetto* (2000, originally for television but now in a stage version called *My Son Pinocchio: Geppetto's Musical Tale*) and *Enchanted* (2007, lyrics only). The stage musical *Captain Louie* (2005) is another work for youth.

Schwartz has approached new genres since the huge success of *Wicked*. His son Scott Schwartz, a theatrical director, wrote a play called *My Antonia* based on Willa Cather's famous novel. For this the composer wrote a score of incidental music, which premiered with the play in 2004. The following year Schwartz's score for the Danish musical *Mit eventyr* (*My Fairytale*) appeared, a project that has been translated into English and played in California in 2011. Finally, Schwartz accepted a commission to write an opera for Opera Santa Barbara in 2006, resulting in *Séance on a Wet Afternoon* (2009), based upon a British film noir by the same name. The Santa Barbara premiere was followed by a run at the New York City Opera in spring 2011.

Schwartz's work and reputation are international. His first professional work, *Godspell*, found considerable success in Europe, and other shows, such as *Pippin*, *The Baker's Wife*, and *Children of Eden*, had brief runs in London. His greatest international success has been *Wicked*, which has played in London since 2006 and in various cities in Germany, Japan, Australia, and in Helsinki.[1]

Most of Schwartz's best-known shows are still important. Songs from *Godspell* remain famous and the show is produced on a regular basis. Along with *Hair* and *Jesus Christ Superstar*, *Godspell* has become an icon of its generation. *Pippin* remains part of the repertory and songs such as "Magic to Do" and "Corner of the Sky" are easily recognized. The show's theme of youthful exploration and finding oneself is universal and helps keep the show fresh. A Broadway revival opened in April 2013. Although popular at the time, the success of *The Magic Show* was as much dependent upon the impressive illusions by star Doug Henning as it was upon the musical that surrounded it; the show has fallen out of the repertory. *Wicked* has tapped into an enormous well of fans because of its clever take on *The Wizard of Oz* and message about feminine companionship and "girl power," irresistible marketing hooks. The show boasts several numbers that have become standards, such as "Defying Gravity," "Popular," and "For Good," and the score would seem destined to become Schwartz's most popular. Now in his midsixties, Schwartz remains active managing old properties and pursuing new projects.

Schwartz, Critics, and the Tony Awards

As will be shown in surveys of critical opinion of Schwartz's shows, his works have usually not been a major hit with critics, either in New York or London. It is a complicated situation that defies easy explanation; indeed, it is difficult to summarize the varied reactions of fifteen or twenty critics to any single musical, and even flops often get a few positive reviews. Early in Schwartz's career he became disenchanted with critics and stopped reading them after a show opened, saving such perusal for the moment that he might be revising a work. At that point he reads all reviews at once to see if there are common themes that might benefit his knowledge of an audience's reaction.[2] A provocative aspect of Schwartz's career has been how many critics pan his most popular shows, highlighting what seems to be contrasting taste between the audience and some reviewers. He has hardly been alone in this phenomenon in the last four decades because Andrew Lloyd Webber, who wrote several hugely popular shows, has often been the general target of critical slings and arrows. Perhaps critics and the average member of an audience simply do not look for the same things? This phenomenon as it applies to *Wicked* is approached in detail in my last book,[3] but an important part is perhaps that audiences buy original cast recordings and the music becomes part of their playlist, reinforcing their positive feelings about the show. A critic sees the show once or twice and reviews it, meaning that the "glow" the score might bring to an audience member outside of the theater is not part of the critic's experience.

Another oft-noted aspect of Schwartz's career, until recently, had been his failure to win a Tony Award. With the 2013 revival of *Pippin* winning for Best Revival of a Musical this is no longer the case, but none of his other shows have ever won for Best Musical or Best Score. Before further consideration of Schwartz's shows and the Tony Awards, we should take note of his history with various awards.

Tony Award
    2013—Won Best Revival of a Musical for *Pippin*
Drama Desk Awards
    1971—Two citations for Most Promising Composer and Most Promising Lyricist for *Godspell*
    1978—Won Best Director for *Working*
    2004—Seven citations for *Wicked*, including for Best Musical, Best Lyrics, and Best Orchestration
    2013—Won Best Revival of a Musical for *Pippin*
Academy Awards
    1995—Best Score for *Pocahontas* (music by Alan Menken; lyrics by Schwartz) and Best Song for "Colors of the Wind" from *Pocahontas*
    1998—Best Song for "When You Believe" (music and lyrics by Schwartz) from *The Prince of Egypt*
Grammy Awards
    1971—Two as producer and composer/lyricist for the original cast recording of *Godspell*[4]
    1995—One for "Colors of the Wind" from *Pocahontas*, the best song specifically written for a film or television show (music by Alan Menken; lyrics by Schwartz)

2004—One for the original cast recording of *Wicked* (producer and
composer/lyricist)
Songwriters Hall of Fame (2009)
Schwartz won the twelfth Richard Rodgers Award for Excellence in Musi-
cal Theater (2009)
American Theatre Hall of Fame (2010)

Schwartz has been critical of the Tony Awards for their outsized influence,[5] an opinion that crystallized in 1978 when the producers of *Working*
rushed the show to Broadway in order to qualify for the Tonys that year. As
reported in Chapter 7, the show had opened in Chicago, and as director and
one of the adaptors of the book, Schwartz had labored there with the expec-
tation of several more weeks for fine-tuning at the Arena Stage in Washington DC. The producers cancelled that run, over Schwartz's objections. He
tried to finish the show in rehearsals and twelve previews in New York, but
it ran only twenty-four performances. It is easy to see Schwartz's longtime
criticism of the awards as sour grapes, but he did watch the industry's Tony
lust help ruin a show on Broadway that has since had a useful life.

Awards shows engage public interest and spawn debates about relative
merits of various nominees. Tony nominations and wins are major parts of
Broadway advertising, and they help a show run longer. Like any such award,
however, the honor depends on many variables. For example, the quality of
the competition in a given category each year varies significantly, such as in
1958, when for Best Musical the committee had the difficult choice between
The Music Man and *West Side Story*. Meredith Willson's valentine to his
home state of Iowa won by a single vote.[6] Given their widely contrasting
natures, comparing the shows was problematic. In 2004, Schwartz's *Wicked*
competed with *Avenue Q* in a number of categories, and the clever puppet
musical won Best Musical and Best Score. The shows have little in common
in terms of size, intention, or the type of story told. When one uses the Tony
Awards as a measure of Broadway success, subjectivity and serendipity must
be considered.

Schwartz's record of Tony nominations for Best Musical, Best Score, and
Best Book (for his adaptation of Studs Terkel's book into the script for *Working*) are as follows:

Best Musical, 1973: *Pippin* nominated; the winner was *A Little Night Music*
Best Score, 1973: *Pippin* nominated; the winner was *A Little Night Music*
Best Score, 1977: *Godspell* nominated; the winner was *Annie*

Best Book, 1978: *Working* nominated; the winner was *On the Twentieth Century*

Best Score, 1978: *Working* nominated; the winner was *On the Twentieth Century*

Best Musical, 1987: *Rags* nominated; the winner was *Les Misérables*

Best Score, 1987: *Rags* nominated; the winner was *Les Misérables*

Best Musical, 2004: *Wicked* nominated; the winner was *Avenue Q*

Best Score, 2004: *Wicked* nominated; the winner was *Avenue Q*

In the 1973 Tony Awards, *Pippin* and *A Little Night Music* basically split the awards for musicals. *A Little Night Music*, following closely on the heels of the admired Stephen Sondheim/Hal Prince shows *Company* and *Follies*, won Best Musical and Best Score. Much of the acclaim for *Pippin* was for Bob Fosse's direction and the production, along with star Ben Vereen. Schwartz was working on his second show, probably never a serious threat to Sondheim for Best Score. *Godspell* was nominated for Best Score in 1977 because the show had moved to a Broadway theater for the end of its initial New York run, and Schwartz's songs had been popular for several years. *Annie* was the Tony juggernaut that year, winning seven, and *Godspell* was only nominated for Best Score. Competition for *Working* in 1978 for Best Score and Best Book was steep, including the collaboration of Cy Coleman, Betty Comden, and Adolph Green in *On the Twentieth Century*, which had a healthy run of 449 performances, unlike *Working*'s brief Broadway appearance. *Rags* received nominations in 1987, but it was puny competition for *Les Misérables*, which won eight Tonys. *Wicked* and *Avenue Q* each won three Tonys in 2004, with Schwartz's show winning Best Leading Actress, Best Set Design, and Best Costume Design and *Avenue Q* winning for Best Musical, Best Score, and Best Book. Consideration of success at the Tony Awards must be part of a balanced view of any noted figure.

The Development of a Broadway Composer/Lyricist

Stephen Schwartz wrote the score to *Godspell* just after he turned twenty-three, and by the time he was twenty-six he had *Godspell* running off-Broadway and *Pippin* and *The Magic Show* in the midst of long Broadway runs. It was a spectacular start to his career, one that he prepared for from a young age. Detailed consideration of Schwartz's work in this study will begin with his activities as a student at Carnegie Mellon University between 1964 and 1968. His childhood and early education have been covered well by Carol de Giere; material germane to his development in musical and theatrical endeavors will be summarized here.

Born in New York City on 6 March 1948, Schwartz and his family then lived in Paris, France, where his father attended graduate school from 1949 to 1951. They returned to New York City, and in 1954 bought a house in Roslyn Heights, east of Queens on Long Island. His father worked for the U.S. Navy and later independently in the manufacture of electric signs, and his mother taught preschool. Neither parent was a musician, but Schwartz's mother liked to sing around the house and play recordings. As de Giere reports, Schwartz showed early interest in a recording of Mussorgsky's *Boris Godunov* that he heard while still in France, foreshadowing his later interest in opera. He wrote songs from an early age and put on little musicals with the help of his younger sister Marge. His Broadway ambition was inspired by a neighbor, George Kleinsinger, who composed the score to *Shinbone Alley* (1957), a show about Don Marquis's characters Archy and Mehitabel that ran for forty-nine performances. Schwartz's parents encouraged Stephen's musical and theatrical pursuits, taking him to see a number of Broadway shows and purchasing him original cast albums.

Schwartz's musical development came in years of piano lessons, capped by four years of piano, theory, and composition study at the Juilliard School of Music Preparatory Division between 1960 and 1964.[7] Composers that Schwartz remembers playing on piano included J. S. Bach, Beethoven, Chopin (whom he reports he did not have an "affinity for"), Rachmaninov ("which I loved"), Bartók ("which I liked very much"), Kabalevsky, Prokofiev, Debussy (whose music Schwartz played "a lot"), Schumann (to whom "he never really warmed"), Mendelssohn ("some of which I like a lot"), and a bit of Liszt. Schwartz remembers Romantic music was never his favorite, an opinion that sparked laughter when he expressed it to his pre-Juilliard piano teacher, who told him: "Because you're the most Romantic student in style I've ever had. You manage to make Bach inventions sound romantic!" As will be shown in later chapters, the music that Schwartz learned through a number of these composers influenced his compositions.

For Schwartz's composition lessons at Juilliard, he remembers writing a woodwind quintet, and part of his preparation was detailed study of Paul Hindemith's *Kleine Kammermusik*, Op. 24, No. 2. Schwartz primarily observed how Hindemith wrote for the instruments. Such assignments constituted the largest part of Schwartz's organized music education beyond piano playing. He has made use of these early studies throughout his career. A musician with an excellent ear and keyboard skills and the ability to discern what makes most any style tick, Schwartz learned popular music by listening to recordings and experimenting at the piano, forging his personal style by combining this with his knowledge of classical music. Given Schwartz's status as one of the early Broadway composers to embrace fully the musical styles fashionable among the younger generation, his personal encounter with popular musical styles of the 1960s was a significant part of his music education.

Carol de Giere accounts for Schwartz's growth in literary areas, making a case for where he developed his love of language and ability to write lyrics.[8] His parents are both articulate, and their son enjoyed difficult puzzles. Schwartz read voraciously, showing a love for mysteries by Agatha Christie, and films have been an interest throughout his life. As a teen Schwartz was especially partial to the work of Ingmar Bergman. He was active in theatrical productions at Mineola High School as an actor and musician, working on his first original musical there. Schwartz started kindergarten at four and skipped a year of primary school, making him two years younger than others in his class. Between his age, somewhat short stature, intelligence, and outspoken nature, Schwartz faced alienation and bullying in high school, but had friends among like-minded students.[9]

Only fifteen years old when applying for college, Schwartz received rejection letters after applying to Harvard, Yale, and Oberlin. His father met Broadway lighting designer Jo Mielziner while working for the 1964 World's Fair and spoke of his son's frustration with finding postsecondary education in drama. Mielziner suggested Carnegie Institute of Technology (soon to be called Carnegie Mellon University), which had a well-established program in theater. They accepted Schwartz as a playwriting major; he later switched to directing.[10]

The Pittsburgh Years

Schwartz's work at Carnegie Mellon allowed him to experience every aspect of the theater. A hint of his multifarious activities appears in program books from the department, which produced six main stage productions each year and twenty-one one-act plays. Main stage productions tended to be cast with juniors and seniors, and one-act plays were student projects, such as senior and master's level directing projects. The following is a selected profile of what Schwartz took part in at Carnegie Mellon.[11]

During his first year, he wrote songs for a version of *As You Like It*, directed by Lawrence Carra, and appeared on stage playing the mandolin.[12]

As a sophomore, Schwartz took part in three main stage productions in various capacities and acted in four one-act shows. For *Hotel Paradiso* by Georges Feydeau and Maurice Desvallières (21–30 October 1965), directed by Lewis Palter, he was in charge of sound. On 13 December, he played Dubois in Molière's *The Misanthrope*, a master's project directed by Jean-Bernard Bucky. On 5 January 1966 he was the Vice President in *The Apollo of Bellac* by Jean Giraudoux, directed by Franklin Lindsay. For the main stage production of *The House of Bernarda Alba* by Federico García Lorca (7–15 January 1966), directed by John Ulmer, Schwartz wrote music under the pseudonym he used his first three years of college: Lawrence Stephens. He served on property crew for Shakespeare's *Richard III* (1–12 March), directed by Lewis Palter. Schwartz also acted in two student-directed plays, playing Galy Gay in Brecht's *The Elephant Calf* (9 March), directed by David Greene, and appeared as an actor (there are no named roles) in Michel de Ghelderode's *Christopher Columbus* (16 May), directed by Charles Newman.

Schwartz's principal activity for the department during his junior year was to write music for the main stage production of Richard B. Sheridan's *The Rivals* (20–29 October 1966), directed by Word Baker. He appeared in the pit as a musician with a wig and in eighteenth-century garb, playing his music. Schwartz fondly remembers this production and has reused music written for it in later scores.[13]

During his senior year, in December 1967 and January 1968, Schwartz served as stage manager for Elmer Rice's *The Adding Machine*, directed by Lawrence Carra. On 11 March 1968, he directed his senior project in the Studio Theater: *The Diary of Adam and Eve* by Jerry Bock and Sheldon Harnick. This was the first act of *The Apple Tree*, which had played on Broadway in 1966 and 1967. The choice shows Schwartz's interest in contemporary Broadway shows, and it is interesting to note, in light of his *Children of Eden*, his experience with this musicalization of the story of Adam and Eve.

Schwartz was not the only student writing music for plays within the department.[14] Ron Strauss, a Carnegie student with whom Schwartz collaborated on the Scotch 'n' Soda production of *Pippin, Pippin* (see later discussion), was music director for at least one main stage production and wrote a score for Ibsen's *The Doll's House*. Other student composers who wrote music for departmental productions included David Spangler (another Scotch 'n' Soda creator) and Peter Finch.

Schwartz states that the Scotch 'n' Soda productions at Carnegie Mellon constituted some of the highlights of his college days. For four years he worked on original musicals, and for each he wrote at least part of the score. The Scotch 'n' Soda Club formed in 1938, succeeding other student dramatic organizations. According to sources at the university archive, the group's yearly shows were especially popular in the 1950s and 1960s, and the music written for them gradually became more like contemporary American popular music. Other former members of the club include such figures as Frank Gorshin, Barbara Feldon, and Gerald Adler.[15] Performances took place on a collapsible stage in the ballroom at Skibo, the old student union, and vanity long-play records of music were pressed. These discs are available at the Carnegie Mellon library. Carol de Giere has covered a number of details of the Scotch 'n' Soda shows in her biography; comment here will mostly be confined to the music.[16] In an interview Schwartz offered previously unavailable information on the shows, especially about jointly written scores.

The Scotch 'n' Soda shows took place late each spring semester, but writers were chosen the previous year. Iris Rainer Dart (later author of the novel *Beaches*) had won the previous year's competition with *Whatserface* and had worked on songs with Michelle Brourman, who became a friend of Schwartz's and later served as dance arranger for *Working* (1978).[17] In fall 1964 the songs for *Whatserface* needed work, and Schwartz became involved. The plot involved a cleaning woman at an advertising firm who became a spokesperson, and the show ran from 1 May to 6 May 1965.[18] Working as Lawrence Stephens, Schwartz was listed as a writer and played piano in the orchestra. The 1965 yearbook praised "Larry S.'s exceptional musical score,"[19] and the review in the *Tartan*, the student newspaper, stated, "The music is really superb, the chorus numbers amazingly good if not technically perfect."[20] The recording reveals music that might have been composed by Jerry Bock or Jule Styne, a score by young songwriters who knew contemporary Broadway.[21] Schwartz stated about the score that "you can so hear Jule Styne, how much it was influenced by *Funny Girl* and *Gypsy* and their structures," and he also spoke of his love for songs by Jerry Bock.[22] Schwartz remembers writing the music for the following songs: "Ding! Dong!" "As a Failure I'm a Great Success," "Dreams," "They All Come Around," "We're Rich," "Big Shot—Whatserface" (a self-attribution Schwartz is somewhat less certain about), "What Has She Got," and "Up to the Top."[23] He does not remember who wrote lyrics for which songs. For Schwartz, the songs "As a Failure I'm a Great Success," "They All Come Around," and "Up to the Top" are the strongest indications of Styne's influence.[24] The overture includes rumba rhythms and other lively effects, and after a trip through the show's principal tunes, it ends with a Gershwin-like moment in the piano, probably played by Schwartz. "Ding! Dong!" is a jaunty march, and "As a Failure I'm a Great Success" is a clever ballad.

Iris Rainer Dart and Schwartz wrote *Nouveau*, the next year's show, with Lawrence Stephens writing the music. Schwartz acknowledges that Iris Rainer Dart worked on the lyrics with him, but he could not say who wrote which lyrics.[25] He was assistant director of the production, played in the orchestra, and served as one of the music directors. The plot had to do with the West Coast art scene, ambitious artists, and a fickle public. The production created indelible memories, as may be seen in letters in the university archives from cast members written thirty years later as alumni prepared a retrospective of Scotch 'n' Soda shows.[26] Schwartz's music and lyrics for *Nouveau* are the work of a talented youth whose compositional and lyrical styles were still based on those of 1960s Broadway.[27] There were only a few signs of Schwartz's later popular sensibilities. The show opens with "Pace," a number like "Tradition" from *Fiddler on the Roof*, where the audience meets all of the major characters in descriptive solos amidst interesting choral writing. Major musical influences appear to be Jerry Herman and Leonard Bernstein. Other possible models fly by in subsequent numbers. "Ability" is like a Kander and Ebb soft-shoe, and "Pals" recalls Cole Porter. "There's a New Day" is in a fast four with isolated rumba rhythms as a crowd badgers a wealthy patron into backing a new artist. Like a few other songs in the score, this includes brief quotations of famous works, such as Beethoven's "Ode to Joy." "Where Do We Go from Here?" carries what might be Bernstein's influence with interesting chromatic turns at the ends of lines, and there are clever rhymes. One problem is high writing for female voices, which obscures the text. A funny song is "Noblesse Oblige," sung by the wealthy patron. Schwartz uses the chorus like Gilbert and Sullivan, repeating punch lines just sung by soloists. The score also includes a fugue called "The New Society," which the composer reused in 1974 in *The Magic Show* as "Goldfarb's Variations."

As Carol de Giere describes the genesis of *Pippin, Pippin*, the next year's Scotch 'n' Soda show, Schwartz discovered that music major Ron Strauss was working on a musical based loosely on the life of Charlemagne's son Pepin.[28] He convinced Strauss to let him help, and Lawrence Stephens became involved as an orchestrator, one of the writers, director, and choreographer. Strauss and Schwartz collaborated on the score. The musical numbers were as follows, including Schwartz's recollections as to what each man wrote. (Those left blank for an attribution are ones where Schwartz could not remember who wrote.)

Act 1
Overture
"To Be a King"

"Goodbye, Yesterday"—Strauss
"Run into Your Arms"—Strauss
"Father Said"
"Victorious"—Schwartz
"They Will Listen to You"
"I Don't Owe You a Thing"—Schwartz
"Begging Milady's Pardon"—Schwartz
"A Simple Dance"—Schwartz
"While You Were Away"
"Easy to Be Happy"—music by Strauss, lyrics by Schwartz
"Pippin, Pippin"—music by Strauss, collaborated with Schwartz on lyrics

Act 2
"The Next King"
"The Next King" (reprise)
"Come with Me"—music by Strauss, lyrics by Schwartz
"Somebody Loves You"—Schwartz
"Preparations"—Schwartz
"My Son"
"Kyrie"
"Soliloquy"—Schwartz
"Finale" (based on "Pippin, Pippin," as earlier)

The plot had to do with Pippin's attempt to overthrow Charles and prevent his half brother from succeeding their father, but his efforts separate him from the woman he loves and doom him to life in a monastery. According to the school newspaper, Schwartz believed that *Pippin, Pippin* was "more of a strict book show" with music added to advance the plot rather than "music to which a play has been added." The same article suggests that the music carried the "texture of the ninth century" and included contrast between "the cool formality of the court with the warm liveliness of the country."[29] The score does include a few numbers that sound rustic, such as "A Simple Dance" and "Come With Me."[30] Among the most effective tunes are "Victorious," with its driving eighth-note patterns and a sensibility that resembles Orff's *Carmina Burana*; "I Don't Owe You a Thing," which features a rumba rhythm and an accompaniment of moving eighth notes; "Begging Milady's Pardon," an argument between two female characters with clever rhymes and patter sections; "Pippin, Pippin," a good duet between the lead characters with effective counterpoint; "Somebody Loves You," which carries strong influence from Bernstein; and "Preparations," which develops into five-part counterpoint. Schwartz commented that the show's ethos was like James Goldman's play *The Lion in Winter*,[31] a far cry from what *Pippin* became on Broadway.

During his senior year, Schwartz made his Scotch 'n' Soda contribution an opera. With songwriter David Sheridan Spangler he wrote *Twice Upon a Time*, two one-acts. Schwartz, now working as "Steve Sandford," wrote *Voltaire and Witches*.[32] He commented on his inspiration in an interview: "I was reading Voltaire and I liked witches and so I just made something up that combined them. It was all very collegiate, about [the] Apollonian versus Dionysian, and you can see that someone was taking [a] drama course and philosophy."[33] The contrast between the two acts could not have been greater, because Spangler's show, *That Is the Question*, or *All's Well That Ends*, was a farce set in Shakespeare's England. Schwartz reported to a *Tartan* reporter that he had not planned to write an opera, but the show did not seem to require dialogue, and he was "hung-up on opera."[34] There are effective moments in the music to *Voltaire and Witches*, but the young composer again tended to write parts for sopranos that were so high that the text was obscured.[35] The "Incantation" is majestic, in duple meter with a modal melody, reminiscent of Prokofiev's *Romeo and Juliet*. "Death to Arouet" is primarily a recitative but very dramatic, and the "Trio" is conceived operatically. Overall, the score reminds one in turns of Puccini, Prokofiev, Bernstein, and Copland, along with eighteenth-century musical ideas.

Schwartz believed that his experience with *Pippin, Pippin* during his junior year carried the seeds of his future career. He tried to convince Ron Strauss to go to New York City to find a producer and adopt it for Broadway. Strauss was not interested, but Schwartz plowed ahead, finding work fairly quickly as an artist and repertory agent for RCA and landing as his agent Shirley Bernstein, sister of Leonard, a connection that provided Schwartz with the opportunity to write the English lyrics for Bernstein's *Mass* in 1971. Shirley Bernstein helped Schwartz meet producers with *Pippin*, bringing the young songwriter into contact with Edgar Lansbury and Joe Beruh, who passed on *Pippin* but later hired Schwartz to write a new score for a show called *Godspell*.

CHAPTER TWO

~

Godspell

Those of us of a certain age remember that Stephen Schwartz's catchy score to *Godspell* seemed to be everywhere in the 1970s. The show's origins, however, began with director John-Michael Tebelak, and many others played major roles in its development. Some of that story will be told here with major emphasis placed on the music.[1]

Origins in Pittsburgh

In 1967, the Carnegie Institute of Technology in Pittsburgh merged with the Mellon Institute to become Carnegie Mellon University. The Drama Department had been part of Carnegie Tech since 1914. *Godspell* began as the graduating project for John-Michael Tebelak (1949–1985), a master's student in directing from the Cleveland area. When conceiving his project in fall 1970, he was every inch a hippy. He attended an Easter service at Pittsburgh's St. Paul's Cathedral not long before he worked on *Godspell*, but he felt unwelcome and while exiting was stopped by a policeman and searched for drugs, an experience that inspired a script meant as "a statement against the organized Church—an indictment of it for keeping religion so serious and removed from people."[2] The script that Tebelak produced was mostly from the Gospel of St. Matthew, in the King James Version. Another major inspiration was telling the story with clowns, from the suggestion of Harvey Cox in his *The Feast of Fools*, who spoke of "Christ the Clown."[3] Tebelak was influenced by Peter Brooks's play *Marat/Sade* for its use of clown outfits

15

and the wire fence that surrounded the stage,[4] and perhaps by *Paul Sills' Story Theatre*, which opened at the Ambassador Theatre in New York City on 26 October 1970. The small cast took multiple roles as they told stories, myths, and legends with pop songs accompanied by a band.[5]

The cast and crew for *The Godspell* (its original name) at Carnegie Mellon were drawn from the student body: Andrew Rohrer (who played Jesus), Mary Mazziotti, Martha Jacobs, Robin Lamont, Robert Miller (later known as Bob Ari), Sonia Manzano (later María on *Sesame Street*), Stanley King, Randy Danson, James Stevens, and David Haskell (who played John the Baptist/Judas). Tebelak asked the cast to improvise much of the show, building an ensemble through theatrical exercises conceived by Jerzy Grotowski and others.[6] Original cast members remember a chaotic atmosphere in early rehearsals, somewhat caused by the director's poor communication skills. Tebelak's drug problem was not a secret, and it perhaps compromised his ability to work with the group. Even with the initial frustration, however, some cast members knew Tebelak from previous projects and could reassure their colleagues.

Few details exist on *The Godspell* in its initial manifestation. The cast remember some specifics, but their experience became confused if they were also in the La MaMa version of the show, and some went on to the Cherry Lane Theater premiere. A number remembered the fence behind them on the stage. It cut off all entrances, so actors went through the audience.

The Godspell was a huge success at Carnegie Mellon. It was performed as many as four to six times, and the audience grew from word of mouth.[7] It was a musical, unusual for Carnegie Mellon, where the department favored spoken dramas. The show's score was by Duane Bolick, a friend of Tebelak's from the Cleveland area. According to the program, the musicians were Bolick on keyboards and Cpt. Horton on organ, but a recording from the original production also includes drum set.[8] Several original cast members praised Bolick's music. Most of the texts were from the Episcopalian Hymnal, which Tebelak reportedly found in the attic at his family home in Cleveland.[9]

A recording exists from the live performance of 14 December 1970. It has been circulated among members of the original cast and others, and Peggy Gordon from the La MaMa and Cherry Lane versions made it available for this study. The selections include the following:

"Pre-Show Music"
"Announcement" (Jewel Walker)
"Pre-Show Music, continued"
"Prologue" (fragment of seven seconds)

"Prepare Ye the Way of the Lord" (David Haskell et al.)
"Save the People" (Andrew Rohrer)
"Day by Day"
"Bless the Lord"
"All Good Gifts"
"Sermon on the Mount" (Andrew Rohrer)
"Intermission Jam Session (part 1)"
"Intermission Jam Session (part 2)"
"Intermission Jam Session (part 2, cont.)"
"Turn Back, O Man" (Robin Lamont, Robert Miller)
"Instrumental"
"On the Willows"
"Instrumental"
"Oh God, I'm Busted" (Andrew Rohrer)
"Prepare Ye the Way—Reprise (Finale)"
"Exit Music"
"Post Show: Turn Back, O Man"
"Dialogue Excerpt: Hypocrites"

Duane Bolick was a rock and jazz pianist who provided a serviceable score with tunes that tended to be repetitious. The recording demonstrates that this was not a musically talented cast. The strongest singer was Robin Lamont, who performs the solo in "Turn Back, O Man." Andrew Rohrer, who played Jesus, sounds competent on a few of his solos.

Bolick and his band demonstrate a wide stylistic range, from soft rock to an edgier sound, with jazz, funk, and electronic sounds that resemble synthesized music by Morton Subotnik and other composers of the late 1960s. The latter appears in the "Pre-Show Music," where amplified piano combines with electric organ and drum set. Such sounds, along with soft rock on piano, pervade the remainder of the "Pre-Show Music." "Prepare Ye the Way of the Lord" is a rock march, sung by the ensemble, with David Haskell as John the Baptist preaching over it. "Save the People," in four, begins with a noodling piano accompaniment and moves to a stronger rock beat, the Hammond organ sounding like 1960s soul with wide vibrato. "Day by Day," like the Schwartz version, is repetitious, here with a catchy tune stated over a rock beat, accelerating toward the end during raucous celebration. "Bless the Lord" is in a funky four with effective instrumental fill-ins by piano and organ. "All Good Gifts" demonstrates Bolick's melodic sense, but it is also one of the more repetitious tunes. "Sermon on the Mount" is chanted by Rohrer over a sort of doo-wop vocal accompaniment with body percussion and bluesy harmonica. The "Intermission Jam Session," underscoring talking throughout, is in three sections that include piano jazz, funky material, soft rock, bluesy jamming, and a short section of almost classical organ before the second act starts. "Turn Back, O Man" is one of Bolick's strongest melodies, and Robin Lamont sings it effectively with her folksy alto. Much of Bolick's "Turn Back" is based on an ostinato of three chords. The instrumental selection that precedes "On the Willows" begins in a relaxed fashion, building to considerable energy at the end while alternating between minor tonic and a minor dominant chord. "On the Willows" is less successful, marked by poor ensemble singing, and the instrumental number that leads to the crucifixion is mostly arpeggios in the piano with a few sound effects from the organ. "Oh God, I'm Busted," based on call-and-response between Jesus and the rest of the cast (not unlike Schwartz's comparable tune when Jesus is on the cross), includes convincing instrumental rock sounds as Jesus approaches his death. "Prepare Ye the Way" follows immediately as a reprise, sounding over loud applause and with singing voices barely audible over the instruments. "Exit Music" is mostly jazz piano, some of it perhaps based on "Prepare Ye." The crowd apparently called Robin Lamont back to sing "Turn Back," which she did far from the microphone. The disc concludes with seven minutes of dialogue that sounds similar to what was done in the off-Broadway production. It is mostly Andrew Rohrer performing one of Jesus's major speeches that includes material that Schwartz later set in the song "Alas for You." Rohrer presents the monologue deliberately with reactions from the cast, apparently striking the stage.

The Transfer to La MaMa

The show's fortuitous introduction to the New York City theatrical community took place at the legendary La MaMa Experimental Theatre Club, founded by Ellen Stewart in 1961 as a venue for works by emerging artists. *Godspell* played there from 24 February to 6 March 1971.[10] Stewart learned about *Godspell* from Leon Katz and Rina Yerushalmi, a former student of Katz's who had done a production at La MaMa and went on to be a noted director in Israel.[11] Stewart told Tebelak that he could present the show at La MaMa that winter.

Tebelak attempted to take his cast of Carnegie Mellon students to New York City for several weeks. It proved difficult because drama faculty members disliked the prospect of losing them. With several actors dropping out, Tebelak scrambled to assemble his La MaMa cast and crew. Among the new actors he asked were Peggy Gordon (who had left Carnegie Mellon after her second year[12]) and recent graduates Gilmer McCormick, Herby Braha, and Stephen Nathan. Nathan had worked with Tebelak and was a good friend, and Tebelak asked him to play Jesus at La MaMa.[13]

Another friend that Tebelak brought into *Godspell* at this point played a major role in its continuing success. Nina Faso had graduated from Carnegie Mellon in 1970 and was working in theater in San Francisco.[14] She had learned about Tebelak's project from her brother Laurie Faso, a student at Carnegie and later an actor in the show in New York. Tebelak called Faso in San Francisco and asked her to come manage the stage, one of her specialties.

Faso remembers that there really was no technical staff at La MaMa, so she did everything with the cast and anyone else they could find. Peggy Gordon reports that the cast gathered in New York City on 18 January 1971.[15] They had the luxury of more than six weeks to rehearse and flesh out their improvisations, and what emerged guaranteed the show's future.

Tebelak retained Duane Bolick's score at La MaMa, but it was a different band. The director knew three young musicians, the Quinn brothers, from Cleveland, who now lived near New York. They formed a trio of two guitars, Richard and Doug, and a drummer, Marty. All three went on to musical careers. Peggy Gordon recalls that two songs were added at La MaMa: her "By My Side" and "The Raven and the Swan."[16] The former provided a strong musical moment in the second act before the crucifixion sequence. "The Raven and the Swan" was a ballad written and sung by Jeffrey Mylett.

Lansbury, Beruh, Duncan, Schwartz, and the Cherry Lane Theatre

A future *Godspell* production in New York City depended upon one or more producers coming forward. With several offers to choose from, Tebelak selected Edgar Lansbury and Joseph Beruh. Lansbury (Angela Lansbury's brother) was a designer who met Beruh when they worked on a show together at the Cherry Lane Theatre, and later they formed their production team with the assistance of Stuart Duncan, who put up the money for them to start an office at 1650 Broadway; later they bought out Duncan and his rights. Beruh was an alumnus of Carnegie Tech and knew theater faculty member Larry Carra, and Lansbury remembers that Carra helped lead them to *Godspell*.[17] Actor Charles Haid, another former Carnegie student who had worked with Lansbury and Beruh, also told them that they needed to see it. Lansbury and Beruh thought the time was ripe for a biblical story. As Lansbury states, "It had the potential of being a very moving experience. It told a wonderful story and the music was not really up to what we felt it should be, which is the reason we thought of Stephen Schwartz."[18] Tebelak stated in a 1973 interview that he had wanted a new score as well because the one they had "didn't have variety." He liked the idea that Schwartz should write the new score because he had known his work at Carnegie Mellon.[19]

Lansbury and Beruh had met Schwartz through his agent, Shirley Bernstein. Schwartz played the existing score to *Pippin* for them, and they were not interested in that show, but Lansbury recalls that "we were very impressed . . . he was such a terribly young fellow."[20] As de Giere has reported, Lansbury and Beruh asked Schwartz to come see *Godspell* on the last night that it played at La MaMa (also the songwriter's birthday), and he quickly agreed to write a new score.[21]

The move to Cherry Lane was difficult because it involved the new songs and replacing actors and the Quinn brothers. Schwartz insisted on recasting in favor of stronger singers; Jimmy Canada and Tina Holmes from the La MaMa troupe were replaced by Lamar Alford and Joanne Jonas. As de Giere reports, Schwartz agreed in early March to have the new score ready for a May opening at the Cherry Lane, meaning that he had about five weeks before they started rehearsals.[22] Schwartz now acknowledges that he would never try to write a score in such a short span of time.[23]

Schwartz did not wish to replace all of the songs from the La MaMa production. He liked "By My Side" by Peggy Gordon and Jay Hamburger, and told Tebelak, "You really don't want to change that song!" He thought it was possible that he could write something as good but saw no reason to bother.[24] Lansbury and Beruh agreed; Gordon remains surprised that such a young composer was willing to use her song. She still earns royalties from it.[25]

Lansbury recalls that Schwartz quickly became a major figure in the show's development for its Cherry Lane opening: "He just took charge of the whole thing. He has such a good theater sense and he worked with John-Michael on the book and straightening that out."[26] Schwartz also found a musical director who helped teach the cast the new songs and took part in musical staging. While he worked at RCA, Schwartz had met Stephen Reinhardt, a dancer who wanted to get into music. He brought some songs he had written to Schwartz, who decided to record demos. Nothing came of that, but Schwartz asked Reinhardt to work on *Pippin* with him, and they began to collaborate. Schwartz mothballed that project while he wrote the songs for *Godspell*, and the first that Reinhardt heard of that project was when Schwartz played the songs for him and asked him to lead the band and direct the show's music. Reinhardt had never done anything like it, but, as de Giere reports, Schwartz had confidence in him and Reinhardt accepted the opportunity.[27] One thing that drew them together was their similar styles of piano playing, a trait on which they agree.[28] This was significant because Reinhardt improvised the piano accompaniments from lead sheets; nothing more was written down until the show became a hit and other companies were being formed.

The memories of those involved in rehearsals before the Cherry Lane opening—while not always consistent—paint a picture of a fun, chaotic period, when the rougher La MaMa version was transformed into a more conventional musical with a commercial score, while trying to retain as much as possible of Tebelak's original vision. There is no question that the show changed in April and May. Lansbury observed the creative process and recalls, "As far as I was concerned, I liked everything that was happening. Stephen's influence upon the shaping of the show was quite crucial. John-Michael Tebelak who wasn't particularly well in some respects—you know, did contribute his concept. . . . It was great experience, seeing it all take shape."[29]

Schwartz reports that he worked smoothly with Tebelak. They had known each other at school, but Schwartz graduated in 1968 and did not know about *The Godspell* in December 1970. Schwartz states that Tebelak was clear from the first meeting as to what the songs would be, and reports that the director was "in some instances specific about the feeling that he wanted. For instance, when we talked about 'On the Willows,' he said he wanted the feeling to be 'oceanic,' to sort of wash over the audience, and that was influential, obviously, on the tone of the music."[30] Schwartz also consulted with Tebelak about new songs that he thought should be added, such as musicalizing the "Prologue" (not part of the original score) and what had been Jesus's monologue toward the Pharisees, which became "Alas for You." Schwartz also suggested the song "All for the Best," as a way of demonstrating the special relationship between Jesus and Judas and rendering more tragic the show's conclusion. Tebelak agreed. Schwartz reports,

> He was pretty much always in agreement. There were really no major collaborative disagreements that I can recall at all. When we got into the theater, because he had basically staged the show already, he was very open to my saying "This needs to be shorter" or "Can't this be cleaned up?" He sort of gave way to me on musical staging because that was something I had experience with and he really didn't.[31]

Schwartz notes that Tebelak seemed to become nervous about the show as opening night approached and stayed away from the theater for about a week, leaving Schwartz "to sort of polish and finish things up," but he asserts that he did not originate any "staging concepts . . . other than choreography," such as in "All Good Gifts" where he set up an idea modeled on the end of the film *The Seventh Seal.*

Schwartz and Reinhardt taught the new songs to the cast. Reinhardt remembers how they worked on the "Prologue," where cast members portray Socrates and other philosophers. Schwartz set to music their speeches from the La MaMa version. In a Cherry Lane rehearsal, Schwartz played and sang the various solos to the individual cast members. The tiny theater had no place for Reinhardt to work on a solo with the actor, so he took them outside on the sidewalk and helped them with the tune unaccompanied. When songs had harmonies, Reinhardt recalls a similar process, rehearsing the group.[32]

Schwartz appears to have coordinated the efforts at musical staging, but Reinhardt, with his background in dance, was also involved. The entire cast made suggestions about the dancing, meaning that it turned into things they could do well, since many of them had little dance training. The only real dancer in the cast was Joanne Jonas.

The Cherry Lane rehearsals and improvisations were led by Tebelak and Schwartz, but each member of the cast played an important role and Nathan recalls that the actors felt a sense of ownership about *Godspell.*[33] Nathan suggests that the proceedings were "a bit frightening" to the producers, who expected "a little more polish and . . . professionalism" than the types of antics that helped form the show. Nathan specifically recalls a dress rehearsal when Lansbury and Beruh said that Sonia Manzano, who played the sexy clown and sang "Turn Back, O Man," should not be covered from the neck to her feet, but the cast refused to change it and threw the producers out of the theater. Nathan says, "They didn't realize that there was something hilarious about a sexy clown that's not showing skin." Another time the producers wanted to see a run-through so they could give the cast notes, but the actors refused. Nathan thinks they were probably more cooperative at other times, but their "first instinct" was to possess the show as much as possible. As has been often reported, the cast received a cut of the show's gross. Lansbury states that the producers awarded the cut in recognition of the role that the cast played in creating the show in the context of a production that had a strong box office from the moment the show opened at the Cherry Lane on 17 May 1971. Members of the cast, however, remember that the show was not doing very good business at first and the cut was awarded so they could be paid lower salaries. It is a controversial part of the show's history. Many conflicting statements were made in interviews, but cast members received substantial sums for years after the show opened.

Lansbury offers useful perspective on the show's growth after it became well established at the Cherry Lane. He remembers "great support" from radio and television commentators, along with some religious leaders. *Godspell* outgrew the Cherry Lane by that fall, and in October the show moved to the Promenade on Broadway between Seventy-sixth and Seventy-seventh Streets.[34] (A detailed synopsis of the show as it existed at the Promenade in 1974 is available online.[35]) Lansbury and Beruh founded the Promenade, leasing space for ten years in the hotel located on the property. Lansbury designed the theater with 398 seats in the semi-round along with an architect, and Jules Fisher, a prominent Broadway lighting designer, helped with the lighting board. Their first show there, *Promenade* (1970), gave the theater its name.

As new companies of *Godspell* were launched, they rehearsed at the Promenade. Lansbury reports that, rather than forming only touring companies (a more usual procedure), they assembled sit-down companies for several American cities. A press release from the time that *Godspell* moved to Broadway in June 1976 effectively summarizes the extent of the show's reach. When *Godspell* left the Promenade, it was the third-longest-running off-Broadway show in history after *The Fantasticks* and *The Threepenny Opera*. There had been eight sit-down companies in North America: New York, Boston, Washington, Los Angeles, San Francisco, Chicago, Miami, and Toronto. *Godspell* was now the longest-running show in Boston's theatrical history, and the show later returned. There had been a two-year national tour by another company and "bus and truck" tours to smaller cities and universities for four years. Numerous companies played internationally, including in London, an English tour (managed by a young Cameron Mackintosh), Paris (directed by Nina Faso), a French tour, Hamburg, Copenhagen, Belgium, Amsterdam, Italy, Melbourne, Sydney, South Africa (where *Godspell* was the first integrated musical), Rio de Janeiro, and Buenos Aires.[36] The show's financial success was phenomenal: in an advertisement in the *Wall Street Journal* in September 1974, Lansbury and Beruh announced that *Godspell* had made $4,150,000 in profit (4,000 percent), meaning that an original $5,000 investment had paid back $195,972.[37]

Lansbury commented on the end of *Godspell's* initial life in New York. After running for a bit more than five years off-Broadway, they decided to take the show to a Broadway house, the Broadhurst, with a sort of all-star cast, including Lamar Alford, Robin Lamont, Elizabeth Lathram (an original understudy at the Cherry Lane), Laurie Faso, and Don Scardino (who had frequently played Jesus at the Promenade). The show ran at the Broadhurst until 13 September 1976 and finished its Broadway run at the Plymouth (to 9 January 1977) and Ambassador (to 4 September 1977).[38]

Reviews

Several members of the *Godspell* creative team and cast in interviews mentioned the show's reviews. They generally remember positive commentary, but some recalled Clive Barnes's negative impression in the *New York Times*, countered twelve days later in the same publication by Walter Kerr's favorable notice. Stuart Duncan, one of the show's producers, wrote about this event in a web column in 2004, recalling that Kerr's wife, Jean, saw the show with her children the same night that Barnes did. She disagreed with Barnes and prevailed upon her husband also to review the show. Duncan remembers that Jean Kerr phoned the producers and told them to wait for a more favorable opinion from the *Times*.[39]

Barnes's consideration of *Godspell* was unusual, beginning with his admission that he found "the whole premise rather nauseating." He declared "naive and platitudinous" the show's concept and notion of "Jesus's being a regular fellow," also believing the "eclectic" music to be "the best part of the entertainment."[40] Stephen Nathan was outraged by the review "because it was an admission of a narrow-minded perception that should have alerted him to send someone else to review the show."[41] He sent Barnes a letter stating his views, signing a neighbor's name to it. Soon thereafter Lansbury and Beruh told the cast that Barnes would reconsider *Godspell* on his WQXR radio show. Nathan recalls that Barnes read his letter and partially retracted his review, admitting that the show was joyful.

Walter Kerr's consideration of *Godspell* appeared on the front page of the *Times* arts section on Sunday, 30 May 1971. He provided a friendly, detailed description, explaining several significant moments. He noted that the creators incorporated a number of different effects and theatrical styles, all in an effort to renew perceptions of the biblical stories "that will make the too-familiar become active again, alive on its toes and happy to be up there." Kerr did feel that *Jesus Christ Superstar* was better, especially at portraying the serious aspects of the story.[42]

Many reviews appeared in print or were heard on radio or television the same day that Barnes's review appeared, the day after *Godspell*'s opening. Lee Silver of the *Daily News* described the show as "cheerfully irreverent, spirited, loving, sprinkled with wry humor and bolstered with a good selection of songs—rock, folk, country and pop," all worked "neatly" around Jesus's teachings.[43] Jeffrey Tallmer's review in the *Post* was a rave: "A thing of joy. Youthjoy. Which I'd believed I'd had enough of, in the theater. But last night . . . I found I was wrong."[44] Allan Wallach of *Newsday* admired the show's thrust and Schwartz's music, but thought the score of *Jesus Christ Superstar* was superior.[45] Emory Lewis of the *Record* called Tebelak's work "astonishingly inventive" and the score "magnificent."[46] William Raidy, reviewing *Godspell* for the *Long Island Press* and *Newark Star-Ledger*, said the show "is intelligent, imaginative and indeed a blessing!" with "some truly beautiful music."[47] Edward Sothern Hipp, writing for the *Newark Evening News*, also found "joy" in the story-telling and "jubilation" in the music.[48] Joseph H. Mazo of *Women's Wear Daily* disagreed with the majority, thinking the show charming but little else, and "in the theatre, charm is not enough."[49] In a review that appeared the next day, Lee Mishkin told the readership of the *Morningside Telegraph* that much of *Godspell* is "a little disconcerting" in its blend of religion and popular effects.[50]

Creators and cast members recalled that the immediate reaction on radio and television was positive, and their impressions were correct. John Schubeck of ABC-TV was rapturous: "I tell you not since 'Follies' has a musical affected me so. It is stupendous. Utterly captivating." Other raves or mostly positive reviews ("an exceptional piece of work") came from Richard J. Schulern (working for WCTC AM-FM, WCBB AM, and WGSM AM-FM), Mary Campbell (Associated Press), David Goldman (CBS Radio), Alvin Klein (WNYC), Leonard Probst (NBC-TV), Leonard Harris (CBS-TV), Peggy Stockton (WMCA), and Jack Gaver (United Press International). Martin Bookspan, airing a review for WPIX-TV on 17 May, was one of the few radio or television reviewers to pan the show: "a sophomoric attempt 'to envelope its audience with a message of joy, communication and renewal,' to quote a production note."[51]

Over the course of the next few weeks local journals and national publications included commentary on the show. Dirk Brukenfeld of the *Village Voice* was devastating concerning the show's contrast between mood and material: "The performers become not zanies but stupids, and their simple clowning not only palls but makes a destructive contrast with the underlying reverence."[52] He also thought little of the music. In *Cue*, Marilyn Stasio loved "Tebelak's energetic and inventive direction" and "Schwartz's tuneful, buoyantly cheerful rock score and his marvelous arrangements," but she disagreed with the assumption that contemporary youth was "a viable parable" of Christ's life.[53] Edith Oliver in the *New Yorker* penned a rave: "a touching, resourceful celebration of theatre itself, and, especially when one considers the inexperience of the players, it is well executed by all concerned."[54] John Beaufort in the *Christian Science Monitor* also admired the show's "whole catalog of styles and influences" and said the "results are by turns comic, touching, rambunctious, quietly legiac [sic], pointedly moral, and withal innocently pious."[55] The unsigned review in *Time* took a historical perspective, stating that *Godspell* "suggests what the best of medieval morality plays must have been like."[56] The critic concentrated on the audience's reaction, mentioning those weeping and a Roman Catholic who thought it was the best mass he had attended in years. John Simon of *New York* also commented on the show's variety: "*Godspell* is part clown show, part minstrel show, part vaudeville, part *Hair*, and it works on all those levels and several more of its own."[57] The *Variety* review, by Sege, included the forecast of a "fair run," but the critic said the production was "not very professionally done" with the singing "lackluster, and the acting emphasizes a cloying disingenuous quality." Although the critic called the music was the "best part," he felt it "isn't very good."[58]

The show's transfer to Broadway in June 1976 spawned another set of reviews, and some critics took the long view after five years of *Godspell*. Martin Gottfried, writing for the *New York Post* on 23 June 1976, said that he never had liked the show, admitting that he left at intermission at La MaMa in 1971. He concluded, "The show has no thrust, no continuity, no musical sense." He regretted that the musical staging did not involve the songs, but appeared instead in "the corps movements that were worn even when this show was new."[59] Richard Eder of the *Times* was another critic who noted the show's balance between zaniness and seriousness, finding the first act "still fresh," but the betrayal and crucifixion "doesn't work as well." He thought the reason is simple: "The music thins out and the players must do their best with a dramatically unprepared gloominess."[60] *Variety* sent Hobe (Hobe Morrison) to the Broadway premiere; he also noted the show's varied tone. The critic thought the first six or so musical numbers "are on a primary school level of clowning," but later Tebelak and Schwartz "succumbed to the drama of the story . . . and particularly the last four or five numbers command attention."[61] Alan Rich, writing in *New York*, felt that *Godspell* had made the transfer still worthwhile: "It is no mean tribute that it has come to Broadway with all its good things intact." Five years had been kind to the show, and Rich found it "a . . . rather illustrious, cultural artifact."[62]

It is hardly surprising that critics tended to mention the show's variety of moods. The majority of the parables appear in the first act, and no matter how serious the story, most are treated with a degree of hilarity or silliness. Even decades later this remains a potentially difficult mixture. The comic antics of the first act precede the solemnity of betrayal and crucifixion. Schwartz has suggested that the special relationship between Jesus and Judas as seen in "All for the Best" is designed to make the betrayal all the more horrifying, but it is difficult to prepare the audience for the tonal change in the second act.[63] One could argue that this is a central part of the Christian message: Jesus's death was unwarranted except as a way of taking on the world's sins. The creators of Godspell avoided such a religious and theological perspective, but some might read that into the show.[64]

The Godspell Film

Although many musicals do not appear as films until their original New York run is over, Edgar Lansbury quickly wanted to make a film of Godspell.[65] Very soon after getting productions launched in numerous cities, he spoke to a friend, television director David Greene. He asked Greene to come to London and see the show. Greene was attracted to the property. They began to try to sell the project, but found little interest among Hollywood studios. Lansbury recalls one poor offer from an independent concern. Their break came when the head of London's Columbia studio saw the show and wanted to make the film, allowing the film a major Hollywood release. Lansbury notes that the director hatched the idea that they would shoot sequences at iconic locations all over Manhattan. The result was a film that stayed true to the concept of the Cherry Lane show—with parables and music interspersed to capture the essence of Jesus's message, then leading to betrayal and crucifixion—but all of this played out in modern, empty New York City, as if these ten people were its sole residents. Lansbury still likes the concept but admits that the film was commercially unsuccessful: "I think the movie is terrific and very true to the original material, but it didn't do well. It was too strange for most people."[66] Of the songs in the original score, "We Beseech Thee" and "Learn Your Lessons Well" are not sung in the film, but sound instrumentally. Schwartz wrote "Beautiful City" for the film, a song that has become quite well known in the intervening years and that appeared in the 2011–2012 Broadway revival.

John-Michael Tebelak was a stage director, so it is hardly surprising that Lansbury brought in a director familiar with camera work. Lansbury suggests that Tebelak and Greene worked easily together, but others involved with Godspell say that Tebelak was uncomfortable. Carnegie Mellon drama professor Leon Katz reports that Tebelak was removed from the set for insisting on changes "because he wanted his own piece to be filmed."[67] Robin Lamont, in the film's cast, recalls that Tebelak knew little about the technical aspects of making a film, and Greene was less knowledgeable about the improvisation that helped form casts for the show, so she believes that Tebelak and Greene worked together, but she also thinks that Schwartz was more important in the *Godspell* world as a director than Tebelak was at that point.[68] Lansbury recalls that Schwartz was actively involved with the film as well.[69] (The composer appears in a cameo role as a customer being served coffee in the prologue.) Joanne Jonas, also in the cast, stated, "John-Michael had a bit of a challenge with shifting from an abstract location to a real one and dealing with some of David Greene's choices. That's why it was so important to make it look like we took over the city for the time Jesus was working with us, so it kept the abstract in focus."[70] Tebelak, in an uncredited role, served as the voice of the Pharisee monster, certainly one of the more unusual scenes in the film.[71]

A number of those involved in the Cherry Lane version of *Godspell* worked on the film. David Haskell reprised his role as John the Baptist/Judas, and the cast also included Gilmer McCormick and Jeffrey Mylett, in addition to those named earlier (Jonas and Lamont). Lynne Thigpen, who started her career in a *Godspell* production before later appearing in Schwartz's *The Magic Show* and *Working*, also appeared. Among the keyboard players on the soundtrack were Stephen Schwartz, Stephen Reinhardt (also associate musical supervisor), and Paul Shaffer from the Toronto production. Three members from the band at the Cherry Lane—Jesse Cutter, Richard LaBonte, and Ricky Shutter—joined them. Nina Faso served as assistant to the producer for the film.

The film of *Godspell* was released on 21 March 1973 with the premiere at Philharmonic Hall, one of the New York sites in the movie. A short item in the *New York Times* from 1 April effectively summarized critical reaction: seven favorable reviews, four mixed, and seven negative. Vincent Canby of the *New York Times* provided a mixed review, noting that the film "reduces the story of Jesus to conform to a kind of flower-child paranoia" that he believes to be passé.[72] He disliked the sweetness, but he found that balanced by the movie's "sophisticated show-biz manner." Canby was especially taken with Victor Garber's portrayal of Jesus as an "engaging minstrel man," and he described the production number of "All for the Best," partly on the Bulova sign in Times Square, as one of the best production numbers he has seen in a long time. He also believed *Godspell* to be a fine portrait of New York City in the summertime. Sege, a *Variety* reviewer who covered the stage show two years before, also wrote a mixed review. He believed that the film retained what was good about the stage version—Schwartz's score and "an infectious joie de vivre"—but also carried the original's "flaws," specifically "a relentlessly simplistic approach to the New Testament interpreted in overbearing children's [sic] theatre style mugging."[73] He found the musical portions "often stunning" and praised the cast as well. Such mixed appraisals seem appropriate for a film that has never been considered one of the great film musicals, but still has its adherents and those who appreciate that the movie is a valentine to New York City.

Music

Schwartz had to write the new score to *Godspell* so quickly that he sought models for most of the songs among repertory that he liked. Schwartz has always been disarmingly frank about his influences; as he has stated,

> Because I had to write the score so quickly, I basically took models of songs I liked and jumped from them. And I can tell you what the influences were. It may be giving away my secrets, but I don't think anything is so close that when people know them they say, "Oh, that's just plagiarized."[74]

His influences and borrowings created songs that bear resemblance to the model in one or two specific areas, but the songs are far from copies of other works. Schwartz was young when he worked on *Godspell*, but he had already been composing for several years. During college he moved from writing in the Broadway idiom of Jule Styne and Jerry Bock to including pop ideas in his music, and then two years in the A&R (artists and repertoire) department at RCA brought him in contact with young pop writers. Schwartz had developed a wide stylistic palette, and with his fine musical ear he knew what musical devices helped to evoke each style. It is such preparation that allowed Schwartz to write memorable songs for *Godspell* relatively quickly, a score that he labels a "pop-pastiche" and what must be considered, along with *Hair* (1968) and *Jesus Christ Superstar* (1971), one of the first early theater scores to embrace rock and other popular musical styles. Tebelak gave him the hymn texts on mimeographed sheets.[75] At the time Schwartz never looked at the Episcopalian Hymnal, but believes that he did perhaps five years after writing the score. We now proceed through the show's score and explore Schwartz's memories and comments on each song, as well as include additional analytical commentary.

Schwartz had little to say about the "Prologue," certainly the score's least-known segment because it does not appear on the original cast album, but a different version appears on track 1 of the new original cast recording (NOCR).[76] (What is described here comes from a piano/vocal score supplied by Schwartz's office.[77]) In essence, the sequence is perhaps Schwartz's most elaborate counterpoint song, an interest that he developed from Irving

Berlin's score to *Call Me Madam*, as described here in reference to "All for the Best." In most such tunes, however, Schwartz combines only two ideas, and in the "Prologue" there are eight separate melodies (some together in duets) placed over the same harmonic progression,[78] all combined to produce the "Tower of Babble" that John the Baptist interrupts with his shofar. Schwartz uses bitonality in the first measure, with F-sharp major placed over E major, an effect that recurs twice in each variation. Socrates begins, singing a pop recitative line over wandering harmonies. The scene's four introductory measures intervene before Thomas Aquinas opens his variation with four measures of a sort of Gilbert and Sullivan patter song followed by a more recitative-like section marked "Romantically" over constant arpeggios. Martin Luther enters immediately in the third variation, singing in square quarter and eighth notes over a German march parody as the theologian speaks of conflicts between nobility and peasants. The introductory music returns before the variation marked "a la Mozart," featuring Leonardo da Vinci and Edward Gibbon. They sing a duet reminiscent of the Classic era, but with more chromaticism. Friedrich Nietzsche follows in the fifth variation where the harmonic rhythm has doubled in speed with an accompaniment somewhat like music of the late Classic or early Romantic eras. Nietzsche sings mostly in whole notes, asking, "What is noble nowadays?" In the next variation the harmonic rhythm returns to its previous rate as the odd couple Jean Paul Sartre and Buckminster Fuller sing in alternation. Sartre intones quarter notes to a march accompaniment while Fuller's music swings in bluesy triplets. The introduction music returns as Fuller speaks over the music, leading immediately to "Tower of Babble."

The next segment opens with the bitonal E against F-sharp, introducing a passage where all of the philosophers sing "Babel, babble" in a jazzy style with constant syncopation and many seventh chords. The repeated chord progression returns with each philosopher singing his own distinctive variation simultaneously. Not all sound at once throughout, and the accompaniment thins out to just punctuation chords as the counterpoint becomes more complicated. In the staging, this contrapuntal confusion is echoed by the philosophers becoming increasingly agitated, dumping rags and other refuse out of garbage sacks and throwing it at each other. Finally the introductory material with its distinct bitonality returns with all singing "Ah." John the Baptist disrupts these opening exercises with his shofar, and sings "Prepare Ye."

Schwartz states that one of his overriding influences at the time was Motown: "Much of what I did in those days in pop was influenced by Motown, because I had fallen in love with the writing of Holland-Dozier-Holland and the songs they wrote for the Supremes and other Motown groups." As will be shown, this influence combined with those from several other pop sources as Schwartz quickly wrote the songs for *Godspell*.

Schwartz does not believe that the song "Prepare Ye the Way of the Lord" had any especially strong influence. With only one line of text, he found himself "just trying to find a way to stretch the line so that it was more singable and memorable on the ear." The words and the song's function suggest a fanfare, but he deemed that treatment too obvious. By using an angular melody and constant rumba rhythm (3+3+2), he created the catchy song that became the show's "hook." Schwartz's timing is impeccable as he moves from the solo presentation to a choral arrangement accompanied by instruments (original cast recording [OCR], track 1, 0'53') making the most of the brief material that he composed. The choral writing is in four parts with a few passing tones; the cast repeats the final section until all have been baptized.

Schwartz's music for "Save the People" was based upon his experience in recording the title song for the play *Butterflies Are Free* (1969), his first Broadway work. Sunbury, his employer RCA's publishing division, asked for a demo recording of the song to stimulate cover versions. Schwartz produced it and asked guitarist Hughie McCracken to play the guitar track. What McCracken played was like the accompaniment that Schwartz wrote for "Save the People," but his song has a different harmonic progression and new melody. The tune is diatonic, in G major throughout, with frequent syncopation. The song ends with a strong choral version set off by instrumental interjections (OCR, track 2, 2'05"), resembling gospel music.

The show's major hit was "Day by Day," which sold well as a single with Robin Lamont as soloist. Schwartz's model for the song was "What the World Needs Now" (1965) by Burt Bacharach and Hal David. Schwartz reacted to the song's waltz meter and Bacharach's use of seventh chords, but Schwartz's uses more minor seventh chords.[79] "Day by Day" also includes chord movement from a minor dominant to major tonic, such as E minor 7 to A major and D minor 7 to G major (see mm. 11–14[80]), which he heard in a number of pop songs at the time, such as "Society's Child" by Janis Ian. The opening triple meter, marked "Easy waltz feel," includes a swinging triplet feel in the bass line. The tune is sixteen measures in length in four different phrases of equal length. Schwartz switches to quadruple meter later in "Day by Day" (OCR, track 3, 1'07"), which he believes gave it "more energy." The text that Schwartz set from the Episcopal Hymnal seemed "sincere" to him, and he heard a similar quality in the Bacharach/David song. Sincerity seemed especially important for "Day by Day" because it is the first song in the show where a cast member sings to Jesus, demonstrating commitment.

Schwartz recalls, "The idea of this song was that by the end . . . it was so simple melodically and chordally, that the audience would be able to sing along, and I am sure that is part of what made it a hit." The audience at the Cherry Lane did not tend to join in the singing, but the composer notes that they did clap in time.

Schwartz wrote all of the songs before the rehearsals started at the Cherry Lane except for "Learn Your Lessons Well," which was for Gilmer McCormick, one of two cast members, including Herb Braha, who did not have songs at that point. Schwartz thought that the stretch without music between "Day by Day" and "Bless the Lord" was too long. "Learn Your Lessons Well" was also an intermission number, which Lamar Alford performed singing and playing the piano, joined gradually by other cast members playing small instruments. The composer does not mention a single influence on "Learn Your Lessons Well," but admits that it sounds a bit like folk-rock and, along with Motown, that was a style that he "really responded to" at the time. He also acknowledges the obvious ragtime influence, heard primarily in the syncopated melody with all of its rapidly declaimed text. It is a sixteen-measure tune in AABA form that includes some of Schwartz's favored minor dominants. The tune features the dotted rhythms of a soft-shoe, but it also includes frequent syncopation. In later professional productions there has been more of an emphasis on a singing cast, and Schwartz reports that the second verse has become an opportunity for "people to rock out." In preparations for the new Broadway production, Schwartz set to music the spoken "Lamp, lamp, lamp of the body, body, body" spoken text (NOCR, track 5, 1'15"), which is in between the verses of "Learn Your Lessons Well" in the script.

As he has stated before, Schwartz said that the model for "O, Bless the Lord, My Soul" was "Save the Country" by Laura Nyro, an influence that he calls "really obvious."[81] He liked the tune's "shuffle feel," and went on to explain that "the thing that Laura Nyro did that completely changed my writing from the moment I heard it were those chords where the bass note is not in the chord," an influence that he believes she took from gospel music. While describing this in our discussion, Schwartz was at the piano, and he played an F major chord with a G in the bass that he described as "just thrilling, musically." Similar chords appear throughout "O, Bless the Lord, My Soul." A difference that Schwartz notes between his song and Nyro's is his use of a minor key (leaning toward Dorian mode), rather than major. Another influence Schwartz took from Nyro was her change of tempos during a song; as Schwartz notes: "One of the sort of tenets of rock music was you would start a rhythm and that's it. It doesn't change." He was especially fond of her album *Eli and the Thirteenth Confession* (1968), which he calls "one of the most brilliant albums ever made." The song "Eli's Coming" featured a constant accelerando that Schwartz used in "Bless the Lord." Although pop singers recorded covers of Nyro's songs, Schwartz listened to her albums and was influenced by her performances, learning the songs off the albums. The soloist in the original production was Joanne Jonas, added to the cast as a strong singer. Schwartz ignored that the original text from the Episcopalian Hymnal suggests a strophic song because that choice seemed "anti-theatrical."[82] He marked his song "Rock with a solid Bass," and the verse is eleven measures long, AAB in form, a segment sung twice by the soloist (OCR, track 5, 0'07"–0'40") before the key changes from A minor to A major for the three-part chorus sung by females over constant driving eighth notes in the bass (0'42") with more voices entering later. The verse returns for two statements with a new text (1'14"), and Schwartz doubles the soloist with the female parts and the men alternate with an accompanying line. The mode changes again for the chorus (1'48"), which has a different text as well, and the song ends with ensemble statements of the title text. The soloist goes up to an a" at the end, one of the highest vocal notes in the score.

Schwartz conceived the dramatic idea for the song "All for the Best." He based it on Irving Berlin's "You're Just in Love" from *Call Me Madam*, which he heard on the radio as a child. He remembers, "It just tickled me so much. It was the first time I heard what you could call pop counterpoint, and I just thought it was dazzling." He went on to explain why he thought this song needed to be added to the show:

> I thought that one of the things I brought to the show was that I was not brought up in this religion. I didn't know these stories, these parables. I didn't have any investment in the story-telling from a proselytizing point of view, so I was just looking at it as a piece of theater, as a story on the stage. And so I talked to John-Michael and said, "Well, look, the major event is in the second act, that Judas betrays Jesus, so we need to set that up in the first act. There has to be something they have to be sort of special friends. Judas has to be more of his main lieutenant, rather than just another one of the apostles." And that's what this song is for. . . . If these guys were named Rick and Joe, and it was about how Joe betrayed Rick in the second act, you would give them a duet in the first act.

Schwartz was not concerned that his model for "All for the Best" was not rock and accepted that it would be accompanied by a small rock ensemble. He believes that the song "seems more like vaudeville than musical theater."[83] Reinhardt recalls that the number included the ukulele because

Stephen Nathan played the instrument, and he helped Nathan learn some of the chords.[84] Schwartz marked the song "Soft shoe tempo," and musically it fits that description throughout with its "boom-chink" accompaniment and frequent quarter-eighth triplets. Jesus sings his thirty-two-bar, AABA segment first over the chord progression (OCR, track 6, 0'03"–1'02"), promising heaven's reward after a difficult life on earth. Judas then sings his AABA chorus in which he comments cynically on the differences between the rich and poor (1'05"–1'37"). Judas's comments are in stark contrast with the song's light character. Jesus and Judas sing the contrapuntal version twice, faster the second time.

Stephen Reinhardt commented on how close the song "All Good Gifts" sounds to Elton John's piano style,[85] but Schwartz states that the actual model was James Taylor's "Fire and Rain." The composer agrees that the song's accompaniment sounds fairly similar to Elton John's piano style (he cites John's "Your Song" as an influence), but the actual model was a guitar song. Schwartz distinguishes between popular songs conceived with piano accompaniments, such as Nyro's "Save the Country," and those written by guitarists like James Taylor. Schwartz, of course, wrote all songs for Godspell with piano accompaniment, but, as we have seen, "Save the People" was modeled after a guitar part. When one listens to "All Good Gifts" next to its model, it does not sound that similar to "Fire and Rain," but Schwartz notes that he changed the mode from major to minor and also altered chords and other elements, and the melodies are different. Schwartz tends to do his own choral arrangements, and this was the case in Godspell. He is not certain what his specific influences as a choral arranger might have been, but he drew upon his knowledge of contemporary popular music. The use of recorder in the song came from Jeffrey Mylett's ability to play the instrument, and Schwartz had always loved how the Weavers used recorder in their folk arrangements, such as "I Know Where I'm Going." Reinhardt remembers that the dance for "All Good Gifts" was performed by the entire cast, and, like most of the other dancing in the show, contributions to the choreography came from everyone.[86] The song is in D major and includes prominent reference to the dichotomy of the blues third and seventh, with frequent use of F-natural and C-natural. The verse is AAB, with an A section of eight measures (OCR, track 7, 0'14"–0'44") and B section thirteen bars in length (0'45"–1'09"). The following recorder solo is derived from the tune, and then everyone sings the verse in three- and four-part harmony before the coda (based on the B section), where the Lamar character sings a powerful solo over the harmonies (2'48"ff).

The text of "All Good Gifts" was from the Episcopalian Hymnal. Schwartz did not set all of the verses; he was selective about which hymn verses he used in a number of songs for *Godspell*. He used the first verse, and then in the production Jesus interrupted the song with his monologue about the importance of storing treasures in heaven rather than on earth. Schwartz skipped to the hymnal's third verse "because that is what it felt like everyone should be singing to him." As noted previously, the songs tend to occur in the show where one of more characters commit themselves to Jesus, and Schwartz states, "This is the moment in the show when all the disciples give over to him."

Schwartz's model for "Light of the World" was "Gemini Childe" by the Mamas and the Papas, a group with which he was "completely besotted" and an influence on how he arranges his choral music. The accompaniment of "Light of the World" has a prominent and repeating "boom-boom-chink" (eighth-eighth-quarter) with the second beats carrying dissonant chords. The original cast's soloist for this song was Herb Braha, who mostly spoke the song, but Schwartz noted that in more recent professional productions that this has become another song where cast members "really rock out." The song is marked "Slow Rock" and Schwartz supplied it with an appropriate bass line based on a hard four beat and rich syncopation in second halves of measures. The two musical segments of the tune form a satisfying musical contrast, with the eight-bar A section (e.g., OCR, track 8, 0'23"–0'40") dominated by nearly constant use of a bluesy G-flat, usually over the tonic of E-flat major. The first three two-bar phrases of A start with a G-flat. In the B section (e.g., 0'40"–0'56") Schwartz modulates to G minor and finally B-flat, then with a melodic A-flat functioning as a blues seventh degree. The B section, however, is emotionally quite different than A, with a text advising the believer to let "your light so shine." Repetitions of these two sections form the remainder of the song.

Reinhardt remembers that soloists in the Cherry Lane production all held microphones, but the chorus had to rely on a floor microphone, a barely adequate solution. As musical director, Reinhardt was in charge of balance, and that was "probably the most difficult part of my job."[87] He had "to try to keep the band in there, really supporting the show, without overwhelming the singing on stage."[88] They acquired the best directional microphones they could find, but with the band above and behind the stage, it was picked up by those devices as well. Reinhardt had to make sure that the band knew when it could play loudly, when to play *sforzando piano* (suddenly loudly and then softly), and when it needed to support the chorus with good presence but not be overpowering.

Schwartz wrote "Turn Back, O Man" in honor of suggestive, bluesy Mae West numbers. The accompaniment is similar to stride piano, foreign to Stephen Reinhardt's experience before he learned the song.[89] The soloist was Sonia Manzano, who turned out to be a better singer than Schwartz had expected, and he placed it in a good key for her. When Jesus starts singing at the verse beginning "Earth shall be fair" (OCR, track 9, 2'17"ff), Schwartz changed the affect completely and modulated up a fifth. The verse is twenty-four measures in length with three eight-bar phrases forming an AAB form. The female soloist and cast enter on the return of the "Slow Cakewalk" (3'02", only so identified at the return). The accompaniment here includes swinging triplets, including in the "striding" left hand, where the strong first and third beats often are tied to the third eighth-note triplet of the previous beat.

Another theater composer who influenced Schwartz was Leonard Bernstein, and the younger musician considers "Alas for You" his tribute to Bernstein in this score. *Godspell* predated Schwartz's work with Bernstein on *Mass*, so this influence was based on earlier knowledge of the older composer's music. Schwartz suggested to Tebelak that "Alas for You" should be added to the show in place of Jesus's long monologue about the Pharisees:

> It was boring to hear him carrying on for five minutes, and so I said to John-Michael, "This is a moment of high emotion for the character—he needs to sing." And basically the rhythm of it just grew out of the words themselves. I had the biblical text in front of me [Matthew 23:13–39] and paraphrased it. . . . I was just thinking of Bernstein in general with the jagged rhythms.

Schwartz admits that Bernstein's version of this song would have been more dissonant, especially on chords such as on the seventh beat of the first measure. At measure sixty-three on the text "Blind guides! Blind fools!" (OCR, track 10, 1'26"), Schwartz hears more of a Sondheim influence, especially in the chordal movement from G-flat/A-flat to F minor/A-flat.[90] He had loved the score to *A Funny Thing Happened on the Way to the Forum* and knows that he saw *Company* not long before he wrote *Godspell*.

Schwartz's admission of Bernstein's song in "Alas for You" is believable given the song's musical style, and he is also correct to say that the older composer probably would have written more dissonant harmonies. There are actually few chords in the song in the first sixty-two measures in which the bass note does not fit in the chord; most such chords with added tones appear between measures sixty-three and sixty-nine under the text "Blind guides! Blind fools! The blood you've spilt on you will fall." This is the start of what could be considered the song's coda, which ends with material returning from the song's opening. Schwartz takes a strong stab at Bernstein's rhythmic practices in "Alas for You" with shifting meters and use of speech rhythms. The song is in the form of AABABC with a brief coda based on A. Each A section is thirteen measures long (e.g., 0'04"–0'21") and the B section ten bars in length (e.g., 0'38"–0'50"). After a two-measure introduction in 7/4, the A section is rhythmically the most irregular segment of the song, with a mixture of measures in 6/8, 5/8, 4/4, and 6/4. Toward the end of the section there are six consecutive bars in 4/4 that sound rhythmically much like Schwartz's other quadruple meter writing in the score. The B section is primarily in 4/4 with frequent syncopation, as is the coda before the last eight measures, which are derived from A. The C section, described earlier for its harmonies, starts at measure sixty-three. Given the emotional load that the song carries, with Jesus railing against the Pharisees, Schwartz provided appropriate music that remains in a pop sensibility. Joseph P. Swain found the song "rhythmically and harmonically imaginative and appropriate for its rather harsh text," but wondered, "Can such passion come from a clown?"[91]

Schwartz worked on the vocal harmonies for "By My Side," but did not alter the duet that included Gordon's melody and Gilmer McCormick's harmony part. He states, "I didn't want to touch it. I loved the song!" Schwartz did try to get Gordon to change the lyric from "I will call the pebble dare" to "Call the pebble death," but she would not. When it came time to produce a score for *Godspell*, Gordon had never actually written the tune down, and Schwartz helped her. At that moment, Gordon remembers that she sang the song incorrectly, and people have sung it that way ever since. Reinhardt recalls that Schwartz wanted the song in D major for its brightness.[92] As Gordon described, "By My Side" is not in any established song form and feels more like a "monologue," the way she describes the poem that lyricist Jay Hamburger asked her to set.[93] The song is through-composed with several motives that recur, comfortably within the feeling of 1960s folk music. Gordon wrote the haunting tune within a narrow range, and the vocal harmonies provided by Gilmer McCormick (years before at Carnegie Tech) and Schwartz add to the appeal.

Schwartz based "We Beseech Thee" on "You Can't Hurry Love," written by Holland-Dozier-Holland for the Supremes. Schwartz reports that he has used the beat of that song a great deal in his career, including for a reporter's chorus in his opera *Séance on a Wet Afternoon*, where it helped set the time period of the 1960s. Schwartz notes, "It was actually not my favorite Supremes song, but I [was] looking for something that would be really up and pop and how to do a big up production number in a pop show—that's what occurred to me, that music." In setting the lyrics from the Episcopalian Hymnal, Schwartz made one of the verses a repeating chorus. The song is in AAB form (e.g., OCR, track 12, 0'07"–0'53") with three eight-bar phrases. Those twenty-four measures sound twice, the first time as Jeffrey's solo and the second with the company participating as a chorus. The A section occurs twice more in three parts (1'41"ff), and then instead of the B section, four members of the company gradually produce four different sounds and imitations of instruments (2'11"ff), which builds to a sudden modulation and the exciting, gospel-like end of the song. Reinhardt describes "We Beseech Thee" as the "10:30 number"—a standard feature of many musicals—providing an emotional lift before the ending.[94] He believes this song plays a major role in the second act, helping the audience to deal with the separation and crucifixion.

As noted earlier, when Schwartz discussed "On the Willows" with Tebelak, the director told him he wanted the song to sound oceanic, like waves, and the cast could not sing at this moment while Jesus says farewell to his followers. Schwartz notes, "I thought of it like a movie where you see action and there is a voice-over song." Schwartz was fond of Stephen Reinhardt's voice and gave it to the music director, much to his surprise. Reinhardt reports that he was not a high baritone, and the song is in the high vocal key of A major because that is what Schwartz wanted for the guitars.[95] His model for the song was the title cut from Judy Collins's 1962 album *Golden Apples of the Sun*, also based around A major arpeggios in the guitar. Schwartz associates keys with certain colors, and one of his major frustrations in the theater is that keys are often changed for cast members during a show's process of creation. In "On the Willows," Schwartz composed a freely flowing melody that sounds over constant eighth-note triplets in the 6/4 meter. It is in AAB form with eight measures in the A section (e.g., OCR, track 13, 0'09"–0'36"). The second time through, A includes an added vocal line of harmony. The B section (e.g., 1'13"–1'58") is eleven measures in three-part harmony with interesting parallel fifths in the vocal accompaniment. The text is loosely based upon Psalm 137, where the poet laments that the Babylonian exile has caused the Jews to hang up their harps because they cannot sing songs of Zion outside of Israel. "On the Willows" instead describes that it is their lives that they hang on the willows. The song's text has little to do with the dramatic situation, but it is an effective moment with the silent stage action.

A prominent feature of the "Finale" is a number of aggressive electric guitar licks, which resemble rock guitar sounds used during the crucifixion scene in *Jesus Christ Superstar*. That score by Andrew Lloyd Webber and Tim Rice appeared first as a concept album in 1970, and the Broadway show did not open until 12 October 1971, five months after *Godspell* premiered at the

Cherry Lane Theater.[96] Schwartz insists that he avoided the recording of *Jesus Christ Superstar* as much as possible:

> I knew of the existence of *Jesus Christ Superstar* . . . the album had just come out, so I knew of it, but I was very careful not to listen to it at all! But not so much as not to be influenced by it, to take things from it. I didn't want to feel limited, thinking, "I can't do that because it's too much like something in *Jesus Christ Superstar*" . . . I was really careful. If ever anyone was playing it, or if it came on the radio, I turned it off. I never heard it until after the show opened.

Schwartz notes that both he and Lloyd Webber took such electric guitar licks from the same sources. Schwartz named Led Zeppelin and Jefferson Airplane, but the latter was his favorite. Schwartz recalls that the guitarist in *Godspell* improvised some of the licks, and he probably played something slightly different every night. The printed score does not include the guitar part, specifying instead piano and organ, with wild instrumental music alternating with Jesus singing his simple dying words from the cross, repeated by the company. The key modulates to B major when the cast starts to sing a simple, folk-like melody to "Long live God," based on the chord changes for "Prepare Ye," which Schwartz then adds in another contrapuntal moment. The music for bows is "Day by Day."

The original cast album of *Godspell* enjoyed considerable success. Schwartz produced the recording, a role in which he felt comfortable after his two years of work at RCA. The original ten cast members and four members of the band recorded the score at a Bell Records studio in May 1971. The album was a major commercial success; it sold more than 180,000 copies in the United States by early June 1972, and it spent months as the only theatrical cast album in the top 100 in sales. In 1971 *Godspell* won the Grammy for Best Score from an Original Cast Show Album[97] (with Sondheim's *Follies* and Rodgers's *Two by Two* among the competition). Albums recorded by other companies included the London cast (also on Bell Records, with David Essex playing Jesus), the German company (Kinney), and the French cast (Phillips).[98]

Godspell Abroad

The efforts by John-Michael Tebelak and the producers to take *Godspell* to England resulted in a three-year run in the West End, several revivals, and a long tour throughout the provinces. Until only a few years before, the United Kingdom's theatrical censorship would not have allowed the production; the ban on biblical subjects on the British stage had only been lifted in 1968 when the Lord Chamberlain ceased his role as theatrical censor.[99] *Hair* opened the next month, updating the British stage quickly.

Tebelak assembled a talented cast in London, including David Essex (later a major pop star) as Jesus, Jeremy Irons (the renowned actor) as John the Baptist/Judas, and others who went on to fine careers in the British theater, including Julie Covington, Verity Ann Meldrum, and Marti Webb. Deryk Pankin was in the show for its entire run, and Robert Lindsay (later of *Me and My Girl* fame) was a replacement in the West End cast. The London and Toronto casts have gone down in *Godspell* lore as perhaps the most talented ever assembled. (The Toronto cast included Eugene Levy, Victor Garber, Andrea Martin, Gilda Radner, and Martin Short, and Paul Shaffer was music director.) Tebelak led his London cast through improvisations with the parables as he had done in New York; press reports and reviews show that this production was prepared for a British audience. In his review in the *Times*, for example, Irving Wardle states that the story of the Good Samaritan was told in "a gushing monologue for an Edinburgh Morningside lady."[100] *Godspell* premiered in London at the Roundhouse Theatre at Chalk Farm on 17 November 1971, a venue that Kurt Gänzl describes as "wilfully fringe-y."[101] A photograph from that production shows that the set design did not include the chain-link fence, but rather there was a white wall at the back of the stage with planks leaning against it, meaning that the actors did use various elements as a movable set, as in New York. Costumes were similar to the clown outfits used in New York.[102]

Godspell was a huge success at the Roundhouse, one of the revered moments in the theater's history. In 1982 Andrew Lloyd Webber was spearheading an effort to save the theater, and he invoked the memory of *Godspell* there as an "extraordinary . . . theatrical experience," also admitting that the space might be less suitable for "more conventional productions."[103] The Roundhouse was only available for the beginning of *Godspell*'s London run; according to the *Daily Telegraph* the show had to leave the theater by 22 January 1972.[104] The archbishop of Canterbury saw *Godspell* at the Roundhouse, afterward meeting the cast.[105]

From the Roundhouse, *Godspell* went to a major West End house, opening at the elegant Wyndham's Theatre on 26 January 1972. *Godspell* took on all of the trappings of a West End hit there, including visits from the royal family; Prince Charles was there soon after the opening.[106] Late in April 1973, Princess Margaret came to *Godspell* for the third time, this time with her husband, Lord Snowden (on his second visit), and their children. Afterward they spent thirty minutes with the cast.[107] In early March 1972, the cast taped a forty-five-minute version of *Godspell* in the crypt at St. Paul's Cathedral for broadcast Easter Sunday on BBC-1's television show *Songs of Praise*.[108] The show closed at Wyndham's on 2 October 1974; *Godspell* had other runs of varying lengths at West End theaters in 1975, 1977, 1978, and 1985.[109]

As in New York, British critics were mixed about *Godspell*, but some raved about it. Irving Wardle in the *Times* took the middle road, clearly enjoying the show but also wondering whether a Martian, converted to Christianity by the show, might then be able to recognize Christianity in a church. He liked Schwartz's score: "The numbers . . . are musically as good as any we have heard since *Hair*. The lyrics are solid gospeling stuff, but simply in terms of sound they have you on the edge of your seat."[110] Felix Barker, writing for the *Evening News*, called *Godspell* an "extraordinary musical charade" and added that it had much in common with "the naïve grotesquerie of the medieval miracle plays." He esteemed the cast highly and said the show included the "best ensemble work I have seen on the London stage."[111] Harold Hobson of the *Sunday Times* called David Essex, who played Jesus, "the best performer in London, the best histrionic, the happiest, and the most moving." He compared the show to Handel's *Messiah* (an institution in England) because both place "the Gospel into a modern idiom" for its time.[112]

Cameron Mackintosh produced *Godspell*'s tour in Great Britain, a saga that lasted for years after the tour started in 1972. The show had multiple runs in many cities, and at times the "Theatre Museum Programme Index Card" collections indicate that there was more than one company.[113] In addition, there were other major tours in the 1980s and 1990s, and there have been many other single productions as well. It would appear that *Godspell* has been as popular in the United Kingdom as it has been in the United States.

Nina Faso spoke enough French that Lansbury and Beruh decided to send her to Paris to direct the French version. Faso reports that they hired a translator for the script, but that person did not work out, so she did much of it herself. (Much of the text could be taken out of a French Bible.) In an interview, Faso commented that she "should be resting on her laurels" for successfully directing the show in French while in her early twenties.[114] Stephen Reinhardt worked with the French cast on the music. The show enjoyed great success in Paris. In some other European countries the show caused controversy, such as in Roman Catholic Spain where it faced a serious challenge from the censors.[115] In Breda, the Netherlands, the Dutch Reformed Church tried to ban the show because it might offend the faithful.[116]

The Broadway Revival of 2011–2012

An effort to bring *Godspell* to Broadway had begun as early as 2007 (my research for this book included the fascinating experience of watching some auditions for the show on 17 January 2008, in anticipation of a summer opening), but the opening was postponed, and producers abandoned it in August after losing a major investor in the face of the slumping economy.[117] The effort came to fruition in 2011 when *Godspell* opened at the Circle in the Square (in the same building as *Wicked*) on 7 November (after thirty premieres that had started on 13 October).[118] As had been the case three years earlier, the director was Daniel Goldstein and choreography was by Christopher Gattelli. The show's critical reaction was mixed and it ran 264 performances, closing on 24 June 2012.

On 24 May 2012, *Godspell* drew a good crowd. Playing Jesus at that point was Corbin Bleu, famous from the *High School Musical* films. The cast's energy level was exceptional, the source of Charles Isherwood's main complaint in his *New York Times* review, where he compared the production to "a bunch of kids who have been a little too reckless with the Red Bull."[119] However, *Godspell* is hard to imagine without a perky young cast, certainly what Tebelak chose and prepared in productions that he directed. As the theater's name implies, it is in the round, which works well for *Godspell*. Scenic designer David Korins made fascinating use of trapdoors, which opened up to provide a pool of water for baptisms, dry ice and interesting lighting to form the communion table, and many small doors with trampolines for each cast member in the aerobic staging of "We Beseech Thee." The cast's improvisations during rehearsals had brought a myriad of references to popular culture into telling the parables.

Schwartz's score came into this production more or less intact, but there were many changes that would be noticed by any member of the audience who knew the original cast recording. Michael Holland prepared new orchestrations for two guitarists, one musician doubling on guitar and keyboard, bass, drums, and the conductor, who also played piano and keyboard. The musicians were spread out among the audience. Holland updated the show's sound with more aggressive use of guitars and a funkier sound overall, and completely changed the focus of the accompaniment for several songs. "Turn Back, O Man," for example, took on a completely different cast, with less emphasis on piano and a distinctive Hammond organ sound from synthesizer. "Alas for You," a piano tune in the 1971 production, was accompanied in this production mostly by guitars. Some new music that Schwartz wrote for the production, as noted earlier, was the text that starts "The lamp of the

Signs for two Schwartz musicals in the same building in May 2012: *Wicked* in the Gershwin Theatre and *Godspell* in Circle in the Square. *Photo by Paul Laird*

body . . . ," the central section of "Learn Your Lessons Well." He also inserted "Beautiful City," written for the film, before "On the Willows," and reprised "City" in the finale in counterpoint with "Prepare Ye." The production's cast recording transmits a fine impression of the show's music.

A Final Word on *Godspell*

Although the show began as a product of the counterculture, time and tradition have made *Godspell* part of the theatrical mainstream. Such movement was perhaps inevitable as it moved from the Café La MaMa to an off-Broadway location and started a long run, but the process was assisted greatly by Schwartz's popular score. As a teenager involved in a Protestant church in New Jersey while the show was in its original run in the 1970s, I know that friends wore out their LPs of *Godspell*, and the score's appeal has not dimmed appreciably. As is the case with many musicals, the score is far better known that anything that takes place on stage during the show, and at this point detailed aspects of Tebelak's work are not well known. Despite the work of his collaborators, *West Side Story* today is associated primarily with the name of composer Leonard Bernstein; similarly, this chapter might have been called "Stephen Schwartz's *Godspell*."

CHAPTER THREE

~

Leonard Bernstein's Mass

A high-profile project early in Stephen Schwartz's career was his composition of the English lyrics for *Mass* by Leonard Bernstein, a work that Jacqueline Kennedy Onassis commissioned the famed composer/conductor to write for the opening of the John F. Kennedy Center for the Performing Arts in Washington DC.[1] The premiere was 8 September 1971. It became a controversial piece covered widely in the press, partly because of the celebrity composer and the association with the Kennedy family, but also because of the musical and dramatic content, which confronted diverse aspects of American life and politics. (The controversy reached the FBI after Bernstein visited Father Philip Berrigan in prison to consult about *Mass*, and J. Edgar Hoover falsely warned Attorney General John Mitchell that Bernstein had invited Berrigan to supply a subversive text for the work.[2]) Schwartz played a crucial role in the work's development, but at the time his participation was overshadowed by Bernstein's large public persona and the event's notoriety.

Bernstein routinely had too many irons in the fire—in his case, one might have noted multiple fires—and *Mass* was only one of a number of compositions that he finished at the last moment. His procrastination in writing *Mass*, however, was extraordinary. After resigning as music director of the New York Philharmonic in 1969, he collaborated for three months with Franco Zeffirelli on a film about St. Francis of Assisi, but departed from the project over creative differences. The project eventually became *Brother Sun, Sister Moon* and some of the music that Bernstein had written for it appeared in *Mass*.[3] Guest conducting and a Japanese tour with the New York

45

Philharmonic consumed Bernstein through the end of summer 1970, when he promised a bedridden Roger Stevens—the Kennedy Center's director recovering from a heart attack—that he would finish *Mass*.[4] Bernstein finally got down to serious composing at the MacDowell Colony in December 1970, but his theatrical piece still lacked a dramatic thrust. The project's director, Frank Corsaro, left after a conference with Bernstein in January 1971, and from February to early May Bernstein was in Europe conducting.

Bernstein was soon desperate to finish *Mass*, and needed assistance on the English lyrics that would provide commentary on the Latin lyrics and relate the show to contemporary America. Through his sister Shirley Bernstein, a theatrical agent with Stephen Schwartz as a client, he saw *Godspell* and met its composer/lyricist.[5] Bernstein and Schwartz perused the compositional sketches of *Mass*, and soon thereafter the older composer called his sister to say, "Oh my God, this is it. Now I can finish *Mass*."[6]

According to Schwartz, he first met Bernstein in late May or early June, and they embarked on a frenetic collaboration.[7] Incredibly, Humphrey Burton has reported that they drafted the show over the next two weeks.[8] Bernstein outlined for Schwartz his multiple intentions for the work.[9] He wanted to write a Requiem for John F. Kennedy, but he chose to set the Mass instead of the Requiem Mass. An opponent of the Nixon administration and Vietnam War, Bernstein wanted to address contemporary events and problems, and he also was interested in reflecting upon contemporary unrest in the Roman Catholic Church as reflected in the efforts of Daniel and Philip Berrigan.[10] In addition, Schwartz listed theological questions that piqued Bernstein's interest: "What are we confessing to? Do we still have the capacity to feel guilty? What is holiness? Do we believe?"[11] Not surprisingly, Bernstein had trouble working all of these competing themes into the piece. Schwartz reports that when he came aboard, the work was in "shards."[12] As they started work, Bernstein told Schwartz that *Mass* would include stage musicians, a dance group, and street people. He showed Schwartz what was written: most of the first twenty minutes, the taped segments, the chorale "Almighty Father," some of the early devotional material, and settings of most of the Latin texts. Alongside a few other sections, Bernstein had also started "A Simple Song." He had briefly collaborated with Paul Simon on the Zeffirelli film, bringing from the young songwriter the quatrain that begins, "Half of the people are stoned . . . ," which Simon presented to Bernstein for use in *Mass*.[13]

Schwartz helped conceive the dramatic structure: "I think through the years that that's been a strength of mine, the ability to give a structure and a coherent narrative to the pieces I'm working on. They're not always obvious stories."[14] He found that writing *Mass* was similar to creating a Broadway show. Schwartz described what he believes he contributed in terms of dramatic structure:

> I think I was able to help him structure the concept that he had in a way that had some kind of dramatic thrust. . . . He had a basic idea of something he wanted to do, musically and from a content point of view. What became clear when I began to work with him was how to take all of these pieces and put them together in some sort of coherent whole. Yes, I did contribute that.

The Celebrant became their central figure.[15] This priestly figure possessed at first what Schwartz described as pure, simple faith. As the show progresses, the Celebrant suffers through increasing objections from his congregation and is weighed down by more and more trappings from the established church, symbolized by his gradual changing from a simple robe to elaborate vestments, presented to him by the dancers who function as acolytes. The Celebrant comes to represent the status quo, and the congregation eventually opposes him. The climax is "Fraction," a mad scene for the Celebrant. He destroys the vessels holding the bread and wine, demonstrates his doubts in parodies of many motives and lines from the show, and finally exits. The "happy ending" is prompted by a rebirth of faith as the youngest member of the cast sings a few phrases from "A Simple Song." The entire ensemble joins in, reestablishing the community and a sense of innocence. After arriving at this basic plot and structure, Bernstein and Schwartz placed interruptions and tropes with English texts. Schwartz has compared the plot of *Mass* with that of *Godspell*. Both concern a community that forms around a charismatic leader who disappears, and in both shows the leader returns in peace.[16]

The Bernstein Estate has embraced Schwartz's role in fashioning the dramatic progress of *Mass*, as may be appreciated from written material on the show at www.leonardbernstein.com, which describes the "fully staged, dramatic pageant" that Bernstein and Schwartz conceived.[17] The source notes the mixture of liturgical Latin with English texts of various levels of confrontation as drawn from the "Jewish practice of debating and arguing with God."

Schwartz described their harried work on *Mass*. They wrote much of it in Southern California, where a revival of *Candide* also commanded Bernstein's attention. Schwartz described his hikes through the Hollywood Hills, looking every inch the hippy, shirtless and with long hair, singing silently as he considered possible lyrics for the preexistent music while drawing suspicious eyes from police.[18] Schwartz had two awkward moments with his dog while working on *Mass*. While at Bernstein's home in Fairfield, Connecticut, his pet stole a piece of bacon from the hand of one of Bernstein's children, and then it did its business on the carpet in Schwartz's room at the Watergate Hotel shortly before the premiere.[19] He spent the hour before he met the Kennedy family cleaning the carpet.[20]

Schwartz commented on the sequence of their work: "We went more or less in order." The schedule that Bernstein's procrastination had forced onto the project did not allow for revisions. As Schwartz said,

> What happened was the entire work, from a lyric point of view, is first draft. As soon as a piece was completed to some sort of satisfactory end, we moved on. And there really was not the time to go back and improve the work. I mean if you are working on the simplest Broadway show, for instance, one would go through workshops and readings and developmental stages. Songs would be in and songs would be out and lyrics would be rewritten and revised, and that never happened with *Mass*.

Schwartz remembers alterations to *Mass* lyrics—especially to "Fraction"—between the Washington premiere, the original cast recording, and a performance at the Metropolitan Opera House in June 1972. A listener following the score with the original recording will note such changes. Once those revisions were complete, Schwartz at the time considered it finished.

When Schwartz noted the continuing popularity of *Mass*, he decided to revise his lyrics. This decision was partly driven by a symposium on the work sponsored by the Columbus Pro Musica Chamber Orchestra, which included his participation.[21] In retrospect, Schwartz considered himself "a little young and a little callow to deal with the subject matter" when he wrote the lyrics in 1971. He defines the writing of lyrics as more a craft than an art and has found that one improves at it with time. Schwartz admits that he wrote the texts for *Mass* "under factors that were less than ideal," and more than thirty years later he could approach the task with greater skill and confidence. He stated, "This [his lyrics] could be better and it would be nice to try to bring the English texts up to the level of the music in places I feel they're not." Schwartz resolved to revise his lyrics without changing Bernstein's music:

> One of my charges to myself is not to change a single note of music, including scansion and emphasis so that the lyric can be sung to the music exactly as written, even in places where Lenny slightly changed timing on things, added a sixteenth note or extended a note to accommodate a lyric. Because he is not around, I am honoring those choices.

He proposed his idea to the Bernstein Estate, and they expressed their interest. He later shared his suggested revisions with Jamie Bernstein Thomas, the composer's eldest daughter, who selected what she liked; Schwartz estimates that she accepted perhaps 60 percent of his revisions. The new lyrics sounded first in a Hollywood Bowl production of 19 August 2004.[22]

Schwartz's revised lyrics for *Mass* include the following numbers:[23]

Trope: "I Don't Know"
Trope: "Easy"
Trope: "Half of the People"
Trope: "Thank You"
Epistle: "The Word of the Lord"
Gospel-Sermon: "God Said"
Trope: "Non Credo"
Trope: "Hurry"
Trope: "World without End"
Trope: "I Believe in God"
Trope: "I Go On"
"Agnus Dei": "Dona Nobis" section
"Fraction"

This was not a limited revision on Schwartz's part. He went over all of his lyrics with a close eye for improving overall effect, addressing sections that he thought could be improved. In some, such as "The Word of the Lord," his revisions were extensive, including entire stanzas. A stanza's role in the song did not change, but Schwartz used different imagery and varied language to achieve a similar effect, also sharpening the message. He did not make as many changes in "Easy," where in some stanzas altering a few choice words improved the effect. The seventeen-page document of lyric changes in *Mass* that Schwartz prepared in 2004 includes over 2,500 words, some merely headings, titles, or brief instructions as to where in a piece a change begins, but mostly new lyrics for a show that Schwartz had last worked on more than thirty years before. These changes fit right into his life's work: Schwartz is a composer/lyricist who has shown extraordinary willingness to delve into "finished" works and revise them. The changes that he agreed on with Jamie Bernstein Thomas remain available for use in performances of *Mass*, but they do not appear in the online version of the score available from Boosey & Hawkes.[24] One should note that the lyrics in that full orchestral score are not entirely the same as they are on the recording that Bernstein made in 1971,[25] and there are other variants on the 2009 recording that Marin Alsop conducted with Jubilant Sykes as the Celebrant.[26] Clearly Schwartz's lyrics for *Mass* have remained more of a work in progress than one might have suspected. His 2004 revisions were used in a version of *Mass* at Northwestern University in late November 2009. In a brief review of the production, Schwartz noted the improvement in his lyrics, especially in "The Word of the Lord" and "I Believe in God" from the "Confiteor" section.[27]

Schwartz recalled many useful memories of writing the original English lyrics for each song and the order that he and Bernstein worked on numbers in *Mass*. In our interview, Schwartz offered a fascinating account of a young lyricist collaborating with a more seasoned composer. The lyricist worked from Bernstein's compositional sketches, and sometimes Bernstein would change music to accommodate lyrics. As has been reported concerning Bernstein's work with Stephen Sondheim on *West Side Story*, Schwartz and Bernstein relaxed during breaks with word puzzles.[28] The older composer introduced Schwartz to crypto-crossword puzzles.

As Schwartz noted, their work progressed on *Mass* more or less in the order of the movements. Bernstein had started "A Simple Song"—an innocent number that interrupts the taped cacophony that opens the show—before Schwartz entered the project. Schwartz estimates that Bernstein wrote over half of the song's lyrics, which are primarily paraphrased from Psalms. Bernstein already had included the Latin word *lauda*. The suggestion that Schwartz made that he recalls most vividly was changing "love is the simplest of all" to "God is the simplest of all"; he found "love" to be "off message." He also simplified other phrases.

The "Prefatory Prayers" are primarily in Latin, but they also include an English segment ("Here I go up to the altar of God . . .") that Bernstein wrote; in his music he tends to illustrate the text's ascending imagery with rising scales. The words of the next major English text, "Almighty Father," are also the composer's work. It is a peaceful, unaccompanied chorale that returns at the show's closing.

The first English trope of the "Confiteor" is "I Don't Know," to which both men contributed. It opens with a bluesy intensity and then moves to more of a rock beat, but it includes the cross-accents and shifting meters one often hears in Bernstein's music. Before Schwartz was on the scene Bernstein had conceived the title and drafted some of the "syllogism-like" statements (such as "What I say I don't feel"). Although Schwartz usually worked with music that Bernstein had already composed, the lyricist does not specifically remember if all of the music to "I Don't Know" existed when he started to work on the song. Concerning the collaboration, Schwartz states, "In general the music was there; there are a couple of places where the words came first."

(The only movements where he remembers the words coming before the music were "The Word of the Lord" and "Fraction," both considered later.)

Schwartz wrote the majority of the text for "Easy," the next trope of "Confiteor." It is a composite segment that includes material from "I Don't Know," male and female blues singers, and interruptions from the setting of "Confiteor" that opens this section of *Mass*. The music that Bernstein wrote for "Easy" seems to emanate squarely from his Broadway muse.

As previously noted, Paul Simon wrote the first quatrain "Half of the People," a trope for the "Gloria." Schwartz wondered whether Simon might have written more than just the first four lines; Schwartz certainly appears to have worked on the song as well because he included it in his 2004 revised lyrics.[29] Bernstein accesses a variety of styles in this trope, from a jazzy groove to a restrained funk.

Schwartz wrote all of the lyrics of the next trope, "Thank You." He offers, "That is the one that I most remember wandering around Beverly Hills, trying to come up with words to that music." His choice of the word *wandering* is telling, because Bernstein's music for the section also has that quality, a combination of declamatory writing and nostalgic yearning close to the composer's slow movements in concert music. That movement's affect must have constituted one of Schwartz's tallest orders for *Mass*, but his lyrics are apt and sensitive.

Schwartz wrote the words to the "Epistle: The Word of the Lord" and gave them to Bernstein to set. They did the piece late in the collaboration, after "Fraction." He found Bernstein's music for the "Epistle"—based on the style of the *Nueva Canción*, "Versos por la sagrada escritura" by Chilean songwriter Violeta Parra—beautiful and completely unexpected. Schwartz wishes that after Bernstein had written the music he had reworked the lyrics to fit the music better, which Schwartz did in 2004. "The Word of the Lord" is unlike anything else that Bernstein included in *Mass*, combining a precise approach to speech rhythms, an exorable forward motion, and an unusual musical style. The monologues added between verses were derived from letters that Bernstein obtained from an unknown source; Schwartz believes that they discussed which letters to use.

The music and Bernstein's initial work on lyrics for the "Gospel-Sermon" existed before he started collaborating with Schwartz. The song includes a constant alternation between 2/4 and 3/8. Schwartz believes that Bernstein conceived the music from the rhythm of the lyrics: "Basically what Lenny did was say, 'God said, let there be light. And there was light.' It made its own rhythm." Schwartz recalls toiling over the quatrains on pages 140–41 of the published score. He was not sure whose idea it was to pronounce the g of *gnats* (p. 137), but he thinks that he wrote the word and mentioned to Bernstein that the audience might have trouble understanding it. Then perhaps Bernstein suggested enunciating the g, a playful touch in an irreverent, jocular song.

Tropes play a large role in the "Credo" section. Bernstein developed the concept for the first, "Non Credo," but Schwartz wrote the lyrics for this declamatory, sermon-like piece that features interaction between a defiant baritone and male chorus. The next trope, "Hurry," includes two distinct musical ideas—one dissonant and confrontational and the other more like one of Bernstein's hopeful Broadway ballads. The next, the exciting "World without End," which also combines two varied musical ideas, is another song for which Schwartz added lyrics to the music. He states, "It is one of my favorite things, musically. I really like it." The final trope in the Credo is the rock-like "I Believe in God." Bernstein wrote its lyrics; Schwartz describes it as one of the score's more problematic songs. In 1971 he found it dated as pop music because Bernstein parodied songs from the mid-1960s, but, as will be described later, Schwartz believes this is no longer an issue.

Following "The Lord's Prayer," the Celebrant sings the trope "I Go On," the moment that Schwartz believes the Celebrant starts to doubt his faith. Here Bernstein approached the kind of profound and reserved music heard in "Candide's Lament" from *Candide*. Schwartz commented on his original lyric for "I Go On" after revising it in 2004: "Actually I quite like that lyric, though I think it is slightly over-rhymed. . . . I retreated into poetry in a couple places where it would be better, actually, to deal with the reality of the situation." Schwartz may have had second thoughts about his original lyrics for the number, but the range that he showed here early in his career was notable.

Bernstein wrote the English lyrics that appear with Latin and Hebrew words in the "Sanctus," which opens with play on solmization syllables and their homophones: "*Mi . . . Mi . . . Mi* alone is only me" (pp. 200–201 of the published score). Schwartz consulted with Bernstein on all of the English texts, and he might have contributed to a line or two of this song, but it is mostly Bernstein's work. With all of the plays on words, Schwartz deems it "quintessentially Lenny." The music is also pure Bernstein, combining an easy lyricism with fetching fluidity of meter.

In our interview, Schwartz described the large dramatic load carried by the scene with the "Agnus Dei" and "Fraction," noting that they show "the whole structure of the piece and the character of the Celebrant and what happens to him and how everybody turns on him and the sort of disintegration of the congregation, until he has his own mad scene."

Schwartz wrote the "blues stanzas" for the confrontational "Agnus Dei," where Bernstein recapitulates music from earlier in the show, such as "I Believe in God" and other movements. He wrote fresh music for the blues stanzas, using a repetitive, strophic structure with ever-increasing dissonance and complexity as the message of Schwartz's stanzas become more strident. "Fraction," the Celebrant's mad scene, originated with Schwartz's lyrics: "I wrote it as a sort of big, stream-of-consciousness monologue and he set a lot of it. Some of it he used, some of it he didn't use. We talked about it . . . it kind of went back and forth, but it began by my presenting him with a big monologue." "Fraction"—at over fourteen minutes long, the score's lengthiest segment—is through-composed. They discussed the concept of recapitulating text and music from throughout the show for dramatic purposes, and Schwartz repeated earlier lyrics in his draft of "Fraction," but Bernstein structured how the music returns in the scene and added puns such as "day" (rather than the Latin *de*) to *profundis* (p. 252, m. 268 of the published score).

"Fraction" is the show's last major English text. "Pax: Communion," following the flute solo, opens with "Sing God a secret song," followed by Latin text and the concluding chorale in English, reprised from earlier in the work. Schwartz helped conceive the end of the piece as part of the scenario, but the movement is Bernstein's work. He returns to the innocence and music of "A Simple Song," gradually spreading it throughout the ensemble.

The details of preparing and premiering *Mass* are now a blur for Schwartz, but he notes, "I was around a lot." There were meetings with director Gordon Davidson, choreographer Alvin Ailey, and set designer Oliver Smith, and Schwartz participated in important discussions on the production, such as how to use dancers as the Celebrant's acolytes. Meryle Secrest reports that the entire production team, except Bernstein, considered the show too long. The composer allowed them to experiment with cuts at the dress rehearsal, but afterward he ordered them all restored.[30] Schwartz believes that something like that occurred, but remembers no details.

For Schwartz, Bernstein's music for *Mass* has "come into its own" because "time has been very good to the work." Bernstein combined popular and classical styles and Schwartz believes that "time has proven that Lenny was ahead of the curve," placing him in "the vanguard as to what has happened in classic music." Some critics after the premiere disliked Bernstein's synthesis,[31] but his combination of divergent sides of his musical personality could be seen as part of a larger trend in classical compositions of the twentieth century to mix obvious references to vernacular music with more traditional sounds and techniques of concert music.

Schwartz, a young composer of music based on popular styles when he worked with Bernstein on *Mass*, commented on the older musician's vernacular music in the work and on possible continuing relevancy of earlier perceptions:

> I don't think that's the thing [composing rock music] at which he was strongest, to be honest. I feel at the time there was something a little "retro" about the pop music he was writing in the '70s for something that was being seen in 1971 . . . [but] I feel time has been very kind to it. It doesn't matter anymore if something is a little '60s. Who cares? It all has become American pop of a certain time . . . of the past. I feel that it fits very well with the rest of the music: the folk influences, the Broadway influences, and the classical influences, and even the twelve-tone stuff he did in *Mass*. All of it seems much more of a piece than I think it did in the '70s. And one of the reasons is that how contemporary, or not, the pop writing was in 1971 is no longer of issue.

Schwartz offers the following overall appraisal of *Mass*: "If I have a reservation about the piece to this day, I do think it is too long and I do think that certain parts overstay their welcomes. [But] I think *Parsifal* is too long, too!" He noted at the Columbus symposium that he finds the three "Meditations" in *Mass* troublesome because they slow the dramatic momentum. He pronounces the movements lovely and realizes that Bernstein wanted to give the audience an opportunity to ponder the show's content, but it is fairly clear that, if he had the power, he would cut the "Meditations."[32]

Schwartz's collaboration with Bernstein gave him a better understanding of the older composer's music: "Obviously from having worked with him—although it was a brief time—it was an intense time, and an intimate time. I really got to know his approach to music as it stood at that time of his life and I think I internalized it to a certain extent."

The older composer had a large influence on Schwartz's music, as he admits, "I can hear a lot of influence of Lenny in my work. I think that would have been true had I worked with him or not. I am such an admirer of him! His approach to rhythm was very influential on me, not just in *Wicked*, but a lot of work I've done." (Bernstein's influence on Schwartz is considered in detail in Chapter 5 on *The Magic Show*.) As we have seen, however, Schwartz was also a bigger influence on Bernstein's *Mass* than has heretofore been noted.

CHAPTER FOUR

~

Pippin

Stephen Schwartz originally went to New York City hoping to develop *Pippin, Pippin* into a Broadway musical. *Godspell* came first, but he remained committed to the Scotch 'n' Soda show he did at Carnegie Mellon with Ron Strauss. *Pippin* became the project that showed Schwartz the process of mounting a show in New York. *Godspell* had been more like young people putting on a show with a basically friendly creative process and everyone offering suggestions. As Schwartz worked with producer Stuart Ostrow and director/choreographer Bob Fosse, the rules changed. Fosse did not welcome input from writers into his areas of purview, and he would change whatever he could about a book or score. Schwartz's battles with Fosse are legendary, but despite the show's tempestuous creation, it was one of the greatest hits of the 1970s, running 1,944 performances. It remains a popular rental property and a revival opened on Broadway in April 2013.

In her biography, Carol de Giere provides a good overview of *Pippin*'s creation from Schwartz's perspective.[1] The story's outline will be presented here with reference to de Giere's account and other sources. Schwartz took *Pippin* to New York without Ron Strauss, who maintained a conception credit and would receive a percentage in any production. Schwartz became a client of agent Shirley Bernstein, who helped him shop the show around to producers. David Merrick took an option on it in 1969, dropping it when a writer failed to produce a workable book.[2] Through Bernstein, Schwartz met writer Roger O. Hirson. The composer/lyricist played some songs for Hirson, and they agreed to collaborate. Schwartz thought that Hirson "had the right sort of absurdist tone."[3] By this point, the show had changed from a medieval royal court drama to a tale about a young man searching for meaning in life.

An Early Script

An early version demonstrates what the show was like before Stuart Ostrow became producer.[4] (Versions of the script that date from after Ostrow's involvement include his name and address on the title page, and this one does not.) The plot and songs of this version will be recounted briefly here. The first number is the familiar "Corner of the Sky," where Pippin announces his search for meaning in life. He sees his father, Charles, on his fourth day back from the University of Padua. Charles and Pippin sing "Welcome Home" as part of a brief conversation. (A bit of "Welcome Home" remained in later versions.) While being dressed, Pippin describes Peregrinus from ancient Greece, who lived an extraordinary life and then died spectacularly from self-immolation. Lewis, Pippin's half-brother, enters, singing "Going against the Visigoths." Pippin discovers how close warrior Lewis has grown to their father. Fastrada, Lewis's mother, enters. She plans for Lewis to become king after Charles instead of Pippin. After verbal jousting between Pippin and Fastrada, she sings a bit of "Welcome Home." Pippin decides to join the army; Charles tells Pippin to get a helmet and they march off with puppet soldiers. The king sings "War Is a Science" with Pippin twice interrupting him. Charles wants Pippin to pray with him, and once the war starts it ends almost immediately with dismembered puppets littering the stage. The cast sings "Glory," but Pippin is too horrified to utter a peep; Charles tells him that a prince must sing. What follows is a scene between Pippin and a disconnected head from the opposing army, which survived into the Broadway version. Pippin sings a short reprise of "Corner of the Sky" with the words changed for the dramatic situation.

The script includes no numbered scenes, but the stage direction states that the scene changes to the country with peasants playing instruments. The song is "Simple Joys," a version of which remained on Broadway. Pippin visits his grandmother Berthe and asks her to go to a peasant's wake, but she refuses and sings "Just No Time at All." Pippin leaves as the song continues and goes to the wake. He meets Gisela, with whom he leaves to make love. Later, peasants assemble for work and Pippin tries to help, but cannot perform the tasks.

Pippin has deserted the army, and the king's soldiers arrive to arrest him, but peasants fight them off. Pippin sings "With You" to Gisela, attempting to declare his love, but she keeps talking about a pig she just saw slaughtered. Pippin tells her that she should never speak again and sings "My Life with You," which becomes a duet. Pippin is in love, but Gisela finds Pippin strange.

The repulsed soldiers return to court and Charles sends fierce men to put down the revolt; they leave court singing a ballad. When they come upon the peasants, they are again singing "Simple Joys" before the soldiers kill them. Berthe advises Pippin to return to the king, but he decides to lead a revolt against his father and sings a song of resolve that was perhaps titled "To Save Tomorrow."

Fastrada, Pippin's stepmother, comments on her double-dealing, acting like she supports Pippin while trying to maneuver her son Lewis onto the throne. Pippin calls a meeting of the barons to incite a revolt, but they all leave. One returns and tells Pippin he will support him and that others will follow, but the baron then reports to Fastrada about Pippin's activities. Fastrada talks to Charles but does not inform him of Pippin's plot; Charles says that his rebellious son will only be received at court on bended knee. Pippin meets Fastrada and asks her when Charles will go to Arles to pray and how he will be guarded. She understands that Pippin intends to commit regicide and discloses the information.

Pippin finds Charles praying in Arles. They engage in dialogue much like that which appears in the Broadway version before Pippin stabs his father. He sings a song not found in later versions with lyrics that might have been titled "Nothing Will Ever Be the Same." Pippin speaks with some peasants, and then Fastrada and Lewis pledge their allegiance. Berthe comes to crown her grandson, and various groups dispute in song about who will first pay homage to Pippin (perhaps "I Will Be First"). The argument continues as Pippin tries to decide what to do, and then he faces a headless man who asks that his body be restored. The groups sing "Decide"; Pippin dismisses everyone so that he may pray. He returns to Charles, removes the dagger, and restores him to life. Charles orders the hanging of anyone who cannot explain his presence at Arles. Pippin asks that his life be spared, and Charles sentences him to continue living, "the cruelest punishment of all." Alone, Pippin concludes this version with a reprise of "Corner of the Sky."

Moving Forward

Shirley Bernstein secured an appointment for the songwriter to play what existed of the score for Stuart Ostrow, who had produced *1776* (1969). Ostrow was looking for a show for the young generation, and, after hearing "Corner of the Sky," he thought Schwartz might be the right songwriter, especially when he learned that Carole King was one of his major influences.[5] Both Schwartz and Ostrow report that they worked with Hirson on the script and score for *Pippin* for a year, and Schwartz recalls that at that point he worked well with Ostrow. Like *Wicked* producer Marc Platt, according to Schwartz, Ostrow was "a producer who was very smart and very interested in structure and material, etc."

Schwartz believes that the search for a director began before Ostrow entered the project. He remembers trying to involve Hal Prince before meeting Ostrow. Prince was not interested but advised making the first act the entire show, a notion that Schwartz and Hirson adopted, as has been recounted by Carol de Giere.[6] When Prince heard the story (at a point before the script described earlier), it still involved the kind of court intrigue that was part of *Pippin, Pippin* at Carnegie Mellon. Prince was more interested in Pippin's personal journey, the direction in which the show moved in rewrites. Pippin's assistants in his quest are Players who try to urge him to commit a spectacular suicide. Scott Miller has suggested that these Players—in fact, every other member of the cast—are all inside of Pippin's head, voices with which he wrestles as he contemplates ending his life.[7]

With Ostrow involved, the team offered *Pippin* to directors Joseph Hardy and Michael Bennett, who both turned it down. Schwartz was especially disappointed that Bennett declined the show. Schwartz remembers that Bob Fosse was the fourth or fifth director that they approached. He had just directed the film of *Cabaret* (released 13 February 1972[8]), and Schwartz reports that he had seen *Godspell* and liked the show. The director had no other project at the time. The prospect excited Ostrow, who praised Fosse's "very personal vision" that "would deliver the score I loved and overcome the dramatic problems Roger Hirson, Stephen and I could not solve during the pre-production year."[9] Ostrow has reported that Fosse "never trusted the *Pippin* writing";[10] in November 1972 Fosse called the material first presented to him as "small-scaled . . . and fey."[11] Miller has suggested that Fosse's staging was purposefully antagonistic to the script and songs, including musical stagings designed to make fun of the songs.[12] Fosse changed the show's tone, as Ostrow states, "from a sincere, naïve, morality play to an anachronistic, cynical burlesque."[13] Fosse was not the first Broadway director who changed a show's book, and, as may be seen in Carol de Giere's account, he did not spare a collaborator's feelings.[14] According to Ostrow, Fosse and Schwartz first clashed during auditions, when the director wanted to hire dancers who could not sing back-up vocals to Schwartz's satisfaction. The producer backed Fosse, establishing the pecking order among the creators.[15]

Schwartz looks back on *Pippin* as a learning experience, acknowledging that much of what Fosse did was brilliant, but he was frustrated by the director's verbal limitations:

> What I wish had been possible, for Bob, was for him to be able to articulate what it was he was trying to accomplish, in the way that Joe Mantello [director of *Wicked*] can articulate why he thinks something should be, because Joe is very verbal. I didn't agree with everything Joe said, but I understood what he was trying to accomplish, and more often than not, he was persuasive, and we could discuss it. Bob just did these things and it was hard to understand what it was he was trying to achieve. . . . And part of that was because, in some places, he did it very well, and in some places he did it not very well. . . . He couldn't articulate what he was trying to accomplish, because he was just not a verbal guy.

Schwartz acknowledges that *Pippin* worked, but calls the Broadway version "a bit of a hodge-podge," a situation that might have been avoided "if we'd been able to work together in a different way." Fosse's vision for *Pippin*, according to Schwartz, was a "tension between dark and light." Schwartz and Hirson shared this conception to a sufficient extent that Fosse was able to superimpose his own stamp and allow for the show's great success.[16]

Fosse brought to *Pippin* his distinctive choreography and dependence on dance as a narrative element.[17] As was his wont, Fosse made *Pippin* a sexy show in terms of costumes and actions of female dancers (especially in "With You"[18]) and in the portrayals by homosexual male dancers. In an interview from 1973, Fosse said that *Pippin* was the first show in which he did not insist that these performers act manly. He thought that it gave the musical "another dimension" but was not certain if his "idea of gay liberation would work with all musicals."[19] According to Scott Miller, sexual content during the Finale was quite prominent, with members of the cast rubbing their bodies and some simulating masturbation as they contemplated Pippin's potential self-immolation. Miller states, "Like the bulk of the show, sex was a barely concealed subtext to everything that happened."[20]

The casting process changed the show's content because Fosse brought in Ben Vereen. Schwartz says everyone was "completely blown away" by Vereen's audition, but the book did not include a part for him. Although Fosse claimed credit for inserting the role of the Leading Player,[21] Schwartz reports that Hirson helped form the idea and they all agreed to it. Hirson combined the Old Man, who performed some of the Leading Player's functions and sang one song at the end of the show, with a few minor characters to produce the Leading Player. The Old Man's song was "Magic to Do"; Schwartz took that text and quickly wrote the new version for Vereen to open the show. Schwartz does not remember the original song well but describes it as "sort of spikier and not as pop." Schwartz also rewrote "Simple Joys" for Vereen and wrote "On the Right Track" for Vereen and John Rubinstein, who played the title role. The song "Glory" existed before Vereen's casting, but Schwartz rewrote it for the Leading Player. Schwartz states that he did not really know to write the songs specifically for Vereen's voice because he was too young and inexperienced.

The show's final punch line was a source of considerable tension. Fosse had already made *Pippin* more sophisticated and raunchier, and John Rubinstein told de Giere that Fosse got nervous about any sweetness that remained during the Washington tryout period, worrying that cynical New Yorkers would dislike the show.[22] One of his new changes was to Pippin's final line, when he has accepted domesticity with Catherine and her son. He said that he felt "trapped, but happy." Fosse deleted the last two words. Schwartz calls this "a huge bone of contention." When Schwartz went to publish the script with Hirson, they reinserted the words, a move that Ostrow opposed. This led to arbitration over the Australian rights for the show, a case that Hirson and Schwartz won because they own the script's copyright.

In more recent years, the authors changed the ending to one that Schwartz believes Fosse would appreciate. Schwartz discovered the possibility in a London fringe production at Bridewell Theatre in the 1990s. He was in London, and a group led by director Mitch Sebastian asked permission to make this change because British child labor laws required there be three young boys to play Theo, Catherine's son. They made him a teenager, and at the end they had him start to sing "Corner of the Sky," meaning Theo was just starting his search. Schwartz notes, "It's really dark in a wonderful way when all the people come creeping back and start gesturing to Theo and trying to seduce him. That's why I just know that Bob would have loved that." This is now the ending to the show.[23] Discovery of this ending raised Schwartz's comfort level with Fosse's darker vision. With other changes, Schwartz believes that he and Hirson have managed "to realize more successfully—and I think more tastefully—what it was Bob was after." It is not possible to trace the history of this "new" ending without consulting scripts from different periods, but one from 1 April 1976 (about a year before the end of the Broadway run) includes an ending with Theo starting to sing "Corner of the Sky."[24]

Ostrow had difficulty raising money for *Pippin* and spent liberally from his own funds.[25] On 13 September 1972, *Variety* stated that the budget had been set at $700,000, but that was later cut by $200,000, an adjustment assisted by the Kennedy Center's guarantee against losses during the four-week tryout in Washington.[26] Schwartz reports that one could see the budget's impact in the scenery. Major investors were Motown (who released the original cast album), the Kennedy Center, Belwin Mills, the Shubert Organization, and Ostrow. Hirson received 2 percent of the gross before the show paid back its investors (2.5 percent after payback), and Schwartz received 4 percent (later 4.5 percent). Payback took place on 24 February 1973, four months after the show opened.[27] When *Pippin* closed in June 1977, the profit had been $3,318,415.[28]

Pippin is famous as the first Broadway musical to use television advertising, an innovation that seems to have significantly helped increase attendance. The musical opened on 23 October 1972 to mostly good reviews, but Grubb reports that business grew soft not too long after opening.[29] It ran through the first season and in the spring won five Tony Awards (best actor, scenic design, lighting design, choreographer, and director). Stuart Ostrow remembers the ads started in 1973,[30] and a report in the *New York Times* from 17 August 1973 stated that the television campaign had worked so well that he planned on quintupling his advertising budget in the new season.[31] Ostrow produced commercials of dance moments from the show for $6,500 to $8,500 each and at one point had allocated $61,000 for buying television time, spending $16,000 to $17,000 per month for commercials shown during the popular shows *Maude*, *Columbo*, and *Sanford and Son*.[32] Producers took note, changing forever the way shows were advertised.

The show's design elements were a major part of its success. Tony Walton's sets and Jules Fisher's lighting created eye-popping concepts, especially the famous disembodied hands at the opening.[33] Costume designer Patricia Zipprodt provided between seventy and seventy-five costumes based on an eclectic approach, from "20th Century thrift shop" to "dance hall girls in 19th Century bloomer and corsets."[34]

Pippin was Schwartz's first New York show with professional orchestrations. Fosse chose Ralph Burns, whose orchestration credits included *No Strings*, *Golden Ray*, *Funny Girl*, *Do I Hear a Waltz?*, *No, No, Nanette*, and *Illya Darling*, and he also worked with Fosse on the film of *Cabaret*. Burns was a jazz pianist who had played and arranged for Woody Herman, Charles Barnett, Benny Goodman, and Red Norvo.[35] Schwartz reports that he liked Burns as a person, but was not sure he understood the score, especially the pop elements:

I thought tonally he didn't quite get it, and the orchestration as it played in the theater is different than what's on the record. I eliminated a lot of stuff for the record. I just didn't feel it was pop enough in its sensibility. It was too brassy and too Broadway-esque, and it sort of straddled the line between pop and Broadway in a way that made it, to my ears, seem old-fashioned.

Schwartz believes that Burns was most successful with ballads, but the pop music "needed to rock out a little more." He does not think that the sound design and use of microphones possible in Broadway theaters at the time would have allowed the musical to sound like what is on the album. The sound designer was Abe Jacob, whose popular music credits included *Hair*, *Jesus Christ Superstar*, and concerts with Peter, Paul and Mary, The Mamas and the Papas, and others.[36] For a production of *Pippin* by Deaf West in Los Angeles in 2009, directed by Jeff Calhoun, Schwartz let Steven Landau do new arrangements that might capture the show's spirit a bit more accurately. However, any musical relying on pop sounds as much as *Pippin* would require new orchestrations in a new professional production that many years after the Broadway premiere. Schwartz, for example, remembers the Hammond organ in the original production, which was "so much of the period," but out of place today. Orchestrations for the Broadway revival that opened in late April 2013 are by Larry Hochman.[37]

Carol de Giere has described how the rift between Fosse and Schwartz continued through the Washington tryout,[38] but the songwriter wrote "Extraordinary" and "Love Song" there. Complicated business dealings preceded Washington. The show was originally supposed to be at the National Theater, owned by the Nederlanders, but Roger Stevens of the Kennedy Center invested and guaranteed the show against losses, so the show moved.[39] A contract dispute with Kennedy Center musicians cancelled that booking, and they moved the tryout to the Shubert Theater in Boston, then back to the National Theater.[40] The dispute was resolved and *Pippin* returned to the Kennedy Center, with previews from 16 to 20 September 1972 and the run lasting until 14 October.[41] The Washington program reveals the musical numbers at the time included "Magic To Do," "Corner of the Sky," "Welcome Home," "War Is a Science," "Glory," "Simple Joys," "No Time at All," "With You," "Spread a Little Sunshine," "Morning Glow," "On the Right Track," "Kind of Woman," "Marking Time," "Just between the Two of Us," and the "Finale." Later changes included "Extraordinary" replacing "Marking Time" and "Love Song" substituting for "Just between the Two of Us." Schwartz recalls that "Marking Time" did not work for Rubinstein, "was not high-energy enough," and was "sort of pop-poetic lyrically rather than theatrical."

Washington critics received *Pippin* warmly. Richard L. Coe, writing for the *Washington Post*, noted the production's variety, citing the presence of elements from "magic shows, minstrelsy, 19th century vaudeville, 20th century music hall, organ music from the soap operas," and also described the eroticism in Fosse's dances. Coe found the work of Hirson and Schwartz "immensely resourceful."[42] Richard Lebherz of the *Frederick News Post* was full of praise for the music and Fosse's production, and stated that the "book . . . has wit, wisdom, and life to it," and he also commented on what he saw as a continuity in Schwartz's shows: "Pippin takes up where 'Godspell' left off."[43]

Mick reviewed the Washington premiere for *Variety*, praising what he saw and heard: "Stephen Schwartz's music and lyrics are so tuneful and polished, and the production so dazzling and varied, that 'Pipin' [sic] is neither pretentious nor precious."[44] The critic loved Fosse's staging and choreography.

Music

Unlike *Godspell*, the majority of which Schwartz composed in about five weeks, he wrote songs for *Pippin* over about four years. No music from the college version remained in the Broadway show. Schwartz sees the songs for *Pippin* as different from *Godspell* because they are more involved in storytelling. According to the composer/lyricist, the songs for *Godspell*—most with lyrics from hymns—"supply emotional signposts" for the show. He has likened writing the earlier score to "putting together a record album or a concert . . . in terms of the flow of it." The exceptions are "Alas for You" and "All for the Best," for which Schwartz also wrote the lyrics. These two songs are more like those for *Pippin*, which the composer sees as more theatrical. What follows is a summary of Schwartz's comments concerning each song in *Pippin*, in addition to musical description. Carol de Giere also addresses aspects of these songs, especially concerning their creation.[45]

"Magic to Do" is one of several songs from *Pippin* that became popular with young listeners.[46] As reported previously, an earlier version existed for the character the Old Man, and Schwartz rewrote the music for Ben Vereen. It helps to establish the show's promise of surprises. In the opening moments, the Leading Player performed magic tricks. Schwartz describes the second version as "kind of dark and definitely pop-influenced." The tune represents what he calls his "singer/songwriter period, but it's a little darker than pop songs in terms of its harmonies." Schwartz helps express this darkness by playing with an ambiguous blues third. The song opens in A minor, but Schwartz makes considerable use of major mode with many melodic C-sharps, always returning to C-natural. Combined with Schwartz's usual syncopation and repeated gestures in the bass, there is plenty of a pop nature (including the Hammond organ set on *molto vibrato* at the opening). The show's creators also use the song to introduce the main characters by having them sing appropriate lines, such as Charles, who promises battles (original cast recording [OCR], track 1, 1'49"–1'53").

The well-known ballad "Corner of the Sky" is the title character's first song, and Schwartz believes that it shares a musical sensibility with Pippin's other numbers: "young and wide-eyed, a bit naïve, sort of folk-rock." He acknowledges that the *Pippin* score, like that of *Godspell*, shows his strong influences from the period, including Joni Mitchell, James Taylor, and various Motown figures. *Pippin*, however, is the first of Schwartz's scores where he musically linked a character's songs. A possible influence that Schwartz cites on the title character's songs is Joni Mitchell's "Both Sides Now." "Corner of the Sky" is one of the earlier songs that he wrote for *Pippin*. Carol de Giere has recounted the story of its creation, involving a car trip to Washington when Schwartz's wife, Carole, suggested the image of how "cats fit in the windowsill," making possible other discoveries, such as "children fit in the snow."[47] (Many singers have instead informed audiences that cats and children "sit" rather than "fit," which still bothers Schwartz. The errors unfortunately appear in the published score.) Before the show reached Broadway, Schwartz rewrote one verse of "Corner of the Sky" to make it more like the typical "I want" song for major characters early in a book musical. The song returns several times. Schwartz made use of the reprise under the influence of Jule Styne's "I have a dream" motive in *Gypsy*. Schwartz believes that this small gesture toward musico-dramatic unity is less sophisticated than what he did later in *Children of Eden* and *Wicked*.

"Corner of the Sky" demonstrates Schwartz's considerable skill in writing pop tunes. The form is a simple eight-measure verse (OCR, track 2, 0'23"–0'45") followed by a ten-measure refrain split into two phrases of four and six bars (0'45"–1'10"). Pippin soars into the highest range yet heard in the song on the words "Got to find my corner," followed by the delayed resolution on "of the sky." The form remains the same through all three verses. Schwartz bases the accompaniment on the noodling sixteenth notes that were ubiquitous in piano-based pop tunes in the 1970s. Harmonies are predictable but effective. It is easy to see why "Corner of the Sky" became one of the most popular tunes to emerge from a Broadway show during the decade. Mark Grant uses an example of the song's melodic rhythm (compared to Stevie Wonder's song "Overjoyed") to demonstrate that Schwartz "is an unheralded Broadway revolutionary" for the way that he combined "the notated backphrasing of melodic rhythm that was characteristic of recorded Motown music" with the eight eighth-note beats typically heard in rock in the late 1960s.[48]

"Welcome Home," a song mentioned previously in the early script before Ostrow became involved in the show, was a minor song in the Fosse version of *Pippin* and does not appear on the OCR. It is in two separate sections in a scene with dialogue, painting a picture of Pippin's unusual family. Schwartz encourages a feeling of oddness with unexpected meters. Much of the song is in 5/4 divided at the eighth-note level into 3+3+2+2, with the occasional measure in 11/8 (3+3+3+2). Charles demonstrates his lack of real concern for Pippin, and the audience meets Fastrada and Lewis and senses their transparent ambitions.

Charles's "War Is a Science" features Pippin's well-intentioned (but embarrassing) interruptions as he tries to convince himself of war's glory. Schwartz's model was a Gilbert and Sullivan patter song, such as "I Am the Very Model of a Modern Major General," but his tune is more chromatic. Schwartz thought the song type fit the character: "It seemed to give you who Charlemagne was and it was fun, the idea of each of the major players doing what is essentially a vaudeville turn. . . . And that was his, and he was sort of the patter-song guy." As writing progressed this scene came to include more music. Charles had spoken his battle strategy in earlier scripts, but Schwartz musicalized much of it, albeit with the "singer" often speaking. The songwriter reports that military terms in the lyrics came from Hirson. The accompaniment is like that often heard in operatic recitative, in the piano version with chords in the left hand and a simple countermelody in the right. The "Cake Walk" that opens the scene sounds like music for a vaudeville routine, with a repetitious, syncopated melody, predictable harmonies, and an accelerando. The three main musical sections of "War Is a Science" following the introduction include Charles's recitative (OCR, track 3, 0'28"–0'50"), the patter song (0'50"–1'26"), and Pippin's march (1'26"–1'54"). The recitative opens with a classical-sounding melody and simple chords with a few added tones (played by synthesized harpsichord). Schwartz's patter song draws only its basic idea from Gilbert and Sullivan, because the tempo is not that fast. Chromatic touches and modal shifts lend Charles's military planning a tentative air. Pippin interrupts his father twice with his march, marked "Quasi 'March of Time,'" written in a Sousa-like character with dotted rhythms, piquant melodic chromaticism, and trumpet flourishes. When the chorus concludes the scene with another version of the same music, it ironically prepares the scene for Pippin's dispiriting military campaign.

"Glory" became the music for one of Fosse's dance sequences. As de Giere reports, the original song's model was Carl Orff's *Carmina Burana*. Schwartz notes, "There was a lot of sort of medieval things—or meant to feel medieval—in the show . . . particularly stuff that was written early for the show, and then got . . . made jazzier or poppier . . . when Bob came in." "Glory" was for choir, but it became Vereen's solo, with ensemble entering later. Schwartz changed it when Fosse asked for a stronger rhythmic element to assist with the choreography. While working with dancers on the "Manson Trio," Fosse used "Come On, Baby, Let the Good Times Roll" as a dummy tune; Schwartz wrote music with a similar meter. According to Schwartz, Fosse did something like this when he choreographed "All That Jazz" for *Chicago* (1975), meaning that Schwartz's music also resembles the later song by Kander and Ebb.[49] "Glory" is marked "Polite Acid 4"; Schwartz has no idea who added that or what it means. At that point his understanding of the Broadway process did not include proofreading the piano/vocal score.

Although not heard on the recording, "Glory" opens with brief reference to "Magic to Do" and its promise of battles. The number juxtaposes two musical ideas that help project one of war's simple facts: victory might mean slaughter on both sides. Schwartz follows "Magic to Do" immediately by two measures marked "Moderate Jazz 4," the material of which accompanies the principal part of the song. Schwartz interrupts this with the idea that opens this track on the recording: four statements of the tune's title over synthesized organ (marked "church sound") that approaches the exultation of sections of *Carmina Burana* (OCR, track 4, 0'00"–0'15"). The driving accompaniment in the next six measures of the score (mm. 9–14) does not appear on the recording, where organ chords continue through new material and a repeat of the opening. The return of the somewhat jazzy accompaniment concludes the introduction and moves into the sinister main section (0'44"ff), where aspects of war ("blood," "steel") are treated ironically in minor keys. The accompaniment does change at times, such as the soft-shoe dotted rhythms in the "Shout it out" segments (e.g., mm. 53–57, 1'42"–1'55"). "Glory, Part 2" follows immediately, presenting, as noted earlier, the meter of "Come On Baby, Let the Good Times Roll" (2'29"–3'46"). This is the "Manson Trio" (named for the famed mass murderer) where Fosse reduced the horror of war to a hat and cane routine. Restrained scoring for electric piano and occasional drumsticks struck together adds to the mockery. "Glory, Part 3" (3'46"–4'29") returns to material from the first segment presented dramatically for a big finish, but it is not all on the recording. In the score, Pippin's march from "War Is a Science" returns in "Victory Underscore," and then Pippin reflects briefly on his disappointment in military life with a reprise of "Corner of the Sky."

As noted previously, Schwartz wrote "Simple Joys" for Vereen. The composer calls it a "very high-energy guitar song," making his common distinction between keyboard-based popular songs—such as "Corner of the Sky" and "Morning Glow"—and songs written with guitar accompaniment. Actor John Mineo accompanied "Simple Joys" with guitar on stage. For the recording, Schwartz added more instruments. The song places Schwartz firmly in the period because there are moments that might have been written by any number of singer/songwriters from James Taylor to Carole King, or even Richard Carpenter. In F-sharp minor and A major, the song has a verse of 32 measures (ABAB; OCR, track 5, 0'36"–1'21") with a shorter chorus of eight measures (two similar four-bar phrases, 1'22"–1'32") and a concluding phrase of 12 measures filled with memorable images (such as "left-handed flea," 1'32"–1'52"). In both minor and major modes, Schwartz makes use of the lowered seventh as a substitute dominant chord, similar to many folk songs.

The number that caused the most comment among reviewers was "No Time at All," a sing-along that Schwartz wrote soon after he went to New York, perhaps as early as 1969. The word *granny* appeared in the lyrics before Irene Ryan—famous as Granny on television's *The Beverly Hillbillies*—was cast. Schwartz suggests that word spawned the notion of hiring her to play Berthe, Pippin's grandmother. Schwartz considered changing the word once they had hired Ryan, but others liked the association. Schwartz based the sing-along idea on concerts by the Weavers that he attended as a child. Ostrow remembers that the song stopped the show.[50] *Pippin* was Irene Ryan's Broadway debut, but she had played the Palace in vaudeville. The part of Berthe had originally been intended for a large actress, and Ryan weighed only ninety-five pounds. Because she was elderly, Ryan's understudy had to be at the theater each night instead of just calling in to see if she might be needed.[51] Ryan died on 26 April 1973 and was replaced by Dorothy Stickney.[52] Ryan received a posthumous nomination for a Tony Award as best featured actress in a musical.

"No Time at All" is extraordinarily catchy. The repeated chorus is eight measures long with the melodic outline of the first two measures immediately repeated with different rhythms for new text. Berthe sings three other sections. Her opening recitative (OCR, track 6, 0'03"–0'38") sets up the remainder with especially clever lyrics in the last phrase.[53] The verse, which Berthe sings several times (first time: 0'38"–1'09"), is sixteen measures long, AABC. Chords in each of the first two phrases move from C to B-flat major, another song that invokes folk music with the lowered seventh. The choruses (first time: 1'09"–1'24") become increasingly bawdy. Schwartz modulates to A major for the chorus, prepared suddenly by a G-sharp in the accompaniment under a G major chord, drawing everyone into the sing-along. There is also an eight-bar bridge (such as mm. 64–71, 2'18"–2'32") that can be primarily spoken and includes a jazzy accompaniment.

Another song that Schwartz wrote for *Pippin* soon after graduating from college was "With You," sung at his wedding in 1969. The song's meaning changed with Fosse's participation. It was a love song that Pippin sang to Giselle, but with Fosse, Pippin sang "With You" before an orgy. He leaves his moment of sexual experimentation feeling unfulfilled. The song's tone fits the title character at his most innocent. Schwartz crafted a lovely melody in AABA form (OCR, track 7, 0'15"–2'25") with a longer B section (9+9+12+9 bars). The second segment of the B section (1'35"–1'54") takes the singer into a high tessitura and sets up the return of A in a low range (1'55"ff). The introduction of "With You," not heard on the OCR, has a folksy feeling with soprano recorder playing a tune that alternates between raised and lowered sevenths, and then the Leading Player recalls the text from "Magic to Do," as we now have "sex presented pastorally." This ironic stance is confirmed by raucous dance music that follows for the orgy (not on the OCR). Part 1 concludes with the tune converted into a waltz played by strings and celesta, but jazzier music soon intervenes (m. 59). Part 2 opens with a sarcastic march tune whistled first by men on stage and played by various instrumental combinations. In m. 120 there is a burlesque of part of "With You" sung by the men to "bup bup bup bah," and the segment concludes with rapid sixteenths. Part 3 (marked "Gisella") is a series of variations over a funky bass line, marked in m. 180 "quasi Joe Cocker" (a British rock and blues singer). Following this dance sequence, there are brief musical segments called "Bad News Clues," underscoring an exchange between Pippin and Leading Player as the title character decides to become a revolutionary, followed by "Pippin the Politico," based on "Corner of the Sky" but treated as early jazz and marked "quasi Red Nichols 5 Hot Pennies" (a jazz figure whose career began in the 1920s).

Fosse and Ostrow asked Schwartz to write "Spread a Little Sunshine" for Leland Palmer, cast as Fastrada. (In several places the published score of the song carries the date 22 September 1972.[54]) The song sounds classical in places, and Schwartz reports that it was a "send-up of sort of Bach . . . based on all those years of Bach inventions I played." The marking, which Schwartz did not provide, is "quasi Mozart." The song is a waltz, and he chose the triple meter "just to refresh the ear because so much of the show is in 4/4." Schwartz did not think that the song worked very well: "It's a lot of stage time for a character we don't really care about." The three verses are a small part of the number, where Fastrada works toward getting her son in the line of succession ahead of Pippin. Underscoring for dialogue in the score precedes material heard on the recording, where the song opens with straight eighth notes reminiscent of Bach's minuets (OCR, track 8, 0'00"–0'11", returning after refrains), but the designation is a "moderate waltz," and the accompaniment confirms this. The naïve affect contrasts with Fastrada hatching her plot. The melody bears folk traits with repeated motives and a flat seventh chord as a dominant substitution (as may be seen in m. 29, for example). The verse is two phrases (AA', 8+7, first heard: 0'13"–0'32"), followed by a sixteen-measure refrain (0'32"–0'53", basically 4+4+4+4). There is a great deal of music for underscoring and dancing after the third verse, much of it still in triple meter, but the ending is in 4/4, again with classical references.

Schwartz remembers that "Morning Glow" came to represent a sense of hope for young people: "It's an anthem about someone who believes he can change the world, and now everything is going to be better. It's a point of view that's very much part of the anti-Vietnam [War] generation." The composer notes the similarity between "Morning Glow" and Sondheim's "Our Time," the finale of *Merrily We Roll Along*, where the characters are youngest. As Schwartz states, "That's the one place where I feel he [Sondheim] was trying to channel that kind of young, hopeful, naïve [feeling]. . . . It's very appropriate for that point in *Merrily*. They are all at the stage where Pippin is in the show."

"Morning Glow" follows "Chapel Underscore" (not on the OCR), during which Pippin confronts his father in Arles and, temporarily, kills him. The chapel music includes a simple melody in a narrow range and predictable harmonies. In m. 9, Schwartz introduces an ominous figure on A, a dotted quarter followed by an eighth note and half note, which builds tension until Pippin stabs Charles. The title character sings briefly to a declamatory, modal melody about his shaking hand and future possibilities. The orchestra introduces "Morning Glow," and Pippin sings the first verse, the song's start on the recording. As noted earlier, Pippin's music has a surface similarity, and this carries the freshness and innocence one hears in "Corner of the Sky." The verse is twelve measures long, three four-bar phrases. The first phrase (mm. 14–17, OCR, track 9, 0'14"–0'22") includes an introduction of the primary idea spread over a major ninth, all presented over two statements of the two-measure vamp that preceded the tune. The second phrase (0'23"–0'31"), in a higher range, lyrically announces the possibility of sweeping change. The final phrase (0'32"–0'39") confirms that feeling. The choral harmonies that are part of the remainder—which includes eight measures of transition (such as mm. 44–51, 1'18"–1'34")—help make "Morning Glow" one of the score's highlights. The next two brief numbers include underscoring from the previous song as Pippin starts his disappointing rule as king. "Charles Resurrection," based on "Chapel Underscore," then provides

atmosphere for Pippin's second meeting with the headless man and his re-
trieval of the knife to resurrect Charles.

Schwartz cites "On the Right Track" as a successful collaboration with
Fosse. The director found the song difficult to stage and asked Schwartz to
remove every word that he could, leaving what Schwartz calls "these strange
little, 'jaggedy' sections." In sung sections, he deleted text for a few beats at a
time and there is a dance break in the score that might have once had text,
but it does not appear on the OCR. When Schwartz produced the recording
he added more jazzy seventh and ninth chords than heard in the theater, noting, "I associate those sorts of chords with a kind of cynical sophistication."
This is similar to the affect of "The Pursuit of Excellence" in *Children of Eden*.
Schwartz is not a big jazz fan, but he knew Dave Brubeck's work in the 1950s,
especially the album *Take Five*, which his parents owned.[55] Schwartz reports
that there was an earlier number in *Pippin* perhaps called "On Your Knees,"
when the show was two acts and ended with Pippin entering a monastery. It
was still in *Pippin* after Fosse came aboard, but they cut the song and "that
idea got folded into 'On the Right Track.'" The music of "On the Right
Track" includes jazz ideas along with Schwartz's favorite Motown sensibility.
This may be heard distinctively at m. 35 (OCR, track 10, 1'25"), when the
Leading Player has completed his first verse and backup singers enter. The
time signature for the song is 4/4, but Schwartz set it with a jazzy swing and
wrote most of it in 12/8.

For a solo for Jill Clayburgh's character, "Kind of Woman," Schwartz
turned to the model for "Day by Day" in *Godspell*: Burt Bacharach's popular
waltz "What the World Needs Now." Schwartz hears country influence in
"Kind of Woman," a style he does not often use. (Schwartz reports interest
in more recent country music, represented by such artists as Trisha Yearwood
or Mary Chapin Carpenter.) The country influence is muted in "Kind of
Women," a pop waltz set in a low range for Jill Clayburgh and three backup
singers. Several brief phrases begin on second beats, and the declamation
bears a strong feeling of speech rhythms, especially in mm. 28–32 on the
text "conservative with a budget, liberal with a meal" (OCR, track 11,
0'45"–0'52").

In the score, "Kind of Woman" follows "There He Was," Catherine's brief
song where she describes finding Pippin and bringing him home. Schwartz
is not sure if the song survived in the original Broadway version. It does not
appear in the show's song listing on the *Internet Broadway Database* or in the
Broadway programs consulted for this study.[56] Following "Kind of Women,"
the score includes two brief incidental pieces: "Theo's Cue" and "Hearth
Incidental."

The song "Extraordinary" replaced "Marking Time" during the Washington tryout. Schwartz modeled the song on "I'm the Greatest Star" from *Funny Girl*, music by Jule Styne. Schwartz states, "Though it's pop in its musicality, it's a really classic '60s musical theater style structure, you know, from me being a kid and going to see all of those shows." He begins with the "less driving statement of the theme" than Styne and moves into the middle section. Styne used a *tresillo* (3+3+2) rhythm there, as did Schwartz (OCR, track 12, 1'07"ff), and the song concludes with a return to the theme, this time set to a more driving beat. The opening section is AABA, primarily eight bars per section except for a slight extension of the last A as Pippin emphasizes that he is "*very* extraordinary" in mm. 31–35 (0'58"–1'02"). Schwartz based the opening of each A section on a D-flat arpeggio that he quickly repeats (0'00"–0'03"), but he does this over a B-flat chord, making the A-flat for that chord a blues seventh. The rich syncopation in the melodic line and swinging accompaniment make for a jaunty tune that sets Pippin's delusions in high relief. Schwartz's middle section is only ten measures long (1'03"–1'23"); he complicates the *tresillo* in the accompaniment with quarter-note triplets and eighth notes in groups of four in the nearly spoken vocal line, providing rhythmic complexity that functions somewhat like the "dogfight" in a march, building tension before the final section. The final AABA (1'23"–2'30") is marked "Straight, Driving Rock," an appropriate musical cognate to Pippin's anger.

The next song in the score is "Prayer for a Duck" (not on the OCR), where Pippin tries to help Theo's sick pet. It is a simple D major melody over a chordal organ accompaniment. Schwartz based this music upon a tune sung at a monastery in an earlier version of the show, perhaps called "On Your Knees," which, as noted earlier, had been deleted. Schwartz remembers it in the gypsy run-through in New York, but it was cut before they went to Washington. Schwartz reused that tune in "Prayer for a Duck" because of its religious nature.

As Pippin and Catherine discover each other romantically, there are two musical excerpts, neither on the OCR. The first, "Intro to Bed," is what the script identifies as changing from "romantic to corny passionate." It is a wandering melody with hints of "Love Song." The "Bed Music" that follows is full of energetic, militaristic rhythms as Pippin and Catherine joyously consummate their relationship after an unsuccessful first attempt.[57]

Schwartz wrote "Love Song" late in the show's creation, replacing "Just between the Two of Us." The composer calls "Love Song" "a breakthrough . . . for me musically." In the same way that he acknowledged Bernstein's influence in the uneven rhythms and constantly shifting meters of "Alas for

You" from *Godspell*, Schwartz applied similar procedures here in a slower, lyrical tune. In "Love Song" he approached the sensibility of some of Bernstein's songs from *Mass*, such as "Thank You" and "Hurry," where shifting meters are also part of a lyrical statement.[58] Schwartz also considers "Love Song" a breakthrough "because it's a song that's not really modeled on anything. It came from the emotion of the moment, and I wasn't trying to be pop or write anything that could be lifted out of the show, or whatever." "Just between the Two of Us" was more of a pop tune. Schwartz further reflects on "Love Song": "This is the music that came out, and I was sort of surprised at myself, for not staying in one time signature. I know when I wrote this it felt as if I had taken a step forward as a theater composer." Schwartz considers this an important song because the audience must believe that Pippin and Catherine are in love.

"Love Song" bears an unusually disarming honesty for *Pippin*. As noted, the title character's songs are naïve, showing that he must mature. The callowness of "Corner of the Sky" becomes clear during its reprises, showing what Pippin gradually learns. "With You" seems downright clueless when followed by an orgy. He sings "Morning Glow" in a flush of excitement after killing his father. "Extraordinary" is an angry boy's rant. In "Love Song," Pippin finally finds adult emotions, and the song is graceful. In the eight-bar verse, heard three times (mm. 11–18 [OCR, track 13, 0'13"–0'30"], 24–31, 47–54), Pippin and Catherine exchange images of love with his concern involving communication ("talking 'til dawn") and hers the physical ("lavender soap and lotions"), but their unanimity of feeling is clear in shared melodic material, such as frequent evocations of D-flat, the lowered seventh in E-flat major. The overall form of the song is ABABCAB with a coda. The B sections (such as mm. 19–23, 0'30"–0'43") are simple, with the text showing self-awareness as they sing a "love song" and of their satisfaction with simple vocables ("la, la"). Pippin sings the C section (1'16"–1'34"), which is in 4/4 with Schwartz offering gestures from his typical pop style, a fine foil to the remainder of the song. The coda (2'11"ff) includes additional play with the D-flat and "la, la" chorus, bringing the song to a peaceful close. Pippin, however, has a relapse, singing "Corner of the Sky—Last Reprise" (not on the OCR) as he leaves Catherine and Theo and goes off again in search for something more.

Catherine sings "I Guess I'll Miss the Man." As Scott Miller has pointed out, the song title tends to be absent from programs because the Leading Player does not want it performed. He has been maneuvering Pippin toward suicide, and this song shows Catherine's feelings for the title character.[59] Schwartz describes the song as "Pippin-esque," demonstrating his influence on Catherine. Schwartz wrote this as a guitar song; the accompaniment includes fillers and countermelodies by solo instruments. The tune captures Catherine's honesty and world-weariness. Interruptions from the Leading Player, who tells her to stop singing in a script from 2005,[60] do not appear in the score. The song is in AABA' form with fourteen measures in the A sections and eight in the B. The range is an octave and a fourth from f-sharp to b'; Schwartz makes effective use of the highest note in the sixth measure of each A section, jumping from f-sharp' to b' each time (first time: OCR, track 14, 0'17") that Catherine provides unpleasant details about Pippin.

Schwartz went through a number of possible finales for *Pippin*. An early song, when the players tempt the title character to immolate himself, was "One Glorious Moment." Schwartz finally decided to base the show's finale on the kind of material that he used to close the recording of *Godspell*, what he calls "a maniacal 'Day by Day.'" He places the first solo verse in triple meter, uses the chorus to accompany on the second verse, and then goes to 4/4 and repeats the idea several times. This introduces Pippin's final solo, where he wonders about his quest. The stage version was much different than what is on the recording, which includes none of the Leading Player's spoken interjections during Pippin's final solo. On stage this scene resembled the finale of *Damn Yankees*, where Mr. Applegate hurls abuse at Joe Boyd and his wife as they sing their final duet. The OCR gives little idea as to the show's ambiguous ending, when the Leading Player strips away the production elements.

The finale opens with the Leading Player's version of "Think about the Sun" in triple meter, punctuated by birdcall-like gestures from piccolo and oboe. The tune has a gospel tinge and becomes a full revival song with driving beat and clapping when it changes to 4/4 (OCR, track 15, 1'29") and the choir enters, urging Pippin to jump in the fire. The segment ends with a dissonant choral treatment of two lines from "Corner of the Sky" (3'22"–3'35"), prompting Pippin to muse about what he has wanted in life (3'49"ff). He realizes that the closest he has come to happiness has been with Catherine. The melody tends to move in eight-bar phrases (sometimes with extensions) constructed from a single motive, where each two-measure subphrase starts on the second beat of the quadruple meter with a similar rising gesture.

Reviews

Reviewers in New York loved Fosse's direction and choreography but were mixed about other aspects of the show. Clive Barnes, writing for the *New York Times*, missed no opportunities to praise Fosse's contributions. He called *Pippin* a "commonplace set to rock music," but that music is "somewhat characterless" with "a few rock ballads that could prove memorable."[61] Barnes, however, thought that Fosse took "a painfully ordinary little show and launches it into space." Douglass Watt of the *Daily News* compared the show's concept to *Dude*, which had bombed a few weeks before, but liked that *Pippin* was "tongue-in-cheek" with "a becoming thread of sincerity."[62] He thought Schwartz's songs "charming" in a score that "rocks, croons, dances and, in general, floats the proceedings most attractively" with "superb orchestrations." Watts found the lyrics "equally engaging." He praised the song "No Time at All," and lauded Fosse's contribution. Richard Watts, critic from the *New York Post*, wrote a rave: "There is such humor and wealth of imagination in the book, score and brilliant production that I can't believe it could possible fail."[63]

Martin Bookspan, who disliked *Godspell*, positively reviewed *Pippin* on opening night for WPIX-TV, Channel 11. He said the creators "have combined to produce a prodigious work," admitting that it was difficult to catch everything on one viewing, but he was "tremendously impressed."[64] Edwin Wilson of the *Wall Street Journal* was enthralled, describing it as "what the American musical should be: using the vast resources of dance, music, scenery, and lighting we have developed to serve an original idea."[65] He praised Schwartz's "fresh" score.

As more reviews appeared, a wider spectrum of opinion appeared. Martin Gottfried of *Women's Wear Daily* disliked the show. He reserved some of his strongest venom for the music, which he called "wildly erratic, ranging from pseudo-Bacharach to the anonymous show tune."[66] He also took issue with Schwartz's lyrics, which he called "an uncanny example of a man not understanding his own beats." Hobe Morrison, writing for *Variety*, praised the "brilliant production" but described a "routine and cluttered story" and "passable songs" that were "not particularly memorable."[67] Walter Kerr, in a review published four days later in the *New York Times*, raved about *Pippin*, including Schwartz's score. He praised the "trippingly bitter tunes" that can be "busy as raindrops hitting tin roofs" or end with a "sharp halt as though an anvil had finished them."[68] He described the score as "perky, driving, and—fortunately—nearly omnipresent."

Reviews followed in a steady stream. Helen Kruger of the *Chelsea Clinton News* loved Fosse's contribution, hated Hirson's book, and called the music "sluggish" but with "bright and intelligent" lyrics.[69] Julius Novick of the *Village Voice* called it a "hackneyed, mush-headed, pseudo-serious story" told with "the most aggressively up-to-date, sleek, chic, pseudo-innovative showmanship." He admitted that it would probably be popular, despite the "thundering excess of stupidity" from both the main character and writers.[70] Brendan Gill called *Pippin* "simultaneously a great show and a poor musical" with undistinguished music and lyrics and a "skimpy book."[71] Rex Reed, reviewing the show for the *Sunday News*, had huge praise for Fosse and the cast, less for the ending and book, but he found the score more interesting than *Godspell* with Schwartz providing "a cornucopia of music from traditional show tunes to the hot tempos of rock."[72]

The nation's major news magazines published reviews of *Pippin* on 6 November. T. E. Kalem of *Time* believed that many would enjoy the show because of its "splendiferous theatricality," although it failed to rise to the "pinnacles of the art of musical comedy."[73] He loved the eroticism, dancing, songs, and female dancers "that the gods of Olympus might ogle." He portrays Fosse as a great American builder, like those who "flung railroads across a continent." Jack Kroll of *Newsweek* thought that Fosse's contribution made the show worthwhile; the music and lyrics were "high octane and quick-evaporating."[74]

John Simon of *New York* was unimpressed with the music, believing Schwartz to be more comfortable in "the miniature of *Godspell*."[75] The distinguished Harold Clurman in the *Nation* described *Pippin* as "rapid, banal scenes relieved by the physical splendor of spectacle."[76] He saw "clever ploys" but also "inner emptiness" and thought that Fosse's production helped "one forget that most of the lyrics and music are vapid."

Three national forums offered later views of *Pippin*. Tom Prideaux of *Life* saw the show in line with Broadway's movement to the youth market, but with a more conventional approach than in *Hair*. He described it as the premiere Broadway attempt by "old-time show-biz experts" to work "with rock-style music and expressing a youth-cult point of view. The fusion is fruitful and overdue."[77] Henry Hewes of the *Saturday Review* thought the show "so relatively joyless" and the score worthy of only faint praise, but said Schwartz had to be "above average" as a tunesmith if he could "write a show stopper like 'No Time at All.'"[78] John Beaufort's review in the *Christian Science Monitor* appeared in late December. He found problems with the script toward the end but enjoyed the production elements and thought the show "enjoys the advantage of music and lyrics by Stephen Schwartz, who more than fulfills the promise he showed in 'Godspell.'"[79]

Pippin Abroad

Stuart Ostrow and Bob Fosse went to London to work on the West End version of *Pippin*. Schwartz was unavailable and did not wish to be involved.

It was unsuccessful, and Schwartz attributes that to what he believes is an essentially American story about a young man searching for his place in life. He also wonders if *Pippin* perhaps would even appeal to those who live with an actual monarchy. The songs were the same as in the New York version and the Leading Player was Northern J. Calloway, Vereen's standby in New York who later played the role there. The press was for the most part unimpressed by *Pippin* in London, often enjoying the production but not the writing. Jack Tinker in the *Daily Telegraph* stated, "The book begs to be forgotten. The songs don't hang around too long in your head." An audience, member, however, would "come away whistling the production and humming its tricks."[80] The show had a short run in the West End, and *Pippin* has not proven popular with the British in regional theaters.[81]

As noted earlier, Schwartz worked on the *Pippin* in Melbourne, Australia. Kenn Brodziak (1913–1999), a major Australian producer who had brought *Godspell* there,[82] owned the rights for his country along with Schwartz, and they made the show more like Schwartz's conception, with the Leading Player less important than the title character.[83] The show opened at Her Majesty's Theater in Melbourne in March 1974 with the roles of Pippin and Catherine played by Johnny Farnken and Colleen Hewett, the latter known in Australia as "the *Godspell* girl" for her recording of "Day by Day." Director and choreographer was Sammy Bayes, and the order of songs was similar to that on Broadway. Clive Barnes visited Australia in the summer of 1974 and declared that the production there was "just the shadow of the original."[84]

Pippin on Video

The available video of *Pippin* was produced for the series *Broadway on Showtime* in 1981, directed by David Sheehan.[85] Filming took place at a theater in Hamilton, Ontario, and the cast included Ben Vereen as the Leading Player, William Katt in the title role, Martha Raye as Berthe, and Chita Rivera as Fastrada. Reviewing the video for the *New York Times* in 1984, John J. O'Connor found the show dated, saying that the music and book "fairly reek of the flower-child innocence and anti-war sentiments of the previous decade."[86] From the perspective of three decades later, it is useful to have Vereen's energetic, soulful performance recorded for posterity. Katt was an appropriately naïve brat as Pippin, and Chita Rivera brought about as much to the circumscribed role of Fastrada as might have been possible. Martha Raye's brief turn as Berthe works, and Ben Rayson was excellent as Charlemagne. Leslie Denniston provided the right mixture of charm and confused motives as Catherine. The production's credits for stage director and choreographer went to Kathryn Doby, who appeared in *Pippin* on Broadway as a Player and served as Fosse's assistant. The video is "Based on Bob Fosse's Original Staging & Choreography," a worthwhile document to have on video, and the production must have been similar to what one saw in the Broadway theater with set designer Tony Walton, costume designer Patricia Zipprodt, and lighting designer Jules Fisher each repeating their Broadway credits. The ending seems to indicate that Fosse's hand extended into this production because Pippin says that he feels "trapped" rather than "trapped, but happy." There are differences between this production and what happened on Broadway—Catherine, for example, does not sing "I Guess I'll Miss the Man" after Pippin leaves—but it is a worthwhile source for one studying the show.

The 2013 Broadway Production

Originating with the American Repertory Theatre of Cambridge, Massachusetts, *Pippin* returned to Broadway in spring 2013. It remains a show that

The Music Box, with the revival of *Pippin* playing there in May 2013. *Photo by Paul Laird*

seems to benefit from a production "hook"—like Fosse's idiosyncratic real-ization in 1972—to succeed at its highest level. Here the producers added a myriad of circus acts. Gypsy Snider of *Les 7 doigts de la main* created the circus effects, collaborating with director Diane Paulus and choreographer Chet Walker to make the show a busy feast for the eyes, especially during musical numbers. Playing the show in a circus tent that opened to the audience, the Players danced, sang, and executed spectacular acrobatics and circus tricks involving climbing poles, hanging from swings, balancing acts, tricks on large balls, hula hoops, knife-throwing, and other amusements. The show also included magic, such as the Leading Player levitating Arthur's body in a shroud after Pippin murders him and making it vanish (one of Doug Henning's tricks in *The Magic Show*) and a large box used during Fastrada's "Spread a Little Sunshine" where characters disappear, re-materialize, and others come and go. Chet Walker's choreography was "in the style of Bob Fosse," and the war sequence included Fosse's original "Manson Trio." Other major dance sequences, such as the implied orgy in "With You," also are redolent of Fosse.

Schwartz's score basically remained intact, but in some numbers the stage activity was so frenetic that the music almost became part of the background. Larry Hochman provided fine new orchestrations for two keyboard players (upright piano and synthesizer), two reed books, trumpet, trombone, vio-lin/viola, cello, guitar, bass, drums, and percussion. Pianist and conductor Charles Alterman sat with his upright instrument just below stage level, and the remainder of the orchestra was below the stage. The cast, including several Broadway notables, performed numbers effectively. Patina Miller was a wonderful vocal and dancing presence as the seductive Leading Player, while Matthew James Thomas was appealing in the title role as an actor and singer, especially in "Love Song," which he performed with Rachel Bay Jones as Catherine. A trio of well-known actors included Terence Mann as a commanding Charles, Charlotte d'Amboise as a sexy Fastrada, and Andrea Martin as a funny Berthe.

The omnipresence of circus acts appeared in the opening number "Magic to Do," establishing the production's visual tone. Pippin's "Corner of the Sky" helped set up his character, and the song's multiple reprises. Schwartz changed the lyrics significantly for "War Is a Science."[87] In this version it became the patter song that Schwartz intended when Charles condemned Pippin for interrupting him before the last verse and announces that he must finish quickly, which Mann did with aplomb. "Glory" and the war segment included the requisite solo and choral passages, but the circus atmosphere minimized any feeling of horror. Pippin's encounter with a talking head ap-

pearing about the rim of a wooden chest was effective, especially soon thereafter when someone pushed the head into the chest and carried it away. The
staging of "Simple Joys" was very busy with many ring tricks. "No Time at
All," the sing-along, should be one of the production's highlights, and it was
with Andrea Martin playing to the audience, removing her dress to reveal a
brief circus costume. She sang some of the song dangling in various positions
from a man on a trapeze, including upside down. "With You," the sweet song
that Fosse staged as an orgy, received the same treatment here, first with just
a few dancers and finally with such effects as the Leading Player entering,
dressed as a dominatrix, on top of an animal cage carrying two women. Pippin entered the cage for implied sex. Fastrada's "Spread a Little Sunshine"
was an extended circus act that opened with Charles throwing knives around
her and the box she had stood against becoming the port of disappearance
and entry for several characters. It was one of the songs where music took a
backseat, especially during the dance as Fastrada changed her costumes three
times with astonishing rapidity. "Morning Glow" served as the Act 1 finale
when they crowned Pippin; the Leading Player sang a bit of "Magic to Do"
before the conclusion to indicate that the Players are making progress toward
their promised finale.[88]

Act 2 opened with another frenetic circus scene, accompanied by music
earlier associated with Charles, now for the new king. After Pippin failed
as monarch, he declared his frustration to the Leading Player, who led him
through the duet/dance, "On the Right Track." Catherine sang "Kind of
Woman" as she supervised Pippin being put to bed, finally with three female back-up singers. Pippin was all over the stage during "Extraordinary,"
interacting angrily with the cast dressed as farm workers, pigs, and chickens.
"Love Song" started with Pippin accompanying alone on guitar; later the orchestra entered, finally fading to only the pit guitarist, and then Pippin took
over with the accompaniment to finish the song. As usual, "I Guess I'll Miss
the Man" was not listed in the program because it is not part of the Leading
Player's plans. Catherine began tentatively and unaccompanied with the
Leading Player yelling at her, but Catherine finally stated that she did have
a song there and the orchestra joined her. The finale was musically similar
to the original version. The plan for Pippin to immolate himself was enacted
literally, with him on a trapeze over a flaming cauldron; he abandoned the
effort to screams of "compromiser!" The furious Leading Player had the cast
tear down the circus tent and props for many of the tricks, in addition to removing costumes for Pippin, Catherine, and Theo. The adults left the stage,
but Theo stayed to poke around the scenery and finally started to sing "Corner of the Sky," bringing the Players back on the stage for their new target

to the music of "Magic to Do." Playing for full houses in the spring of 2013, *Pippin* won the Tony Award for Best Revival of a Musical, Schwartz's first show to win the award in such a major category. It also won for lead actress (Miller), featured actress (Martin), and director.

Conclusion

With *Godspell* and *Wicked*, *Pippin* remains part of the trio of shows that form the most famous part of Schwartz's Broadway legacy. When one considers the show's history, the initial version on Broadway was only partially what Schwartz and book writer Roger O. Hirson had thought it might be because of the huge role played by Bob Fosse in shaping it. Given the varied approaches advocated by director and writers, it might seem surprising that *Pippin* was a success at all. A more predictable outcome might have been something like the initial failure of *Candide* in 1956–1957, where at least part of the problem was the disparity in tone of Lillian Hellman's cynical book and Leonard Bernstein's ebullient score. Despite the show's difficult conception, however, *Pippin* carried a number of qualities that contemporary audiences could appreciate. Stories of a young person's personal search for fulfillment were ubiquitous in the 1960s and 1970s, combined here with Schwartz's winning tunes and Fosse's ability to create eye-popping dances and surprising theatricality. Fosse was not a versatile director and choreographer, but he manipulated *Pippin* into something that he could deliver with his characteristic verve. Given the show's success in its day and continuing life—including the successful new Broadway run—clearly the difficult collaboration bore fruit. *Pippin* is the sum of its parts, the totality of which somehow came together in the extraordinary imagination of Bob Fosse.

CHAPTER FIVE

~

The Magic Show

Beginnings

Producers Edgar Lansbury and Joe Beruh, after *Godspell*, were keen to work again with Stephen Schwartz. They had considered the possibility of a show based around magic,[1] and in late 1973 they heard from Marvin Krauss about a magic show with rock music in Toronto.[2] The show, at the Royal Alexandria Theatre, was called *Spellbound* and starred illusionist Doug Henning, a young, talented, charismatic Canadian magician.[3] The producer was Ivan Reitman, later a Hollywood movie mogul. In December 1973, Lansbury and Beruh went to see the show along with Nina Faso and Stephen Schwartz.[4] They were impressed but believed that it would require a new book and score for Broadway. Initially dubious, Schwartz was taken with Henning's illusions and agreed to do the musical as long as it would be produced during the current season, meaning that it would need to open within six months. Schwartz had seen *Pippin* take five years to reach Broadway from the time of the collegiate version, and he also experienced the rapid creation of *Godspell* at the Cherry Lane Theater. In addition, he had already committed himself to *The Baker's Wife*.[5] At this point he sought a smaller project, noting in an interview, "It was a slight idea; it was fun. I just didn't want to spend a year and a half of my life on it."[6] Schwartz states that he did not feel rushed on *The Magic Show* because he chose the schedule. He clearly does not consider it to be one of his better conceived shows because he has allowed it to fall out of the repertory; it can no longer be rented from Music Theatre International, but given the expensive machinery needed to produce the illusions,

81

few theaters or groups would try it. The show's creation, with book writer Bob Randall, director/choreographer Grover Dale, and Henning, happened quickly; Schwartz now admits that the short schedule might not have seemed ideal, but he also is not sure how much better the show could have been if they had spent longer writing it. Despite any questions on its creation, the run of over four years (1,920 performances) constituted Schwartz's third consecutive hit. *The Magic Show* appealed to audiences, mostly because of Doug Henning's extraordinary illusions. Schwartz wrote some fine songs, especially "Lion Tamer" and "West End Avenue"—and one can observe interesting growth in his use of meters in the score—but most reports on *The Magic Show* indicate that audiences came more to be astounded by magic than for the music or drama.

Producer Edgar Lansbury and director/choreographer Grover Dale have provided worthwhile accounts of putting together *The Magic Show*; useful secondary summaries have come from John Harrison and Carol de Giere.[7] Once Lansbury and Beruh saw *Spellbound*, they negotiated with Reitman and Henning to bring the show to Broadway.[8] Lansbury, Beruh, and Schwartz convinced them that they would need a new book and score. Lansbury remembers that Henning was protective of his illusions and believed that nobody else could perform them, but when he left the New York production the show ran on with another actor taking his part, and there was also a touring production. Lansbury was in California shooting a film for most of the show's rehearsal period, but he remembers returning to New York before a publicity stunt at Grand Army Plaza where Henning and actress Dale Soules performed an illusion from the show, said to be in honor of the centenary of Harry Houdini's birth.[9] Lansbury was pleased with both the writing and the show's cast, and remembers, as in *Godspell*, that Schwartz was involved in every aspect of the production. Lansbury and Beruh tried to arrange a London production with Cameron Mackintosh as the British producer, even having the script rewritten to take place in an English club and adjusting the songs for a British audience, but the effort bore no fruit. Given recent changes in performance of magic, exemplified by David Copperfield and his splashy Las Vegas shows, Lansbury expressed doubts as to whether what happened in *The Magic Show* would be successful today. He unsuccessfully tried to pursue producing a version of *The Magic Show* in Las Vegas through the William Morris Agency.

Grover Dale wrote a humorous essay on the show's creation for the souvenir program book.[10] Joe Beruh called Dale in January 1974 to ask him to go to Toronto and see Henning's show. Dale was amused that they intended to make a musical starring someone who had not trained in acting, singing, or dancing, and the first rehearsal was scheduled for 1 April, although they lacked both a book and a score. Beruh assured Dale that the magic was worthwhile, however, and Dale agreed to go to Toronto, partly because he needed the work. As Dale put it, "We went. We saw. We were amazed. We were dismayed."[11] (Dale's final reaction perhaps referred to Henning's lack of typical Broadway talents.) A few days later Dale met Schwartz and discovered that they had similar ideas on how to craft a musical around Henning's act. The plot included four main characters, with the "dream girl" played by Dale's wife, Anita Morris.[12] Dale notes that the creators advised Henning to eschew his usual "rock star" outfits and appear in casual dress, a striking change from the magician's traditional tuxedo.[13] After Lansbury and Beruh told Dale and Schwartz how little money they would probably be able to raise, Dale said he would require a simple set and Schwartz asked for an accompanying ensemble of only seven musicians; other collaborators also kept expenses down.[14] Bob Randall, author of the play *2 Rms Riv Vu*, agreed to fashion a script around Henning's illusions and Schwartz's songs,[15] a task that Dale reports took "less than eight days."[16] According to Harrison, the hardest aspect of the book was deciding how Henning's character would take revenge on the other magician at the end; Schwartz did not believe that they ever fully worked out that part of the plot.[17] The producers allowed rehearsals to begin before securing even half of the funding, and Dale remembers being harried: "There wasn't time to 'redo' anything. We were working at top speed."[18] They lost one week replacing an actor who had infectious hepatitis. The production arrived at the Cort Theater on 5 May 1974; Dale remembers a blur of activity before first previews and the premiere on 28 May.[19] A press release stated that previews began on 14 May 1974; it also provided the names of some of Henning's illusions: "The Floating Woman," "The Mis-Made Girl," "The Neon Tubes," "The Bed of Horrors," "ESP," "The Zig-Zag Woman," and "Beauty into Beast."[20]

Schwartz retains some specific memories on creating the show. He notes that Henning was "a real, original personality," and Schwartz enjoyed being part of one of the first Broadway musicals to feature magic. His credit line for *The Magic Show* read "songs by" rather than "music and lyrics by" because Schwartz did not really think of his work as forming a score, describing the show as "some songs and this magic act," but he did craft songs to appear in specific places in the plot. Schwartz comments on the challenge and delight he found in writing the show:

What was fun about writing *The Magic Show* was that Doug didn't sing—couldn't sing . . . and we tried to figure out how to incorporate them into a story so that they became the musical numbers. It was really fun—it was sort of like doing *Crazy for You* and being given all of these Gershwin songs and figuring, "How are we going to put a story around these songs?" Except they were magic illusions instead.

The story takes place in a club called the Top Hat in Passaic, New Jersey, owned by Manny (played by Robert LuPone). A female singing duo (Cheryl Barnes, Annie McGreevey) and a fading, alcoholic magician named Feldman (David Ogden Stiers[21]) that work there are seeking their big break, which might occur when they are visited by Mr. Goldfarb, an important agent. The club's owner hires a stellar new magician, Doug Henning. His assistant is a tomboy named Cal (Dale Soules) who has a crush on him, but Henning has never really noticed her. The resentful, older magician tells him that he has no style; in response Henning causes a beautiful woman, Charmin (Anita Morris), to materialize. Cal becomes jealous and manages to get Henning's character to fall in love with her. He turns Charmin into a lion that Cal can tame, because her fondest wish is to have such an animal act. On Broadway the show was done without intermission. As Schwartz notes, "It's not a great, deep plot, but then neither is *Crazy for You.*" For Schwartz the show was at least as deep as *42nd Street* and was an excuse to bring magic to a Broadway musical. He likens it to something like the Disney shows now on Broadway, which can be enjoyed by children and also be of interest to adults, but *The Magic Show* was much less expensive to put on than a typical Disney musical.

The Music

Schwartz wrote several of his songs to be used with illusions, such as "Lion Tamer," sung by Cal on a platform twenty feet above the stage just before Doug suspended her over a sword.[22] "Charmin's Lament" was sung by Anita Morris just after Doug had conjured her up. In "Two's Company," Doug performed a trick with Cal as the female singing duo called her the "third wheel" now that Doug had Charmin. Cal was prone on a table and Doug covered her with a cloth before levitating her. The end of the song includes the lyrics "at the count of 1, 2, 3," and on the next beat Doug grabbed the cloth as Cal disappeared.

Schwartz began *The Magic Show* with the notion that he should use "tricky meters" (such as complex and mixed meters) as a musical cognate for illusions, perhaps continuing from "Love Song" in *Pippin* and remembering "Alas for You" from *Godspell.* Schwartz did not carry this intention throughout the entire score of *The Magic Show* but, as will be shown, the composer went beyond typical meters associated with popular music in *The Magic Show*.

Consideration of songs from *The Magic Show* in our interview led us into Schwartz's use of speech rhythms, another feature that became more frequent in his songs for this show. Schwartz spoke of his interest in speech rhythms; by the time he was working on *Séance on a Wet Afternoon* he found himself writing into the score "parlando," or in the rhythm of speech. He considers such rhythms basic to his work: "I guess part of it is because, for me, it's an extension of the dramatic story-telling. I think most of the contemporary theater writers tend to write in speech rhythms." He mentioned Bernstein and Sondheim as other exponents of the ideal. Schwartz does not believe that this was always the case in American theater music, noting, "Jerome Kern tended to do the whole-note thing . . . where he stretched time more melodically." When composing, if lyrics exist before the music, Schwartz finds himself following the text's implied rhythms, but often he writes both at once, meaning that the melodic line can be bent to freshly written lyrics. Several songs in *The Magic Show* open with recitative, where one expects rhythms close to those of speech, but Schwartz also made this choice in sections with a stronger sense of meter, such as in "West End Avenue." This is more the rule than the exception in *The Magic Show*; such precision in rendering speech rhythms becomes more difficult when music exists before lyrics, which is how Schwartz has usually found himself working with other composers. Generally Schwartz finds it "slightly more difficult to be the lyricist," but it is also "nice to have a collaborator to fall back on."

Songs for *The Magic Show*, like *Godspell* and *Pippin*, offer a tour of popular musical styles. Schwartz admitted this in an interview the summer after the show opened, stating that he consciously wrote songs in different styles while "keeping in mind the musical accompaniment necessary to help create the magical illusion."[23] In our interview, Schwartz described what he considers Bernstein's strong influence in some songs for *The Magic Show*. We noted in the previous chapter that Schwartz considers "Love Song" from *Pippin* "a breakthrough" where he acknowledges Bernstein's influence on constantly shifting meters.[24] Schwartz further accessed for *The Magic Show* what one might call his "inner Lenny" in "Lion Tamer" and "West End Avenue."

"Lion Tamer" is in a deliberate tempo and fairly consistent 7/4 with strong, marked rhythms. Schwartz typically separates the meter into 3+4, with the triple often subdivided into two dotted quarter notes in both the melody and bass. Much of the melody is conjunct, but Schwartz also draws upon perhaps another Bernstein influence with angular melodies, especially at the ends of phrases. Bernstein showed a strong predilection for disjunct melodies, such as in "A Simple Song" from *Mass*. In terms of its lyricism and 7/4 meter, "Lion Tamer" resembles the opening of Bernstein's "Oh, Happy We" from *Candide*. Schwartz reports that the older composer liked "Lion Tamer." After seeing *The Magic Show*, according to Schwartz, Bernstein remarked, "That song is going to step out."

"West End Avenue" is more energetic than "Lion Tamer." It is primarily in 7/4, but there are also sections of shifting meters, especially between 9/8 and 3/4, the kind of rhythmic interest that Bernstein loved to bring to his music, such as in the second movement, "Profanation" of the Symphony No. 1, *Jeremiah*. Like 7/4 measures in "Lion Tamer," "West End Avenue" includes the basic rhythm of two dotted quarter notes in the opening triple subdivisions. There are also 8/4 bars that start with similar gestures. The song's melody is mostly conjunct and bears a rich sense of syncopation. The harmonies at times tend toward the dissonant, especially at the end with a number of added tone chords as the singer holds a b' against alternations of an F major chord and a G chord with C in the bass, another element that sounds a bit like Bernstein. Even the song's topic takes on an odd Bernstein resonance because his shows often involved New York City.

The following musical numbers were included in the Broadway version of *The Magic Show*, performed by the named members of the cast:

"Up to His Old Tricks"—Entire Company
"Solid Silver Platform Shoes"—Dina, Donna
"Lion Tamer"—Cal
"Style"—Feldman and Company
"Charmin's Lament"—Charmin
"Two's Company"—Dina, Donna
"The Goldfarb Variations"—Dina, Feldman, Donna, Manny, and Charmin
"Doug's Act"—Doug
"A Bit of Villainy"—Feldman, Dina, Donna
"West End Avenue"—Cal
"Sweet, Sweet, Sweet"—Charmin, Manny, Mike, and Steve
"Before Your Very Eyes"—Dina, Donna, and Feldman

As noted earlier, the orchestra was only seven musicians: two keyboard players, two guitarists, bassist, drummer, and percussionist. The conductor/keyboard player was Stephen Reinhardt, also music director of *Godspell*; Paul Shaffer (music director of *Godspell* in Toronto) played the other keyboard. As in *Godspell*, the orchestra was on a high platform against the stage's back wall. Reinhardt recalls that the show's music was "more pianistically challenging" than in *Godspell*, but the musicians with whom he worked were "more experienced."[25]

The following description of songs from *The Magic Show* is based upon the original cast recording (OCR) and published *Vocal Selection* [*sic*], the printed musical source used in the following analysis.[26] The opening number, "Up to His Old Tricks," demonstrates Schwartz's pursuit of heightened rhythmic interest. The OCR begins with a drum roll under noodling on the piano and tinkling from the mark tree before one hears the introduction provided in the published version (OCR, track 1, 0'51"ff). Although primarily in common time, the introduction includes measures of 3/4 and 5/4, and Schwartz's opening gesture in the right hand is 3+3+3+3+4 in eighth notes over the first two measures. Each group of three is a quick alternation from one note to its lower neighbor and back, and then two more measures, the first a rumba rhythm (3+3+2) and then a concluding 3/4 measure with a descending eighth-note arpeggio that leads to the entire gesture's repetition. It is a distinctive opening that carries a hint of Bernstein. The segment returns several times during the song. The A section, repeated with different text (first verse, track 1, 1'02"–1'34"), is in four phrases, aabc (five bars+6+5+10). It is mostly conjunct and harmonically predictable, but with lively rhythms notated primarily in 4/4 and 2/4. The text comments on the excitement of magic, and specifically "Doug, the magic man, up to his old tricks." Schwartz's contrasting B section (2'12"–2'54") begins as the second time through A cadences straight into the new 3/4 meter, where soloists refer to specific tricks and the chorus speaks exclamations ("Hooray! Ooh!"), all over a simple waltz accompaniment. The vocal line here tends toward the disjunct and the overall feeling is similar to 3/4 sections of "At the Ballet" from *A Chorus Line*, which postdated Schwartz's song by about a year. The published version of "Tricks" then returns to the introductory gesture and concludes with bc of the A section with new text in b (track 1, 4'10"–4'54"). Before this concluding material on the OCR there is primarily instrumental music to accompany an illusion (2'54"–3'32") that sounds a bit like vaudeville, but with the more interesting rhythmic material heard elsewhere in this song and then the chorus commenting that the illusion was "fun" unless you "know how it's done." The next section (starting at 3'32") is also reminiscent of vaudeville, and the chorus sings with an underwater effect.

Schwartz returns to his rock roots for the first female duet, "Solid Silver Platform Shoes," marked "Fifties rock ballad" in the score. He reports that an influence here was a cover of "Mockingbird" (an old folk song) performed by James Taylor and Carly Simon in a straight-ahead rock version with

Taylor and Simon singing the same lyrics but to different rhythms. Schwartz mimics this exciting effect in the main section of "Platform Shoes" (track 2, 0'48"–1'30"), and it works well on the OCR (where the two vocal lines could be mixed), but he admits that it was difficult to understand the lyrics from the stage. The songwriter reports that the two sleazy nightclub singers performing the song had huge hair and shoes with very high platforms, looking like Donna Summer in the 1970s; the feel of "Solid Silver Platform Shoes" falls somewhere between 1950s rock and the sound that one associates with Summer's disco hits. The A section (0'00"–0'48"), in F major, is a driving 6/8. The melody line operates in a narrow range over constant eighth note chords in the right hand. The B section is the segment inspired by the Taylor-Simon rendition of "Mockingbird." Schwartz manages a visceral affect with both singers tearing into two verses of varied and alternating material in F minor in which they tout the benefits of having "a solid gold record and solid silver platform shoes." A brief, contrasting section, C (1'30"–1'44"), largely homorhythmic and in parallel thirds and sixths, leads to a return of B (1'44"–2'00"), followed by an instrumental interruption (2'00"–2'24") based upon B that is not in the published version. A version of B with more of the energetic counterpoint concludes the song.

Stylistically nearly the antithesis of "Solid Silver Platform Shoes," "Lion Tamer" helps delineate Cal's character, showing that her desire for this unusual profession would be a preface to learning how to deal with men. The song's simple earnestness places her far from bitter machinations elsewhere in the plot. The rhythm and meter were considered earlier; it is notable how much of the song is based upon that basic rhythmic idea. That, combined with economic use of motives, lends the song a satisfyingly taut structure. The form is ternary, with a repeated first section following a short introduction (track 3, 0'11"–2'00") that includes fairly simple harmonies in the prevailing F major, but the composer does make a foray to A-flat in the sixth measure, moving back quickly to C through a D minor seventh chord. The central section (2'00"–2'31"), based on the same material, reveals Cal's intention to confront men. As she announces this, Schwartz abandons septuple meter and inserts two bars in common time. The segment begins in E minor and moves unexpectedly to A major at the conclusion after we reach the surprising word *men*, setting up the tonic D minor that opens the closing A. Cal admits that this is her first prayer, and Schwartz ends with a plagal cadence (like the "A-men" of a hymn) in C major.

The older magician Feldman sings "Style" in mockery of Doug, finding unacceptable his casual dress and demeanor. Sung by David Ogden Stiers on the OCR, it is an exercise in name-dropping and feigned elegance. The lyrics include mention of such figures as Rex Reed, Jascha Heifetz, Conrad Hilton, Joanne Woodward, and others, and Schwartz also used French to help set the mood. There is, however, an ironic touch because in places Feldman and his backup ensemble chants or sings "Alouette, gentil Alouette, Alouette, je te plumerai," hardly a true indication of savoir faire. Schwartz notes that he "doomed" himself with the song because it became popular, and as singers perform it in revues they feel that they must update the names, meaning, for example, that "Conrad Hilton" might become "Paris Hilton." Schwartz states, "I somehow thought it would be like 'You're the Top,' you know, and no one would care. Cole Porter is referring to people and things [they haven't heard of]. Nobody knows who many of those people are anymore." "Style" opens with recitative that Stiers mostly speaks, and then Schwartz provides the indication "Reggae," identifying the song's basic beat and feeling. The songwriter reports his fascination with the drum loop in the hit song "I'll Take You There" (1971) from the Staple Singers, and for "Style" he "expanded out of it" in establishing the song's groove (track 4, 0'31"–0'40"). Schwartz alternates a nine-measure refrain (0'40"–0'58") with other material, all of it sounding appropriate within the song's ambience, including the jaunty bass line, Hammond B-3 insertions during rests in the vocal line, and female backup chorus.

Schwartz continued his chameleon-like stylistic transformations between songs in "Charmin's Lament," where he ambled into the world of country rock, inspired by performer Anita Morris's roots in North Carolina. Charmin laments her "obvious femininity" because magicians constantly summon her for sexual release. The lyrics are clever, drawing on the kind of euphemistic imagery one often encounters in the blues ("I'll appear before a genie/Who wants me to roast his weenie"), presented here with a country twang, slide guitar, and appropriate percussion. At one point Doug assures Charmin that she misunderstands his intentions because he wants to saw her in half, another reason for her to lament.[27] After the recitative, Schwartz provided four verses in predictable, four-measure phrases with various endings and a coda with opportunities for country yodels and bluesy melismas.

"Two's Company" is the song that Dina and Donna sing to Cal as Doug levitates her off a table under a cloth. As noted earlier, her subsequent disappearance was timed to take place just as they counted to three at the end of the song. Schwartz marked it "Blues ballad" and calls it an example of "doing my Irving Berlin thing again" with two tunes placed in counterpoint. Dina opens with a sixteen-measure idea with four phrases of equal length (aabc) that Schwartz infuses with blues notes and places in a swinging 12/8. Donna's tune is a jazzy patter song of thirty-two bars, also in four-measure phrases, with Dina's idea placed against it in augmentation. Schwartz's inspiration for the song was partly a member of the accompanying instrumental ensemble:

> It sounded to me like something that would be played while people were having a drink, and it had that attitude, but I actually wrote that song, particularly that part of it, because Paul Shaffer, I knew, was going to do the keyboard, and he could do all that cool, kind of jazzy improvisation, and so I did that for Paul, and I gave it to him with the basic chords, which are jazz chords, and just said, "Do your thing!"

The version of "Two's Company" on the OCR includes interpolated piano solos, presumably played by Shaffer, that are not in the published score.

The next song placement involved four characters (Feldman, Dina, Donna, and club owner Manny) reacting to the impending visit of Mr. Goldfarb, an agent. Schwartz made a musician's association: since "Goldfarb" sounds like "Goldberg," he decided to write a Bach-like fugue. He had written one while a student in the Juilliard Preparatory Division and used it for a song in *Nouveau*, which Schwartz worked on at Carnegie Mellon (see Chapter 1). He had wanted a fugue for a song called "The New Society," sung by wealthy art patrons in a gallery, and he recycled his Juilliard exercise. He used the same music with a different text for "The Goldfarb Variations," a number that contrasts strongly with the show's other songs.

The next two numbers, "Doug's Act" and "A Bit of Villainy," did not appear on the OCR or in published selections. The first was musical underscoring for a twenty-minute segment where Henning performed magic tricks involving prestidigitation that were not worked into the plot. David Spangler, the dance arranger, assisted Schwartz on this number.[28] "A Bit of Villainy" was a brief vocal introduction and underscoring for another illusion, this performed as part of a fantasy sequence where Feldman, Dina, and Donna imagine disposing of Doug. The staged illusion appeared to be anything but a fantasy, as it looked like they chained Henning up and dropped a bed of spikes on him, after which Doug appeared safely elsewhere on stage.

"West End Avenue," described earlier as a song that shows Bernstein's influence, is sung by Cal, who feels no longer needed after Doug has conjured up Charmin.[29] The lyrics speak of how she tried to get away from her old neighborhood, but now she will return. The demanding rhythms and active accompaniment make the song a tour de force for a pianist; Schwartz once met a musical director who had been an accompanist, and the man punched him on the arm, stating, "That was for making me sight-read 'West End Avenue' at all those auditions." Schwartz remembers that he wrote the song quickly, lyrics and the music simultaneously. The song features strong rhythmic and motivic unity and is in an overall AABA' form, but material from A occurs often in the B section. Cal states what was her resolve to get out of the neighborhood in the first two sections, which are identical musically, and in the B section she admits that her life has not worked out the way that she had hoped, and she regrets her return home in A'. The jaunty rhythms seem a bit ironic when compared with the rueful affect, but it is also one of Schwartz's most tautly conceived songs.

"Sweet, Sweet, Sweet" was Anita Morris's solo dance number. Schwartz admits that it was in the show on the slim pretext that she needed to encourage Henning to seek revenge on Feldman, Dina, and Donna. Schwartz spoke about the type of music that he chose: "It was sort of the dance music rhythm of that period, which was also what Marvin Hamlisch was jumping from in the dance music for *A Chorus Line*." Indeed, sections of "The Music and the Mirror" from Hamlisch's slightly later score sound very much like "Sweet, Sweet, Sweet" in terms of instrumental choices and musical effects. Both numbers are creatures from the 1970s that orchestrators might choose to revise today, but the vocal portion of the song does not sound dated. It starts somewhat like a recitative, but intended more for singing than the opening of "Style," and Morris sings every note. After she announces that the three little words one must remember are "Revenge is sweet," Schwartz launches into an exciting section (track 9, 0'45"ff) designated "Moderately slow rock" that begins with a repeated section dominated by six rapid pick-ups to several of the measures, often on a g-natural headed into a tonic A minor chord, playing consistently with the modal sound of rock. In the next section (1'40"ff) Schwartz builds on the same idea of six rapid pick-ups, but makes each phrase a bit longer, sometimes with quick rumba rhythms (3+3+2 in sixteenth notes) in the prevailing quadruple meter. A lengthy dance portion sounds on the recording before a short vocal coda based on a similar idea for soloist and men's chorus ends the song.

The musical's finale was "Before Your Very Eyes," a number where Schwartz perhaps returned to what was on his mind when he wrote *Godspell*. Indeed, the songwriter states, "That ['Before Your Very Eyes'] was really straight Motown in terms of the drum rhythm . . . what I call 1–4 drumming where there's a hit on every single beat. . . . If you listen to early Supremes records, that's what the drumming is like." The dramatic context is Doug's revenge on Dina and Donna. As they sing "Before Your Very Eyes" for Mr. Goldfarb, Doug uses magic to distract them, but afterward all ends happily. As Schwartz offered, "It's that kind of show." The form is a simple AABA and the text is primarily like that of a typical pop love song, but with some lyrics that invoke magic imagery. The song includes a prominent clap track, like some songs in *Godspell*.

Other songs have been associated with *The Magic Show*. David Koyle, a Canadian, freelance television director, met Henning and became interested in filming a staged version.[30] The project was completed in 1981. They filmed it at Queen Elizabeth Theatre at Exhibition Place in Toronto with direction by Norman Campbell and musical numbers and dances staged by Sammy Dallas Bayes. It was shown on the Canadian Broadcasting Corporation (CBC) in 1982 and never released in theaters, but today is available on DVD.[31] Schwartz earlier had told parties interested in reviving *The Magic Show* that he thought it needed a new book and he wished to compose new songs,[32] so rewriting took place for the filmed version. Jerry Ross wrote the new book based upon the same story. Schwartz replaced four songs: "Solid Silver Platform Shoes" with "It's Gonna Take a Magician," "Charmin's Lament" with "Admired from Afar" (which Schwartz likes), "West End Avenue" with "Where Did the Magic Go?" and "A Bit of Villainy" with "A Round for the Bad Guys" (Schwartz calls the latter "a much better song"). According to Harrison, Schwartz believed that "Charmin's Lament" was "too bawdy for what had become a family show," and other songs he wanted to make less dependent on New York for their appeal (explaining the departure of "West End Avenue") or he needed to update references (such as the lyrics of "Style").[33] Compared to the Broadway production, this filmed version included a fuller orchestra with added winds and strings. The musical numbers in the film include the following:

"Up to His Old Tricks"—Ensemble
"It's Gonna Take a Magician"—Dina, Donna, Van Zyskind (the other magician)
"Lion Tamer"—Cal
"Style"—Van Zyskind and Ensemble
"Two's Company"—Dina, Donna
"Admired from Afar"—Charmin
"A Round for the Bad Guys"—Van Zyskind and Ensemble
"Where Did the Magic Go?"—Cal
"Right before Your Very Eyes"—Dina, Donna, Van Zyskind
"It's Gonna Take a Magician" (reprise)—Dina, Donna
"Admired from Afar" (reprise)—Charmin
"Lion Tamer" (reprise)—Ensemble
Bows: "Up to His Old Tricks" (reprise)—Ensemble

The film convincingly presents Henning's extraordinary illusions. Some occur during songs and the remainder with underscoring, including several that were not in the Broadway production.[34] Didi Conn makes an appealing Cal, and although it is interesting to have Anita Morris as Charmin on video, she does not sing the number that she sang on Broadway ("Sweet, Sweet, Sweet" was cut) and only has a brief solo dance during the song "Admired from Afar." The bumbling magician in the production, played adequately by Jon Finlayson, is named Van Zyskind. Overall, this version of *The Magic Show* seems a bit forced, but it cannot be compared to the original. Harrison believes that Henning and Schwartz, as they tried to improve it, "lost sight of the fact that the show's greatest appeal was its innocence."[35] Whatever the case, the film disappeared from sight until its DVD release in 2000.[36]

The Magic Show played on Broadway for over four years, but it has not often been produced since it closed in 1978 and the national tour ended, meaning that its songs have not been heard nearly as much as those from *Godspell* and *Pippin*. Although *The Magic Show* is one of Schwartz's lesser-known collection of songs, it includes several numbers of high quality.

Reception

The reception of a musical is a complicated phenomenon that can only be imprecisely assessed through reviews, consideration of commercial success, and anecdotal evidence, but the case of *The Magic Show* seems fairly clear. The commercial success, with a run of 1,920 performances (28 May 1974 to 31 December 1978)—including 920 repetitions after Henning left—was undeniable.[37] When it closed, it was the thirteenth longest running musical ever.[38] Toward the end of the run, *Variety* reported that the profit had been over $1 million and that touring versions had made money.[39] Apparently the Shubert Organization, which owned the Cort Theater where the show played its entire run, believed that *The Magic Show* might still have some "legs" in October 1978 after attendance had started to dip; the corporation underwrote losses in return for a share of future profits.[40] *The Magic Show*, however, closed at the end of the year.

With few exceptions, critics found Henning and his illusions extraordinary, but they were less sanguine about the remainder of the show.[41] Creators knew that magic would dominate and conceived other material as a vehicle for Henning's talents. A questionable book or unmemorable songs were more forgivable than poor presentation of the illusions. A survey of critical opinion effectively documents contemporary appraisal of *The Magic Show*. We will approach these published reactions to the show, as in other chapters, in chronological order. There was no shortage of critics at the premiere; Harrison reports that 600 press outlets were invited, and 400 members of the audience on opening night had press passes.[42]

The morning after opening night, 29 May, the major New York dailies and *Variety* weighed in on the show. Clive Barnes, writing for the *New York Times*, gave it an "adulterated rave." Henning was "terrific" but the musical was "awful." Barnes had no idea how any of the tricks were accomplished, but the songs "all sounded much alike" and Randall's book "was not clever enough to be camp and not smart enough . . . to be silly."[43] Douglas Watt in the *Daily News* found Henning "gifted" but did not think that he rose above the "slapdash affair" around him. Watt called Randall's book "flimsy" and gives Schwartz the backhanded slap that he "has been engaged to write some songs." The critic expressed some praise for "West End Avenue," but "Style" "doesn't have enough of it."[44] In his review in the *New York Post* Richard Watts spoke admiringly about Henning through most of the review and praised David Ogden Stiers and Dale Soules as actors, but said that one does not "have to bother" with the book and there is little that he could say about the songs because the lyrics "were inaudible." The show, however, was "a lot of fun" because of the magic.[45] Longtime *Variety* critic Hobe Morrison found the show "utterly inconsequential" but "diverting," and believed that it might provide the first hit at the Cort Theater in years. Morrison described Henning as "an expert magician" and offered that the songs "tend to sound alike" and were "quickly forgettable."[46]

The next day, 30 May, Martin Gottfried published his reaction in *Women's Wear Daily*. He was agog about the magic, but thought that with Henning's lack of stage presence he should have remained behind the scenes. For Gottfried the main problem was the book, which he called "probably the worst story you could imagine for a magic show." Unlike some critics, Gottfried noticed the variety of styles in Schwartz's music, but he found it "disorganized" while showing "some quality" when one got past the excessive amplification.[47] The *Christian Science Monitor*'s John Beaufort offered his opinion on 31 May, praising many elements but believing that "this novel piece of showmanship doesn't quite come off." He described the music as "pleasant enough and not overly amplified." Randall's plot was "accommodating," staying out of the way of Henning's illusions.[48]

Reaction continued into June from weekly journals and other sources. Ross Wetzsteon of the *Village Voice* provided the delicious detail that Henning, through a crack in the curtain, could be seen jumping for joy at the opening night ovation. Wetzsteon was fairly sure that he saw how several tricks were done, but he also believed that Henning's future career was assured. He thought that Randall and Schwartz must have planned their contributions "over a hurried lunch," and dismissed aspects of the show as "Seedy Sondheim."[49] Lillian Africano, writing in the *Villager*, deemed the show a "fullblown frolic" for the magical component, but as a musical "sluggishly earthbound." The book "isn't bad," but the songs "have a recycled sound," too close to those of *Godspell* and *Pippin*.[50] On 8 June Edwin Wilson offered an evaluation from his perch at the *Wall Street Journal*, rhapsodizing about the magic, but severely criticizing the book and songs, suggesting that Henning should have made them disappear early in the show.[51] Noted Broadway critic Walter Kerr wrote a review for the *New York Times* the next day, echoing the popular line and almost entirely concentrating on the magic, but noting that he saw Anita Morris's legs "skip away" from the cage when she seems to be turned into a cougar. Kerr mentioned the "feeble story" and "gratuitous and even monotonous songs," like Wilson suggesting that Henning should have made both vanish.[52]

Reviews appeared in three major weekly journals on 10 June. Brendan Gill of the *New Yorker* took equal delight in describing the magic and skewering the book and music, effectively summarizing his thoughts with the line "a first-rate magician has a lot to lose and nothing to gain from allowing himself to be encapsulated in a fifth-rate musical."[53] T. E. Kalem in *Time* covered the same territory, going so far as to suggest that the songs (which he attributes erroneously to both Schwartz and Henning) "seem to have been composed under water and piped directly from the ocean floor in all their gurgly indecipherability."[54] *Newsweek*'s Jack Kroll offered similar thoughts, basically ignoring the book and music, dismissing them only as a "semi-musical comedy format."[55] John Simon piled on in *New York* a week later, again describing how Henning manages to amaze everyone while tossing barbs at the "dry, wizened book" and "lackluster lyrics and tunes."[56]

Theatrical reviews have seldom been good places to look for solid information and informed opinions about a show's score, and, as described earlier, *The Magic Show* included effective songs and examples of competent craftsmanship. Robert Adels wrote mostly about the score in a review in *Record World* from 22 June, demonstrating a sophisticated interest in what Schwartz tried to accomplish. He opened by citing the effective television commercial that was helping to fill the Cort Theater, and called the musical "a family show."[57] He stated that the cast was just then in the process of recording the original cast album at A&R Studios, which he expected to be "the most long-awaited Broadway album of the season." For Adels, Schwartz's score was "more than serviceable," landing somewhere between *The Fantasticks* and *Hair* in inspiration. He predicted that some songs in *The Magic Show* might become huge hits like "Day by Day" and "Corner of the Sky." Adels found "Lion Tamer" the "most accessible song," but he also had specific praise for the following: "Sweet, Sweet, Sweet" as effective in the funky "Shaft" tradition; "Before Your Very Eyes" as a chameleon that might prove popular with the young crowd; "Solid Silver Platform Shoes," which he described as "specifically written as a Bette Midler parody"; "West End Avenue," with a story that could be told in any contemporary American city; and "Two's Company," which "successfully deals with the psychological components of a relationship." The critic was not troubled by the thin plot, because one is too busy trying to understand the illusions. He clearly thought the show would become a hit.[58]

Two reviews that appeared in July blew hot and cold about Schwartz's music. Richard Philip, writing for *After Dark*, wrote a positive appraisal of the show, especially the songs. He praised Schwartz's "flare [sic] for New York–type lyrics," such as the rhyme of "gay bars" and "Zabars" in "West Side Avenue," part of "the plangent, often memorable score." He lauded Anita Morris in "Charmin's Lament," calling it a "show-stopper."[59] In *Show Business*, Debbi Wasserman stated that *The Magic Show* does not have "outstanding book or memorable music or a polished cohesive production."[60]

This survey of seventeen reviews demonstrates that the "received opinion" on *The Magic Show* was consistent praise for the amazing illusions and criticism, and sometimes outright dismissal of the book and score. The plot, however, was literally conceived around the list of illusions, and those that did not fit in the plot occurred in the segment called "Doug's Act." Most Broadway musicals do not include such an important element besides story, music, and dance. If Randall's book was poorly received, he accomplished the intention of crafting a plot that tied the show together. Schwartz's songs were unappreciated by some, but in retrospect we can come closer to evaluating the score.

The Magic Show in Other Locations

The show's popularity dictated the formation of a touring company, and evidence remains of performances of *The Magic Show* in various cities in the Northeast between 1975 and 1979.[61] Some of these were part of an organized tour run by the Broadway producers, but others might have been local efforts. A Lansbury-Beruh-Reitman touring version of the musical played at the Shubert Theater in New Haven, Connecticut, from 4 to 16 February 1975. This was while Henning was still in the show at the Cort Theater; he trained Peter DePaula to perform his illusions.[62] As on Broadway, the touring version was staged by Grover Dale. It also ran at the Forrest Theater in Philadelphia.

Joseph Abaldo played a minor role and was DePaula's understudy; Pippa Pearthree played the role of Cal.[63]

Joseph Abaldo offered a brief interview for the radio series *This Is Broadway* in 1978.[64] Abaldo stated that he was first hired to be an understudy for eight months on the national tour after demonstrating his ability to sing, dance, and act; his audition for the magical portion of the lead role included showing that he could walk on a high platform without fear. Then he met Henning, with whom he worked extensively on performing the illusions. Abaldo had always been interested in magic, and he worked with Henning for two years before going on in the role, which he performed for more than two years on Broadway and then in productions in a number of other cities. He reported that everyone involved in the production signed an agreement that they would not divulge any of Henning's secrets.

The Magic Show appeared in a production at the Studio Arena Theater in Buffalo, New York, in 1976. The program reports that the production was "Restaged for Studio Arena Theatre by Jay Fox," who served as assistant to Grover Dale and dance captain on Broadway. Abaldo was the lead; the program stated "Magic by Doug Henning." Unlike the New York City production, this was in two acts, and musical numbers appear to have been similar except for the finale, which in Buffalo was a reprise of "Solid Silver Platform Shoes." The production was before Abaldo took over for Henning in the Broadway production; Henning's last performance was 31 October 1976.[65]

A production of *The Magic Show* took place in Detroit at the Fisher Theater from 1 to 19 August 1978. Edgar Lansbury produced the show along with Robert S. Fishko and Irving Siders, and magic credit again went to Doug Henning. The lead was Robert Carello, and the orchestra included Doug Quinn on guitar and Marty Quinn on percussion, two brothers who played in *Godspell* at the La MaMa in 1971.

After *The Magic Show* closed on Broadway at the end of 1978, Abaldo went on another tour. It played at the Westport County Playhouse in Connecticut in July 1979, reviewed positively by Sarey Bernstein in the *Westport News*.[66] The show was at the Pocono Playhouse in Pennsylvania from 9 to 14 July, at the Ogunquit Playhouse in Maine from 23 to 28 July, and at the Guild Hall in East Hampton, New York, from 1 to 4 August, where they also added an extra matinee.

Conclusion

In the context of Stephen Schwartz's career, *The Magic Show* was an anomaly: a commercial success that yielded little in terms of his career legacy. Except for a few songs that have remained in circulation, little of Schwartz's work on the show has had any staying power. The show remains unavailable for rental, but, as previously noted, the huge expense for illusions made it very unlikely to have been a popular choice for regional or amateur companies.

In his biography of Doug Henning, John Harrison tries to place the show within a historical context, noting that musicals such as *Hair, Jesus Christ Superstar, Godspell,* and *Pippin* helped change the American musical theater, making possible *The Magic Show* and other unusual properties.[67] The shows that he names were preceded by *Cabaret* and others, which had already helped replace what might be called the "Rodgers and Hammerstein model" with new ideas and different types of dramatic creativity, but *The Magic Show* was unique because its conventional Broadway side was a shell for Henning's illusions. *The Magic Show* did not change the history of the Broadway musical, but, as Schwartz noted earlier, it was a true family show, unusual on Broadway before Disney's participation in the medium began in the late 1980s. Harrison also offered this point and states that *The Magic Show* and Doug Henning were important parts of reinvigorating magic in popular entertainment.[68]

CHAPTER SIX

◠

The Baker's Wife

No project of Stephen Schwartz's life better illustrates his tenacity than *The Baker's Wife*, which he worked on with book author Joseph Stein and other collaborators for nearly three decades before it arrived at a point where the writers considered it finished. The saga began with a long pre-Broadway tour in 1976 that never opened on Broadway, and did not end until the production at Paper Mill Playhouse in Milburn, New Jersey, in 2005. Schwartz's son Scott once commented that his father had worked on the show his entire life, and the composer/lyricist has described *The Baker's Wife* as "an enormously tortuous process."[1] That difficult slog, however, bore fruit. Many musicals that close before making it to New York or have disappointing runs on Broadway are never heard from again. Schwartz and Stein, however, never gave up on *The Baker's Wife*, and they finally produced an entertaining show with both heart and brains. Gordon Greenberg, a director who entered the process for the last five years or so of the show's development, calls *The Baker's Wife* a "terrific" show that "can take its rightful place beside other classic musicals."[2] That may go a bit far for some commentators, but Greenberg is correct when he compares it to "classic musicals," because *The Baker's Wife* carries that quality, espousing traditional values and a somewhat realistic feeling. It is very different from Schwartz's first three shows and a fine example of his compositional range.

The Original Production

Carol de Giere told the story of the show's initial creation and its ill-fated tour in 1976 in her biography of Schwartz,[3] but included little material about subsequent developments, especially the 1990 production in London when director Trevor Nunn assisted Stein and Schwartz in reconsidering their approach. Coverage of the initial touring production, therefore, will be minimized here and based primarily upon interviews with Schwartz and Stein. Important later productions at the York Theater in 1985, the aforementioned West End version in 1990, and later productions at Goodspeed Opera House in East Haddam, Connecticut, in 2002 and Paper Mill Playhouse in 2005 will demonstrate continuing collaboration. These latter versions will be approached through interviews with the writers and Greenberg, and comparison between an early script and the show at the Paper Mill will provide bookends to show how the musical changed over the years.

Schwartz lunched with playwright Neil Simon in 1974.[4] Simon pitched ideas for musicals, but none resonated with Schwartz until the end of the meal with the mention of Marcel Pagnol's 1938 French film *La femme du boulanger*. Schwartz has always had a soft spot for France and its culture because his family lived there when he was very young while his father pursued graduate studies. Schwartz bears a few memories from that time. His parents continued for years to play their recordings of Edith Piaf, Yves Montand, and Charles Aznavour, and his mother sang French folk tunes. Schwartz was interested in the story of *La femme du boulanger*, and began work on a musical adaptation with Simon under the eye of producer David Merrick, who had acquired the musical rights to the film shortly before Pagnol's death in 1974.[5] (Merrick's first success as a producer had been *Fanny* from 1954, based upon a trilogy of Pagnol films.) Because Merrick had released Schwartz from their contract on what became *Pippin*, the songwriter owed Merrick his work on a show. Schwartz and Simon had barely started when the playwright moved to California to be with his wife, Marsha Mason.

Schwartz's agent, Shirley Bernstein, connected Schwartz with another of her clients, writer Joseph Stein (1912–2010), who wrote the books for *Fiddler on the Roof* (1964) and *Zorba* (1968), among other shows. Carol de Giere reports that Shirley Bernstein made the introduction, and Stein remembers that he probably met Schwartz shortly before they started work on *The Baker's Wife*. (Merrick was perhaps involved in establishing this pairing as well; he had previously worked with Stein as a "play doctor" on *Jamaica* in 1957 and as book writer on *Take Me Along* in 1959.[6]) Stein, no stranger to musicals with an ethnic twist, liked the story for *The Baker's Wife*, as he stated in an interview in 2007:

> What attracted me, and still attracts me, is it is a very fascinating, romantic story with a very important basic theme, with a colorful background, colorful area in which to work, and also with very attractive characters and with relationships that were intriguing. In other words, it had all the positive elements that I look for in a musical, and it had situations that called for musicalizing. So it had everything.[7]

Work appears to have proceeded smoothly. Stein reported that they met to "rough out an outline of the plot" and decided which moments seemed to require songs. Stein stated, "I literally do not remember any point at which we were at odds." (Schwartz and Stein both offered that they became very good friends, remaining so to the end of Stein's long life.) Pagnol's film is a delightful period piece, one of the classics of the French cinema. It tells a deceptively simple story about a small hamlet in Provence where the baker has committed suicide, and villagers await his replacement. A middle-aged baker and his young wife arrive. His baked goods are superb, but his wife runs off with a local man, and the baker becomes despondent and stops working. The villagers, who are well-rounded characters in the film (with screenplay by Jean Giono), have never gotten along, but they work together to bring the couple back together. Gordon Greenberg notes that the film's character types became archetypal in French films.

The adaptation presented major challenges. The plot and its ambience were quintessentially French but had to be presented to an American audience. No matter how likeable he might be, the baker is a cuckold, traditionally a figure of derision. Without careful treatment, none of the three principals would be sympathetic. The man who steals the baker's wife must be sufficiently appealing to understand why she might take up with him. The villagers might be interesting personalities, but they probably would not carry a show with three unlikable main characters.

Stein felt that they could capture the tone for an American audience. He said that they tried "to be true to the feeling of the show. It was a universal feeling." Stein noted that a man abandoned by a woman that he loves and trying to hold everything together could be described as "enormously human. You have to put it in terms of that particular environment and for these people."

The collaboration might have been without rancor, but Schwartz reports that there were different approaches: "We actually have fairly different artistic sensibilities and . . . they seemed to be two different shows, the score and the book."[8] Resolving these differences only started to become possible when Trevor Nunn became involved in the late 1980s.

In the late nineteenth century and early twentieth century, long tours for shows that also played on Broadway were common, but few modern shows have been developed on such odysseys. Even out-of-town tryouts in just one or two cities have become rare, so the story of *The Baker's Wife* being doctored in the midst of a six-month tour is unusual for the 1970s. David Merrick, one of Broadway's most flamboyant figures, planned it. Stein remarked that it lasted "something like forever!" and Schwartz called it "legendary" because Merrick fired and replaced leads, the director, and the choreographer, among other figures.[9] According to a schedule in a script that David Rounds, one of the cast members, later donated to the New York Public Library, the tour was to proceed as follows:[10]

> 2 May to 26 June, Dorothy Chandler Pavilion, Los Angeles (premiere was
>   11 May)
> 28 June to 14 August, Curran Theater, San Francisco
> 16–22 August, St. Louis Municipal Opera, St. Louis
> 23 August to 11 September, Shubert Theater, Boston
> 13 September to 2 October, Forrest Theater, Philadelphia
> 4 October to 13 November, Kennedy Center Opera House, Washington
>   DC
> 15 November, New York City

The itinerary, however, changed. For example, sometime in August the company returned to New York for two weeks of rehearsal with the new director, John Berry, and then another week of rehearsal in Boston before opening there in September, rather than the August date listed earlier.[11]

Stein and Schwartz were uncomfortable with aspects of the project. Stein remembered, "Our vision of the show became increasingly distorted as we got into production, unfortunately. Other people were making contributions that seemed to be at variance with what we had in mind." Merrick prevailed in choosing the leads, which included Topol as the Baker, or Aimable (Schwartz called this "one of the disastrous choices"); Carol Demas as his wife, named Geneviève; and Kurt Peterson as the young lover, Dominique. Stein loved Topol as Tevye in the London production of *Fiddler on the Roof* and in the film, but he "had some questions as to whether he was right" for Aimable. Stein said that they considered Zero Mostel, who had "an earthier quality," but Mostel declined.[12] The first lead replaced was Carol Demas, by

Loni Ackerman,[13] and her by a young Patti LuPone, whom Schwartz had seen in *The Robber Bridegroom* produced by John Houseman's The Acting Company. Although he had been urged often to replace Topol, Merrick did not hire Paul Sorvino for the role until the tour was four weeks into its last stop in Washington. The first director was Joseph Hardy, about whose work neither Schwartz nor Stein were happy. As previously noted, John Berry replaced him during the summer.[14] De Giere reports that the show had three different choreographers during the tour.[15] Merrick dumped the first set of orchestrations (by Thomas Pierson) and hired Don Walker to redo them.[16] Another problem was the set, which Stein described as "too musical comedy and not earthy and simple." The designer had been the legendary Jo Mielziner, who died in March 1976 before finishing the work; his assistants completed what turned out to be a ponderous set.[17]

Schwartz and Stein both described a worthwhile moment that came out of all of this angst when Jerome Robbins came to see the show in Los Angeles. Stein had worked with him on *Fiddler on the Roof*, and asked him to take a look. Schwartz recalls, "We were desperate to have him work on the show but he didn't get to be Jerry Robbins by being dumb—and I think he saw in its current state and with its current team that it was fairly irreparable." Robbins made some suggestions, however, the most important concerning the show's opening. Stein remembered Robbins saying, "We don't really know where we are. You have to tell us musically." Stein went on to say, "Jerry was great on openings." (Indeed, Robbins was famous for crafting the brilliant openings for *A Funny Thing Happened on the Way to the Forum* and *Fiddler on the Roof*.) Schwartz noted that he had written an opening number called "Welcome to Concorde," a "kind of a fast, French-style waltz" for the ensemble. Robbins suggested that they "should open in a much simpler and folk-oriented way" with one character leading the audience into their French world. Robbins had liked the performance by Teri Ralston as the café-owner's wife and said, "Why don't you start with that girl and have her sing something?" Schwartz continued, "That's when I wrote 'Chanson,' which remains to this day one of my favorite songs that I've ever written. And full credit to Jerry Robbins—he didn't tell me what to write—but he led me to that."

Working on a show produced by Merrick was challenging. He involved himself in every aspect, including offering strong opinions about songs. He wanted "Meadowlark" deleted so badly that in Washington he had the parts taken from the music books in the orchestral pit and returned with them to New York. According to Kissel, Merrick and his general manager Helen Nickerson thought the song was "too sensitive" for the "vulgar" wife.[18] The music director informed Schwartz, who worked through his agent to point out that Merrick could not do this, and the song was restored.

Despite the problems, Merrick intended to open the show in New York in November. Neither Schwartz nor Stein wanted a show in that shape to open on Broadway, and they credit their agent, Shirley Bernstein, with stopping it.[19] Other sources state that Stein and Schwartz invoked a termination clause in their contracts, but either way the touring production of *The Baker's Wife* died in Washington DC on 13 November 1976.[20]

But that was not the end. After seeing the show in Boston, Bruce Yeko suggested that Take Home Tunes, a recording company he owned with his wife, Doris Chu, issue an LP. In order to make the project affordable, they worked only with songs sung by the three principals and "Chanson." Schwartz assembled a list of what he considered the best songs, which were never all in the show at the same moment.[21] The project preserved much of Schwartz's score with fine performances by Paul Sorvino, Patti LuPone, Kurt Peterson, and Teri Ralston. As Schwartz says, the recording would "become a cult hit." The songs on the recording included the following:

"Chanson"—Denise
"Merci, Madame"—Aimable, Geneviève
"Gifts of Love"—Aimable, Geneviève
"Proud Lady"—Dominique
"Serenade"—Dominique, Aimable, Geneviève
"Meadowlark"—Geneviève
"Any-Day-Now Day"—Geneviève
"Endless Delights"—Dominique, Geneviève
"If I Have to Live Alone"—Aimable
"Where Is the Warmth?"—Geneviève
"Finale (Gifts of Love)"—Aimable, Geneviève

De Giere reports that Schwartz began to fill requests for sheet music, and some songs were published.[22] Schwartz notes that three of the songs written for Geneviève ("Meadowlark," "Gifts of Love," and "Where's the Warmth?") became the most popular, and listeners also noticed "Chanson." But Schwartz returned to the three songs "that Patti sang. They're the most emotional. They're the ones that in writing them I really tried 'method' writing, to apply instances of my own life . . . something I could feel intensely enough to allow the emotion to come through, and I think that spoke to people."[23]

Musical theater performers sang them at auditions for such influential figures as director Trevor Nunn, who regularly heard auditions through the

1980s as he found cast members for such shows as *Cats* and *Les Misérables*. The album helped keep *The Baker's Wife* alive, but Schwartz reports that it also sent them down the wrong path because what seemed right was to feature the principals in future productions, and the show's eventual salvation was in the villagers.

The York Theater Production, March to April 1985

The first major production after the 1976 tour took place in March and April 1985 at the York Theater, which at the time was at 2 East Ninetieth Street (Church of Heavenly Rest). Schwartz and Stein reworked much of the show for this production and Schwartz directed. The leads were Jack Weston (Aimable), Joyce Leigh Bowden (Geneviève), and Kevin Gray (Dominique). Besides the principals, there were only ten other cast members (plus Pom Pom, the cat), demonstrating how Stein and Schwartz placed more of the show in the hands of the principals. (The 2005 Paper Mill production had fifteen cast members beyond the three leads.) The songs at York included the following:

Act 1
"Chanson"—Denise
"Voilà"—Aimable, Geneviève
"Bread"—Villagers
"Proud Lady"—Dominique
"Gifts of Love"—Aimable, Geneviève
"Chanson" (reprise)—Denise
"Serenade"—Dominique, Phillipe, Aimable, Geneviève
"Meadowlark"—Geneviève

Act 2
"Any-Day-Now Day"—Aimable and Villagers
"Chanson" (reprise)—Denise
"I Could Never Get Enough of You"—Geneviève, Dominique
"Feminine Companionship"—Marquis, Simone, Inez, Nicole, Aimable
"If I Have to Live Alone"—Aimable
"New Musketeers"—Marquis and Villagers
"Where Is the Warmth?"—Geneviève, Aimable, Denise

As may be seen, of the fifteen songs (including reprises), only five included substantive participation by anyone but the three leads and Denise.

Stein called this production "very unsuccessful." He characterized the lead, Jack Weston, as "not right," and continued, "It was one of these uneven productions. Some of it was really quite wonderful. A lot of the music was beautiful . . . some scenes also worked well . . . but somehow it didn't hold together properly." Stein suggested that part of the rewriting was because of the York Theater's small size, and the orchestra was only four musicians (arranged by David Siegel and Kevin Stites[24]). Newspaper reviews report that show ran from 20 March to 14 April, and Stein stated that the production was probably thought to have been commercially successful, "but it was not to our satisfaction."

Reviews were mixed, to the negative side, but there were positive comments and one rave. Most critics found Jack Weston wanting as Aimable, but there was praise for most other cast members. Stephen Holden in the *New York Times* thought that "the show's deficiencies suffocate its fragile charms." He cited Stein's "crude, connect-the-dots book" and Schwartz's "awkward, plodding direction," but found the score included "some of Mr. Schwartz's most captivating tunes."[25] Don Nelson in the *Daily News* stated simply, "C'est pretty bad." He disliked many things, but allowed that without "Stephen Schwartz's bittersweet music and lyrics, the evening would have been interminable."[26] Clive Barnes was brutal in the *Post*: "It is one terrible musical."[27] Howard Kissel (at *Women's Wear Daily*), however, called it "marvelous" and said "Schwartz's score is certainly his most intelligent, dramatic and melodic." He praised Schwartz's direction and concluded that it was "the first show this season worthy of being called a Broadway musical."[28] John Beaufort of the *Christian Science Monitor* found the production "charming, intimate" and mentioned the "serviceable libretto and a particularly lovely score."[29] Terry Miller of the *New York Native* was insightful, pinpointing a central problem: the song "Proud Lady" made Dominique unlikable, and that renders Geneviève and Aimable unsympathetic. He also offered, "We are treated to some fine Schwartz songs, but they seldom seem to be on speaking terms with Joseph Stein's book."[30] Writing for *Stages*, Debbi Wasserman described Stein's book as "less adept" than his fine work on *Fiddler*, and noted the following about the score: "Stephen Schwartz's French Boulevard-styled songs, except for one self-consciously smutty one, go along with the flavor of the period film."[31] The "smutty" song was almost surely "Proud Lady."

Trevor Nunn Steps In: *The Baker's Wife* in the West End, 1989–1990

One of the most prominent directors of musicals in both the West End and on Broadway since the 1980s, Nunn became director of the Royal Shakespeare

Company in 1968 at the age of twenty-eight, leading it for eighteen years. His memorable production of *Nicholas Nickleby* (West End, 1980; Broadway, 1981) saved the company financially and prompted Andrew Lloyd Webber to ask Nunn to direct *Cats* (West End, 1981; Broadway, 1982). Nunn subsequently worked on *Les Misérables*, *Starlight Express*, and *Aspects of Love*. Nunn apparently knew nothing about *The Baker's Wife* from its initial tour in 1976, but, as noted, in the 1980s he began to hear songs from the show in auditions. Nunn has recalled, "Every now and again a particularly haunting song would leap out from the stage. . . . Every time I asked where these amazing tunes came from the answer was, *The Baker's Wife*."[32] Later in the 1980s Nunn saw Pagnol's film on television and resolved to do a production of the show. He told more than one story about contacting Schwartz and Stein, but worked with them on revising the book, and suggests it took some cajoling: "They needed persuasion. . . . It was a wound they didn't necessarily want to reopen. . . . What I asked them to do was go back to their original intentions."[33]

Stein and Schwartz credit Nunn with changing their approach. Stein recalled that Nunn "wanted to spend some weeks going over the material from the very top and he suggested that we work at his home . . . outside of London." He summarized Nunn's basic thrust:

> Trevor's main approach is to make the play about the people of the village, all of them as individuals rather than, as I suppose it was in the first production, as chorus. . . . He wanted the sense, the smell, the feel, the tone of the French village on that stage. And that's what he worked for really, and much of the rewrite was in that direction.

Stein stated that he rewrote extensively for London, "mainly in terms of clarifying each of the characters, not only the two or three principals, and their relationships to each other basically and to the village and to each of the village people and how they felt about each other." Nunn thought that the story was "simple," comparing it to "Chaucer, with a moral intention and much delight in human foible," but one must render "the simplicity believable, amusing and moving," carrying "naturally into song."[34]

Schwartz also worked hard for the London production. Nunn noted that Schwartz came "ready to throw out anything,"[35] and with the new focus on the villagers, there would be new numbers. The five new songs that Schwartz wrote included "If It Wasn't for You," "Plain and Simple," "Buzz a-buzz," "Look for the Woman," and "Romance."[36] (Schwartz believes that the decision to place "The Luckiest Man in the World" and "Feminine Companionship" in close proximity, making them a single musical scene, was made in

London.[37]) The majority of numbers in the York Theater production were also heard in the West End. The production included new orchestrations by David Cullen, whose earlier credits included *Cats*, *Starlight Express*, and *Phantom of the Opera*.[38] Schwartz told a reporter that he had wanted "something with its own distinctive sound, something very French" that would reflect the types of music he drew from in writing the score.[39] Schwartz told the same reporter that he wanted to minimize electronic sounds. (This is slightly different and more restrictive than the explanation Schwartz provided in an interview for this study, as will be shown later in the musical analysis.) The orchestration that Cullen provided included the following instruments (grouped by players): flute/piccolo/recorder, oboe/English horn, clarinet/flute/tenor sax, bassoon/shawm, horn, harp, accordion, percussion, viola, cello, bass/bass guitar, and two keyboard players (with surely one synthesizer). Trevor Nunn appreciated Schwartz's contribution, stating, "Schwartz hasn't yet tried anything approaching the complexity of Sondheim, but his sheer facility is at Sondheim's level."[40]

Nunn raised money through his company, Homevale Limited, making *The Baker's Wife* its first project. After a workshop, Nunn arranged for a provincial run in October to November 1989 in his hometown, Ipswich (Suffolk), in the 400-seat Wolsey Theatre.[41] Nunn has described the show at the Wolsey for Carol de Giere, noting that the theater's thrust stage allowed the action to be close to the audience. He remembered nightly standing ovations.[42] Nunn allowed the show to run at its full length at Ipswich, waiting to make cuts during London previews to see the West End reaction. Previews started at the Phoenix Theatre on Charing Cross Road on 16 November 1989, and the premiere was 27 November. The three principals were Alun Armstrong as Aimable, Sharon Lee Hill (Nunn's wife at the time) as Geneviève, Drue Williams as Dominic, and Jill Martin as Denise. The entire cast included eighteen actors and the cat. Nunn assembled a team that he had worked with on several productions, including John Napier as set designer, David Hersey as lighting designer, and David Toguri served as the choreographer. The songs were as follows:[43]

Act 1
"Chanson"—Denise
"If It Wasn't for You"—Teacher, Priest, Marquis, and Villagers
"Merci, Madame"—Aimable, Geneviève
"Bread"—Villagers
"Gifts of Love"—Geneviève
"Plain and Simple"—Aimable, Geneviève

"Proud Lady"—Dominic
"Look for the Woman"—Teacher, Marquis, Claude, Barnaby, Antoine, Casimir, Pierre, Doumergue, Philippe
"Chanson" (reprise)—Denise
"Serenade"—Dominic, Philippe, Aimable, Geneviève
"Meadowlark"—Geneviève
"Buzz a-buzz"—Aimable, Marquis, Philippe, and Villagers

Act 2
"Chanson" (reprise)—Denise
"If It Wasn't for You" (reprise)—Priest, Teacher, Marquis, and Villagers
"Any-Day-Now Day"—Aimable, Villagers
"Endless Delights"—Dominic, Geneviève
"The Luckiest Man in the World/Feminine Companionship"—Claude, Village Men, Marquis, Simone/Inez, Nicole
"If I Have to Live Alone"—Aimable
"Romance"—Denise, Hortense, Therese, Simone, Inez, Nicole
"Where Is the Warmth?"—Geneviève
"Gifts of Love" (reprise)—Geneviève, Aimable
"Chanson" (reprise)—Denise, Aimable, Geneviève, Villagers

The Baker's Wife only ran fifty-six performances in the West End, closing on 6 January 1990. Stein described the West End production as "lovely" and remembered good reviews, believing that it failed because it lacked a real star. (Stein perhaps ignored here Alun Armstrong, who enjoyed a long career in British theater.) Stein also recalled that Nunn "insisted on some things that didn't work and one [unnamed] member of the cast was really unfortunate," but Stein called it "a giant step forward, though there were certain weaknesses that we saw even then." Schwartz's evaluation had mostly to do with the length: "There were some casting issues—but the major thing wrong with it was it was simply too long, and we cut a good half hour to forty-five minutes. It's not a big enough story to justify being almost three hours long." Nunn told de Giere that the theater ruined the show. The Phoenix was the only one available, and there the entire show had to take place on the stage, removing the audience from the action. He also disliked the title, which tells one little about the show.[44] For that season, however, *The Baker's Wife* was nominated for an Olivier for Best New Musical. The winner was *Return to the Forbidden Planet.*

Reviewers were somewhat positive. Michael Coveney of the *Financial Times* called it "a near decent musical with about one and a half good songs," and offered the aromatic detail that during "Bread" a yeasty smell was pumped out into the theater. Of the cast he liked most Armstrong as Aimable, but his overall tone was lukewarm.[45] Writing for the *Times*, Irving Wardle was mostly positive, noting "the piece may be a throwback to the days of musical comedy, but it is a fine piece of stagecraft and it tells a true tale." He praised most aspects, including the score.[46] John Peter, while reviewing a number of new West End shows for the *Times*, was generally positive, calling it "a charming, robust, enjoyable, and intimate musical" in which the score and orchestrations "evoke the cheery rum-ti-tum of 1930s and 1940s French popular music."[47] Matt Wolf, writing for the *Chicago Tribune*, saw Nunn's love for the material, was mixed about Stein's book, and found Schwartz's score "the show's greatest strength." Wolf does wonder, however, if *The Baker's Wife* might not be "that good, solid show that resists all efforts to make it great."[48] Sheridan Morley noted in the *Times* that four musicals closed in the West End over Christmas and briefly into the New Year, but *The Baker's Wife* "was by far the most distinguished."[49]

Goodspeed Opera House (2002) and Paper Mill Playhouse (2005)

Both Stein and Schwartz described the next important developments in bringing *The Baker's Wife* to its final form to be productions directed by Gordon Greenberg at the intimate Norma Terris Theatre (235 seats) of Goodspeed Opera House in East Haddam, Connecticut, in 2002 and at the Paper Mill Playhouse in Milburn, New Jersey, in 2005. Greenberg is a director who has figured prominently in Schwartz's career, and an opportunity to speak with him offered a detailed look at his role in the development of *The Baker's Wife*. The Goodspeed production played from 7 November to 1 December 2002, with Lenny Wolpe as Aimable, Christiane Noll as Geneviève, Adam Monley as Dominique, and Gay Marshall as Denise.[50] The songs were as follows:

Act 1
"Chanson"—Denise
"If It Wasn't for You"—Villagers
"Merci, Madame"—Aimable, Geneviève
"Bread"—Villagers
"Gifts of Love"—Aimable, Geneviève
"Proud Lady"—Dominique
"If It Wasn't for You" (reprise)—Villagers

"Chanson" (reprise)—Denise
"Serenade"—Dominique, Phillipe, Aimable, Geneviève
"Meadowlark"—Geneviève
"Any-Day-Now Day"—Aimable, Villagers

Act 2
"Chanson" (reprise)—Denise
"The Luckiest Man in the World"—Claude, Marquis, Nieces, and Men
"Feminine Companionship"—Claude, Marquis, Nieces, and Men
"If It Wasn't for You" (reprise)—Priest
"If I Have to Live Alone"—Aimable
"Romance"—Women
"Where Is the Warmth?"—Geneviève
"Gifts of Love" (reprise)—Aimable, Geneviève
"Finale"—Company

The Paper Mill Playhouse production began previews on 13 April 2005, running 17 April to 15 May.[51] Lenny Wolpe again played Aimable with Alice Ripley as a sexy and vulnerable Geneviève, and Max von Essen as Dominique. Gay Marshall reprised her role as Denise. Christopher Gattelli served as choreographer, and David Cullen's orchestrations from the London production remained. The song list at the Paper Mill was the same as at Goodspeed. Reviews were excellent. Writing for the *New York Times*, Naomi Siegel raved about every aspect of the show. She praised Alice Ripley for "her brand of spice and heat" to the title role and also lauded the other principals, concluding, "After 30 years of fine tuning, Messieurs Stein and Schwartz will have the lovely little musical they always wanted."[52] Schwartz considers the Paper Mill version of the show "definitive."

Stein and Schwartz revised the show substantially for both Goodspeed and Paper Mill. Stein recalled that they "worked to make the characters as clear as possible and their relationships with each other, as husband and wife, or as friends with each other, . . . or as friends in the village . . . and to make sure the scenes had that kind of purpose." Their intention was to proceed further down Nunn's road, and Greenberg noted, "I fit into his plan because I felt the same way." Greenberg continued, "My sort of next goal for the show was to make sure that every character was treated as a full human being and functioned at the top of their intelligence at all times."

Greenberg saw Pagnol's film and noted the story's depth, deciding like Nunn that the show's star needed to be the village. He compares Geneviève's arrival there to throwing a pebble in a lake and watching rings emanate out from the center and change everything. He encouraged the writers to make the title character "more likable"; if Aimable is to be a sympathetic character, the same must be true of the woman he loves. They moved the song "Gifts of Love" back a few scenes to demonstrate earlier in the show "what makes their relationship work." Geneviève is pleased with their new home: "Every aspect of the house is a gift for her, and you see they have this loving, joking, symbiotic relationship that works for them." The creators also added other small actions she performed in the village that made her more sympathetic. Greenberg did not want the age difference between Aimable and Geneviève to be so large that the audience could not understand it, so he favored her to be in her late thirties, "at the end of her string of options." Aimable is safe, and Dominique is her midlife crisis.

Greenberg pushed to make Dominique someone the audience might see as more complicated and likable than the typical home wrecker. The director states, "We made 'Proud Lady' an ode to love—he's Romeo, he's in love with love." He has never seen anyone like Geneviève before, so changes in his song and the dialogue made him "more vulnerable and younger and a little more desperate." Dominique's sincerity makes his tryst with the baker's wife a bit "more respectable," a perception that Greenberg found important.

Greenberg provided insights into several specific aspects of the productions. He considered the London production "very big . . . Trevor Nunn-sized!" They cut some characters and songs, perhaps thirty minutes total. He believes an important touch they added was when Hortense, wife of Barnaby the butcher, at the end leaves her abusive husband. It gave the plot more of a sense of realism and the character of Hortense "a thorough and fully developed arc." (Schwartz remembers discussing this addition with Stein and advocating for a "dash of bitters" at the end.) This is after Hortense has spoken out at the town meeting—a moment that always got a positive reaction—and now the audience can imagine her better future. As Denise sings "Chanson" the final time, the lyrics offer her the chance to stay or leave her husband, but Claude (whose relationship with Denise is problematic) appears on his knee with a rose; Denise accepts it and stays. (Schwartz notes that this addition took place in a Woodstock Opera House production in Woodstock, Illinois, where director Paul Lazarus conceived the moment. The composer/lyricist found it attractive and insisted that it remain.) Greenberg's research took him to the Provençal town of Le Castelet, where Pagnol filmed his outdoor scenes, and he also managed to meet Pagnol's printer. Greenberg developed his production from these materials and the film *Chocolat*, which includes several of Pagnol's character types. Of his actors, Greenberg specifically commented on Lenny Wolpe as Aimable, whom he described as a "warm and winning man" who an audience loves. He chose Gay Marshall for the role of Denise, an American actress who lived in Paris, where she played Grizabella in *Cats*.

Greenberg worked on *The Baker's Wife* for about five years, and he considered it time well spent:

> In the end, it was one of the most joyous and lovely collaborations I've ever had, with both of them. Stephen has become a close friend and a mentor in a lot of ways, but I learned more about the craft of structuring a show and the music and story-telling and theater in general from Stephen, probably, than anyone else.

Greenberg believes that the show has a future, even if he is not certain where that might be: "I think ultimately that it would find an audience, and could, because it has such quality and speaks to themes that I think appeal to people, today especially."

Concerning the Paper Mill version, Stein stated that they both "are quite proud of and I don't want to change it at all." When considering the show's completion, Schwartz reflected back on Trevor Nunn's contribution: "It's hard to overemphasize how important he was. He came, he got us excited about the show again and he showed us the way to make the show work. Even though we didn't entirely succeed with him, he restarted the engine."

The Baker's Wife at the Paper Mill Playhouse: What the Audience Saw

The New York Public Library Theatre on Film and Tape Archive includes a complete recording of the Paper Mill production from spring 2005. What follows is a detailed description to document the show's finished version.

The curtain rises on buildings in the Concorde town square, with villagers sitting at café tables and a guitarist strumming. Denise, who opens as narrator, begins speaking in French, but English follows quickly. It is afternoon, and the village awaits their new baker's arrival. The last baker died six weeks ago. Denise, waitress of the café that she owns with her husband, Claude, sings "Chanson." The Teacher reads the village's only newspaper, and the scene turns into an argument over when the new baker might arrive. The Teacher and Priest debate faith versus reason, which becomes "If It Wasn't for You." Another point of contention arises when the Marquis enters with his three "nieces," inspiring the Priest to berate him for cavorting about with his personal harem. By the end of the song there is a general hubbub with singers in counterpoint and some people on chairs, gesticulating wildly. The baker, Aimable Castagnet, and his young wife, Geneviève, enter; the Marquis mistakes the young woman for his daughter. Aimable and Geneviève soon thereafter enter their new home as the set turns around to reveal the bakery. Aimable, deeply in love, worries when his wife does not answer from upstairs, and then he lovingly massages her tired feet. Aimable exuberantly sings "Merci, Madame," much of it addressed to his wife through their cat Pom Pom. Aimable puts the cat out and sings, "I will try to make you happy." It becomes a duet, and they dance a polka, an undertaking that exhausts the baker. He sends his wife to bed while he lights the oven.

The third scene opens as the cock crows. The villagers sleepily enter the square, some in nightclothes, propelled by the heavenly aroma of baking. "Bread" sounds in brief phrases from each rhapsodizing villager. Aimable and Geneviève open the door as the set revolves, and all enter frantically. The baker holds a baguette overhead like communion bread and shares it. The song ends with Aimable on the table in triumph with baguettes pointed up at him from each hand. The Marquis makes a large order with his "nieces" present, precipitating yet another argument. Further discussion involves the baker and wife, with questions about how they met and how long they have been married.

In the next scene, Geneviève waits upon customers, including Dominique, the Marquis's chauffeur. He distracts her. Dominique is infatuated, first thinking she is the baker's daughter, and asking her for a date even after she tells him she is Aimable's wife. Their clear attraction makes counting loaves into Dominique's bag a chore. Aimable enters, and Dominique says if he were married to Geneviève he would watch her closely. When he asks Aimable if he is ever jealous, the baker answers that other men should envy him. Dominique leaves, and Aimable tells Geneviève he loves her; she will not say it. Left alone, she sings "Gifts of Love," revealing her ambiguous feelings about Aimable, and her strong memories of her married lover before she became the baker's wife. Aimable joins her in a duet from the bedroom upstairs, neither aware of the other.

The following scene is several days later, back in the village square. Pom Pom is on the roof and four men argue over what to do. Geneviève comes out and sees her cat and asks if any might be able to fetch her, but all refuse, except Dominique, who has entered. He fails and apologizes to Geneviève, now alone with him. His hand is scratched and she touches him, but soon thereafter discourages him, saying she will not hurt her husband. Dominique says he understands, and Geneviève leaves. He launches into "Proud Lady," showing his infatuation.

Three weeks later, villagers discuss matters in the café, including the difficult marriage between Claude and Denise. Geneviève and Aimable enter, and the town drunk, Antoine, asks obnoxious questions about their age difference; Dominique, who has entered, drives Antoine away. Geneviève objects to his interference; all three leave in a huff. Those who remain briefly reprise an earlier song but it is now "If It Wasn't for Her," showing their dislike for Geneviève.

The set revolves to the bakery. Geneviève tells Aimable he does not know people or really know her, but he assures her that the next day will be better. Denise appears on her balcony and sings a bit of "Chanson." Dominique arrives at night with a guitarist to sing "Serenade" for Geneviève, ostensibly honoring Aimable for his delicious bread. The song becomes a quartet. Geneviève asks her husband to make them leave, and he goes downstairs to thank them and give them pastries. Dominique climbs to the balcony to beg Geneviève to leave with him, and they kiss. Aimable misses this exchange, and he tells Geneviève that it is so late that he will just take a nap downstairs before he must rise to work. Left alone, Geneviève sings "Meadowlark." She expresses her frustration with the brazen Dominique and tells a story about a meadowlark that dies because it does not take its one last chance to find love. She sings longingly about this "beautiful young man" and decides to leave with him.

Morning dawns. Villagers come to the bakery and find Aimable asleep with bread burning. The baker misses Geneviève and the men suspect what might have happened. The Marquis comes to speak with Aimable alone, leaving the villagers to gossip. The Marquis comes out to announce that Geneviève and Dominique have left together in his car. Aimable sadly drinks a bottle of cognac at the café. Antoine, ever the provocateur, asks Aimable how it feels to be a cuckold, but the baker announces that his wife has gone to visit her mother. He drunkenly sings "Any-Day-Now Day" about his wife's return as the villagers try to convince him to return to baking. The finale includes a brief reprise of "Bread" as they take Aimable back to the bakery, where dough hangs from the ceiling and loaves are burned.

As the opening of Act 2, villagers lament their lack of bread, and Denise reprises part of "Chanson." The Teacher enters and wonders if Aimable might be ill, so he leads a few men to the bakery. Aimable is asleep in his dough vat, and the men try to raise his spirits by recounting the vagaries of married life in "The Luckiest Man in the World." The Marquis enters with his "nieces," and they sing "Feminine Companionship," offering Aimable intimate company. Tunes combine and a production number ensues. The old spinster Thérèse has gone to get the Priest because of what she perceives as immorality at the bakery; an argument ensues that ends with Aimable throwing out everyone. In the next composite scene, Aimable is in the background working angrily, with exaggerated motions, as Dominique and Geneviève dance in the foreground to the music of "Meadowlark," representing their lovemaking.

The scene changes to the church with all of the villagers except Aimable. The Marquis suggests that they divide into pairs to go looking for Geneviève and Dominique. He pairs people who do not get along, and an argument ensues. The Priest condemns Geneviève, singing "If It Wasn't for Her" with new lyrics suggesting that her sins are unforgivable. Aimable enters and apologizes for his outburst in the bakery. He says that he is not a cuckold because his wife has not deceived him; he knew she was not an angel, but he gambled on her and lost. He offers his life savings to the Marquis as reimbursement for the automobile. He leaves, and the villagers become sympathetic. The men pair off to look for Geneviève, but only after Hortense—married to the domineering Barnaby—yells at her husband and the other men that they need to stop haggling and help.

In the next scene, Aimable is in his bedroom—where Geneviève sang "Meadowlark"—singing "If I Have to Live Alone." He lived for years by himself and asks that his "scars harden like stone."

The women are at the café. They toast Hortense for speaking up, and sympathize with Geneviève since she has sought "Romance," a song that offers a cynical look at older men and souring marriages. It becomes a humorous dance, and toward the end Denise reprises a bit of "Chanson," recalling the happy times of her marriage. One of the pairs out searching, Claude and Barnaby, who had not spoken in years, enter as friends, more interested in each other than their lack of success in finding Geneviève. Another formerly antagonistic pair enters drunk. Antoine comes in saying that he has seen Geneviève and Dominique. He tries to tell the story loquaciously, but is compelled to spit it out. After an argument over who should go speak with Geneviève, Denise finally suggests that the Marquis, Priest, and Teacher go together, and they do.

The next scene is in a hotel room in a nearby village. Geneviève and Dominique are in bed. They have clearly enjoyed each other physically, but besides that they are poorly matched. Dominique falls asleep, and she sings "Where Is the Warmth?" concluding, "My beautiful young man, good bye!"

In the next scene, the Marquis, Priest, and Teacher find Geneviève. She is uncertain how she can return to Aimable, but they convince her to try, each saying things that seem out of character. The men go back to the village and ask everyone to leave the square so that Geneviève may return without embarrassment. Thérèse, however, wishes to confront the sinner. The Teacher tries to drive her off by making insincere romantic advances, and he is horrified when she invites him to her house the next day. Denise runs into Hortense and learns that she is leaving Barnaby.

The set revolves to the bakery; Geneviève enters to find the dinner table set for one. She wants to tell him the truth and he does not wish to discuss it. Pom Pom enters for the first time in days, and Aimable berates her for leaving, asking if she went with some tomcat and calls her a slut. Continuing to communicate through Pom Pom, he tells her to depart now if she is going to leave again. Geneviève says, "She will not leave!" beginning the rapprochement. She sings "I will try to make you happy" from "Merci, Madame," and it becomes a loving duet. Aimable realizes that he must start the bread, and Geneviève offers to light the oven and says that her name is Madame Castagnet, a title she had asked Aimable not to use earlier.

Denise returns and reprises "Chanson," with Aimable and Geneviève each singing a line. Denise comes to a line about whether a person might want to leave or not—clearly considering Hortense's example—and her husband Claude is there with a rose and a smile. She stays, and all of Concorde sings "Chanson" on "la."

Glimpses of *The Baker's Wife* on Tour in 1976: An Early Script

David Rounds (1930–1983) played the Priest in *The Baker's Wife* on the 1976 tour, and he donated his script to the New York Public Library.[53] Study of this source makes possible an accounting of aspects of the show that differed from what one sees and hears in the present version, along with hints of the arduous process that Stein and Schwartz endured.

The opening song "Welcome to Concorde" includes lyrics that demonstrate the town's friendly name is a lie. The Teacher has tried to model logic and reason but hates his position. The Priest returned to his hometown for his ministry but is horrified by all the sin. Men and women lament their unhappy marriages, but there is also a verse about their village's beauty. The script notes that the song ends the first time on "a terrible discord," but the Marquis suggests they try the chord again, and he directs as they sing a consonance just as the baker and his wife arrive. (A revision to this scene from 18 May 1976 includes another song before "Welcome to Concorde" in which villagers sing about cleaning the bakery for the new baker and backstory about the baker who died, with disagreements between villagers.) After a welcoming speech from the Marquis, Aimable and Geneviève enter the bakery, and the Teacher in an aside calls Aimable a fool for having such a young wife. The couple sings a song that was perhaps called "A Little Taste of Heaven" (later replaced by "Merci, Madame") where they comment on two other towns where they have lived. Aimable sings what was pleasant about each town, and then Geneviève states why they left. The main point of the song, like its successor, is for Aimable to try to cheer up Geneviève. Aimable recalls their past and his wife participates reluctantly, finally asking him to "stop it" when he asks why a "sweet young pie" would agree to marry "a stale old crust." She sings that she had thought he might let her sleep and goes to bed as he lights the stove. Aimable goes to the café for a coffee and notes the town's lack of good humor, informing them that he will bake the finest bread they have ever tasted as long as they do not upset Geneviève. (In a revision from 18 May 1976, Aimable has this discussion with villagers just after his arrival while he is in the café with his wife.) She sees Aimable at the café, knowing exactly what he is doing, and sings "Gifts of Love," with Aimable singing in counterpoint from the café. The song is different than versions available on recordings. Geneviève regrets that she cannot return his kindnesses and admits that she needs to make the best of her marriage. Counterpoint continues with her husband still in the café, with her trying to make "gifts of love" for him and Aimable requesting that the town do the same for her. After Geneviève calls to him, Aimable enters the bakery to start his night's work and sings that he is king of his kitchen and cannot help being in paradise as long as Geneviève loves him.

At the beginning of the next scene, the villagers sing a version of "Bread" with many lines that appear in later versions, but Aimable has a section (later deleted), repeated by the ensemble, in which he compares baking bread to making love. The Marquis and his handyman, Dominique, enter, and the driver immediately falls in love with Geneviève, ending the scene with the first, more arrogant version of "Proud Lady."

Scene 3 is in the café as the town drunk, Antoine, bothers Aimable and Geneviève. Dominique intervenes, to the resentment of the baker's wife. What follows, later cut, is an argument between Aimable and Geneviève where she reveals her exhaustion with his pet names and failure to notice what goes on around him. He counters that she is upset because of the scene in the café and because her cat, Pom Pom, is missing. In a 1 June 1976 revision, this scene includes more backstory on the town's unhappy citizens.

Scene 4 is the song "Serenade," the lyrics of which were later substantially rewritten. In this version it is Geneviève who brings éclairs to Dominique and his companion, Raoul, and sings of her anger with her suitor in a trio with him and her unknowing husband. Dominique kisses her and says that he will be at the church waiting for her in one hour. After he leaves, Aimable says that he will sleep the last few hours downstairs next to the oven. His wife sings "Meadowlark" and departs.

Scene 5, ending the first act, finds three villagers coming to the bakery, where they smell something burning. Aimable says his wife allowed him to oversleep and looks for her. He suggests that she has gone to visit her mother. The Marquis enters to say that Dominique has run off with his car and Geneviève. Aimable does not want to believe this, but offers the Marquis money to help pay for the car. Aimable tries to bake but is distracted. He goes next door to the café to drink. Antoine asks him how he likes being a cuckold. The Priest tries to help Aimable pray to St. Cecilia, the village's patron. The baker gets drunk and sings "Any-Day-Now Day" as he ignores his ruined bread. The villagers conclude the act singing "Oh, what a day!" In a revision from 2 June 1976, different events include a more extensive drunken scene for Aimable. Villagers escort the drunken baker back to his lodgings and find the bakery in disarray. They sing about the mess and how this is the funniest thing to happen in their village in forty years.

As Act 2 opens, the villagers sit around singing of their lack of bread. A possible title for this song might have been "Something's Got to Be Done." The teacher discovers the bakery closed, and the women sing "Romance" with different lyrics than later versions. The focus elsewhere on stage is a seedy hotel where Geneviève and Dominique sing "Endless Delights," and then an immediate return to the café for more of "Something's Got to Be Done." "Endless Delights" returns along with dialogue that shows that Dominique has no plans for Geneviève except for physical passion, and then we return to the café as the women sing more of "Romance." (An undated revision includes new lyrics for both "Romance" and "Endless Delights.") Male villagers go to the bakery to encourage Aimable, but all he wants to do is rest in his dough trough. In "The Luckiest Man in the World" they sing about the problems of marriage, and during the song the Marquis comes with his "nieces" to offer one to Aimable. Each niece sings a few lines, and the Priest enters. A revision from 6 April 1976 is three trios singing different material in counterpoint, and Aimable orders everyone to leave. He sings "If I Have to Live Alone." The script includes many revisions to this scene. Stein and Schwartz were clearly struggling with the tone of "Endless Delights" and dialogue between Geneviève and Dominique, ranging between discussions of past lovers and Geneviève wondering what Aimable might be thinking. There are also varied revisions for the men, encouraging Aimable to start baking again, including one moment when he says that he will "do something." They leave and he starts to hang himself, but they return and stop him.

In Scene 2, Barnaby beats a drum to announce a town meeting called by the Marquis. In Scene 2a, everyone but Aimable is there. Tempers are short, but an Old Maid suggests that they divide into pairs to try and find Dominique and Geneviève. Aimable enters to say that he will resume baking, but he is angry about what some say about him. He leaves and villagers start to pair off, but they learn that Raoul has known all along where they went. The group decides that the Marquis, Teacher, and Priest should go speak to Geneviève, each saying things in reconciliation that seem out of character.

In Scene 3 in the hotel room, Geneviève and Dominique continue to have communication problems. He goes back to sleep, and she sings "Where Is the Warmth?" and leaves. He awakens, clearly relieved.

Scene 4 is in the village square. Barnaby announces that Geneviève is returning and asks that the square be cleared so that she need not be embarrassed. Everyone seems friendlier. An undated revision has the Old Maid wanting to stay and confront her, and the Teacher makes a false pass at her as in the final version. Geneviève enters, led by the Priest.

The next scene, marked as "7," is similar to Geneviève's return to Aimable in the current version, but she sings a brief reprise of "Gifts of Love." He says that she can go to bed, but she wants to stay and light the oven for him.

The Music

The sources for this description and analysis include the recording made after the 1976 tour, the London cast recording, and a piano/vocal score that bears a 1990 copyright date for lyrics and a 1993 date for the book. The intention of this section is to document Schwartz's thinking about the music as related in an interview and provide a brief analysis of each song based on this score. With what was available for this study it is not possible to provide a full history of each song, but it was an arduous process to get the score to where it is today. Stein recalled, "We fiddled around with almost every one of the songs before we got it into the shape it is in now." In our interview Schwartz described a number of ways that individual songs changed. Lists of songs from various productions appear earlier, and we begin this section with a table that compares song titles as they appear on each recording (see Table 6.1). As previously noted, the 1977 recording included only music for the principals, while the 1990 recording was a full original cast recording for the West End production.

Table 6.1. Songs on the 1977 and 1990 Recordings of *The Baker's Wife*

1977	1990
Act 1	Act 1
"Chanson"	"Chanson"
	"If It Wasn't for You"
"Merci, Madame"	"Merci, Madame"
	"Scene"
	"Bread"
	"Scene 2"
"Gifts of Love"	"Gifts of Love"
	"Plain and Simple"
"Proud Lady"	"Proud Lady"
	"Look for the Woman"
"Serenade"	"Serenade"
"Meadowlark"	"Meadowlark"
	"Buzz a-buzz"
Act 2	Act 2
	"Chanson"/"If It Wasn't for You" (reprises)
"Any-Day-Now Day"	"Any-Day-Now Day"
"Endless Delights"	"Endless Delights"
	"The Luckiest Man in the World"
	"Feminine Companionship"
"If I Have to Live Alone"	"If I Have to Live Alone"
	"Romance"
"Where Is the Warmth?"	"Where Is the Warmth?"
	"Scene—Pompom's Return"
"Gifts of Love" (finale)	"Gifts of Love"/ "Chanson" (reprises)

As is his wont, Schwartz has been open about his compositional process for *The Baker's Wife*. Various versions of the story have appeared elsewhere,[54] but this is how the composer/lyricist recounted his pre-compositional process in our interview. He cited four primary influences on the score: French folk songs from tune books that he owns and that he remembered from his childhood; recordings by such French cabaret singers as Edith Piaf, Yves Montand, and Charles Aznavour represented in his parents' record collection (Schwartz "particularly responded to" Piaf); music from French films scored by Georges Delerue, such as *Le roi de couer* (The King of Hearts, 1966); and the music of Debussy, Ravel, and Satie. As the composer stated,

> Before I started writing I listened to a lot of Piaf and . . . Delerue scores, and I played a lot of Debussy, Satie, and Ravel, but mostly Debussy. I just actually spent a month . . . playing that on the piano, and also going through the

French folk music. . . . And then when I started to write, I put all that away but those chords were in my fingers.

Unlike *Godspell*, where Schwartz based each song on a favorite tune, he usually did not try to isolate single influences for songs in the score for *The Baker's Wife*, instead stating that his four models "influenced all of the tunes."

Schwartz admits that this show, after *Godspell*, *Pippin*, and *The Magic Show*, was "a real departure of musical style." He felt like he was going back to how he wrote music "before the pop infusion in college." He was not seeking to do something completely different but responding to the story of *The Baker's Wife*, and clearly "it would be weird to write pop, contemporary music for something set in France in 1935." The composer/lyricist believes that this show has the feeling of perhaps Rodgers and Hammerstein, and he notes that Stein participated in that era.

The low, rich voice of Edith Piaf resonated strongly with Schwartz. Among female soloists in the show, every voice is that of a mezzo-soprano or alto Broadway belter. Schwartz states that this was not conscious, but he "never thought of . . . high voices for the kind of French stuff that I was writing." He wanted to avoid French operatic or theatrical models such as Gounod and Offenbach, but there is an ensemble soprano for high notes in choruses. There are places in the score where one hears motivic unification, where music from one song reappears at a dramatically opportune moment, but Schwartz notes that he did that a great deal more in *Children of Eden*, *Wicked*, and *Séance on a Wet Afternoon*.

Schwartz believes that the simple waltz meter of "Chanson" came from his love for French children's songs, and while he admits that the song carries a Piaf feel, he hears more Debussy. One might imagine Schwartz thinking of the "Sarabande" from Debussy's *Pour le piano*, but the simple harmonies of "Chanson" seem more reminiscent of Satie's *Gymnopédies*. Schwartz hears a strong Delerue influence starting at m. 57 (London original cast recording [LOCR], 1'16"ff); there is a major stylistic change as the accompaniment thickens and chords include more added tones. Schwartz remembers that Teri Ralston in 1976 sang the song in G major, but he likes it lower; it is in E in the 1990 score. The extensive use of harp and accordion in the orchestration was Schwartz's idea, a combination that he likes. He cast the song in AABA form, but with A stated first with French text as an introduction. That is immediately translated into English for the "first" A. The Delerue segment is a varied B (twenty-four measures), and then an extended return of A (thirty-two measures) where the text confirms the song's (and show's) message that life can change for the better. The song concludes with a short coda. It is an effective opening number that takes the audience directly to Provence in the mid-1930s.

The original opening number, also for full ensemble, was "Welcome to Concorde," which Schwartz considers a Ravel-like waltz. For the West End, following Nunn's dictum that "the town was the central character," Stein was writing personalities more like folk characters. Schwartz wanted his new song, "If It Wasn't for You," to start "on a guitar" and "feel like some folk tune." This required simple harmonies, but Schwartz includes piquant added tones. The song includes rounds that use the basic tune, such as the four-part round at the end (LOCR, 2'40"ff), designed to make the villagers "sound childish, like 'Row, Row, Row Your Boat.'" While we discussed the song, Schwartz was at the piano and played an incipit of a French folk song that he remembered like the 6/8 ditty that he wrote for "If It Wasn't for You." The Teacher opens the song with the basic melodic material as he advises the Priest, "since you do not think," to take Descartes's advice and disappear. The Priest admits to the same tune that loving his neighbor would be easier "if it wasn't for you!" Their following duet of mutual complaining includes sweet, ironic harmonies (LOCR, 1'05"ff) over a jaunty recorder accompaniment.

Schwartz admits that he emphasized one influence in "Merci, Madame": "Now that's French music hall—you're really in Piaf land!" This tune, rewritten for the London production to show how happy Aimable and Geneviève can be together, is primarily in a rollicking duple meter. Schwartz spoke mostly in the interview about the chorus that begins with the title text (LOCR, 0'51"–1'07"), noting, "You can just hear an accordion doing an obbligato over it." He mentioned specifically as a French cabaret sound his repetition of an a' in the melody on the downbeat of measures thirty-six to thirty-eight ("*home* for us, Pom *Pom* and I a-*gree*," 0'56"–0'58") over changing harmonies, the last two with the a' as a dissonance. Several elements, however, recall French music hall, forming one of Schwartz's best imitations of a style outside of American popular music. After an opening, rhythmic recitative, Schwartz proceeds through the verse and refrain of the tune twice with a short break for Aimable as he picks up the cat and sings a bit of the tune on "Rowr." He breaks the second time through the refrain just before the end for a modulation from C to D-flat, when Aimable turns serious and promises to try to make Geneviève happy (LOCR, 1'55"ff). Schwartz feels here the influence of Debussy and Delerue with unresolved dissonances and melodic notes repeated as nonharmonic tones over other chords, and the noodling eighth-note accompaniment that was typical of Delerue in his scores for *Shoot the Piano Player* (1960) and *King of Hearts* (1966). The tune concludes with a return of the duple meter material and a dance.

The opening of "Bread" channels Debussy, as villagers enter enraptured with the aroma. Five voices enter in turn on the notes of a C-sharp diminished chord, proceeding finally to a fully diminished seventh chord that twice descends chromatically (LOCR, 0'00"–0'24"). The main melody is like a slow soft-shoe, but Schwartz also hears the influence of Delerue and the French music hall in it, especially when ninths and sevenths occur between the melody and bass notes in measures eight to ten (LOCR, 0'26"–0'32"), inspired by a passage from *Shoot the Piano Player*. The main melody is nineteen measures (ABAC) with interesting chromatic touches and chords outside of the key of A major, such as the E-flat arpeggio Schwartz used to set "What is so luscious" (LOCR, 0'40"–0'42"). A clever rhyme with "luscious" follows with "as a brioche is?" complemented by Schwartz's harmonic slide from an E-flat arpeggio to D major, the latter over a B-flat in the bass. The passage starting at m. 43 (LOCR, 1'54"ff) where villagers interchange quick comments, Schwartz based on "Sounds of Selling" in *She Loves Me* (Jerry Bock and Sheldon Harnick) where the listener keeps dropping in on comments from various shoppers, but he also hears some Bock of *Fiddler on the Roof* because the music is folk-like. Schwartz noted that the lyrics to "Bread" changed several times as he got to know the characters better, concluding, "One of the fun things about this show is there's never really a chorus number where anyone has to drop his character and just be a chorus member. They're always playing themselves."

Schwartz acknowledges that "Gifts of Love" underwent many changes, including versions as a solo for Geneviève and as duet for the couple. The version considered here, heard in London, was the wife's solo. After a brief introduction recalling "I will try to make you happy" from "Merci, Madame," Schwartz used a musical form of AABCA. He opened in his favorite key of D-flat, modulated to F at the end of the second A section as Geneviève starts to remember her previous lover (LOCR, 1'27"), and then returned to D-flat when she vows to live as happily as she can with Aimable (LOCR, 2'43"). Schwartz states that he "finally put together my favorite version of it. I think it's one of the best melodies I've ever written. I mean it's really a flat-out romantic melody." When accessing his romantic muse, Schwartz frequently refers to influence from Puccini, which he did for this song as well, stating "I was just trying not to be too Italian." When describing Puccini's influence, Schwartz cited the opening gesture of the A section (LOCR, 0'29"–0'32"), where Geneviève sings an octave from g to g' with an intervening a-flat over the same pitches in the accompaniment, a gesture that beautifully evokes her ambivalence. Schwartz thinks that the song's biggest "Puccini moment" is his setting of "each day the first thing that I see" (LOCR, 0'46"–0'51").

(When Schwartz played the section from memory during the interview, he embellished his melody a bit as he sang it and made it sound even more like Puccini.) The tune makes one recall the lushness of some of Andrew Lloyd Webber's songs, but Schwartz first wrote this in 1976, before *Cats* or *Phantom of the Opera*, scores by Lloyd Webber that some compare to Puccini. Schwartz remembers liking a version of the song where Aimable joined in (probably unheard by his wife) during the middle section as Geneviève remembered her former lover, and another version was that described earlier from the 1976 tour when the song was a duet as Aimable sat in the café addressing the villagers. Schwartz notes that "Gifts of Love" has moved progressively later in the show. Once after "Merci, Madame," Nunn moved it later "because he realized that that was too soon and you weren't invested enough in her and she just seemed like a sourpuss." As previously noted, in versions with Greenberg, the song was "triggered . . . by Dominique . . . and of course that makes it really ambiguous because she's singing about her husband but you've just seen her really resisting her attraction to this other guy. And so I think now finally its placement in the show earns the ambiguity of the music."

"Proud Lady" is a tour de force for the baritone who plays Dominique, as may be seen on YouTube in Max von Essen's fine rendition in the Paper Mill production.[55] The music does not appear to have changed much over the years; the recorded examples from 1977 and 1990, for example, despite different texts, are quite similar musically. Stein reported that he did not agree with Schwartz on the emotional content of "Proud Lady." In the original version Dominique is flip and arrogant, and Stein later wanted him "to be genuinely for the first time in love with a woman." Schwartz reports that at first he was

> thinking of it more satirically and more objectively, and I made a mistake. I always liked it a lot musically, but what happened when the character was self-aware . . . when he ends singing "I'm in love for the twenty-third time" [as Dominique did in the original version], that self-awareness, even though it's a great last line for doing the song in a cabaret, undercut the story. . . . If she falls in love with him, then she's a fool [when she] leaves, and the baker's pining over her, then he's a fool, and the house of cards collapses. Joe saw that sooner than I.

Schwartz notes that it was Trevor Nunn who got him to understand the problem with "Proud Lady," so the songwriter rewrote the lyric for London "and got it almost right," and then finally fixed it for the Paper Mill production. The title portion of the song (LOCR, 0'55"–1'26") is a bolero, a tribute to Ravel. The accompanying rhythm bears resemblance to the ostinato rhythm in Ravel's famous work, and David Cullen's orchestration adds to the effect. The song's form is ABCBCA. The opening and closing sections are energetic and expectant, establishing Dominique's high emotional state. The B section (e.g., LOCR, 0'25"–0'54") is more restrained, rapid recitative where Dominique continues his reverie and plans for the seduction. The C section is the bolero, which returns briefly later. Schwartz also reports that David Merrick did not like the song and it got cut fairly early in the tour, but Schwartz put it on the original recording.

Schwartz wrote "Look for the Woman" for London in reaction to a request from the director: "Trevor had wanted me to do for London a sort of men's counterpart to 'Romance,' so I did this but when I saw it on stage it just felt like . . . it really doesn't work." It took place after the confrontation in the café between Geneviève, Aimable, Antoine, and Dominique. At Paper Mill Schwartz turned his song of village antagonism into "If It Wasn't for Her," a brief reprise that establishes that the town wants to blame things on Geneviève. Schwartz likes the music to "Look for the Woman" with a number of ninths in the melody above the bass and other dissonances, but he believes, "We just didn't want to hear from them [the men] at that point. The story had started to move along. It wasn't telling us anything we didn't already know." They made the song shorter in London. It is a sort of ironic soft-shoe in F minor that one can hear on the LOCR, but it is no longer in the show.

During the "Serenade" Dominique and his companion Philippe, a guitarist, come at night ostensibly to sing for the wonderful baker, but the lyrics are an elaborate pass at Geneviève, which she understands. Aimable is oblivious. Schwartz states of the introduction: "This is really flat-out Debussy." Dominique sings his opening on "Ahh" accompanied by guitar, harp, and other instruments (LOCR, 0'44"ff), where Schwartz applies an inspired mixture of chromaticism and whole-tone gestures in the vocal line and rapid noodling in the harp to set an exotic mood, lightened later (LOCR, 1'10") when Dominique sings recitative perhaps inspired by French cabaret music, accompanied by accordion. It is this quality that develops into the song's main portion, but Schwartz's Debussyian opening sets the scene beautifully. Schwartz pointed out that the guitarist sings as well just before Aimable and Geneviève sing their responses, making the song a quartet (LOCR, 2'48"ff), what Schwartz correctly calls "a very operatic moment. You can see the composer who someday had aspirations of writing opera!" Schwartz combines the delicate serenade with the married couple's prosaic entrances. The chromatic and whole-tone gestures reappear at the end as Dominique implores Geneviève to run away with him. In the London production, the scene opened with a brief reprise of part of "Chanson," sung by Denise.

"Meadowlark" is one of Schwartz's most popular songs. As noted earlier, Merrick did not want it in the show. Carol de Giere provides a story as to how Schwartz wrote it and his reluctance to show it to others because it felt too personal,[56] but in our discussion the songwriter was less confessional. He was simply trying to get inside the character and look for similarities in his own life, concluding, "A lot of this show is method writing." The song's parable "just came" to Schwartz, and about the whole work he states, "Every now and then you get a gift from the universe. This song wrote so quickly, and I never rewrote it." Once, to address Merrick's annoyance, Schwartz shortened it (the full tune is over six minutes), but it did not work as well.[57] Schwartz believes that the main musical influence came from Impressionism, especially Ravel. Certainly the opening several measures smack of the exoticism of either Debussy or Ravel, with little motives like those famous in such works as Debussy's *Prelude to the Afternoon of a Faun*. As Geneviève's recitative begins, Schwartz's marking is "Driving"; the constant, accompanying triplets provide considerable forward motion. The main portion of the song includes music for a verse (LOCR, 1'21"–1'45") and a refrain (LOCR, 2'06"–2'35"), the verse music usually stated twice before the refrain. The momentum and accompaniment gradually becomes more insistent with constant eighth notes, often in patterns of three, syncopated in relation to the alla breve meter. The bass line varies, but often includes a *tresillo* pattern. Certainly some of "Meadowlark" can be attributed to Schwartz's French models, but the feeling and sound of this tune also seems associated with the composer's accustomed contemporary language with close attention to vocal writing and an over-arching lyricism, not unlike what one hears in "Corner of the Sky" from *Pippin*.

How to end Act 1 and begin Act 2 were two of the knottiest problems for the collaborators. In the York Theatre version in 1985 Act 1 concluded with "Meadowlark" just before Geneviève bolts. Schwartz wrote "Buzz a-buzz" for the West End version when Trevor Nunn was pushing for more involvement of villagers. Schwartz wrote it in the town's folk style, not unlike "If It Wasn't for You" with its 6/8 meter and simple, jaunty feeling, but in "Buzz a-buzz" one hears more dissonance and unexpected silences in the vocal lines filled by similar motives in the instruments. An effective moment occurs when the Marquis pumps Philippe for information about where Dominique has gone and what he took with him (LOCR, 2'25"–2'54"). The rests before Philippe's brief entrances are filled with a revolving instrumental ostinato that makes his reluctant replies more humorous. The passage concludes with the Marquis singing "And with?" several times on expanding intervals, trying to get Philippe to say that Dominique is with the baker's wife. He whispers it, the

Marquis demands again, and Philippe sings it loudly. It is part of an effective musical scene that Stein and Schwartz ultimately found unnecessary. As Schwartz states, "When Joe and I were compressing the show it felt as if the ship had sailed and really we wanted to jump story more quickly, that we didn't need to see them gossiping—we get it!"

The result after London was moving the song "Any-Day-Now Day" from early in Act 2 to the finale of Act 1. Schwartz describes it as "a joyous song filled with rage," where Aimable takes "great revenge on all these townspeople." Aimable is drunk and sings in the style of a Parisian cabaret. As Schwartz states, "This is as Edith Piaf as it gets." At the song's first real cadence on the title text (LOCR, track 2/2, 0'34"–0'36"), the music seems headed for a resolution on the tonic of C, which occurs in the bass, but Aimable sings an a, perhaps confirming his doubts about his wife. After Aimable sings the full tune (LOCR, track 2/2, 0'44"–1'08"), the villagers pester him about baking and the song becomes a duet or a trio. Once Aimable again finishes his ditty, he remembers his work, and starts to sing "Bread" (LOCR, track 2/2, 2'04"ff), mocking the villagers as they lead him back to his bakery and find it in disarray, singing their observations to the same tune. The song concludes with Aimable performing a slow version of "Any-Day-Now Day," threatening to cease his baking as the villagers despair that this is the worst thing to happen in their town in forty years. Schwartz enjoys the song's irony and multiple layers, stating, "One of the things I love about The Baker's Wife is how subtextual so many things are, that a lot of times people are saying one thing and feeling something else, and . . . hopefully the music is telling you something else."

Act 2 now opens with "Chanson," and Schwartz finds the song's reprises delightful: "One of the things I like about the structure of the show now is that it opens with 'Chanson' one more time through and then throughout we sing the entire song one more time though broken up." The next return of "Chanson" as the show's finale was Trevor Nunn's decision, replacing "Gifts of Love" and just a brief reference to "Chanson." Schwartz clearly agrees, stating, "He didn't get to be Trevor Nunn by accident." In some earlier versions at this point there was a reprise of "If It Wasn't for You."

The first new musical moment in Act 2 is the combination of "Luckiest Man in the World" and "Feminine Companionship." Schwartz wrote "Luckiest Man" first, then replaced it with "Companionship," and for London they decided to combine the numbers into a single scene. The composer/lyricist calls them "two French music hall numbers," firmly rooted in the 1930s with the continuing "implications of can-can" from the nineteenth century and a deliberate bow to what Maurice Chevalier might have sung. Earlier descriptions of similar tunes render close attention to the music of these songs redundant. "Luckiest Man in the World" is based on a series of jaunty four-bar phrases with playful melodic skips, some insinuating chromaticism, and bits of syncopation. Schwartz treats the main tune imitatively at one point (LOCR, track 2/4, 1'29"ff), similar to the round in "If It Wasn't for You." "Feminine Companionship," which follows "Luckiest" immediately on the London recording, includes a familiar but effective treatment of the title text, mostly in half notes and sung by female trio in close harmonies (before the Marquis begins the main segment), but most of this suggestive tune is in the dotted eighths and sixteenth notes of a soft-shoe. Schwartz points out as a French element his repetition of melodic and harmonic elements in spots with a number of ninths in the chords (LOCR, track 2/5, 0'26"–0'30"), and Cullen's orchestration of both tunes enhances the Gallic feeling. Schwartz emphasized his inspiration from Chevalier: "When the show's performed in heaven and you can choose from anybody, we'll ask for him to be the Marquis."

Aimable's solo for Act 2 has usually been "If I Have to Live Alone," which appeared on the original 1977 recording. Schwartz opened the accompaniment with what he likes to call "the music box sound," which he describes vividly: "To me it feels icy and cold, and this little glistening, bell-like sound just kind of goes right through it and then people sing over it, and I just love that and I've done it a lot." The orchestration features high metallic sounds such as glockenspiel and an appropriate synthesizer setting. (One hears a similar accompaniment at the beginning of "I'm Not That Girl" from *Wicked*, where Elphaba sings softly but with deep emotion.) Schwartz remembers changing a section of the melody in response to a request from Trevor Nunn. One can hear the change by comparing the two recordings, where in the earlier version on the text "and there's time enough has flown" (mm. 10–11) the vocal line descends (1977 recording, 0'31"–0'35"), but Nunn thought "it got too low and too lugubrious." The melody ascends and stays in the singer's middle tessitura in the later version (LOCR, track 2/6, 0'45"–0'51"). The song is in AABA form and based mostly on short phrases, especially at the beginnings of sections, causing an improvisatory, confessional quality.

"Romance," written for the London production, is another number for the villagers. Schwartz comments, "I really like this moment. You know, I think that balancing the show and giving the village women more of a voice also really makes a difference in the show." The song provides major moments for Hortense and Denise, allowing the audience to consider their individual stories. The song is a tango that sets a humorous, cynical text, long enough and with sufficient variety to feel like a musical scene. Schwartz makes three musical references to earlier material. The opening includes Dominique's vocalise from the beginning of "Serenade"; the gesture returns several times in "Romance." As the ladies continue their tirade against men (LOCR, track 2/7, 1'22"ff), a section of "If It Wasn't for You" (LOCR, track 1/2, 0'52"–1'09") returns, ending with "if it wasn't for men." At this point the melody of "If It Wasn't for You" is in a dotted rhythm rather than 6/8. Denise has a solo moment later in the song that references melodic gestures from "Chanson." Schwartz cites Bernstein's influence in tying all of these melodic snippets together, noting, "It's intentional but not calculated . . . I just tried to let it happen organically."

Another song that has been in the show since the 1976 tour is "Where Is the Warmth?" Schwartz remarks about what the song says about Geneviève: "Some people have criticized the show for her being too intelligent and too self-aware and they've said, 'You know, a character like that, she should leave him and go to the Sorbonne.' I understand what they mean, but I still think it's more interesting when she has a brain."

This song seems within character for the woman who already has expressed herself through a parable in "Meadowlark," and here she separates the passion that she has experienced with Dominique from their lack of personal connection. The vocal melody is declamatory, sounding regretful and lacking the impact of true vocal climaxes until the end when she says goodbye to her "beautiful young man" (LOCR, 2/8, 2'41"–2'–52"), sung to the same motive heard in "Meadowlark" (LOCR, 1/12, 5'52"–6'04"). The form is AABA' with a brief coda. The accompaniment of "Where Is the Warmth?" is contrapuntal, carrying the feel of French neoclassical scores from the 1920s and 1930s by such composers as Milhaud and Poulenc.

"Endless Delights" was a song that Dominique and Geneviève sang in their lover's retreat. Schwartz calls it the score's most "Georges Delerue [song] of all" and is fond of it, but "it never, ever worked . . . and Trevor couldn't make it work." Schwartz wrote another, satirical version of the song for *Snapshots*,[58] a revue based on his songs, but Schwartz has strong feelings about banishing "Endless Delights" from *The Baker's Wife*: "The audience doesn't want to hear from these two people at that point. . . . And it gives away too much, that the cracks in the plaster are already beginning to show, then it gives away the ending." The versions on the two available recordings are substantially different, each in Schwartz's French mode and both "kind of wistful and full of regret." The song was fraught with problems of tone from the beginning, with Stein remembering discussions over how cynical it should be and how the addition or subtraction of various words changed its meaning. Schwartz still receives requests from directors to restore the song, but he refuses. The moment in Act 2 in the current version to remind the audience that Dominique and Geneviève are enjoying each other is a cross-over of the two dancing while Aimable throws the villagers out of his bakery after "Feminine Companionship."

Schwartz had long used "Gifts of Love" as the finale for *The Baker's Wife*, and Nunn urged its expansion for the London production. The composer/lyricist calls it his "most Puccini-esque, most 'Nessun dorma' type tune" with sections where he wants to hear a sixty-piece orchestra. In the current version Aimable and Geneviève complete their moving duet, and then Denise returns with another reprise of "Chanson," interrupted by her husband on his knees with a rose. She concludes, with Aimable and Geneviève singing a few lines, and the entire cast sings "Chanson" on "la." The show ends differently on the LOCR, with a choral treatment of part of "Chanson," demonstrating yet another change that Schwartz and Stein made to their show over the years. The charming musical that exists today is a monument to their extraordinary persistence, and the assistance of Nunn and Greenberg.

CHAPTER SEVEN

Working

Unsuccessful on Broadway, *Working* is yet another show in Schwartz's output reworked after its initial run, since produced often by professional and amateur companies. Unlike *The Baker's Wife* and *Children of Eden*, successful revisions took place on *Working* soon after the Broadway production closed on 4 June 1978, and subsequent changes have produced two, newer versions. *Working* is the only musical in his output that Schwartz directed from its conception until the initial run closed on Broadway, and it is also unique in his career because of the number of songs in the score written by other artists, a step that Schwartz initiated because of the wide variety of personalities and ethnic groups represented in the cast. He knew that he had colleagues who could more naturally write songs for some characters, and he spread the work around to such masters as James Taylor, Craig Carnelia, Micki Grant, and others. This chapter will provide a brief history of the show's creation based upon an interview with Schwartz with some details filled in from Carol de Giere's chapter on *Working*, which provides good coverage on the show and its creation.[1] This consideration will also offer a summary of the critical reaction of the unsuccessful Broadway run in 1978, and include description of the songs that Schwartz wrote for the project.

From Book to Show

In 1974 Studs Terkel (1912–2008) published *Working: People Talk about What They Do All Day and How They Feel about What They Do*, a voluminous

set of transcribed interviews primarily with blue-collar workers.[2] He surely
never thought that it might become a source for a musical theater piece.
Schwartz quickly discovered the book through a brochure from the Book-of-
the-Month Club; he was intrigued by an excerpt about a telephone operator
who loved it when a customer asked her about her day.[3] As Schwartz said
in our interview, "That little thing really triggered the whole idea for me. A
person that I had just thought about as a function, as part of the machine,
the phone company. I never thought of operators as individuals [that] were
having, maybe, a tough day."[4] In the same way that other ideas for musicals
have suddenly hit Schwartz, he immediately decided that the book might
make an interesting show and sent his agent, Shirley Bernstein, looking into
the rights. As de Giere reports, Schwartz went to Chicago to persuade Terkel
to agree to the project. The writer was "astonished," but saw that Schwartz
had a "vision," and gave his permission for the adaptation.[5]

The composer/lyricist wanted his friend Nina Faso to work on the project
with him. She recalls that he asked her to read the book, and her reaction
was overwhelmingly positive. They immediately began to discuss their favorite characters.[6] Faso served as Schwartz's associate director for *Working*;
in various listings she shared credit for the adaptation with Schwartz, but
in others Schwartz incorrectly receives sole credit. They went through the
book, looking for segments and characters that seemed appropriate for dramatization. After editing those interviews, Schwartz and Faso gathered actors who had been in a company of *Godspell* or someone else that they knew
and worked sections with them, perhaps twice per week for three hours at a
stretch. As Schwartz stated in our interview, "It was completely developed
by workshop."[7] Carol de Giere reports that the actors who assisted with the
workshops included *Godspell* veterans Robin Lamont, Gilmer McCormick,
Jeffrey Mylett, Laurie Faso, and Lynne Thigpen, at the time in the cast of *The
Magic Show*.[8] Nina Faso has commented on the abundance of material that
did not appear in the show, including, for example, a segment on "Husbands
and Wives" and scenes involving sports figures. She specifically remembers
sessions when they conceived the section on supermarkets and migrant farm
workers. James Taylor was present with a melodic idea, and Matt Landers
and Graciela Daniele wrote the lyrics, producing the song "Un mejor día
vendrá."[9]

In order to make depictions of workers as realistic as possible, they took
field trips to visit such places as a firehouse, steel mill, and supermarkets,[10]
a process that Schwartz remembers remaining a part of the show's developmental process all the way through the Chicago tryout period and with the

original cast in the New York City area. Nina Faso has special memories of their firehouse visit, watching Schwartz try on equipment.[11]

Another question was how the show might be framed, providing a central idea that would tie together what could be seen as unrelated segments. Schwartz recalls that during the Chicago tryout period the script included the Ringley family, characters who would return at various points.[12] Schwartz removed the idea in New York but recalls, "I should have cut it after Chicago. It was clear it wasn't working." *Working* opened in Chicago at the Goodman Theater on 5 January 1978 and ran for one month.[13]

Schwartz came upon the idea for *Working* the year that *The Magic Show* opened, and his realization for the new show was delayed by *The Baker's Wife*, which consumed much of 1975 and 1976. As de Giere reports, the bitter experience of the latter show inspired Schwartz to retain as much control over his new project as possible, including directing, script, and score.[14] Writing the *Working* script became an all-consuming project that was not resolved for the New York run until the show opened.[15] Interest in reality spilt over into writing songs as well, arguably the least "real" part of a musical, but Schwartz emphasized the continuing interest in making the show feel like the lives of the characters:

> We . . . really tried to make this a nonfiction musical, as much as possible; we tried to stay true to the words of the characters that we were musicalizing, not superimpose our own inventions and our own impressions, but to let them speak through their own words—basically, exactly what Studs did. I think [in] the original, frankly [more] than we are now. But with the original, any time we had to write two lines simply to make a transition from one thing to another, it was agonizing for us. . . . And now, even with the '90s version and the new version, we don't make up characters. We go and do interviews, and then we edit these. We do exactly what Studs did. . . . Everything in the show remains basically something that someone actually said. We have done the fictional thing of making composite characters on occasion. For instance, the iron worker from New Haven, that I talked to and the original steelworker, they are combined into a character. But that seems fair—we're a little less doctrinaire now about hewing the line, but we're still basically trying to make this nonfiction.[16]

As director and working on the book, Schwartz already had monumental tasks for *Working*. It is hard to imagine that he could have written the entire score, but that was his original intention.[17] The wide range of ethnic groups and types of characters in the various monologues demanded songs in a number of styles, a task that Schwartz could certainly have approached, but he decided to pursue another path. As he told de Giere, he was working on a song for the parking lot attendant and found himself trying to compose in the style of Micki Grant, and finally it seemed logical to see if she might be interested in writing the number.[18] They met and Schwartz heard the kind of music from her that he wanted; the concept of multiple songwriters for *Working* was born.

Schwartz continued meeting with songwriters "who seemed to me might be appropriate, and we talked individually about what they might be interested in. In some instances I had a thought for them, and they often would say, 'I'm interested in such and such a character.'" The songwriters who contributed songs that opened with the show in New York were Schwartz, Grant, Craig Carnelia, Mary Rodgers (with lyrics by Susan Birkenhead), and James Taylor. Their experience at writing theatrical songs varied considerably. Grant had already composed the scores for *Don't Bother Me, I Can't Cope* (1972) and *Your Arms Too Short to Box with God* (1976).[19] After those two hits she wrote the songs for the short-lived *It's So Nice to Be Civilized* (1980). Mary Rodgers, nearly a generation older than Schwartz, is part of a Broadway royal family along with father Richard Rodgers and son Adam Guettel. Before *Working* her Broadway career had included the music for *Once Upon a Mattress* (1959), songs for *From A to Z* (1960), and music for *Hot Spot* (1963). Later she did additional music for *Side by Side by Sondheim* (1978) and some songs for *The Madwoman of Central Park West* (1979). Craig Carnelia had written numbers for cabaret performances before Schwartz approached him, and after *Working* he collaborated on scores for three shows that had limited success: music and lyrics for *Is There Life after High School?* (1980), and lyrics only for *Sweet Smell of Success* (2002) and *Imaginary Friends* (2002). James Taylor, one of the most celebrated singer/songwriters of his generation, has written little music for theater, with no previous Broadway experience before *Working* and only one show that included some of his songs afterward: *Chita Rivera: The Dancer's Life* (2005). Susan Birkenhead also had not written for Broadway before *Working*, but since she has written lyrics for *King of Schnorrers* (1979), the highly successful *Jelly's Last Jam* (1992), *Triumph of Love* (1997–1998), and *High Society* (1998).

Schwartz shared Terkel's book with the other songwriters, who conceived ideas for numbers. Schwartz's favorite song in the show is Taylor's "Millwork," and he reports it was "totally James's idea. It never occurred to me that might be a musical number. He just wanted to do it."[20] Micki Grant came up with the idea of a song about cleaning women when she visited a rehearsal in Chicago and thought the show needed something about domestic workers.[21] Schwartz worked with songwriters individually as he assembled the score; they never met as a group except on opening night. Schwartz discussed their songs with them, but did not edit them. He encouraged his collaborators to attend rehearsals, especially as the cast worked on their material, and de Giere reports a moment when James Taylor asked the accompanying instrumentalists if they could bring more "funk" to "Brother Trucker."[22] Schwartz reports, "They basically gave me the songs and I used them. You know, I might ask for certain things, but in the end, they were their songs."

In the same way that Schwartz often wrote songs for a show that later got edited or removed, such also happened with numbers by his *Working* collaborators. He reports, for example, that they went through several versions of "Just a Housewife," the first few with music by Mary Rodgers and lyrics by Susan Birkenhead.[23] Schwartz had asked them to write for the song placement because they were married women with children, but ultimately Craig Carnelia managed to provide the song's feeling of quiet desperation. The following songs became the core of the first successful version of *Working*, appearing on the original cast recording (OCR):[24]

"All the Livelong Day"—Stephen Schwartz
"Lovin' Al"—Micki Grant
"The Mason"[25]—Craig Carnelia
"Neat to Be a Newsboy"[26]—Schwartz
"Nobody Tells Me How"[27]—Mary Rodgers and Susan Birkenhead
"Un Mejor Día Vendrá"[28]—James Taylor (Spanish lyrics by Graciela Daniele and Matt Landers)
"Just a Housewife"—Carnelia
"Millwork"—Taylor
"If I Could've Been"[29]—Grant
"Joe"[30]—Carnelia[31]
"It's an Art"[32]—Schwartz
"Brother Trucker"—Taylor
"Fathers and Sons"[33]—Schwartz
"Cleanin' Women"—Grant
"Something to Point To"—Carnelia

(The OCR also includes Carnelia's "Hots Michael at the Piano,"[34] cut before the Broadway opening, and Schwartz's "I'm Just Movin',"[35] added in 1999.)

A "nonfiction" musical needed a certain musical approach, and the same was true for the choreography, which could not trivialize the typical actions of various types of workers while also providing the kind of dancing expected by Broadway audiences. Schwartz first started working with Graciela Daniele, who served as choreographer for the initial production in Chicago. She (and Matt Landers) wrote the Spanish lyrics for James Taylor's song "Un mejor día vendrá." Daniele left the show to honor her commitment to do musical staging for the musical revue A History of the American Film, which ran for twenty-one performances on Broadway in March to April 1978. Schwartz replaced Daniele with Onna White (1922–2005), veteran choreographer of a number of Broadway successes such as The Music Man (1957), Mame (1966), and 1776 (1969). Schwartz reported that he "really missed" Daniele as they went to New York, although he also noted that White "did an OK job. She was certainly a very talented choreographer, and nothing against her, but there was something about the collaboration with Graci that was working really well, and I really regretted not having her."[36]

The orchestrator for Working was Kirk Nurock, described by Schwartz as "one of those pop/rock guys who could . . . straddle the world of pop and folk music and more Broadway-esque music." Nurock has had a varied career as a jazz pianist, composer, and arranger, among other musical positions. He performed varied musical tasks for several short-lived Broadway musicals between 1973 and 1984.[37] Schwartz liked Nurock's orchestrations for Working. Stephen Reinhardt again served as musical director, as he had for Godspell and The Magic Show. He reports that he led a "small ensemble" in Chicago in the pit (unlike Godspell and The Magic Show, where the band was on a platform at the back of the stage), and then in New York, after Nurock completed his orchestrations, Reinhardt conducted the orchestra in the pit, for him "a totally new craft." Reinhardt remains grateful for how Schwartz entrusted him "with each new level of difficulty" as he directed music for Godspell, The Magic Show, and Working.[38]

Working, encompassing a number of different workplaces, provided interesting problems for set design. One of Schwartz's first notions was that they needed to evoke Chicago; he mentioned the common phrase one hears about "the city that works" and a few choice phrases from Carl Sandburg's famous poem, "the whole hog butcher to the world image. Chicago just feels like that." Scenic designer David Mitchell went about Chicago taking photographs "to try to make it have that feel, in an abstract way." Schwartz describes the Broadway set as uncomplicated, but with "big elements." As the director remembers, "It was pretty spare, actually, but there were things that were complicated about it in its spareness. It had pallets . . . that were mechanized so they could move up and down and you could deliver different people and pieces of scenery that way." In his review in the New York Times,

Richard Eder described the set as "high red girders" with scenes of working and the city projected around them.[39] One of Schwartz's favorite moments in terms of set and costume design took place in the finale, the song "Something to Point To," which opens with the lyric "See that building . . . ," an opportunity for the laborers to show pride in what they create. The cast performed most of the song in white costumes inspired by George Segal's white sculptures and tableaux, but these costumes easily tore away, allowing each toward the end of the song—when singing "By me!"—to appear quickly in color versions of their costumes, concluding the show with a stirring splash of colors made possible by costume designer Marjorie Slaiman.

Schwartz's original agreement with his producers was that the show would run at the Arena Stage in Washington DC, before opening in New York. Those in charge, however, decided to go straight to Broadway so that the show might qualify for the Tony Awards that year, a move that began Schwartz's antipathy toward the awards.[40] Schwartz's notes, "We weren't ready. The show was too long and there were things in it that didn't work. . . . We didn't have time to fix it, and some of it I blame myself for, for not being more ruthless sooner. But some of it I blame the producers for because they went back on what I had been promised."[41] By this point Schwartz had stopped reading reviews of shows at the time they were published, but he did go back and review them once further work started on the show after its disappointingly short run in New York.[42] He found a substantial number of writers who felt that the show might have worked if it were shorter, and he decided that the critics "stood in, in some ways, for the audience—that felt the show could have worked but it was just too damn long. They were right! It wore out its welcome."

Working is an engrossing, challenging evening of theater. Studs Terkel's interviews include considerable rawness as people express unvarnished emotions about their work, from pride of accomplishment to resentment of what might be perceived as lowly roles in the world. Terkel set the tone for his book in the first paragraph of his introduction, where he states, "The book, being about work, is, by its very nature, about violence—to the spirit as well as the body." He also identifies "daily humiliation" as a pervasive theme.[43] Schwartz's show includes an older primary school teacher who is angry about the new requirements of her position, a depressed housewife, a bored and desperate millworker, a retiree trying to find meaning in life as a widower, and a newspaper copyboy who seethes with anger.[44] Evocative songs assist with the overall effect, but it is a heavy emotional load, balanced to an extent by such delightful moments as a parking attendant who adores his work, a mason who derives satisfaction from the permanence of his creations, an energetic newsboy who revels in throwing his products at floppy bushes, a waitress who finds her work to be an art, and a stirring finale. The realism that is *Working* demands delicate, careful balance, the kind that Schwartz has tended to find in his career through a process of trial and error before an audience. Without the opportunity to finish the pruning and editing, especially the crucial winnowing it down to an ideal length, the New York run suffered.

Critical Reception

New York critics found things to like in *Working*, but overall print reviews were disappointing, and as a group they surely contributed to the show's quick closing. A common theme was that the show was too long—as seen earlier, Schwartz now agrees—but most writers praised the cast and several appreciated Schwartz's direction. Judgments about the music were mixed. Of the seventeen reviews consulted for this study, only two could be called raves; the others range from critics who basically liked what they saw but believed the show was too long and/or lacked focus to those who condemned the idea of turning Terkel's book into a musical.

Working opened on 14 May 1978, and reviews appeared in major New York dailies the next morning. Richard Eder of the *New York Times* lauded the "absolutely first-rate cast" but for him the conception was "out of focus," partly because the portrayals of various laborers work on paper but not on stage, where they seemed "dramatic fictions" that are "usually too frail" and "overburdened."[45] Eder praised a few songs by James Taylor but described the others as "musically uninteresting" with lyrics that are "trite and sentimental." The critic thought that Schwartz's direction was "magnificent." Writing for the *Daily News*, Douglas Watt thought that the show needed editing: "If all of 'Working' were up to its best moments, [it] . . . would be one of the niftiest and most refreshing shows of the season."[46] Unfortunately, however, for Watt, it was too long and Act 2 was problematic, despite a fine cast and what he considered the show's positive message. Clive Barnes of the *New York Post* panned *Working*: "Basic honesty and banality are the two qualities of this show."[47] He appreciated the "good cast" but overall described the show as "a personal reminiscence interupted [sic] by the occasional feeble song."

Another noted New York critic, Howard Kissel of *Women's Wear Daily*, was only marginally more positive when his review appeared the next morning. He called *Working* "an odd combination of authenticity and show business."[48] He found the best moments to be dramatic monologues with some songs that "give this sprawling subject some focus," naming "The Mason" and "Just a Housewife." Despite what he saw as a few attempts to organize the show, he noted that the good parts were handicapped because "the show has no shape." Kissel described *Working*, along with the contemporary *Dancin'* and *Runaways*, as shows inspired by *A Chorus Line*, but he preferred the "sense of momentum" in Michael Bennett's famous show.

Hobe Morrison, the longtime critic for *Variety*, provided a mostly positive appraisal on 17 May. In one of his typically thorough columns, Morrison mentioned the "excellent" cast and appreciated the score that included "no outright clunkers" with some songs that "give the impression of being minor gems."[49] He found *Working* to be "a highly unusual, provocative and amusing show with a topically pertinent theme," and suggested that it might have a long run. The critic briefly compared the Chicago and New York versions of the show, noting that since the Windy City run that the songs "American Dreaming," "Nobody Goes Out Anymore," and "The Working Girl's Apache" had been removed, and "The Mason," "Husbands and Wives," and "Cleanin' Women" had been added. Rex Reed, writing another review of the show for the *Daily News*, raved about *Working*, calling it a "rich, fertile cornucopia of lives set to music" and "much of it immensely moving, all of it terrifically original in concept, beautifully and artistically performed."[50]

The last review consulted from opening week appeared in the *Soho Weekly News*, penned by Gerald Rabkin. He compared the show to *Runaways*, noting that the creators of both fumble the balancing act of trying "to reconcile experimental seriousness with the obligation to amuse."[51] He did not think that efforts of the multiple songwriters produced a cohesive score, and questioned whether the show should have even been attempted. Rabkin offered the useful detail that some of Terkel's monologues had already appeared in New York earlier in 1978 in The Talking Band's *Worksong* at Theatre for the New City.[52]

Numerous additional reviews appeared between 25 May and 8 July. Leo Shull of *Show Business* found *Working* to be "the most extraordinary combination of story, songs, lighting, movie-sets & props I have ever seen."[53] His approbation continued as he called the show, "stunning and magnificent." In a review that appeared in the *East Side Express*, Leah D. Frank was far less sanguine, citing the show's "deep, all-consuming regret and dissatisfaction with life."[54] One of her overall judgments was typical: "*Working* merely succeeds in elevating the ordinary to the commonplace." Marjorie Gunner of the *Nassau Star* offered a mixed review, finding the show "endless" but "boasting some excellent talent."[55] With careful editing, she thought *Working* had a future off-Broadway. Barbara Lewis in the *New York Amsterdam News* on 27 May had lukewarm impressions, noting that it "features songs and vignettes that communicate a poignant human dimension," but she also suggested that the show could have ended after Act 1, despite some good moments in Act 2.[56] Walter Kerr weighed in from his august perch at the *New York Times* on 28 May, two weeks after opening. He described the show in some detail and appreciated the cast, but had little to say about the music while noting that the songwriters retained simplicity in the lyrics, following the plainness of Terkel's interview subjects. His overall judgment of the show was provocative: the musical was "life dramatized,"[57] and that quality was destined to fail because the stories were not meant as theater to begin with, a condition that could be applied to many stories that have been musicalized.

Three reviews from well-known publications appeared on 29 May. The *Village Voice* sent Erika Munk, who clearly disliked musicals and went expecting to hate the show, but then "kind of liked it."[58] Although *Working* would have been dismissed downtown for a myriad of problems in attitude ("shallowness, gimmickry, and ostentation" and soft-pedaling racism and sexism), Munk admitted that for a Broadway show it is "socially useful and generally amusing," and it should certainly run when one considers the competition. *Time*'s T. E. Kalem, in a mostly negative review, decided that the "problem is that the characters are not doing their jobs but talking about them."[59] For him *Working* was a "confessional musical," like *A Chorus Line* and *Runaways*, with songs written by too many artists "to possess a distinctive signature." Brendan Gill of the *New Yorker* found turning Terkel's book into a musical a "bizarre notion" and resented that "the message of the show is so relentlessly upbeat" and that most songs "are far too sweet for their own good."[60] In a review that did not appear until 8 July, more than a month after the show closed on 4 June, veteran critic Martin Gottfried published a comparison of several recent shows in *Saturday Review*. He called *Working* "an intelligent musical, dealing with a substantial subject and providing that quality so rare on Broadway: contact with reality."[61] He thought the weaknesses included "no dynamics or tension" and that the show petered out in Act 2, but he lauded the directing, composing, and lyric writing, crafts that he saw on the decline in contemporary Broadway. John Simon (frequently scornful of Schwartz's efforts) in *New York* took issue with the entire conception: "It is a distinctly clever attempt to do the impossible," but "common sense . . . would have told one to desist."[62] He did praise aspects of the show, like the way that Schwartz connected the vignettes together and most of the cast and production values.

This is a revealing set of reviews. As previously noted, Schwartz confirmed from them that the show was too long. Many critics liked the cast, production values, and direction. Several described how *Working* fit into its period by presenting a number of unrelated stories tied together by a central theme, a trend launched by *A Chorus Line* (1975) and continued by *Runaways* (1978). A fascinating aspect of the reviews is the widely varied perception of the show's overall mood, with some writers finding it too depressing and others irritated at what they saw as its unfailing cheerfulness. Such opinions aside, the show does portray a wide range of emotions. *Working*, in revised forms, has become a successful property,[63] but these reviews help explain its short life on Broadway in 1978.

A Rapid Fix

Unlike some other shows in Schwartz's output, which he worked on for years with collaborators after an initial failure, successful revisions for *Working* took place soon after it closed on Broadway. Paul Lazarus (born 1954), who has enjoyed a distinguished career as a director in theater, film, and television, saw the show during its brief New York run and approached Schwartz about doing the next production at Dartmouth. He had some ideas on how to make the show work better, as Schwartz recalls:

> I had known Paul because he had a radio show in New York where he interviewed writers. . . . And we sat down and we talked about the show, and I said that I felt that one of the reasons it hadn't worked was because it was too long, but I wasn't sure about what to lose and what to cut, and he had ideas about re-arranging things. It was his idea—the thing that I most remember because it worked immediately, and I learned a lesson from it—it was his idea to flip the order of "Cleaning Women" and "Fathers and Sons." They were originally in the opposite order and neither of the songs particularly worked . . . as well as I anticipated they would.

The original order of the segment was Schwartz's song "Fathers and Sons" followed by monologues for the newspaper copyboy and a tie salesman,[64] setting up "Cleaning Women," what the director identified "as the 11:00 number . . . this big rock 'em, sock 'em number right before the end." Lazarus recommended switching "Father and Sons" and "Cleaning Women" while leaving the monologues in place. Schwartz reports that change helped the show because "Fathers and Sons" "sort of leads you home. It . . . starts to tie up the show emotionally, and by having 'Fathers and Sons' . . . lead almost immediately into 'See That Building' [the finale] it just was very powerful all of a sudden."

Schwartz was disgusted with the Broadway scene after his difficult experience with *The Baker's Wife* and the failure of *Working*. As Carol de Giere has shown, the composer/lyricist spent much of the next three years with his family, entering a sort of retirement at the age of thirty.[65] His huge early success gave him financial freedom, but clearly a project that he saw to before his period of reflection was fixing *Working* with Lazarus and getting a version ready for the production at Dartmouth. The changes were successful; as Schwartz recalls, "Once the show got fixed, which was more or less immediately afterwards, it always worked from that point on."

Video Version and Updates

The Educational Broadcasting Corporation and Community Television of Southern California produced a video version of *Working* in 1982 to be shown on *American Playhouse*, presented by Thirteen/WNET New York.[66] Schwartz directed the video along with Kirk Browning (1921–2008), a prolific television director and producer. Valente Riolo was associate director, and Nina Faso was credited as assistant to directors and co-adaptor of the property with Schwartz. Other creative credits included musical staging by Sammy Bayes, music direction by Stephen Michael Reinhardt (Schwartz's frequent collaborator), orchestrations by Tom Pierson, musical supervision by John Adams (now famous as the composer of *Nixon in China* and other operas), and executive producer was Jac Venza. The production was only eighty-eight minutes long but included twenty-seven total segments, fifteen of which are a full song or brief musical number. Several of the songs were shortened for this version. The list of segments along with the impressive cast was as follows:

> Introduction; Main Title—"All The Live Long Day"—Ensemble
> The Steelworker—monologue—Barry Bostwick
> Parking Lot Attendant—"Lovin' Al"—Scatman Crothers
> The Editor—monologue—Barbara Browning
> The Secretary—monologue—Vernée Watson
> The Corporate Executive—monologue—Jay Garner
> The Newsboy—"Neat to Be a Newsboy"—Billy Jacoby
> The Schoolteacher—"Nobody Tells Me How"—Barbara Barrie
> The Supermarket Checker—"Treasure Island Trio" (brief)—Carole Schwartz
> The Supermarket Bagger—monologue—Bill Beyers
> The Farm Worker—"Un mejor día vendrá" (mostly as underscoring)—Fausto Barajas
> The Gas Man—monologue—Charles Haid
> The Housewife—"Just a Housewife"—Beth Howland

The Call Girl—monologue—Barbara Hershey
The Millworker—"Millwork"—Eileen Brennan
Montage—"If I Could've Been"—Ensemble
Studs Terkel—monologue
The Waitress—"It's an Art"—Rita Moreno
The Operators—monologues—Lynne Thigpen, Edie McClury, Didi Conn
The Trucker—"Brother Trucker"—James Taylor
The Retired Man—"Joe"—Charles Durning
The Fireman—monologue—Matt Landers
The Cleaning Woman—"Cleanin' Women"—Patti LaBelle
The Salesman—monologue—Mark Neely
The Copyboy—monologue—David Patrick Kelly
The Steelworker—"Fathers and Sons"—Barry Bostwick
Montage—"Something to Point To"—Ensemble

The video demonstrates the creative approach that Schwartz and Faso took to *Working* and confirms the show's challenging, direct nature. Promotional materials packaged with the DVD portray it as a sociological document, a descendant of Marc Blitzstein's *The Cradle Will Rock* (1937). *Working* lacks the overt political punch found in the famous Federal Theater Project work, but it shares *Cradle's* call for the dignity and worth of the common worker. The video carries the look of a documentary and the cast is believable and appealing, but some of the songs are performed without style or grace. Barry Bostwick is fine as the steelworker who sings "Fathers and Sons" toward the end, and Scatman Crothers works well in "Lovin' Al." Other memorable musical performances include Rita Moreno in "It's an Art," James Taylor appearing to sing his own song "Brother Trucker," and Patti LaBelle singing "Cleanin' Women." Schwartz's wife, Carole, appears convincingly as the supermarket checker. Studs Terkel makes a number of appearances, several times serving as the agent for continuity, as the next worker starts to tell his or her story. Movement between segments works well in the video, sometimes with an actor suggesting a thematic connection at the end of a scene that leads to the next. At other times there is a simple cut, but in monologues the medium renders the show a bit strained. These brief speeches are presented without underscoring, raw and brutally honest. The monologues seem all the more stark when compared with segments where characters sing, which often include underscoring for some spoken lines. Monologues without underscoring would not seem so stark in a stage version, but the close-ups make the show feel more like a film with its separate expectations.

As *Working* has remained popular for over three decades, it has required updates that take into account changes in the workplace. Nina Faso reports that she has spent hours on the telephone with Schwartz over the years working on revisions.[67] When one strives for more realism than ordinarily found in a musical, it would be awkward to try and let the show become a period piece like *Oklahoma!* or *My Fair Lady*. Schwartz spoke of a new version prepared in the late 1990s,[68] and another that he did with director Gordon Greenberg for a May 2008 production at the Asolo Repertory Theater in Sarasota, Florida, the version currently available. Greenberg designed a production for a cast of only six actors, adding the complication of costume changes as they decided the order of the segments, the step that Schwartz believes makes or breaks the show. Lin Manuel Miranda, the composer/lyricist of *In the Heights*, wrote new material for *Working*, including a song about a delivery boy on his first job. This replaced "Lovin' Al," sung by the parking lot attendant, which Schwartz believed had "dated a bit." In our interview Schwartz expressed the hope that Miranda might write another song, which he subsequently did.[69] Greenberg conceived the Sarasota version as one act and about ninety minutes of material. Schwartz shared some details of their deliberations: the trucker had been cut, but then they restored the segment with James Taylor's song; they removed the migrant worker "because that's really '70s"; the newsboy had been replaced by a supermarket checker, but that has since been removed because Schwartz thought the song was too much like his "It's an Art." Schwartz believes that several of the show's "classics" remain: the opening, the disgruntled teacher, the housewife, the mill worker, "If I Could've Been," the mason, the retiree, the waitress, "Fathers and Sons," and the finale "Something to Point To." He says that these are "the songs that really are the ones that people identify with the show. We're trying to do a show that doesn't feel dated, if we can, but also isn't so of the moment that next year this version will be dated." It is his hope that this version of *Working* might remain viable for about a decade. Since the Sarasota run, it has played at the Old Globe in San Diego in March 2009, the Broadway Playhouse in Chicago in February 2011, and at the 59E59 Theaters in New York in December 2012. Greenberg directed *Working* in each location.[70]

Stephen Schwartz's Songs for *Working*

Schwartz's songs that made a major mark in the Broadway version of *Working* were the opener "All the Live Long Day," "Neat to Be a Newsboy," "It's an Art," and "Fathers and Sons." For the 1999 version he added "I'm Just Movin'."

Schwartz took the title for "All the Live Long Day" from "I've Been Workin' on the Railroad." Some of the lyrics came from Walt Whitman's famous poem "I Hear America Singing."[71] Schwartz used a few lines from the poem; it was a worthwhile inspiration because Whitman spends most of it naming workers who sing. "All the Live Long Day" includes sung or spoken references to a number of characters, giving it the feeling of other famous introductory numbers to Broadway shows—such as "Tradition" from *Fiddler on the Roof* or "Comedy Tonight" from *A Funny Thing Happened on the Way to the Forum*, both shows directed by Jerome Robbins—where the audience meets a variety of characters and situations, establishing the show's intention and mood. Schwartz might have been influenced by Robbins; as reported in the previous chapter, Robbins made important suggestions on how to open *The Baker's Wife*. As they performed "All the Live Long Day," the cast climbed around on the show's title in large red letters.

The score for *Working* consulted for this study was published in 1978 with notations in it indicating that it postdated the 1978 Dartmouth production. The first segment of the opening song is for unusual percussion instruments, including typewriter, metal pipes being pounded together, and releases of steam, marked in the score as "in lieu of taped opening."[72] The first 0'47" of the OCR includes such noises placed in juxtaposition with actors speaking of workplaces. The tune starts at 0'48" in a "Funk Four" with a characteristic bass line, building out of the rhythm set by the pipes. Schwartz sets brief quotations and paraphrases from Walt Whitman's poem over the basso ostinato, finally at 1'46" allowing sung lines to become background over which voices start speaking as representatives of professions portrayed later in the show. This cacophony is suddenly interrupted (at 2'04") with a bluesy verse with funk accompaniment over which a man offers to sell his story of working at a store. For a million dollars, he would quit his job. A counted measure of four (2'28") opens the refrain, where Schwartz references "I've Been Working on the Railroad" ("Just like the song say, All the livelong day"). Another verse (with chorus complaining about working issues, such as the arrival of a Monday) and refrain follow. A disco instrumental passage intervenes (3'47") for dancing, preceding a choral treatment of motives from the refrain (4'07"), which closes the number. It is reminiscent of many 1970s funk treatments, such as parts of "The Music and the Mirror" from *A Chorus Line*.

Schwartz conceived "Neat to Be a Newsboy" as what he called "kid/pop; it was just supposed to sound like a little kid." He based the lyrics on Terkel's three interviews with paperboys,[73] but made the character in the show younger than the twelve- to fourteen-year-olds in the book and avoided the negativity that dominates the third interviewee's comments. Schwartz compared the accompaniment to Beatles songs with "repeated chords" in the right hand that sound on most quarter notes beats in the quadruple meter over a syncopated bass line. The songwriter cited the style as well in "Popular" from *Wicked* and "No Time at All" from *Pippin*, and the songs at times do sound very similar. The verse of "Newsboy" is an AAB (8+8+4). The refrain is quick and feels like a fast soft-shoe, dominated by long-short triplet rhythms and effects in voice and orchestra that represent movement in the bushes that child loves when he throws the paper in them. (Terkel's interviewee insists that he would then fish the paper out of the bushes and place it on the porch.[74]) The refrain is CC' and a delightful confection, but with fairly rapid text to be presented, a task that the young Matthew McGrath did not perform with success. (Some critics noted how unintelligible his lyrics were, but apparently his physical approximation of the word *sproing* with his body was something to behold!) It is a conventional song for Schwartz, but effective in its place.

Schwartz managed one of his more memorable, dramatic numbers in "It's an Art," his paean to waitresses largely based on this profile in Terkel's book.[75] The waitress (named Dolores Dante) emphasized her Italian heritage, piquing the interest of opera lover Schwartz. The similarities between Dante's interview content and Schwartz's song are especially close. A moment that jumped off the page for the composer was her description of speaking "sotto voce" (softly), emphasizing her family's nationality with a term one encounters in operatic scores. Schwartz set out to write an "Italian waltz" for her, the model being "Sempre libera" from Verdi's *La traviata*. In an interview involving the show *My Son Pinocchio: Geppetto's Musical Tale*, for which Schwartz also wrote an Italian waltz, Schwartz admitted that his efforts in the genre are more based in folk melodies than the vocal gymnastics of opera, but certainly the accompaniment of "It's an Art" is strongly reminiscent of "Sempre libera," and both melodies include typical rhythmic gestures associated with the waltz and show a tendency toward conjunct motion. The basic verse (first time, 0'03"–0'33") is an aabc, each section an eight-bar phrase. Following the first two verses Schwartz introduces contrasting material where he quotes themes from the classical repertory, followed by the refrain in cc'd (8+8+7) form. The first two quotations are sung on vocables, including the theme from the opening of "Un bel di, vedremo" from Puccini's *Madama Butterfly* (0'33"–0'36") and the opening of Act 2 from Tchaikovsky's *Swan Lake*, as the swans swim on the lake (1'30"–1'35"). Just before the Puccini snippet the waitress has compared the subtlety of one of her motions to something "near oriental," perhaps prompting Schwartz's thoughts of *Butterfly*. Following the second refrain (with new lyrics) Schwartz introduces new material as the waitress states her feelings about tips, offering that a customer can satisfy her with a coin, which makes her feel like Carmen, the gypsy.[76] The composer invokes the spirit of Spanish music as heard in Bizet's opera (2'11"–2'24"), first with descending chromatic motion in the vocal line, evocative harmonic motion, and castanets. One more verse and refrain with some additional music under spoken material complete the song, a chorus joining the soloist in the final refrain, calling for service as she finishes her song. It is one of the more uplifting moments of the show, celebrated with a delightful musical élan.

Parental feelings resonate deeply with Schwartz, appearing in a number of his shows, most prominently in *Children of Eden*, but *Working* includes one of his clearest evocations of the theme. He calls "Fathers and Sons" a "very personal" song that he had written for the show, inspired by Terkel's interviews but not directly taken from one, so the songwriter was going to remove it. Nina Faso insisted that it belonged, and Schwartz finally agreed.[77] (Faso noted that much had to be cut from the show, but not "Fathers and Sons," because "that was what the whole play was about: posterity."[78]) Schwartz reports that a mistake in the original production was not giving the song to Mike the steelworker, a character with whom the audience identified deeply. When Paul Lazarus suggested that the position of "Fathers and Sons" be switched with "Cleanin' Women," they also gave the former song to Mike. It carries a prominent, driving piano accompaniment that alternates between an eighth-note line with syncopations and half-note chords. It opens in F-sharp minor and stays there for much of the song, befitting the nostalgic tone as a father thinks about how quickly his son grew up. "Fathers and Sons" feels like a plainspoken country song. The form includes three verses separated by two refrains (ABABA). The verses are aa'bb in form and present a progression of sentiment, the father moving from remembering his son at age three and one-half in the first verse (0'18"–1'02") to considering his own father and their relationship in the second (1'47"–2'33"), and then musing on the speed that life passes and how he has worked for a better life for his son (3'26"–4'18", with additional instrumental accompaniment and backup singers). The refrains end ruefully in F-sharp minor and the song overall in A major, but the modulation is not a catharsis. Any parent can appreciate the speed with which a child's life passes by, and Schwartz captured that spirit in one of the show's more thoughtful songs. Schwartz also wrote the music to a minor piece in the 1978 version of *Working*, the "Treasure Island Trio," where he worked with Graciela Daniele on adding some realistic work movements into the choreography.

For the 1999 version of *Working* Schwartz adapted the music to "I'm Just Movin'" from the supermarket checker dance (arranged by Michelle Brourman, whom Schwartz had known at Carnegie Mellon) from the Broadway run into the song.[79] Here the songwriter returns to the Motown roots that partly began his professional musical theater career with *Godspell* in 1971. The bluesy, syncopated melody, backup singers, and driving accompaniment bear more than a whiff of the Holland-Dozier-Holland hits from the 1960s, here setting lyrics about the checker's love for her work with reflections on the job's difficulties. The song is, like the character, honest and genuine.

Such truthfulness explains much of the appeal of *Working*. The workers from Terkel's book come alive on stage, warts and all, expressing feelings of pride, drudgery, satisfaction, anger, hope, and despair. Some of these vignettes explode into song and dance, an unrealistic conceit for those who tire of musical theater, but a satisfying bit of artistry for those willing to accept the possibility that these emotions warrant melodic relief. Critics who saw the influence of *A Chorus Line* here were onto something.[80] Michael Bennett and his collaborators worked from life stories of Broadway dancers, and Schwartz and Faso mined Terkel's interview transcripts from many professions. The Broadway results could not have been more different—6,137 Broadway performances to 24—but *Working* remains a regular in local and regional theaters.

CHAPTER EIGHT

~

Rags

The Show's Genesis

When working on Broadway, Stephen Schwartz has usually served as both composer and lyricist. The only Broadway project for which he has written exclusively words is *Rags*, a 1986 musical that played only four performances in August 1986. His involvement in this show, with original story and book by Joseph Stein and music by Charles Strouse, began in early 1982. In addition to writing lyrics, Schwartz directed the first workshop and codirected the show with Charles Strouse after the dismissal of their first director during rehearsals. *Rags* remained a project worthy of rethinking in subsequent productions, but, unlike *The Baker's Wife*, *Rags* perhaps has not reached a finished form. We begin with Schwartz's thoughts on its creation, followed by additional material drawn from interviews with Stein and Strouse, and newspaper accounts.

Referring to an important stage in the development of *The Baker's Wife*, Schwartz stated that "*Rags* needs the equivalent of Trevor Nunn."[1] This would be a director who brings a fresh eye on the material. Schwartz believes in the quality of much of the work, but he thinks that it needs to be submitted to another knowledgeable party. He noted that writing *Rags* was "a bit of a truck without a driver, and that's always problematic." The problems were not based on personality clashes, because, as Schwartz stated before Stein's death, "Joe, Charles, and I like each other very much, like working together," but they possessed "I wouldn't say very different visions, but different enough that the show needs somebody fresh and dramaturgically smart, who can come in and say 'OK, this is what we're doing.'" Schwartz noted that there have been a number of regional productions of *Rags*, some "enormous successes," but none has yielded what he believes to be the completed version.

Schwartz admires Strouse's work for *Rags*: "I'm in awe of Charles's music for that show. I don't think I could ever have done what he did." An oft-cited aspect of the show's music was casting opera star Teresa Stratas as the lead, but Schwartz does not believe that the role requires such a voice. He has nothing but praise for Stratas in *Rags*, calling her "wonderful." Schwartz emphasizes that the issues with *Rags* were elsewhere. Comparing it with a show that was successful at the time but is now commercially unavailable, Schwartz asserts, "The reason that [*The*] *Magic Show* works and *Rags* doesn't is that the structure of *Magic Show* works. So the fact that some of writing was pretty inferior didn't matter. All of the writing in *Rags* is better."[2]

Joseph Stein reported that he had been approached "dozens of times" about doing a sequel for *Fiddler on the Roof*, but he felt he "had told that story and that story was finished."[3] As the son of immigrants, Stein became intrigued by the immigrant experience, first as a screenplay. When Lee Guber, son of Russian immigrants (and who, with Shelly Gross, operated Westbury Music Fair and Valley Forge Music Fair[4]), saw the draft, he suggested that Stein make it into a musical.[5] Stein remembered that he presented the idea to Schwartz, with whom he had worked on *The Baker's Wife*, and together they approached Charles Strouse (composer of *Bye Bye Birdie*, *Applause*, and *Annie*) about writing the music. Stein said that he would have been enthusiastic about Schwartz writing both music and lyrics, but he thought that Strouse "was much more familiar with that period."

Strouse remembered that he loved the original script, and he described the show as a continuation of *Fiddler on the Roof*, a historical period that had always fascinated him. He believes that Stein's book "caught that feeling of the terror [of the immigrants] and the cynicism of Americans towards these people."[6] Strouse has always thought that critics of *Rags* "gave short shrift to the book." He emphasized the significance of the Triangle Shirtwaist Factory fire in 1911,[7] and credited Stein with showing how some immigrants had difficulties in the United States.

Contrary to Stein's account, Strouse said he started work on the score for *Rags* with Hal David, famous for lyrics he wrote to tunes by Burt Bacharach. Strouse and David were friends and had worked together a bit on another show. They collaborated on two songs for *Rags*, but Strouse thought that Guber was afraid that they were the start of "more of a pop score" and did not capture the story's Jewishness. Strouse noted that one of the tunes actually remained in the show. According to Strouse, Guber suggested Schwartz as a possible lyricist, and the composer welcomed the idea. He had met Schwartz through previous professional contacts. Strouse knew that Schwartz had worked with Leonard Bernstein on *Mass*, and he "felt flattered that he would do this with me." Strouse was impressed with Schwartz's lyrics for *Rags*: "Stephen took to it and I thought captured a part of his emotional life that I had never seen. . . . He really dug in and was very moved by what we wrote."

Stein had completed the story's initial treatment before Strouse and Schwartz came aboard. Stein remembered that the three met often as they developed the project. Details of the long collaborative period are sketchy, but they first announced the show in summer 1982, possibly for an opening the following winter.[8] In early 1983, the *New York Times* reported that the opening would be delayed until perhaps the following season,[9] and in September 1983 the *Daily News* said that the show might be close to production.[10] In March 1984 they held a workshop and Carol Lawton reported in the *Times* that the creators were considering whether to rewrite or go into production.[11] Demonstrating Broadway's harsh economic reality, the producers raised $300,000 for the workshop alone.[12] The decision was to rewrite, helping to delay the production for two years.

Nina Faso reports that she was also involved in *Rags* during the developmental period, working with Schwartz on directing it and taking part in workshops.[13] From an immigrant family, Faso notes that she told stories about her grandparents that appeared in the show. They reached a point where Schwartz did not feel that he could continue directing, and his decision to remove himself, which also cut out Faso, became a major point of contention between them for several years. As a female director in the 1980s, Faso faced considerable prejudice, and *Rags* was her last real chance to work on Broadway.

While Schwartz and Stein remembered the collaboration on *Rags* as smooth and friendly, Strouse indicated that they had moments of disagreement:

> They're both very dominant personalities, and I would say if there's a question of giving in, it would be Joe who would give into Stephen more. Stephen is very dominating, and I spent a lot of time in that show feeling that they were dancing, the two of them all the time, and I was in the background with the orchestra.

Schwartz and Stein both stated that they were good friends, but Strouse remembered that "Joe and Stephen fought a lot." As far as his direct collaboration with Schwartz on the songs, Strouse insisted, "We always had a merry time of it. . . . He is so musical, which helps me a great deal, and I have a pretty good ear for lyrics—I write them myself."

Despite their strenuous efforts, the problems with *Rags* could not be remedied in its first production. As Stein put it, "We had the usual out-of-town problems, but they were not soluble." The book continued to change throughout the Boston tryout period, and the New York opening was delayed for two weeks so that replacement director Gene Saks could make more adjustments. The previous director was Joan Micklin Silver, who had directed the film *Hester Street* (1975), concerning immigrants from the same period, and had also directed musical theater. Stein said that "she was at a loss" in dealing with musical rehearsals, and Strouse thought she "got mired into a director's need to read the script and she would have the actors read the script sitting around a table for days and days, and then for a week." The actors wanted to know when they would get started on the music. Strouse noted that the actors helped force the change in directors. Silver later said that the creative team had originally intended "to make a musical drama but the producers lost confidence in the nature of the material and fell back on the traditions of musical comedy."[14] Silver left the show toward the middle of June, as reported by *Variety* on 18 June 1986.[15]

The lyricist and composer succeeded her. Strouse said that they could do this because most of the score was finished. He remembered that they took over about the time that *Rags* went to Boston, where the show ran from 23 June to 19 July.[16] Schwartz and Strouse took no directorial credit, wanting to avoid the stigma of "directed by the authors." He admitted, however, that "everything is public in musicals, and it was known that she was canned and we took over." At the time, *Variety* reported that Schwartz succeeded Silver as director.[17]

Schwartz and Strouse were only interims; the search for another director continued, but they had trouble agreeing on someone. Media reports named several possible figures. A story about male lead Larry Kert in July said that Arthur Laurents came in and made suggestions.[18] There were numerous reports that Jerome Robbins was asked to direct the show, but he declined.[19] In a *Newsday* story that announced that Gene Saks was becoming the director, James Lapine was mentioned as one who considered taking the position.[20] Strouse did not think that Saks worked out very well, and he also recalled that Stratas disliked working with Saks and would have preferred having Strouse and Schwartz continue to direct. According to Strouse, they wrote one song under Saks's direction: "What's Wrong with That?"

Saks has commented on his work with *Rags*. Coming into a show that was in trouble so late in the game can be a thankless job. He attempted "to clarify the story so people knew what was going on, but by clarifying it, I probably took away some of the camouflage that covered its deficiencies. Basically, Teresa Stratas *was* the show. But as written, Rebecca was not a character but an all-purpose symbol, and that's always deadly."[21]

Teresa Stratas, as the lead, Rebecca Hershkowitz, dominated. Many reviewers loved her, but the creators did not agree on her appropriateness. Stein stated, "We had a very exciting, very talented, and, I think, totally miscast leading lady." She was in her forties when she played the role, and Stein "had envisioned her as a young, timid, insecure, frightened immigrant," and he did not see the role as meant for a "diva." When Stratas was ill at the beginning of the Boston run, her understudy Christine Andreas went on, and Stein found her "terrific!" In contrast to Stein's apprehensions, Strouse enjoyed his opportunity to compose for a renowned opera singer whose abilities "ran the gamut of styles." He recalled,

> I got so that I knew her voice well, and I would say, "Let's lower that a half-step," or something, and she'd say, "No, we do it just where you did it, because you must have heard something because you started on the F-sharp." But I said, "Your voice is so much stronger down there. If I lower it just a little bit, you'll still have that note." But she wouldn't do it.

Strouse does not remember whose idea it was to approach Stratas, but he played for her what existed of the score and she liked it. Stratas had never been on Broadway and had turned down operatic roles since 1983 because she was taking care of her ailing father. Impressed with her cabaret work and renown as a Kurt Weill specialist, Strouse observed that she could sing in a jazz style, encouraging him to write "Blame It on the Summer Night." Schwartz expressed his admiration for Stratas the actress: "She has a combination of vulnerability and inner strength—like the immigrant women." Certainly a drawback with Stratas was her tendency to miss performances, necessitating an effective stand-in like Christine Andreas. The producers paid Stratas handsomely with a weekly guarantee of $25,000 and 3 percent of the show's net profits.[22]

Boston

Both Stein and Strouse emphasized how successful *Rags* was in Boston. Stein was "proud" of the show there, despite what he saw as the wrong lead actress and a set that "had lost all sense of intimacy." Strouse remembered large audiences in Boston and good reviews. The *Times* reported that the weekly gross in Boston grew from $170,000 to $420,000.[23] In addition to Saks becoming director, Ron Field replaced Kenneth Rinker as choreographer while in Boston. The producers wanted to stay in Boston and continue to work on the show, but there was a previous booking at the Shubert Theater.

Several Boston reviews were raves. Writing in the *Manchester Union Leader*, Bob Hilliard was effusive: "'Rags' will rate as one of the delights of the stage. This is a story of the heart, compellingly told in word and song."[24] Arthur Friedman, critic for the *Boston Herald*, praised "a deeply felt story by Joseph Stein, a rich and varied score by Charles Strouse, and haunting lyrics by Stephen Schwartz."[25] Arnold Howard in the *Boston Jewish Times* was more circumspect, but he praised the "clever" sets, "ingenious" structure of the ensemble numbers, and Rebecca's "strongly defined character." Although impressed with Christine Andreas's performance, he promised another review when Teresa Stratas returned.[26] Jon Lehman of the *Patriot Ledger* did a second review after Stratas's return, and he described her as a defining difference: "Without her, it is a nice little musical. With her, it has the potential to become the best Broadway show since *La Cage aux Folles*."[27] Jay Carr filed a second review for the *Boston Globe* when Stratas returned and found her "a giant" who "not only dwarfs the huge and unalluring Statue of Liberty upstage in her big finale—she renders it virtually invisible."[28] Carr also noted that the show was changing substantially during its Boston run.

New York

Rags was set to open in New York on 7 August, but the premiere was postponed three times to give Saks more time.[29] Previews started on 5 August, and opening night was 21 August.[30] Late summer is an unusual time to open a major musical, but the *Times* reported that was when Stratas was available for a one-year contract, and Stein had other commitments later in the year.[31]

The demise came swiftly. Stein stated that it was brought on by "mixed reviews, but mixed on the bad side because the *Times* was bad." The producers had already spent $5.3 million, and the mixed reviews probably would not have encouraged a sufficient number of patrons to attend. Audience reaction in Boston and New York had seemed exciting enough to suggest positive word of mouth, but that required advertising and staying open with small audiences until enough people had heard about the show from friends. In a meeting on Friday, 22 August, the day after the show opened, the producers estimated that it would cost at least $1 million to make a television commercial, purchase air time, and pay expenses while they waited for results. The weekly break-even point was $285,000, a difficult amount to reach with disappointing ticket sales.[32] The decision to close seemed inevitable. Guber first informed Stratas, who offered to waive her salary, and then he went to the cast, who agreed to do the same, but Actors Equity would not allow it. After the Friday evening performance, the cast decided to organize a demonstration after the Saturday matinee.

What followed sounds like a scene from a Broadway musical. Lonny Price, who played Ben, exhorted the audience after the Saturday matinee to march with the cast down to the TKTS booth at Duffy Square, resulting in a media sensation. Stein was in upstate New York and saw coverage of the procession on television news. The demonstration had the desired effect because all 784 leftover tickets for that evening's performance were sold, resulting in the demonstrative, full house heard in the Theatre on Film and Tape archive videotape at the New York Public Library. The excitement prompted the producers to make another effort to find money to keep the show open, but they were unsuccessful.[33] Rags closed.

The show was not a favorite of critics, and some reveled in their pans. John Simon, writing in New York, suggested that the show was such a bomb that it "should have been detonated underground somewhere in Nevada."[34] Douglas Watt of the Daily News found the proceedings "mournful."[35] Michael Feingold, one of two to review the show for the Village Voice, described moments of real appeal, but asserted that "Rags ultimately lives up to its name, a bagful of shmattes . . . all jammed together without regard for sense or style."[36] The Variety reviewer Togi lamented that the show failed "to deliver any true impact," despite "an ambitious score, slick staging, and a solid performance" by Stratas.[37]

Frank Rich's New York Times review was thoughtful. He praised Stratas but felt the show did not live up to her "voice and spiritual fire blast."[38] Her role, however, was only a "symbol," as were most characters in a show that tried "to cover so much ground." He praised Strouse's score, but thought that Schwartz's lyrics "contain few surprises." He considered the cast "competent and predictable," and had faint praise for most production elements.

Positive reviewers admitted that there were difficulties, but the show had admirers. Clive Barnes of the New York Post was thrilled with Stratas, saying that she "commands the night," and he also admired the remainder of the cast.[39] He praised the "high seriousness" of Strouse's score, which he heard as "unlike anything he has attempted before." In Schwartz's lyrics he heard "easy, unforced wit and genuine poetic feeling," and Stein's book told a "sweepingly panoramic story." He found the show "too predictable . . . too sweet," but cast and score carried the day. Writing the other Village Voice review, Julius Novick realized the show suffered from "evasions, implausibilities, uncertainties, crudities," but its themes reminded him of Dickens.[40] This Jewish reviewer respected the effort, wishing that his two-year-old daughter were old enough to see it and appreciate what her ancestors went through.

Charles Strouse thought that critics reviewed his score positively, and several did. It is a lively mixture of Jewish, folk, ragtime, and jazz elements from the early decades of the twentieth century. Strouse was not present at the demonstration led by the cast down Broadway, and he related why:

> I wasn't there because I was too hurt. I felt that it . . . represented not only some of the best work I had ever done and Stephen had ever done, but it was a particularly bad blow for me because my background in music had been a serious one and this was one of the few things I had done where I had tried to bring it together. I wasn't George Gershwin by any means, but I felt that it made a synthesis of the kinds of backgrounds that I had had.

Strouse, Schwartz, and the Score

As Strouse and Schwartz collaborated, the composer usually wrote a tune first, and then Schwartz added lyrics.[41] Strouse found that his wordsmith was a "very expressive judge of what he wanted, a reactor . . . I can remember getting the tune of [he sings a bit of 'Greenhorns'] and his coming up with 'Greenhorns.' I wasn't even that familiar with the word *greenhorn*." Strouse listened to a great deal of music from around 1910, some on original discs, and he began to notice how Jewish much of it sounded, including "all the riffs that clarinet players would play. . . . It was a crossover. The Jews as well as the blacks contributed to this thing we call jazz." Strouse found some typical klezmer gestures to be close to early jazz, not unlike the plaintive sound of "the Jewish crying. . . . It was something I tried to capture in the piece a lot."

Strouse achieved a wide range of musical expression in *Rags*. "Penny a Tune," "Hard to Be a Prince," and "Kaddish" effectively access various Jewish musical styles, and "Penny a Tune" takes the listener on a journey from klezmer music to popular American music. There are also strong Jewish musical references in other songs, such as "Easy for You." In addition to sections of "Penny a Tune," Strouse works with ragtime and early jazz in "Greenhorns," "Blame It on the Summer Night," "Rags," and "Cherry Street Café." A dramatic song early in the show that blends Jewish music and ragtime is "Brand New World." "Three Sunny Rooms" opens the verse in a Jewish vein, but the chorus could be an Italian street song or French cabaret tune. "Blame It on the Summer Night" smacks strongly of Gershwin with a delightful melody coupled with instrumental interjections from 1920s and 1930s jazz, sounding a bit late for the show's 1910 ambience. "For My Mary" is Strouse's tribute to a song for Irish tenor with a sentimental melody and waltz meter. "I Remember" is like an Eastern European folk song, and "Yankee Boy" is a mixture between ragtime and patriotic tunes. "Children of the Wind" and "Bread and Freedom" are the sort of dramatic pop anthems common in musicals in the 1980s. Other songs that seem to be in more conventional Broadway styles are "What's Wrong with That?" "Uptown," and "The Sound of Love." A distinctive song is "Wanting," a duet between Rebecca and Saul, each singing alone on a separate place on the stage. The undulating accompaniment and motivic melody are reminiscent of Sondheim.

Schwartz's lyrics for *Rags* were the subject of diverse comments from reviewers, but the subtlety of this craft is hard to evaluate on the basis of one or two hearings. There are few places in *Rags* where Schwartz demonstrates the kind of poetic or rhyming virtuosity that one associates with Lorenz Hart or Ira Gershwin at their wittiest (rhyming "luminous" with "one of us" in "Blame It on the Summer Night" is a fine moment), but the songs help tell the story and/or develop characters. Any lyricist would be challenged when dealing with the richly syncopated melodies that Strouse wrote for his ragtime-inspired numbers, such as "Rags." Schwartz penned a number of lines for the descending, syncopated line that dominates Bella's lines, capturing her profound frustration. Schwartz managed a triple rhyme ("run to where . . . everyone to wear") at the end of the first two lines, a virtuosic touch:

> This land of freedom we had to run to where
> Now we're free just like everyone to wear
> Rags.[42]

An example of Schwartz's work with vivid images in *Rags* appears in the introduction of "Children of the Wind" (in the version that exists on the recording), when Rebecca describes escaping a pogrom with her son David. In two short stanzas, sung to the music of "I Remember," Schwartz paints the pogrom ("Flames are on the hillside/Blood is in the streams"), Rebecca's anguish at watching her son injured ("David, did they hurt you, darling?"), their flight ("Sneaking past the border/In the silent snow"), and her determination to find her husband, Nathan ("Well, we made it here from Danzig/What's another mile or so?"). Schwartz pithily presents the story's stark emotions with evocative images, rather than narrating. Effective moments late in each stanza are his repetition of words at line endings (*darling* and *Danzig*).[43] His lyrics in this introduction contrast with the subsequent hopefulness that follows in the chorus of "Children of the Wind."

Schwartz's manner with rhyming appears in "What's Wrong with That?"—an ironic song for Nathan and the Tammany Hall crowd that demonstrates their corrupt and violent nature. The lyricist provides constant rhymes, basing many on the words *that* and *Nat* (a shortened form of Nathan's name). The clipped nature of these rhymes lends the song a falsely jocular air and emphasizes how Nathan has assimilated by shortening his name from Nathan Hershkowitz to Nat Harris.

Schwartz's lyrics help develop character and make a poetic contribution in the introduction to "Uptown." Nathan expresses shame at his ethnicity as he describes how wealthy New Yorkers feel about poverty-stricken Jews. Strouse wrote a disturbing, noodling accompaniment that punctuates Schwartz's rhymed dialogue. Schwartz paints the situation with odors and sounds ("With the noises of their wheedling/And the smell of rotting meats"). The segment is brief, but it persuasively explains why Nathan wants to move to a better neighborhood.

In "Wanting," Schwartz builds much of this wonderful duet between Rebecca and Saul from one- to five-word lines that capture both their mutual attraction and recognition that these feelings are impractical. When their individual words combine into a duet, the result is magical.

In our interview, Strouse offered useful comments on several songs and scenes. The creators struggled with how to start the show. They placed the immigrants in the ship's hold, or starting at Ellis Island, and they also labored over when the main character, Rebecca, should meet her friend Bella. The song "I Remember" was performed by an immigrant in the ship's hold as a tribute to their homeland. Schwartz liked the song, and it grew on Strouse, but he also believed "there was a long time there in the hold of the ship." They wrote a song for Rebecca and Bella called "Don't Forget Me" that the composer wanted to cut because they could emphasize the female friendship late in the show. Strouse thought that the show took off when the immigrants landed and the Americans sang "Greenhorns"; otherwise it took too long for the show to get to the apartment and the songs "Brand New World" and "Children of the Wind."

For Strouse one of the score's special songs is "Blame It on the Summer Night," sung by Rebecca when she realizes that she has fallen in love with Saul, the union organizer. "Blame" replaced a song called "Up until Today." Strouse describes the music: "It changed from like a Jewish tune into a jazzy tune. It's nothing the audience realizes, but it's very important that this was a transitional period in her life as well as in American music." Her first marriage had been arranged, and now, with Nathan missing and a new love interest, "it was actually the time that she felt sex for the first time, the first time America was happening to her." Stratas performed the piece on a nearly bare stage in duet with a clarinetist next to her, Strouse's idea.

In a number of versions of *Rags*, the second act opens with the chorus "On the Fourth Day of July," a song that Strouse dislikes. He stated, "It came out a little, the way composers can, screwed up in intention. Three feel, instead of a march feel, although we used it as a march, too." Schwartz liked the song, and the creators moved it around in the show. Strouse noted jocularly, "I think I probably wanted to write something that would be 'God Bless America'—wouldn't we all?"

Another song that opened the second act in several versions of *Rags* was "The Cherry Street Café," which Strouse based on jazz and the type of songs heard in burlesque. He liked the song but reports that his collaborators did not. The song became background, diegetic music for the café scene, where, in various versions, either Nathan and/or Rebecca meet his political boss in an effort to impress him, or Nathan meets Rebecca's friends.

According to *Newsday*, a major point of contention between the three writers and the producers was the funeral scene, where Rebecca sings "Kaddish" for Bella with her friend's father, Avram. The producers polled audience members in Boston, trying to find ammunition to get the song removed, but reportedly the audience thought it should remain.[44] They did remove the scene at one point during the New York previews, but it was reinstated the next performance. The creators deleted the scene in more recent versions.

The Development of *Rags*

Since the original Broadway version of *Rags* there have been many smaller productions. Stein estimated that he wrote about twenty scripts for the show, but a full analysis of those sources goes well beyond the scope possible here. We will instead consider what played on Broadway in 1986 through a detailed synopsis and then consider some recent developments in work on the show that proceeded for decades. Details on the development of various scripts in the 1980s and 1990s are available online.[45]

The Original Show

The version of *Rags* that played on Broadway in August 1986 is available in the Theatre on Film and Tape Archive at the New York Public Library for the Performing Arts at Lincoln Center. The staff must have worked feverishly to secure the proper permissions and make the physical arrangements to record for posterity a show that only lasted for three days and four performances.

Act 1 opens at Ellis Island in 1910, with an immigrant singing "I Remember," a lament of lost homelands. Rebecca Hershkowitz looks for her son, David, who has wandered off. Immigrants who have qualified for entrance into the United States get into a "barge" on stage, which moves them past a large Statue of Liberty; they disembark at the Battery as Scene 2 opens. Two Americans sing "Greenhorns," sarcastically recognizing how immigrants grease gears in the capitalist machine. Rebecca seeks her husband, Nathan, who came six years before. She sings lines about this during "Greenhorns," but he is not there. The musical segment ends with all singing "Long live America!" An immigration official notices that Rebecca is an unattached female attempting to enter the country, which is against the law, and he starts to push Rebecca and David toward the barge to return to Ellis Island. Bella, a young woman who does not know Rebecca, intervenes, convincing her father, Avram, to lie that he is Rebecca's uncle. Avram reluctantly takes responsibility for Rebecca and David while fretting that he had to leave his son Herschel at home. Ben, a young man with whom Bella fell in love on the ship, finds her, but is only able to learn that they will be on Suffolk Street. Avram does not approve that Ben has rejected his Jewish identity and will not tell him the address of his brother-in-law's apartment, where they are headed. As they make their way toward the Lower East Side, Avram and Rebecca sing what becomes "Brand New World," telling their children to "open your eyes" and "now it belongs to you."

In Scene 3 they arrive at the Cohens' tenement apartment, where Rebecca and David also receive lodging. Rebecca wonders where her absent husband is. David tries to sleep and Rebecca sings to calm him, a continuation of "Brand New World." They look out the window and see unfamiliar sights.

In Scene 4 Rebecca searches for Nathan. She finds his landlord and a neighbor, who say that Nathan has gone to Buffalo. She places an advertisement in the paper for Nathan and consults with a social worker. They cannot help find Nathan, but offer an orphanage for David while Rebecca looks for work. Rebecca reacts passionately, recalling the pogrom that drove them from Russia. Alone with a spotlight, Rebecca sings "Children of the Wind," where she recounts their terrible experiences and hopes for a brighter future.

Scene 5 features "Penny a Tune," through which the audience meets the pushcart merchants that Avram and David join, the sweatshops where Rebecca finds work, and klezmer musicians. Most of the cast sings lyrics specific to each situation. Rebecca leaves David with Avram, who wonders aloud to his absent son Herschel how a scholar ends up selling from a cart. Rebecca is at Mr. Bronstein's shop, where Saul, who Bronstein fired, has returned to organize the workers. Rebecca becomes his obstacle because she needs employment and will not join his effort to close the shop on Sunday. Bella sews at home while singing how Ben will find her and marry her. Ben works unhappily in a cigar factory. Back at the pushcart, David learns to haggle with customers and Avram discovers that he must pay a protection racket. Rachel, another seller, learns with interest that Avram is a widower.

In the next scene, Saul confronts Rebecca. He explains the union, but Rebecca wishes to avoid complications. He sings the introduction to "Easy for You," saying that in this country one improves things by making trouble. As the song continues, Saul and Rebecca disagree but also become mutually attracted. "Easy for You" continues off and on as Rebecca and David see Saul often. He teaches them to read English, constantly preaching socialism. The scene ends with Rebecca reprising for David the "belongs to you" segment of "Brand New World."

In Scene 7, Saul takes Rebecca and David to the Yiddish theater, where they experience a mixture of Shakespeare's *Hamlet*, Zionism, and audience participation, including the song "Hard to Be a Prince." Later that evening in Scene 8, Rebecca and Saul are alone. She describes her husband, trying to avoid romantic entanglements, but Saul attempts to kiss her. She demurs and Saul respectfully leaves, leaving Rebecca on a dark stage with a clarinetist. Together they perform the jazzy "Blame It on the Summer Night," Rebecca's confession of love.

In Scene 9, Rebecca and Bella are in the Cohens' apartment. Bella is lonely and asks Rebecca to help her find a job in a sewing shop. Ben finds her, arriving with a gramophone as a gift and painting a false, rosy picture of his work situation. He plays the Irish song "For My Mary" on the machine, and it becomes a duet as Ben changes the words to describe Bella. They waltz awkwardly as Avram and David enter. The father senses that Ben has lied to his daughter and asks him to leave. The Cohens return and a general argument ensues, causing Bella to flee. Avram catches her in Scene 10, and Bella sings "Rags," frustrated about how he will not allow her to leave home and experience America; all she sees are the rags that she wears and sews together. She runs all the way to Fourteenth Street, where she watches a fantasy dance of rich New Yorkers. In the final verse of "Rags," Bella acknowledges that these people will never accept her because she is "just one more Jew in her rags."

In Scene 11, we meet Nathan, who works for Tammany Hall. He is at Pat's Tavern, in a meeting with party boss "Big Tim" Sullivan and two associates. They sing "What's Wrong with That?" explaining what steps they are willing to take to maintain electoral superiority. Nathan seeks a position as ward leader. Someone reads Rebecca's newspaper advertisement, and the scene ends with Nathan leaving to find his family and singing what he is willing to do to get this job.

Scene 12 takes place back at Suffolk Street on 4 July. There is a small marching band, an entertainer on stilts, and flags as the crowd sings "On the Fourth Day of July." Rachel and Avram are at their pushcarts discussing Bella; Rachel hints at her marital availability. Avram leaves to check on Bella. A thug comes to collect protection money, but David refuses to pay, singing lines that he has learned from Saul, who is with Rebecca off to one side. Thugs return and beat David, relenting only after Rebecca pays them. Rebecca blames Saul for the attack and rejects him. In the act's final scene, Nathan finds his family and together they sing "In America," with Nathan promising that they will not be hurt again.

After an "Entr'acte" based on "Blame It on the Summer Night" and "Greenhorn," Act 2 opens on the roof of the Cohens' tenement building, where everyone is watching fireworks. Nathan sings a bit of "On the Fourth Day of July." He is a politician, working the crowd. Rebecca brags that he is about to be named ward leader, but Nathan says nothing. He announces a change of his name to "Nat Harris" and sings "Yankee Boy" about how he will succeed in the United States. David joins his song.

Rebecca takes David to bed and returns to Nathan in the next scene. He castigates her for mentioning the ward leader position before he has the job. Rebecca does not understand, but Nathan tells her that Jews are despised in the United States.[46] He has no trade, but his ability to make people like him means he can make a living in politics. He sings "Uptown" with Rebecca, where they express their hope for financial success so that they can move farther north. The song concludes with Rebecca reprising a bit of "I Remember" about their life in Russia. Rebecca shows Nathan the money she has saved, which he takes so he can get a new suit. Saul comes to ask how David is doing after the attack and learns that Rebecca's husband has arrived. She says good-bye to Saul, and they sing the duet "Wanting" from two parts of the stage, lamenting their feelings for each other.

Scene 3 opens with Avram and Rachel at their carts. Avram says that his son, Herschel, is coming, and Rachel notes that she has a niece he might like. Bella comes to announce that Rebecca has found her a job in a shop; she ignores her father when he tries to send her home. Avram regrets how hard it is for a man to raise a daughter, and Rachel offers to help. In the song "Three Sunny Rooms" she lays out a scenario for their possible happiness at her apartment. Avram is unsure, but then he joins the song and they become engaged.

In Scene 4, Ben is having difficulty selling gramophones. David is there and records his voice. When they replay it, passersby become interested and Ben learns how to sell the machines in "The Sound of Love." Bella enters and finds Ben recording a violinist and an Italian tenor. David leaves Bella and Ben together for a reprise of "For My Mary." They go off with hands clasped.

Scene 5 is at the Lower East Side Democratic Club, where Nathan and Rebecca enter with new clothes. She meets Big Tim Sullivan, charming the party boss, and then leads the Jewish portion of the ethnic dances that are part of the "Democratic Club Dance." Sullivan names Nathan ward leader. David dashes in to tell Rebecca there is a fire at Bella's shop, and Rebecca leaves hurriedly.

Scene 6 opens before a frame of a building with red lighting effects for flames. Bella has jumped from the building and died, and the "Kaddish" prayer for the dead starts immediately. The background disappears as men sing the prayer, joined by Rebecca.

Back at the Cohen apartment for Scene 7, Rachel and Avram have married, but Avram grieves for his daughter and is unresponsive as his wife helps him pack. They are surrounded by Jack, Anna, Rebecca, and David. Ben comes to say good-bye because he is moving to Boston. He tries to speak with Avram. Ben learns that Avram has mentioned returning to Russia. Ben tells him that he needs to live his life because that is what Bella would have wanted. The older man wishes Ben good luck before he leaves and begins to pack.

At Bronstein's shop, the boss discourages discussing the fire. He yells at Rebecca, and she responds by leaving with her sewing machine because she pays Bronstein for its use, asserting that she has purchased it. Others go on strike with her, singing the union song "Bread and Freedom." Scene 9 is later that day at Union Square, where Saul leads the demonstration. Nathan enters and urges Rebecca to leave, telling her that hoodlums will be coming to break this up. The musical scene that follows, "Dancing with the Fools," includes Rebecca's reprise of "I Remember," as she ponders her future, and Nathan sings Rebecca's lullaby to David from the first act, trying to calm her. As Rebecca sings, Nathan no longer understands her. He asks what has happened, and Rebecca answers, "I don't know, America!" Rebecca steps on the speaker's stand to tell her story as Nathan leaves.

The final scene opens on Suffolk Street with a reprise of "Brand New World" from Rebecca and David. The two men who sang "Greenhorns" at the opening of the show appear for a reprise as the scene changes to Battery Park with new immigrants, including Herschel, whom Avram greets.

All leave the stage except Rebecca, who reprises "Children of the Wind" in front of the Statue of Liberty. David enters; she kisses him and points to Miss Liberty.

At the end of this performance, Lonny Price (Ben) announced to the audience that this was the last scheduled performance. He invited them to join the cast in their parade down Broadway. He said that they hoped to reopen in a few weeks.

A Memo from Schwartz to Stein, 7 April 2005, and a Script from January 2007

Within Joseph Stein's voluminous collection of *Rags* materials, there is a printed copy of an e-mail message from Stephen Schwartz, dated 7 April 2005, with a summary of Schwartz's feelings on how the show might be revised. It is a fascinating and detailed glimpse inside this collaboration. In the e-mail, Schwartz wants "to return to our early impulses about the show . . . and then incorporate some things we have learned."[47] He suggests starting with an immigrant singing "I Remember," and then go straight to Ellis Island, deleting all scenes on the ship. The audience would meet Rebecca and David during "Greenhorns," as she announces that she is to meet her husband. Bella would rescue them without previously knowing Rebecca, and they would get to know each other as Avram goes off to ask directions. Ben would then interrupt them, singing "Yankee Boy," moved from where Nathan sings it in the second act. Schwartz states that this was the song's original placement; the lyricist begins the memorandum by stating that he was working from the Broadway script (which he misdates as April 1984), as well as an earlier version from sometime in 1984 and an undated script with many notes that he thinks might have been for the American Jewish Theatre production in December 1991. Bella, Rebecca, and David would be minor participants in the song's performance. Schwartz would retain the brief, sung passages that Avram and Rebecca direct to their offspring as they leave the Battery area with a brief reprise of "Greenhorns," and then go directly to the Cohens' apartment, where Rebecca would sing the lullaby to David, and they would perform "Brand New World." Rebecca would go to the newspaper office and social worker, but she would not sing "Children of the Wind" there, instead proceeding to where she leaves David with Avram and goes to find work. Schwartz wants to use "Penny a Tune" more or less how it exists, but wonders if the order should be adjusted, especially when Rebecca finds employment. He wants to delete what he terms "omniscient commentary" in the lyrics, such as where the klezmer musicians are encouraged to play for various characters. He then sees the first act playing about as it exists through the songs "Easy for You," "Cheer Up, Hamlet" (probably an alternate title for "Hard to Be a Prince"), "Blame It on the Summer Night," "For My Mary," and "Rags." Schwartz would also like to make Saul "more idiosyncratic," perhaps "find the humor in his single-minded socialism." He does not believe that the scene with Nathan and the Tammany Hall crowd should be in the first act; he likes Stein's original thought to have Nathan appear unexpectedly at the end of the first act. Schwartz believes that Act 1 should end with the final scene as it has often been written ("On the Fourth Day of July" with the crowd, David resists paying the extortion and gets assaulted, and Rebecca sends Saul away), but that then Rebecca sings "Children of the Wind" followed by Nathan's entrance, and then she sings a bit more of the same song.

Schwartz wants to see Act 2 open on the tenement roof with Nathan there, but Bella has not returned from running out in Act 1 and everyone is worried. When alone, Rebecca and Nathan sing "Uptown," and then Nathan leaves and Bella comes out of hiding to ask Rebecca's help in finding a job. Bella sings a short reprise of "Rags." Rebecca and Bella would tell Avram about Bella's desire and go act on it, leaving Avram and Rachel to do the "Three Sunny Rooms" scene. As Schwartz continues to tell it, Rebecca and Bella look for work, and they encounter Ben selling gramophones. Schwartz suggests that they cut "The Sound of Love," and with a scene they can imply that Ben and Bella continue to see each other. After she helps Bella find a job, Rebecca runs into Saul, who wants to unionize that shop. They perform a scene that already exists in the second act in another context, and sing "Wanting." Back with Nathan, Rebecca and her husband go to the Democratic Club, and there Schwartz favors the placement of "What's Wrong with That?" in a version that involves Rebecca. Schwartz then believes that Act 2 should remain similar to its current state, but he also answers what appear to have been several questions among the creators. He wants Ben to remain the person who tells the mourning Avram that he must continue to live his life, and he wants Saul in the last scene as well so that Rebecca can decline to follow him to his next stop as union organizer. He also asserts that the last scene should not be a long succession of farewells. The remaining musical numbers in Act 2, as Schwartz sees it, are "Kaddish," "Bread and Freedom," "Dancing with the Fools," and the finale of "Greenhorns" and "Children of the Wind."[48] Several of Schwartz's suggested changes appear in an official script from the Rodgers and Hammerstein Library with revisions from November 2005.

For the three primary creators, however, *Rags* still had not reached a form they could finally accept. In interviews in December 2007 and January 2008, both Stein and Strouse told me that there had been another recent revision.

The final script from Stein's collection consulted for this study bears the notation "Jan. 2007" on the title page. It includes profound changes, including a new title: *Brand New World*. Along with the script is a list of the most important changes in this new rendering, some of which had appeared in the last version, and others that had appeared throughout the show's history: There is no prologue on the ship; the show starts at Ellis Island. Bella does not know Rebecca before she saves her. Anna and Jack share fewer lines about having to open their home to Rebecca and David, and Rebecca never finds Nathan's landlady to find out where he has gone. The audience never sees Bella doing piecework in the apartment with Anna, and she does not sing to Anna about Ben in "Penny a Tune." Ben also does not appear struggling to work in the cigar shop in that scene. They cut the song "Easy for You." The list also states that Bella now sings "Rags" with Rebecca instead of Avram and that the song has changed musically at the end. The scene between Saul and Rebecca in the last scene of Act 1 has been shortened, and the list reports there is a new song ending the act. As will be seen in the following discussion, this is not the case in this version. "Yankee Boy" has been moved back to the second act (a change only found in the previous version), and the songs "Kaddish" (along with the fire scene) and "Dancing with the Fools" have been deleted. The list also notes that there were numerous other brief cuts in the script. The scenes from the January 2007 version are as follows:[49]

Act 1

Scene 1—On Ellis Island, the barge goes to the Battery, and Bella saves Rebecca. They get acquainted while Avram asks directions, and Ben comes over to see Bella. Avram will not tell him their address. The songs are "Greenhorns" and "Open Your Eyes (Now It Belongs to You)."

Scene 3 [*sic*]—At the Cohens' apartment, they reluctantly offer lodging to Rebecca and David, who sing "Brand New World." Rebecca goes to the newspaper to place an advertisement so Nathan can find them, and then she goes to the social worker; she leaves angrily and sings "Children of the Wind."

Scene 4—On the street, Rebecca leaves David with Avram, and they sell goods from a cart provided by Jack. Mike, the gangster, collects protection money, and Avram meets Rachel. During the song "Penny a Tune," Rebecca finds work at Bronstein's shop and David learns to haggle.

Scene 5—At Bronstein's sweatshop, Saul comes to try to organize the workers. Rebecca refuses to join and thwarts his effort.

Scene 6—Saul confronts Rebecca, at first without success, but he yells after her when she leaves that her boy will end up an ignorant immigrant just like her, and Rebecca goes to Bella to ask what she should do. Bella encourages Rebecca to learn English, and she returns with David to Saul to do so. There are sung lines in the scene by Rebecca, David, and Saul, most of which were part of "Easy for You" in earlier versions.

Scene 7—The scene in the Yiddish theater is more or less as described earlier with the song "Hard to Be a Prince."

Scene 8—Saul interprets *Hamlet* in a socialist fashion for David's edification, and then the boy goes to bed. Rebecca and Saul briefly discuss her husband and arranged marriage while he tries to find the courage to say how he feels, and they kiss. Saul leaves and Rebecca sings "Blame It on the Summer Night."

Scene 9—Bella has repaired Rebecca's dress so she can look nice to go out again with Saul, and Bella is cool to Rebecca because she has the freedom that Bella lacks. Ben arrives, and the scene described above ensues with "For My Mary." Avram and others arrive and the argument takes place that drives Bella away.

Scene 10—As it appears in the script, this plays similarly with Avram and Bella singing "Rags"; a rag-seller enters. A written note, however, states that Rebecca will replace Avram (as noted earlier) and the scene will be revised.

Scene 11—The chorus sings "On the Fourth Day of July," and Rebecca tells Saul she is worried about Bella. David resists paying protection money, and thugs return to assault David. Rachel pays to stop the beating and turns on Saul. She sings "We Didn't Come to America to Be Hurt Again," and Nathan finds Rebecca and David at that moment. He sings "Nothing Will Hurt You Again."

Act 2

Scene 1—The entr'acte is "On the Fourth Day of July," and the chorus opens the scene with different words appropriate to evening fireworks. Nathan and Rebecca are together on the roof; he starts to sing "I Remember Summer Evenings," and then stops as David enters, apparently feeling better. Nathan sings "Yankee Boy," and it becomes a family trio. Avram, Jack, and Anna join them, and Rebecca brags that Nathan will be named ward leader. Nathan takes Rebecca off by herself and upbraids her for assuming that he has the job, and they sing "Uptown." Bella comes to Rebecca and asks for her help in finding a job.

Scene 2—Anna and Rebecca go to Avram at his pushcart and tell him that Bella is getting a job. Avram and Rachel sing "Three Sunny Rooms" and become engaged.

Scene 3—Rebecca and her friend Rosa exit Bronstein's shop and run into Saul, who asks about David, and then gets upset when he learns that Nathan works for Tammany Hall. They sing "Wanting."

Scene 4—David brings Bella to a street where Ben sells gramophones. Ben agrees to come to see Bella and her father on Saturday, and to wear a hat. Bella sings a verse of "Rags" about how she will not allow her life to be "thrown away like rags."

Scene 5—At the East Side Democratic Club, Nathan brings Rebecca, and she helps charm Big Tim Sullivan. The three sing "What's Wrong With That?" but Rebecca is uncomfortable with the implication that violence could be used against strikers. Sullivan names Nathan ward leader, and David comes and gets Rebecca because Bella's shop is on fire.

Scene 6—At Bronstein's shop, Rebecca remains upset about Bella's death in the fire. She leads a strike and the scene closes with workers singing "Bread and Freedom."

Scene 7—The song continues into the labor rally at Union Square, where Nathan tries to separate Rebecca from her colleagues, warning her that thugs will be coming to break up the strike. Rebecca and Nathan only speak, but the song "Bread and Freedom" flows through the scene.

Scene 8—This is primarily the scene in the Cohens' apartment described earlier for this place of the show. Saul is going to Boston to organize workers, but says that he might return to New York to be with Rebecca and David.

Scene 9—At the Battery, Rebecca, David, Avram, and Rachel greet Herschel, Avram's son. The Americans sing "Greenhorns" and Rebecca, followed by the entire cast, sing "Children of the Wind."

Conclusion

Rags has a complicated plot that includes more than one major theme (immigration, exploitation of immigrants by capitalist forces, unionization, political corruption, etc.), causing one to wonder if there is too much to the story for it to be a successful musical play. It is no more complex, however, than *Les Misérables*, a sprawling tale with a number of major characters and several important themes. The show that inspired *Rags*, *Fiddler on the Roof*, has four couples and a number of important characters, but the only major themes of the show are tradition versus generational change and anti-Semitism or, more generally, a racial majority that persecutes a minority. Perhaps a problem with *Rags* is the number of societal themes that it involves, because it is certainly not the only show where there are many characters to develop and for the audience to follow.

Rags has its strengths.[50] Stein's story is dramatically interesting with satisfying interaction between several characters, and the various stories overlap effectively. Much the story seems plausible. One need only hear the recording starring Julia Migenes as Rebecca to note that Charles Strouse wrote a fine score with memorable melodies and an effective survey of musical types from the turn of the twentieth century. Schwartz's lyrics help move the story along and define the characters while including poetic and charming use of language. Problems with the show, besides the plethora of major themes, might include its often pessimistic tone, some characters who seem more like symbols than flesh-and-blood people (compare, for example, Rebecca from *Rags* with Tevye from *Fiddler*), and scenes like the Yiddish theater that add little to the plot and present the audience with yet another idea to understand and interpret. Much of the necessary craft is there, but the show's relative failure remains. If writing good musicals were simple and predictable, however, more would succeed. *Rags* is one of many examples in the history of the American musical theater where talented artists collaborated, working with their best intentions, but magic did not inhabit the result. What makes *Rags* unusual is how long their collaboration continued, and perhaps the willingness of the creators to share its story with others.

CHAPTER NINE

~

Children of Eden

Although it has not yet had a Broadway run, *Children of Eden* is popular among school, community, and religious groups. It is Stephen Schwartz's favorite work in his output,[1] partly because of his fondness for the theme of relationships between parents and children. Based on the first ten chapters of Genesis, *Children of Eden* provided Schwartz with another opportunity to develop a fresh approach to familiar stories. It is his only show with the character of a pageant, including a chorus of Storytellers and children who play the animals that Adam and Eve name in Act 1 and that board the ark in Act 2. Finally, *Children of Eden* is another of Schwartz's shows that took years to complete, more than a decade between the mid-1980s and the final version performed at the Paper Mill Playhouse in Milburn, New Jersey, in 1997. His primary collaborator was John Caird, a British director and writer most famous as codirector and cowriter of *Les Misérables* with Trevor Nunn.

Family Tree

In the mid-1980s Schwartz received a commission to write a piece for a Roman Catholic youth festival "Youth Sing Praise" at Our Lady of the Snows in Belleville, Illinois.[2] About the same time, he was contacted by production designer Charles Lisanby concerning a project based on Genesis. Lisanby had served as art director for the video version of *Working* (1982), which Schwartz directed. The designer wanted to cover Adam and Eve through Noah and the flood, an idea he first conceived for the Crystal Cathedral in

Amphitheater at National Shrine of Our Lady of the Snows, Belleville, Illinois, where *Family Tree* premiered in 1985. *Photo by Paul Laird*

Garden Grove, California (for which a script survives from 11 July 1985), and later rethought for a possible summer show at Radio City Music Hall.[3] The familiar material suggested to Schwartz a show about parents and children. The first parent is God, but there was no effort to portray a deity on stage in the original production, where Schwartz remembers God as rumbles of thunder. Schwartz's take on Genesis was casting Eve and Cain as "sort of heroic rebels as opposed to disobedient bringers down of humanity."

The show became known as *Family Tree* and premiered at Our Lady of the Snows in 1985; Schwartz remembers working on it for less than one year. It was in an outdoor amphitheater (see photo). Schwartz recalls that Noah's rainbow was accomplished with helium-filled balloons behind the stage area that flew skyward at the right moment. The composer/lyricist notes that most of the songs that he wrote for *Family Tree* remain in the show in some form, but no full script for the original version was available for consultation. It is not possible to establish with certainty the identity of every song, but between Schwartz's memory and the partial script described here, it would appear that versions of the following songs were sung: "Let There Be," "The Naming," "Grateful Children," "Lazy Is the Lion" (later cut), "The Spark of Creation," "In Pursuit of Excellence" (as a solo, rather than in the later ensemble arrangement), "Good Help Is Hard to Find" (for Adam and Eve, later cut), "World without You," "Close to Home," "Lost in the Wilderness" (not the version heard today, but what was sung in London in 1991), "What Is He Waiting For?" "The Hardest Part of Love," "Ain't It Good?" and "In the Beginning."

An undated script of Act 1 by Lisanby survives in Schwartz's papers. Schwartz believes that it dates from after the initial production when they were developing the show into a full-length musical, before John Caird took over as the book writer. The following outline summarizes the action in each scene and identifies the songs.

Chapter 1: The scene in which God creates the world is entirely the song "Let There Be."

Chapter 2: In the Garden of Eden, there are three scenes. In the first, God is heard speaking, waking Adam and Eve for the first day. They identify the animals in "The Naming" and close in prayer with "Grateful Children." In the second scene, Lucifer, also only heard, speaks to Adam, telling him that the function of humans is to ask questions. In Scene 3, Eve returns from gathering berries, telling Adam that she found a barrier at the end of the garden that she walked along until she returned to the place where she had started. Adam, busy counting insects, is not interested. Eve sings "The Spark of Creation" about what seems to be her divine desire to learn. Adam and Eve find themselves complementary and sing "Made for Each Other."

Chapter 3: The serpent enters the garden and tempts Eve to take fruit from the Tree of Knowledge with "In Pursuit of Excellence." She joins the song and takes three apples. In the next scene, Adam arrives home for dinner finding Eve wearing clothing and offering a new recipe: apple pie. She is reluctant for him to eat the pie, however, and Adam figures out what has happened. He quickly eats it and tells her why in "In a World without You." In the next scene, a fiery angel tears off the serpent's arms and wings. The animals say goodbye to Adam and Eve, who leave the garden, which is surrounded by fire.

Chapter 4: This is a representation of Adam's family fending for themselves twenty years later. Eve removes a thorn from Abel's foot. Cain has been disappearing for days at a time. Adam enters, and the couple and their younger son have dinner and sing "Close to Home." The lyrics comment on their hard lives, but they are proud of their accomplishments. Cain enters with a bird that he killed. Angry about how his parents lost Eden, he sings "Lost in the Wilderness." Cain has seen footprints of other people and hopes to find them. Against his father's wishes he leaves; Abel follows. In the next scene, Abel catches up with Cain and tries to stop him. Adam enters and knocks Cain down. Cain picks up a rock to hit his father, but Abel gets in the way and Cain kills him. Adam carries home his son's body and the devastated Cain sings, perhaps a segment of "Lost in the Wilderness." The final scene of the chapter occurs years later. Eve delivers a monologue that tells the remainder of the story. Cain never returned. She had another son, Seth, and later Adam died. Seth ran away and returned with a wife and family, with whom Eve now lives.

The fifth chapter includes only the song "Generations of Adam."

This partial script may have been John Caird's introduction to *Family Tree*; it includes two pages of notes in what the director identifies as Charles Lisanby's handwriting. Lisanby apparently took notes while Caird commented. Caird praised the opening of "Let There Be," but once Adam and Eve appear he wondered how they could engage in clever wordplay before they have eaten of the Tree of Knowledge. He questioned several individual lines and situations, such as Cain's burning anger at his parents' expulsion from Eden. If they had not left paradise, Cain might never have been born. Showing his director's imagination, Caird suggested that all of the animals that appeared had to produce splendid effects, which he sought in the 1991 West End production.

A New Collaborator

Schwartz and Lisanby naturally desired a successful professional launching of *Family Tree*. Carol de Giere reports that Radio City Musical Hall declined it.[4] Schwartz decided that they needed a director, and he wished to work with someone responsible for *The Life and Adventures of Nicholas Nickleby* (New York, 1981), codirected by Trevor Nunn and John Caird. Schwartz considered the play "the greatest thing I'd ever seen," and he did not really believe that he would interest Nunn, so he approached Caird. Born in 1948, Caird studied acting at the Old Vic Theatre School and in 1977 began a long-time association as a director with the Royal Shakespeare Company (RSC). Nunn was artistic director, resulting in their association on *Nicholas Nickleby* and later *Les Misérables*, for which Nunn and Caird codirected and cowrote the book. In musical theater, Caird had also directed Andrew Lloyd

Webber's *Song and Dance* (London, 1982), and he has been busy in other musical theater and operatic projects since.

Schwartz found Caird working in Boston and invited him to his house in Connecticut to discuss *Family Tree* and hear the songs. The songwriter sent the director a script before their meeting; the following note is extant from 8 December 1987: "Enclosed is the current draft of Act 1 of *Family Tree* and a synopsis of Act 2. I look forward to seeing you Sunday. Enjoy the drive."

Caird knew some of Schwartz's songs from auditions, singling out "Where's the Warmth?" and "Meadowlark" as two favorites.[5] Caird liked what he heard that day and joined the project. The extent of his involvement by 18 February 1988 is clear in a fax from Schwartz where he mentions names of possible producers and notes that Lisanby is busy with the Academy Awards broadcast, but that he soon would be in New York for a few days, after which he hoped they could send Caird some material. They would all gather in London after the Oscar broadcast in April.

A package that Schwartz sent to Caird on 20 March 1988 included a description, lyric sheets, and demo tape of the fifteen numbers for Act 2, but Schwartz reported no work completed with Lisanby. The songwriter acknowledged that this was a huge amount of music for one act. Without Act 2 existing as a script, he had worked far ahead of Lisanby. The songs included the following (with a paraphrase of Schwartz's brief description):

"I Wish You'd Change Your Mind/Civilized Society"—Noah pleads with God and we meet the evil society that will be destroyed.

"Colloquy"—Mama Noah sorts through what will go on the ark with Anah, a young woman that her son Japheth left when he ran away to be a sailor.

"Do-It-Yourself"—Noah's other sons, Shem and Ham, struggle with their wives to build the ark, a comedy number to establish the need for Japheth.

"Prayer"—a reprise of "Close to Home" from Act 1; Japheth returns.

"Family Dancing"—Japheth's memory of the night he left, renewing his conflict with Noah.[6] Schwartz notes that it includes motives from Act 1.

"The March of the Animals"—an instrumental arrangement of "The Naming" for when the animals come to the ark.

"Smile to Beat the Sun"—Japheth and Anah discover they are still in love.

Song of conflict between Noah and Japheth yet to be written that would reprise material from the conflict between Adam and Cain in Act 1. Japheth will not marry Anah, as his father has ordered.

"The Flood"—instrumental and choral number yet to be written.

"What Is He Waiting For?"—the people on the ark are wondering when God will make the rain stop, and Noah and Japheth still fight.

Possible quartet for Noah, Mama, Japheth, and Anah about the need to resolve conflict.

"Letting Go"—Noah realizes that he must let Japheth follow his own free will.

"Ain't It Good?"—Mama's gospel number of triumph when Noah and Japheth resolve their fight and the rain stops.

"Come Home to Me"—They are waiting for the dove to return; possibly sung by Mama or Anah.

"In the Beginning"—Finale

Schwartz continued work on the score, sending Caird a new song on 20 April 1988. It was a duet between Mama Noah and Anah sung between "Smile to Beat the Sun" and "The Flood," replacing the earlier "Colloquy."

Joint work started among the three collaborators, but Caird soon discovered that "the book was not at all adequate as a response to the songs or the framework." He tried to rework it, but found himself writing it. Schwartz's letter to Caird from 16 June shows that problems had arisen with Lisanby. The composer had been trading messages with orchestrator Michael Starobin, but he was reluctant to work further on music until Lisanby wrote more. He mentions a workshop planned for September and urges Caird to work with Lisanby to resolve their "stalemate," believing that if they can produce an act that works, Schwartz could do whatever might be necessary to make songs work. The composer/lyricist then looked past the writing, suggesting that once they have enough of a script and score that they needed to find a producer. Caird sent Schwartz a brief response, commenting that his counsel was "very wise" and that he would call Schwartz from Los Angeles when he was with Lisanby, a visit that took place for several weeks in Los Angeles in fall 1988.[7]

Caird asked for recognition as coauthor, which Schwartz thought was reasonable, but Lisanby refused. Caird offered to withdraw, noting, "It wasn't a ploy; it was a simple decision. I couldn't go forward more or less writing it and not be credited, or have my work acknowledged." The disagreement gradually involved lawyers. A letter from Schwartz to Lisanby on 29 November 1988 stated that he was invoking the thirty-day cooling-off period previous to dissolving their partnership, but also urging Lisanby to reconsider and suggesting that it would be an honor for him to be coauthor and designer of a possible RSC production. He mentioned slow progress on Act 2, and stated that Caird had written half of the act in four days. Caird informed his lawyer by letter on 8 February 1989 that joint work with Lisanby had ceased, and he was proceeding solely with Schwartz on a show now called *Children of Eden*. Caird's papers include notice of a suit filed by Lisanby's lawyer on 6 April 1989.

According to a letter that Schwartz sent to Caird on 26 June 1989, the arbitration with Lisanby and his lawyer would take place on 25–26 July 1989. He wanted Caird to send the most recent script so that he could forward it to Lisanby and show how far they had progressed since Lisanby and Caird stopped collaborating. The American Arbitration Association decision, rendered 25 August 1989, stated that Schwartz owns music and lyrics; Lisanby owns the spoken texts and titles *Family Tree*, *The Glory of Creation*, and *Genesis: From the Top*; and Schwartz could not remove any further texts from Lisanby's work. The concept is jointly owned and the project will always carry the credit line "Based on a concept by Charles Lisanby." Lisanby continues to receive a 15 percent cut of the royalties whenever the work is performed.

Schwartz's letter to Caird from 14 December 1988 outlines possible future plans. While still hoping that Lisanby perhaps might be involved, this letter showed how Schwartz and Caird were ready to proceed without him. Schwartz calls Caird the "book writer," but hopes that the director had spoken with Lisanby. The letter includes Schwartz's thoughts on a Guildhall School of Music and Drama workshop, with his hopes that they might work on larger numbers. He was coming to London the week of 16 January to present his work to the RSC and speak with potential directors (perhaps Caird was thinking of just writing the book?) and choreographers, and he wanted to meet with experts on ethnic instruments, most likely to learn something about the world music Schwartz hoped to reflect in his score.

Material consulted in Caird's papers demonstrates the extent of his early work on the project.[8] A spiral notebook includes Caird's detailed description of possible events for Act 2, where focus remains on Shem, Ham, and their wives bumbling through trying to build the ark and the young woman who marries Japheth was still named Anah. (Later she was called Yonah.[9]) It includes "suggestions" in jest, such as Scene 6 when Caird muses that Anah might sing "Don't Cry for Me, Mama Noah," a humorous reference to *Evita*. Caird's notes for the next scene were as follows:

Scene 7—boat-building in w/ Noah, Shem, Ham, Mama, Aisa, and Sheba— <<"Do It Yourself">> sung by quartet of S, H, A, & S—Noah leaves to water horses—Shem and Ham try to build the ark—chaos—their wives are no

help—despair!—bits of ark are assembled and collapse at the end of the song—
S & H not really believing in the flood, or the women?

As work progressed, the writers realized that they did not need to drama-
tize the ark's construction, instead concentrating on family relationships.
The next list in Caird's notebook includes a proposed twenty-six songs for
Act 2—a huge number—with indications of which Schwartz still needed to
write. A number of those so indicated Schwartz had written by the time of
his March 1988 letter, meaning that this list dates from earlier. There is also
a list of scenes for Act 2 that indicates which might have been written by
Caird and which by Lisanby.

Children of Eden: The Final Form

Caird and Schwartz embarked on a joint venture that lasted for a decade as
they wrote the version for the West End in early 1991, continuing through a
number of productions with bouts of rewriting before the final version played
at the Paper Mill Playhouse in late 1997. The show's development can be
viewed through correspondence, draft scripts, and commentary gained in
interviews with Caird and Schwartz, but first we view the final destination
through this synopsis of the show's current script. (Note: The acts are not
divided into scenes.)

Act 1
One flame is lit, and gradually more candles and lanterns appear. The Storytellers, or chorus, become visible. A small child sounds a trumpet, and they
sing "In the Beginning," joined by Father. He concludes the act of creation
with the Garden of Eden and first couple, singing four lines of the title song
"Children of Eden." The Storytellers sing that everything was "Perfect."
Eve shows her curiosity asking about the glistening Tree of Knowledge, and
Father loses his temper, causing Eve to cry. Father distracts her by suggesting
they name the animals ("The Naming"). He tells them it is time for them to
sleep, and they sing their prayer "Grateful Children." Father looks at them
fondly as they sleep and sings "Father's Day."

During the next sequence the Storytellers narrate, declaring sporadically
that each day was perfect. Adam and Eve discover how they were created for
each other physically, and Eve's curiosity takes her to the Tree of Knowledge.
She runs to Adam, eager to show him that everything grows darker and the
tree glows when one approaches it. Adam sees the mystery but has no further interest, leaving Eve to work on his list of bugs. Eve sings "The Spark

of Creation." Five Storytellers form a Snake and pique Eve's interest with questions before singing "In Pursuit of Excellence," noting that the tree's fruit will provide answers. Eve eats after the Snake leaves, and the Storytellers declare "The End of a Perfect Day." Adam enters; Eve has made apple dishes for dinner. She offers him juice, but stops him from drinking it. Adam realizes what has happened as the Storytellers sing that they heard Father walking in the garden. They hide, but Father comes to them and knows what Eve has done. She is excited about what she knows and sings "I can see," based upon Father's "Let There Be," but he answers in song that she knows too much and must leave Eden. He offers another wife to Adam, who dislikes losing Eve. Father counters that staying with Eve means Adam would never see Father again. Adam sings "World without You" about his choice, including material for Father and Eve. Adam bites the apple and Father and the Storytellers drive them from the garden, cursing them to bear their own children and blasting away Eden with a bolt of lightning. Adam fashions a walking stick from what is left of the Tree of Knowledge, and as they walk away the Storytellers sing "The Wasteland," narrating their trek and the birth of two children.

Cain and Abel are ten and eight, offering a sacrifice at an altar with Adam, singing new words to "Grateful Children." Eve interrupts with dinner, and Cain questions when they might return to Eden and what is above the waterfall. Adam makes his children promise that they will never go beyond the waterfall, but Cain is curious. Eve reprises "The Spark of Creation," realizing that she has passed on her questioning nature to Cain. Her children grow to ages seventeen and fifteen during the song, and they are alone on stage. Cain has packed to leave and wants Abel to accompany him. Abel prays at the altar, singing "Grateful Children," and Cain sings that they must make a life for themselves, leading into "Lost in the Wilderness." He convinces Abel, but Father appears. He accepts Abel's grain offering and stops him from calling his parents. Cain is defiant, even as Father offers to return and bring them wives. Cain sings some of "The Spark of Creation" and leaves. Father makes Abel promise not to tell his parents that he was there and sings that he is now Father's hope. Adam and Eve return and are furious that Cain has fled; they remember an earlier moment by singing "Close to Home" with younger versions of Cain and Abel.

Cain returns excited, reprising music that Eve sang earlier when she told Adam about the Tree of Knowledge. The whole family follows Cain to his discovery, the Ring of Stones, narrated by Storytellers with another verse of "The Wasteland." Cain, Abel, and Eve are excited, starting a musical scene with material from "The Spark of Creation" and other songs. Adam interrupts, saying that they should return before it rains. Cain implores him to listen, but Adam tears into his son, insisting that Cain cannot see the dangers, which Adam experienced when he came here himself and saw the people dancing among bones. Eve is hurt that Adam had never told her that. Cain wants to leave forever with Abel, but Adam tells Abel if he leaves that he will never see his father again. Abel's answer is what Adam sang earlier when trying to choose between Father and Eve. Cain taunts his father with the news of Father's visit, but Abel refuses to confirm it, and Cain tries to leave. Adam slaps him, and Cain picks up a rock to strike his father. Abel tries to restrain his brother, and Cain kills him. He yells that Adam should have died and flees. The Storytellers sing another verse of "The Wasteland" as Eve begs in song for her son to live. Adam carries Abel's body away, and Eve follows. As Cain runs, Father sings "The Mark of Cain" with the Story-tellers, cursing him and his progeny and striking Cain with a lightning bolt to mark his forehead. The segment ends with more verses of "The Wasteland."

The act concludes with Eve's monologue. She asks Father what happened to Cain, but receives no answer. Eve describes how Adam kept waiting for Cain's return. Adam and Eve had another child, Seth, who ran away at seventeen and returned with a wife; Eve recently had her first great-grandchild. One day, while working in the fields, Adam collapsed and died. Suddenly there is music, like that heard earlier in Eden, and Father comes on stage. Eve, only hearing his voice, learns that she will die soon and that Cain is alive and found some happiness. Eve announces to her family that this will be her last harvest, and leads singing of "Children of Eden."

Act 2

The ensemble presents "Generations of Adam," naming the family's succession from Seth to Noah, passing Adam's staff until it rests with Noah. He converses with Father about the ark's completion date and whether his sons have married. Noah reports that Shem and Ham have, but Japheth has turned down the wives selected for him. Father says that the woman must be chosen soon, or Japheth will go on the ark alone. Noah asks when animals might arrive, but Father tells him to finish the ark and wait. Noah confronts Father with "The Gathering Storm," which includes Noah's "I Wish You'd Change Your Mind," but Father will not be deterred. His sung response dwells on the evil of the Race of Cain. Only Noah and his family remain unblemished. Father disappears in a rumble of thunder.

The Storytellers sing a stanza as the scene changes to outside Noah's house, where sits the prow of a huge wooden boat. Noah concludes the musical moment by singing as he pounds in the last peg. "A Piece of Eight"

starts immediately. The Storytellers sing most of it, with characters jumping in with their lines. The family customarily sets seven places for dinner
(Noah, Mama, three sons, two wives), but tonight the eighth place is for
Japheth's intended. The chorus introduces Yonah, the family's servant and
a daughter of the Race of Cain. The Storytellers describe each couple's arrival and the family blesses their meal with "Grateful Children." Yonah sits
alone. The eighth chair remains empty until Noah asks if the girl is coming.
Japheth fetches Yonah. The song ends, and Noah reminds his son that he
cannot marry her. Japheth protests and runs away. Animals start to arrive
to the music of "The Return of the Animals." The animals dance and play,
and then Storytellers briefly describe the situation before Noah sings some
of "Children of Eden," acknowledging human blame for ruining their habi-
tat. He asks the animals to sleep. Meanwhile, Yonah has packed her things
to leave. Noah apologizes that she cannot be on the ark and leaves. Yonah
sings "Stranger to the Rain," acknowledging her family line. Japheth enters
and says that he has found a place for her to hide on the ark. She protests,
but Japheth insists that God must be wrong about her race. He sings "In
Whatever Time We Have," opening with a line from "How could I live in a
world without you?"—Adam's song in the first act. Yonah joins the song, and
Japheth insists that she hide on the ark before the family wakes up. There is
thunder as Father appears, singing material from "The Gathering Storm" as
he sees the Race of Cain boarding the ark. Father and the Storytellers declare
the beginning of "The Flood."

Forty days pass and Noah's family cannot understand why rain continues.
They sing "What Is He Waiting For?"; morale and supplies are low. Shem
suggests that there is plenty of food, but Mama answers they will not kill any
animals. Noah hears nothing from Father. Japheth goes to Yonah, who has
not yet been discovered; she insists that she needs to reveal herself. Japheth
considers that dangerous and leaves. Yonah goes out on deck, takes one of
the doves out of a cage, and sings "Sailor of the Skies" (which includes some
of "Children of Eden"), commissioning the bird to find them hope. Father
watches silently as the dove flies away. Shem and Ham are on deck, and
Yonah allows herself to be discovered. The sons fetch Noah. Shem and Ham
want to throw her overboard, but Japheth appears intending to defend her
to the death. Noah strikes Japheth, who picks up Adam's staff and is ready
to hit Ham, but Yonah runs between them. Japheth returns the staff to his
father and says that he will share Yonah's fate. Mama orders everyone but
her husband below. Singing from "The Spark of Creation," she insists that
Noah must solve this alone. She goes below. Noah sings an excerpt of "World
without You," not wishing to decide between his son and Father; "The

Hardest Part of Love," about how difficult it is to watch a child grow up, follows. Father joins him, remembering his disappointment in Eden, but Noah cannot hear him. They finish the song together. Noah pounds on the deck with his staff. The family gathers as Storytellers sing "Words of Doom." Noah tells Japheth and Yonah to hold his staff, and marries them. Noah answers protests from his other sons and sings how they need to reconcile in "The Hour of Darkness." Noah wipes the Mark of Cain from Yonah's forehead, kisses her, and hugs Japheth. Yonah sings an excerpt from "In Whatever Time We Have"; the family joins. The dove returns, bearing an olive sprig. Stars become visible, and the rain stops. Mama leads "Ain't It Good?" and Noah asks Father for a sign that he will never again destroy the world. A rainbow appears. The ark lands, and each son with his wife declare that they will take a portion of the animals in one direction to make their new lives. Japheth states that he and Yonah will search for Eden; Noah gives him his staff. The family embraces as Father sings "Precious Children" from above before the ensemble finale, "In the Beginning," which ends with "Children of Eden."

The New Collaboration

Caird and Schwartz described their work in interviews. The director started over on the script, writing a first draft at Schwartz's house, where he stayed for weeks at a time. Schwartz has noted Caird's wide musical knowledge and that the director/writer "had a lot of input" on the songs. Schwartz recalls, "We did lots of research. We had so much fun!" Caird believes that their collaboration worked because "neither of us had much ego about our individual contributions." Caird observes the show's importance to his collaborator: "He works on them [musicals] when he loves them and *Children of Eden* he's had an incredible soft spot for. . . . It's the stuff about fathers and children that's so central to his deepest preoccupations."

Writing a musical about Genesis also resonated deeply for Caird, who had been "steeped in the Bible" by his father, a prominent Congregationalist minister and Oxford theology professor. The director has always been "fascinated by the inconsistencies in the different creation myths" as well as father-child relationships that provide the show's core theme, especially parental expectations of family loyalty that "children cannot sustain." Other favorite issues for Caird included "the theological problem of the silence of God" and God's relationship to the pain one inevitably suffers. One also must explain what follows Genesis, especially what happened after the Flood. The conclusion that Caird and Schwartz reached in *Children of Eden* is that humans are on their own. Caird could not accept the "ghastly paternalism" inherent in the Fall of Man story, suggesting that "if the Tree of Knowledge is forbidden, let's start by assuming that it's a bad thing that it was forbidden. If the forbidding of the fruit was not a good idea, if parents shouldn't do that to their children, then why should the children be punished?" If humans are born curious, why would we not try to learn? Caird and Schwartz wanted to remove the entire blame from Eve's shoulders.

Research in Caird's personal archive yielded a profusion of materials, rendering possible a description of the writing of *Children of Eden* that is far more detailed than can be presented here. We will therefore look at the show's creation in vignettes, pausing for detailed looks at various scripts, pieces of correspondence, and other evidence in order to sample what transpired during the collaboration.

The show's early form in the Schwartz/Caird era may be seen in an incomplete script draft dating from 21 February 1989, described here in terms of action and songs.

Act 1
Scene 1—After "Let There Be," Adam and Eve appear and begin "The Naming" with the animals. They sing "Grateful Children" before sleeping, and we understand that God—who does not appear as a character in this version—has told them to avoid the Tree of Knowledge. They arise for another day, and Adam counts animals while Eve sings "The Spark of Creation." The Snake appears and sings "In Pursuit of Excellence," causing Eve to take the apple. Adam returns home and finds Eve frightened; he sings "How Can I Live in a World without You," describing the garden's beauty and his love for Eve. He eats the apple before they leave the garden accompanied by nightmarish animals and music.

Scene 2—It is twenty years later. Abel, age ten, scares a dinosaur away from their cave. Adam enters, bearing harvested corn, and shows Abel a snail. Cain, who is seventeen, arrives and argues with his father. Cain expresses his feelings in "Lost in the Wilderness." Cain exits; Adam and Abel return to naming this type of snail, but Eve is worried that Cain might never return. The three sing "Close to Home" about family rituals.

Scene 3—Abel is alone at home and Cain arrives, excited. Their conversation reveals mutual regard and a sibling rivalry. Eve and Adam enter, furious at Cain for his week's absence. Cain sings excitedly of the "Ring of Stones," proof that other people exist. (The action that follows appears on a fax that Schwartz sent to Caird on 21 February 1989.) Schwartz describes how Cain wants to meet these people but Adam forbids it. Cain tries to leave but Adam knocks him down. Cain picks up a rock; Abel runs in front of his father, and Cain kills his brother. The grieving parents cradle Abel's body, and Cain cries out to God for forgiveness.

Scene 4—Cain exits and Adam carries Abel's body offstage. The remainder of the scene is Eve's monologue about the rest of her life, the content of which is the same as the show today, but God never appears. Eve leads the cast in singing "Children of Eden."

Act 2

Scene 1—During the song, "Generations of Adam," his staff is passed from father to son until it comes into Noah's possession. He bows at an altar to tell God that the ark is completed, but one of his sons, Japheth, has been away for two years. Noah begs God to cancel the flood or at least postpone it for his son and all humanity. A song for chorus, "Cutthroat," describes evil in the world and why God has decided to destroy it, while Noah suggests reasons to spare it.

The act continues with ideas added and deleted, a script in the midst of creation. What appears to be the next scene begins with the vista behind Noah revealed: He is high on a mountainside with the ark's prow to one side. We see part of a stone house and a group awaits him: his wife, Thulah (she is unnamed in Genesis, and in most later versions of *Children of Eden* is Mama Noah); their sons Shem and Ham; and their wives, Asah and Sheba. (At one point there was a family meal, later deleted.) Noah drives the last spike into the ark, and they sing "Ship-Shape" before eating dinner, assisted by their servant, Anah. Some want her on the ark, but Noah reminds them, singing that she is of Cain's race. They sing "Bless Our Home" to the tune used for prayers in Act 1, and Anah, eating alone, sings some of the counting song heard in "Close to Home." Mama sets a place for Japheth in hope of his return, and she sings that he might be distant or "Close to Home." Noah meets a rich man who hopes to purchase a place on the ark, and suddenly pairs of animals arrive, a comedy and a dance sequence set to "The Arrival of the Animals." Noah informs the animals of what will happen. Anah brings in the pair of doves and sings "I'm Not a Stranger to the Rain." Japheth arrives, expressing his love to Anah. He sings a song with no obvious name, beginning with how something was missing in his travels, and he has returned to love her. She tells him that his father will never allow them to be together, but he challenges her to express her feelings, and she joins the song. In the next scene we see Anah asleep in Japheth's arms, and he tells her to stay hidden. The rain has started, and there is considerable confusion as the family sees Japheth. Mama hugs him and then hits him for the worry he caused. Noah wants everyone to get ready, but Mama is upset that Anah cannot come. Japheth declares that she will. Noah knocks him down and Japheth arms himself with a board, but Anah runs between them. Japheth carries her onto the ark and Noah laments that he has failed God. The world drowns as the ark rises with the flood. This draft ends here.

Another draft script dated 1 May 1989 includes a few interesting moments and insertions of possible reprises. The "Ring of Stones" scene was changing, some of the dialogue to be added later. The intention remains that Cain has found evidence of other people and wants to meet them. Adam intervenes, and Abel dies in the fight. This script also includes Japheth reprising "Lost in the Wilderness" (sung by Cain in Act 1) in Act 2, Scene 2 and bringing back the tune of "In Pursuit of Excellence" for "In Pursuit of Permanence," sung by Noah's family below on the ark while the patriarch considers what to do about Japheth and Anah.[10]

Undated sources include information about possible alternative avenues. A script from Act 1 that perhaps dates from when Lisanby was still involved, or shortly after his departure, includes what are probably Caird's suggestions for possible songs that never appeared, including one perhaps called "Footprints," sung by Cain concerning evidence of other people around the Ring of Stones. Other notes suggest Abel singing a prayer ("Help Me, Father") as he goes to try and bring back the fleeing Cain and then Adam's possible song to God as he carries Abel's body back home. This script, including only Act 1, also refers to Eve, in her last scene, speaking of "generations of Adam" as a family tree grows from the stage. Someone, however, deleted "Generations of Adam" here and added "Children of Eden" lyrics. Another script presents evidence of Caird suggesting changes to Schwartz's lyrics, urging him to avoid clichés and use specific images. Once, Schwartz wrote "Life can be a battlefield" and Caird requests that he instead work in something about the ark.

Toward a Possible London Opening

A letter dated 13 July 1989 from the RSC to William McDonald of Upstart Productions—a company formed to produce *Children of Eden*—announced that a complete script draft and tape of ten fully orchestrated songs would be ready by the first week of September, and that RSC director Terry Hands would decide what role his company might play in producing the show by 28 July. (At that point, Hands decided that the RSC would participate.) John Napier, an important West End set designer, joined the project.

A draft script from 4 October 1989 demonstrates new thinking from Schwartz and Caird. God ("Father") is now a corporeal presence who interacts with other characters, but not as much as he did when the show opened in the West End more than a year later. After Adam and Eve sing "Grateful Children," Father returns to erect the Tree of Knowledge, warning them to avoid it. Eve falls for the snake's temptation and Adam figures out what has happened; he sings "World without You," acknowledging that he does not want to leave her, and eats the apple before Father returns.

Considerable rewriting had taken place in the confrontation over the Ring of Stones. After Cain describes it, Adam admits that he had been there, surprising Eve because he had never told her. Cain tempts his mother to come and see it, and Eve asks him not to force her to make that choice, a familiar stance for characters elsewhere in the story. Cain decides that he will go and find the other people, and Abel wants to go with him. As Adam tries to stop them, Cain accidentally kills his brother.

In Act 1, Scene 4, Father's presence has changed Eve's final monologue. Eve calls to Father, asking if it is time for her to die. He answers that her life will end soon. She asks if Cain is alive and if he found any happiness, and God says that he did. When Eve thanks Father, he replies, "No thanks to me." This exchange remains in the show today, but Eve only hears his voice.

The 4 October 1989 script opens Act 2 with "Generations of Adam," as most versions of the show do, but from there the act proceeds differently. Noah divides his lands among his sons and announces the wives that he has chosen for them. Shem and Ham are grateful, but Japheth rebels and sings "Bound for the wilderness"—like Cain in Act 1—as he runs away.

Scene 2 starts here much as Act 2 does today, with the ark's prow visible and God asking why it is not finished. Noah sings "I Wish You'd Change Your Mind" while the ensemble presents "Civilized Society," now cut. "Ship-Shape" remained, but they removed it after the West End run. The family's servant is now named Yonah. Japheth returns and takes her on the ark as the flood starts, over Noah's objections. Animals gather. Songs through the floods include "Close to Home" at the dinner table, Yonah's "I'm No Stranger to the Rain," Noah presenting a version of "Children of Eden" to the animals explaining how humans have ruined their home, Japheth and Yonah singing "In Whatever Time We Have," Noah crying out what Cain intoned after killing Abel in Act 1 ("Oh God, turn back the time/Give me this day to live again/Or let me die!"), and the chorus singing contritely as they realize that all will drown. Of these songs, "Close to Home" has been cut and Japheth and Yonah now run onto the ark without the confrontation with Noah, so the patriarch need not sing about Yonah on the ark. The flood is declared today musically by Father and announced by Storytellers with no chorus appearing to apologize for misdeeds.

Like the current script, the 4 October 1989 version mentions no change of scene as the script jumps to forty days later and Noah's family waits for the rain to stop as supplies run low, singing "What Is He Waiting For?" Noah sends a raven flying off in hopes that it will return with some hope, but it does not. Yonah sings "Dove Song" (later "Sailor of the Sky"), sending a dove out to search for land, and it returns as in the current script. Shem, Ham, and their wives sing material from "Civilized Society" before suggesting that Yonah needs to be removed from the ark. The remainder of the act bears considerable similarity to the current show.

An article in the *Financial Times* on 20 January 1990 stated that the RSC would produce *Children of Eden* along with Upstart (run by Patricia Macnaughton) at the cost of £700,000. It would run over Christmas for eight weeks at the Barbican.[11] Much of the remainder of the article concerns the RSC's financial problems. In our interview Caird reported that the prospect of *Children of Eden* in an RSC production "did not really go too far" because the 1990–1991 season was cancelled by Thatcher-era budget cuts. Indeed, an article from 19 July 1990 in the *Times* reported that the RSC had pulled out of *Children of Eden* because of cost-cutting measures, and Caird had resigned as an associate director from the RSC with the departure of his boss, Terry Hands.[12] Caird announced in the same source that *Eden* would open before Christmas in a West End theater.

Schwartz had doubts about proceeding to the West End. He was not sufficiently comfortable that they knew what they were doing with *Eden*, and Caird himself was concerned, but they were convinced to plunge ahead by the noted designer John Napier, who thought he had seen other successful shows in similar shape this far in advance of a West End opening. Schwartz did not believe that they had managed a sufficient number of workshops, but they had interest from producer Patricia Macnaughton. Caird reports that it was a joint decision to move to production.

Another draft script survives from 19 March 1990, which included several noteworthy changes. When Father presents the Tree of Knowledge in Act 1, Scene 1, he seems downright reckless, bringing the tree out of the ground in front of Adam and Eve, admitting its beauty, but ordering them to avoid it. In response to Eve's questions, he states that the tree bears his knowledge, which they may not possess. Adam sings brief warnings to Eve about her curiosity and the need for obedience, and Father sings that there are things he knows better than they do because "you're newer here than me," an admonition that remained in the show through a number of versions. This segment occurs here after "The Naming."

Scene 3, the confrontation between Adam and Cain, has become a duet in this draft, with Adam playing the parental role that Father did earlier with Eve, suggesting there are things that a child cannot know. Cain leaves after singing "Lost in the Wilderness," momentarily a duet with his father, and then Adam and Eve sing "Close to Home," remembering when Cain was younger and things were easier. The remainder of this act and Act 2 include little that is surprising.

Another script survives from 4 July 1990, the typed version from 19 March 1990 with that date crossed out and the new one entered. The newer version includes many handwritten emendations. Act 1, Scene 1 has not changed substantially since March, but there has been considerable work on Scene 2. Eve runs in singing about something "that will astound" Adam, the way she still addresses her husband as she comes to get him and show him how the Tree of Knowledge brightens when you approach it. There is more here about her encounter with the Wall of Trees. As usual, Adam is unimpressed, but he actively tries to dampen Eve's curiosity, singing a few stanzas of moralizing. In later versions Adam remains concerned about Eve's curiosity, but does not lecture her.

Some of the material added to this script came from a fax that Schwartz sent to Caird on 25 June 1990. (There are several such faxed sheets in this cobbled-together script.) Among the ideas that did not remain long in the show was collaboration between Cain and Abel as the older brother stayed away from home. Abel brings Cain food, and it is clear from dialogue that they have met like this before. Cain pulls out a knife so that the brothers can swear a blood pact about leaving home together, establishing how close they are and making the murder all the more shocking, an idea that the writers later deleted.

Act 2 in this script includes new material that, if it had remained, would have sent *Children of Eden* off in different directions. Early in the act, a faxed sheet includes Noah stating that he has called his family together to divide up his lands and announce wives for his sons. The chorus—called Angels here (later Storytellers)—sings "Beyond, beyond" (heard from Eve in Act 1) in reference to Japheth, who resists Noah. (It is clear that "Beyond" and its music was already a recurring motive.) The script follows Japheth's journey. He encounters people who speak different languages. He climbs through the set trying to escape the cacophony but the voices just become louder. He tries to sleep with his hands over his ears, but the noise reaches a "deafening climax," and Japheth disappears into the darkness. Father appears above and silences everyone when he starts singing "Degenerations," setting up the flood.

The script also includes a fascinating addition just before "The Return of the Animals." Father arrives disguised as an old man wanting to go on the ark. Noah refuses, pointing out that their own servant Yonah may not because she descends from Cain. Father remarks that Noah's god appears to be cruel; Noah admits that might appear to be the case. Father also speaks to Yonah, asking where she will go. She replies that she will be in the deepest valley, where the flood will strike first. Noah comments on Yonah's lack of fear; she says she only fears for Noah's venture on the ark. The rich man who had tried to buy his way onto the ark in Lisanby's version had become Father coming to Noah in disguise to test his resolve, a scene later cut. Japheth returns and the act proceeds much as in previous versions, but after Japheth takes Yonah aboard the ark Noah cries out to Father, "My shame is more than I can bear," tying him to Cain's feelings in Act 1. As the waters rise, this script describes people climbing through the set with their possessions, fighting for higher positions. The world drowns and the script states that the audience sees bodies suspended in water, an interesting staging problem. The act proceeds similarly to previous versions with perhaps more explanation of actions. Caird's papers include another script from just a week later, 11 July 1990, a typed version of what was just described.

The London Production

The production team held cast auditions through the summer. In an undated communication from Schwartz to Caird, the songwriter mentions Carol Woods-Coleman, an African American actress who worked both on Broadway and in the West End in the 1980s and 1990s, and he also wonders about Rae Dong Chong as a possibility for Eve, believing that she could sing well. Martin Smith had auditioned, and Schwartz thought that he would be "terrific" as Adam from a musical standpoint, as he stated in another undated fax to Caird. Schwartz left "looks, age, personality and marquee values" of the possible actors up to Caird and the producers in London, but he wanted input as to their singing ability.

From the start they sought a multiracial cast. African American actor Ken Page, famous for his work in *Ain't Misbehavin'* and as Old Deuteronomy in the New York production of *Cats*, was Father, raising objections from British Equity because he was not British. According to *Variety* on 17 September 1990, the British Equity panel accepted Page in the role, but they also suggested that two Japanese actors who had been hired for singing some songs in close harmony could perhaps be cast from the field of British actors.[13] The show's main cast members were as follows:

Ken Page—Father
Martin Smith—Adam
Shezwae Powell—Eve

Richard Lloyd-King—Snake
Adrian Beaumont and Shion Abdillah—Cain, at various ages
Ramilles Corbin and Ashley Walters—Abel, at various ages
Kevin Colson—Noah
Earlene Bentley—Mama Noah
Craig Pinder—Shem
Ray Shell—Ham
Anthony Barclay—Japheth
Hiromi Itoh—Aysha
Ruthie Henshall—Aphra
Frances Ruffelle (Caird's wife at the time)—Yonah

Caird stated that they did not set out to create a megamusical, but it was a large production with a cast of thirty-eight and Schwartz's score (orchestrated by David Cullen) was played by twenty-three musicians, including didgeridoo.[14] They had ten weeks of rehearsal, longer than usual.[15] John Napier's set, made from eight tons of steel, was an inverted globe about thirty feet tall. Actors climbed on it and traversed two walkways that stretched across the stage and projected into the audience.[16] The budget was £2.2 million, jeopardized when the RSC pulled out and left a £500,000 hole, plugged by Japanese businessmen.[17] Later an American investor withdrew, removing another £400,000; enough money remained but there was no cushion. Caird at one point reportedly dipped into his own pocket to pay salaries.[18] Geordie Greig stated that they needed twenty-four weeks of sellouts to recoup costs, and a run of ninety-eight weeks to pay back investors if they only averaged half of the house.[19]

Caird admits that the show was "huge and ambitious," set at the Prince Edward Theatre before its refurbishment by Cameron Mackintosh. The director called the house a "big barn," and *Children of Eden* was "essentially quite a small, familial story." He continued, "I think the charm of the story got lost in the expanse of the space we were in." Caird also recalled the effective choreography, devised by Matthew Bourne before he became famous as a ballet choreographer and musical theater director.[20] Another problem, according to Caird, was that *Children of Eden* is more of an American show. The Bible is more important in the United States than in England, occupied by what Caird calls "rather a godless race." He also finds his own country more skeptical about musical adaptations than Americans, especially those based upon famous texts. The show opened on 8 January 1991, nearly the eve of the First Gulf War, accompanied by a serious dip in theater attendance.

Caird's candid evaluation after the show's London closing included possible improvements. He thought that it was too long, noting, "We'd fallen in love with too much stuff." An expendable song he named was the close harmony quartet "Ship-Shape" (in the style of Manhattan Transfer) performed by Shem, Ham, and their wives. There was also backstory early in Act 2 that could be deleted. Caird recalls that he made a number of changes with Schwartz before discussions started with other collaborators, and he notes that they continued "tweaking" the show for years, even after the Paper Mill version in 1997.

The souvenir book from the London production included photographs that give an impression of the production's visual impact, featuring the efforts of designer John Napier, lighting of David Hersey, and costumes by Richard Sharples. Father wore a costume that mixed a business suit and robe, while Adam and Eve, before eating of the Tree of Knowledge, had on flesh-colored shirts with anatomical features drawn on them. Other characters were in a mixture of period and modern dress, such as Adam and Cain wearing pants but with cloths draped over their torsos. Dress became more modern in Act 2 with Noah in shirt and pants with suspenders, for example. Several years before the staging of *The Lion King*, animals for *Children of Eden* were made possible with spectacular costumes and puppetry, such as a skeletal rhinoceros shape with two people under the costume, and a woman dressed as a florid peacock. The huge metal globe figured in the production in a myriad of ways, and lighting effects distinguished various sections of the globe, with, for example, brown light on the lower level and blue lights higher, designating heaven.

Extant correspondence and financial information track the show's decline. A letter from producer Patricia Macnaughton to Caird from 26 February 1991 confirmed that he had agreed to waive his royalties and directorial fees, and that they negotiated a rent reduction from the Prince Edward Theatre. The weekly grosses started in January around £80,000, falling to as low as £54,000 in February and sometimes less than £40,000 in March. The overall gross was a bit over £1 million.[21] A fax that Schwartz sent to Caird on 21 March indicates that he had heard from his agent Shirley Bernstein that the show would close on 7 April. Schwartz, however, stated that he had "lost none of my belief in the show" and plans were underway for new versions of *Children of Eden*. Early in the run there was talk of an American film with interest from Paramount and 20th Century Fox, but the notion died.[22]

Critical response to *Children of Eden* in London was disappointing. Of the twenty-one reviews surveyed, fifteen were mostly or entirely negative, four mixed, and two positive. The show's dramatization of Genesis inspired

some critics to imitate the King James Bible, with perhaps the most outrageous such review written by Michael Coveney of the *Observer*: "And Caird
knew his wife Frances Ruffelle and she created some songs as Yonah, wife of
Japheth, and they were good but not that good."[23] Jack Tinker of the *Daily
Mail* echoed a number of his colleagues when he wrote, "It is that feeblest
of things, just well-intentioned."[24] Paul Taylor of the *Independent* suggested
that the show's only religious element would have been experienced by investors: "If you had money in it, your thoughts would be turning purposefully
to prayer."[25] Charles Osborne, writing for the *Daily Telegraph*, said, "*Children
of Eden* is mildly and fitfully entertaining," but he was unimpressed.[26] Clive
Hirschhorn in the *Sunday Express* offered that the creators "begat a stinker,"[27]
and Michael Church in the *Independent on Sunday* penned a sarcastic pan:
"As drama it's a shambles; musically it's a ragbag; there's no sex, no wit."[28]
One of the few positive voices came from Michael Darvell in *What's On*.
Darvell started by stating his dislike for recent musicals, listing short-lived
shows and *Miss Saigon*, but he praised most aspects of *Children of Eden* and
referred only to Schwartz when he wrote, "With *Children of Eden* I have to
admit that he has done a thoroughly professional job of adapting the first
book of the Bible."[29] Such a positive notice is a useful reminder that almost
every musical generates a variety of opinions.

Children of Eden after London

Caird and Schwartz started working on rewrites before the show closed on 7
April 1991. A new script had been produced that bears the date 18 March,
and it included minor changes. Act 1 was truncated a bit, but the essential
story was familiar. In Act 2, Noah does not sing "I Wish You'd Change Your
Mind" to Father while that ensemble renders "Civilized Society." Noah's
prayer instead comes later, where Father expresses his disappointment on
how long the ark has taken to build. Much of the remainder of the act is
similar to previous versions, with some rewriting.

Previous reference to Schwartz's fax to Caird on 21 March 1991 involved
the show's imminent demise in London. Just two sentences later, Schwartz
anticipates "much happier outcomes in future productions." He mentions a
possibility in La Jolla, California. Shortly thereafter, Schwartz sent another
fax to Caird, reporting on his meeting in La Jolla, which included the company's artistic director, Des MacAnuff, later well known.[30] Schwartz had left
them a copy of the script from a New York reading (an event that is otherwise undocumented) and a demo tape. He reports that they were pleased that
Eden was unfinished, and they were considering it. Schwartz had also met

with a friend at San Diego State University to plant the seed for another possible production or workshop. Schwartz noted that he had a telephone call upon his return to New York from director Ernie Zulia, who was at a regional theater in Virginia. Schwartz knew him to be "an excellent director." This connection resulted in the next production of *Children of Eden*.

A fax from Schwartz to Caird on 25 June, including a proposed outline, suggested a major change for Father. The composer/lyricist thought that the character either needs to become "the focus of the evening," or eliminated as an onstage presence, as was the case when Lisanby was involved. Schwartz preferred the former because "he is the only character common to both acts and one of the only characters who changes."[31] He also wanted to use the Angels (later called the Storytellers) more to help tell the story. The outline that Schwartz enclosed with the fax shows extensive brainstorming, helping to lead *Children of Eden* in a new direction. The outline includes much new thinking. "Grateful Children" had always ended the first segment of Act 1. Schwartz wanted to add a song for Father as he watches his children sleep, resulting in "Father's Day," which he wrote that summer.[32]

An example of how Schwartz tried to challenge their assumptions and previous work on the show came when he approached the expulsion scene in his lengthy fax:

> 10. "The Expulsion"—sans ballet (though I still like the idea of the ferocious animals). Much more challenge of God's behavior by Eve; really confront the issues—why is he making such a big deal about their disobedience and gaining knowledge? Raise issue of free will—why did Father put that in us? Because we're made in His image? Does he want us to choose to obey him? We need to make it clear this is the issue here, and we need to confront it in a non-hackneyed way.

Schwartz's outline introduces a number of new ideas, appearing to change the discussion of several significant details. He advocates that Father join in "The Naming," helping to bring that scene into its final form. He also suggests bringing Father into the scene before Adam eats the apple, raising the level of confrontation and making explicit the scene's parallels with other pivotal moments involving Adam, Cain, and Abel, and later Noah and Japheth. A suggested addition of a scene between Father, Cain, and Abel where Father prevents them from calling their parents inserts Father more firmly in the second half of Act 1 and deepens the rift between Adam and Cain. Father's subsequent cursing of Cain after he murders Abel is another divine appearance in Act 1 and makes the Mark of Cain all the more vivid as Yonah's problem in Act 2. Schwartz included several philosophical questions about Father's silence in the second half of Act 2 as Noah's family sings "What Is He Waiting For?" The writers did not elect ultimately to explain Father's silence, but such questions show the depth of their discussions. Schwartz suggested that the violent confrontation between Noah and Japheth begin like the parallel moment in Act 1: Noah strikes his son, as Adam does Cain, but Japheth refuses to strike back and allows his father to decide what to do. The final version is different, with Yonah intervening and Japheth returning the staff to Noah and stating that he will share Yonah's fate, whatever it might be. Mama Noah frames the choice starkly for Noah before she leaves him alone on deck. This allows Mama Noah to sing a reprise of "The Spark of Creation." By all appearances, Schwartz's fax from 25 June 1991 was a crucial moment in the show's history.

Schwartz's outline also suggests that actors should play analogous characters in both acts, combining the roles of Adam/Noah, Eve/Mama Noah, and Cain/Japheth. This was first done in the Virginia production in November 1991. The director there, Ernie Zulia, strongly favored the concept.[33] Schwartz explained in an interview that he thought that it gave the show a greater sense of cohesion and helped the audience connect parallel themes between acts.

A few sources survive from the work session that Schwartz and Caird had late that summer, including a folder that identifies the dates as 9–19 September 1991. A draft of a script from 9 September 1991 was available for study through the point where Adam with Cain and Abel make a sacrifice to Father at their altar in the Wasteland. Given the 25 June fax already reviewed, there is little in the script that is surprising. There is a list of songs in Caird's hand that does not include "A Piece of Eight," which Schwartz wrote that fall. Caird's list includes "Japheth and Yonah" and "Noah's Refusal," replaced by "A Piece of Eight." The new script, probably prepared for rehearsals in Roanoke that fall, also clarifies the double casting.

Ernie Zulia was associate artistic director of the Mill Mountain Theater in Roanoke, Virginia. The first musical that he ever directed, as a senior in college, was *Godspell*. Later, with collaborator Frank Bartolucci, he assembled a revue of Schwartz's songs called *Magic to Do*, premiered by the Cincinnati Playhouse in the Park during summer 1979. The revue then ran in Boston at the Charles Playhouse, and went on to Ford's Theater in Washington DC under the title *Day by Day*. Zulia and Schwartz became friends. When the director arrived in Roanoke, he wanted to revive his Schwartz revue. The composer/lyricist sent his latest songs in about 1990, including the score of *Children of Eden*. Zulia revised the revue, incorporating material from *Chil-*

dren of Eden, which he thought included some of Schwartz's "most beautiful, probing, inspiring kind of songs."[34] Zulia was surprised when *Eden* failed in London, and, along with Mill Mountain artistic director Jere Lee Hodgin, asked Schwartz about including it in their new season. Zulia thought it would help that Roanoke was "off the beaten path," providing a "low profile production" that would allow trying out revisions. Schwartz and Caird agreed. The composer recalled that it was Zulia "who had the vision on how he wanted to do the show." Caird remembers help from Hodgin, but Zulia made a stronger impression: "Ernie was very, very energetic and persuasive in getting us to rethink certain things. You don't need to bully Stephen and myself to rewrite and rethink, but Ernie was very generous in allowing us the space to do it."

Schwartz and Caird spent two weeks in Roanoke, and the summer before the show's run there they had meetings with Zulia at Schwartz's home in Connecticut and in North Carolina. The production was nothing like what occurred in the West End; Zulia remembers "developing and creating a whole production concept that was going to shape the show." Among the major changes were the double casting and rewriting "In Pursuit of Excellence." The former change allowed Zulia to hire better actors and addressed another of his major concerns:

> I really felt the show was suffering from being two one-acts rather than a full evening. By double casting, we were able to get the audience invested in the characters and their epic human journey in Act 1, so they could be more connected and more profoundly affected by the resolution delivered in Act 2. The universals in each story were emphasized and the double casting made them resonate on a deeper level.[35]

Among the cast members were Bill Nolte (a Broadway veteran) as Father, Cass Morgan (one of Schwartz's favorite singers) as Eve/Mama Noah, Craig Wasson (star of the film *Body Double*) as Adam/Noah, and Paul Anthony Stewart as Cain/Japheth. Zulia conceived a stark production in modern dress with simple stage pieces, such as a raked disk in the center where most of the acting took place. The director's desire was to "deliver the heart of the show and let the strength of the cast . . . and storytelling move center stage." The cast was large: fourteen principals, thirty-two in the choir of Storytellers, and about twenty-four children, who played the animals. He stated, "My task was to create an epic and then achieve a very intimate story in the middle of it." Some of the epic quality came from keeping choir and dancers on stage whenever possible, letting each fulfill a number of functions.

There were moments for Zulia that felt like madness before a Broadway opening. For example, while working on the new song "A Piece of Eight," Schwartz gave Zulia the song's lyric so that he would have something to work with in his staging, but the composer did not complete the music until four days before they opened. The director worked from the text's rhythm, admitting, "That was kind of exciting!" The orchestra was about eight musicians with orchestrations prepared by music director David Caldwell. *Children of Eden* ran for a month in Roanoke and did well at the box office. Zulia remembers exuberant standing ovations and calls it "one of the most satisfying directorial experiences I have ever had." He now teaches at Hollins University in Roanoke and remains associated with Mill Mountain Theatre.

Schwartz and Caird continued revising *Children of Eden* through various regional productions. In a 1997 article that appeared in the *Cleveland Plain Dealer*, Schwartz told reporter Linda Eisenstein that the writers had participated in eight productions of *Eden* at regional theaters since the show closed in London, and this article names yet another production, the show's Ohio premiere at the Cleveland area Jewish Community Center Halle Theater.[36]

Caird's papers include documents that continue to illustrate the rich history of *Eden*'s creation. One develops a sense for the continued detailed nature of their work from a three-page list entitled "Children of Eden/To Do—30 Nov. 1992" (see Textbox 9.1). Clearly the result of a lengthy meeting between the two writers concerning the latest script, the list shows that the writers wrestled with many matters, but by this point most tasks involved aligning parallel moments in the show, a character's momentary motivation, verses, small musical segments, and lines, rather than scenes or the order of events. A few larger questions were asked in the document—such as the first entry for Schwartz as he rewrote passages in "Let There Be"—but here, one year after Roanoke, they were mostly polishing. As one reads this document, it is almost possible to hear Schwartz and Caird sparring, challenging each other's work and urging the other to reconsider material, some of which had been in the show for years. Some suggestions recorded here did not remain in the show; "Close to Home," for example, was not ultimately replaced by "Family Prayer." Almost five years, and many additional rewrites, remained before the Paper Mill production in 1997.

Schwartz and Caird next prepared for a workshop in spring 1993 at Playwrights Horizons, off-Broadway in New York City. In a fax that Schwartz sent Caird on 28 February 1993, the composer/lyricist reported the director would be Kirsten Sanderson and the New York Choral Society would supply the twenty-four Angels. Collaborators at Playwrights Horizons believed that the second half of Act 1 and Act 2 were strong, but work remained on the

Textbox 9.1
"To Do" List by Schwartz and Caird, 30 November 1992

Children of Eden
To Do—30 Nov. 1992

Act One

1. "Let There Be"
   Stephen: Write verses for Father
      Focus more on Father's motivation—what does he want in creating Man? What does he expect?
      Should some of this material be handled after the number, before waking Adam and Eve?
      Perhaps there should be some lines to the Angels leading to first statement of "Children of Eden"
   John: Line for Father after "Light," such as "Hmmm . . . Not much to look at, is there?"
2. Pages 4 to 6
   John: Look at rewritten lines
   Stephen: Consider cutting "Out of chaos" motif
3. "Grateful Children"
   Stephen: Consider cutting or rewriting second verse if we're losing "Speak to me" section from "Hardest part of Love" . . . unless we're putting back second verse on page 23.
4. Page 11
   Stephen: Add beats after "I think he's got my nose"
      Shorten music at end of "Father's Day"
      Improve music for "Perfectly Happy"
5. Page 12
   John and Stephen: Strengthen and clarify Adam's reaction to discovery of Wall of Trees
6. Snake
   John: Snake's questions need to be more challenging and "scientific"—like A Brief History of Time
   Stephen: Rewrite lyric to intro to clarify what Snake means by "excellence"
      Cut "If you stay ingenuous" couplet?

7. Pages 18 and 19 (lead up to Adam eating apple)

John: Look at rewritten lines and let's discuss this scene – it seems too short and not focussed [sic] on Father enough; we really need to deliver this scene philosophically

Stephen: Lengthen build into "Oh, my garden"

8. "Expulsion"

Stephen: Cut or shorten "Oh my children that I love so well" section?

Add Angel chorus to some lines as emphasis

John: Does Eve need another line or two after ". . . my children of Eden?"

9. First "Wasteland" scene

Stephen: Put "Wasteland" into third person throughout?

Replace second verse of prayer to Father?

Cut "Close to Home" and replace it with "Family Prayer"

John: Add material for Adam on page 23 to establish his motivation for this section more strongly (strengthen "If we're good")

Increase the mystery about going beyond the waterfall; arouse audience curiosity

10. Transition to grown-up Cain and Abel (page 26)

John: Add a brief exchange between Adam and grown-up Cain to establish their relationship (Instructions to Cain and Abel)

Stephen: Improve "dark inclination" lyric

11. "Lost in the Wilderness"

Stephen: Rewrite so this functions more as a song; perhaps *start* it with "Spark of Creation" reprise into "Beyond"

12. Grandfather scene

John: Establish "Grandfather" idea sooner

It's a tough jump from the "wives" moment to Cain defying Father; it happens too quickly

We need a better build to the "Lost in the Wilderness" reprise

Lengthen Abel's "Don't go, Cain" line

Stephen: Improve the end of the scene musically

13. Page 31

John: Clarify and strengthen Adam's reaction to Cain being gone; raise the mystery of the waterfall again?

14. "Ring of Stones"

    Stephen and John: Adam's position is unclear; clarify why he's so opposed. Should Father be present, watching? If not, why not?

    John: Make Adam's line on 34 "You will never see us again"

        Make clear Adam is actually preventing Cain from going—earlier he says "If you go" so it's not clear exactly what's happening—clarify the physical reality of the scene

15. "Mark of Cain"

    Stephen: Add Angel chorus for emphasis

16. Older Eve (Page 37–38)

    John: Speech till Father comes feels just slightly too long, but where to cut?

        Interchange "to remember Adam . . . and to give thanks to you, Father" to help Father's entrance

    Stephen and John: Make more of moment when Father returns.

Act Two

1. "Generations"

    John: Note this is now led by Eve

    Stephen: Improve music of "And Noah in his turn"

2. Page 44 (Noah/Father scene)

    John: Look at rewritten scene

        Is it clear why Noah can't see Father?

        Strengthen lead-in to "Civilized Society"?

        Note cuts in "Civilized Society"

3. Pages 52 to 53 (Noah/Japheth confrontation)

    Stephen and John: Improve end so it feels more finished, or cut in more abruptly with appearance of snake – it's in the middle now

    Stephen: go up musically on "gives us life once more"

4. Lullaby to the animals/ "Stranger to the Rain"

    Stephen: Raise key of Lullaby—it's too low

        End "Stranger" musically

5. Japheth and Yonah

    John and Stephen: Father needs to be present—does he speak or just watch?

    John: Is scene slightly too short?

> Stephen: First verse of "In Whatever Time" should be completely rubato, conversational
> 6. "The Flood"
>   Stephen and John: Is there a less melodramatic way to get into it than Father's "No"?
>   Stephen: Add Angel chorus for vocal emphasis
> 7. Dove song
>   John: Clarify Yonah's "I know what I have to do"
>   Stephen: Song feels truncated now; add bridge?
> 8. Page 65 to 66 (Family confrontation)
>   John: Does this need to be musicalized so it's more like "Ring of Stones"?
> 9. "Spark of Creation" reprise/ "Hardest Part of Love"
>   Stephen: Lyric for "Spark of Creation" reprise is too sentimental—toughen it up ("The spark of creation—That's all you've got left now")
>   Stephen and John: Should we cut the "Grateful Children" intro at top? . . . song feels too long
> 10. "In the Beginning"
>   Stephen: Write 8-part chorale for "Now at this dawn"
>   Change "knife" to "knives"?

difficult Eden segment—no surprise to Schwartz. He had also done a fifteen-minute presentation to The Directors Company, another New York theater, and they seemed interested. Schwartz had rewrites for Caird and reported that he would spend all of March on *Children of Eden*, except for one song he needed to write for Disney. Schwartz's interest in revisions appeared again in a fax from 10 March, where he again considered why Father might place the Tree of Knowledge in Eden, wondering if it might have been "a test of their love, which is of course a very dysfunctional thing for a parent to do."[37]

Caird's contract with Playwrights Horizons allowed for rehearsals starting on 13 April, with the performance 26 April. The company's artistic director was Don Scardino (a frequent Jesus in *Godspell* in New York in the 1970s). The cast included Bill Nolte as Father, Stephen Bogardus as Adam/Noah, Cass Morgan as Eve/Mama Noah, and Paul Anthony Stewart as Cain/Japheth. The production script, dated April 1993, included a number of changes, such as "Blind Obedience" becoming a separate song from "A Piece of Eight," and "Dove Song" renamed "Sailor of the Skies." In Act 1, Adam's family prayer was removed in the "Wasteland" segment, and Cain convinced Abel to run away with him before Father appears. Act 2 was more settled and Caird worked on minor matters. Yet another script extant from the next month (May 1993) includes few surprises, but the Tree of Knowledge's presence corresponds with Schwartz's recommendation from March: Father places it there and tells Adam and Eve that it is not good for them.

Caird wrote Schwartz on 9 November 1994 with various tweaks. He was thinking, for example, about how Eve would have realized after eating the apple that she could have her own children with Adam, meaning that animals did not have to be like their children. Caird had wanted her to tell Adam this before he ate the apple, and in the current script she does not say this until Father has arrived and they are both tugging at Adam's loyalty. The author also sent a dummy lyric that Schwartz could rewrite. Schwartz returned a fax on 13 November stating that his initial reaction to Caird's changes were positive, but he did wonder if the material about animals as children "gets over-ecologically-conscious in spots."[38] He had sent the changes on to Wichita for a production about to occur there.

Caird saw the second performance in Wichita and went on to Los Angeles, from where he sent notes on the script to Schwartz on 14 December 1994. It is a telling communication: a writer reacting from the audience, several times mentioning that there were too many beats in a line or the tone of a line needed adjustment. Schwartz answered Caird's fax four days later, saying that he liked the changes and would place them in the script. Schwartz also sent suggestions concerning the scene where Adam and Eve discover each other sexually. Schwartz sent yet another fax about that scene just six days later, on Christmas Eve, with a completely different version.

Caird had concluded his letter asking Schwartz what had happened with the "Disney angle," and Schwartz answered that he had spoken to Disney executive Jeffrey Katzenberg, who wanted to see the script and hear the demo tape for *Children of Eden*. Schwartz was also working on speaking with Michael Eisner and hoped that Katzenberg, Eisner, and David Geffen would come see the show in Riverside, California, late in 1995. Nothing ultimately came of this possibility.

Schwartz sent Caird a fax on 17 October 1995 that included a draft script of a revised opening and demo tape for a new song. The script draft includes notes from Caird to Schwartz, meaning that the book writer had sent it to the composer, who apparently returned it with the lyrics for a new song, "Good." This represented a detour for Act 1 with ideas that did not remain in the show. For example, after Adam and Eve meet Father they learn that their purpose in life is to be good and grateful. Adam sings "Good," a witty exploration on how one can live in such a manner. It remained in a script from September 1996, but later disappeared. Eve decides that being grateful should not be hard, initiating the singing of "Grateful Children." Productions that occurred about this time included Riverside, California, in December 1995, at the Las Vegas Academy of Performing Arts in April 1996, and a workshop and performance in Lincoln, Nebraska, in June 1996. Caird and Schwartz tended to be involved with these events.

At the 1996 National Alliance for Musical Theatre Festival of New Musicals, *Children of Eden*, directed by Scott Schwartz, was one of the featured works (along with *Thoroughly Modern Millie* and other works). The festival is an important opportunity for shows to be vetted by potential producers, and de Giere notes that this production led to the 5 November to 14 December 1997 version at the Paper Mill Playhouse.[39] Starring Stephanie Mills and Adrian Zmed, *Children of Eden* was an unqualified hit at this important regional house, and an original cast recording followed from RCA.[40] Since then the show has seen many productions through licenses from Music Theatre International (MTI). A letter to Caird from Steve Spiegel, president of MTI, dated 16 March 1998, stated that since *Eden* had been released to Secondary Marketplace in 1997 that there had been over 100 separate productions in churches, universities, and high schools.

Given the Paper Mill Playhouse's proximity to New York City in Milburn, New Jersey, the New York press joined New Jersey colleagues in reviewing that production. Peter Filichia, writing for the *Newark Star-Ledger*, described the show as "one of the most intelligent and profound musicals ever written."[41] He offered that *Eden* "will make you take a second look at your views on religion and parenthood." He called the score "percussive, melodious and haunting" and commented on the wide variety of musical inspirations. Alvin Klein of the *New York Times* was derisive, stating that "Mr. Schwartz has turned one of the greatest stories ever told into one of the silliest musicals in memory."[42] He complained of "a Disneyfied score" and found no tune comparable to Schwartz's best efforts in other shows. He also panned Caird's book. Linda Armstrong of the *New York Amsterdam News* lauded the "lovely family musical production" with "an innocence about this production which touches the heart."[43] *New York Post* critic Clive Barnes praised the score's "sometimes heart-piercing lyricism," especially in Act 1, and he labeled Caird's book "carefully yet persuasively dramatic," but he thought the two acts "bisect rather than fuse" and the "results are basically unwieldy."[44] Writing in *Variety*, Robert J. Daniels wrote a rave, citing, for example, "the most ambitious and impressive score to date by Schwartz, and it is spiced with a variety of jubilant tunes, haunting melodies and sensitive lyrics."[45]

Caird remains "very happy" with how *Children of Eden* was produced at the Paper Mill. He believes, along with Schwartz, that they have "arrived at something that was pretty much director-proof. It had become itself in a way that was going to allow it to grow up and leave home." Caird notes that he and Schwartz are "quite fierce" with directors who want to make changes: "We think we know better because any suggestion from a director—a little tweak here or a little tweak there that might be a good idea—is always something that we have already tried and rejected!"

The Music

Stephen Schwartz finds his compositional voice "more unified" in his later shows with "more of a classical sensibility," less varied than his early shows: "In *Godspell*, each song is a pop pastiche. In a way, it's what Andrew Lloyd Webber did when he was a similar age when he wrote *Joseph and the Amazing Technicolor Dreamcoat*, which is also pop pastiche, where every number is defined as the French number, the country-western number."

The score includes more music than any of Schwartz's other shows (except his opera *Séance on a Wet Afternoon*); the Paper Mill original cast recording (OCR) includes two compact discs, and major segments of the plot develop mostly in song. The rich use of the chorus of Storytellers renders the show's structure different than any of his other shows, in places approaching an oratorio in effect, but with important distinctions. Choruses in classical oratorios usually provide group commentary, less often serving as narrator. Schwartz's chorus often serves a narrative function, frequently condensing aspects of the story into less time than it would be required with stage action, and adding dramatic weight. An example would be in Act 1 when Father has banished Adam and Eve from Eden. The Storytellers recount Adam fashioning a walking staff from the blasted Tree of Knowledge, and how when they looked back that the entrance to the garden had disappeared. The Storytellers, with chorus and soloists, render vividly the difficulties that Adam and Eve face in "The Wasteland." Schwartz became fond of choral recitative while working on *Eden*, adding a substantial amount between the London and Virginia productions. He cites no clear model for these passages, but Schwartz has been arranging much of his own choral music since *Godspell*.

An influence on Schwartz as he considered the extensive choral role in *Children of Eden* was *The Gospel at Colonus*, an updated version of three plays by Sophocles that starred Morgan Freeman and was on Broadway in spring

1988.⁴⁶ Schwartz was fascinated by the gospel choir in bleachers around the area where action took place. In his review of *The Gospel at Colonus*, Frank Rich started with the major presence of gospel music and singers in the show, praising the music by Bob Telson (lyrics, book, and direction by Lee Breuer) and performances by gospel singers.⁴⁷ Schwartz is not certain that the show's score provided him any musical influence, but the concept was "a jumping-off point" for *Children of Eden*. Schwartz admits that *Eden* was "conceived as semi-oratorio," and we discussed possible classical influences, such as Mozart's *Requiem*, Handel's *Messiah*, Verdi's *Requiem*, Haydn's *The Creation*, and J. S. Bach's *St. Matthew Passion*, models for Schwartz more in terms of concept than in musical aspects, and classical oratorios are usually performed in concert versions. Schwartz is willing to admit that he felt influences in writing *Children of Eden*: "This was more everything just conglomerating in my head and coming out as 'This is how I hear this.' There are all sorts of influences throughout."

John Caird was less comfortable with comparing *Children of Eden* to oratorios. The only places where he saw this as a possibility was in the opening and closing numbers, "Let There Be" and "In the Beginning/Children of Eden"; at other points he described the music as "almost operatic." Caird does not remember discussing oratorios with Schwartz when they worked on the show, but he notes that they did discuss various styles of choral music and musical models, including Bach, Mozart, Stravinsky, and Bernstein. Ernest Zulia was more interested in comparing *Eden* with an oratorio, calling it "a postmodern Broadway oratorio." With action in the middle of the stage and a choir singing around it, he conceived it as different than conventional musical theater.

In an interview with Mark Steyn that corresponded with the opening of *Children of Eden* in London, Schwartz cited another, surprising influence on the show's structure: *Sweeney Todd*.⁴⁸ The composer/lyricist compared it with Sondheim's show because *Children of Eden* also includes far more music than one finds in a typical musical and both move unexpectedly between music and dialogue. Again, like Sondheim in a number of his shows, Schwartz also tried to make less use of predictable song forms in *Eden*.

Schwartz is accurate when he states *Eden* includes more music than one expects in the average Broadway score. Besides *Sweeney Todd*, other apt comparisons include *Candide* and *The Most Happy Fella*. The former constitutes Leonard Bernstein's operetta score that can include about two hours of music (depending upon the version), and the latter Frank Loesser's show that comes as close to opera as one tends to find in the musical theater.

Textbox 9.2: Occurrences of Selected Motives in Stephen Schwartz's Score for *Children of Eden*

Each motive appears in a separate listing to allow the reader to trace it through the musical. A brief statement explains the dramatic reason for its occurrence at that moment. This analysis of Schwartz's use of motives was performed from a piano/vocal score published by Music Theater International in an unspecified year, but it includes "Good," meaning that it dates between October 1995 and late 1997. (Schwartz first suggested "Good" in a fax to Caird from 17 October 1995 and it continued to appear in a script from September 1996, but it had been cut by the time *Children of Eden* played at the Paper Mill Playhouse in late 1997.) The other important source for this analysis was the Paper Mill OCR, which corresponds to the undated score in many details. Since the recording is available and no full piano/vocal score for the show has been published, the motives are identified by the names of tracks in the score and the time indices where they begin in each track ("1/5" refers to disc 1, track 5). Which act a motive appears in may be determined by the disc number, where Act 1 appears entirely on the first disc and Act 2 on the second.

Motive 1: First three syllables of "In the beginning" at opening of "Let There Be" set to ascending perfect fourth followed by ascending perfect fifth (1/1, 0'00")

   Recurs in finale "In the Beginning" as opening vocal motive (first occurrence: 2/17, 0'11") and often throughout song

Motive 2: From opening of "Let There Be," bitonal (could also be analyzed as octatonic) material sets text "without form, void, darkness" (1/1, 0'28")

   Recurs with same text at end of "The Flood" (2/8, 2'55")

Motive 3: "Let there be" set to three descending stepwise pitches (1/1, 1'53"), sometimes immediately repeated one fifth lower

Recurs in "The Spark of Creation" briefly (1/7, 1'41") and then more definitively (1/7, 1'55") as Eve claims to have inherited some of Father's creative spirit

Recurs in "Childhood's End" as Eve sings "I can see, I can see" (1/10, 0'31") to Father, using his motive just after she states "I can see what you can see."

Father answers her with Motive 3 setting "You are a child no more" (1/10, 1'08")

Recurs instrumentally in "The Hour of Darkness" (2/14, 1'47") as Noah's family sees stars

Motive 4: Accompaniment pattern in "The Naming" with eighth notes based on perfect fifths and octaves with notes *do-so-do* (1/3, 0'03")

Similar accompaniment recurs at opening of "A World without You" (1/11, 0'08"), sounding often at various pitch levels

Motive 4a: Rising fifth prominent in Motive 4 accompaniment pattern appears prominently in melody of "A World without You," such as on "half my heart is yours" (1/11, 0'13")

Rising fifth recurs several times in melody of "A Ring of Stones" as Cain wonders about finding people who built Ring of Stones (1/17, 2'01")

Motive 5: Melody from opening of "The Naming" ("Come and gather in the meadow," 1/3, 0'08")

Recurs in a transformation in "The Return of the Animals" (2/4, 0'28"), where thirds that dominate the melody in "The Naming" recall original but now in 6/8 meter

Original motive from "The Naming" recurs in "Noah's Lullaby" at beginning (2/5, 0'00") and end (2/5, 0'52")

Motive 6: Chant-like setting on single pitch of "Oh, Father, for all we have received, we thank you" in "Grateful Children" (1/4, 0'00")

Recurs in "A Piece of Eight" as prayer sung by Noah's family (2/3, 2'31")

Motive 7: Setting of "your grateful children" based on ascending major second and then ascending and descending perfect fifth (1/4, 0'16") in song "Grateful Children"

> Recurs at same pitch level when Father sings "Ungrateful children!" (1/12, 0'40") in "The Expulsion"
>
> Recurs one-half step lower as Abel prays to Father and makes his sacrifice at beginning of "Lost in the Wilderness" (1/15, 0'04")
>
> Recurs at same pitch level as last occurrence as Father starts to sing "Precious Children" (2/16, 0'06"), a tune largely based on "Grateful Children"

Motive 8: Setting of "That's what it means to be a Father" that ascends a third in stepwise motion and then descends an octave stepwise and in skips (1/5, 0'23") in "Father's Day"

> Recurs as Cain verbally attacks Adam for trying to keep Abel from leaving with Cain (1/17, 5'06") in "A Ring of Stones"
>
> Recurs as Father sings motive when he mourns what he has done (2/8, 2'19") in "The Flood"

Motive 9: Stepwise setting that ascends total of a fourth and descends to opening pitch on "Oh, I will be their teacher and I will be their guide" (1/5, 0'41") in "Father's Day"

> Recurs on setting of "Children, that I love so well, what wrong you do to me" (1/12, 0'06") in "The Expulsion" as Father prepares to drive Adam and Eve away and destroy Eden
>
> Recurs transformed as setting of "children that I love so well, my heart is dark and cold" (2/8, 1'47") as Father mourns what he just did in "The Flood"
>
> Recurs without transformation in accompaniment (2/12, 0'09") and as setting of "son of mine I love so well, and oh, the toll it takes" (2/12, 0'19") in Noah's song "The Hardest Part of Love," and heard often in remainder of song
>
> Recurs as instrumental closing to Father's brief song "Precious Children" (2/16, 0'33")

Motive 10: Setting of "And the night was perfect" has distinctive rising fourth in "Perfect" (first occurrence: 1/6, 0'00")—in undated score this song is called "Perfect—Part 2" because there is an earlier song ("Perfect—Part 1") using this music

  Recurs often in song (e.g., 1/6, 0'51") to help show predictability of life in Eden

Motive 11: Rhythm of eighth note and two sixteenths with similar melody appears instrumentally and in vocal lines as Eve comes running to take Adam to see Tree of Knowledge (1/6, 1'46") in "Perfect—Part 2"

  Recurs in accompaniment as Father comes to discover that Eve has eaten apple (1/10, 0'01") in "Childhood's End"
  Recurs as Cain comes to get his family at start (1/17, 0'02") of "Ring of Stones"

Motive 12: "Beyond" sung by Eve to rising, melismatic motive (first time with text, 1/7, 0'07") at beginning of "The Spark of Creation"

  Heard in female voices in "Perfect" (1/6, 2'15") just before "The Spark of Creation" (1/7)
  Word recurs on long note value (1/13, 0'42") in "The Wasteland," not unlike long note that Eve sings word on in "The Spark of Creation" (1/7, 0'41"), here mocking her as she leaves Garden of Eden, showing contrast to what she had thought might have been "beyond"
  Original rising motive that Eve sings recurs instrumentally in "A Ring of Stones" (1/13, 0'39") just as Cain bring his family to place
  Word *beyond* recurs on a long note value (1/15, 0'42") in "Lost in the Wilderness"—not really a musical motive but word's repetition seems dramatically important
  Similar setting of "Beyond" sung by Yonah (2/10, 0'39") in "Sailor of the Skies"

Motive 13: Leap of major seventh and return to opening pitch (*do-ti-do-ti-so-do*) on "The spark of creation" (first occurrence: 1/7, 1'08") in

"The Spark of Creation"—answered instrumentally soon thereafter in eighth notes

> Recurs in "The Spark of Creation (Reprise 1)" (1/14, 0'45") as Eve worries that she has passed her curiosity onto Cain
>
> Cain sings the text "spark of creation" set to transformed motive as he leaves Father and Abel in "Lost in the Wilderness (Reprise)"—not on OCR
>
> Adam sings the *ti-do-ti* on "bravery," perhaps mockingly on the text "look at the lesson our bravery taught us" (1/17, 4'06") in "A Ring of Stones"
>
> Recurs in "The Spark of Creation (Reprise 2)" (2/11, 0'16") as Mama Noah urges Noah to look inside himself for what must be done about Japheth and Yonah on ark
>
> Recurs instrumentally (only in the undated score) at opening of "Precious Children"—does not sound on OCR

Motive 14: Energetic opening melody of song "The Spark of Creation" (first occurrence: 1/7, 0'47")

> Recurs in "The Spark of Creation (Reprise 1)" (1/14, 0'15") as Eve worries that she has passed her curiosity onto Cain
>
> Recurs in "A Ring of Stones" (1/17, 1'03") as Cain rhapsodizes in A major about his discovery; Eve then sings theme in her original key (from 1/7) of D-flat major (1/17, 1'30"); Cain sings more text set to that melody later at end of song (1/17, 2'20")

Motive 15: Descending, stepwise melody on "Oh, Father, please don't make me choose . . ." (1/11, 1'05") in "A World without You" that continues through additional phrases in some occurrences (perhaps related to Motive 18: "Lost in the wilderness")

> Recurs in "A Ring of Stones" (1/17, 4'49") as Abel pleads with Cain not to make him choose between leaving with him or staying with parents—music that follows instrumentally in score is what Father sings in earlier scene about pain that choices cause, but that is not heard on OCR

Recurs in "The Hardest Part of Love" (2/12, 0'00") as Noah begs Father to not make him choose between Japheth and what he considers his duty to Father

Motive 15a: Disjunct setting of "how could I live in a world without you?" in "A World without You" (first occurrence: 1/11, 0'27")

Recurs in "In Whatever Time We Have" (2/7, 0'10") as Japheth explains his feelings to Yonah before they start their duet

Motive 16: Choral and orchestral setting of "now and forever will it burn!" concluding with long bitonal chords introduced by sixteenth notes under "burn" at end of "The Expulsion" (first occurrence: 1/13, 1'36")

Bitonal long chords introduced by two sixteenths recur several times in "The Mark of Cain" (1/19, 1'04", 1'09", 1'48", 1'54", 2'00")
All of Motive 16 recurs in "The Flood" (2/8, 1'27")

Motive 17: Bass line and melody associated with "The Wasteland," including slow, modal march (1/13, 0'00") and pop-based segment with solos or chorus of Storytellers over distinctive bass line (1/13, 0'43")

Second idea recurs as Storytellers narrate family's trip to Ring of Stones (1/17, 0'18")
Same idea recurs without bass line after Abel dies, a duet with Eve as she begs for Abel to live (1/18, 0'05")
Recurs as Storytellers sing more of this narrative material with bass line after Father has cursed Cain (1/19, 1'13")

Motive 18: Descending, stepwise setting of "Lost in the wilderness" (first occurrence in "The Expulsion" when Father sings "Live in the wilderness"—1/12, 0'43"), perhaps related to Motive 15: "Oh, Father, please don't make me choose . . ."

Recurs with text "Lost in the wilderness" in "The Wasteland" (1/13, 1'39")
Recurs on same text in "The Wasteland" (1/13, 2'21") after announcement of Abel's birth

Recurs often in song "Lost in the Wilderness" (first occurrence: 1/15, 1'08")

Recurs in score as Cain reacts to meeting he and Abel have with Father, cut before Paper Mill production

Recurs in "A Ring of Stones" (1/17, 4'09") as Adam responds to Eve's concern that he had not told her of his earlier visits to Ring of Stones

Recurs at end of "The Death of Abel" (1/18, 0'29") sung by soloist who was singing material from "The Wasteland"

Recurs in "Children of Eden" (1/20, 2'17")

Recurs slightly transformed in "Sailor of the Skies" (2/10, 1'10") as Yonah urges the dove to "Fly far as wings can fly"

Motive 19: Three descending stepwise notes on *fa-mi-re* initially setting "close to home" in "Close to Home" (first vocal occurrence, 1/16, 1'28")

Recurs in "The Hour of Darkness" three times as Noah calls for family to reconcile (2/14, 0'25")

Motive 20: Song "Children of Eden" (first occurrence on OCR: 1/20, 0'42") as finale of Act 1—in current script earlier in act four lines occur in "Let There Be" at opening of act and Father sings a snippet of it to Abel as he calls him hope for future, but these are not on OCR

Recurs instrumentally toward end of "The Return of the Animals" (2/4, 3'42")

Recurs when "Noah's Lullaby" (2/5, 0'16") is based upon "Children of Eden"

Recurs briefly as an opening motive of the song with original text (2/10, 1'03") in Yonah's "Sailor of the Skies"

Recurs with original text at end of finale "In the Beginning" (2/17, 4'33")

Motive 21: Ascending, stepwise setting of "This is the last chance I will give" (2/2, 1'15") in "The Gathering Storm"

Recurs in "The Flood" (2/8, 0'02") as Father sees Yonah go on ark and prepares to destroy world

Motive 22: Conjunct melody in alternating 6/8 and 3/4 that forms main section of "Stranger to the Rain" (first occurrence: 2/6, 0'10") as Yonah explains her parentage and reduced expectations in life

Recurs with new text in "Sailor of the Skies" (2/10, 0'30") as Yonah launches dove that she hopes will assist those on ark

Motive 23: Song "In Whatever Time We Have" (first occurrence: 2/7, 0'27") is love duet between Japheth and Yonah

Recurs in "The Hour of Darkness" (2/14, 0'38") after Noah marries Japheth and Yonah and family seeks reconciliation

Schwartz has stated on numerous occasions that *Children of Eden* was the first show where he pursued the systematic use of musical motives to help unify the drama. As noted in previous chapters, one finds intentional recurrence of musical material in his earlier scores (some were noted, for example, in *The Baker's Wife*), but Schwartz's real efforts with the concept appear in the scores to *Children of Eden*, *Wicked*, and *Séance on a Wet Afternoon*. Since Schwartz worked on *Eden* for more than a decade, he had plenty of time to consider ways to tie his score together. As seen in Textbox 9.2, there are more than twenty musical ideas that recur in the score, offering a satisfying web of musical and textual allusions.

Recognition of some of these motives calls for additional comment. The bitonal/octatonic material of Motive 2 to set such ideas as "without form, void" associated with the time before creation places Schwartz in the company of composers like Franz Joseph Haydn, who used dissonance and chromaticism unusual for the 1790s in his "Representation of Chaos" in his oratorio *The Creation* (1798). The recurrence of Motive 5 from "The Naming" in "The Return of the Animals" is not exact, constituting one of Schwartz's more distant musical relationships in the score, moving from a march-like opening in quadruple meter to a dance in 6/8 where the melodic thirds of the earlier song sound in a new context. The chant-like setting of Motive 6 for a prayer is a typical gesture in music from many traditions, previously heard on Broadway in "Sabbath Prayer" from *Fiddler on the Roof*. Motive 12 more refers to recurrence of the word *beyond*, which Schwartz sets distinctively for

Eve toward the opening of "The Spark of Creation." When the word returns from Cain and Yonah the composer sets it differently, but the word is too important in the score to ignore the subsequent references. In Motive 13, Schwartz's setting of "The spark of creation" functions as a traditional leading motive, sounding each time that Eve and Mama Noah sing the song and providing an energetic musical representation of Eve's curiosity. Motives 15 and 18, although they start and end on different degrees of the scale, might be musically related because they set related concepts: the options that characters choose, and it is the choice that Adam made that caused all to be "lost in the wilderness." The efforts that Schwartz clearly made to provide a sense of musico-dramatic unification to his score is impressive and places him alongside such Broadway composers as Leonard Bernstein and Stephen Sondheim, and others who thought more about a score than simply writing effective but unrelated songs for a show.

One commonly thinks of Schwartz as a composer who makes rich use of a variety of pop styles; world music is an infrequent influence for him. This changed to an extent in *Children of Eden*, where he cites African music and calypso. The former appears in "The Naming" where the mallet percussion bears a strong African stamp, and "A Piece of Eight" is a calypso number both in terms of the rhythmic basis, much of it heard in the bass line sung on vocables, and the interplay between soloists and chorus. On the OCR the chorus in this number sang with a tone quality like one sometimes hears in African music. The mallet percussion in "The Naming" also appears in the opening "Let There Be" (1/1, 1'44") as Father starts to create. Schwartz included Orff xylophones in the show after discovering them through his children's school music programs. The composer was delighted: "It was one of the most magical sounds I'd ever heard!" Schwartz apparently brought his own Orff xylophones for the West End production, at one point asking Caird in a fax to please bring them back to him on one of his trips to the United States.[49]

Schwartz and Caird told much of their story during musical sequences, and Schwartz found himself writing more solo recitative than he had in most previous scores. He was assisted by the similarity of recitatives to traditional verses for Broadway songs, which often are not in a strong meter and approximate speech rhythms. Schwartz noted this when describing writing recitatives for his later opera, *Séance on a West Afternoon*: "[When] it came time to work on *Séance*, everybody was saying to me, 'The hardest thing of opera writing is all the recitatives; it's not the arias, it's the recitatives.' But it came very naturally to me; it didn't feel difficult to do because I was so used to doing it." Several representative examples of Schwartz's recitatives for *Children of Eden* appear in "A Ring of Stones" (1/17). An appreciation for the amount of recitative in the score is one point that will emerge in the following brief descriptions of the show's numbers. This description is tied to time indices from the OCR.

The most distinctive aspect of "Let There Be" is the opening (Motive 2), which might be described as bitonal or octatonic. Schwartz makes interesting use of the relative dissonance in the section, until the choir whispers "light" (1/1, 0'57"). An accompaniment of rapid sixteenth notes then enters, probably played by synthesizer, introducing Father's description of his dream, where he speaks of "whirling shapes" and other wonders, inspiring him to create. The sixteenths gradually fall into the background, replaced at 1'44" by Orff xylophones and other percussion instruments. As Storytellers join Father, Schwartz establishes interplay between soloist and choir that one often hears in oratorios, an effect that is strongest in this movement. At 2'50" Father starts to name many of the individual things that he creates over an active bass line, soon thereafter rejoined by mallet percussion and building to the end of the section. At 3'33" Father declares, "It is not enough," joined by the shimmering sixteenths from his description of his dream. The creation of humans, his "children," occurs with recapitulations of material that have already been heard.

The song "Good" appears in the piano/vocal score from 1995–1996, but it was soon cut. Here Adam expresses his desire to fulfill his part of the bargain by obeying Father's will. Schwartz marked the song a "Fast Shuffle" and filled it with dotted rhythms and syncopations, the feeling of swing jazz. At one point the Storytellers enter as backup singers. It is delightful, but it adds nothing to the show in terms of plot development and Adam's loyalty to Father could be established more briefly in dialogue.

Schwartz managed the exotic, somewhat African sound of "The Naming" through use of Orff xylophones, repetitive melodies based on similar motives and a limited set of pitch classes, and effective use of modality in both melody and harmony that starts on E but migrates to A. The lowered seventh occurs frequently in both melody and harmony. The A section (1/3, 0'08"ff) sounds twice at the opening of the song and returns at the end; the middle sections include comparable rhythmic motion with similar melodic ideas, usually stepwise or in arpeggios. Schwartz designed the A and B sections to be sung in counterpoint, which occurs at 1'15".

The brief prayer that Adam and Eve sing, "Grateful Children," introduces Motives 6 and 7. Motive 6, the repeated notes at the start of their prayer, opens as a recitative over held chords, changing to constant, arpeggiated sixteenth notes as they start to sing the lyrical portion. The melody is largely disjunct with emphasis on triadic motion, providing the contented affect that the moment requires.

After Adam and Eve fall asleep, Father looks at them with great pleasure, a moment understood by any parent. These "children," however, are adults, and their fall from grace will come shockingly quickly. The innocence of "Father's Day," therefore, is a double-edged sword, showing Father's naïve happiness and providing ironic contrast for what is to come. The song is in 6/8, a choice of meter that Schwartz affirms with nearly constant sixteenth notes in the accompaniment. He contradicts the 6/8 in a number of places with speech rhythms in the vocal line, such as quadruplet eighth notes over half of a measure on "I *think she's got my* nose" (1/5, 0'09"). It is a moment of melodic repose in the story and provides a useful study of one side of Father's character. The introduction of Motive 9 also provides one of Father's most important recurring musical ideas.

Caird and Schwartz clearly wish to show that the "Fall of Man" was inevitable because curious humans could never be satisfied with Eden's unchallenging life. Schwartz demonstrates this effectively in the music for "Perfect," where the frequent use of Motive 10 on text that declares day after day "perfect" quickly becomes staid and uninteresting as the melodic snippet ingeniously provides no forward motion or excitement. Some interest arrives briefly when Adam and Eve discover the physical possibilities in their relationship (1/6, 0'15"), presented in choral, solo, and duet recitatives, but Motive 10 soon returns, and even the introduction of sex is not enough to make Eden bearable. Eve goes to the Tree of Knowledge, but she does not sing until she runs to get Adam with Motive 11. Adam only speaks about how he is trying to place the insects in alphabetical order, confirming his lack of imagination. The choir resumes its recitative, taking them to the Tree of Knowledge and closing the segment with Motive 12 (1/6, 2'15"), setting up Eve's next number.

The material that ties "Perfect" to the next number, "The Spark of Creation," is entirely dialogue. Caird and Schwartz struggled mightily with this scene, at some points having Adam sing of his discomfort with Eve's interest in the forbidden tree. In the end, however, they let Adam simply note that the tree glistens more when one approaches it and the rest of the world appears darker, but he remains more interested in his list of insects and leaves Eve at the tree. She opens her song with sinewy melismas, Motive 12, reveling in the word *beyond* and its meaning. Following the introduction (1/7, 0'47"), the song unfolds frenetically, capturing her restlessness. The first statement is an AABC; all material later in the song is based on these sections with a slight variant at the coda (2'42") when Eve remarks that she is not a "crustacean" and has interest in things that lie "beyond." Schwartz makes rich use of *tresillo* rhythms (3+3+2 in eighth notes) in the prevailing duple meter, but also often pairs measures and creates a driving 3+3+3+3+2+2. The accompaniment is dominated by acoustic guitar.

"In Pursuit of Excellence" is unusual for Schwartz. Jazz is not one of his major musical interests, but he clearly associated close harmonies, swinging dotted and triplet rhythms, and the rich chromaticism heard here with the snake's slick sales job. The overall style is close to songs sung by Manhattan Transfer around 1980. The song starts with a childhood taunt set in a bitonal context with the melodic C major against E-flat major in the accompaniment (1/8, 0'00"). Schwartz admits that his interest in bitonality has grown as his career has progressed, and while it is not that common in his show music, he used it fairly often in *Séance on a Wet Afternoon*. At the end of the verse on the vocable "dum" (2/8, 0'37"), Schwartz builds an augmented chord on E-flat with an added F and A (or an F maj/min7 chord without the C but with G and B), another of the composer's interesting augmented mixtures that he favors when requiring an unusual harmony.[50] As the main portion of the song starts (0'42"), Schwartz liberally accesses traits named earlier with a few brief instrumental breaks, especially for clarinet and piano. His witty adoption of the jazzy style and the scene's staging, where the snake is formed by singers connected by long stretches of fabric, forms one of the memorable moments in *Children of Eden*. "Ship-Shape," which appeared in the London version of the show in Act 2 but, as previously noted, was cut soon thereafter, was in a similar style.[51] Written for Ham, Shem, and their wives to celebrate their successful construction of the ark, Caird says that "Ship-Shape" was "absolutely brilliant . . . sensational . . . very funny," but it was a "stand-alone number" that did not contribute to the story. That song's musical effectiveness helped inform Schwartz how he wanted to revise "In Pursuit of Excellence" for the Virginia production. He changed it from a jazzy solo to the quartet, along with changing some lyrics.

Solo and choral recitative dominate both "The End of the Perfect Day" and "Childhood's End," important musical scenes that include several repeated motives. The confrontation between Father and Eve in the second number sets up this emotional dynamic for later when Adam fights with Cain and Noah with Japheth. "Childhood's End" segues directly into "A World without You," shifting the main focus to Father and Adam, who is trying to decide whether or not to eat the apple.

Adam sings basically the same material to Father and Eve in turn, interrupting Father when he tries to invite his son to stay with him. The leaps of a perfect fifth on "half my heart is yours" (1/11, 0'13"), designated earlier as

Motive 4a, add greatly to the song's emotional appeal. When Adam goes to Motive 15 in the B section (1'05"), he introduces material that returns in the show's two later confrontations between parent and child, deepened here by Father's note that with choices one finds pain (1'20"). He blames Eve for introducing pain into the garden. Adam tears into his wife, demanding to know if she might want to relive the day and make a different decision, but changing to a less confrontational affect later in his line. Eve, challenged and conflicted, answers in a low range, nearly chanting on the same pitch, that she loathes the pain but would not want to return to her former state, a strangely neutral response in an emotional number. Adam returns to the opening music (with ornamentation on the OCR), declaring his love for Eve and intention to remain with her. Adam's solo lines include a number of stepwise descents from *sol* to *do*, not unlike Motive 18, occurring here well before Cain introduces that motive, but in a different rhythm. The gestures might be related because Adam's choice here guarantees that all are "lost in the wilderness."

"The Expulsion" reveals Father's other side, the violent streak that allows him to destroy the world in Act 2. Schwartz marked the opening "Ominous, subdued," and the melodic material is from Motive 8, first heard in "Father's Day." It is a recitative that becomes more lyrical as Father rhapsodizes about the beauty that he created with the Garden of Eden (1/12, 0'21"). Once Father sings Motive 7 on "ungrateful children" (0'40"), the mood has changed, confirmed by the first occurrence of Motive 18 on the text "Live in the wilderness" (0'43"), descending from *sol* to *do* over bare fifths and octaves. Father's recitative to the end of the song is punctuated powerfully by Storytellers, concluding with the terrifying image of Father's sword forever burning in place of Eden. Schwartz's accompaniment to the final, long note on "burn," in addition to the sound of thunder, is declamatory, with sixteenth notes introducing long, bitonal chords of E minor and D major, an idea that returns briefly in "The Mark of Cain" and more prominently in "The Flood," other numbers where Father shows his anger.

"The Wasteland" sounds here for the first time and becomes the most important recurring song with which Storytellers, in chorus and as soloists, narrate the plot. The chorus sings two verses in minor keys over tonic pedals, the first in E-flat minor and the second modulating up one step to F minor. It is a slow march in quadruple meter with strong melodic emphasis on the tonic. Lowered sevenths in both melody and accompaniment provide a modal cast. The Storytellers's last word is *beyond*, mocking Eve. As the choir concludes, a prominent line of eighth notes begins in the electric bass, always resting on the first beat but otherwise sounding throughout the measure. It features mostly stepwise motion, a constant musical reminder of the "wasteland" each time it occurs. There are six verses for soloists in various combinations based on two different melodies with the similar bass line. The soloists, singing more or less in the Motown style that Schwartz made a bedrock of his style in the early 1970s, narrate the births of two children, the land's monotony, and the hardness of their lives. Motive 18, "Lost in the wilderness," sounds from a soloist at 1'39" and from several singers at 2'21".

"The Spark of Creation (Reprise 1)" is musically similar to the song's first occurrence, again in D-flat major and based upon Motives 13 and 14. The opening oboe solo is angular and provides arpeggios that form bitonal structures over the harmonies, concluding on D and A major. Schwartz moves directly to D-flat major for Eve's entrance, using a different accompaniment than the last time the tune sounded, helping to illustrate Eve's worries that she has passed her curious nature onto Cain.

"Lost in the Wilderness" shows Cain's anger, sung to Abel as he tries to convince his brother to leave home with him and search for other people. It opens with Abel singing "Grateful Children" (Motive 7) as he makes a sacrifice to Father over the sixteenth-note accompaniment associated with the melody. Cain joins him in counterpoint with aggressive, syncopated material from 0'08" to 0'19". Abel argues, suggesting that their isolation might be "God's will," but Cain wonders if they have "been conned" and urges Abel to follow him "beyond" (Motive 8), holding the note out before the main portion of the song starts. This is a guitar tune in G major with active accompaniment. The A section (0'51"–1'07") is angry, highly syncopated, and mostly in a low range, moving from E minor to G major. The B section (1'07"–1'25") is the chorus with two statements of Motive 18 and a higher tessitura. The two sections repeat with different words. The contrast of C (2'07"–2'23") is less in musical style than imagery, with Cain asking Abel if he has ever wondered how the eagle "got to be so free," reminding one of the chorus from "Corner of the Sky" in *Pippin*. "Lost in the Wilderness" concludes with a return of the chorus (B, starting at 2'23"), but with moments for Cain in his higher register because of anger and frustration.[52] In the score from 1995–1996 and the show's current script, Cain reprises some of this song as he reacts negatively to Father, making use of Motives 18 and 13 ("The Spark of Creation"). The scene also included Father singing to Abel, to the tune of the title song "Children of Eden" (Motive 20) how he was now Father's future hope. The 1995–1996 score includes a section where the Storytellers join in with another verse of "The Wasteland," commenting on Cain's lonely flight and concluding with Motive 18. These last three small segments do not appear on the Paper Mill OCR.

After Cain leaves, Abel, Adam, and Eve sing "Close to Home." It opens with a recitative for Adam (0'00"–0'30") that was part of the reprise of "Lost in the Wilderness" in the 1995–1996 score. He ruefully remembers when Cain was a boy and how happy they were. "Close to Home" was not part of the 1995–1996 score, but a version close to what is on the Paper Mill OCR appears in the *Children of Eden Vocal Selections*.[53] The song, not surprisingly, is in D-flat, Schwartz again writing in his favorite key when considering a theme that he loves. We first hear young Cain and Abel softly singing their counting song (0'32"–0'46") in Adam's memory, an idea that appeared in various guises during the show's long genesis. Adam and Eve think back on their lives together since leaving Eden and rededicate themselves to each other, singing primarily in a low tessitura over an active accompaniment of constant eighth notes, with some interjections of the counting song from the now grown Abel. The title text tends to occur on *fa-mi-re*, emphasizing the second degree of the scale while anticipating the tonic, a feeling strongly underlined in the last two statements when the E-flat sounds over a D-flat9 chord (a gesture that also occurs several times earlier in the song), finally resolved in the counting song's return. Schwartz has stated that "Close to Home" is his favorite song in the score.

The dramatic climax of Act 1 occurs during and just after "A Ring of Stones," a musical scene where Schwartz recalls several motives. The scene opens with Motive 11 (0'02"–0'17"), Cain singing music that earlier described his mother's excitement about the Tree of Knowledge. The family must walk to the Ring of Stones, necessitating a return of "The Wasteland" material (0'19") as Storytellers enter with yet another verse for narration. Once they arrive, Cain introduces his discovery with Motive 14 (1'03") from "The Spark of Creation." Cain's material is in A major, but when Eve sings that she "can feel the old tingling" (1'30"), Schwartz modulates to D-flat, her key. Soon thereafter (1'37") the composer modulates once again, to A-flat major, as Eve, Cain, and Abel speculate about the discovery. The music here is new, primarily rising gestures as each makes suggestions, becoming more recitative-like at 2'01" when Cain introduces Motive 4a with the prominent ascending fifths that Schwartz places on three consecutive rhymes ("and skill," "but still," "until"). The three family members come together on an ensemble setting of "giant stones" just before Cain again briefly recalls Motive 14 (2'20") followed by a descending line from *fa* to *ti* on "We are not alone," perhaps from Motive 18. The track continues into what Schwartz called in the 1995–1996 score "Clash of the Generations" (2'31"), mostly in recitative with music changing subtly with the drama. At 2:48 Adam berates Cain, accusing him of wanting to destroy everything that they have accomplished since Eden. His revelation that he has been to this spot but not told anyone causes dissension, and Schwartz builds the scene through more recitative and spoken dialogue over music, or melodrama. When Eve questions Adam's bravery (3'57") the music becomes more melodic, and Adam defends himself by noting that their bravery was their undoing, leaving them "lost in the wilderness" (Motive 18, 4'09"). Cain leaps on that and announces that Adam can stay where he is, but he and Abel will go find other people. Adam warns Abel that if he leaves he will never see his father again, prompting Abel to sing Motive 15 to his brother (4'49"), from Adam's earlier plea in Eden. Cain's answer (5'06") is based on Motive 8, music that had only been associated with Father. Music stops as Adam slaps Cain, and events quickly escalate to Abel's death, without music.

The brief "Death of Abel" is a combination of a solo male Storyteller singing another verse of "The Wasteland" (Motive 17), without its characteristic bass line, and Eve simply chanting that Abel "must not die." The verse of "The Wasteland" ends with Motive 18, "Lost in the wilderness." The selection's chordal accompaniment includes bitonality.

In the 1995–1996 score, "The Mark of Cain" opened with Storytellers singing a verse of "The Wasteland," but in the Paper Mill script Father starts the number by yelling Cain's name, heard on the OCR over rapid material similar to what accompanies "No Good Deed" in *Wicked*. The effect is a frenetic, accompanied recitative, punctuated by backup singing from Storytellers, who later sing another verse from "The Wasteland." The orchestral chords from Motive 16 appear several times in the number (1'04", 1'09", 1'48", 1'54", 2'00"), tying it to "The Expulsion" and "The Flood."

The Act 1 finale, "Children of Eden," is the song's first full statement; excerpts sound earlier in the act, but they are not on the Paper Mill OCR. In what has become a cliché for Eve, the number is in D-flat major. Eve sings the first time through as a solo (0'42"). It is in AA'BA" form with AA' remaining in D-flat major and a modulation to E major for B, where Schwartz derived material from A. He uses a common tone modulation, making the A-flat at the end of A' become a G-sharp in the E major chord. The B section carries a change in affect as Eve asks later generations to excuse the errors of their parents. Schwartz returns to D-flat major for the final A", moving from a G-sharp minor triad as a minor enharmonic dominant to D-flat. The chorus enters with Eve singing over it in a gospel fashion as they repeat the entire song to close the act.

Act 2 opens with "Generations," an African-inspired number marked "Tribal dance feel" during which Schwartz made use of his Orff xylophones and other percussion. He establishes the rhythmic underpinning at the outset and maintains it throughout while various soloists and Storytellers perform a constant call-and-response to make their way first through the generations that followed Cain, and then Adam's descendants. The harmonies are almost entirely tonic and dominant.

"The Gathering Storm" is a compound number that includes Noah's plea to Father, asking him to change his mind about destroying the world, and Father's stern answer. Noah sings briefly and lyrically over a repetitious accompaniment of eighth-note arpeggios with prominent harp, piano, and winds. It is modal on F with lowered sevenths, and largely pentatonic. Father's response (starting at 0'41") is mostly recitative as he states how he has waited for his children to be "good and grateful" and then moves to stern threats about how he will let Noah's family survive, saying, "This is the last chance I will give." The mention of "grateful children" (0'59") is not set to Motive 7. The stark ending is reflected in the sudden cadence where D major resolves directly to E-flat major.

In "A Piece of Eight," where Japheth announces his choice of a bride, the family becomes four complete couples. Schwartz perhaps made the leap to "pieces of eight" and their relationship to piracy and the Caribbean, and he was inspired to use a calypso beat. This song frames other material as Schwartz and Caird craftily work through aspects of the plot. The first 0'26" is choral and solo recitative in which Storytellers and Noah announce the ark's completion. The calypso section that follows carries the designation "Bright, rhythmic" and is in a fast two. Basses in the chorus spend much of the song singing a characteristic pattern on vocables. The Storytellers serve as narrators and characters make short entrances as needed. The chorus steps in with delightful, syncopated punctuations at various points when providing names or repeating an important point (e.g., 0'38" on "Yonah was her name"). As the seven members of the family have gathered for dinner they sing a prayer (2'31") to Motive 6, a segment that Schwartz develops into a brief chorus with Yonah singing lead on two entrances as she prays by herself at another table. The family starts their meal and Japheth's intended fails to show. When he ends the mystery and names Yonah at 3'23" the calypso accompaniment ceases and the chorus sings the same melodic material over chords, setting up the final calypso section (3'56") as Storytellers describe the confusion. Noah asks others to leave and speaks to Japheth, singing a brief recitative called "Blind Obedience" in the 1995–1996 script in which he recalls Father's order that the Race of Cain must be avoided.

"The Return of the Animals" follows almost immediately. Schwartz commented upon the influences of Orff and Hindemith here, and it includes two motives from elsewhere in the score. The piece carries several stylistic qualities that remind one of Orff, including multiple repetitions of motives, layering of various ostinati, and occasional modal qualities. In places one also hears mallet percussion that might include Orff xylophones. Schwartz insistently emphasizes the 6/8 meter, like one might expect from Orff. The composer's naming of Hindemith as an influence is more problematic, but he hears it "in all the open fourths and fifths," a quality he remembers from Hindemith's music. As noted in Textbox 9.2, the opening of "The Naming" appears in "The Return of the Animals," with parallel thirds from the opening of the accompaniment in that song becoming repeated melodic thirds, as heard for example at 0'28" and in other places. The melody in A Aeolian that enters at 1'23" also bears resemblance to sections of "The Naming." Schwartz brings in Motive 20 ("Children of Eden") at 3'41", just before the end of the dance. Animal sounds also appear on the Paper Mill OCR.

"Noah's Lullaby" bears the title "Naming Reprise and Noah's Lullaby" in the 1995–1996 score, a more accurate appellation. It opens with brief reference to "The Naming" as Storytellers announce the full gathering of animals, and the material recurs instrumentally at the end. Noah sings once through the "Children of Eden" melody with melodic and harmonic alterations (Schwartz opens the passage in F major, but ends the melody in C-sharp minor) as he apologizes for humans spoiling the environment and wonders about taking the animals back to Eden.

"Stranger to the Rain" is Yonah's defining musical moment. The title is misleading, because the actual line is "I am not a stranger to the rain." At the end of the third verse she promises "to dance before the lightning, to music sacred and profane," an indication of the spirit she will bring to her death. Schwartz placed this song in D-flat major, perhaps tying Yonah's fresh, young spirit to that of Eve in Act 1. The tune is in ABC form, eight measures in each section, stated four times but with variations in the vocal line and elsewhere in the last two sections. Metrically it is a constant alternation between 6/8 and 3/4.

With the relationship between Japheth and Yonah setting up the central conflict of Act 2, a memorable musical moment between the two is necessary. Schwartz provided it in "In Whatever Time We Have." After Yonah sings "Stranger to the Rain" and starts to leave, Japheth tells her he will hide her on the ark. Japheth starts the song with a brief, defiant solo in C-sharp minor questioning the "thunder of fathers," but he quickly softens his mood and sings Motive 15a (2/7, 0'10") with Adam's text from Act 1: "How could I live in a world without you?" As the main body of the song starts, Schwartz presents the primary motive on the title text (0'27"), which sounds at least once in almost every phrase. The basic rhythm is in two-measure chunks with six eighth notes followed by a whole note. The duet portion at first sounds in different rhythms in counterpoint, but most of the last twenty measures are homorhythmic, representing the couple's complete agreement.

The song concludes and Japheth urges Yonah to follow him onto the ark as Father appears above. Thunder rumbles and music for "The Flood" starts. Father observes Yonah boarding the ark, but does not prevent it. Instead, he commences with the flood, opening with Motive 21 ("This is the last chance I would give") intoned in the dark key of E-flat minor. The recitative that follows is derived from Motive 21, followed by chorus (2/8, 0'27") calling for water from "heaven and fountains of the deep," singing in block chords. An ostinato in eighth notes commences (0'43") over which the chorus declares "Open" alternating with Father's spoken pronouncements. Father leads the Storytellers in an angry, oratorio-like passage that ends with Motive 16 in a powerful parallel moment with "The Expulsion" from Act 1. The number continues with a recitative from Father where he bemoans how old he feels after destroying the thing that he had loved. It includes Motive 9 at 1'47" and Motive 8 at 2'19". The selection concludes with Motive 2 at 2'55", recalling the show's opening now that the earth is again "without form, void."

The audience does not see Noah, his family, or the animals board the ark. The act skips to forty days later and the rain continues. "What Is He Waiting For?" is a brief song of two strophes separated by the family's expressions of impatience, hunger, and discontent. It opens with a repeated b" that would seem to represent the rain. The piece is recitative-like but lyrical, in E minor, with frequent use of the lowered seventh and metric shifts.

Japheth brings a plate of food to Yonah. She wonders aloud if her presence has prolonged the rain and caused Father's silence. She wants to disclose her presence, but Japheth considers it too dangerous; he leaves. Yonah asks Father if she is the problem, but hears nothing. She releases a dove to go find land and sings "Sailor of the Skies," a number that Schwartz makes largely a reprise of earlier musical material. The opening recalls Japheth's angry introduction to "In Whatever Time We Have." She charges the dove to help them, the music then quickly changing (2/10, 0'30") to the title portion of the song, more or less a reprise of Motive 22 from "Stranger to the Rain," but also including a lengthy setting of "Beyond" (Motive 12, 0'39"). This portion of the song, like Yonah's earlier solo, is in D-flat major. "Sailor of the Skies" continues with a modulation to G-flat major and reprise of Motive 20 ("Children of Eden"), stated here over a *tresillo* rhythm. Schwartz then includes Motive 18 ("Lost in the wilderness") on the text "Fly far as wings can fly" (1'10"), setting up the final hopeful cadence.

Yonah allows herself to be discovered, and a scuffle breaks out. Japheth goes to strike Noah with a board and Ham intervenes. Yonah stops Japheth, ending the violence, but leaving Noah with a tough decision. Mama Noah orders everyone below and confronts her husband, forcing him to admit that he has not heard from Father since before the rain. With a brief reprise of "The Spark of Creation" (Motive 13), she urges Noah to look inside, make himself the father now, and decide how to proceed.

"The Hardest Part of Love" follows, opening with Noah singing Motive 15, a section that also occurs at the end of the reprise of "The Spark of Creation." Noah faces the show's third difficult choice, and Schwartz associates all three moments with Motive 15 (here, 2/12, 0'00"). The main portion of the tune starts at 0'09" (with an instrumental version of Motive 9 from "Father's Day," the song's principal building block). It is in three verses in AAB form with the A section based on Motive 9 and new material in the B section. Noah sings of how he has tried to help Japheth, but all assistance has been refused. Father joins the song at the end of the second verse, but Noah cannot hear him. Father sings both A sections of the third verse and comments upon his changing relationship with his children. They sing B, the refrain, together. It is an important moment for both characters as Noah decides through the song that he will be merciful to Japheth and Yonah, and Father apparently decides to leave his children alone and henceforth let them make their own mistakes.

Schwartz emphasized the significance of Noah's impending decision with the choral recitative "Words of Doom," a brief choral recitative in B minor. In a scene that changed often during the show's writing process, Noah brings everyone onto the deck and marries Japheth and Yonah, admitting to Shem that he did so without Father's permission. The script reports that Father sports a "faint smile" and then he turns away as Noah sings the opening of "The Hour of Darkness," a recitative in D-flat major where he asks the family to reconcile. At 0'25" Noah sings "here and now, every one of us, reconcile" with emphasis on three statements of Motive 19, originally heard setting the text "close to home." After Noah wipes the Mark of Cain from her forehead, Yonah starts to sing "In Whatever Time We Have" (Motive 23, 0'38"), gradually involving the whole family. High above them, Father turns around and releases the dove, which flies to the family with an olive sprig.

Ham notices that the stars have come out, and what was a desperate situation only moments before gives way to general rejoicing. Schwartz intended "Ain't It Good?" as homage to the "black church," opening with a solo for Eve but then initiating a full gospel treatment. Schwartz wrote the song in A minor and C major, harmonically far from the D-flat major that occurs so often in the score's numbers sung by females. In the 1995–1996 score this appears as a piano lead sheet with nothing more than chord symbols, designed for a keyboard player who can improvise in that style. Schwartz notes, however, that the accompaniment has since been written out, as it is in the published *Vocal Selections*.[54]

The ark lands on Mount Ararat. Noah's three children announce which direction they will go to live, with Japheth stating that he and Yonah will seek Eden. Noah gives them Adam's staff and asks them to plant it when they find Eden and let it grow so that descendants can eat of the Tree of Knowledge. Father sings "Precious Children," based mostly on "Grateful Children" (Motive 7), an admission that Father cannot hold them in a "prison made of gratitude." In the 1995–1996 score, Motive 13, "The Spark of Creation," appears instrumentally three times at the opening of the song, but this is not on the OCR. The tune concludes with an instrumental version of Motive 9 (2/16, 0'33"), now that the deity has discovered what it truly "means to be a father."

"In the Beginning" follows directly. Schwartz and Caird made the show's ending a bit like the end of Wagner's *Ring*, where the gods are destroyed and humans are left to their own devices. Father does not cease to exist in *Children of Eden*, but in "Precious Children" he removes himself from the human equation and, with a rainbow, satisfies Noah's request for a sign that he will never destroy the world again. Noah pointedly calls it "our world." During the show the human race has grown from the child-like Adam and Eve to a state where Noah can rub away the Mark of Cain.

The finale carries strong resonance of Leonard Bernstein's music, especially the finale of *Candide*. The opening motive (ascending *sol-do-sol*) is the same as in "Make Our Garden Grow," and in both songs the motive appears a number of times. Bernstein's finale also progresses deliberately, grandly, sung by various characters and finally everyone. The messages of the songs are related because both groups announce that they will work things out for themselves, and Schwartz's song also refers to a garden when Noah's family comments on how "lovely was the world we had in the beginning." "In the Beginning" is AAB (A is based on Motive 1, from the show's opening), sung twice, and then Father enters (1/17, 3'20") and elements of A and B appear in solo and varied choral statements before the first AA' of "Children of Eden" (Motive 20) recurs at 4'33", tying this finale to that of Act 1. Schwartz's choral writing in the finale is most effective, returning the show in its conclusion to the feel of an oratorio.

As Schwartz's favorite among all of his scores, and one that he lavished attention on for about a dozen years, we should pause and consider his overall accomplishment in *Children of Eden*. The show is produced often and speaks to many. A number of its songs demonstrate Schwartz's gift for writing memorable melodies in a contemporary style, especially "Father's Day," "The Spark of Creation," "A World without You," "Lost in the Wilderness," "Children of Eden," "Stranger to the Rain," "In Whatever Time We Have," and "In the Beginning." Many Broadway shows include numbers that access stylistic signifiers of a particular musical style, and Schwartz does this in *Children of Eden* with generalized reactions to African music in "The Naming" and "Generations," calypso in "A Piece of Eight," and gospel in "Ain't It Good?" There are moments where modern styles more associated with concert music appear, such as the octatonic/bitonal writing heard in association with the text "without form . . . void," and he approaches Orff's musical style in "The Return of the Animals." Numbers also demonstrate Schwartz's ability to write for talented popular singers, most prominently heard on the Paper Mill OCR in the work by Stephanie Mills as Eve/Mama Noah. The show's extended birthing process allowed Schwartz to find many opportunities for musico-dramatic unification through the repetition of motives, and, as has been shown, he did this extensively in *Children of Eden* for the first time in his output. The score includes connective tissue in solo and choral recitatives that keep the plot moving forward. The many verses of "The Wasteland" in Act 1 play a strong narrative role and tie together various events. Schwartz approaches an operatic mentality with the amount of music in this score and the seriousness of many of the scenes. John Caird, a constant ear and critic in the process, also deserves some credit for the score's effectiveness.

A Full-Orchestral Epilogue

On occasion one hears Broadway scores performed with larger accompanying ensembles than are possible in a pit, and the experience often awakens in one the realization of how many compromises in orchestration become necessary because of the size of pits and budgets. Shows from Broadway's "Golden Age" of the 1940s and 1950s certainly benefit from larger string sections and fuller scoring in the winds, but the effect carries over as well into more recent scores that include a wider variety of musical styles. Manfred Knaak, a German arranger, produced orchestrations for *Children of Eden* in 2010 for a fifty-five-piece orchestra, and this version was staged at the Kansas City Music Hall in July 2011.[55] The director was Charles Piane, and the cast was led by Nathan Granner as an imposing Father, Adam/Noah played by Cary Mock, and Eve/Mama Noah by Erikka Dunn. The Storytellers included twenty-four singers and the vocal forces also included a community chorus and the Kansas City Boys Choir and Kansas City Girls Choir. The large orchestra was on stage with the action occurring around it and chorus members and others on three levels of platforms on the back and to the sides. Although one might wonder if such a production is economically viable (and there were problems making it work in Kansas City), the full orchestra added satisfying body to the entire score, including numbers based on pop styles. Such an ambitious production helps demonstrate the following that *Children of Eden* has gained among the musical theater audience. It remains unusual to see a musical gain such a following without a Broadway production and its high-profile OCR, but Stephen Schwartz and John Caird achieved something singular with *Children of Eden*, a theatrical monument to dogged perseverance.

~

CHAPTER TEN

Animated Features for Disney and DreamWorks

By the early 1990s, Stephen Schwartz's greatest success as a theater composer was more than a decade in the past. He had invested several years on *Children of Eden*, but so far had little to show for it in terms of material success. In a development that he could not have predicted, Schwartz next found success as a lyricist working with composer Alan Menken for Disney animated features in the mid-1990s on *Pocahontas* (1995) and *The Hunchback of Notre Dame* (1996), and a few years later in the first animated feature from DreamWorks, *The Prince of Egypt* (1998). Although Disney took umbrage at Schwartz working for their rival, they invited him back to work again with Menken on *Enchanted* (2007). As will be shown, Schwartz took his customary role in these projects, influencing aspects beyond just the songwriting.

Pocahontas (1995)

Alan Menken had been composer for Disney's animated features *The Little Mermaid* (1989), *Beauty and the Beast* (1991), and *Aladdin* (1992). He had written songs for the first two of those films with longtime collaborator Howard Ashman and started *Aladdin* with Ashman, who died of complications from AIDS in 1991. Menken wrote the remainder of the feature's songs with Tim Rice, but the British lyricist's home in London made it difficult for him to work with Menken, who lives outside of New York City. As Carol de Giere tells it (in her useful coverage of *Pocahontas*), Disney wished to find new songwriting talent, and they contacted Stephen Schwartz the year that Ashman died.[1] According to de Giere, after *Working, Rags,* and *Children of Eden*—none of which worked well in their initial runs—Schwartz had decided to quit theater and was taking courses in psychology at New York University.[2]

At the urging of Mike Gabriel, who became the film's codirector, Disney had decided to make their thirty-third animated feature a treatment of the legend concerning John Smith and Pocahontas in Jamestown, Virginia. This was the company's first such movie based upon a historical figure. Kevin Bannerman, the film's director of development, conceived the idea of asking Schwartz to write the lyrics.[3] Disney brought Menken and Schwartz together, and they decided that they could collaborate. Menken has commented that their work included moments of tension because Schwartz is also capable of writing music, and Menken has had experience with lyrics.[4] They both wanted to go to the keyboard at times, but they arrived at a working strategy.

Carol de Giere credits *Pocahontas* with reviving Schwartz's career. As shown in Chapter 9 on *Children of Eden*, Schwartz continued working on the show with John Caird through the 1990s, but he does not appear to have been working on new theatrical projects in the early part of the decade. The success that Schwartz found with the three animated features in the 1990s, along with continued work on *Eden*, provided his professional bridge to writing *Wicked*.

With the huge success of recent animated features, Disney Films was riding high, confirmed by the blockbuster hit *The Lion King* (1994). Michael Eisner took over the reins of the Disney Corporation in 1984 and brought in Jeffrey Katzenberg to run the film division, which became successful with popular live action and animated features. Much of the work on *Pocahontas* was done before Katzenberg left Disney over a dispute with Eisner in fall 1994. Corporate interest in the film surrounded the theme of promoting understanding between different groups of people, but the film included violence and threats of greater conflict, and the romance between Smith and Pocahontas ends unhappily. Schwartz, as usual, became heavily involved in the storytelling: Bannerman reports that he spent a week with one of the screenwriters and helped work out the overall themes of tolerance and cooperation. De Giere describes a Los Angeles meeting with *Pocahontas* directors where they decided which parts of the story might work best as a song.[5] Schwartz's research included the Disney-sponsored trip to Jamestown in June 1992 where the lyricist soaked in the atmosphere and bought tapes of Native American music and English sea shanties and other music from the early seventeenth century that helped inspire numbers in the film.[6] Schwartz modeled his writing of lyrics for people of other ethnicities on that of Oscar Hammerstein 2nd and Sheldon Harnick.[7]

The legend of romance between John Smith and Pocahontas is probably fictitious. Settlers from the Virginia Company landed in the Tidewater region, occupied by the Powhatan confederation of tribes led by Chief Powhatan. His daughter, Matoaka, also known as Pocahontas, was perhaps ten to twelve years old when she met John Smith, a leader of the settlers. He reported in his own chronicle that she saved his life before he was to be executed by her father, but many doubt this story.[8] The Disney storytellers crafted their own story, as is admitted by Roy Disney early in "The Making of *Pocahontas*," released with the film in the tenth anniversary DVD.[9] In the commentary track available with the DVD, codirectors Eric Goldberg and Mike Gabriel and producer James Pentecost several times mention their extensive research, which probably influenced their depiction of Native American life and other aspects, but little of the film is recognizable as history. Pocahontas here is a free-spirited woman, perhaps eighteen to twenty-two years old. She is athletic, spiritual, and decidedly curvy. Her father wants her to marry the warrior Kokoum,[10] but she shares with John Smith the tendency to wander away off alone, and they meet and fall in love. Complications caused by the greedy Governor Ratcliffe, convinced that there must be gold in Virginia, lead to conflict, but war is averted when Pocahontas saves Smith just before he is executed. Hoping to provoke battle, Ratcliffe tries to shoot Chief Powhatan; Smith is wounded as he takes the bullet instead. The tale includes the far-fetched notion that Smith can only be saved by returning to England, and he shares a tearful farewell and lingering kiss with Pocahontas. The film's world features high rock cliffs, mountains, and waterfalls, hardly resembling the flat coastal plain of Tidewater Virginia.

Disney pulled out all of the stops with beautiful animation, famous vocal talent, and fine realization of the music. The speaking voice for the title character was Irene Bedard, a Native American whose hair and facial appearance seems to have been the model for the animators, with singing by Broadway veteran Judy Kuhn. Mel Gibson voiced John Smith, singing credibly. David Ogden Stiers provided the voices for Governor Ratcliffe and his assistant, Wiggins, and, in a major coup, Oglala Sioux activist and actor Russell Means spoke and sang for Chief Powhatan. Means praised Disney's approach and sense of realism in "The Making of *Pocahontas*." Linda Hunt was the voice of tree spirit Grandmother Willow, Pocahontas's spiritual advisor. Menken's music was orchestrated and conducted by Danny Troob, and David Friedman did the vocal arrangements and conducted the songs. Other music credits included arrangements for the songs by Troob and Martin

Erskine and additional orchestrations by Michael Starobin and Douglas Besterman. The film was a success commercially[11] and won two 1995 Academy Awards, both for its music: for Best Song ("Colors of the Wind") and for Best Score of an Original Musical or Comedy.

The songs that Menken and Schwartz wrote for *Pocahontas* consume about twenty-two of the slightly less than eighty minutes of the film; much of the remainder includes orchestral underscoring that Menken often based upon his songs. Segments with sung material on the DVD include the following:

"The Virginia Company"—0'12" to 1'49", 5'08" to 5'37", and 43'49" to 43'53"

"Steady as the Beating Drum"—5'36" to 7'23" and 12'03" to 12'27"

"Just around the Riverbend"—12'55" to 15'09"

"Listen with Your Heart"—17'04" to 18'07", 32'13" to 33'21", and 48'36" to 48'44"

"Mine, Mine, Mine"—25'54" to 28'48"

"Colors of the Wind"—39'23" to 42'47", melody presented with "ah" in the choir over orchestral scoring 77'52" to 78'38", and sung by Vanessa Williams under the second part of the closing credits

"If I Never Knew You"—62'43" to 65'52", 76'21" to 76'38", and sung by John Secada and Shanice under the first part of the closing credits

"Savages (Part 1)"—66'37" to 68'11"

"Savages (Part 2)"—69'23" to 70'24"

"The Virginia Company" introduces the English as they begin their adventure. Two reprises have to do with violence they intend to visit upon Native Americans. Menken's music sounds like it might have been based upon recordings of English sea shanties.[12] Its most important segment is an eight-bar phrase in march meter with triadic and conjunct material in G major and jaunty dotted quarter notes at the beginnings of measures. Schwartz began his lyrics with the recognition that they set sail in 1607 and filled much of the remainder with stories of great riches that awaited the men (as he notes they have been told by their employer), along with ironic recognition that most of the riches would go to the Virginia Company. The refrain of "glory, God and gold and The Virginia Company" tells the brief story for the ethnocentric British settlers. The lyrics change in reprises, concerning how they will kill Native Americans, but with the same refrain.

"Steady as the Beating Drum" serves as the main title as well as a musical introduction to the Powhatan. Menken and Schwartz took a page from the openings of many musicals by describing community life in song. The composer hewed closely to standard Hollywood musical signifiers for Native Americans, composing a mostly pentatonic melody set primarily to rhythms based upon steady eighth notes, accommodating Schwartz's wordy text. Following an opening presumably from a Native American language, Schwartz leads with the title text and then moves to such images as a cedar flute, change of seasons, clarity of water, fish and crops, and calling upon the Great Spirit to help them maintain their traditions. As noted earlier, Schwartz claimed to be channeling Sheldon Harnick (and Hammerstein) when writing for another ethnic group, and what he created with Menken here is a brief but convincing Native American "Tradition," Bock and Harnick's ingenious opening of *Fiddler on the Roof*. Chief Powhatan sings the brief reprise five minutes later, urging Pocahontas to marry Kokoum.

According to the commentary track, "Just around the Riverbend" was one of the first three songs that Menken and Schwartz wrote.[13] Carol de Giere reports that Schwartz's wife Carole devised the notion that Pocahontas has had a recurring dream that suggests something coming her way (one of several *West Side Story* resonances in the film), paving the way for her "I want" song.[14] De Giere also notes that "Riverbend" at first did not resonate with Disney executives, causing Menken and Schwartz to write another that fell away; revisions of "Riverbend" brought about its successful reconsideration.[15] Directors and producer on the commentary track offered that this song was difficult to animate, and Schwartz's text, including Pocahontas's feelings and natural imagery, clarifies the challenges. She considers herself a poor candidate to settle down with the steady Kokoum.[16] In "The Music of *Pocahontas*" Schwartz stated that this was a tune where lyrics took a backseat to the music, one of Menken's more original tunes for the film. Moving mostly in eighth notes and with lively syncopations not heard in music for other Native American characters, the melody includes a few repetitive "hooks." When she refers to Kokoum, Menken used nearly straight eighth notes. The most important repeated material is the lively setting of the title text, but Menken also wrote a number of statements of *do-ti-do-la* high in Kuhn's range, each one with rhyming lyrics that challenge the status quo ("I look once more . . . beyond the shore . . .").

After "Riverbend," Pocahontas pulls her canoe up to a giant willow tree, where she consults Grandmother Willow, who embodies Native American beliefs in spirits of nature. Pocahontas describes her quandary about Kokoum and her dream about a spinning arrow; Grandmother Willow answers that she will counsel her like she once did Pocahontas's deceased mother. The song "Listen with Your Heart" is a simple tune in G Aeolian with a gapped scale. The "Voice of the Wind" joins in as a soft choir, directing Pocahontas to look for clouds, which turn out to be the sails of the English ship. After opening vocables, Schwartz's lyrics strangely seem to mimic a Romance language ("Que natura"), but he settles into simple advice based upon the title text. Colored leaves, representing Pochahontas's mother's spirit, appear prominently here and throughout the film.

"Mine, Mine, Mine" makes explicit English greed. Governor Ratcliffe urges his men to dig for gold that he assumes will be found, while John Smith goes exploring to find natives in a land that he intends to "claim" and "tame," all the while watched stealthily by Pocahontas. Menken marked his tune "Madrigal style," but the triple meter feels closer to dance songs one might associate with the decades around 1600. This song includes Schwartz's cleverest work in the film, such as delightful rhymes that describe Ratcliffe's overweening ambition ("The king will reward me,/he'll knight me . . . no, lord me!"). Smith's lines tend to be less witty, more functional. It becomes a major production number with Jamestown settlers turning over dirt and cutting down trees at a horrifying rate, the men of the chorus turning the words *dig* and *diggedy* into a refrain. Alternations between Ratcliffe's paean to greed and Smith's astonishment at the world he explores speed up as the song reaches its climax and the contrapuntal closing.

"Colors of the Wind" is one of the most popular songs to have emerged from Schwartz's Hollywood work. Menken and Schwartz suggested the song placement and wrote this first. Directors and producer on the commentary track insist that "Colors" helped define the film's "heart and soul."[17] In "The Making of *Pocahontas*" Schwartz states that he is fond of the song "because we were able to say something in an unexpected but very simple way," and in "The Music of *Pocahontas*" he offers that here the music and lyrics are in balance, without one element dominating another. Carol de Giere reported at length on "Colors," including how they worked on it and the source of some of Schwartz's images in the lyrics. She also included facsimiles of some of Schwartz's notes.[18] Schwartz began "Colors" with a few draft ideas for lyrics, and then Menken wrote the melody with Schwartz listening at the piano and making suggestions. Schwartz added lyrics before a session together where they refined it. Menken began the opening recitative simply, in D minor. A modulation to D major precedes the start of the main portion, which is in the form of AABAAB' with a short, closing tag. Menken makes fine use of basic building blocks: movement between tonic and submediant chords and a pentatonic melody, mostly in eighth notes, but with a satisfying sense of pacing and a number of moments when Judy Kuhn soars into a higher tessitura.

Schwartz's lyrics for "Colors of the Wind" demonstrate the Native American sensibility that he sought, but his intentions were more artistic than realistic. In the first two A sections he presents what Pocahontas sees as John Smith's wrong-headed beliefs about land ownership and usage, contrasting them with her knowledge of nature and greater tolerance. The second A section includes the powerful "you'll learn things you never knew you never knew." The first B section presents possible Native American images; Schwartz admitted to de Giere that he based "the blue corn moon" on aspects of his research, but that phrase was his own.[19] The remainder of the song all has to do with Pocahontas's side of the issues with a plea for tolerance in the B' section as she sings "for whether we are white or copper-skinned." When they finished the song, Menken and Schwartz produced a demo with Judy Kuhn, and in due time Disney decided that her voice matched Irene Bedard's.

The commentary track revealed one song placement that was abandoned. They had planned a song for when Pocahontas and Smith met in the glade, just before Kokoum attacks his rival and one of the settlers stalking Smith kills Kokoum. The directors and producer reported that they tried three or four songs at this point, including "In the Middle of the River," but finally decided that the story could not be stopped for a song.

The love song was supposed to be "If I Never Knew You," sung by Pocahontas and Smith after he had been captured by her people. Most of the animation had been completed when, as the commentary reports, they ran into problems with how the scene played for test audiences. Younger children were not interested—hardly surprising, given the adult nature of the song's emotions—and the audience of teens was "giddy."[20] Menken reports in the video "The Making of 'If I Never Knew You'" that he was the first to suggest that they cut the song, although the melody sounds often in the orchestral underscoring.[21] Disney decided to restore the song for the DVD release in 2005. Menken wrote an AA'BA melody that includes solos and a duet. It is a sweet melody that transmits longing and passion, feelings that Menken artfully produced by initiating many measures with a dissonance in the melody and including a number of large leaps. Schwartz's lyrics are effective but conventional given the sentiment of the song. In the B section, when Menken's melody changes character completely, the lyrics elegantly mention the "fear . . . rage and lies," overcome by the "truth" in her "eyes."

Governor Ratcliffe seizes upon Smith's capture and fans the flames of war among the settlers while Powhatan calls for his tribe to attack the settlers at dawn after Smith's execution. Menken and Schwartz grabbed this moment for "Savages," which occurs in two parts. The first includes opposing camps, and in the second Pocahontas offers hopeful counterpoint as she runs to prevent Smith's execution. On the commentary track the two directors and producer compare the end of "Savages" to the "Tonight Quintet" in *West Side*

Story, which aptly applies to the entire tune. Menken does not work with the same level of dissonance as Bernstein did, and the regular quadruple meter of "Savages" is more consistent than the meter in "Tonight," but Menken manages a sense of breathless, forward motion in a melody conceived in short, energetic bursts. His setting of the title word on a rapid, descending fifth is a powerful refrain. Schwartz has both the settlers and Native Americans paint their opponents in stark terms, assuming that the others must be destroyed because they are different. Ratcliffe, for example, sings "They're not like you and me which means they must be evil." The lyrics set up the battle, but also the path to defuse the violence, which is accepting the need to reach out and learn about another group of people. In the second part Pocahontas becomes the plucky force for good, singing as she runs about the terrible power of hatred and war and calling upon the forces of nature to bring her success. The song is predictable, but carefully wrought in both music and words.

The process of making *Pocahontas* for Menken and Schwartz was not unlike that of a stage musical, and each of their songs contribute to the forward progress of the story. "Colors of the Wind" became one of the iconic Disney songs, and this project—despite any objections one might have to the film's treatment of history or its characters—earned Schwartz two of his Academy Awards.

The Hunchback of Notre Dame (1996)

The second animated feature that Alan Menken and Stephen Schwartz scored for Disney was another unusual project for the company. Victor Hugo's *Notre Dame de Paris* (1831), written by the great French writer to stir public interest in the Parisian cathedral's restoration, is an adult work that ends violently. The animated film tells a substantially different story that turns the hunchback Quasimodo into a hero and unites the soldier Phoebus and gypsy Esmeralda. Claude Frollo, the villain who has served as Quasimodo's stepfather, dies in a fall from a cathedral tower while trying to kill Quasimodo and Esmeralda. In Hugo's novel, Esmeralda is hanged, Phoebus becomes engaged to another woman, Quasimodo throws Frollo from the tower after seeing Esmeralda executed, and many years later a hunchback's skeleton is found in her casket.

Carol de Giere's account of making *The Hunchback of Notre Dame* includes emphases on the problems of adapting a serious story with several dark themes, the joint work of Menken and Schwartz, a research trip to Paris and how it inspired the lyricist, and details on creating some songs.[22] As had been the case with *Pocahontas*, Jeffrey Katzenberg was chair of Disney Studios during most of the production of *Hunchback*. The film's directors were Gary Trousdale and Kirk Wise, both veterans of *Beauty and the Beast* (1991), and Tab Murphy was lead writer. The spectacular animation in *The Hunchback of Notre Dame* was a tour de force executed by an army of Disney and contract artists; one can learn about the challenges of making the film in "The Making of *The Hunchback of Notre Dame*" and the audio commentary available on the DVD from producer Don Hahn and directors Trousdale and Wise.[23] Vocal talent included Demi Moore playing Esmeralda, Kevin Kline rendering Phoebus, and Tom Hulce serving as the voice of Quasimodo, among a number of other well-known talents. The film was fairly successful, but not a blockbuster like *Pocahontas*.[24] Disney animated features include cute sidekicks, and for *Hunchback* these were three outrageous gargoyles who usually exist in Quasimodo's imagination, but they are full participants in the final battle. Their voices were provided by Jason Alexander, Charles Kimbrough, and Mary Wickes, and the jocular nature of their work with these characters provided Menken and Schwartz with the possibility of one silly song in "A Guy Like You."

Menken and Schwartz wrote eight songs that became part of the film, and, as will be shown here, they wrote more than one possibility for some placements. The appearance of each song in the film may be found in the following timings in the DVD:

> "The Bells of Notre Dame"—0'54" to 6'26" and 83'49" to 84'52"
> "Out There"—12'13" to 16'24"
> "Topsy Turvy"—20'49" to 26'04"
> "God Help the Outcasts"—35'49" to 38'32"
> "Heaven's Light/Hellfire"—46'10" to 51'20" ("Heaven's Light" portion
>   briefly reprised from 60'33" to 61'06")
> "A Guy Like You"—56'24" to 59'05"
> "The Court of Miracles"—67'50" to 69'31"
> "Someday" (under the credits)—84'56" to 89'06"

These songs represent a bit more than thirty minutes of *Hunchback*, and "Someday" plays as the credits roll. Menken also worked on the underscoring, and his music for the entire film was orchestrated by Michael Starobin with additional efforts by Danny Troob. Schwartz not only wrote the English lyrics but also received credit for adapting Latin lyrics that appear at appropriate moments. The actors who provided the voices usually also sang, but Heidi Mollenhauer sang in place of Demi Moore. The voice-over for the song "Someday" was recorded by the group All-4-One. Observations and analysis of individual songs here have been buttressed by material provided by de Giere and information from the DVD audio commentary track.

The DVD audio commentary included considerable information about the process that resulted in "The Bells of Notre Dame" as the film's prologue.[25] The first conception was apparently that it should be spoken, and the creative team tried scripts with live actors, but Schwartz suggested that a song could develop the backstory for Frollo, the Parisian minister of justice. He accidentally kills Quasimodo's gypsy mother while chasing her for the bundle that she was carrying. He discovers that the bundle is a disfigured child, whom he is about to drop in a well before being stopped by one of the cathedral archdeacons, who tells Frollo that the child may grow up at the church but his penance will be serving as the child's stepfather. Commentators on the DVD suggested that Menken's chase music was influenced by Mozart's *Requiem* because they had used that as background music in one of their test scenes. The song is sung by Clopin (voiced by Paul Kandel), a puppet master who lives among the gypsies at the Court of Miracles. He becomes a narrator for parts of the film through his participation in this song, "Topsy Turvy," and "The Court of Miracles." Another indication of Schwartz's participation in the storytelling was described in the DVD commentary, when the soldier Phoebus defies Frollo and douses a torch in water rather than setting fire to a house. Schwartz suggested that the scene be portrayed so that the audience would not know what Phoebus would do until he puts out the torch.[26]

Menken's music for "The Bells of Notre Dame" includes a recurring refrain in triple meter with repeating material in D minor and ambiguity between minor and major dominants, a modal and medieval gesture. The dramatic chase, mother's death, and discovery of the disfigured baby play out before the cathedral over choral singing of a Latin text (from the first two stanzas of the "Dies irae," perhaps a textual influence from Mozart's *Requiem*) that Menken sets with a pounding quarter-note beat and modal inflections over brief pedal points and wandering harmonies. There are also recitative-like passages for Frollo as he reluctantly accepts responsibility for the child and muses that he might someday be of use. Schwartz conceived a number of verses to Menken's basic triple meter tune that provide backstory and continually return to the song's title. The first verse describes the omnipresence of church bells in Parisian life, as members of various professions work to their clanging. The second verse starts the story of gypsies coming up in a boat by night as Frollo and his men wait to entrap them, the segment ending with the topical allusion to Frollo's "clutches," which were "as iron" as the bells. Following the textual invocation of the "Dies irae" ("Day of wrath, day of judgment") just before Frollo considers throwing the baby in a well and concluding with an instrumental reference to the song "Hellfire," later associated with Frollo, Menken returns to his triple meter refrain, here with text for the archdeacon as he calls Frollo to account for the mother's death and his intention to murder the child, texted by Schwartz with a dollop of righteous indignation (including the rhyme of "qualm" and "Notre Dame"). Menken brought back here music like that from the chase, but calmer, as the narrator comments on Frollo's sudden fear of judgment, inspired by the eyes of statues on the cathedral's façade. In words and two brief recitatives Frollo agrees to help raise the child, as long as he lives at the cathedral, with "Hellfire" motives separating sung passages. Clopin concludes the song with a short segment of the triple meter refrain with new lyrics that question which person in the story is a monster and which is a man.

Carol de Giere reports that Menken had a tune that he liked when they started work on *Hunchback*, two notes that suggested the words *out there*, a logical thing for Quasimodo to sing as he looked down from his tower.[27] The research trip that Schwartz took with the production team to Paris in October 1993 allowed him to sit in one of Notre Dame's towers and contemplate what Quasimodo might have seen in 1482.[28] The song opens with Frollo reminding Quasimodo that the wicked world will not understand his deformities and that he must stay in Notre Dame, discouraging him from enjoying the Feast of Fools. The music and text of this recitative-like passage moves toward longer lines, finally with Quasimodo imitating Frollo and admitting his monstrous appearance. Schwartz's lyrics are cutting and concise, demonstrating Frollo's brutality and Quasimodo's helpless acquiescence. The segment is mostly in C-sharp minor, a dark key that sees Frollo leave. An unprepared modulation from that key down to C major prepares Quasimodo's hopeful portion of the song, demonstrating his desire to join the world. He opens with recitative, followed by an expansive, flowing melody. Menken frequently used two half notes separated by a descending minor seventh ("out there"). Schwartz's lyrics are dominated by Quasimodo's observations of everyday people going about their business as he climbs all over the cathedral. It is his "I want" song, a hopeful moment in a dark story. Quasimodo obviously intends to go "out there" for the Feast of Fools.

"Topsy Turvy" is the major production number, one that the DVD commentators suggested they worked on for most of the three years that it took to produce the film.[29] The song frames the myriad of activities that mark the Feast of Fools. Schwartz told de Giere that he read Hugo's *Notre Dame de Paris* a number of times, especially as source material for this song and others.[30] In addition to the dizzying array of characters and activities, the song carries a significant plot load, introducing Esmeralda as a dancer and how she interests the three main male characters with her tame pole dance and brings Quasimodo into the celebration as he is crowned King of the Feast. Menken abandoned intentional "medievalisms" in "Topsy Turvy," writing a smarmy tune in quadruple meter with frequent ascending chromatic gestures and nervous rhythms that sound like Kurt Weill. The dissonances can be striking, especially the usual setting of the title text, a B major chord with an added sixth and ninth. The major singer is Clopin, presenting Schwartz's rapid, descriptive lyrics that trip along over repetitive music, a necessary part of a segment with rapid visual cuts between various activities. The lyrics move between Clopin egging on decadent activities (like *Cabaret*'s emcee) and explaining what is transpiring. Schwartz's rhyming patterns are fairly predictable, but without the song's explanatory lyrics, following this scene would be difficult.

Esmeralda seeks sanctuary from Frollo in Notre Dame Cathedral and briefly converses with the archdeacon. She rails against people who hate those who are different, and the priest suggests she consult with a higher power. The gypsy sees other praying and sings "God Help the Outcasts." This was the first song written for this placement, the second being "Someday," which is more like an anthem of hope than a prayer.[31] The film's creators decided that they wanted the religious song in the cathedral, leaving "Someday" to underscore final credits. "God Help the Outcasts" is plain in structure, opening with a brief recitative where Esmeralda wonders if God might listen to a gypsy, and then moving two times through the simple verse (each including two eight-bar phrases, AA') that frames a central portion where parishioners pray selfishly. In contrast, Esmeralda asks for nothing for herself. Menken's melody is mostly a descending, stepwise line in triple meter with constantly moving eighth notes accompanying. Schwartz wrote four dignified, rhymed couplets for the main tune that express Esmeralda's feelings.

The next song, the composite "Heaven's Light/Hellfire," is based upon the stark juxtaposition of Quasimodo wondering if Esmeralda might actually love him, and Frollo pondering the same question in lustful nightmares. He desires the girl but considers her a witch, deciding that she can either burn or give herself to him. Frollo's portion is filled with disturbing images that would terrify many young viewers. Schwartz reported to de Giere his appreciation that Disney allowed them "so much creative freedom" in "Hellfire," a portion based in concept upon the end of Act 1 of Puccini's *Tosca* where Scarpia considers his evil plans against the sound of a church choir.[32] "Heaven's Light" and "Hellfire" are separated by the archdeacon leading monks in chant; the text is "Confiteor deo omnipotenti," which Schwartz took from the prayer of sinfulness from the Extraordinary Form of the Roman Rite.[33] Latin phrases continue in counterpoint to Frollo's self-righteous declarations. According to the DVD video commentary, animators redrew Esmeralda's comely form as Frollo imagines it in the flames to make sure that she appeared dressed, a concession to the film's G rating.[34]

Menken's tune for Quasimodo's "Heaven's Light" is a sweet concoction in F major in AA'B form. Pairs of bars occur throughout with the first of each starting with an eighth rest and including mostly fast notes and a second measure that often includes a whole note. The constant initiation of phrases with rests gives the tune a breathless quality, and Schwartz's lyrics add to the effect with AA' built upon Quasimodo's observation that he has often watched loving couples walk together and acknowledging that he has never expected to have such a relationship. At B, Schwartz introduces the "angel" (Esmeralda), who has given Quasimodo hope that he might find "heaven's light." The lyricist made almost every rhyme in the song work with "light." "Heaven's Light" recurs briefly later in the film with new lyrics to express Quasimodo's anguish over seeing the love between Phoebus and Esmeralda. The film's creators considered placing a song there for the lovers, but they decided that the focus needed to stay on Quasimodo.[35]

The transition to Frollo's portion is through the Latin text named earlier. Menken's setting sounds like harmonized chant. Once Frollo's recitative section begins the music builds into a passionate segment at the text "like fire, hellfire," reminiscent perhaps of Mussorgsky's *Night on Bald Mountain*. This occurred earlier in the underscoring when Frollo was about to throw the infant Quasimodo into the well. "Hellfire" includes pounding eighth notes in the accompaniment with Frollo's short motives sung between Latin phrases in the choir. Schwartz chose liturgical phrases that mirror Frollo's agony over his sinful thoughts such as "mea culpa" ("my fault") and "Kyrie eleison" ("Lord have mercy"). The song's English lyrics are some of the darkest that Schwartz has written and surely helped inspire the nightmarish animation of Frollo's visions. Schwartz told de Giere that Frollo was the character that he has most enjoyed writing for.[36]

Five minutes after leaving Frollo's tortured lust is the film's silliest song: "A Guy Like You." The three gargoyles try to convince Quasimodo that Esmeralda must love him because he is unique. They introduce a variety of fanciful, sophisticated situations, including a gambling table, barbershop, and piano with candelabra (worthy of Liberace), balanced with sight gags. Menken's music carries a feel of a Parisian cabaret song at the opening, a recitative-like idea in quarter note triples that contrasts with a later march-like figure, two sections that alternate. Schwartz's lyrics wittily approach the issue from a variety of angles, obviously providing grist for the animation mill.

Schwartz told de Giere that some of his inspiration for the next song, "The Court of Miracles," came from his repeated consultations of Hugo's original novel.[37] The film's creators were not originally certain what to do with this part of the story. Menken and Schwartz wrote two love songs before the creators settled on the current ghastly gigue during which Clopin sentences Phoebus and Quasimodo to death by hanging for finding the gypsy and brigand hideout.[38] The other two songs were called "The Court of Miracles" and "As Long as There's a Moon" ("Gypsy Wedding Song"), but both placed too much emphasis on Phoebus and Esmeralda.[39] Menken's sinister music is in minor keys and 6/8 with frequent chromaticism, and Schwartz joined the nefarious fun by providing Clopin and his minions with lyrics that vividly describe the mortal danger that Quasimodo and Phoebus have found. For example, Schwartz compares the court's residents with "hornets protecting their hive." Clopin is about to hang the two heroes before Esmeralda stops him.

There are no songs for the next fourteen minutes as the plot progresses to the next morning. Frollo has Esmeralda ready to be burned as a witch in front of Notre Dame, but Quasimodo rescues her and a battle for the cathedral ensues, resulting in Frollo's death, Phoebus and Esmeralda being reunited, and Quasimodo being declared a hero. Clopin reprises "The Bells of Notre Dame" with a version of the lyrics that concluded the tune at the film's opening. It becomes the choral finale with Frollo's "Hellfire" music making its final appearance, now in a major key. As the credits roll, All-4-One sings "Someday" in a splendid pop performance, perhaps in hope that it might receive an Oscar nomination for Song of the Year. The score was nominated, but did not win. "Someday" is a fairly conventional call for future hope when, for example, "life will be fairer." Menken provided an attractive tune in 12/8. Menken and Schwartz wrote nine additional songs for the story when it was produced in 1999 as a German-language live staged version called *Die Glöckner von Notre Dame*. The show ran for three years in Berlin. Schwartz's English lyrics were rendered in German by Michael Kunze, and James Lapine wrote the book.[40]

The Prince of Egypt (1998)

After writing lyrics for *Pocahontas* and *The Hunchback of Notre Dame*, Disney offered Schwartz the opportunity to provide words and music for their next animated feature, *Mulan*, a Chinese story. As de Giere recounts, Schwartz went on the team's research trip to China in June 1994 and wrote two songs.[41] In the meantime, however, Jeffrey Katzenberg had left Disney and started the competitor, DreamWorks, with Stephen Spielberg and David Geffen. They chose to make their first animated feature on the story of Moses, and Katzenberg offered Schwartz the opportunity. The composer/lyricist saw no reason why he could not finish *Mulan* and then work on the new project, and signed a contract. Michael Eisner at Disney, however, made Schwartz choose between the films. Schwartz disliked the pressure and went with DreamWorks.[42] The songs that he wrote for *Mulan* disappeared from the film.

Schwartz was not at first excited about the story choice of Moses, but Katzenberg, Spielberg, and Geffen explained their take on the story, focusing on Moses and his transition from someone who grew up at the pharaoh's court to the leader of the Hebrew people.[43] Schwartz was concerned about his involvement in yet another biblical project, but this story sounded attractive and he joined the project. Hans Zimmer, composer of scores for many films (including *The Lion King*), agreed to provide the orchestral score, which used Schwartz's themes.

The film more or less follows the biblical narrative on Moses's life from his birth until God presents him with the Ten Commandments. The sole writer given credit for the story is Philip LaZebnik, and the directors were Brenda Chapman, Steve Hickner, and Simon Wells. The creators admit at the opening that "artistic and historical license has been taken." The first major change is at the outset. The book of Exodus opens with everyone in Egypt under pharaoh's edict to kill every new baby boy. Moses's mother, Jocheved (named in Exodus 6:20 and Numbers 26:59), hides her boy for three months and then places him in a basket among the reeds on the Nile. The baby's sister watches her and sees the pharaoh's daughter find the baby and realize he is Hebrew. The sister offers to find a Hebrew women to nurse the child, and fetches her mother. Later Moses lives at the palace as the pharaoh's grandson. That is all Exodus reveals about Moses until he kills an Egyptian beating a Hebrew slave, flees Egypt, and ends up in Midian. In *The Prince of Egypt*, the story's opening is changed to where Moses is found by the pharaoh's wife and raised as brother to Rameses, heir to his father's throne, allowing an exploration of their fraternal relationship. When Moses returns from Midian, his brother has assumed the throne and leads Egypt through the plagues. He is despondent over his son's body, who dies in the last plague, when he tells Moses that the Hebrews may leave. After leaving the palace, Moses breaks down in tears after seeing his brother so grief stricken. The brotherly relationship adds considerable personal drama.

Much of the remainder of the plot deals faithfully with the essence of Moses leading the Hebrews out of Egypt, but many details in Exodus 1–15 are glossed over. One change includes reducing the role of Moses's brother, Aaron, who served as spokesman for the reluctant leader. The plagues that God inflicts upon the Egyptians are simplified, presented as brief images in a song that maintains focus on Moses and Rameses. In the biblical account Moses at first just seeks permission to take his people into the desert to offer sacrifices to God, but the pharaoh will not allow this and God makes him stubborn while visiting one plague after another on Egypt. Once God kills the firstborn children and initiates the celebration of Passover, the pharaoh tells Moses and his people to leave, but then pursues them toward the Red Sea, resulting in the final Egyptian debacle. In *The Prince of Egypt*, Moses only asks Rameses to "let [his] people go." Tzipporah, Moses's wife, goes with him to Egypt in both Exodus and the film, but she appears often in the latter and is barely present in the Bible after Moses arrives in Egypt. At the conclusion Moses descends from the mountain with the Ten Commandments, a story that does not appear until Exodus 34. Nothing from Exodus 15 to 34 appears in the film.

DreamWorks added to the film's impact by hiring noted actors to voice the characters. For most roles there was a speaking voice and a different singing voice with attempts made to match quality and timbre, a point raised in the DVD audio commentary.[44] The main roles included Val Kilmer as Moses and God, Ralph Fiennes as Rameses, Michelle Pfeiffer as Tzipporah, Sandra Bullock as Miriam, Jeff Goldblum as Aaron, Danny Glover as Jethro, Patrick Stewart as Seti, Helen Mirren as the Queen, Steve Martin as Hotep, and Martin Short as Huy. Among the singers were Amick Byram as Moses, Sally Dworsky as Miriam, Ofra Haza as Jocheved, Brian Stokes Mitchell as Jethro, and Linda Shayne as the Queen. Pfeiffer, Martin, and Short did their own singing. The film was extremely successful.[45]

Music plays a huge role in *The Prince of Egypt*, both in Schwartz's six songs and Hans Zimmer's extensive orchestral score. Focus here will remain on Schwartz's songs and how they help convey the drama. Each song in the film appears on the DVD at following timings:

"Deliver Us"—1'36" to 8'12" (includes Jocheved's "River Lullaby," which appears separately on the recorded soundtrack, and a segment that briefly reprises when Miriam sings to Moses, 21'35" to 22'07")
"All I Ever Wanted"—22'11" to 24'20" (reprised by the Queen to Moses, 28'28" to 29'00")
"Through Heaven's Eyes"—38'59" to 42'04"
"Playing with the Big Boys"—54'36" to 56'36"
"The Plagues"—65'13" to 67'42"

"When You Believe"—77'25" to 81'49" (reprised by Mariah Carey and
Whitney Houston under the credits)

Important musical assistance came from orchestrator Bruce L. Fowler,
with additional orchestrations by Ladd McIntosh and Yvonne I. Moriarty.
Recordings took place in London with such groups as the Boy Choristers
of Salisbury Cathedral. After the performance of "When You Believe" by
Mariah Carey and Whitney Houston under the end credits, one hears "I Will
Get There" by Diane Warren sung by Boyz II Men.

Schwartz's songs consume about 21:30 of the running time, including
interruptions for dialogue. "Deliver Us" presents the suffering of the Hebrew
slaves and the journey of baby Moses into the pharaoh's household. "All I
Ever Wanted" depicts Moses realizing that he can no longer be happy at the
pharaoh's court now that he knows he is Hebrew and sympathizes with their
plight. "Through Heaven's Eyes," sung by Jethro as he welcomes Moses to
Midian and used in a montage to show his acceptance there and his marriage to Tzipporah, introduces for Moses God's significance in their lives
and makes plausible his acceptance of divine direction at the burning bush.
"Playing with the Big Boys" is sung by Egyptian priests after God has turned
Moses's staff into a snake. They demonstrate that they, too, can perform
magic in this over-the-top, villainous song. As previously noted, the film
covered the plagues quickly in a song. "When You Believe" is the inevitable
celebratory song after the Hebrews are allowed to leave Egypt.

"Deliver Us" provides an impressive opening, both in terms of music and
animation. De Giere reports that Schwartz decided early on how to open the
film, knowing that his song must show the Hebrews in cruel bondage.[46] It is
the first song that he wrote. We see Moses's mother, Jocheved, desperately
setting her baby in a basket to float down the Nile. The song's running time
includes dramatic underscoring for the basket's harrowing trip down the Nile
to the palace. Preceding the song is a trumpet solo on a theme associated
with Jocheved, and Moses's Hebrew past.[47] Schwartz based it upon a variant
of what some call the Jewish scale (*do, ra, mi, fa, sol, le, te, do*; heard in "Hava
Nagila"); instead of the augmented second between *ra* and *mi*, however,
Schwartz substitutes *re*, a note that only occurs once when the tune cadences
on the dominant. Moses's mother (performed by Israeli singer Ofra Haza)
and sister Miriam later sing the theme. Whether or not the second degree
of the scale is flatted seems less significant than the overall exotic sound.
(While on the Egyptian field trip, Schwartz notes that he purchased recordings of modern popular Arabic music that inspired him to "work within a
specific scale,"[48] probably meaning this one, aspects of which appear in some

later songs.) Schwartz opens the melody with what sounds like a major-minor seventh arpeggio (*do-mi-sol-te*), introducing a searching quality that lasts through the three phrases and fourteen measures. The trumpet is unaccompanied. The melody includes a descending fifth between *me* and *le* just before the dominant chord that precedes the E minor of the song's opening, implying a Phrygian cadence.

What follows is a slow march as we watch the Egyptians forcing the Hebrews to make bricks. Schwartz includes melodic touches that might be called Jewish signifiers and also works with his trademark syncopation. It is a wide-ranging tune in regular phrases (ABCC', sixteen bars of 4+4+4+4). Moses's mother opens what becomes the second verse with lyrics in Hebrew offering comfort for her baby,[49] continuing onto recitative-like material in English before the chorus returns with "Deliver Us," the lyrics slightly different. During that chorus, Jocheved hurries with her children down to the Nile while avoiding Egyptian guards. Placing the basket in the river and Moses's sister Miriam following it on the banks requires three statements of the opening melody, two sung by Jocheved and one by Miriam. The first is the mother's last lullaby to her son, recalled by Miriam as an adult to show Moses that he is Hebrew. His mother then addresses the river, requesting a safe journey. Hans Zimmer underscored the opening of the basket's journey with Jocheved's theme, Ofra Haza singing over it dramatically. At the conclusion of Miriam's innocent passage, noting that Moses has been found by the Egyptian Queen, she invites Moses to some day return to the Hebrews and deliver them. The segment concludes grandly with chorus and orchestra.

Schwartz reported to de Giere his dramatic story of inspiration for "All I Ever Wanted," sung by the devastated Moses once he has found out that he was originally son of an enslaved Hebrew. While on an excursion down the Nile on the DreamWorks field trip in late 1995, Schwartz noted the play of moonlight and flashlights on columns at the temple of Kom Ombo, inspiring the scene of Moses bearing a torch as he tried to assimilate the news of his birth.[50] (In the film Moses runs through the palace with a torch looking for painted images of the murdered Hebrew babies.) Schwartz told de Giere that he conceived there a musical theme reminiscent of Philip Glass that became the song. The inspiration from minimalism is clearly the energetic, repetitive accompaniment. Moses has run into Miriam and Aaron, and his sister assumes that he has learned of his heritage, but Moses has not and rebuffs her angrily. As he turns to leave she sings her mother's lullaby, which immediately strikes a chord with Moses. He flees and Schwartz's relentless accompaniment of triplets in 4/4 begins. The song focuses on Moses and his past, showing that he can no longer be happy now that he knows his people are slaves. Schwartz filled the lyrics with images of the life that Moses had known (a posture also adopted by the animators as he returns to his room in the palace), allowing him a farewell to the glory of his previous life. Based on a classic song form (AABA'), Schwartz wrote in unbalanced phrases (6+6+12+11) that match the character's uncertain emotional state. The melody traverses a perfect eleventh, at times rapidly, giving further airing to his wild emotions. The rapid ascent in the first measure across a minor ninth occurs a number of times, balanced by a scale-wise descent on each statement of the title text that sounds in eighth notes until Schwartz augments it to quarters in the last statement. The song's harmonies are notable simple, primarily triads without sevenths, approaching the diatonicism often associated with Glass. The Queen's brief reprise of material from the song follows four minutes later, but she never sings the title text and the accompaniment is chordal, without the triplets. She counsels Moses to forget what he has learned and be content in the role that he has always lived. As he hugs his mother, the orchestra plays some of Jocheved's lullaby, the music that accompanies Moses down another path. Music from "All I Ever Wanted" returns in "The Plagues."

After accidentally killing an Egyptian guard who was whipping a Hebrew slave, Moses flees into the desert, joining a Jewish tribe at Midian led by Jethro. Years pass before his encounter with the burning bush, during which Moses marries Tzipporah and learns about his heritage. The film's creators wrestled with this song placement, wondering what should be emphasized. Schwartz told de Giere about three songs that preceded "Through Heaven's Eyes."[51] The first was "All in Your Attitude," offering Jewish humor about poverty, followed by "Don't Be a Stranger" and "One of Us," but he still failed to capture the moment. Schwartz recalls that Katzenberg suggested a song from Jethro about his philosophy. Both de Giere and the DVD commentary track state that codirector Steve Hickner remembered the anonymous poem "The Measure of a Man" (reproduced by de Giere along with the lyrics to Schwartz's song[52]), which inspired "Through Heaven's Eyes." Schwartz notes that he changed the poem's images to things that Midianites might have understood, but this appears to overstate the poem's importance in inspiring the song.[53] In "The Measure of a Man" the spotlight is on one's character, but Schwartz translated this into the possibility of improving oneself by looking through God's eyes. Schwartz provided Jethro with a satisfying progression of ideas, beginning with how a thread in a tapestry cannot appreciate its role in the larger work and proceeding through a number of images that show how small objects and acts play into larger schemes. The lyrics deepen as the songs proceeds, ranking it with the finest of Schwartz's serious works, such as heard in *Children of Eden* and *Wicked*.

The song's music includes references to the scale described earlier, especially the lowered seventh and second degrees, each applied ambiguously. The overall form of "Through Heaven's Eyes" carries a strophic feel, but Schwartz keeps it irregular, allowing the character, sung gloriously by Brian Stokes Mitchell, the leisure to develop his ideas. Jethro sings in shocked response to Moses's claim that he has done nothing in his life that merits honoring. Jethro states that Moses helped Tzipporah escape from Egypt (she had been captured and offered to Moses as a concubine) and that he saved three of his other daughters from brigands when he arrived in Midian. The song becomes an elaborate introduction for Moses into life in Midian with three musical sections, each basically stepwise and full of rhythmic verve in the prevailing quadruple meter. Jethro sings (four measures) in a low tessitura as he offers situations where something small must recognize its part in the greater whole. After two statements of A in E major, the song climbs toward the higher tonic in the B section as the lyrics move toward the title text. A dance segment set to sung vocables by the choir, which functions as C, follows the first "verse" as we watch Moses gradually enter his new community. Jethro's second segment begins up one half step and is longer, but based on A and B. At the end he urges Moses to join in their dancing, aided by Tzipporah and quickly resolving their courting. The next dance segment is up another full step to G major, but it does not remain there long as Schwartz executes a quick move back to E before Jethro sings a brief coda.

After meeting God in the burning bush, Moses returns to Egypt with Tzipporah. De Giere notes that Schwartz and Hans Zimmer went to Las Vegas for a break and saw a show by animal tamers Siegfried and Roy, inspiring them to consider a scene with Egyptian magicians that demonstrated how "showmanship, pomp and pretension" might take the place of actual content.[54] This occurs just after Moses has shown God's power by putting down his staff, which turns into a cobra. The directors on their DVD commentary suggest that "Playing with the Big Boys" began as comic relief, also noting the influence of Siegfried and Roy, with the animation even including showgirls singing the names of Egyptian gods. As the conception progressed, however, it became darker with Zimmer providing new orchestrations that fit the mood.[55] The directors note that Schwartz suggested that it should be clear that the magic the Egyptian priests were doing should seem fake.[56] They are portrayed in high camp, one even commenting "They love it!" as the courtiers cheer them. Toward the end, the cobra formed from Moses's staff gobbles up the snakes produced from sticks by Hotep and Huy (as stated in Exodus), but in a corner, almost unobserved. The directors comment that they did not want it to be too obvious at this point in the film that Moses was in charge.

Such variety of tone also appears in Schwartz's song, which he conceived in full "bad guy" mode. One is reminded here of songs that Schwartz wrote for *The Magic Show*, especially "A Round for the Bad Guys" from the video version. In "Playing with the Big Boys," Schwartz again uses chromatic alterations in the melody that signify Middle Eastern roots and help tie together the film's songs, especially a lowered second degree and augmented seconds. It opens with eight measures of recitative in A minor with distinctive use of quarter note triplets that helps mask the quadruple meter until the penultimate bar in eighth notes, which presents the notion that Moses will now see real power. The song is in AA' form with a brief coda, with A' presented a fourth higher. Before the second verse the magicians and their assistants chant the names of Egyptian gods, as in the opening, and then modulate to the dark key of E-flat minor for the varied conclusion. Most of the lines state the title text, but when other thoughts appear they are short and have precise rhymes, some a bit far-fetched ("Horus . . . before us . . . splendorous"), which help the song sound overwrought.

Presenting the plagues described in Exodus was a major challenge. According to the DVD commentary, the creators began with images of the plague and underscoring, but decided to focus on the deteriorating relationship between Moses and Rameses.[57] Carol de Giere reports that Schwartz tried to write a song about the plagues, but it became too repetitious, so he instead focused on the brothers (and writer Philip LaZebnik credited Schwartz with that discovery). Zimmer suggested that they return to the music of "All I Ever Wanted."[58] Schwartz also reported that studio head Katzenberg was becoming concerned about the film's cost and ordered that the plague sequence should not last more than 2:30.[59] Schwartz adapted "All I Ever Wanted," writing lyrics for Moses and Rameses that recall their shared past and current conflict, and added repetitious choral material that names aspects of the plagues with many statements of "thus saith the Lord." Along with Zimmer's dramatic orchestrations, many sound effects, and animation effects, "The Plagues" is a memorable scene.

Moses is disconsolate as he makes his way back to the Hebrew quarter after seeing his brother with his dead son. Tzipporah hugs him, and Miriam— revered in the Bible for her hymn to God after crossing the Red Sea (Exodus 15:20–21)—starts "When You Believe," which, along with a joyous song in Hebrew, takes Moses and his people to the Red Sea. Carol de Giere reports that the idea for this song came to the directors while in the Sinai Desert.[60] The English portion divides into two parts. The eight-measure opening includes two-bar phrases and rests in D minor with rising fifths from d to a and then c to g, emphasizing the lowered seventh. The lyrics describe the Hebrew slave experiences and their prayers for deliverance, ending with the powerful idea that they had already moved mountains "before we knew we could." The refrain follows immediately. It is only ten measures long and in a simple aa' (4+6) form. The phrase "when you believe" occurs three times in the ten measures, and the rhyme with "achieve" makes the "-ieve" sound dominate the passage. The lyrics also offer the notion that "hope is frail" but "hard to kill," again commenting on what the Hebrews had felt for years. Schwartz's melody includes common gestures in F major with moves toward D minor. Now Tzipporah sings, joined by Miriam for the remainder of the verse and through the refrain. During the refrain's repetition, which modulates up one step to G, the great mass of people begin to move. A small child (another of Zimmer's suggestions[61]) starts to sing the Hebrew song, a happy confection in G major. The text, recommended by a rabbi who consulted on the film, came from the "Song of the Reeds," said to have been sung by the Hebrews after crossing the Red Sea.[62] "When You Believe" later returns, now in a triumphant A major for large chorus and orchestra. The studio version of the song during the credits features pop divas Whitney Houston and Mariah Carey.

Thus, in this animated musical film for which Schwartz wrote both music and lyrics, we find that he was again involved decisively in determining the motivations of characters and details of the plot. Each of Schwartz's songs plays a significant role in the film's effect and characterization. Moses's story, for example, begins with Jocheved's and Miriam's portion of "Deliver Us," and "All I Ever Wanted" confirms his happiness in life at the Egyptian court, returning in "The Plagues." "Through Heaven's Eyes" moves Moses into the orbit of his new family at Midian and sets up his receptiveness to God in the burning bush. "Playing with the Big Boys," while humorous, establishes the misplaced confidence of the pharaoh's court and rectitude of Moses's mission, while "When You Believe," which starts as Miriam tries to cheer up Moses, becomes the song of the triumphant Hebrews.

Enchanted (2007)

Schwartz's third Disney project was the successful *Enchanted*, Disney's clever tribute to their long history of animated musicals that also evokes other iconic Hollywood musicals.[63] Working again with Alan Menken, Schwartz crafted lyrics that made a strong contribution to the film's reflexivity. One sees allusions to *Snow White and the Seven Dwarfs*, *Sleeping Beauty*, *Mary Pop-*

pins, Cinderella, The Little Mermaid, Beauty and the Beast, and even such non-Disney films as *The Sound of Music. Enchanted* also features a sassy, modern take on the genre's conventions, especially after Giselle arrives in New York City.

Carol de Giere interviewed Schwartz about *Enchanted,* offering the text in an appendix. Schwartz reports that the film's screenplay was in a substantially finished form before they started the score. Director Kevin Lima and scriptwriter Bill Kelly had already decided where some of the songs would be, but they also allowed suggestions from the musical team. The five songs that they wrote appear below with time indices of when each can be seen in the film:

"True Love's Kiss"—2'19" to 5'43", 7'07" to 7'50", 50'28" to 50'30", and 69'17" to 69'44"
"Happy Little Working Song"—26'20" to 28'19"
"That's How You Know"—47'41" to 51'55"
"So Close" (called "The King and Queen's Waltz" in the film)—80'13" to 84'03"
"Ever Ever After"—95'56" to 99'03"

Lima and Kelly decided to begin the film with a song in the animated land of Andalasia, for which Menken and Schwartz wrote the saccharine "True Love's Kiss." The script included a scene where Giselle would call forth the kinds of animals available in New York City—flies, rats, pigeons, and cockroaches—to help her clean Robert's apartment, but Schwartz is not sure whether or not they had decided that a song like "Happy Working Song" belonged there. He reports that the musical team suggested adding "That's How You Know" to a scene that already existed and also helped decide its context in the relationship between Robert and Giselle. The placement for "So Close" at the ball was not only in the script, but the title had already been chosen. Schwartz reports that the final number "Ever Ever After," sung as a voice-over by Carrie Underwood, was something that he lobbied for strongly, insisting that *Enchanted* needed to end as a musical to underscore the happiness that each of the main characters has found.

Schwartz discussed the "pastiche" nature of the score with de Giere, describing an overall scheme where the songs progress from typical Disney fare of the 1930s to the modern world. Given the story, this seems with hindsight like a natural gesture for Menken and Schwartz to have pursued, but the lyricist reports that the process "wasn't conscious from the very beginning."[64] The score's progression from fantasy to reality provides the film with a satisfying musical arc and parallels the story, a feature that will be approached in more detail later as we consider music and lyrics. In some ways the five songs are a surprisingly small part of the movie, sounding for only about eighteen minutes total (and even those excerpts are interrupted by dialogue and action), but tunes recur in the orchestral underscoring.

Schwartz notes that "True Love's Kiss" was inspired by the classic Disney animated features such as *Snow White* and *Sleeping Beauty*, but that he and Menken also "made fun of it a bit."[65] The song operates on two levels. Children respond to the sweetness and innocence, but those with more sophisticated sensibilities cannot miss the sentimental overplay and statement that finding love results in a physical relationship that Schwartz's lyrics treat ironically, suggesting that only lips of lovers touch. Menken wrote a simple melody in C major and quadruple meter based upon wide, ascending leaps and conjunct descents, moving to a triple meter when Giselle invites forest animals to help her complete the statue she is making of the man who recently appeared in her dreams. The forest animals answer and come running in E-flat major, singing part of the song as a waltz before the return of the opening key, and later the original time signature, as Giselle and her friends finish the first part of the song. Elements of the song return over the next few minutes as the scene plays out with Giselle escaping a troll and falling literally into Prince Edward's arms.

Schwartz's lyrics, in tandem with Disney's animated action, play a major role in developing the song's two levels of understanding. The innocent opening recitative includes cutesy, spoken lines from two bunnies (like Thumper in *Bambi*) and two birds (like Cinderella's friends in that classic film, the opening scene of which is referenced throughout this segment of *Enchanted*). The disgusting troll with his runny nose provides some of the fun that the *Enchanted* animators made of earlier Disney features. After Giselle falls in Edward's arms he starts to sing the song again, this time with the lyrics referring to finding the one who completes the lover's duet, redolent for musical theater fans to the song "Ah! Sweet Mystery of Life" from Victor Herbert's *Naughty Marietta*, where the condition of love truly is finishing the lover's song.

As Schwartz told de Giere,[66] "Happy Little Working Song" is a satirical look at Disney working songs, specifically "Whistle While You Work" from *Snow White*, which also includes animals that help cleaning up. One also hears echoes of "Spoonful of Sugar" from *Mary Poppins* and "A Dream Is a Wish Your Heart Makes" from *Cinderella*. Giselle cleans Robert's dirty apartment, but with rats, pigeons, cockroaches, and flies. Menken's song is in quadruple meter and primarily diatonic, but with enough melodic leaps to help provide the requisite perkiness. Schwartz's lyrics are carefully chosen, mixing the sentiment of a cheerful laborer with such messy references as "crud" and "stubborn mildew stain," and managing some clever rhymes ("determine . . . vermin"). For a moment, Giselle looks out the window in hopes that Edward will arrive soon, which occurs as Menken modulates from D major to F-sharp major and Schwartz temporarily places Giselle's thoughts on a loftier level.

"That's How You Know," which takes place in Central Park, unites revelers of all ages and diverse races in what Schwartz compares with huge production numbers in old-time Hollywood musicals.[67] He told de Giere that the number's model moves forward to later Disney animation features, specifically referencing the calypso feeling of "Under the Sea" from *The Little Mermaid*,[68] but it also recalls ethnic numbers in *The Lion King* and other films. In "That's How You Know" Menken combined rhythms and a counter-melody that sound like calypso, brought alive with steel drums and other Caribbean instruments. Although artless simplicity in lyrics can be difficult to manage, Schwartz provided just that, mixing statements of how a woman might wonder if a man loves her with suggestions of what type of actions might confirm that fact. Rhymes are usually of a common variety, but one can admire "mind reader" and "lead her."

The next song, "So Close," occurs diagetically as Jon McLaughlin sings it with the orchestra playing at the ball. The conductor calls it "The King and Queen's Waltz" and asks that everyone dance it with someone they did not attend the ball with, allowing Edward to dance with Nancy and Robert to finalize his bond with Giselle. The song is in 4/4 with prevailing triplet motion, hardly making it a waltz, and couples clearly dance in quadruple meter. Schwartz told de Giere that the conception of "So Close" was based upon the Menken's title tune of *Beauty and the Beast*, partly because director Kevin Lima wanted to reproduce in live action the spinning camera angles made famous as the Beast and Belle dance.[69] The lyricist further reports that the director asked that the last line of the song be "So close and still so far," because this appears to be the final moment together for Robert and Giselle. Menken wrote a flowing tune with a wide range that takes the tenor to a d-flat"; McLaughlin negotiates any note that is a b-flat' or higher with a colorless falsetto. Robert, played by Patrick Dempsey, sings some of the lines quietly to Giselle, a moment that Schwartz fought for because the actor did not wish to sing.[70] Schwartz's lyrics convey the song's dual message. He relies less on rhyme here, but does say "happy end" rather than "ending" to align with "pretend," and there are a few other prominent rhymes.

"Ever Ever After" completes the chronological journey that Menken and Schwartz embarked on in this score, bringing them to the "present" with a country/rock song written for pop diva Carrie Underwood to sing as a voice-over. During this song Edward and Nancy fall in love and rush off to animated Andalasia to get married and other minor story points resolve. Robert and Giselle find happiness in Manhattan. Menken wrote a typical pop ballad with rich syncopation in the melody and some large, effective ascending intervals, obviously working carefully with Schwartz in terms of when to bring the title text in, which happens often. The accompaniment includes a pulsating rumba rhythm (3+3+2) and throbbing eighth notes in the bass line, imparting great energy. Schwartz's lyrics include references to "story book endings" and "fairy tales," certainly appropriate for *Enchanted*, but then he moves into the real world. As the A section repeats he calls for the initiation of a new trend of one's "heart on your sleeve," the posture that Giselle has affirmed for the entire film. Despite the fun that the movie's creators have with the Disney canon throughout, *Enchanted* ends with two couples living "happy ever after."

The five songs that Menken and Schwartz wrote for *Enchanted* play varied roles in the story-telling. "True Love's Kiss" introduces Giselle's deep desire for a man and becomes "her song" with Edward, recurring a few times. Its final statement in counterpoint at the end of "Ever Ever After" brings the score full circle and transfers its "ownership" to Giselle and Robert. "Happy Little Working Song" is not crucial to the story but serves up one of the film's best "tributes" to earlier Disney films. "That's How You Know" is a production number and barely impacts the plot, but it is charming. "So Close" becomes the song for Robert and Giselle and renders the ball as one of the film's most important musical moments. "Ever Ever After" ends the film with music and accompanies efforts to tie up loose ends, not essential to the plot but helpful to the overall effect.

CHAPTER ELEVEN

~

Geppetto Becomes My Son Pinocchio: Geppetto's Musical Tale

Geppetto (2000), which premiered on *The Wonderful World of Disney*, is Stephen Schwartz's only television musical. He later joined with collaborator David I. Stern in turning *Geppetto* into *My Son Pinocchio: Geppetto's Musical Tale*, a children's show conceived for community and regional theaters. Intended for a cast of seven adults and an unstated number of children, the project's stage version is simple and unpretentious and shorter than the first act of many musicals. Like many such properties, however, the script includes elements for potential adult interest, and the integration of plot and music is carefully wrought. Adapting *Geppetto* for stage took place during the research period for this study, allowing this chapter to include observations of Schwartz in the process of working and collaborating.

A Television Musical

The show's history begins with the Disney television production, which partly emanated from the personal experiences of book writer Stern. He had worked with Schwartz earlier in the 1990s on *Snapshots*, which Stern wrote with Michael Scheman. Stern was assistant to lyricist and director Richard Maltby Jr. and Scheman was a production assistant for the musical *Nick and Nora*; Stern met Scheman during the production. *Snapshots* is billed as a "musical mosaic." Scheman conceived the idea and pitched it to Stern, who had already written the Rodgers and Hammerstein revue *Some*

Enchanted Evening. Stern conceived the idea of making *Snapshots* a combination of book show and revue. They wrote it after gauging Schwartz's interest, and he became more involved once they got to the workshop stage. Stern and Scheman wrote their story about a middle-aged couple reviewing their personal history through photographs. Within this framework they sing a number of Schwartz's songs, and for some Schwartz wrote new lyrics. The show has been performed in regional theaters throughout the country.

Stern then involved Schwartz in what started for him as a personal project. Stern's father died in 1996, forcing him to move home to Atlanta for a few months. Stern found this to be life changing, bringing him to new realizations about who his father had been, and showing him how little he had really known him as a person. About that time, Stern also read *Pinocchio*. He found himself pondering, "How did Geppetto end up inside the whale?"[1] Stern noted that Geppetto had prepared Pinocchio poorly for meeting the world: "He basically gives him an apple and sends him off." By the end, however, Geppetto has gained better parenting skills that Stern assumes developed during the father's "separate journey." The writer reports that the remainder of the story for the television musical followed from that realization.

Schwartz states that Stern first shared this idea with him when the two were at a workshop for *Snapshots* at the Virginia Stage Company in Norfolk in about 1997. Schwartz explains it as a story about a "father becoming a father," in which the familiar story would be told from Geppetto's viewpoint.[2] Stern's proposal appealed to Schwartz on at least two levels. The composer has often worked with the theme of parents and children, especially in *Children of Eden*. The other level would be Stern's unusual take on an iconic tale, the likes of which Schwartz also experienced in several of his shows. Schwartz believes that such an approach "allows . . . a writer to deal with themes and make points more succinctly because the very unusualness of the take on a familiar story makes its own point."

Stern was interested in turning his vision into a stage musical, but Schwartz was more intrigued by a musical for television. They pitched the idea to Disney in 1997, which at the time was in the process of producing what became successful new television versions of Rodgers and Hammerstein's *Cinderella* (1997) and *Annie* (1999). As Schwartz remembers, "they bought it immediately" as an episode of *The Wonderful World of Disney*.

Schwartz's previous work with Disney had been as a lyricist with composer Alan Menken on *Pocahontas* and *The Hunchback of Notre Dame*; later they collaborated on *Enchanted*. Schwartz has enjoyed his work with the large media and entertainment corporation: "I have always had a very good experience working with Disney. . . . From my experience, they are tough to negotiate with in terms of your contract, but once you have a deal with them they treat you very well and I've found that they have great respect for writers."

In the process of creating *Geppetto*, Schwartz felt similar to his Broadway work: "I had pretty much as much autonomy as doing a theater piece."

Disney gave Schwartz and Stern specific instructions that would allow the musical to fit into the two-hour format of *The Wonderful World of Disney*. The show has a seven-act structure, allowing for commercials, and the musical came to eighty-nine minutes of running time. The cast included several well-known television actors: Drew Carey as Geppetto, Julia Louis-Dreyfus as the Blue Fairy, Brent Spiner as Stromboli, Rene Auberjonois as Professor Buonragazzo, and pop star Usher Raymond played the Ring Leader. The writers retained their unusual viewpoint; as Schwartz stated, "We keep the camera on Geppetto instead of moving with Pinocchio." Geppetto follows the puppet, desperately trying to find him, finally catching up with him at Pleasure Island before they are swallowed by the whale. In the process, Geppetto learns more about being a father, and when the Blue Fairy turns Pinocchio into a real boy they are ready to settle down to a family life with a child who knows that his actions can bring consequences and a father who realizes that boys do not always behave.

In writing songs for *Geppetto*, Schwartz felt strongly that he needed permission to use some of the famous songs from the animated feature, especially "When You Wish Upon a Star" and "I've Got No Strings" by composer Leigh Harline and lyricist Ned Washington. Schwartz considers both masterpieces of their type: "These two songs are as perfect as songs can be for what they are supposed to do." Disney actually does not own the rights. Schwartz's lawyer was able to secure rights for both songs from the widow who owns them. She had steadfastly refused to grant Disney the right to use the songs in a stage version of *Pinocchio*. Schwartz notes, "We will be eternally grateful to her. Both of these songs are intrinsic to the score."

Schwartz stated that the original animated feature was based strongly on German models in its style of music and animation. Although he needed his new songs to be part of the world that people knew from the film, Schwartz wanted them to sound more Italian because of the story's location. This was clearly destined to be, like *The Baker's Wife*, a score where Schwartz stretched his compositional wings past the pop styles that appeared with such profusion in *Godspell*, *Pippin*, and *The Magic Show*. The two songs borrowed from the iconic *Pinocchio* animated feature belonged in the great American songbook tradition of the first half of the twentieth century, a style that Schwartz often approximated in his score. He wrote the following new songs: "Toys," "Empty Heart," "And Son," "Just Because It's Magic," "Bravo,

Stromboli," "Satisfaction Guaranteed," "Pleasure Island," and "Since I Gave My Heart Away."

Schwartz based four of these songs on Italian models. "And Son," a duet for Geppetto and the newly animated puppet, serves to show Geppetto's pride in his work and his desire to pass his business onto Pinocchio. Schwartz considers the piece an Italian waltz, a designation that will be approached later when we see how Schwartz replaced the song for the stage version. "Bravo, Stromboli" is a parody of Rossini's famous rapid arias from *The Barber of Seville*, which Schwartz admits he first got to know in the Bugs Bunny cartoon *The Rabbit of Seville*. Schwartz asked Martin Erskine, who did the orchestrations and musical underscoring for the television version, to use Rossini's orchestra for the accompaniment, which Erskine did most effectively. Schwartz captures his model beautifully, with rapid repeated notes and triadic melodies as Stromboli, an unsuccessful puppeteer, reveals his delusions of grandeur. "Satisfaction Guaranteed," sung by Prof. Buonragazzo, concerns the character's ability to produce artificial "perfect children" in his mysterious machine. Schwartz used as a model the Italian folksong "Funiculi, Funicula," and his song is also an energetic march in duple meter. For "Pleasure Island," Schwartz listened to scores that Nino Rota wrote for Federico Fellini's films, such as *8 1/2*. The song is another march, but in quadruple meter, and with a good bit of chromaticism, perhaps reflecting the place's nature. This is, after all, where boys are encouraged to be badly behaved so they will turn into jackasses.

Schwartz's other four songs are closer to traditional Broadway fare, or at least pop ballads. "Toys," a production number that introduces Geppetto's popularity among the local children, is a peppy march with a diatonic melody that moves between notes of the tonic triad. Schwartz seems to remember basing the song on what he regards as an Italianate chord progression, but it is also the type of melody often heard in his Broadway scores. The song includes three versions with different melodies sung by Geppetto, the children, and their parents that are combined in counterpoint at the end. As shown in this study, Schwartz tends to place at least one counterpoint song in each show. The ballads "Empty Heart," sung by Geppetto to the inanimate Pinocchio about his longing before the Blue Fairy appears, and the finale "Since I Gave My Heart Away" are effective, lilting tunes in Schwartz's best manner, the latter with several especially catchy phrases.

"Just Because It's Magic" is Schwartz's tribute to various songs by Rodgers and Hart. It has a vaguely chromatic, cloying melody, and resides in a minor key. The Blue Fairy and Geppetto sing the song, commenting variously on her spell's effectiveness. It concludes with a contrapuntal section. Schwartz remembers having to write more than one version each of the songs "Just Because It's Magic" and "Satisfaction Guaranteed," and perhaps he replaced other songs for *Geppetto* as well, but he notes that the show "wasn't like a Broadway project where you write at least twice as many" songs than end up in the score.

Schwartz was not entirely pleased with *Geppetto*. He recalls: "I was a little disappointed. . . . For various reasons there were things about the final product that I thought didn't quite capture the fun and imagination that the subject matter potentially had."

Geppetto Moves to the Stage in Kansas City

Four years passed during which Schwartz collaborated with Winnie Holzman and others to bring *Wicked* to the stage. In about 2004, he was at a meeting with Music Theatre International (MTI), which licenses most of his shows. One of their representatives expressed a desire for more family shows with casts of several adults and an unspecified number of children. The composer/ lyricist suggested *Geppetto*, which he thought could be adapted fairly easily to fit the need. MTI showed immediate interest, presenting Schwartz with several requirements: a length of about one and one-quarter hours, a maximum of seven adults, and scenes for groups of children. David I. Stern approved, and MTI secured Disney's interest in turning the television show into a stage musical. Schwartz found Disney Theatrical Productions "enormously supportive" as he worked with vice president Steve Fickinger.

As Schwartz and Stern considered their rewrites, MTI and Disney looked for a theater for a workshop. MTI had worked successfully with the Coterie Theatre in Kansas City, Missouri, in 2003–2004 on a family version of *Seussical* by Lynn Ahrens and Stephen Flaherty. The Coterie, an Equity house based in Crown Center south of downtown Kansas City, was founded in 1979. Their home is an oblong, black box theater with the stage on one of the long sides, jutting slightly out into the audience and a total capacity of 280. In 1990 the director became Jeff Church, a Colorado native who earlier had served as playwright-in-residence at the Kennedy Center Theatre for Young People in Washington DC.[3] Church was gratified to see the Coterie become a workshop site for new family musicals, such as *Seussical* and *The Dinosaur Musical* in 2004–2005.[4]

Church first heard about the project from Tim McDonald of MTI. The licensing agent could not tell him at the time if Schwartz would want to be involved or not, and the stage script did not yet exist. The director ordered the compact disc to *Geppetto* and called McDonald two days later to give him his assent. He remembers hoping that the project would not "break the bank."

Schwartz and Stern now needed to figure out how to adapt a television musical for the stage. Schwartz did not think it would be difficult because a script and songs already existed and the two versions would be about the same length. They soon realized, however, that they needed a new framing device. The storybook they used to set up the story, fill gaps, and close the show would not work. Stern explains some of the basic differences between writing for film and stage:

> Core differences between movies and stage . . . have to do with the strengths of the media—movies being more of a "show me" medium, and stage more of a "tell me" medium. The easiest example would be: if I have two characters talking and one is wearing a tie that the other gave him, and if it's important that we know that—in film we would cut to a close up of the tie, then a close up of the character's reaction. On stage, since we can't really see those reactions (or the tie, for that matter), the character would have to say something like, "Hey, is that the tie that I gave you?" in order for us to notice it.

Stern notes that they decided to frame the show with the Blue Fairy. Schwartz says that it was Stern's idea, and they focused on the conflict between Geppetto and the Blue Fairy. It is the toymaker's contention that he wished for his heart to be filled, and the fairy produced a "defective" living puppet. Schwartz finds the framing device "very clever" and "much of the fun of the show," wishing they had thought of it for the television version; "that's why the stage show is so much better." Schwartz also enjoys Stern's "amusing take" on the Blue Fairy, who is "smug and very sure of herself." Another part of the framing device for *Disney's Geppetto & Son* is a "time machine" that takes the audience from one flashback to another, realized on stage with a time machine and actors singing "Rise and Shine" while appearing to be clockworks.

Stern and Schwartz prepared a draft script and sent it to Jeff Church in February 2006. Church had cast the show in January without a script. The writers continued work into March with the workshop scheduled in Kansas City for late that month, and a reading with audience on 26 March. They took a new version of the script with them to Kansas City. Church remembers the first rehearsal: "The actors were all milling about outside here, and Stephen was inside the room. Finally our executive director said, 'You know, you have to go in there sometime.' Because they were all white with fear, like pale." Church reports, however, that Schwartz worked well with the cast, offering suggestions that were "very practical, nothing to be scared of. He doesn't make any decisions that are coming out of left field. The decisions seem absolutely appropriate."

The 26 March workshop was a success with the audience, who applauded it warmly. Those creating *Geppetto & Son* were pleased. Schwartz noted that the "basic form and basic structure and basic theatrical device worked," but at the same time "some places seemed short-changed . . . others overdone."

Schwartz and Stern now had to decide what changes to make. Stern believed that they needed to replace "And Son," which no longer moved the story forward, and they needed to cut running time. The first raised dramatic and musical issues. In the television show that song had helped the audience learn about Geppetto's parental attitude, but in the stage version much of that had been expressed in his initial argument with the Blue Fairy. What was needed now was a song that showed Geppetto's apparent happiness at having a son, but also his high expectations for Pinocchio. This song became "Geppetto and Son," written for the summer workshop.

Like "And Son," the new song is what Schwartz classifies as an Italian waltz, which he had approached before in "It's an Art" in *Working*. He described "It's an Art" as "sort of Verdi-esque," but Schwartz wrote "more folk-style tunes" for *Geppetto*. Schwartz added, with a giggle, that he also used as a model the Dean Martin hit "That's Amore" (music by Harry Warren and lyrics by Jack Brooks, recorded by Martin in 1953). Schwartz noted that he replaced "And Son" with another waltz partly because there is little else in triple meter in the show, and, "as any composer writing a long-form piece with several individual numbers, you try to have variety."

Jeff Church commented on the nature of the changes after the March workshop. Sections were consolidated to use time more efficiently, especially early in the show when Geppetto introduces Pinocchio to his town. The cuckoo clock and song "Rise and Shine" became more specifically a time machine, causing tighter sequences with village fathers and at the school. Church also notes that Stromboli now enters the story later, and the plot now goes further in the direction of Geppetto's major disappointment being that Pinocchio does not wish to be a toy maker. Church also noted a dramatic tightening of the arguments between Geppetto and the Blue Fairy that helped show more precisely the development in toymaker's character. The audience discovers that the Blue Fairy "was right all along," but the audience also notices her feeling of self-importance. Church liked how Schwartz and Stern dealt with the Pinocchio story overall, noting that they have "both deepened it and darkened it a tiny bit."

Another place where Schwartz and Stern noticed a dramatic problem was between Geppetto and Pinocchio, because their rapprochement at the end of the show seemed forced. They tightened up the whale scene and Schwartz wrote a short reprise of "Geppetto and Son," allowing their hug at the end of the show to seem "earned."

Stern and Schwartz wrote the show "in one," meaning that there would be a front drape that opens and closes with scenery changed behind it for the next scene. Church and Coterie set designer Gary Wichansky retained much of the in-one feeling, but altered it as they crafted the show's design. They made the set a cuckoo clock with a drape for the in-one scenes in the center, and side panels with large gears. Between the side panels was a centerpiece from which was suspended the curtain; a large clock was in the middle of the centerpiece. In niches around the set were various toys, representing Geppetto's profession, which could be removed by characters when necessary. The central portion of the stage was a turntable, which made possible the cuckoo clock's motion.

Some scenes that could not be easily staged, such as the Blue Fairy flying in or Geppetto and Pinocchio being swallowed by the whale, were done with shadow puppets behind the "Magic Mirror," located behind the main curtain when needed. There were several imaginative props, such as a long red tongue that rolled out from the central portion of the set when Geppetto and Pinocchio are in the whale. The whale is also represented with teeth and a uvula on the curtain behind the action. Pinocchio's nose grew as a shadow behind the Magic Mirror when the puppet tickled the back of the whale's throat.

Although they had trouble dealing with how much the production should look like Disney, Church and his designers had drawings to show Schwartz, Stern, and Fickinger at the March meeting. After seeing a drawing of the cuckoo clock, which also functions as Geppetto's toy shop, they objected to showing the toy shop at the opening of the show when the Blue Fairy was on stage alone. The solution was to put a blue, confetti drape over much of the set that disappears quickly when the Blue Fairy waves her magic wand to start the flashbacks that Geppetto requested, and the toy shop appears. Another part of the Coterie's conception was that Pleasure Island would look a bit less like the "Bowery Boys," as one sees in the animated feature, and more like circus roustabouts, with a touch of what Church calls "delinquents through time," grabbing elements of young, undesirable characters from various times and places. The set was also draped in lights for the Pleasure Island sequence.

After the March reading, Stern and Schwartz did their rewrites and produced a rehearsal script. Schwartz notes that he had no contact with Jeff Church and the Coterie Theatre after finishing that step until June. Church

Charles Fugate, Geppetto; Alex Peterson, Pinocchio. *Photo courtesy of the Coterie, Kansas City, Missouri*

and the Coterie, of course, were busy with the remainder of their season, which concluded with *Geppetto & Son* from 27 June to 6 August. Disney changed the title of the musical to *Disney's Geppetto & Son*, necessitating changes in the posters and other publicity, but also clarifying provenance and inspiration. Steve Fickinger supervised a national publicity campaign and an extensive article appeared on *Playbill.com* on 27 June that included information on the show's conception and the creative intentions.[5] In the main roles, the Coterie Theatre's production included Jessalyn Kincaid as the Blue Fairy, Charles Fugate as Geppetto, Alex Peterson as Pinocchio, Ben Gulley as Stromboli, Damron Russel Armstrong as Professor Buonragazzo, and Justin Michael Van Pelt as the Pleasure Island Ringleader. Church reported that the cast included six professional actors, three interns, and nine children. There were two pit musicians on piano, synthesizer, and percussion. Church managed to defray some of the expenses by securing a $22,000 grant from the National Endowment for the Arts.

Once Church had the rehearsal script, the writers gave the director free rein to "play with" the show. For example, in one scene in Act 1 Church added Pinocchio putting down "My Goodbye Letter" and running away from the toy shop while the Blue Fairy sings "When You Wish Upon a Star." Schwartz and Stern retained the scene. Although Church knew that the show was to flesh-out the character of Geppetto, he wanted to make sure that some of the basics of Pinocchio's story remained. He said, "I think the staging director of the musical wants to try to always remember who the audience is, and my audience, at least half is going to be kids. I want to make sure we don't forget Pinocchio in this."

The next major step in the show's genesis observed for this study was the first preview on Tuesday, 27 June, and the rehearsal that afternoon that took place with Schwartz and Stern. There the writers made the majority of their cuts, some that they had decided upon before arriving in Kansas City and others that they conceived that day. The show's actual premiere took place on Friday evening, 30 June; the Coterie's schedule called for four previews with rehearsal after the first three afternoons for cuts and polishing.

On 20 July 2006, I attended a performance of *Disney's Geppetto & Son* to see what the show was like after they froze it at some point during previews week. The first act was forty-two minutes and the second act thirty-two minutes, so they had brought the show in at just under the seventy-five minutes requested by Music Theatre International.

The Kansas City press covered *Disney's Geppetto & Son*. Robert Trussell attended the show for the city's main newspaper, the *Kansas City Star*. The critic knew the Coterie's work well and concentrated as much on the well-known local actors as the show itself. He began the review with effusive praise for Jessalyn Kincaid, describing her as so natural for the part that her dialogue sounded almost improvised. He called the show "by turns charming and hilarious," and noted that Stern and Schwartz "address the story's emotional arc straight-on," but also allow for "honest human behavior."[6] He named the songs retained from the 1940 animated feature, but also stated that "Schwartz's original compositions have a charm all their own." Trussell's final judgment was that "This show has a future."

Alan Scherstuhl reviewed the show for the *Pitch*, a local weekly that extensively covers arts and entertainment. Scherstuhl loved the local cast and the Coterie's work, but was less sanguine about the show itself. He noted the show's "distinguished pedigree" with Schwartz's score, but thought that it "might seem like Disney's attempt to milk an old property for community-theater dollars."[7] His major complaint was Stern's script, which he found shallow and filled "with that sub-*Mad* sarcasm common to too many fairy-tale updates." He praised director Jeff Church and his designers and the entire cast, especially Jessalyn Kincaid and Damron Russel Armstrong as Professor Buonragazzo.

The national website TheaterMania.com sent Steve Walker to *Disney's Geppetto & Son*. Walker offered a mixed review, describing moments where the show "positively glistens," but others "as wooden as the legendary puppet at its center."[8] He praised some of the actors, again especially Jessalyn Kincaid and Alex Peterson, but found that other characters lacking. The critic blamed Stern's book for not having a sufficient sense of connection between the scenes and Church for his casting choices of adult actors, but noted that Schwartz's "music and lyrics give the piece its surface charm."

In the end, the Coterie Theater workshop of *Disney's Geppetto & Son* bore theatrical fruit. Schwartz reports that there were workshops subsequent to Kansas City, with an especially important one taking place at the StarStruck Performing Arts Center in Stuart, Florida, in July 2009, organized by MTI and Disney. A major effort there for Schwartz and Stein was to make cuts in the show for a "junior" version, and they also decided to add "four younger girls called the Fairies-in-Training, who are always with the Blue Fairy and sing with her."[9] The Fairies-in-Training have also taken over other duties, such as singing "Rise and Shine" as the clock operates, showing the passage of time.[10] These young shadows for the Blue Fairy worked so well that the creators added them to the standard version. Disney then asked for additional revisions on the junior version, and Schwartz reports that there have been test productions in the schools. The junior version was released in fall 2012. As marketing campaigns began for these various productions and workshops,

Schwartz reports the discovery of a general ignorance of Geppetto's identity as Pinocchio's father. The problem remained even when there was a picture of his long-nosed, wooden son on the poster.[11] For marketing purposes they decided that a new title was indicated in which the son's name appeared, and they settled on *My Son Pinocchio: Geppetto's Musical Tale*. Although more cumbersome than *Geppetto & Son*, Schwartz reports that this change has been successful. As one may note on the MTI website, various community and children's theaters around the United States have performed both the standard and children's version (*My Son Pinocchio Jr.*).[12] Considerable interest in the show could be documented through a web search in summer 2013. Schwartz was sanguine about the future for *My Son Pinocchio: Geppetto's Musical Tale*, especially the junior version.[13]

CHAPTER TWELVE

~

Wicked

Clearly Stephen Schwartz's most famous recent musical must be represented in this study, but the need for extensive consideration of the show's creation and its music is mitigated by my book *"Wicked": A Musical Biography* (Scarecrow Press, 2011), made possible by fortuitous access to primary documents. This current volume was the first book started, but it was interrupted when what was intended to be a chapter on *Wicked* grew into a single volume. This current chapter includes a brief overview of *Wicked*'s creation and its music with references to my previous work. Other important sources on *Wicked* include books by Carol de Giere and David Cote.[1]

Wicked is based upon Gregory Maguire's novel by the same name.[2] Maguire brilliantly inverted L. Frank Baum's Oz, perhaps the most important fantasy in the American imagination, making the Wizard an evil interloper from another world and the Wicked Witch of the West (named Elphaba) his misunderstood enemy. Glinda is Elphaba's friend and an important ally for the Wizard who plays a bigger role in the play than she does in the novel.[3] Schwartz first heard about the novel in late 1996 and over the course of the next few years identified Winnie Holzman as a book writer who could convincingly render young female characters, convinced Marc Platt of Universal Studios—which held dramatic rights for the novel—that *Wicked* should be a stage musical rather than a film without music, and helped Maguire reach the same conclusion.[4] The show's development took place through copious writing and rewriting between 1999 and the opening in late 2003, and a series of workshops and readings in New York and Los Angeles between 2000 and 2003.[5] With Schwartz and Holzman regularly hearing their material performed by professionals as part of the creative process, members of the cast started to fall into place. Kristin Chenoweth played Glinda in two readings around a workshop in February-March 2001 and remained in the role thereafter, substantially altering the way that they wrote the character.[6] Idina Menzel joined the project as Elphaba in October 2001 and had a similar influence on her character's development and the later music that Schwartz wrote for her.[7] Other members of the cast were assembled over the months before the show opened, some just before the final rehearsal period in New York. They included Carole Shelley as Madame Morrible, Norbert Leo Butz as Fiyero, Michelle Federer as Nessarose, Christopher Fitzgerald as Boq, William Youmans as Doctor Dillamond, and Joel Grey as the Wizard.

A crucial member of the creative team was director Joe Mantello, who came aboard in July 2001 after a difficult search that involved a number of the prominent Broadway musical directors.[8] In addition to being a major presence in the auditions, staging the show, and assisting the actors in exploring their characters and making choices on how to present material, Mantello led the design team in assembling the memorable production.[9] His lieutenants were set designer Eugene Lee, lighting designer Kenneth Posner, sound designer Tony Meola, costume designer Susan Hilferty, makeup designer Joseph Dulude II, wig designer Tom Watson, and choreographer Wayne Cilento. Mantello's background is in acting and directing, meaning that a choreographer was needed not only for dancing but also to assist with staging the musical scenes. Nobody would mistake *Wicked* for a dancing show, but Cilento worked extensively with Mantello toward a state where "you don't know where the direction starts and the choreography ends."[10] The choreographer's work is obvious in numbers like "Dancing through Life," but Cilento's influence is present whenever the chorus is on stage and in many other situations. The show takes place in another world, and Cilento made his choreography help create its style, noting "that everything I did would have to be a little bit strange."[11]

Wicked is a huge production, and Mantello was concerned that every element would not come together seamlessly. Schwartz, on the other hand, was more concerned about the writing and wanted to conclude the workshops with an intimate production of the show somewhere outside of New York, after which he and Holzman could rewrite as necessary. Mantello finally convinced the creative team that they needed a full-scale production out of town to make sure that all design elements were desirable and compatible.[12] This resulted in a run at the Curran Theater in San Francisco in June 2003. Schwartz accepted this choice with the proviso that they would shut down the production during July and part of August to give them a chance to do their revisions, a choice that producer David Stone told Schwartz cost $1.5 million to keep everyone under contract for that period.[13]

After securing rights for Maguire's novel, Schwartz and Holzman had to decide what story they wished to tell. The novel is a dark tale and many aspects of the story changed in the musical, partly because a Broadway audience would never have warmed to a musical that closely followed Maguire's plot. Schwartz and Holzman took Maguire's characters and the basis of his story and crafted their own story, including such profound changes as keeping Glinda's significant presence in the plot throughout (making the show a tale of the two young women) and allowing Elphaba to survive at the end so that she could be with Fiyero. Schwartz prepared a scenario for the show in September 1998 that already included a surprisingly close outline to what happened in the show that opened five years later,[14] but changes that did take place were difficult to finalize and included surprising detours. The first act was the stickler, especially the plot-heavy sequence that finally became "Dancing through Life" and trying to decide what Elphaba's grand cause would be that would place her in conflict with the Wizard. The creators finally decided that she would be an advocate for Talking Animals, who were being persecuted by the Wizard and his minions. This decision gave final shape to the role of Doctor Dillamond and how Elphaba would become an outlaw. Schwartz and Holzman, however, tried to maintain focus on the two women and their friendship, even as other momentous events take place. Revisions, mostly in the first act, took place through the summer of 2003 and right up until the show opened, and continued beyond the time that *Wicked* had been installed as a Broadway hit. When the original Wizard, Joel Grey, an old hoofer, left the show and singer George Hearn entered the role, the writers made changes that took into account their different stage personas, and later changes were made for other actors in the role. Incredibly, one can find emendations in a script dated 5 December 2006, more than three years after the show had opened in New York. Schwartz has always been ready to revise his shows, but his work on *Wicked* with Winnie Holzman seems especially relentless given its immediate status as a hit.

Schwartz's compositional process in *Wicked* can be described in considerable detail—more than for most other shows in this study—and what emerges in the lengthy chapter on music in *"Wicked": A Musical Biography* is a composer/lyricist who often reacted to a problem by revising or rewriting a song. As demonstrated in detail in a textbox toward the beginning of Chapter 5 in my previous book, the following song placements had especially arduous histories.[15]

Act 1

"Opening"—at least four versions exist of various lengths

"The Wizard and I"—wrote an entirely different song called "Making Good" for which lyrics and melodic line existed by 30 August 2000; wrote "The Wizard and I" in October/November 2002 and there were later revisions

"What Is This Feeling?"—original song was "Bad Situation" (two versions), then "Far Be It from Me," and two versions of "What Is This Feeling?"

"Something Bad"—replaced "As If by Magic," which occurred later in the act and also involved Doctor Dillamond

"Dancing through Life"—earlier songs for the placement included "Who Could Say No to You?" (30 August 2000), "Easy as Winkie Wine" (undated), "We Deserve Each Other" (12 March 2001, and segments stayed in the show), "The Emerald City Stomp" (21 November 2001), "Which Way's The Party?" (two versions exist and aspects appear in sources between 20 July 2002 and 31 March 2003), and "Dancing through Life" (lyrics appear in script from 28 July 2003)

"A Sentimental Man"—final version was a conflation of this song and another called "The Chance to Fly"

"Defying Gravity"—placement was originally two songs: "For Goodness Sake" (lyrics existed on 30 August 2000) that was deleted and lyrics for "I Hope You're Happy" existed in a script from 12 March 2001, and a few lines from it became part of "Defying Gravity"

Act 2

"Thank Goodness"—preceded by "Happy Healing Day" (lyrics in script from 12 March 2001), some lyrics of which appeared in "Thank Goodness" (lyrics in October 2002 script)

"Wicked Witch of the East"—preceded by "Step by Step by Step" (lyrics and vocal line existed 30 August 2000) and "We Deserve Each Other" (lyrics in 12 November 2001 script); final scene emerged late, much of it in 16 September 2003 script included elements that had existed for months, especially material from "We Deserve Each Other"

A number of songs not mentioned here also went through extensive revisions as Schwartz and Holzman continued to tweak their work. What could be gleaned of Schwartz's creative process and revisions from the drafts, scores, and scripts consulted for the study appears in *"Wicked": A Musical*

Biography, offering extensive documentation of what Schwartz went through writing a score for a musical play that took five years to complete.[16]

Schwartz decided to craft for *Wicked* a thematically unified score, a process that he had explored completely for the first time with *Children of Eden* and that he considered crucial when writing his opera *Séance on a Wet Afternoon*. The musical styles that he brought together for the songs in *Wicked* vary considerably, some of them chosen to help describe a character. The Wizard's songs, for example, including "A Sentimental Man" and "Wonderful," carry touches of ragtime and vaudeville music, placing him in that era in the United States. "Dear Old Shiz" sounds like a creaky school song, "Popular" verges on a country sound in places, and the stylistic catalog continues. The composer tied this together with recurring motives and powerful reprises.[17] The two most important motives appear in the opening number. The first, sounding immediately, describes Elphaba as "Wicked," or at least that is how she comes to be identified. Based here in A minor, it is several loud chords in a high range set to a syncopated rhythm. Schwartz took the material from the accompaniment of "As Long as You're Mine" (a song that he wrote in the 1970s), which Elphaba sings with Fiyero in Act 2. The theme's identification with Elphaba becomes obvious during her birth (original cast recording [OCR], track 1, 4'53"ff), and it recurs several times as Elphaba takes her forced trip to the dark side, such as in the first scene with the Wizard as she finds out that her magic has painfully provided wings for many monkeys (not on the OCR) and in Act 2 in "No Good Deed" as she screams Fiyero's name (track 16, 1'59"ff).

The second important motive is "Unlimited," Elphaba's motto and hopes for her future (OCR, track 1, 0'39"–0'54"). Schwartz opened the theme with the first seven notes of "Somewhere over the Rainbow." The rhythm disguises the connection, and he continues the motive with fresh material that is similarly romantic. The theme follows Elphaba on her journey, starting during "The Wizard and I" (her "I want" song, track 3, 3'39"ff), as she tries to enlist Glinda in her mission during "Defying Gravity" (track 11, 3'00"ff), and in "For Good" (track 18, opening) where she must admit to Glinda that she is "limited" and her friend must finish the job of taking Oz back from the Wizard. There are other motives, but these two have the most significant roles in tying the score to the plot.

Schwartz used reprises intelligently in *Wicked*, usually small sections of songs in dramatically sensitive places, a process that becomes more frequent toward the end of the show. For example, after Elphaba and Glinda sing "For Good," the remainder of the show includes the following repetitions of earlier material:[18]

"The Melting" (no. 26 in the score, not on OCR) opens with a bit of "No One Mourns the Wicked" and proceeds through the "Unlimited" motive as Elphaba melts and finally an instrumental setting of part of "For Good."

"A Sentimental Man—Reprise" (no. 27, not on OCR) begins with a pre-recorded excerpt from the Wizard's seduction song to Elphaba's mother in the opening number (track 1, 4'12"ff) as he realizes his paternity, and then he sings a bit of "A Sentimental Man" followed by instrumental underscoring from "A Sentimental Man" and "Wonderful" as Glinda relieves him of power and he leaves dejectedly.

The "Finale" (no. 28, not all of which is on the OCR) repeats twenty-four measures of the opening number (track 1, 1'00"–1'29") that includes bitonal instrumental music and choral settings of "Good news! She's dead!" As Fiyero reaches the castle and retrieves Elphaba, the underscoring includes "As Long as You're Mine," "For Good," and the "Wicked" motive. The instrumental material that opens the "Finale" on the OCR is from "The Wizard and I" (setting the lyrics "a celebration throughout Oz," reprised in "Wonderful") and "For Good—Intro" ("Now it's up to you"), and then the ensemble enters with "No One Mourns the Wicked," material of which dominates the remainder while Glinda and Elphaba reprise a bit of "For Good." The final segment is the same as from the opening number, an evocation of the tritone that closes Bernstein's score to *West Side Story*,[19] tying Schwartz's score for his musical play to one of Broadway's iconic works and recognizing the older composer's profound influence on his music.

A place where Schwartz reprises a larger chunk of a song in *Wicked* is "I'm Not That Girl," sung by Elphaba in Act 1 when she realizes that Fiyero, for whom she has developed feelings, is in love with Glinda.[20] The tables have turned in Act 2, and the brief reprise of an A section of the original AABA tune comes from Glinda, who has just seen the man she was about to marry fly away with Elphaba. It is perhaps the ideal musical gesture for the moment and a powerful reminder of what music can do in a well-crafted musical play.

The principal orchestrator of Schwartz's score was William David Brohn, who has enjoyed a long career on Broadway and in related fields.[21] *Wicked*, however, includes a number of songs that depended upon the sounds of popular music, meaning that a substantial portion of the musical arranging required close attention to the guitars, bass, drum kit, and synthesizers in a style with which Brohn has not had wide experience. Therefore, the orchestration of *Wicked* began with Stephen Oremus, the show's music supervisor, and Alex Lacamoire, assistant music director, working with Schwartz on scoring each song for the two guitars, bass, drums, and most of the material for the three keyboards.[22] (Oremus worked with Schwartz on the score from September 2000 on, playing the piano at each of the workshops and assisting with keyboard arrangements and vocal scoring. Lacamoire also helped with incidental music and other aspects, but Oremus notes that Schwartz approved every note in the score.[23]) Much of this pop scoring took place during the summer of 2003, and then they shared this material with Brohn, who added parts for the other musicians, with assistance from Andy Barrett who programmed the synthesizers. The orchestra in the Broadway pit was twenty-three musicians, including two violins, viola, cello, two trumpets, two trombones, two horns, four reeds, three keyboard players, two guitars, bass, drummer, another percussionist, and harp.[24] The reed players, guitarists, bassist, and percussionist each played more than one instrument—sometimes far more—widely enriching the palette available to Brohn and allowing the *Wicked* orchestra to imitate a symphony orchestra (such as in the ballroom introduction to "Wonderful" [track 13, opening]) and produce a wide variety of popular sounds, such as the bubblegum rock of "Popular" and the disco-inspired sounds of "Dancing through Life." Both Schwartz and Brohn believe that they broke new ground in *Wicked* with the ways that various guitars and synthesizers were integrated into the orchestrations.[25] The initial orchestrations were for the Broadway production, with changes made for London and touring versions, and the orchestra became smaller as the tours continued with synthesizers being used to make up for the removal of acoustic instruments.[26] In Japan, the initial production in Tokyo included an eighteen-piece orchestra, but in Osaka the accompaniment was prerecorded and the show functioned without a conductor.[27]

The critical reaction to *Wicked* was mixed.[28] Critics often singled out for praise were Chenoweth and Menzel, and many liked the aspects of the production, but some of the most prominent reviewers were negative about the book and score. Many critics praised what Holzman and Schwartz brought to the production, but the public approval of the show has outstripped what one would expect if only the reviews were consulted in assembling a reception history for *Wicked*.

Indeed, the show has become an international phenomenon. The Broadway production surpassed 4,100 performances in September 2013 while still drawing nearly full houses.[29] The first national tour began in 2005 and the second in 2009, both continuing in 2013.[30] There have been lengthy sit-down productions in Chicago, Los Angeles, and San Francisco. It opened in the West End on 27 September 2006 and continues to run in 2013, and versions based on translations of the Broadway version have also played in various cities in Germany, Australia, Japan, and the Netherlands.[31] The first production that was not based on the Broadway production opened in Helsinki in August 2010. Some perspective is required—in terms of international success and length of runs, *Wicked* has yet to rival *Les Misérables* or *The Phantom of the Opera*—but it is by far Schwartz's most successful musical and the major international hit in the genre for the beginning of the new century.

CHAPTER THIRTEEN

~

Séance on a Wet Afternoon

The genesis of this study occurred between 2005 and 2007, when Stephen Schwartz's career took a fascinating turn. When asked about future major projects in 2005, with *Wicked* ensconced at the Gershwin Theater, Schwartz did not report interest in more Broadway musicals, but noted that he might be interested in writing an opera.[1] This was not a simple decision. Opera and musicals like *Wicked* are cousins, but their cultural niches and accompanying expectations significantly differ. Contemporary operas sell tickets to a different public than do Broadway musicals, and different critics review them. Composing an opera placed Schwartz in the crosshairs of commentators who tend to doubt that a creator of popular theatrical scores would have the musical gravitas to write a successful opera.

Schwartz had experience with classical genres. He studied classical piano as a child and loves opera. Our discussions drifted into classical music, and he has a good understanding of past styles. Despite the strong influence of folk music and various types of pop, Schwartz has stated that "classical remains my music of choice."[2] When describing orchestration for *Wicked*, Schwartz requested that passages sound like classical orchestration, such as a scene in Mussorgsky's *Boris Godunov*.[3] Schwartz has also made use of classical influences in his shows, especially *The Baker's Wife*, *Children of Eden*, and *Wicked*.

Schwartz, however, found composing an opera to be a hugely different task than writing a musical, especially conceiving melodies for operatic voices and orchestrating, a task that he shared for *Séance on a Wet Afternoon* with William David Brohn, orchestrator of *Wicked*. Schwartz admitted in

277

late 2008, when he had been working on the score for more than a year, "I didn't really know that much about opera voices from a technical point of view when I began this, so this has been a crash course, and I'm learning about where they sit comfortably."[4] In interviews, Schwartz also described with relish what he was learning from Brohn about orchestration.

Schwartz is accustomed to collaborating on musical theater pieces, and he found writing an opera to be "lonelier,"[5] partly because he served as his own librettist. He did, however, work with fellow creative spirits. In addition to Brohn, Schwartz sought assistance from his son Scott, the opera's stage director, who served as dramaturge and sounding board for libretto and music. Valéry Ryvkin, who conducted the premiere at the Opera Santa Barbara, was a useful source on how to notate classical music, on writing for singers, and the operatic world. Schwartz also collaborated with his main singers— especially Lauren Flanigan and Kim Josephson—allowing them to tell him what would work best in their voices and changing vocal lines according to their suggestions. Another important figure was executive producer Michael Jackowitz, upon whom Schwartz depended to coordinate activities on both coasts.[6] Jackowitz is a producer of musical theater both in California and New York and for national tours, and he continues to promote possible new productions for *Séance on a Wet Afternoon*.

Jackowitz has written that he attended New York City Opera performances with Schwartz between 2000 and 2003, and was surprised by the Broadway figure's knowledge of classical music.[7] They spoke about a possible opera from Schwartz. Jackowitz arranged a commission for his friend after moving to Santa Barbara. The producer sold Opera Santa Barbara general director Steven Sharpe and his board on the idea before pitching it to Schwartz. After attending a Opera Santa Barbara production of Puccini in winter 2006, Schwartz accepted their commission, the funds provided by a local couple. The composer chose the film *Séance on a Wet Afternoon* and spent three years conceiving the libretto, writing music, testing his material in workshops, and taking a crash course in orchestration with Brohn.[8] Scott Schwartz, working with noted designer Heidi Ettinger, supervised the conception and construction of the set. All of these preparations were for a run that lasted three performances because the Opera Santa Barbara could only sell that many tickets. Although the premiere was not in a major operatic center, Schwartz's name drew attention and national reviewers attended. How Schwartz and the opera made it to that point is a compelling story, told here primarily through the eyes of Schwartz and his collaborators.

The Libretto and Its Models

Schwartz wrote the libretto first. The story involves a medium, Myra, and her easily manipulated husband, Bill, kidnapping a wealthy couple's daughter and holding her until the police would be flummoxed. At that point Myra would emerge, use her "powers" to help find the girl, and become famous. Things go wrong and the girl dies. Schwartz knew the story from Bryan Forbes's 1964 film, which starred Kim Stanley and Richard Attenborough. Schwartz stated in an interview, "There are so many reasons why I thought this was a good subject for an opera: the story, the atmosphere, the characters, the age of the leads, which . . . makes available roles to people who are too old now to be doing Musetta [in Puccini's *La bohème*] anymore."[9] The story includes psychological drama,[10] a compelling plot, and memorable characters. The composer/librettist's models were the film and its predecessor, Mark McShane's 1961 novel by the same name.[11] Schwartz acquired rights for both novel and film, basing his work primarily on Forbes's screenplay. He said that the libretto was 75 percent based on the film with the other quarter emanating from the novel or his own ideas.[12]

McShane filled his novel with detailed descriptions of Bill, Myra, and their crime. Myra works as a medium and cherishes her ability; McShane states that she seldom actually finds contacts in the afterlife, running her séances with sensitivity and mind-reading ability. The novel includes no mention of a dead child who serves as Myra's conduit to the afterlife, part of both film and opera. Bill is convinced of his wife's gift and conceives "The Plan." They believe that nothing will go wrong because Myra has envisioned their success, but after Bill successfully kidnaps the girl and picks up the ransom money, little goes right. Compared to the opera's characters, McShane's Bill and Myra are mostly concerned with themselves. Myra is unsympathetic, with no concern for the child and little for her husband. Her sanity in the novel is never in doubt, unlike in the film and opera. In the novel, Bill is concerned about their victim's welfare and grieves for the child when he accidentally kills her, but his personal comfort and hopes for "The Plan" are more important.

There are other significant similarities and differences between novel and opera that illuminate how Schwartz adapted the story. The novel opens with Myra and Bill executing "The Plan"; there is no opening séance as in the opera. In the opera Bill is a henpecked husband, but in the novel he is an equal participant in the abduction. He is not healthy in any version, suffering from severe asthma and other disabilities. In the novel, Myra plays a nurse and is the only person who interacts with the child (named Adriana, as in the opera); Bill stays out of sight and does not impersonate a doctor, a role he performs in the opera. In the novel Myra manipulates the child and strikes her when necessary. She does not appreciate children and "could never understand why they acted so childishly."[13] Myra's interactions with the child are different in the novel than in the opera because Adriana is only six; in the opera, where she must sing, Schwartz presents her as a twelve-year-old. (When asked about this in an interview, the composer was surprised to be reminded that Adriana was only six in the novel, correctly remembering her as older in the film, where she might be nine or ten.[14]) Bill and Myra in the novel read the newspaper each day to see if they are getting publicity, an interesting parallel to Schwartz's three scenes with reporters. When Myra takes breakfast to Adriana the first time, as in the opera (where Bill joins her as the doctor), she tells the "patient" that she has German measles; the child responds, "Had it." Myra changes it to "double German measles," pleasing Adriana when she tells her that the disease is "very special."[15] Myra goes to the Clayton's house (Adriana's parents) in the novel to tell them about her "dream," the content of which is similar to the opera. In the book Myra senses Mr. Clayton's strong psychic abilities (something that Schwartz had her comment on in an early version of the libretto), although Clayton is unaware of his powers; however, as in the opera, Mrs. Clayton is more interested in what Myra has to say, and Mr. Clayton is skeptical of her.

The police play a more prominent role in the novel. After Myra returns home from the Claytons, police are sent to check her out there, and the couple remains silently inside until the police leave. Soon thereafter Bill, losing his nerve, suggests that they take Adriana somewhere and call the police to say where she is. As in the opera, when Bill makes a similar suggestion, Myra insists that "The Plan" continue. In a long sequence in the novel of which Schwartz made no use, Bill hides the drugged Adriana in the sidecar of his motorcycle and drives her all over town the next day so that she will not be in the house when the police return. He also picks up the ransom money at the Piccadilly Circus Underground station. Bill runs out of gas on his way home and is assisted by a policeman, who accepts Bill's explanation that the noises coming from his covered sidecar are caused by two cats. While they are gone, Myra showed another policeman their empty house.

Myra holds her usual Wednesday afternoon séance, and in book, film, and opera, Rita Clayton attends. Myra tells her that Adriana is safe and will be found the next day, but Adriana wakes up and hears her mother. Trying to silence her, in the novel Bill clumsily smothers the child, very different than the reason she dies in the opera. At the moment of her death, she takes over Myra's consciousness and the medium screams "Die!" (This also occurs at the end of the opera's first act, when Myra follows Arthur's lead in using the word, foreshadowing her insistence early in Act 2 that Arthur wants Adriana to join him in death.[16]) Later in the book, Myra is pleased that she was able to sense what happened in the other room. Bill lies to Myra, telling her that Adriana died falling out of bed. They decide that Bill will take Adriana's body to some woods and place it near a landmark where Myra can "sense" it, but when he arrives at the location Boy Scouts are nearby; they find the body immediately as Bill scuffles with one of the adults. After Bill arrives home, Myra is distraught about their frustrated plan. She calls Mr. Clayton to provide her "vision," but when she calls the newspaper, they already know about the body. Myra hopes to plant the money and "predict" where to find it, but she learns that Mr. Clayton and another policeman named Watts (the inspector's name in the opera) are coming for a séance, prompted by their suspicion. Myra discovers that Watts has great psychic presence, and she is anxious for the encounter. She quickly goes further in the next realm than she ever has. Adriana speaks through her, exposing the plot and her murder.[17] As in the opera, Watts asks Bill where the money is. The novel ends with Myra confirming her psychic accomplishment with Bill, who congratulates her. Mr. Clayton continues to hold Myra's hand, staring at her.

The screenplay of *Séance on a Wet Afternoon* (1964) includes many lines that appear in the opera libretto, and others that inspired Schwartz to write arias. Notable differences, however, exist between film and opera, especially the ending. The creators of the film did not want to conclude as darkly as the book: the abducted girl survives, rendering the final séance almost meaningless. It is a major disappointment in what is otherwise a gripping film noir. An overview of the black-and-white film will show what Schwartz used in his opera, and how the opera differs from the film and novel.

Like the opera, the film opens with a séance. Schwartz instills his longer scene with character development and humor. Once alone, Myra and Bill go to Arthur's room, where Myra talks about "The Plan" and how the room looks like a hospital. Early in the film she seems disconnected from reality; Myra is less delusional at the opening of the opera. In the film they go downstairs to the living room, where Myra puts on her record (a movement from Mendelssohn's *Hear Our Prayer*), later turning it off but arguing with Bill that he must have done so. The scene's dialogue includes ideas that appear in the opera: disputing Bill's doubts about "The Plan," saying how much her husband needs her, noting how "We've had so much sorrow" (a major lyrical moment for Myra in the opera), and saying how she performed as a psychic for her family as a child. She mentions that Arthur conceived "The Plan," but the boy never appears in the film. Bill allows that he "mustn't disappoint" Arthur, a line that also appears in the libretto.

Forbes showed the abduction in the film; the victim's name is Amanda Clayton. The film's next scene involves the ransom note, which Schwartz placed before the kidnapping. Myra asks Bill to read it. The letter's text is different than what Schwartz used, but in both versions they edit it and Myra insists that they must threaten to kill the girl if the family fails to follow instructions. Myra cuts off a lock of Amanda's hair and brings it to Bill, who is preparing the note with letters cut from the newspaper. She finds him reluctant, but if he agrees with the ends, then he must support the means, a line that also appears in the opera. She makes Bill say that he loves her and needs her and that he wants her to return safely from mailing the letter, also in the opera. After she leaves, Bill calls upon God and Jesus to intervene, which Bill sings loudly in the opera.

The newspaper arrives the next morning, and they find a small story about the missing girl. Myra's first interaction with Amanda in the film includes several lines that are in the opera. Bill watches Myra through a hole in the wall and confronts her for not telling Amanda that she would be going home soon, but Myra responds that he does not understand how adaptable children are, like Arthur was at the same age, another of her delusions.

Myra goes to the Claytons' house to describe her "dream," a scene that bears resemblance to what Schwartz set. After she leaves in the film there is a brief scene between the Claytons that does not appear in book or opera. Back home, as in the book but not the opera, the police visit Myra and Bill, but they turn out the lights and the police leave. Bill goes to their victim dressed as a doctor in both film and opera, and she tells him he does not smell like a doctor because he carries no odor of peppermint. As he returns to Myra, Bill suggests that they return Amanda now because the police will return, but Myra has already figured out what to do, and she tells her husband, "I have to do this little lie, Bill, so they can hear the whole truth." Schwartz turned this line into one of Myra's major arias.

On the Underground, Bill looks at Clayton's classified ad in the paper that tells them he has received the ransom note, and later he phones Clayton with instructions. As the police rush to the phone booth where they traced the call, Bill gets on a bus.

The next day Bill takes Amanda, drugged, with him in the covered sidecar of his motorcycle. The film follows most of the sequence of events as in the book, switching between Bill picking up ransom money and Myra showing an inspector through their empty house. Upon Bill's return, Amanda is running a temperature—a departure from the novel—and Bill thinks they should call a doctor. Myra mocks her husband, speculating on what they might tell the doctor. They buy medicine the next day.

Myra insists on holding her usual Wednesday séance, and Mrs. Clayton attends. As in the opera, Myra considers this useful. Bill stays in the room with Amanda, who calls out, but Bill does not smother the girl. During the séance, Myra stands up, collapses, and says, "Die!" This seems unmotivated in the film. Before she leaves, Mrs. Clayton tells Bill that his wife made her hopeful when she came to share her dream, the same reason that she seeks out Myra in the opera.

Myra has recovered from collapsing after everyone has left, and she has wonderful news for Bill, prefacing it by saying, "It is so bright after a séance. Brightness seems to fall from the air." Schwartz used this idea in Myra's opening aria in Act 2. She announces that Arthur wants Amanda to die and stay with him. Bill confronts Myra in the film, asserting that "The Plan" was her idea and not Arthur's, who was stillborn. Like in the opera, he forces Myra to admit this, but she defiantly insists that she sees Arthur and speaks with him. (In the opera this exchange occurs after Myra murders the girl.) Bill left Amanda's door unlocked and she comes out, seeing that this is a house, not a hospital, and also seeing Myra and Bill without their masks. Myra tells Bill that he knows what he must do, and then they will be "safe forever."

At this point the film departs from McShane's novel by allowing the child to survive. Some might prefer this ending, but the chilling conclusion of the novel (and opera) occurs as Myra has her first successful contact with a dead spirit in the final séance, when her victim exposes the crime. By comparison, the film's dénouement lacks cohesion. After Myra tells Bill that he must ensure their safety, we see him laying Amanda's motionless body in a misty forest. Scouts and a leader around a campfire are nearby. The film returns to the house with a silent Bill listening to Myra; prompted, he again tells her that he loves her. Three policemen arrive. Superintendent Walsh informs Myra that he is interested in psychic phenomena and convinces her to hold a séance. From an unknown source, Myra reveals the crime. At the end, Myra pretends that she holds a baby. Walsh asks Bill where the money is, and Bill tells him where and says he left Amanda where the scouts would find her, and asks if she is well. Walsh nods his head. Myra asks Bill if she did "it right," and Bill assures her that she did. Here the film ends, without a suggestion as to how Bill managed to deceive the perceptive Myra.

Schwartz says his changes to the screenplay included material "I invented because I was changing the story, or it's stuff that I lyricized by giving it more of a song structure or aria structure."[18] Schwartz decided that his lyrics should include rhymes, but not the profusion found in his musicals. The decision to move the story from London to San Francisco occurred because Schwartz did not wish to deal with English accents and colloquialisms, meaning that he needed an American city "with lousy weather."[19]

The first libretto available for this study dates from September 2007, by which time Schwartz had experienced a workshop of Act 1 at the Seagle Music Colony (described later). In this source, Schwartz identified Act 2 as a "rough draft" and "pre-libretto." Most of the action in this version remained in the opera, but the order of the events proved flexible; by the time Schwartz finished a version dated December 2008, the scene structure was significantly different. This is summarized in Table 13.1, a comparison of these two librettos. There were no substantive changes to Act 1, but Act 2 remained a work in progress.

More specific comparisons between the two librettos demonstrate other ways that the opera changed. The more assertive Bill of McShane's novel mostly disappeared in the film until the confrontation over Myra wanting to murder their victim, and Schwartz also made Bill pliable in his relations with Myra. Schwartz added a note of hesitance for Bill after Myra sings "One Little Lie," placing "(after a moment's pause)" (2008 libretto, p. 11) before Bill asks when Arthur wants "The Plan" to start. In the earlier libretto (2007, p. 13), during her first act duet with Arthur, Myra showed more doubt about her psychic abilities, stating that she has "never been good when tested"; Arthur reassures her. That duet was designed to humanize Myra,[20] but Schwartz made her more certain of herself in the final version. Scenes 2 and 3 with reporters and Adriana and Myra in the "hospital" room were tightened up between the two librettos with lines reordered and repetitions deleted in Scene 2 and the order of the dialogue changed in Scene 3. Scene 4 at the Claytons saw several alterations between the two versions, such as polishing lyrics for the quartet "Awful/Careful/Heedful/Hopeful" and various details cut. The reporters' material in Scene 5 changed between the sources with unnecessary lines removed (2007, p. 35). In Scene 6, the second séance, Schwartz tightened up the lyrics to "Lucky," and Myra makes Bill say "I love you" before he goes to be with Adriana during the séance (2007, p. 39), deleted by 2008. There were also a few changes in the séance to add to the drama and changes in stage directions because the conception for the stage set had changed. In the film and earlier libretto, Arthur's room and the séance room are next door to each other, but now Adriana is upstairs.

As may be seen in Table 13.1, similar events occur in Act 2 in both versions of the libretto, but the scene order and arrangement changes. In the 2007 libretto, Schwartz placed most of the action in Scene 1, including Bill taking Adriana's body to Glen Canyon. Spreading the action out more evenly adds to the dramatic tension, especially as Bill leaves Adriana unconscious from chloroform in his effort to fake her death. Scene 3 is at the Claytons, and then Myra finds Adriana alive in Scene 4 and smothers her.

Bill then confronts Myra, which belongs later in the act than in Scene 1, as it appeared in 2007.

A few details illuminate other important ways that Act 2 changed during these fifteen months. Schwartz added Myra's opening solo "Brightness Falls" in Scene 1, inspired by a line in the film, as noted earlier. An indication of how advanced Schwartz was on major set pieces by the fall of 2007 is that there were only small changes in Bill's aria "You Didn't Know Her" by the end of 2008. The main change occurred in the second verse, where Bill observed in 2007 (p. 52) that Myra was "fragile" when he tried to leave her, a word that Schwartz removed. Mrs. Clayton's aria "Wondrous Things" changed more, becoming less verbose but conveying a similar sense. In 2007 (p. 59) she describes her belief in psychic "phenomena" that her husband does not accept, but by late 2008 (p. 52) this had been simplified to her belief "in the miraculous," caused by her love for her daughter.

The third libretto available for this study was from May 2009, representing a fairly final version. Comparison of this libretto with December 2008 yielded only five minor changes. After Bill has ushered attendees of the opening séance out of the house, Schwartz added in the stage directions that Bill should stand in the rain, "as if gathering his courage" (2009, p. 5). Bill knows that he is about to discuss "The Plan" with Myra, and Schwartz wanted the audience to sense his reluctance. In Act 2, Scene 3, as the Claytons and Watts debate whether or not they should attend Myra's séance, Schwartz inserted two lines for Mrs. Clayton where she tells her husband that the last séance gave her some hope, and a bit later she wonders what Myra meant when she said "Die" in the second séance (2009, p. 54). These additions more precisely define Mrs. Clayton's feelings before she sings "Wondrous Things." In Act 2, Scene 3, when Myra discovers that Bill did not kill Adriana, she becomes angrier in the later libretto (2009, p. 57) and reminds herself that he let Adriana see his face. Arthur reappears and offers to help her finish the task, which refocuses Myra. At the beginning of Scene 6, Myra is more agitated in 2009 than in 2008 when she cannot sense Arthur's presence (2009, p. 63), putting on her favorite recording to seek tranquility. She sings "Empty" (deleted after Santa Barbara) and goes to Arthur's room, more activity before Watts and the Claytons arrive. (Work continued on this segment with a new aria that Schwartz wrote for the New York premiere in 2011, described later.) After Watts and the Claytons arrive, Myra stalls until Bill returns, because she has not yet heard near what landmark he has left the body. Schwartz added to Myra's lines, and she says to those awaiting the séance, "And this is so important, everything needs to be right" (2009, p. 64). She pleads that Bill is always in the house for séances. In the 2008 version, she stated simply,

Table 13.1. Scene Comparison of Schwartz's Librettos for *Séance on a Wet Afternoon*, September 2007 and December 2008

Libretto, September 2007	*Libretto, December 2008*
(Act 2 identified by Schwartz as "rough draft" and "pre-libretto")	
Act 1	Act 1
Scene 1—Myra and Bill's house	Scene 1—Myra and Bill's house; similar events and material
Séance 1; Myra and Bill discuss "The Plan" ("'Tis My Faraway Laddie"—Irish tenor and "One Little Lie"—Myra); Myra discusses her hopes for fame with Arthur ("It's Always Been True"—duet)	
Scene 2—reporters describe abduction of Adriana; acted out by Bill, Adriana, and Clayton family chauffeur	Scene 2—similar events and material
Scene 3—Arthur's bedroom	Scene 3—Arthur's bedroom; similar events and material
First interaction between Myra, Bill, and Adriana; Bill goes to kitchen and prays for Myra to be stopped	
Scene 4—Claytons' mansion	Scene 4—Claytons' mansion; similar events and material
Claytons and Inspector Watts argue over lack of leads; Myra arrives and tells her "dream"; "Longfellow" (Bill as the abductor) calls ("Awful/Careful/Heedful/Hopeful" follows); Claytons sing "Adriana"; Watts ushers Myra out ("Truth to Tell")	
Scene 5—outside Clayton mansion	Scene 5—outside Clayton mansion; similar events and material
Reporters (with Bill singing about his reaction) describe exchange of ransom	
Scene 6—Myra and Bill's house	Scene 6—Myra and Bill's house; similar events and material
Myra expresses happiness over their progress and cares for Adriana ("Lucky"); Séance 2 with Bill upstairs calming Adriana ("All through the Night"); séance ends with Arthur shouting "Die!" through Myra	

Act 2

Scene 1—Myra and Bill's house
Myra tells Bill that Arthur wants them to murder Adriana; Bill "agrees" but tries to fake her death ("You Didn't Know Her"); Myra finds Adriana alive and murders her as Arthur urges her on; Bill discovers body and confronts Myra, forcing her to admit that Arthur was stillborn; Bill takes Adriana's body to Glen Canyon; Myra phones Claytons

Scene 2—Claytons' mansion
Claytons and Watts debate Myra's offer of special séance (Mrs. Clayton sings "Wondrous Things")

Scene 3—outside Myra and Bill's house
Reporters comment on new developments, such as psychic entering case

Scene 4—Myra and Bill's house
Myra is agitated because she cannot sense Arthur; Claytons and Watts arrive for special séance; Séance 3 where Adriana speaks through Myra and reveals her murder; Myra and Arthur happily together at the end

Act 2

Scene 1—Myra and Bill's house
Myra appreciates the clarity of the air after a séance ("Brightness Falls"); Myra tells Bill that Arthur wants them to murder Adriana; Bill goes to Adriana; Myra phones Claytons

Scene 2—Myra and Bill's house
Bill goes to Adriana and tries to fake her death ("You Didn't Know Her")

Scene 3—Claytons' mansion
Claytons and Watts debate Myra's offer of special séance (Mrs. Clayton sings "Wondrous Things")

Scene 4—Myra and Bill's house
Myra finds Adriana alive and murders her as Arthur urges her on; Bill discovers body and confronts Myra, forcing her to admit that Arthur was born dead; Bill takes Adriana's body to Glen Canyon

Scene 5—outside Myra and Bill's house
Similar events and material as 2007, Scene 3

Scene 6—Myra and Bill's house
Similar events and material as 2007, Scene 4

"This is so important" (2008, p. 59). It is with such tweaking and honing that Schwartz gradually completed his libretto.

Composing the Score

Schwartz found himself writing music for his opera with different methods. For musical theater, he tends to improvise at the piano; he states, "Actual songs exist in my fingers and my head before they get written down."[21] In my book "Wicked": A Musical Biography, consideration of music included handwritten drafts of songs, but Schwartz reports that he only wrote down a song, or a section of it, once he had figured most of it out at the piano. With computers and software, Schwartz often skips the handwritten version and plays the music into the computer. Sometimes when he starts a project, Schwartz has an idea for a recurring motive that he will write down.

The way that he wrote Séance on a Wet Afternoon he calls "the exact opposite" of his musical theater practice, because he conceived the music at the piano and wrote down almost every note.[22] Either Schwartz or a copyist then entered the piano/vocal score into the computer. A major part of the newness in operatic composition for Schwartz was composing for a different type of voices. He described the challenge in November 2008:

> From the point of view of vocal writing, it has felt much more like terra incognita than I anticipated. . . . It's much more technical. . . . The voices make very different demands from musical theater and I really had to learn about that. There's the issue of the passaggio [the range between chest and head voice] and the tessitura is completely different—I don't ever think about that working in musical theater. . . . I know if you need to hear the singer over the orchestra, you can just boost the mike.[23]

Clearly Schwartz's process of writing vocal music changed, and he often made adjustments according to feedback from singers.

From the beginning the composer intended to unify his score dramatically with various motives. He stated, "That's the fun thing about writing opera: you just keep recycling the motives."[24] His manipulation of motives in the opera is "more elaborate" than in the shows, such as Children of Eden and Wicked.[25]

As noted in Chapter 6, as Schwartz prepared to write the score for The Baker's Wife, he listened to and played music by Debussy, Ravel, and others. In preparing to write Séance he was less deliberate about his models, because in the earlier show he simply wished to evoke France.[26] The first musical influence that Schwartz identified for *Séance* was for scenes where reporters proclaim the latest headlines. He wanted their music to sound like pop in 1962.[27] (These scenes are marked by strong rhythms with syncopation and simple, angular melodies, but dissonant harmonies; one would not immediately compare it to rock and roll from the time.) Schwartz remarked that his principal influences for the remainder of the opera were "not clear to me at all," but he studied many operas "to listen to how the voice is set, just from a technical point of view."[28] Schwartz hears in his score influence from some of his favorite composers, including Ravel, Debussy, Puccini, Mussorgsky, and Prokofiev, as well as American composers: "The Bernstein influence is obvious, and you know I'm a big minimalist fan, so there's Philip Glass and John Adams."[29] An opera composer that Schwartz paid considerable attention to was Britten, especially how he wrote for voices. Schwartz remembers listening to *Peter Grimes* and *Turn of the Screw*, and he learned more from the latter, noting, "I felt that the vocal writing for the kids in *Turn of the Screw* is just too difficult . . . so I've tried to be careful to make Arthur's and Adriana's material easier to sing."[30] In order to help children's voices be heard, Schwartz tried doubling with offstage voices, but finally settled upon a microphone for the singer onstage, which allowed them to sound ethereal, perhaps like ghosts, a state that describes Arthur throughout and Adriana in the last scene. While Adriana remains with the living, Schwartz used light orchestrations.

Schwartz found his experience in musical theater a useful starting point, especially in terms of structuring and developing the story. Since he has been such an active contributor in plot discussions, Schwartz feels "a confidence that I really know how to use music to tell a story. . . . And I know how to structure a story so that it will function theatrically."[31] A challenge in operatic writing for Schwartz was deciding which lines should not be set to music; as he noted in an interview, he tried to avoid setting something like "Please pass the milk," believing that some material needed to be spoken and not emphasized musically. The largest segment of the opera that is spoken is when Bill reads the ransom note in Act 1, Scene 1 over underscoring.

Since Schwartz worked with some singers on their parts and made changes according to their suggestions, selection of performers became part of the compositional process. He stated, "We sort of accrued our cast."[32] Schwartz found singers with assistance of Santa Barbara opera director Valéry Ryvkin, and they consulted with stage director Scott Schwartz. They interested Lauren Flanigan, veteran of more that 100 roles for major opera companies,[33] early in the process, and Schwartz "basically wound up writing it [the role of Myra] for her."[34] Flanigan has made a specialty of singing operatic premieres; her presence raised the project's stature and provided Schwartz with a distinctive muse. As will be explained further in the segment based on an interview with Hila Plitmann, Schwartz knew this soprano and invited her to join the project. Baritone Kim Josephson, who sang for years with the Metropolitan Opera and premiered a major role in William Bolcom's *A View from the Bridge*, was recommended to Schwartz; Ryvkin agreed that he was a fine addition. Other principals auditioned, and cast changes occurred as workshops moved between coasts and Schwartz and Ryvkin heard new singers. By November 2008, Schwartz reported that most of the major singers had been selected for the premiere.[35]

Schwartz considers himself fortunate to have had the chance to develop *Séance* through workshops.[36] The first one, Act 1 only, took place at Seagle Music Colony at Schroon Lake, New York, in July 2007. Schwartz was there for rehearsals and worked with singers, and his son served as stage director. The work was paired in performances with Gian Carlo Menotti's *The Medium*, which also includes séances, madness, and murder. Singers at Seagle are advanced undergraduates and graduate students and they acquitted themselves competently with Schwartz's score, but he was not writing for young voices. The original plan was to return to Seagle the next summer with the entire opera, but Schwartz needed to work with professional singers.

This became possible with two workshops produced by American Opera Projects (AOP), an organization that fosters contemporary dramatic vocal music. Based in Brooklyn, AOP sponsors developmental workshops and readings for several works each year, placing them in front of an audience in concert versions with minimal accompaniment. The first workshop for *Séance*, Act 1 only, took place at locations in Brooklyn and Manhattan on 18–19 January 2008. The second evening was in the Daniel and Johanna S. Rose Rehearsal Studio in Lincoln Center, a packed, overheated room. The conductor was Steven Osgood, and Charity Wicks played piano. After an introduction by AOP executive director Charles Jordan, Schwartz announced, "Immediately after tonight I will be doing my cuts and revisions!" That night it became clear that major segments of *Séance* were already in a fairly finished form, and audience reaction was positive.

The first workshop for Act 2 took place in Val Verde, California, in August 2008 as part of the Musical Academy of the West. Schwartz also worked there for a week on roles with Flanigan, Josephson, and Plitmann, consulting about their voices and where in their ranges various emotional qualities and effects should be placed. The remainder of the singers were students in the Marilyn Horne Academy at the Musical Academy of the West. Schwartz reports that the performance took place before about twenty of the Opera Santa Barbara's principal patrons.[37]

The second AOP workshop, the entire opera, was 21–22 November 2008, again in Manhattan and Brooklyn. The performance in AOP's home borough was at South Oxford Space, a large house with a huge room on the second floor. Valéry Ryvkin conducted, and Charity Wicks was again pianist/music director. Chris Cooley played synthesizer. The performance gave a good indication of the material's dramatic nature, and, like in the Act 1 workshop, one could hear in Act 2 that effective versions of main numbers existed. Schwartz's ability at musical characterization shone toward the end of the opera as all major characters assembled for the final séance and one recurring motive after another sounded.

The first four workshops primarily involved work on vocal lines, but *Séance on a Wet Afternoon* was Schwartz's first professional foray into orchestration, which, as noted, he did with William David Brohn (considered in detail below). Three orchestral readings allowed the composer to hear most of the score at least once. The first took place 1 May 2009 as part of the New York City Opera's "VOX: Showcasing American Opera" series, a two-night event that included excerpts from several new operas accompanied by the New York City Opera Orchestra,[38] including twenty-five to thirty minutes from Act 1 of *Séance*. On 10 July 2009, the Chelsea Symphony in New York City did an open rehearsal of the remainder of Act 1 and some of Act 2. Valéry Ryvkin then led the Opera Santa Barbara Orchestra on 29 August 2009 in a reading of Act 2, providing Schwartz with time for revisions before the next orchestral rehearsal on 19 September.

With the opportunity to interview Schwartz several times during the opera's composition, it was possible to gain a sense of which sections were revised when, and which scenes brought continuing challenges. When we spoke in November 2008, he mentioned that there had been a new version of Act 2 in September that reflected changes made in reaction to Val Verde, and soon after the current workshop he would speak with Scott Schwartz and Michael Jackowitz and revise the entire work again. Of special concern were the first and third scenes of Act 1, "written very early before I really had the whole shape of the opera in view."[39] Schwartz thought that the first scene "gets off to a bit of a slow start and there's material that—now that I have the whole thing—is not so necessary." The scene includes exposition, but Schwartz hoped to move more quickly and make it feel more "like living, breathing human beings." The third scene, with Adriana in bed, needed to be shortened for "both technical reasons and timing reasons." The consistent eighth-note noodling in the accompaniment helps provide the sense of foreboding, what Schwartz called "a motor going underneath," but the first workshop had him thinking about "overall arc of the piece and Adriana's journey." Schwartz thought he knew how to compress the scene. He also mentioned that there were perhaps twenty lines for the singers that he would raise an interval of a third or fourth to place them in better ranges.

In our next discussion, a few months before the premiere, Schwartz confirmed that the majority of his revisions had taken place in Scenes 1 and 3 of Act 1; the most problematic areas in Act 2 had been Scenes 4 and 6. Almost all such changes occurred because "from a storytelling point of view we just weren't moving forward dramatically enough."[40]

After Santa Barbara, Schwartz made one major alteration before the New York City Opera performances in spring 2011, writing a new aria for Myra for the final scene and adding a motive to recurring ideas at the end. He says that an aria Myra sang called "Empty"—when she could no longer sense Arthur's presence after admitting to Bill that he did not exist—"didn't really seem to be serving either the character or the overall musical structure of the piece as well as I thought. It felt like she was missing a final statement to balance out the other two big arias in the second act for two other characters."[41] (He refers here to Rita Clayton's "Wondrous Things" and Bill's "You Didn't Know Her.") In Santa Barbara just before "Empty" there had also been a brief instrumental segment during which Myra ran upstairs, hoping to feel Arthur in his room. The staging was changed for New York when Lauren Flanigan decided that she did not want to ascend the steps. These reasons inspired Schwartz to write a new aria called "Before You," hoping to give Myra more depth.[42] Flanigan became worried about endurance with the demanding schedule of New York performances, so Schwartz noted, "I made adjustments to make it easier for her to sing, and she had some good suggestions about structure and specific notes and passages, as she would. We almost wrote the aria in tandem, in a way." Before New York, Schwartz also worked out a few problems in orchestration and some more of those pesky changes in voice parts so sections "would sit a little higher in various people's voices."

A Project in Orchestration

Schwartz did not know how to arrange his piano score for orchestra. Instead of hiring a specialist—how Broadway shows have been orchestrated for generations—Schwartz resolved to take part by working with William David Brohn, orchestrator of *Wicked*.[43] Brohn has had wide experience on Broadway scores ranging in style from *The Secret Garden* to *Miss Saigon*, and such projects as arranging music from *West Side Story* for violinist Joshua Bell and orchestra.[44] In a three-way discussion with Schwartz and Brohn concerning the *Séance* orchestrations, they were reluctant to state their roles. According to the contract they are co-orchestrators, but Brohn did not embrace that title in our conversation, saying that he was helping Schwartz with it, and the composer said Brohn was the true orchestrator and Schwartz's teacher, but they agreed to "meet in the middle" as co-orchestrators.[45] Brohn believes that orchestration "is not lofty, it's practical," perhaps more craft than art, but an experienced orchestrator possesses vast knowledge and experience.

Schwartz stated that "anything that I'm doing I've got to walk through very carefully with Bill."[46] He showed me a page of piano/vocal score that he had just been consulting about with Brohn, with Schwartz's extensive notes as to which instruments should be used where, including such specific instructions as "second flute to piccolo." Schwartz would then draft the orchestral score and listen to it on Sibelius with Brohn, and they would discuss possible changes. Schwartz compared the experience to attending school.

Brohn has worked with such composers as André Previn, who gives indications of the kinds of things that he hopes to hear, but leaves most decisions up to Brohn, who clearly enjoyed his detailed discussions with Schwartz and did not believe that he made all of the scoring choices for *Séance*. Schwartz's feelings about their work came from one who has collaborated extensively and sees the creative process as joint problem solving:

> I'm completely non-proprietary. . . . All I want is for the piece on every level to be as good as it possibly can be. I'm a believer in Gestalt theory, artistically. I don't care about who gets credit for what. If the piece succeeds, there's lots of credit to go around. If the piece fails, it's the whole famous thing about failure being an orphan.[47]

In a later interview that took place during the opera's premiere run at Santa Barbara, Schwartz further explained the process of orchestration.[48] Schwartz and Brohn saw everything that the other person wrote. Work on a section started with Schwartz playing it on piano, and they decided who would orchestrate it. For those that Schwartz did, as previously noted, they talked through it and the composer took notes. Once Schwartz finished with a section and had it in Sibelius, Brohn came to his house, sometimes for a few days, and they went through his work together and discussed Schwartz's questions concerning voicing, volume, or instrumental choice. When Brohn finished a section, Schwartz often entered his work into the computer and might make changes that he would discuss with Brohn. Given the extent of this collaboration, Schwartz thinks, "In the end it all sounds of a piece because we . . . basically did it all together."[49]

The composer tended to initiate work on set pieces such as arias and ensembles while Brohn worked on "connective tissue," Schwartz's phrase for recitatives and other sections that tend not to include lengthy lyrical passages. Schwartz revealed that he initiated work on Prelude to Act 1, Séance 1, "One Little Lie," and "It's Always Been True" in Scene 1, and Scenes 2 and 5 for reporters in Act 1 ("to establish tone" for Brohn, who did Scene 5 for the reporters in Act 2). Brohn initiated much of Act 1, Scene 3 with Adriana in bed, and Schwartz did most of Scene 4 with the Claytons, including "Adriana," "Truth to Tell," "I Don't Believe in Mediums," and part of Myra's alleged dream, "I Saw a Little Girl." Schwartz cannot remember who started Act 1, Scene 6, but the composer orchestrated Myra's solo "Lucky." In Act 2, Schwartz started work on the Prelude, "Brightness Falls," and the remainder of Scene 1. Brohn worked on the opening of Scene 2, but Schwartz started "You Didn't Know Her" and the scene's ending. Brohn worked on the opening of Scene 3, but the composer contributed Rita Clayton's "Wondrous Things." Brohn started the work for much of Scene 4 and, as noted, did Scene 5. The composer worked on the opening of Scene 6 (the segment "Empty," which got cut before New York), and Schwartz also initiated orchestration on the third séance.

The orchestra for *Séance* at Santa Barbara included forty-six musicians: strings, two harps, two flutes (both at times doubling on piccolo, second flute also playing alto flute), two oboes (second doubling on English horn), three clarinets (third doubling on bass clarinet and baritone saxophone), two bassoons (second also on contrabassoon), two trumpets, two horns, three trombones, one synthesizer (providing piano, celesta, and glass armonica sounds), guitar (both acoustic and electric), timpani, and two other percussionists playing a wide variety of instruments. Schwartz favored a dedicated timpani player and three other percussionists, but three players covered everything. The score includes several scenes with noodling eighth notes—a sound often associated with minimalism—causing Schwartz and Brohn to include three clarinets. The piano is also important in the noodling.

Schwartz discovered that his intentions for the orchestration were mostly realized in workshops with the New York City Opera Orchestra, Chelsea Symphony, and Opera Santa Barbara Orchestra. After VOX, he commented, "The revisions have been relatively easy to make and not terribly extensive; it has gone well and I hope the second act will prove to be about the same."[50] The major problem in most cases had to do with balance between singers and orchestra; Schwartz stated, "I'm really striving to make sure that every word can be heard and understood without having to read supertitles." The greatest care with orchestral volume was necessary when accompanying Arthur and Adriana.

Since Schwartz used motives extensively to help tell his story, he often has the orchestra simultaneously play a different motive than a character sings. This occurred in both *Children of Eden* and *Wicked*, but Schwartz used such counterpoint more often in *Séance*. He said something about the orchestra's role that Wagner might have uttered: "There is no question in my mind that the orchestra's telling the story."[51] While a character offers an explanation, "the orchestra is telling you the emotional truth." Schwartz labels the orchestral part the "subtext."[52]

When *Séance* played at the New York City Opera, there were more strings, necessitating careful work on balance, especially with active material in internal string parts.[53] The only other differences in orchestration in New York were that the baritone saxophone part and timpani players were dedicated chairs.

The *Séance* Production in Santa Barbara

This was the first premiere for the Opera Santa Barbara, and *Séance on a Wet Afternoon* was a large production for them. Schwartz found that the company's "biggest . . . challenge" was just dealing with the event's size, and assembling the production raised "inevitable glitches."[54] One problem was failure of the Granada Theater's new light board, necessitating flying in a technician. A major problem for Schwartz, accustomed to Broadway, was the production schedule.[55] They had three days of technical rehearsals; a typical Broadway show has three weeks. Also problematic for Schwartz was the day off before the premiere. They performed the dress rehearsal in front of high school students, and the show "came off brilliantly," but after a day of rest, typical for opera singers before an opening, the premiere suffered new glitches.[56] Lauren Flanigan had a cold opening night and could not reach her c'", but the remainder of her high notes sounded. Her respiratory distress also was announced at the second performance, but she sounded lovely.

Schwartz found himself working on orchestration to the last moment. Besides copying errors, in places the accompaniment required additional thinning so that voices could be heard, and Schwartz also "beefed up the ending a bit" because he found it "a little thin."[57]

The second performance on 2 October included many successful components. Schwartz wanted the text understood, and from the middle of the downstairs one could follow almost every word without consulting the

Granada Theater, site of *Séance on a Wet Afternoon* in Santa Barbara, California, 2009. *Photo by Paul Laird*

projected text. Much of the score demonstrated Schwartz's sense of lyricism, in recitatives as well as in arias and ensembles. Highlights included Myra's first aria "One Little Lie" and her duet with Arthur "It's Always Been True" from the first scene, and Hila Plitmann was superb in the Claytons' duet "Adriana" from Act 1, Scene 4. Her solo "Wondrous Things" in Act 2 is an elegant explanation to her husband as to why they must go to Myra's séance. A defining moment for Bill is the lovely "You Didn't Know Her" from Act 2, Scene 1, where he explains his youthful feelings for Myra.[58] Only Myra, Bill, Rita Clayton, and perhaps Adriana have sufficient stage time to be developed as characters. Myra is domineering in her scenes with Bill, vulnerable with Arthur, and frighteningly competent in executing "The Plan." Flanigan enriched her character with touches of humor and other unexpected moments, and, despite the ambiguous ending, Myra seemed unhinged from reality at the conclusion. Bill's character is less developed both dramatically and musically, remaining spineless until he tries to save Adriana early in Act 2. His confrontation with Myra in Act 2, Scene 4 carries great musical power.[59] Rita Clayton must show her class's elegance and maternal anguish, and this Schwartz's music effectively does. Some might wish for more depth for Charles Clayton and Inspector Watts, but neither has much stage time. Clayton's anguish was apparent in "Adriana." Watts's best moment was "Truth to Tell," where he thrusts and parries with Myra.

The set and staging were a major part of the show's effect; both will be considered later in the segment on Scott Schwartz. The three scenes for reporters were good examples. Costuming included men in trench coats and ladies in matching period outfits, none in bright colors. Most carried umbrellas. Their stage movement suggested the action, with principals enacting the kidnapping and collection of the ransom money while moving among reporters, who represented the trolley that Bill used as a diversion. The reporters' hubris provided some of the show's humor. Other light moments came in statements by Myra's séance attendees—Mr. Cole's desire to contact his Lhasa apso in the afterlife is very funny—and there were light touches between Bill and Myra.

Singers in Santa Barbara were for the most part outstanding, and also good actors. Lauren Flanigan occupied her character with striking intensity and made this scheming woman, at times, likable. Kim Josephson as Bill held the stage well opposite Flanigan, especially in their confrontation in Act 2, Scene 4. John Kimberling as Charles Clayton sang well; Hila Plitmann as his wife had far less stage time than the two leads, but her Act 2 aria "Wondrous Things" might have been the solo highlight. Craig Hart was excellent as Inspector Watts with a huge, round voice and commanding presence. Aaron Refvem as Arthur was a satisfying combination of innocence and creepiness, and Kelsey Lee Smith as Adriana was believable. In the orchestra most everything sounded in tune and with appropriate timbre and dynamics, completing a respectable presentation of Schwartz's opera.

Schwartz was satisfied with his opera's premiere. He stated that it was the performance that he had "dreamed about," and this cast and production would have pleased him at the New York City Opera. His final statement on the experience combined a reflection on the project itself and a hope for *Séance*'s future:

> I guess I've achieved what I really wanted from it, which was just to do it. But if I have a hope for the future, it is that it has a future, and I'm perfectly happy for that future to be in colleges or in smaller opera companies, or whatever. You just want your work to live.[60]

Josef Woodard reviewed the opera for the *Los Angeles Times*.[61] He considered this a battle between opera and musical theater, and suggested that

Schwartz erred on the side that he knew best, composing "watered-down Leonard Bernstein and modern-day show tune-smithing," when the likes of Britten or Berg might have been more effective. He pointed to Schwartz's inspiration from a film—comparable to a number of recent operas—then faulted how Schwartz set the story with a "feelgood atmosphere." Woodard appreciated singers and production, finally concluding that this might be a good opera for those who dislike the genre and praising Schwartz's "sure skill with a tune and the arc of a dramatic evening."

Bob Verini's review of *Séance* in *Variety* praised how Schwartz combined his knowledge of "Broadway songwriting and Hollywood scoring . . . with a lyrical streak," providing a piece that was "terrifically involving and entertaining" and might even bring "new audiences" to opera.[62] He enjoyed the touches of humor and how appropriate extreme emotions involving the supernatural can be for opera. Verini believed that Schwartz did little that was innovative, but called his melodies "assured, evocative" and noted how some "arias are indistinguishable from stand-alone songs." He praised the opera for its spookiness and similarity to movie thrillers, but Verini was not sure if Schwartz sufficiently explored the relationship between Myra and Bill to explain why he would help her in this scheme. The reviewer appreciated the performers and production.

The composer/lyricist believes that he explained the relationship between Myra and Bill with the husband's Act 2 aria "You Didn't Know Her."[63] Bill also says to Myra in their Act 2 confrontation that he loved her too much. Schwartz did not want to tell the audience everything about Bill; he has a conception of the character and wanted to let others draw their own conclusions. He also will not say whether Arthur actually exists. Schwartz notes,

> I'm happy for people to have their own interpretation. I think that makes a work of art interesting, if there is enough ambiguity that you can . . . have a different opinion about some of what's going on. I think there's a difference between being murky or obscure and being ambiguous. This has ambiguity.[64]

Séance at the New York City Opera

The New York City Opera programmed *Séance on a Wet Afternoon* at a crossroads in its history.[65] The 2008–2009 season corresponded with major renovations at their New York State Theater at Lincoln Center; the company presented operas at other venues. The 2009–2010 season of five operas, led by new general manager and artistic director George Steel, took place in their house, rechristened the David H. Koch Theater. The company's financial difficulties affected their 2010–2011 season, which included only three operas and an evening of monodramas in their main series, but they were committed to recent American opera. In addition to *Séance* between 19 April and 1 May 2011, the main work in the fall was Leonard Bernstein's *A Quiet Place* (1983).

The "biggest disappointment" for Schwartz surrounding the opera's New York City run was that it was not recorded.[66] They had planned to record several performances and splice together a marketable version, but contract problems with stagehands interfered. The City Opera again caused Schwartz to question operatic production schedules because the company took three days off between the last rehearsal and opening night, which Schwartz insists affected quality of the first night.

Séance was effective in New York. At first the orchestra seemed too loud, but after the first scene improved, and singers were for the most part understandable. The second act was a convincing portrayal of Myra's descent into madness. The recurrence of motives in the final séance was effective and it became a true ensemble segment as Myra channels for Adriana, solving the crime. Myra seemed insane at the end as she celebrated with Arthur and a circle of the omnipresent chains descended around them. The auditorium was not full, but there were many in the orchestra and in the centers of the rings. The opera's reception in the theater seemed generally positive.

Anthony Tommasini, reviewing *Séance* for the *New York Times*, gave Schwartz credit for trying, calling the work "a labor of love" from a composer/lyricist who hardly needed to approach opera.[67] Tommasini avoided the possible identity debate for *Séance* (opera versus musical theater) and went straight to the work's quality. Asking whether it is good, the critic says, "Not very, I'm afraid." He found it "thoroughly professional" and that it "held the stage with mostly sure dramatic pacing" in a "striking production," and approved of Schwartz's choice of the story for operatic treatment, the libretto, and the comprehensibility of the text.[68] Tommasini's major problem was the "easygoing and harmonically tame score," which seemed too dependent on Bernstein and Copland. He thinks there are segments of *Wicked* that are musically more interesting than *Séance*, and he criticized a way that Schwartz changed the story, making it at times more about a mother who lost a child and kidnaps another that becomes like her own. (This comment only applies to a short segment; Myra's concern for Adriana is short-lived.) Tommasini also disliked how Schwartz's music often sounded too pastoral, running counter, for example, to Myra's insanity. He found wanting the music for the reporters, and concluded that he liked the work more when the music was less predictable.

The less accessible opera that Tommasini would have wanted Schwartz to write was not a possibility. The composer does not like music that lacks lyricism or that pushes other musical boundaries. As he says, "I don't like that kind of music, so I wouldn't want to hear it, so why would I write it?"[69]

Schwartz decided that the New York City Opera version of the opera represented its completion. He stated, "I feel really good about the piece. I feel I put on stage and in the score what I intended. I love the staging of this particular production. . . . It seems to be communicating to people."[70] The next step was the opera's publication by Boosey & Hawkes, from whom the orchestral score is now available online.[71] Schwartz is uncertain whether he would want to tackle another opera.[72] While almost any piece of musical theater takes two to three years, Schwartz comments that "it was not really the length of time; it was the intensity of the experience." Composing an opera is also "lonelier," with less collaboration when one writes music and libretto.

Collaboration

The observations that follow emanate from interviews with singers Kim Josephson and Hila Plitmann, conductor Valéry Ryvkin, and director Scott Schwartz, shedding further light on how the composer worked with singers, auditions, preparing the work for its Santa Barbara premiere, the set, and stage direction.

Kim Josephson

Baritone Kim Josephson became involved in *Séance* about eighteen months before rehearsals began in Santa Barbara.[73] He was singing in workshops for André Previn's *Brief Encounter* and met Schwartz at the premiere of Jake Heggie's *Last Acts* in Houston in March 2008, when they discussed *Séance*. Josephson's first workshop was at Val Verde, California, in August 2008, and he also sang in the VOX and Chelsea Symphony orchestral readings. What Josephson found "terrific" about his experience with Schwartz was the composer's interest in his voice and "where it might speak the best to make some dramatic point and where it needed to be for a Verdi baritone voice to really be shown at its best." The "Verdi baritone" refers to the range and tone quality heard in the title role of *Rigoletto* and Germont in *La traviata*, which Josephson sang a number of times.

Josephson and Schwartz collaborated at Val Verde. The composer allowed the singer to offer specific suggestions on how sections of the role might work better for his voice. In the confrontation between Bill and Myra in

Act 2, Scene 4, where Bill forces his wife to admit that Arthur was stillborn, Josephson noted that

> a lot of the notes were landing where the voice was already turned and really strong into the head resonance instead of the middle area resonance that he really wanted for the declamation of what Bill was saying. And so I suggested that, if we brought that down a half step or a whole step then the resolution points would be where they needed to be for it to be in the meaty part of the baritone voice.

Josephson believed that Schwartz wanted "this to dig in and really eat her [Myra] up," an effect that would be better realized with the line a bit lower. They tried the lines at both pitch levels; Josephson remembers preferring the whole-step transposition, but Schwartz decided to move segments down by a half step where he heard "the energy it needs," which Josephson believes helped. Bill's major solo in Act 2, "You Didn't Know Her," changed little during the course of preparing the opera; Josephson states, "He seemed to have that just exactly right." Schwartz's memory of their collaboration is that he dropped some passages to a lower key and "worked specific notes with him," but the demanding high notes f' and g' occurred often and the singer believed that all were possible.[74]

Josephson remembers how much Schwartz altered the conclusion, especially when Myra and Bill react to police and press at their house, with many changes taking place between Val Verde and the 2009 premiere. The sextet in the third séance (Myra, Bill, Mr. and Mrs. Clayton, Inspector Watts, Adriana) changed substantially after Josephson joined the project. Revisions were legion: Josephson noted that Schwartz "worked on it consistently, honing it, refining it, and changing things," with much that was new as they started final rehearsals.

Clearly Josephson relished discussing the project with Schwartz, noting, "You could really get in touch with Stephen. Stephen couldn't be more open or more willing to share what his real intent was." The baritone believes that he serves the composer's vision. He notes that *Séance* requires a strong, trained voice, but it is also "totally American" and in its mixture of opera and musical theater Josephson compares it to *Sweeney Todd*. He also mentioned Schwartz's work, similar to Bolcom's *A View from the Bridge*, is what some have called "American verismo," which the singer characterizes as a work "with big tunes and . . . real human emotions in this out-of-control situation—it brings to mind things like *Pagliacci*." Josephson offers the following about the conclusion of *Séance*: "That Schwartz has the magical power to make you feel good that Myra and Arthur are finally together is just too crazy to be believed!"

Josephson had worked with both Laura Flanigan and Valéry Ryvkin before. In 1994 Josephson performed *La bohème* with Flanigan at the Metropolitan Opera, and they have been friends for years. He states, "I find her to be a fascinating performer and I relish working with her at any time." Josephson's association with Ryvkin began in New York City when the conductor labored there as an opera coach.

Josephson vividly described the audience's reaction at the final dress rehearsal. The invited high school students seemed interested, and at the end there was utter silence until the final scene faded to black, and then thunderous applause. He was thrilled to see "young people so moved" by opera.

Hila Plitmann

Soprano Hila Plitmann played Rita Clayton at Val Verde in the August 2008 workshop in California, in the AOP readings in New York in November, and at the Santa Barbara premiere. She is wife of composer Eric Whitacre. Plitmann is known for singing premieres, and she also composes.[75] Whitacre and Plitmann knew Schwartz through mutual friends, composers John Corigliano and Mark Adamo, and Whitacre once presented material he had written for a musical on *Paradise Lost* to Schwartz at an ASCAP (American Society of Composers, Authors and Publishers) workshop.[76] (Plitmann found notable the depth of Schwartz's comments on the show's structure.) About 2006, during a dinner, Schwartz asked if Plitmann might be interested in singing in his opera. Soon thereafter, Schwartz was again in Los Angeles and brought "Wondrous Things." She recalls, "It was very moving. The aria itself is heavenly beautiful and I think he was just happy to be hearing it sung aloud." The soprano does not believe that the aria changed much after that early reading, but Schwartz might have moved some of the melodic material higher because of her comfort in that tessitura. Plitmann believes that Schwartz also showed her what he had composed to that point of the duet "Adriana." The soprano notes that the relatively modest role of Mrs. Clayton could be sung by either a lyric or coloratura soprano. The singer does not remember making suggestions to Schwartz about changes to make the part better suit her voice, admitting, "I'm kind of a shy singer." She also has "deep respect for the creative process and for the creator." (Schwartz did once comment in an interview that Plitmann requested some changes.[77]) She found it fascinating to watch a composer work on a large project through several stages, and described Schwartz as "always willing to learn" and looking for continuous improvement. For Plitmann a distinctive aspect of this opera "is just how beautiful the music is," making for a genial accessibility.

Valéry Ryvkin

Valéry Ryvkin was born in Leningrad, where he fell in love with opera and studied piano. At age eighteen he immigrated to the United States and studied at Mannes and Juilliard, later working as an opera coach.[78] His "conducting came by accident." He took lessons and started to work as a cover conductor, and then directed performances.[79] He guest conducted for the Opera Santa Barbara in the 1990s, and took over the company in 1999, leaving not long after the premiere of *Séance*. The company grew steadily under Ryvkin. At the time of *Séance* a typical Opera Santa Barbara season included two major productions, two shortened operas for children, and opera scenes as part of a young artists program. In 2005 Ryvkin also became artistic director of the Greensboro Opera in North Carolina. For *Séance* he advised Schwartz on aspects of operatic writing, helped choose the cast, and performed innumerable other tasks that involve a company's artistic director.

Séance was the largest project ever for the Santa Barbara Opera in terms of production size or budget. Patrons Richard and Luci Janssen provided the commission fee, and another major gift made possible the sumptuous production, but more money had to be raised. Their 2009–2010 season had been scheduled to include *Séance* and two other major productions, but this proved unworkable; they scaled back to Schwartz's opera and Verdi's *Macbeth* in a coproduction with the Fresno Opera.

Ryvkin reports that Schwartz attended Opera Santa Barbara's production of Puccini's *Suor Angelica* and *Gianni Schicchi* in winter 2006,[80] helping inspire him to accept the commission. When Schwartz finished drafting numbers, he sent them to the conductor. Ryvkin advised the composer on how writing for operatic voices differs from writing for amplified, Broadway voices and notating ideas for classical musicians. (Schwartz described in an interview how Ryvkin helped him distinguish between meters, such as 3/2 and 6/4. The composer stated, "He was so helpful to me there, so that ultimately the score will be conductible by other people, and they won't have to read my mind and I won't have to be sitting in the back of the room taking notes."[81]) The conductor's primary counsel on operatic writing concerned using more melismatic declamation, because Broadway composers tend to write more syllabic vocal music. Ryvkin enjoyed working with Schwartz on his first world premiere: "He's been a fantastic collaborator throughout—easygoing, and yet he knows what he wants." He believes that Schwartz "combines real musical knowledge and literary gifts."

A section where Ryvkin suggested how to notate a passage came in Act 2, Scene 1, where Myra sings to Bill of Arthur's request to murder Adriana. Schwartz had set the vocal passage as 3/8 + 3/8 + 4/4, which Ryvkin described as a "jazzy" idea like one that Leonard Bernstein might have written in *Trouble in Tahiti*. The conductor asked Schwartz to place the passage in 7/4 so it could be conducted as 3+4.

Ryvkin wished to contextualize *Séance* in the repertory. He found the score's greatest strength to be its tunefulness, and he rhapsodized about the opera's accessibility:

> It sounds contemporary, it sounds like it's written now, it's modern. And yet, at the same time, you can actually relate to it. Anyone who likes music, loves music, loves opera, loves something romantic, passionate, etc., can relate to it and can actually realize that it's written for them, and not for a small circle of aficionados or fellow composers, musicologists, or performers.

Ryvkin was intrigued with how Schwartz manages to get the audience to care about Myra and Bill, despite their deplorable activities. The conductor compared it to the empathy that Shostakovich develops for Katerina Ismailova in *Lady Macbeth of the Mtsenk District* and Wagner's sympathetic treatment of a love affair between brother and sister in *Die Walküre*. Ryvkin equates Myra with Katerina, "a vulnerable, incredible female character that one cannot help but love," no matter what she does. The conductor also suggests that Schwartz wrote effective music that humanized Myra not unlike how Wagner's lovely writing helps justify a love that is taboo in almost every culture. Ryvkin especially praises the effect of Bill's Act 2 aria, "You Didn't Know Her."

Reflecting on the experience, Ryvkin believed that everything had worked well with singers and set. Flanigan and Josephson played major roles in their success; the conductor noted, for example, that Flanigan's influence extended beyond her singing and character, such as to how they staged the ending between Myra and Arthur. Scott Schwartz accepted her idea.

The size of the Santa Barbara market limited how many performances they could schedule. After a month of rehearsals, only three presentations were practical, and they only filled the Granada Theater to 90 percent of capacity for the premiere. The second performance was not that full.

Ryvkin enjoyed his collaboration with Schwartz. The composer/librettist gave the performers ample creative space, leaving town for nine days during the second and third weeks of rehearsals. The experience fascinated a musician who has spent most of his career performing music by deceased composers. With a premiere, Ryvkin commented, "You are co-creating . . . because you cannot go and listen to a recording of it."

Scott Schwartz

Séance on a Wet Afternoon appeared in a first-class production that rivaled Broadway standards. A gift from Opera Santa Barbara patrons made possible a nightmarish realization of the house and San Francisco's frequent rain from the dual visions of director Scott Schwartz and designer Heidi Ettinger. Kim Josephson appraised it succinctly: "The house should take a bow!"[82] In both Santa Barbara and New York City Opera productions the compelling set assisted in creating the warped world of *Séance*. Director Scott Schwartz helped shape the final product in terms of set, content, and stage action.

Scott Schwartz, successful director of plays and musicals and Stephen Schwartz's son, started to direct *Séance* during workshops. The younger Schwartz functioned as sounding board and dramaturge.[83] Scott Schwartz saw and heard material during its creation, especially the libretto, and made suggestions, admitting that he did not offer as many suggestions as he might in a musical's development because here music is most of the show, but his father played sections as he finished them and Scott Schwartz offered notes. His father said that it was useful to have "another pair of ears and eyes" while working, and found the director helpful "making sure that the psychology of the story is clear," and in seeing that aspects like Myra's deterioration did not become too repetitious.[84]

As director Scott Schwartz fulfilled the position's traditional roles for *Séance*, working with designers on the visual concept and collaborating with singers on performance choices. A major difference between a new opera and new musical is that text and orchestrations of an opera are finished before rehearsals start, and they change little. Scott Schwartz compared this to directing a classic play, where the text seldom changes.

The director's role in suggesting changes to libretto and music cannot be reconstructed, but there are instances that father and son remember, sometimes with contrasting accounts. Scott Schwartz reports that his father credits him with the conception for "It's Always Been True," the first number between Myra and Arthur. The director considers it one of the opera's best moments and is grateful for the credit, but he does not believe that his suggestion was specific. Myra seems cold and calculating as she discusses "The Plan" with her husband, and Scott Schwartz believes that he described the need for "a moment of vulnerability" for her. In "It's Always Been True" she finds reassurance through Arthur, and the audience starts to appreciate her relationship with this son that she sees. As an example, a suggestion he made about reworking music resulted in improvements to Mrs. Clayton's aria from Act 2, "Wondrous Things."

Scott Schwartz directed the *Séance* workshop at the Seagle Music Colony in summer 2007. It was staged with minimal set, and the director had a week to work. He also directed workshops at Val Verde in August 2008 and in New York City in November 2008, but both involved singers learning notes and at Val Verde changes were being made to music, so his contributions were minimal. These were, however, important events for learning more about the opera and its flow.

Scott Schwartz did not have the kind of input on casting *Séance* as he would expect to as director of musical theater, but he consulted with composer and Ryvkin on choices of singers, encouraging them to hire the best possible actors. Stephen Schwartz expressed his satisfaction with the cast's dramatic abilities, especially his female lead:

> Lauren is a fantastic actress. The three main principals are all very, very strong actors, and they have to be for a piece like this. You don't just stand and sing. This is definitely meant to be a story and a sort of psychological journey and the acting is, I think, as important as the singing.[85]

Scott Schwartz coordinated the production's design. Before he worked on *Séance*, he had been collaborating with famous designer Heidi Ettinger on another project, but that fell through, and he thought that she would be a fine choice for the opera. His father agreed. The director reports that he brainstormed with Ettinger for six months. They studied sources and discussed whether the house should be a large structure or created with set pieces and wagons, moving characters between "rooms" by stage trickery. Scott Schwartz reports that he decided to make the house in one large piece for technical reasons, and it needed to be able to turn and to move up and down stage. In the Granada Theater, the need to move the house limited its rotation to only three visible sides. Ettinger conceived "the brilliant idea" of building the house from translucent plastics, giving it a ghostly appearance with figures visible through walls. Ettinger also suggested hanging chains to represent rain. (Water on the ground was achieved with "puddles" of high-gloss paint.) She built a model of the house that essentially became the set, and discussion continued on how to present the room in the Claytons' mansion and where to put the séance table, which did not fit in the larger house. They hoped to pull the séance room in on a wagon in front of the house downstage, but this was not possible because of limited wing space in the Granada. Ultimately, they set a table in front of the curtain, but a more

The set for *Séance on a Wet Afternoon* production by Opera Santa Barbara, designed by Heidi Ettinger. *Photo by David Bazemore*

satisfactory solution for the séance room was possible at the New York City Opera, where they brought it out of a trap.

Stephen Schwartz reports that he was "kind of a cheerleader" when it came to the set. He has interest in set design, but far more in writing.[86] His participation included visual suggestions in his libretto, and he saw the set design in Ettinger's studio and gave them some notes. He loved the use of chains to represent rain. One decision in which the composer played a major part was how to deal with Adriana's constant presence in the house. Ettinger had what Scott Schwartz called the "cool idea" of having Adriana constantly visible upstairs, but Stephen Schwartz thought this would be a distraction. He suggested that they turn the house to see the bedroom, but that was not possible, so they added a façade for the upstairs bedroom that they brought in from the fly-space when it needed to be covered. The composer/librettist commented that his opera was "staged like a play," different from the level of abstraction one often sees in operatic sets.[87]

Another area in which Stephen Schwartz needed a collaborator was for choreography, especially for the three scenes of reporters, which included extensive stage movement. Matt Williams is a dancer and choreographer who worked with Scott Schwartz when he directed Paul Goodman's *Rooms* off-Broadway,[88] and Stephen Schwartz already knew Williams when his son suggested him as the opera's choreographer. The composer/lyricist calls what Williams did for *Séance* "musical staging," and when auditioning the ensemble they looked for singers who had musical theater experience to allow for proper energy, diction, and "staying on top of the beat."[89]

The Music

The musical sources consulted for this study include seven piano/vocal scores of various sections that date from late 2006 through fall 2010, encompassing early versions that include several set pieces through basically completed scores:

Drafts of sections of Act 1 from late 2006 and 2007
Act 1, December 2006 to August 2007
Act 1, 3 October 2007
Acts 1 and 2, September 2008
Acts 1 and 2, December 2008
Acts 1 and 2 for Opera Santa Barbara, late May 2009
Acts 1 and 2 for New York City Opera, 28 October 2010

An important secondary source on the music is a doctoral document that Charity Wicks wrote at Manhattan School of Music: "An Introduction to and Musico-Dramatic Analysis of *Séance on a Wet Afternoon*: An Opera by Stephen Schwartz" (2011). As music director of the two APO workshops and associate conductor of the Santa Barbara production, Wicks brings a fascinating insider's perspective to her analysis.

One can learn about Schwartz's compositional progress on the opera by comparing the lengths of various segments in the aforementioned sources, the raw data for which are available online where a table illustrates which excerpts appear in each score with an indication of number of pages and measures.[90] Schwartz's work on *Séance* had begun by late fall 2006, when he saved versions of "One Little Lie," "It's Always Been True," "Where Is Adriana Clayton?" and "Adriana." Schwartz first composed set pieces that he could later tie together with recitatives and instrumental music. Working toward his Seagle deadline, Schwartz saved versions of most other materials for Act 1 during winter and spring 2007; the "Prelude" and "Second Séance" finally appeared in early June. Conspicuous material missing from the 3 October 2007 score includes "Truth to Tell" from Scene 4 and "Scene 6, continued," but these selections were not missing from the Seagle workshop because their texts appear in the September 2007 libretto.

Noting the length of each section in various versions provides a crude measure of the size of Schwartz's revisions. It is remarkable that a number of segments changed little in length over three years, including the following in Act 1: "Prelude," "Scene 1, continued," "It's Always Been True," "Adriana," "Truth to Tell," "Scene 6," and "Second Séance." Several segments in Act 2 also changed little in length: "Prelude," "Brightness Falls," "Scene 1," "Scene 2," "Wondrous Things," "Scene 3, end," "Scene 4," "Confrontation Scene," "Scene 5," "The Last Séance," and the "Dénouement." Following are examples of detailed observations of the types of changes that Schwartz made to various sections as he revised.

In shortening the "First Séance," Schwartz changed lines, altered the range of others, introduced more interruptions by Miss Rose (who feels ignored by Myra), and removed some of the medium's passages where she sings "Ah" as she "prepares" to enter the spirit world.

In "One Little Lie," Schwartz excised some lines of dialogue where Myra and Bill discuss phony mediums and at the end of the main tune he significantly reduced the length of a c''' that Myra sings.

In "Scene 1, conclusion," the composer altered Myra's exchanges with Arthur about her doubts in her psychic abilities, becoming the one line "What if it's not true, Arthur?" rather than recalling details of how she has never done well when tested. As shown earlier, Scott Schwartz described the importance of humanizing Myra by expressing her doubts here,[91] but the composer finally decided not to belabor the point.

In Act 1, Scene 2—"Where Is Adriana Clayton?"—between 13 December 2006 and 9 June 2007 Schwartz decided to weave a reenactment of the abduction into the scene with reporters, mostly in dialogue. In the first segment Bill sends the chauffeur off to the headmistress for a nonexistent letter, and later Adriana yells at Bill to leave her alone and he sings that it is "only a game." There are changes to the reporters' lines, but material on which Schwartz based it remains similar. Later he further reconsidered the scene, removing lines and changing melodies.

Between September and December 2008, there were many revisions on Act 1, Scene 3, Myra's and Bill's first encounter with Adriana in their home. Bill has lost his nerve and argues that they should return the child, and Schwartz conflated the material by removing unnecessary details and slight reordering. Bill goes into the kitchen at the end of the scene. He first sings a folk-like song about the rain, which Schwartz shortened by five measures in the later version. Bill then breaks down and calls on God and Jesus to intervene.

Schwartz altered Scene 5 for the reporters between 3 October 2007 and September 2008 in similar ways that he worked on Scene 2, deleting solo interjections of headlines and recomposing, using similar materials that had existed in the first version. The interludes that help tell the story—the narrative of picking up the ransom money and Bill's anguish about seeing Clayton's face—did not change.

"Scene 6, continued" of Act 1 became shorter, and between 3 October 2007 and September 2008 the composer wrote new instrumental music to accompany actions (such as a frantic passage of sixteenth notes as Bill moves nervously around the house before the "Second Séance"), removing yet another passage where Myra forces Bill to express his love, and increasing the melodic range as Rita Clayton enters the house and wonders if she senses her daughter's presence.

Schwartz's extensive revisions also occurred in Act 2, but he composed this act in a shorter span of time, and there were fewer versions available for study. "Scene 3" is the discussion between the Claytons and Watts concerning Myra's special séance. Mr. Clayton argues with Watts about attending; Mrs. Clayton settles the matter by singing "Wondrous Things." Changes in "Scene 3" between September 2008 and 20 May 2009 included deletion of material that had helped frame the argument, but the composer/librettist also inserted new material, such as Mrs. Clayton wondering aloud what Myra might have meant at the "Second Séance" when she said "Die!" Once Mrs. Clayton interrupts her husband and prepares to sing "Wondrous Things," there are few changes between versions.

Act 2, "Scene 6" became longer between September 2008 and 20 May 2009 with the major change being how Schwartz handled Myra's consternation at her inability to sense Arthur's presence. Schwartz wrote "Empty" for the second version, part of a complete rewriting of the scene until the Claytons and Watts arrives. (As noted elsewhere, Myra sang "Empty" in Santa Barbara, but Schwartz wrote a replacement aria, "Before You," for New York.) The remainder of "Scene 6" included minor changes, such as adding a long note on the word "Please" as Rita forces the issue to start the séance, overcoming Myra's reluctance because she has not been able to speak to Bill about where he left Adriana's body.

Motivic Unification

Schwartz made extensive efforts to unify *Séance on a Wet Afternoon* through recurrence of significant motives at dramatically opportune moments. Textbox 13.1 includes identification and explanation of seventeen recurring motives found in *Séance*.

In an interview Schwartz acknowledged his use of noodling eighth notes, similar to what one often hears at greater length in scores by Glass, Reich, and other minimalists. For Schwartz, the eighth notes, identified as Motive 1, appear in tense situations, such as Adriana in her "hospital" room and during the final séance.

Motive 2, first heard as the setting of "It's Always Been True," is, along with Motive 7, "One Little Lie," the ideas most often heard in association with Myra and parts of "The Plan." "It's Always Been True" specifically describes Myra's relationship with Arthur, and "One Little Lie" tends to be associated with what she does to try to become famous.[92] The former, a clear melodic outline with its rising major seventh resolving to the octave and then returning to the first note, sometimes appears in a vocal line with different text. Concerning "It's Always Been True," Schwartz stated in an interview, "That's just me trying to write a really good tune, you know, like a real hook. . . . Myra's emotional heart is placed in that little boy. I was just trying to come up with the most emotional tune of the whole opera."[93] Schwartz compared "It's Always Been True" and Myra's brief setting of "So Much Sorrow" in Act 1, Scene 1 to "really old style operetta" or Puccini.

At the beginning of Act 2, Scene 6, the opening interval is stretched to an augmented octave when Myra cannot sense Arthur after her admission

Textbox 13.1: Occurrences of Selected Motives in Stephen Schwartz's *Séance on a Wet Afternoon*

Each motive is traced in a separate listing with brief statements explaining the dramatic reason for each occurrence. For orchestral motives, the instrument listed is the one that plays the motive first and appears closest to the top of the full score page. Analysis of Schwartz's use of motives occurred from the piano/vocal score dated May/June 2009, the final version prepared for the Santa Barbara premiere. With a published version available online (http://www.boosey.com/cr/perusals/), locations of motives have been identified according to this orchestral score. Schwartz revised the opera between the Santa Barbara premiere and the score's publication, meaning that some cited motives do not appear in the online score. Motives appear here in order of first appearance, and sections of the opera have been identified according to the section's name in the May–June 2009 piano/vocal score. Charity Wicks dealt with repeating motives in her doctoral document; references to her work have been indicated with her name and the page number in parentheses.

Motive 1: Noodling eighth note ostinato (appears at tense moments, such as scenes with Adriana)

Act 1
"Prelude," p. 2, m. 9, flute 1
"Scene 3," p. 186, mm. 936ff, violin 2—begins as Myra prepares to leave "hospital" room
"Scene 3," p. 191, mm. 960ff, violin 1—sixteenth notes (with slashes indicating thirty-second notes) soon before Bill nervously suggests they return Adriana as soon as possible (Wicks, 20, what she calls Bill's "anxiety motive")

Act 2
"You Didn't Know Her," p. 79, mm. 369ff, clarinet 1—becomes part of accompaniment (Wicks, 31, Bill's "anxiety motive")
"Scene 4," p. 135, mm. 611ff, piano—noodling ostinato dominated by "The Plan" (see Motive 5) as Myra wonders if Bill has murdered Adriana

"Scene 4," p. 181, mm. 802ff, clarinets—pattern begins as Bill begins his verbal assault on Myra, reminding her there never was an Arthur (Wicks, 38, Bill's "anxiety motive")

"Scene 6," mm. 1021ff (2009 score)—noodling ostinato begins as Myra wonders if she should go to Arthur's room, where she might sense him (deleted before published score)

"Scene 6," p. 266, mm. 1171ff, clarinets—noodling just before final séance starts, and sounds often in scene

"Scene 6," p. 283, mm. 1240ff, clarinet 1—noodling begins in clarinets as Myra wonders whom she has contacted and Mr. Clayton prepares to express doubts on whether séance should continue

Motive 2: "It's Always Been True"

Act 1

"Prelude," pp. 8–9, mm. 41–42, cello—transformation of theme with deformed intervals (Wicks, 15)

"Prelude," p. 13, m. 58, English horn—motive in its usual form, except does not rise perfect fifth to final long note

"First Séance," p. 20, mm. 85ff, first in flute 1—sounds as Myra speaks with Arthur

"Scene 1, continued," p. 44, mm. 193ff, first in piccolo—sounds as Myra asks Bill if he misses Arthur, and motive occurs three more times in orchestra over next 12 mm.

"Scene 1, continued," p. 50, mm. 222–23, horns—sounds as Myra sings about how much sorrow there has been in their lives

"It's Always Been True," p. 124, mm. 642ff, voice—motive in voice, and it sounds often during aria

"Truth to Tell," p. 300, m. 1488, flute 1—sounds as Watts watches Myra leave Claytons' house

"Scene 6," p. 333, m. 1660, voice and oboe 1—motive used to set "a wonderful son"

"Scene 6, continued," p. 376, m. 1872, violin 1—sounds as Bill reacts in horror to Myra's hope that Mrs. Clayton would be at séance (added after the June 2009 score completed, appearing in published orchestral score)

Act 2

"Scene 1," p. 27, m. 139, flute 1 and p. 27, m. 141, horn 1—sounds as Myra tells Bill that Arthur wants them to murder Adriana

"Scene 4," p. 184, mm. 816ff, voice—Bill sings "It's always been you" to Myra as he denies Arthur's existence, and motive continues in voice and orchestra

"Scene 4," p. 188, mm. 831–32, voice—Myra sings "You don't have to say it" to a transformed version of motive

"Scene 4," p. 190, mm. 839–40, flute 1—sounds after Myra admits Arthur was born dead

"Scene 6," pp. 220–21, mm. 953–55, flute 1—corrupted version with initial major seventh ascent changed to octave, demonstrating that "it is not true" at this moment because Myra cannot sense Arthur

"Scene 6," p. 234, mm. 1030, 1032, 1034, voice and strings—motive sounds three times during Myra's new aria (composed for New York production) as Myra sings "It's never been true" and another line referring to how she does not wish to return to days before having Arthur as companion

"Scene 6," p. 342, mm. 1481ff, flute 1—first of several statements of "It's always been true" motive in orchestra to end of opera

Motive 3: "Ah" (sounds as setting of this neutral syllable in Myra's séances)

Act 1

"First Séance," p. 14, mm. 67ff, voice—sounds often in voice and orchestra

"Second Séance," p. 384, mm. 1916ff, oboe 1—sounds often in voice and orchestra at start of séance (Wicks, 24, suggests that the "Ah" becomes "more maniacal" in the Second Séance)

"Second Séance," p. 397, mm. 1973ff, voice and orchestra—recurs at end of séance as attendees marvel at how vivid this one has been

Act 2

"Scene 6," p. 274, mm. 1203ff, voice—occurs throughout texture at beginning of séance

Motive 4: "So Happy" (primarily associated with Myra and Arthur; set of motives based around four ascending, stepwise pitches, leaps of fifth and sevenths)

Act 1

"First Séance," p. 21, mm. 91ff, flute 1—in orchestra and with falling and rising perfect fifths in voice as Myra assures Mr. Bennett that his dog is happy

"Scene 1, continued," p. 43, mm. 187ff, voice—Myra sings word "happy" three times on descending fifths in reference to Arthur

"Scene 1, continued," p. 50, m. 222, voice—descending perfect fifth as Myra sings "sorrow"

"It's Always Been True," p. 134, mm. 685ff, voice and flute 1—Myra sings "we'll be so happy" and then same motive but with falling major seventh instead of fifth

"Scene 6," p. 328, mm. 1635ff, trumpet 1—sounds as Myra enters Arthur's room, then same motive with falling major seventh

"Scene 6," p. 330, mm. 1645–46, violin 1—sounds as Adriana complains about medicine

Act 2

"Scene 1," pp. 27–28, mm. 143ff, harp 1—sounds in transformed version as Myra tells Bill that they will make Adriana "happy" by killing her

"Scene 1," p. 33, m. 164, voice—setting of "so much more important" is "we are so happy" motive

"Scene 1," p. 37, m. 183, voice—descending perfect fifth as Myra sings "envy" to describe how she would feel toward Adriana after she dies

"Scene 1," p. 41, mm. 208–09, voice—two descending perfect fifths in setting of "Arthur has shown us that, hasn't he?" as Myra reminds Bill that death is a beginning

"Scene 1," p. 43, m. 215, voice—ascending perfect fifth in setting of "envy" as Myra asks Bill if he would envy Adriana after her death

"Scene 4," p. 157, m. 703, voice—descending perfect fifth on "peaceful" as Myra evaluates how Adriana looks after death

"Scene 4," p. 177, mm. 786ff, voice and orchestra transformation of motive as Myra tells Bill how much happier Adriana will be with Arthur in afterlife

"Scene 6," p. 252, m. 1118, voice—scalar passage similar to "we are so (happy)" in setting of "Freedom of the press," perhaps demonstrating Myra's satisfaction that press is involved; ends with ascending fifth

"Scene 6," p. 285, m. 1253, voices—Adriana and Myra talk about how pretty Adriana thinks her surroundings are with descending fifth on "pretty"

"Scene 6," p. 325, m. 1424, voice—Bill agrees that Myra successfully accessed a spirit in the afterlife, or she "did it," with those words sounding on a descending perfect fifth

"Scene 6," p. 340, mm. 1474ff, voice—transformation of "we are so happy" to set Myra singing "aren't we happy?" to Arthur

"Scene 6," p. 341, mm. 1477–78, voices—Myra and Arthur sing harmonization of original version of "we are so happy"

Motive 5: "The Plan" (instrumental idea often associated with "The Plan")

Act 1

"Scene 1, continued," p. 42, m. 185, clarinet 2—sounds as Myra mentions "The Plan" for first time

"Scene 1, conclusion," p. 108, m. 552, clarinet 1—sounds as Myra tells Bill that Arthur wants "The Plan" to start next day

"Scene 1, conclusion," p. 122, mm. 632ff, English horn 2—sounds after Myra mentions "The Plan" and while Arthur reassures her about her abilities

Act 2

"You Didn't Know Her," p. 89, mm. 410ff, bassoon 1—motive appears twice as Bill sings to Adriana that there are "some things even I won't do," meaning that he will not murder her

"Scene 4," p. 135, mm. 611ff, piano—noodling ostinato is dominated by this motive as Myra wonders if Bill has murdered Adriana as promised

Motive 6: "Myra's recording" (sounds first as music that Myra likes to listen to, Schwartz's faux Scottish folk song)

Act 1

"Scene 1, continued," p. 56, mm. 245ff, flute 1—first time Myra plays her record

Act 2

"Scene 4," p. 164, mm. 733ff, piccolo 2 and voice—tenor starts to sing song off-stage and later Myra sings it as she prepares tea just before her confrontation with Bill

"Scene 6," p. 224, mm. 970ff, voice—Myra puts her record on and accompaniment begins, and later melody as Myra uses it to help her sense Arthur

Motive 7: "One Little Lie" (opening motive from Myra's aria in Act 1, Scene 1, p. 77, mm. 356ff)

Act 1

"Scene 1, continued," p. 74, mm. 344ff, English horn 2—sounds as Myra asserts that she will make "The Plan" work by appearing to use her psychic powers

"One Little Lie," p. 87, m. 410, violin 1—motive sounds as Myra provides her backstory; the motive also sounds in orchestra elsewhere in scene

"Scene 4," p. 219, m. 1095, English horn 2—motive sounds as Myra enters the room with Claytons and Watts

"Truth to Tell," p. 291, mm. 1444–45, oboe 1—sounds as Myra feigns surprise that police are interested in her psychic abilities

"Scene 6, continued," p. 377, mm. 1874ff, voice and later in orchestra—occurrence that included more than aria's initial motive, and also presents aria's typical accompaniment, providing musical meaning to Myra singing about Mrs. Clayton attending séance

Act 2

"Prelude," p. 7, mm. 31–32, oboe 1

"Scene 1," p. 33, mm. 162–63, bassoon 1 and mm. 165–66, trombone 1—two occurrences sound around Myra's suggestion that Adriana's death will make kidnapping "much more important"

"Scene 4," pp. 157–58, mm. 706–07, oboe 1—motive sounds after Myra murders Adriana, and then elsewhere in orchestra

"Scene 4," p. 168, mm. 750ff, voice and orchestra—stepwise motion from original "One Little Lie" motive sounds in several parts as Myra tells Bill what they need to do now that Adriana is dead

"Scene 6," p. 242, mm. 1067ff, harps—arpeggiated accompaniment like that heard with "One Little Lie" as Myra ushers in Watts and the Claytons

"Scene 6," p. 269, mm. 1181ff, oboe 1—main motive from aria sounds just as light is turned off to start séance

"Scene 6," p. 282, mm. 1236ff, glockenspiel—probably transformation of "One Little Lie" with descending minor sixth between third and fourth notes changed to descending minor third, which is important throughout scene, perhaps showing how Adriana has taken over Myra's "little lie" by speaking through her

"Scene 6," p. 287, m. 1258—transformed motive with descending minor third sounds in glockenspiel with arpeggiated accompaniment in harp common in "One Little Lie" aria

"Scene 6," p. 304, m. 1331, voices—Mrs. Clayton singing "Adriana, I can feel you" to a new motive with prominent, stepwise outlining of minor third that transformed version of "One Little Lie" features, and then Myra sings something similar to what Mrs. Clayton just sang (mm. 1331–33) ending with transformed "One Little Lie" motive on text "but Dr. Reed wouldn't let me call"

"Scene 6," p. 308, mm. 1346–48, Mr. and Mrs. Clayton—both singing versions of conjunct motive described in last entry, Mr. Clayton's in inversion as he sings "How can I go on without my baby?"

"Scene 6," p. 315, mm. 1374ff, harp 1 and celesta—"One Little Lie" arpeggiated accompaniment sounds as Adriana reports to her mother that she is "happy," but not to descending fifth strongly associated with word (see Motive 4)

"Scene 6," p. 325, mm. 1420ff, clarinet 1—original "One Little Lie" motive sounds as Myra opens her eyes

Motive 8: "Do you love me?" (Myra's question of Bill whenever she needs to finalize something that she wants Bill to do, including an arpeggiated motive with a dotted rhythm, a rising, scale-wise gesture for "Do you love me?" and also at times four conjunct eighth notes forming *sol-fa-mi-fa*)

Act 1
"Scene 1, conclusion," p. 110, mm. 564ff, voice and orchestra
"Scene 3," p. 198, mm. 987ff, voice and orchestra
"Scene 6, continued," p. 358, mm. 1786ff, clarinet 1—dotted
    rhythm with arpeggiated motive appears before transformation of
    rising gesture in horns

Act 2
"Scene 1," p. 48, mm. 238ff, voice and orchestra—recurrence of
    entire sequence with first two motives described above
"Scene 4," p. 146, mm. 658ff, flute 1—"sol-fa-mi-fa" motive sounds
    as Myra rages that Bill promised that he would murder Adriana
"Scene 4," p. 194, mm. 856ff, voice and orchestra—all three motives
    sound as Myra tries to ask Bill if he loves her, but he answers they
    loved each other "too much"

Motive 9: "Arthur's ostinato" (eighth-note passage that sounds when
Arthur appears)

Act 1
"Scene 1, conclusion," p. 117, m. 607, divided between piccolo 2
    and harp 2

Act 2
"Scene 4," p. 148, mm. 665ff, divided between flute 1, piccolo 2,
    and harp 2
"Scene 6," p. 336, mm. 1458ff, divided between flute 1, piccolo 2,
    and harp 2

Motive 10: "Lucky" (material from Myra's aria in Act 1, Scene 6, p.
337, mm. 1675ff)

Act 2
"Scene 4," p. 152, mm. 684ff, voice and violin 1—Myra briefly re-
    prises "Lucky" with violin doubling after Arthur has said the only
    way they can keep Adriana is through murder

Motive 11: "Instrumental opening of Scene 3" (Puccini-like "fate" motive that Schwartz uses often in scenes with Adriana)

Act 1

"Scene 3," p. 157, mm. 811ff, trumpet 1—opening of scene

"Scene 3," p. 165, mm. 854ff, English horn 2—sounds after Myra identifies herself as "Nurse Johnson"

"Scene 3," p. 181, mm. 914ff, bassoon 1—sounds when Adriana asks Bill if he is a real doctor

"Scene 3," p. 188, mm. 942ff, flute 1—sounds just before Bill accosts Myra after she leaves "hospital," saying that they should return Adriana immediately

"Scene 6, continued," p. 359, mm. 1794ff, flute 1—sounds again when emphasis is on Adriana in bed

Motive 12: "Adriana" (material from the duet "Adriana" between Mr. and Mrs. Clayton by this name in Act 1, Scene 4, p. 261, mm. 1302ff)

Act 1

"Scene 3," p. 189, mm. 946ff, violin 1—brief ideas from aria that sound as Myra and Bill discuss Adriana

"Scene 6, continued," p. 363, mm. 1808ff, horn 1—sounds more than once in this sequence as Mrs. Clayton enters Myra's house and wonders if she senses Adriana

"Scene 6, continued," p. 373, mm. 1857ff, flute 1—transformation of motive

"Second Séance," p. 391, mm. 1947ff, voice and flute 1—Adriana sings that she smells her mother and material sounds in orchestra

"Second Séance," p. 392, mm. 1953ff, voice and flute 1—Myra sings material related to séance set to motive, and it sounds in orchestra

Act 2

"Scene 2," p. 58, mm. 284ff, bassoon 1—motive occurs several times as Bill convinces Adriana that she needs to "finish the game" so that she can go home; at times orchestra also plays accompaniment patterns from original duet

"Wondrous Things," p. 125, mm. 569ff, voice—transformed versions of motives from duet as Mrs. Clayton states she believes in miracles

"Scene 6," p. 323, mm. 1412ff—music from duet starts in orchestra as Claytons leave

Motive 13: "Ringing" (rapid repeated notes a minor third apart that occurs when doorbell rings or for another dramatic development)

Act 1

"Scene 4," p. 247, mm. 1235–36, voice—Watts tells Mr. Clayton to answer telephone

"Scene 6, continued," p. 343, mm. 1707ff, bassoon 1—sounds here and often in scene to build musical tension, sometimes in association with doorbell

Act 2

"Scene 1"—in piano/vocal score from June 2009, Bill reacted to Myra's request to murder Adriana by urging himself to think, set to "Ringing" motive, but this was cut before score was published

"Scene 6," p. 249, m. 1101, trombone 2—sounds as Bill enters house to find Myra with Watts and Claytons

"Scene 6," p. 252, mm. 1119ff, trombone 2—sounds as Myra introduces Bill to Watts and Claytons

"Scene 6," p. 260, mm. 1148ff, trombone 1—sounds as Myra and Bill try to get some time alone

Motive 14: "Watts" (dotted eighth and sixteenth patterns with triadic material first heard in Watts's "Truth to Tell" from Act 1, Scene 4, p. 287, mm. 1424ff)

Act 2

"Scene 4," p. 108, mm. 495–96, voice—Watts addresses "*Mister* Clayton" on dotted quarter and eighth notes, a gesture that reappears in segment

"Scene 4," p. 112, m. 518, voice—Watts sings dotted quarter and eighth on "wonder" as he tries to convince Mr. Clayton to allow special séance

"Scene 4," p. 116, mm. 535ff, voice—dotted quarter and eighth notes appear on "humor" and "Mister" as Watts continues to cajole Mr. Clayton

"Scene 6," p. 240, mm. 1060ff, voice—typical rhythm as Watts tells Myra "time is always of the essence" and reintroduces Claytons

"Scene 6," p. 248, mm. 1096ff, voice—Mr. Clayton sings motive from "Truth to Tell" when he sings "Mrs. Foster" as he tries to tell Myra that perhaps they should have not bothered her about special séance

"Scene 6," p. 258, mm. 1141–42, voice—same rhythm returns as Watts sings "*Mister* Foster"

"Scene 6," p. 296, m. 1301, voice—dotted rhythm on word "hospital" as Watts asks Adriana where she was held

"Scene 6," p. 302, m. 1323, voice—dotted rhythm as Watts comments "now we're getting somewhere"

"Scene 6," p. 321, mm. 1401–02, voice—dotted rhythms as Watts announces to other policemen on radio that he will be bringing "Mrs. Foster *out myself*"

Motive 15: "I saw his face" (motive sung by Bill first in Act 1, Scene 5, p. 317, mm. 1572ff, expressing his discomfort at seeing Mr. Clayton's anguish)

Act 1
"Scene 6, continued," p. 358, mm. 1788–89, flute 1—sounds as Bill forgets to put on his mask and Adriana sees his face

Motive 16: "Three half notes" (a rhythm that coincides with "noodling" eighth notes that first appears in Act 1 Prelude [p. 7, m. 31])

Act 1
"Second Séance," p. 405, mm. 2003 and 2008—just before Myra says "Die!"

Act 2
"Scene 6," p. 309, mm. 1350, 1353—as Adriana and Myra recount when Myra said "Die!" in "Second Séance"

Motive 17: "You Didn't Know Her" (material first sounds with this text in Bill's aria by this name in Act 2, Scene 2, p. 73, mm. 344ff)

Act 1
"Prelude," p. 7, mm. 32–34, bass clarinet—first appearance in opera (Wicks, 15)

Act 2
"Scene 1," p. 49, mm. 243ff, horn 1—motive sounds as Myra asks Bill if he loves her (Motive 8) for third time (Wicks, 29)
"Scene 4," p. 159, mm. 711–12, trumpet 1—main motive from aria sounds as Bill unexpectedly meets Myra upstairs after she murders Adriana
"Scene 4," p. 200, mm. 878ff, orchestra—strains from various portions of aria end this scene, such as main motive setting "You didn't know her" in bassoon 1, p. 203, mm. 891ff

to Bill that their son was born dead. Schwartz enjoyed his "discovery" that sounds in Act 2, Scene 4, when Bill sings to the same music "It's always been you," accusing Myra of fabricating her conversations with Arthur.[94]

Motive 3, a convoluted setting of Myra's "Ah" that sounds at the opening of each séance, carries little significance outside of these scenes.

Motive 4, first identified in Act 1, Scene 1 between Myra and Arthur as they sing "We'll be so happy," is associated with Myra, but gradually it takes on a more general meaning. It opens with a scalar ascent and often includes a descent of a perfect fifth on "happy," the latter a gesture that Schwartz sometimes separates from the scalar material, sometimes setting other words. In fuller versions of the motive, Schwartz sets the basic text ("We'll be so happy" or a close variant) to the same stepwise idea but with "happy" on a descending minor seventh. Only the descending fifth, however, appears to carry structural significance elsewhere. In Act 2, as Myra wants Adriana to join Arthur in the afterlife, the descending fifth becomes associated with Myra's passages concerning the girl.

Motive 5, "The Plan," occurs only in the orchestra. It usually sounds in eighth notes with an ascent of a half step, returns to the first pitch, and then rises a perfect fourth. Its two appearances in Act 2 seem especially revealing. In Scene 2 the motive accompanies Bill's admission that there are things that he will not do for Myra, such as killing Adriana. In Scene 4, this motive becomes part of a noodling ostinato when Myra wonders if Bill has murdered the girl.

"Myra's recording," Motive 6, is the faux Scottish folk song that Schwartz wrote to be Myra's favorite music. Schwartz has noted that this tune was intended as "pastiche," perhaps along the lines of "Danny Boy."[95] He did not necessarily intend the perfect fifths that sometimes appear as accompaniment as a reference to bagpipes, but they assist with the effect. Schwartz stated that the song's text carries a vague resonance to the experience that Myra believes she has with Arthur. The song appears in Act 1, Scene 1 as Myra and Bill discuss the ransom note, and it returns in Act 2, Scene 6 as Myra tries to sense Arthur's spirit.

Motive 7, the setting of "One Little Lie," is one of the most important in its frequency of appearance and for what might be its significant transformation in Act 2, Scene 6. Through most of the opera it is Myra's theme and refers to "The Plan." The motive sounds during important steps of "The Plan": her first visit to the Claytons, the initial discussion with Watts, and when Mrs. Clayton attends the second séance. In Act 2 the motive corresponds with Myra's urging Bill to murder Adriana, and it sounds after she kills the girl. Possible transformations of Motive 7 associated with the Claytons and Adriana in Act 2, Scene 6 are summarized in Textbox 13.1 including when the interval between the third and fourth notes changes from a minor sixth to a minor third, perhaps signifying that Adriana takes over Myra's consciousness, turning "one little lie" into "one big truth" that ruins "The Plan." What the Claytons sing are conjunct ideas that might be fill-ins of the new minor third in the transformed motive.

Three musical ideas (described in Textbox 13.1) come together to form Schwartz's treatment when Myra asks Bill "Do you love me?" which constitutes Motive 8. She uses this question to control Bill. Repetition of these musical ideas calls attention to Bill's different response in Act 2, Scene 4 when he tells Myra that they loved each other "too much." Wicks looks at this collection of ideas somewhat differently, likening its triple meter to a slow waltz and seeing it as a major indication of the psychological conditions that seem to beset Myra and Bill, and looking at how these continued exchanges make possible Bill's explosion in Act 2, Scene 4 when he insists that they have loved each other too much.[96]

Motive 9 is an eighth-note ostinato that sounds when Arthur appears. Although it has a different melodic outline than most of the patterns of noodling eighth notes associated with Motive 1, the two ideas seem related.

Motive 10, taken from Myra's Act 1, Scene 6 aria, sounds seldom, but it has one dramatic reprise in Act 2, Scene 4, when she comments that Adriana will be more fortunate after she has joined Arthur in the afterlife.

Reminiscent of Puccini, Schwartz wrote what could be called an instrumental "fate" theme for Act 1, Scene 3 that might be associated with Adriana's inevitable demise. Designated Motive 11, it recurs in Scene 6, again in association with Adriana in her "hospital" bed.

Schwartz derived Motive 12, the primary music associated with Adriana, from the duet "Adriana" in Act 1, Scene 4. He foreshadows the segment in the previous scene as Myra and Bill discuss their victim, and a major reprise of material from the duet sounds in Scene 6 when Mrs. Clayton comes for the séance and feels her daughter's presence. Adriana and Myra sing similar material during the séance. As may be seen in Textbox 13.1, material from the duet sounds three more times at appropriate moments in Act 2, but Schwartz did not choose to use the motive in Scene 6 when Adriana takes over Myra's consciousness. He appears to have based that upon a transformation of "One Little Lie."

Motive 13, "Ringing," sounds in association with doorbells or telephones, but by the end of the opera it seems to represent Bill's sense of danger. (Schwartz calls it the "Danger! Danger, Will Robinson!" motive,[97] referring to the robot's famous line in the 1960s television show *Lost in Space*.) Watts first sings "Ringing" as he tells Mr. Clayton to answer the telephone when Bill calls. The motive then appears in Act 2 in situations that involve Bill and cracks in "The Plan."

Motive 14, associated with Inspector Watts, occurs frequently when he sings, and in Scene 6 penetrates Mr. Clayton's music when he tries to excuse Myra from performing the séance. Watts's theme includes dotted rhythms and triadic material, which Schwartz intended "to sound martial," and then he wanted others, like Clayton, to pick up the material in the last séance when "The Plan" is exposed.[98] The composer went on to describe the feeling that he hoped the motive would "sound . . . [like] someone who had a badge," perhaps showing influence of the famous theme from *Dragnet*. Schwartz spoke of how he conceives the policeman's role:

> The whole point of Watts—I love him as a character—is what he's . . . saying is not at all what is going on in his head. He's much smarter than he lets on. And the music is trying to tell you that. That he is more suspicious of her [Myra] from the get-go than he's letting on.

Motive 15 is minor, but it involves a satisfying recurrence of music related to meaning. He pairs the music in Act 1, Scene 5, to which Bill sings of his anguish at seeing Mr. Clayton's face when he picks up the ransom money, with an orchestral passage heard in the following scene when Bill forgets to wear his mask in front of Adriana.

Motive 16, heard first in the Act 1 "Prelude," corresponds with one of the opera's most dramatic moments: when Myra shouts "Die!" in response to Arthur's use of the word in the séance at the end of Act 1. It recurs in the final séance when Mrs. Clayton recalls the moment.

Motive 17, derived from Bill's aria "You Didn't Know Her," is what Charity Wicks describes as Bill's primary motive for the opera. As she notes, it appears in the "Prelude" to Act 1,[99] and several other places. Its true identity becomes clear in Bill's aria "You Didn't Know Her" in Act 2, Scene 4, and then Schwartz makes effective use of it two scenes later to comment upon Bill's reaction to Myra murdering Adriana. It sounds as Bill unexpectedly encounters Myra upstairs, and then multiple statements of it sound in the orchestra at the scene's end.

Wicks suggests several other interesting associations between musical materials and the opera's dramatic progress. She identifies the pitch class c as related to Myra.[100] It is the only note heard for the first thirteen measures of the Prelude to Act 1, suggesting its importance, and she sings c''' at several significant moments. Wicks also points out the importance of the key of F major in Myra's music, sometimes with leanings toward Lydian mode.[101] She offers musical associations between Bill's breakdown in Act 1, Scene 3 (when he calls for God and Jesus to intervene in "The Plan") and his confrontation with Myra in Act 2, Scene 4, where he accosts Myra with the truth about Arthur. The similarities include the heavy orchestral chords in the accompaniment, and in the later scene the trumpet plays the melody that Bill sang in Act 1.[102] Wicks describes melodic and harmonic associations in the use of the minor second between the end of the Act 1 "Prelude" and the conclusion of the séance that closes the act.[103] Another important relationship between two segments that she notes is between Myra's aria "Before You" (that Schwartz wrote before the New York run) and Bill's "You didn't know her" motive. Wicks suggests that the composer derived the main motive of "Before You" from Bill's material; in both segments the characters reminisce.[104]

Schwartz made some comments in our interviews about his harmonic practice in *Séance*. Building on a type of chord that he used often in *Wicked*,[105] he included a number of augmented triads with added tones in the three séances, noting, "That just sounds to my ears like spooky music, I mean basically you want to be unearthly and unworldly, a little bit, but also unsettled."[106] (In another interview he described his fondness for "tweaked seventh chords," included the augmented triad with an added seventh and a minor seventh chord with a flatted fifth.[107]) The chord that opens the first séance is a D-flat augmented triad over a G in the bass, which he compared to Debussy and Ravel, but primarily the latter. Similar to Debussy's influence on *The Baker's Wife*, Schwartz recalled music that he "particularly liked" by that composer that he played as a student. In general, describing the instrumental music that helps set the opera's ambience, Schwartz states, "One of the lines I've tried to walk here is to be evocative like film music but not have it sound like a movie score."[108]

Schwartz is an intuitive composer, looking for the right sound for a particular dramatic moment or emotion: "It has no basis really in theory. It's just what I like."[109] To be more specific, he states, "I like parallel fifths, I like parallel fourths, I like open-chords in the right hand, I like the third in the bass a lot of times. I just have ways that music penetrates my soul or ear."

The opera's final chord is one of those sounds that has found special importance in his music. In the piano version it was a C major chord in the second inversion with an added F-sharp, emphasizing the major seventh between the G in the bass and the F-sharp on top, but in the published orchestral version the chord has been placed in the root position with a C in the cellos and basses and the F-sharp in a high range. Schwartz describes it as "a little unsettled—it's resolved, but not happily." One thinks back to Schwartz's reference to the finale of *West Side Story* at the end of *Wicked*, where Bernstein's C and F-sharp become an E and A-sharp. In *Séance*, Bernstein's original pitches sound, which the older composer perhaps took from Stravinsky's *Petrushka*.[110] Wicks notes the presence of C in the chord, which she associates with Myra, and she describes the F-sharp as another possible Lydian reference.[111]

A Final Thought: Opera versus Musical Theater

The debate over what separates opera and musical theater will rage endlessly,[112] but perhaps the most useful distinction comes from a composer's intention. With *Séance on a Wet Afternoon*, there is no question that Stephen Schwartz set out to write an opera. He chose a dramatic story with outsized emotions and consciously learned to compose for operatic voices. The use of nearly continuous music and motives to help tell the story contributes to the operatic scope.

In an interview Schwartz described *Séance* as "a hybrid" between opera and musical theater with "storytelling impetus" that "feels more like musical theater."[113] He further explicated the second point: "I think there is a kind of storytelling drive that you find in a few operas . . . *Tosca* certainly has real story-telling." Another aspect of *Séance* that Schwartz considers closer to musical theater is that the piece includes "reliable applause moments." (Or, in Broadway terms, Schwartz said, "We take hands."). Applause after major numbers is common in opera, but the composer believes that it is less common in the genre than it used to be, and some operas include no breaks for applause during the course of an act. It is expected in musical theater.

Schwartz has mixed feelings about the opera–musical theater debate as it relates to *Séance*, perhaps to be expected from a figure that made his fame in the more popular genre and then wrote an opera. At one point Schwartz wondered why anyone really cares what the piece should be called, feeling that it should be decided if *Séance* "works on its own terms." He sees people "try to impose a kind of preconception or theoretical idea about what an opera needs to be. It's so bizarre to me." Schwartz, of course, had his own preconceptions on what opera should be and wrote the work with those ideas in mind. On the larger question concerning opera versus musical theater, Schwartz is gratified that the piece has encouraged debate, but he concluded, "There is no answer, so people can talk about it. But in the end, really, who cares?"

As Schwartz surely realizes, many people care. Musical theater is popular, and people noticed when the composer/lyricist of *Wicked* wrote an opera. His celebrity helped inspire the commission. Generous financial support allowed a quality of production perhaps unlike anything one might expect from the Opera Santa Barbara. The work might have made a bigger splash if the company had been able to give more than three performances, but its profile grew with the longer run at the New York City Opera. Schwartz chose a story worthy of operatic treatment, told the story competently in his libretto, and provided music that merits scrutiny. It is too early to assess fully Schwartz's accomplishment with *Séance*, but the project constitutes a fascinating moment in the career of a composer/lyricist who has traversed an unpredictable journey since writing *Godspell* in 1971.

~

CHAPTER FOURTEEN

Stephen Schwartz's Works outside of Broadway and Hollywood

Although Stephen Schwartz's fame is a function of his larger stage works and Hollywood films, his long career has included several projects with lower profiles. The stage works and recordings described in this chapter, however, speak volumes concerning his personal values as an artist, devotion to certain themes, and desire to collaborate with various people, such as his son Scott Schwartz, a noted theatrical director. Described here are the following: the children's musical *Captain Louie*, for which Schwartz wrote music and lyrics; *Personals*, a musical about personal ads that includes music by Schwartz and others; two recordings that Schwartz made as a singer/songwriter; *Mit eventyr* (*My Fairytale*), a Danish musical on Hans Christian Andersen for which Schwartz wrote songs; and *My Antonia*, a play by Scott Schwartz that includes the composer's only incidental score.

Captain Louie

Although Schwartz has written a number of shows that can be enjoyed by children and young people, his output includes few musicals conceived primarily for such an audience. The only other such work besides *Captain Louie* is *My Son Pinocchio: Geppetto's Musical Tale*, but it also includes adult characters that interact with other adults; *Captain Louie* includes only children (except for the title character's mother, whose lines are delivered offstage[1]) and deals with leaving one's friends and moving to a new neighborhood. Based upon the children's book *The Trip* by Ezra Jack Keats (1978), Schwartz

collaborated with book writer Anthony Stein. The composer/lyricist considered the project because he liked the work of Stein's wife, Meridee, founder
and artistic director of the First All Children's Theatre, a noted repertory
company of young performers in New York City.[2] Anthony Stein is the author of the puppet play *Professor Prattle's Tales of Wonder*, wrote scripts for
children's shows produced by Georgia Public Broadcasting, and was librettist
for *The Prodigal Son*.[3]

As Carol de Giere reports, Schwartz saw Charles Strouse's opera for
children *Nightingale* at the First All Children's Theatre in 1981 and became interested in writing for the ensemble.[4] Meridee Stein notes that she
discovered Keats's book and envisioned it as a children's musical, enlisting
Schwartz in the project.[5] The initial version was *The Trip*, thirty-five minutes
in length, which played in New York City and Washington DC in 1983 and
1984.[6] Schwartz thought the show needed to be an hour in length to be desirable as a licensed property,[7] and Meridee Stein reports that they lengthened
it in 2000.[8] Additions included fresh songs, scenes, and a new character,
Julio. Now called *Captain Louie*, the show played in the initial season of the
New York Musical Theatre Festival in 2004, and then appeared in two New
York productions in 2005,[9] followed by a national tour in 2006–2007. Meridee Stein directed these productions and served as coproducer with various
associates. *Captain Louie* is available from Music Theatre International in the
full version and as the shorter *Captain Louie Jr.*

A brief synopsis demonstrates the placement of Schwartz's songs and how
they help tell the story.[10] Louie has moved with his family to a new neighborhood and has made no friends, heard in the taunts and lament of "New Kid
in the Neighborhood." He retires to his room and imagines that he flies in
his red toy plane to his former neighborhood ("Big Red Plane"), where he
plays with his old friends. During his flight, several apparently sinister creatures wait to trick Louie upon his landing, singing "We've Got a Welcome
for Louie." He finds his old neighborhood empty until dark characters pursue
him in "Shadows." They capture Louie and take him to their lair, where
they frighten him, but he discovers that these scary creatures are actually
his friends in Halloween costumes. They celebrate Captain Louie's arrival
("Trick or Treat"). Julio, a new kid, approaches the gang and they accept him
immediately. They are about to trick-or-treat when Ziggy says that someone
has moved into Louie's old house. Julio encourages them to play tricks on the
recent arrival ("Looza on the Block"), but it turns out that he is the new kid.
The gang wants to go to Ziggy's house, which they have never visited, but
Ziggy resists the idea and confesses that his family lacks money for decora-
tions or candy. Louie leads the gang in sharing what they have to help their
friend ("Spiffin' Up Ziggy's"). Louie takes his friends trick-or-treating on his

plane ("Captain Louie") and then says farewell ("Home Again"). He finds himself back in his room and, with renewed spirit, goes outside dressed in his Captain Louie costume with his red plane and starts to make new friends ("Finale: New Kid in the Neighborhood, Reprise").

Schwartz's songs for *Captain Louie* find him in something like his *Godspell* mode, primarily using pop idioms and rich syncopations.[11] No music director will mistake this for easy music for children or adolescents to sing—there are, for example, many passages with the chorus in challenging close harmonies—but the composer has made the effort worthwhile. The opening "New Kid in the Neighborhood" includes childish chants and taunts and a well-formed melody for Louie, establishing the children's world. "Big Red Plane" takes us into Louie's fantasy, moving from an imaginative opening that appears on the original cast recording (but Schwartz did not publish in the show's *Vocal Selections*) into an energetic ensemble number. The meter changes continuously between 4/4 and 3/4 with some use of 5/4. "A Welcome for Louie" is a brief, creepy musical scene where soloist Mouse and gang members threaten their friend around Louie's short reprise of "Big Red Plane." The menacing mood remains in "Shadows," which becomes a clever "Slow Tango." Schwartz seems to have reached back to Bernstein's *Mass* for some disturbing gestures here, with more than one idea closely approaching choral passages in "Confiteor" of the "Confession" section.[12] "Trick or Treat" is a delightful evocation of this favorite childhood practice, opening with an earnest solo and close harmonies, moving into a "Moderato, Shuffle feel" and, briefly, a slower "Cakewalk." The song returns as the finale. "Looza on the Block" bears the marking "Medium Latin Rock," apparently honoring the Hispanic Julio. "Spiffin' Up Ziggy's" starts out with rap (unusual for Schwartz) as the boy explains his family's poverty and then goes to "Funky, lightly swung 16ths" for the main, choral portion of the song that keeps returning to a riff. The title song is a gospel number and includes a reprise of "Big Red Plane." Schwartz uses multiple modulations to drive the point home. "Home Again," marked "Very gentle, like a music box" and the score's most reflective song, is an attractive waltz. Schwartz used a melodic gesture on the title text reminiscent of how he set the title text in "Close to Home" in *Children of Eden*. The "Finale" is a combination of "New Kid in the Neighborhood" and "Trick or Treat." It is joyful ending to a show that explores typical children's emotions.

Personals

The off-Broadway show *Personals* was the brainchild of three writers—David Crane, Seth Friedman, and Marta Kauffman—who met at Brandeis

University. While still there they noted the humorous, musical possibilities of treating personal ads run by people looking for romance. Their initial effort won the American College Theatre Festival, earning a performance at the Kennedy Center in Washington DC. This began an eight-year developmental process for a show that combines a revue's sketches and songs with characters who tell a continuing story. *Personals* opened off-Broadway at the Minetta Lane Theatre on 24 November 1985 (with a young Jason Alexander in the cast), and ran for 265 performances.[13] The director was Paul Lazarus, who collaborated with Schwartz on the remaking of *Working*. Six composers supplied music: William Dreskin, Joel Philip Friedman, Seth Friedman, Alan Menken, Stephen Schwartz, and Michael Skloff. Frank Rich reviewed *Personals* for the *New York Times* and found the overall idea too thin for an evening's entertainment. He described most of the show's music as "undistinguished soft rock," but allowed that Menken and Schwartz "give their songs (including the opening and closing numbers of both acts) a pleasant showbiz lift."[14]

The three numbers for which Schwartz wrote the music include the openers for Acts 1 ("Nothing to Do with Love") and 2 ("Moving in with Linda"), and the show's finale ("Some Things Don't End"). Lyrics vary in quality, but moments are genuinely funny and touching, and Schwartz's music sets the words comprehensibly and appropriately.[15] Rich noted that the show includes more than a few Sondheim resonances, pointing especially to "Nothing to Do with Love," but the composer/lyricist of *Company* probably would not have used these lyrics in a show. Schwartz's music for the song includes subtle underscoring for dialogue; sung portions resemble bubblegum rock like one hears in "Popular" from *Wicked*. "Moving in with Linda," which Rich praised, presents a ripe situation for musical comedy: Sam is moving into a new apartment with his girlfriend, Linda, but memories, personified by old girlfriends climbing out of his luggage, keep getting in the way. It is a satisfying musical scene that Schwartz enlivens considerably with music that shifts on a dime with the situation. It opens with a light, jazzy feeling as Sam announces that he is moving in with Linda, joined briefly by male backup singers before Elaine enters. She broke up with Sam eight years before and reminds him of their time and physical pleasures in Spain, reflected by Schwartz with a quotation of the famous bass line of "Habanera" from Bizet's *Carmen* and other "Spanish" gestures. Mary Lou arrives in the next piece of luggage. She was homecoming queen in Sam's high school and his biology lab partner. She barely knew that Sam was alive, but she has not left his fantasies, and Schwartz reflects this with gestures from 1950s rock and roll. The next bag brings in Renée, with whom Sam had a messy breakup, and she throws the opening jazzy music back at him with scorn. Sam then takes a phone call from a recent one-night stand before Linda arrives with all of her luggage. The scene closes with a return of the opening music. "Some Things Don't End," the finale, brings the show's book characters to a close. Sam and Claire have just spent the night together, but she wants to run away because she might get hurt in this relationship. Sam attempts to convince her to stay, and quickly the entire cast joins the song. It is an attractive pop ballad over a rock beat for the ambiguous lyrics. This is a funny, cynical show, hard to end positively, but the writers tried with "Some Things Don't End."

Recordings by a Singer/Songwriter

When Stephen Schwartz began his career writing musicals in New York City he was under the influence of popular singer/songwriters like Laura Nyro and James Taylor, in addition to artists associated with the Motown sound. Schwartz based most of his songs for *Godspell* on works by such figures, and influences from these sources have remained in his toolbox. A talented singer and pianist, over the years Schwartz has performed many of his songs for audiences, Broadway producers, writers, actors, and possible investors. In recent years he has presented concerts called Stephen Schwartz and Friends with singers Liz Callaway or Debbie Gravitte and Scott Coulter.[16] Given his influences and customary activities, it seems unsurprising that Schwartz has recorded two compact discs as a singer/songwriter: *Reluctant Pilgrim* (1997) and *Uncharted Territory* (2002).[17] The majority of the twenty-two songs on these recordings have not appeared in Schwartz's dramatic projects and most do not seem to have been removed from shows because they are personal, storytelling songs that set up a scene or emotional space and explore it, not songs that tell about character or advance a plot. In these two albums Schwartz renews his lifelong interest in the role of the singer/songwriter, in the process producing material that his fans will want to experience.

He did not write music and lyrics for all of the songs, as may be seen in the following lists:

Reluctant Pilgrim
"Dreamscape"—music and lyrics by Schwartz
"Crowded Island"—music and lyrics by Schwartz
"So Far"—music and lyrics by Schwartz
"More Than This"—music by Schwartz, lyrics by Dean Pitchford[18]
"Life Goes On"—music and lyrics by Schwartz

"The Hardest Part of Love"—music and lyrics by Schwartz (from *Children of Eden*)
"Prestidigitation"—music and lyrics by Schwartz
"Ten-Day Heartbreak"—music and lyrics by Schwartz
"Code of Silence"—music and lyrics by Schwartz
"Snapshots"[19]—music and lyrics by Schwartz
"Cactus Flowers"—music and lyrics by Schwartz

Uncharted Territory
"Recurring Dream"—music and lyrics by Mary Fahl[20] and Schwartz
"Rewriting History"—music by Schwartz, lyrics by Steven Lutvak[21]
"Worth Waiting For"—music and lyrics by Schwartz
"Cold Enough to Snow"—music by Alan Menken, lyrics by Schwartz (from *Life with Mikey*[22])
"Toxic People"—music and lyrics by Schwartz
"The Roads Untaken"—music by Schwartz, lyrics by Lindy Robbins[23]
"Face of a Stranger"—music and lyrics by Schwartz
"The Line Forms on the Right"—music by John Bucchino,[24] lyrics by Schwartz
"Since I Gave My Heart Away"—music and lyrics by Schwartz (from *Geppetto*)
"Boy on the Roof"—music and lyrics by Schwartz
"Forgiveness' Embrace"—music and lyrics by Schwartz

Comfortable in the recording studio since his early days at RCA, Schwartz produced *Reluctant Pilgrim* with Martin Erskine (who also played synthesizer on the disc) and Schwartz produced *Uncharted Territory* with John Angier, who also was the recording engineer and played some keyboard. Accompaniments are dominated by piano, guitar, percussion, and backup vocalists, but some of the tracks include other instruments. Schwartz's appealing voice is the central presence on both albums, and his fine musicianship is clear throughout. With good intonation and effective use of varied timbres and ranges, Schwartz's singing is touching. He understands how to put over a song in terms of phrasing and timing, and his performances carry the confessional quality that one associates with memorable singer/songwriters.

The material on the albums is varied, both in terms of mood and music. He brings a puckish sense of humor to "Toxic People" and "The Line Forms at the Right" (the latter with music by John Bucchino) and often plumbs the depth of personal feelings derived from relationships, such as in "Code of Silence" and "Boy on the Roof." Some songs are far less predictable, such as "Prestidigitation," which tells a macabre story of an old magician who saves the protagonist from danger by conjuring up a bear-like beast. Some of the songs are based on rock, such as "Worth Waiting For," and others are entirely different, such as "Recurring Dream" (written with Mary Fahl), which is unlike most anything Schwartz has ever written for theater. These two albums provide documentation of a side of Schwartz's creativity that one seldom hears.

Mit Eventyr

Nurtured by common bonds of language and shared values in entertainment, the American musical theater has long been closely related with that of Great Britain. What might be called Anglo-American musical theater has occasionally had influence in other parts of the world, especially in Europe over the last several decades where dramatists and composers have produced shows in other languages based more upon the musical than opera or operetta.[25] Also, as chronicled in this volume, some of Stephen Schwartz's shows have played in France, Germany, the Netherlands, and other countries, and he took part as a lyricist in adapting Disney's *The Hunchback of Notre Dame* into *Die Glöckner von Notre Dame* in 1999, which played three years in Berlin. Schwartz, however, moved into another position in the history of the European musical in 2005 when he wrote songs for *Mit eventyr*, a new Danish musical about Hans Christian Andersen (1805–1875), produced for the bicentennial of the author's birth. Schwartz wrote the songs in English and Adam Price translated them for the production.

Flemming Enevold (b. 1952), a leading Danish musical actor, singer, and director, conceived *Mit eventyr*.[26] His education was at the National Theatre School and Royal Danish Academy of Music in the 1970s, and he has performed in classical repertory at the Royal Theatre. His work in musicals has included appearances in Danish productions of *The Pirates of Penzance*, *Esther*, *The Phantom of the Opera*, *Les Misérables*, and *Sweeney Todd*. He has also cowritten, produced, directed, and appeared in significant Danish musicals. Enevold directed the Gladsaxe Theatre outside of Copenhagen from 1992 to 2006, where the repertory included classical plays and musicals, such as *Mit eventyr*.

The primary book credit for *Mit eventyr* belongs to Philip LaZebnik, with whom Schwartz collaborated on *Pocahontas* and *The Prince of Egypt*. LaZebnik also worked on other Disney and DreamWorks projects and has been active in Europe as a screenwriter and story consultant.[27] He invited Schwartz into *Mit eventyr*,[28] and the writer shared book credit with Enevold, Schwartz,

Adam Price, and Pierre Westerdahl. The show opens with young Hans Christian Andersen at the Royal Theatre in Copenhagen working on an opera libretto for the famous Swedish soprano Jenny Lind. In an experience out of Alice in Wonderland, Andersen goes "through the looking glass" (here, instead, a theatrical trunk), and experiences many of the stories for which he will later become famous. This imaginative journey includes his Shadow and a Boy, who offer insights as opposing sides of Andersen's creative psyche. The Shadow represents the writer's desire to work on serious plays and opera librettos, while the Boy—who has gone into the world to seek his fortune[29]— seems to remind Andersen of the innocence needed to appreciate fairytales. Andersen experiences, among other stories, the Ugly Duckling, the Little Mermaid and her sisters, the Emperor without his clothes, the Snow Queen, and the Princess atop her many mattresses and a pea. The show draws part of its story from the torch that the real-life Andersen carried for Jenny Lind.[30] The actress who played her, Louise Fribo, appears as five fairytale characters and sings several songs. Schwartz has remarked on the show's resonance with *The Wizard of Oz* because in both scenes from real life bookend a fantasy world.[31] Except for a Donizetti aria from *Lucia di Lammermoor* that Jenny Lind sings, the remainder of the music occurs in Andersen's imagination.

Schwartz provided the following songs for *Mit eventyr*:[32]

Act 1
"Bli' hos os" ("Stay with Us")—Andersen, Little Bo Peep (Hyrdinden), Fairytale Characters
"Fader, du var træt" ("Father, You Were Tired")—Boy
"Min rejsekammerat 1" ("Fellow Traveler 1")—Andersen, Shadow
"Rejsekammerat trio" ("Fellow Traveler Trio")—Andersen, Shadow, Boy
"Bli' hos mig" ("Stay with Me")—Princess
"På svanevinger" ("On the Wings of a Swan")—Andersen, Shadow, Boy, and Choir

Act 2
"Synk ned i mit hav" ("Come Drown in My Love")—Little Mermaid and Her Sisters
"Konversation" ("Colloquy")—Shadow, Boy
"Stakkels Andersen" ("Poor Andersen")—Shadow
"Red os" ("Save Us")—Andersen, Shadow, and Fairytale Characters
"Min rejsekammerat 3" ("Fellow Traveler 3")—Shadow
"Det er ganske vist" ("Can You Imagine That?")—Andersen, Boy, and Choir
"Finale" ("Finale")—Jenny, Andersen, and Fairytale Characters

The original cast recording (OCR) includes thirty-four tracks, most of the others incidental music for effects and dialogue, much of which was provided by James Price. There are songs not by Schwartz written for various dramatic situations such as "Andegården" and "Atalante af Arkadien," for which Price wrote the music and Adam Price was lyricist. As is often his wont, Schwartz worked on the choral arrangements along with Jorgen Lauritsen, who also provided orchestrations along with other musicians.

In addition to the Danish OCR, also available for this study was the piano/vocal score of the 2011 production of My Fairytale (the show in English), described later. For one who knows Schwartz's music, the score sounds familiar, and it occupies his usual, wide stylistic range. An aspect of Schwartz's attempts at musico-dramatic unification appears in the reprises and the way a musical style tends to follow a character, especially the Shadow. A most impressive performance must have been that of Louise Fribo in her multiple roles. Her lovely soprano voice is a highlight on the OCR. Performances on the disc are for the most part excellent, providing elegant documentation of the show's premiere at the Gladsaxe Theatre.

Schwartz wrote a tuneful score for Mit eventyr, with somewhat less reliance upon a rock beat than usual. Those orchestrating the score made frequent use of synthesized metallic sounds that perhaps constitute the sonic identifier of Andersen's fairytale world. As will be shown in descriptions of tunes here, the composer included established types of songs familiar in his other productions. Schwartz's opening number, "Bli' hos os," sung by Louise Fribo as Little Bo Peep, Andersen, and the Fairytale Characters, is our musical introduction to the fantasy world. It opens with a lovely soprano line and moves onto pop syncopations over an electronic groove with string countermelodies. The characters beg Andersen to stay with them as a person who can fix things—they lack practical knowledge. The writer explains that he has more important things to do and no time for fairytales. The song ends with Andersen and the ensemble in counterpoint, the characters begging him to stay and Andersen trying to leave. Andersen learns that the characters know of no exit from their world, so his fairytale journey begins. The reprise of "Bli' hos mig" is brief, sung by Fribo as a princess on a music box, accompanied by the requisite tinkly sounds. The princess looks for her prince and wonders if he might be Andersen, but he does not seem sufficiently handsome. The song includes the humorous effect of the music box running down; her helper winds it up so she can finish the song. "Fader, du var træt" is a simple, folklike tune in quadruple meter for the Boy, who mourns the loss of his father. It conveys the innocence of youth with a simple accompaniment, except for some ominous electronic rumblings. The contrast between the Boy and the Shadow's more worldly demeanor appears in a number of the songs. The Boy sings the tune of "Fader" again in "Konversation" with the Shadow in Act 2, opening the song as he plaintively approaches his mother. The Shadow enters after a deceptive cadence, singing faster material as he complains that he must wait for Andersen when they have enough material to write their play. By song's end, the Shadow dismisses his need for Andersen or the Boy, who comments to his mother about the angel that he sees. The Boy's folk-like material contrasts strongly with the speech rhythms that the Shadow sings in alternation and counterpoint, but the Shadow's material more resembles the Boy's by the number's close.

The song that appears most often in Mit eventyr is "Min rejsekammerat," sung three times, first as a duet between Andersen and his Shadow, the latter's musical introduction; the second time as a trio joined by the Boy; and the third time by the Shadow alone. It is a sinister tune, like what one expects from Kurt Weill in Die Dreigroschenoper, with chromatic turns of phrase and the dotted rhythms of a vaudevillian soft-shoe. The Shadow is the darker side of Andersen's character, assuring the author in the first occurrence of the song that he has always kept him "focused on . . . ambition."[33] In "Min rejsekammerat 1" one hears prominent accompaniment from piano, bass clarinet, and synthesizer. "Rejsekammerat Trio" is a brief reprise where Andersen seems pleased to be traveling with companions while they sarcastically mock him. The character of the tune's first occurrence returns in "Min rejsekammerat 3," where the Shadow advises Andersen that he can see his future and it is time to say farewell to fairytales. The Shadow also recalls the tune in the equally creepy "Stakkels Andersen," where the Danish text is attributed to Adam Price rather than Schwartz. Here the wide sonic palette called upon from synthesizer and percussion accompanies the Shadow as he tries to convince Andersen that the fairytales are unworthy of his attention. They are briefly confronted by the Snow Queen, who dissolves with sound effects at 1'15" (track 28), a sign of the Shadow's temporary victory.[34]

The other songs also add markedly to the drama. The finale of Act 1, "På svanevinger," sung by Andersen, Shadow, Boy, and Choir, accompanies Andersen's flight on a large swan, which actually took place on stage.[35] The song is a moving ballad in quadruple meter with an accompaniment of onrushing triplets. Andersen and the Boy sing together, marveling at their ride, but are interrupted by the Shadow, whom they tried to leave behind. "Synk ned i mit hav," sung by the Little Mermaid and her sisters under the sea, moves languidly in 6/8 with soaring writing for solo soprano (up to d'''), backed by women's ensemble. It is marked "Pop Ballad" and includes a subtle rock-like drum track and syncopated metallic sounds from synthesizer, sounding somewhat like a 1950s girl group pining for their boyfriends. The lyrics include erotic imagery as Andersen revels in his imagination. "Red os," performed by Andersen, Shadow, and Fairytale Characters, has the chorus calling imploringly for Andersen to save them as the Shadow tries to convince Andersen to leave. Schwartz marked it "Largo Doloroso." It opens dreamily with a lyrical cello melody followed by the chorus singing on a neutral syllable. The main melody is deliberate, mostly conjunct with rich harmonies. Although it does not sound like the song melodically, "Red os" carries a similar feeling to the music that Jerry Bock wrote for "Sabbath Prayer" in *Fiddler on the Roof*. "Det er ganske vist" is mostly a solo for Andersen on the OCR, becoming a song for the protagonist, Jenny Lind, and the Fairytale Characters in the "Finale." Here Andersen accepts his fate to become a writer of fairytales, offering the images of several. There is a central portion of the song where he returns to reality, set off nicely by Schwartz with a musical change of character, but returning to the original idea with renewed commitment. "Det er ganske vist," marked "Pop Ballad," is a powerful number with a wide tessitura and a lovely motive for the recurring title text, accompanied mostly by piano and strings and later drums. The "Finale" is a beautiful arrangement of the same tune for soloists and chorus, closing with a snippet from the opening song "Bli' hos os."

Stephen Schwartz never expected to hear this show performed in English,[36] but the show's potential appeal proved to be too big of a draw for the California town of Solvang in the Santa Ynez Valley as it celebrated its centennial in 2011. Settled by Danish immigrants, Solvang regards its Danish heritage as very important, and its sites include a park and museum dedicated to Hans Christian Andersen. The performance was produced by the Pacific Conservatory of the Performing Arts, thirty-five miles north in Santa Maria, California, which boasts a strong program in musical theater. Stephen Schwartz's son Scott directed *My Fairytale*, leading a cast of Equity and non-Equity players and students in a production that offered previews at the Marian Theatre in Santa Maria from 12 to 19 August 2011 and then moved outdoors at the Solvang Festival Theatre for a run from 26 August to 25 September.[37] The star was Broadway performer Kevin Cahoon. Schwartz reports that his son thought that the show's music (besides the Donizetti excerpt) needed to begin before Andersen arrives in the fairytale land, so he added "Andersen's Shadow" for the English production. He also noted in the same interview that most of the music in the Danish production also appeared in Solvang.[38] The Solvang production drew attention from critics, such as Stephen Stanley for his website www.stagescenela.com and from the *San Luis Obispo Tribune* and Bob Verini in *Variety*, both reviewing it positively.[39] Now that *My Fairytale* has appeared in an English production, one might expect it to enter the American repertory.

My Antonia

Schwartz's son Scott began to adapt Willa Cather's novel My Antonia into a play while still an undergraduate in psychology at Harvard.[40] Inspired by the famous production of Nicholas Nickleby by Trevor Nunn and John Caird, Schwartz wanted to adapt a "great American novel" for the stage, and My Antonia had entered the public domain in 1993. Schwartz did not realize that Willa Cather had banned dramatizations of her stories in her will before she died in 1947. When he later learned this, he nevertheless continued his effort, but it has inspired him to try to retain as much as possible of the book's spirit.

During the thirteen years that he worked on My Antonia, Scott Schwartz became a noted director, independently from the shadow of his famous father, with whom he chose not to work for the first decade of his professional career.[41] Some of his previous work included a 2000 touring version of Godspell; an award-winning, off-Broadway production of Bat Boy: The Musical in 2001; and a production of William Gibson's Golda's Balcony that played both off-Broadway and at the Helen Hayes Theatre in New York in 2003. His work has not gone unnoticed by his actors. Tovah Feldshuh, who played Golda Meir in Golda's Balcony, stated that Schwartz was "simply one of the best director's I've ever worked with. Period. Exclamation point. He's a brilliant structuralist and his kindness is on a par with his intelligence."[42]

My Antonia, Cather's memorable story about Bohemian immigrants on the Nebraska prairie, has been produced in several different versions. Schwartz staged it in 2002 in the New Plays Initiative of TheatreWorks in Palo Alto, California, and another edition with the same company in spring 2004 with sixteen actors and four musicians for whom his father wrote an incidental score.[43] Scott Schwartz has described that as a "developmental" version of the play.[44] He tried to tell most of the novel's story, but the result caused him to want to simplify the story, which he did in preparing the next version for the Rubicon Theatre in Ventura, California, in spring 2008.[45]

Scott Schwartz did not set out to work with his father when he decided that he wanted an incidental score. He approached Stephen Schwartz to ask names of possible composers, but his father had already seen the play, liked it, and offered to write the music himself. He had never composed an incidental score for a play. Many noted composers have done so, the most famous works in the genre being Felix Mendelssohn's score for A Midsummer Night's Dream and Georges Bizet's score for L'Arlésienne. Mendelssohn and Bizet, however, wrote for orchestra, and Schwartz wrote primarily for piano, bringing harmonica, violin, and accordion in for color. Scott Schwartz found Russian and

Czech poetry that his father used in his score, which includes several songs and provides "an underscore for the entire play."[46] The composer compared this task to "doing a movie score."[47] Schwartz's many short cues for *My Antonia* carry the feeling of nineteenth-century melodrama, a popular theatrical genre where a composer supplied *melos* (short musical sections) that helped tell the story. Given the popularity of melodrama, it seems apt that they adapted this technique into *My Antonia*, a story from the same period.

Stephen Schwartz's office made his score for *My Antonia* available for study. It represents a major effort with sixty-nine cues spread over the three acts and a total of 1,742 measures with a similar amount of music in each act: 577 bars in Act 1, 593 in Act 2, and 572 in Act 3. Schwartz offered musico-dramatic unification, repeating earlier music in many cues. It is largely for piano with isolated use of harmonica, violin, and accordion, but each could easily be played more in a performance. Schwartz is a fine pianist, and this score is idiomatic to the instrument. The score usually transmits only the number of each cue along with the line spoken before and after; occasionally lines spoken during a cue appear. There are five songs. Complete consideration of the score is not possible here, but general comments will be offered.

Schwartz's music demonstrates that several aspects of the show captured his imagination: movement, especially train travel, sometimes represented by a recurring melody; themes associated with various characters, such as one for Antonia; long chords, sometimes bitonal, that can underscore dialogue for extended lengths; work music that occasionally underscores operation of a pump; music that describes natural phenomena, such as rain; and recurring themes from songs. Several of the cues segue directly into each other, meaning that in places the music has an extended presence. At times cues are fairly inconsequential in musical content, surely intentionally, but other cues are very dramatic. Schwartz's musical style here is unusual for him, eschewing a pop sensibility and approaching what one hears in sections of *Séance on a Wet Afternoon*, such as noodling eighth notes that smack of minimalism. Like his larger projects, *My Antonia* carries the feeling of an artist that wants to maximize dramatic effect and tie music closely into the narrative.

Schwartz has commented upon preexistent music and texts that appear in *My Antonia*.[48] At the end of Act 1 (Cue 23), where a hymn was indicated, he inserted the tune "Passion Chorale" by Hans Leo Hassler (1564–1612), famously used by Johann Sebastian Bach in the *St. Matthew Passion* and elsewhere. The hymn reappears at the end of Act 3 of *My Antonia* (Cue 57). Many texts have been set to the tune (the most famous in English is "O Sacred Head Now Wounded"), but Schwartz found it as number 446 in the Episcopal Hymnal (1940) with the text "Commit Thou All That Grieves

Thee."⁴⁹ Schwartz learned the melody when Paul Simon based his "American Tune" on it, and once provided cabaret singer Jane Olivor with an arrangement that combined the hymn with Simon's song. "Commit Thou All
That Grieves Thee" in Cue 23 includes a solo setting with four-part piano
accompaniment much like one expects for one of Bach's chorales; later those
four parts are sung by choir doubled by keyboard.

For the finale of Act 2 (Cue 41), Schwartz used the nineteenth-century
song "When You and I Were Young, Maggie" with text by George W.
Johnson (1839–1917), later set to music by James A. Butterfield (1837–
1891). Schwartz and his son were looking for a song known in Antonia's
day, and this popular tune, published in 1866 by Francis, Day & Hunter,
filled the bill.⁵⁰ The Schwartzes also liked the song's sense of nostalgia
and regret, which fits what is then going on in the plot: Jim, the narrator, is about to leave home and Antonia. In Cue 41, Schwartz states the
first phrase on the harmonica without keyboard accompaniment before
someone sings the tune (and hums a portion of it) with a simple piano
accompaniment.

Scott Schwartz found lyrics to three Bohemian and Russian folk songs
that his father set to his own music, written in imitation of Eastern European folk melodies. The first such text appears in Cue 12. It is Russian, used by
Modest Mussorgsky in a dramatic situation that calls for a folk song in the
1872 version of his opera *Boris Godunov*. (The composer first wrote the opera
in 1868–1869, but that was rejected by the Imperial Theater in St. Peters-
burg, causing Mussorgsky to embark on a massive revision, finished in 1872.
The premiere was at the Mariinsky Theater in 1874.⁵¹) In Act 2 of the 1872
version, Xenia, Boris's daughter, clutches a picture of the deceased Danish
prince that she was to marry. After her brother tries to comfort her, her nurse
takes over the task and sings this nonsensical text, "Kak komar drova rubil,"
which concerns the domestic activities of a gnat and bedbug.⁵² Schwartz's
setting in Cue 12 opens with a short violin melody that sounds a number of
times in the show. The melody for the song is motivic and repetitious as one
expects in a folk song and includes one sixteenth note followed by a dotted
eighth, the reverse dotted rhythms common in Eastern European folk music.
It is in G major, hanging around the tonic most of the time, without any
modal touches. The accompaniment is mostly a "boom-chink" approach in
eighth notes, and Schwartz included another melody for violin on A that
includes ambiguous modal signifiers.

Another text that Scott Schwartz supplied begins "Jtse tak tak ja." He
derived this portion of his play from a moment in Cather's novel where
Antonia describes an old woman, Old Hata, who sang for children. Antonia

and Jim have found a small, green insect, and his chirp reminds the young woman of Old Hata back in her Czech homeland. The tune that Schwartz wrote, appropriate for a folk song, occurs first in Cue 22, but recurs several times in the score. It is in 3/4, but not really in the character of the waltz, especially in the choral accompaniment. The song is in D minor, and it is the opening descending fourth that announces Old Hata when it recurs. Cue 33 ends with a tone cluster in the extreme bass range of the piano, representing a gunshot.

Cue 51 includes the other text that Scott Schwartz supplied his father: "Hospidine pomiluj ny, Jesu Kriste." This Czech text corresponds generally to the Greek *Kyrie eleison* that is part of the Roman Catholic Mass Ordinary: "Lord, have mercy upon us . . ." It exists with a monophonic tune in a medieval manuscript that dates from the end of the tenth or beginning of the eleventh century. Vladimír Stepánek and Bohumil Karásek report that it was well known among the people, sung by armies as they went into battle and by 1346 it had become part of the coronation ceremony for a Czech king, making it something like a modern national anthem.[53] Schwartz's setting for "Hospidine" is perhaps the best of his faux folk song settings here. It is in E minor, opening with a sequential passage in 6/4 and then moving to a conjunct passage in 4/4 with grace notes that sound right out of Bartók. Some of the harmonies include enough added tones to provide just the right amount of spice.

Schwartz's score also included two quotations from themes that he wrote while a college student. Antonia's theme came from a song called "Dream" from *Whatserface*, Schwartz's first Scotch 'n' Soda show, and music that he wrote for the production of *The Rivals* his first year became the theme for Mr. and Mrs. Cutter in Act 3.[54]

The cues described here illustrate how important music is in helping bring *My Antonia* to life on stage, and there are a number of other cues where Schwartz's music seems an indispensable part of a scene. The title character, for example, likes to dance at a time when some did not consider it an acceptable activity for a young woman. While Antonia was working as a hired girl in Black Hawk, an Italian couple opens up a dancing tent where the young people go in the evenings. Antonia is one of the best dancers, becoming fast friends with other immigrant girls who worked in Black Hawk and being noticed by men. The family she works for, the Harlings, finally make her choose between working for them and her dancing, and she leaves to work for someone else, a family she knows is trouble from the beginning, but they will allow her to dance. The dancing tent, therefore, is more than just a pleasant diversion. Schwartz wrote several cues to underscore dances, including, for example, a simple but effective tune in 6/8 in Cue 36a and a waltz in Cue 37 that reappears in 38a and 39; there is a different waltz earlier in the latter cue. How popular Scott Schwartz's dramatic setting of *My Antonia* might become cannot be known, but it is fascinating to see Stephen Schwartz writing incidental music, which is essentially different in intention and execution than his songs for musical plays.

Epilogue: An American Musical Institution: Stephen Schwartz in Revivals and a Pops Concert

The ubiquitous place of music in American life makes it one of our most precious commodities. We commit ourselves to our own playlists and zealously proclaim our allegiance to artists, declaring the venerable ones to be "legends." After a career of more than forty years on Broadway and in Hollywood, Stephen Schwartz has surely reached the status of "legend"—in our era of breathless commercial hype, that might have been guaranteed by *Godspell* or *Wicked* alone. As a composer/lyricist for theater, Schwartz has entered into the pantheon assisted by revivals of his earlier shows and, as proof from the larger culture, in such events as orchestral pop concerts that present retrospectives of his long career.

Revivals of Schwartz's early shows had not occurred on Broadway since they ran in the 1970s, despite the continuing popularity of *Godspell* and *Pippin*. Perhaps *Wicked*'s runaway success has caused such interest, but it was remarkable that these two shows would open at Broadway houses within eighteen months: *Godspell* at Circle in the Square on 7 November 2011 and *Pippin* at the Music Box on 25 April 2013. *Godspell* ran 264 performances, only modestly successful; *Pippin* started slowly and gained momentum when it was nominated for ten Tony Awards, and then it won four Tonys, including Best Revival. As demonstrated in Chapters 2 and 4, the new productions were significant departures from earlier New York versions, but Schwartz's scores remained mostly intact with some changes that he agreed to, including new orchestrations and, for example, using the song "Beautiful City" (written for the film) in *Godspell*. Schwartz's scores help form the identities of *Godspell* and *Pippin*. Whatever success the shows enjoyed on Broadway, producers decided that these shows were worthy gambles in the high-risk competition for the audience's money. Revivals have become evermore popular on Broadway, but it remains no small matter to bring a work back after more than three decades away from the Great White Way. These revivals of *Godspell* and *Pippin* place Schwartz's earlier works in a new, brighter light.

The symphony orchestra plays a unique role in this country—diminished, to be sure, in the last few decades—but most American cities continue to maintain orchestras, even as their core audience ages. Pops concerts have become important parts of orchestral seasons as ensembles search for new audiences and increased relevancy, and often include performers and/or repertory not usually associated with a symphony. The mature popular artists characteristically featured in pops concerts provide nostalgic moments for listeners. Schwartz's entry into this phenomenon demonstrates that nostalgic cravings for some now include his output, just like songs by earlier Broadway masters would have been part of pops concerts in the 1970s and 1980s.

Conductor Steven Reineke conceived "The Wizard and I: The Musical Journey of Stephen Schwartz" for Schwartz's 65th birthday (which was on 6 March 2013) and the tenth anniversary of *Wicked*'s opening. The concert occurred three places during spring 2013: 29 April at Carnegie Hall with the New York Pops, 11–12 May with the Omaha (Nebraska) Symphony, and 16–18 May at the Kennedy Center with the National Symphony in Washington DC. The cast and content of the program varied subtly between performances, and Schwartz only took part in New York and Washington. Performers in Omaha, conducted by Reineke, included Julie Murney (who has played Elphaba on tour and on Broadway), Jennifer Laura Thompson (once Glinda on Broadway), Darius da Haas (Cain/Japheth in the 1997 Paper Mill production of *Children of Eden* and on the cast recording), and Christopher Johnstone (a fine young tenor/baritone with many credits, none previously related to Schwartz). The Omaha Symphony Chorus also took part. It was in the cavernous Holland Performing Arts Center, which on 11 May was perhaps slightly more than half full with an appreciative audience.

The concert opened and closed with repertory from *Wicked*. The program proceeded as follows:

"*Wicked*: A Fable for Orchestra," arranged by Stephen Schwartz and William David Brohn[1]

From *Children of Eden*: "The Spark of Creation" (Murney, later joined by the other three soloists and chorus) and "Lost in the Wilderness" (de Haas)

From *The Baker's Wife*: "Meadowlark" (Murney)

From *The Magic Show*: "West End Avenue" (Thompson)

From *Pippin*: "Magic to Do" (soloists, choir) and "Morning Glow" (de Haas, choir)

From *Godspell*: "Prepare Ye" (Johnstone), "Bless the Lord My Soul" (Murney, Thompson, choir), "All for the Best" (chorus, Johnstone), "Day by Day" (soloists, choir)

Intermission

From *Séance on a Wet Afternoon*: instrumental preludes to Acts 1 and 2

Medley from animated films with choir and soloists:

> From *The Hunchback of Notre Dame* (music by Alan Menken, lyrics by Schwartz): "Heaven's Light/Hellfire" and "Out There" (de Haas)
>
> From *Pocahontas* (Menken and Schwartz): "Colors of the Wind" (Murney)
>
> From *The Prince of Egypt*: "Through Heaven's Eyes" (Johnstone) and "When You Believe" (Thompson)

From *Wicked*: "Popular" (Thompson), "Defying Gravity" (Murney), "For Good" (Thompson, Murney)

From *Mit eventyr*: "Can You Imagine That?" (soloists, choir)

The performers were chatty, especially those with stories to relate about appearing in Schwartz's shows or working with him, and Reineke provided background and commentary. No effort was made at the concert to identify who provided the arrangements for these numbers, but they were uniformly excellent, especially a terrific choral version of "All for the Best." Most performances were worthwhile, and at times they were memorable. Thompson and Johnstone sang all of their numbers well; Thompson and Murney were at their best in the *Wicked* set. The Omaha Symphony and Chorus acquitted themselves well, but the chorus was far above and behind the orchestra, which caused problems with balance and projecting lyrics.

The concert gave a fine look at the full sweep of Schwartz's career and how he has bridged a host of contrasting musical styles in the production of effective theater music that both explains a character's motivation and delights the listener. The audience, much of which was baby boomers and seniors (along with some of the young women who love *Wicked*), enjoyed both the familiar material and lesser-known songs, offering confirmation of Schwartz's status as a composer and lyricist whose varied output and long career justify dedicating a two-hour concert to his works.

What makes a theatrical composer/lyricist an American musical institution? A definition is risky, but one who has had hit shows and films irregularly between the 1970s and 2000s, who wrote the score for the most popular American show of the current century, who has contributed significantly in multiple areas in many successful projects, and who has won numerous awards in both theater and film would seem to qualify. Schwartz has demonstrated his ability to write pleasing, persuasive music in a variety of styles that people want to hear over and over, at least partly because of his gifts as a melodist and excellence in capturing the crucial features of a musical style. The tenacity that he has displayed in trying to make his troubled projects work has been remarkable, and he has been as involved in helping to forge the plots in his shows as perhaps any composer/lyricist in Broadway history. The best shows in which he has been involved, such as *Children of Eden* and *Wicked*, are musical plays with both heart and soul, and include scores that participate fully in telling the story and describing characters. When writing lyrics for music by others, his craftsmanship is admirable. It is this multitalented, inquisitive artist who was honored that night in Omaha, and whose career is far from finished as he starts the second half of his seventh decade.

~

Notes

Acknowledgments

1. Paul R. Laird, "Stephen Schwartz and Bernstein's *Mass*," in *On Bunker's Hill: Essays in Honor of J. Bunker Clark*, edited by William A. Everett and Paul R. Laird (Sterling Heights, MI: Harmonie Park Press, 2007), 263–70.

Introduction

1. Carol de Giere, *Defying Gravity: The Creative Career of Stephen Schwartz from "Godspell" to "Wicked"* (New York: Applause Theatre & Cinema Books, 2008).

2. Paul R. Laird, *"Wicked": A Musical Biography* (Lanham, MD: Scarecrow Press, 2011).

Chapter 1: An Introduction to Stephen Schwartz

1. For additional information on *Wicked*'s international reach, see my *"Wicked": A Musical Biography* (Lanham, MD: Scarecrow Press, 2011), 261–75.

2. Personal interview with Stephen Schwartz in New York City, 1 April 2008.

3. Laird, *Wicked*, 251–60.

4. Between 1965 and 1980, Grammy Awards for self-produced albums included separate citations for artist/composer and producer. See http://www.grammy.com/nominees/search?artist=%22stephen+schwartz%22&title=&year=All&genre=All (accessed 2 February 2013).

5. Carol de Giere, *Defying Gravity: The Creative Career of Stephen Schwartz from "Godspell" to "Wicked"* (New York: Applause Theatre & Cinema Books, 2008), 168.

6. Carol J. Oja, "*West Side Story* and *The Music Man*: Whiteness, Immigration, and Race in the US during the Late 1950s," *Studies in Musical Theatre* 3, no. 1 (2009): 16.

7. The material in this paragraph is derived from a personal interview with Stephen Schwartz in New York City on 19 March 2008.

8. De Giere, *Defying Gravity*, 10–11.

9. De Giere, *Defying Gravity*, 11–12.

10. De Giere, *Defying Gravity*, 12–13.

11. This information emanates from the *Productions* books (which include programs) from the Carnegie Mellon University Department of Drama, available in the University Archive. The book of programs from 1964–1965, Schwartz's first year, was not available.

12. For a photograph of Schwartz in this production, see de Giere, *Defying Gravity*, 14, but she erroneously places the show in the 1966–1967 academic year. The *Drama—List of Productions—1914–1970* in the Carnegie Mellon University Archives states that this production was in 1964–1965.

13. Personal interview with Stephen Schwartz in New York City, 22 November 2008. One of the melodies appeared in his 2008 incidental music score for My *Antonia*. See Chapter 14 for my consideration of My *Antonia*.

14. This information also appears in the drama department's *Productions* books.

15. Historical information on the Scotch 'n' Soda productions appears in the Carnegie Mellon University Archives, *Finding Aids and Inventories for Official University Records*.

16. See de Giere, *Defying Gravity*, 17–27.

17. Personal interview with Stephen Schwartz in New York City, 22 November 2008.

18. The program for each Scotch 'n' Soda show is in the Carnegie Mellon University Archives.

19. Tod Johnson, ed., *Thistle 1965* (Pittsburgh: Carnegie Institute of Technology, 1965), 96.

20. Martha Hodgson, "S'nS Comes of Age in 1965 Production," *Carnegie Tech Tartan*, 5 May 1965, 2.

21. *Whatserface* recording, Carnegie Mellon University Hunt Library Audio Collection.

22. Personal interview with Stephen Schwartz in New York City, 22 November 2008.

23. Notes that Schwartz provided during interview on 22 November 2008.

24. Personal interview with Stephen Schwartz in New York City, 22 November 2008.

25. Personal interview with Stephen Schwartz in New York City, 22 November 2008.

26. Carnegie Mellon alumnus Gerald Adler organized this retrospective, which took place on 26 October 1996. The many letters that alumni wrote to Adler appear in the University Archive, and several mention working with Schwartz.

27. *Nouveau* recording, Carnegie Mellon University Hunt Library Audio Collection.

28. See de Giere, *Defying Gravity*, 21.

29. Sue Attinson, "'Pippin, Pippin' Called Best Collaborative Effort," *Tartan*, 26 April 1967, 1ff.

30. *Pippin, Pippin* recording, Carnegie Mellon University Hunt Library Audio Collection.

31. Personal interview with Stephen Schwartz in New York City, 22 November 2008.

32. In some sources the title is reported as *Voltaire and the Witches*, but the program says *Voltaire and Witches*.

33. Personal interview with Stephen Schwartz in New York City, 22 November 2008.

34. David Crocker, "S'n'S First—Double Feature, Men of Letters Contrast," *Tartan*, 13 March 1968, 5ff.

35. *Twice upon a Time* recording, Carnegie Mellon University Hunt Library Audio Collection.

Chapter 2: *Godspell*

1. A more complete history of the show is available in Carol de Giere, *Defying Gravity: The Creative Career of Stephen Schwartz from "Godspell" to "Wicked"* (New York: Applause Theatre & Cinema Books, 2008), 42–69. The same author is working on a book on *Godspell*. Another worthwhile resource on the show appears in Joseph P. Swain's *The Broadway Musical: A Critical and Musical Survey*, revised and expanded (Lanham, MD: Scarecrow Press, 2002), 295–314.

2. Geoffrey Wansell, "John-Michael Tebelak," *Times* (London), 2 February 1972.

3. Harvey Cox, *The Feast of Fools* (Cambridge, MA: Harvard University Press, 1969). Swain (*Broadway Musical*, 299–300) considers Cox's influence on *Godspell* in some detail, especially in the portrayal of the cast as clowns.

4. De Giere, *Defying Gravity*, 45.

5. Tebelak does not appear to have mentioned this possible influence, but the similarity between *Paul Sills' Story Theatre* and *Godspell* was mentioned by reviewers and publicists from the period.

6. Nina Faso commented to de Giere (*Defying Gravity*, 45–46) on Tebelak's interest in Grotowski, and several actors involved in the original production mentioned in interviews the presence of Grotowski's exercises in *Godspell* rehearsals.

7. Cast members could not remember the number of times they performed the show, and their estimates varied. The Carnegie Mellon program for *The Godspell* included in the Drama Department program books at the Carnegie Mellon Archives reports but one performance, on 14 December 1970.

8. I thank Peggy Gordon, who made an unreleased recording from the 14 December 1970 performance of *The Godspell* available for this study.

9. From "Circus, Spirit, & Rock of Hit Musical to Weave 'Godspell' at Mark Taper/Nov. Opening Set for Sweet Rock Show" (press release), Center Theatre Group Mark Taper Forum, 25 August 1971, consulted in the Billy Rose Theatre Collection at the New York Public Library for the Performing Arts. The hymnal that Tebelak used was *The Hymnal of the Protestant Episcopal Church in the United States of America* (New York: The Church Hymnal Corporation, 1940).

10. See http://www.lamama.org/archives/year_lists/1971page.htm (accessed 3 February 2013). Elizabeth L. Wollman incorrectly states that *Godspell* played at La MaMa for three months and did so with Stephen Schwartz's score. See her *The Theater Will Rock: A History of the Rock Musical, from "Hair" to "Hedwig"* (Ann Arbor: University of Michigan Press, 2006), 87.

11. Telephone interview with Leon Katz, 1 February 2008.

12. Personal interview with Peggy Gordon in New York City, 17 January 2008.

13. Telephone interview with Stephen Nathan, 6 February 2008.

14. Telephone interview with Nina Faso, 6–7 February 2008.

15. Personal interview with Peggy Gordon in New York City, 17 January 2008.

16. Personal interview with Peggy Gordon in New York City, 17 January 2008.

17. Carra directed the Great Lakes Shakespeare Festival in Cleveland, OH, in the summer of 1971, and he asked Tebelak to come and lead a production of *Godspell* that opened on 11 August. This information is available in the Carnegie Mellon University Archive.

18. Personal interview with Edgar Lansbury in New York City, 22 January 2008.

19. Barbara Wilson, "In the Beginning, 'Godspell' Was Matter of Degree," *Philadelphia Inquirer*, 1 April 1973.

20. Personal interview with Edgar Lansbury in New York City, 22 January 2008.

21. De Giere, *Defying Gravity*, 48–49.

22. De Giere, *Defying Gravity*, 49.

23. Personal interview with Stephen Schwartz in New York City, 14 January 2008.

24. Personal interview with Stephen Schwartz in New York City, 14 January 2008.

25. Personal interview with Peggy Gordon in New York City, 17 January 2008.

26. Personal interview with Edgar Lansbury in New York City, 22 January 2008.

27. De Giere, *Defying Gravity*, 52–53.

28. Telephone interview with Stephen Reinhardt, 8 January 2008.

29. Personal interview with Edgar Lansbury in New York City, 22 January 2008.

30. Personal interview with Stephen Schwartz in New York City, 14 January 2008.

31. Personal interview with Stephen Schwartz in New York City, 14 January 2008.

32. Telephone interview with Stephen Reinhardt, 8 January 2008.

33. Telephone interview with Stephen Nathan, 6 February 2008.

34. Elizabeth L. Wollman incorrectly states that *Godspell* played at the Cherry Lane Theater for 2,124 performances. See Wollman, *Theater Will Rock*, 88.

35. My detailed synopsis of *Godspell* from a 1974 performance at the Promenade is available as a PDF at the following website: http://www.music.ku.edu/paul-laird.

36. Gifford/Wallace, Inc., untitled press release, 22 June 1976.

37. *Godspell* advertisement, *Wall Street Journal*, 5 September 1974.

38. http://ibdb.com/production.php?id=3847 (accessed 14 June 2013).

39. Stuart Duncan, "Packet Online" (Princeton, NJ), http://www.zwire.com/site/nyzwire.cfm?.newsid=11169165&BRD=1091&PAG=461&dept, printed from the web on 25 March 2004. Consulted in *Godspell* clipping file in the Billy Rose Theatre Division at the New York Public Library for the Performing Arts.

40. Clive Barnes, "The Theater: 'Godspell,' Musical about Jesus Is at Cherry Lane," *New York Times*, 18 May 1971, 45.

41. Telephone interview with Stephen Nathan, 6 February 2008.

42. Walter Kerr, "Why Make St. Matthew Dance? For the Fun of It," *New York Times*, 30 May 1971, Sec. 2, 1 and 9.

43. Lee Silver, "St. Matthew's Gospel Grooves in 'Godspell,'" *Daily News*, 18 May 1971.

44. Jeffrey Tallmer, "Off-Broadway: Surprise in Nazareth," *New York Post*, 18 May 1971.

45. Allan Wallach, "In Review/Stage: Off-Broadway Gospel," *Newsday*, 18 May 1971.

46. Emory Lewis, "'Godspell' Sings of Jesus—a Jubilant Rock of Ages," *Record*, 18 May 1971.

47. William Raidy, "First Nighter: 'Godspell' Is a Blessing," *Long Island Press* and *Newark Star-Ledger*, 18 May 1971.

48. Edward Sothern Hipp, "'Godspell,' and More," *Newark Evening News*, 18 May 1971.

49. Joseph H. Mazo, review of *Godspell*, *Women's Wear Daily*, 18 May 1971, 12.

50. Lee Mishkin, "The 'Godspell' according to Schwartz," *Morningside Telegraph* (New York), 19 May 1971.

51. All texts of radio and television reviews were accessed at the New York Public Library for the Performing Arts, either in the clipping files of the Billy Rose Theatre Division or in the library's extensive bound scrapbooks of reviews.

52. Dick Brukenfeld, "The Gospel Truth and a Few Fibs," *Village Voice*, 20 May 1971, 55.

53. Marilyn Stasio, Review of *Godspell*, *Cue*, 22 May 1971, 14.

54. Edith Oliver, Review of *Godspell*, *New Yorker*, 24 May 1971, 56.

55. John Beaufort, Review of *Godspell*, *Christian Science Monitor*, 24 May 1971.

56. Review of *Godspell*, *Time*, 24 May 1971, 48.

57. John Simon, "Theater: *The Antigone* and *The Ecstasy*," *New York*, 31 May 1971, 50.

58. Sege, "Off-Broadway Review: Godspell," *Variety*, 2 June 1971.

59. Martin Gottfried, "Will the 'Godspell' Work on Broadway?" *New York Post*, 23 June 1976, 48.

60. Richard Eder, "Stage: 'Godspell' Moves Up to Broadway," *New York Times*, 23 June 1976.

61. Hobe Morrison, "Godspell," *Variety*, 30 June 1976.

62. Alan Rich, "Summer Reruns," *New York*, 12 July 1976, 64.

63. Scott Miller believes that the success of the second act in *Godspell* depends "on how well the emotional ties between Jesus and the disciples are established in Act I." The first act is about "the growth of relationships," while the second act involves " a series of events that follow logically toward a climax and resolution." See Scott Miller, *From "Assassins" to "West Side Story"* (Portsmouth, NH: Heinemann, 1996), 81–83.

64. Swain considers the show from more of a religious angle than most commentators, going so far as to suggest (*Broadway Musical*, 303) that it strongly resembles the Service of the Word from the Easter Vigil, presumably from the Anglican Church, a service that inspired Tebelak to write the show.

65. Lansbury recalled that the local stage producer of *Godspell* in Boston believed that the film's release hurt his business, and Lansbury and Beruh had to pay him off; personal interview with Edgar Lansbury in New York City, 22 January 2008.

66. Personal interview with Edgar Lansbury in New York City, 22 January 2008. An appreciative description of the film appears in Thomas S. Hischak's *Through the Screen Door: What Happened to the Broadway Musical When It Went to Hollywood* (Lanham, MD: Scarecrow Press, 2004), 48–49.

67. Telephone interview with Leon Katz, 1 February 2008.

68. Telephone interview with Robin Lamont, 22 February 2008.

69. Personal interview with Edgar Lansbury in New York City, 22 January 2008.

70. Electronic message from Joanne Jonas McCraty, 16 February 2008.

71. http://www.imdb.com/name/nm0853659/ (accessed 3 February 2013).

72. Vincent Canby, "The Gospel According to 'Godspell' Comes to Screen," *New York Times*, 22 March 1973, 52.

73. Sege, "*Godspell*," *Variety*, 28 March 1973, 18.

74. Personal interview with Stephen Schwartz in New York City, 14 January 2008. In this segment on the music of *Godspell*, all quotations from Schwartz are from this interview unless otherwise indicated.

75. Swain (*Broadway Musical*, 304) provides a table of the sources for the lyrics of each song in *Godspell*.

76. Citations for the two recordings are as follows: Stephen Schwartz, *Godspell: A Musical Based upon the Gospel According to St. Matthew* (Arista ARCD-8304, 1974), and *Godspell: The New Broadway Cast Recording* (Ghostlight Records 8–4456, 2011).

77. The score used for this study was supplied by Schwartz's office: *Godspell Piano Vocal Score. Conceived and Originally Directed by John-Michael Tebelak. Music and New Lyrics by Stephen Schwartz* (New York: Music Theatre International, 1999).

78. Swain describes this as a chaconne.

79. Swain (*Broadway Musical*, 301–02) also covers Schwartz's use of seventh chords in "Day by Day" and their influence on the song's ambiguous key center.

80. *Godspell Piano Vocal Score*, 45.

81. Other commentators have noted Schwartz's debt to figures like Laura Nyro. Writing about the *Godspell* score, Elizabeth L. Wollman has noted, "Its score was reflective of Stephen Schwartz's admiration for singer-songwriters like Joni Mitchell, Laura Nyro, James Taylor, Paul Simon, and Cat Stevens, especially in the largely acoustic instrumentation and its many spiritually introspective lyric passages." See Wollman, *Theater Will Rock*, 87.

82. Swain (*Broadway Musical*, 303–11) considers "Bless the Lord" in considerable detail, comparing the text to Psalm 103 and commenting upon the effectiveness and effect of Schwartz's use of *accelerando* in the number.

83. Stephen Reinhardt contributed the following concerning this song in an electronic message to the author on 9 March 2013: "By the time *Godspell* came along, this vaudeville song, accompanied by a rock band, was very much in the style of Paul McCartney. That's how I thought of it and played it. You had to have your tongue in your cheek, while you rocked."

84. Telephone interview with Stephen Reinhardt, 8 January 2008.

85. Telephone interview with Stephen Reinhardt, 8 January 2008.

86. Telephone interview with Stephen Reinhardt, 8 January 2008.

87. Telephone interview with Stephen Reinhardt, 8 January 2008.

88. In his electronic message to the author on 9 March 2013, Stephen Reinhardt noted that the accompanying band had two phases of rehearsal, one to learn the arrangement and the other for the dynamic levels, which they then adjusted as they started to work on stage.

89. In his electronic message on 9 March 2013, Reinhardt noted that he had to learn stride piano and "pound it into my arms, hands, and fingers." He states that each show he did with Schwartz included songs that he "had to get into the trenches with." In *Godspell* they included the "Prologue," "Turn Back, O Man," and "Alas for You." In *The Magic Show* the difficult song was "A Bit of Villainy," which Reinhardt characterized as "stride on steroids."

90. *Godspell Piano Vocal Score*, 127.

91. Swain, *Broadway Musical*, 312.

92. Telephone interview with Stephen Reinhardt, 8 January 2008.

93. Personal interview with Peggy Gordon, New York City, 17 January 2008.

94. Telephone interview with Stephen Reinhardt, 8 January 2008.

95. Telephone interview with Stephen Reinhardt, 8 January 2008. In his electronic communication from 9 March 2013, Reinhardt reported that he "had to warm up like a singer before Act 2 every night."

96. The coincidence of *Godspell* appearing at about the same time as *Jesus Christ Superstar* created a fascinating moment in pop culture, but Elizabeth L. Wollman has pointed out that several rock groups also recorded songs at the time with religious meaning, including "Put Your Hand in the Hand" by Ocean, "Jesus Is Just Alright"

by the Doobie Brothers, "Signs" by the Five Man Electrical Band, and "Spirit in the Sky" by Norman Greenbaum. See Wollman, *Theater Will Rock*, 87. For a useful comparison of *Godspell* and *Jesus Christ Superstar* from a religious perspective, see Ian Bradley's *You've Got to Have a Dream: The Message of the Musical* (Louisville, KY: Westminster John Knox Press, 2004), 133–44.

97. http://www.grammy.com/GRAMMY_Awards/Winners/Results.aspx?title=g odspell&winner=&year=0&genreID=0&hp=1 (accessed 4 January 2009).

98. Much of the material in this paragraph is derived from Gifford/Wallace, Inc., "High Sales and Musical Honors Afforded 'Godspell' Albums Reflect World-Wide Popularity of Musical" (press release), 5 June 1972. Another Gifford/Wallace, Inc., press release from 22 June 1976 reports that the original cast album had sold more than one million copies. These sources were consulted in the Billy Rose Theatre Collection at the New York Public Library for the Performing Arts.

99. H. L. Spencer, "Behold the Man," program for *Godspell* production at Manchester Opera House, 14–25 August 1990 (Proscenium Publications, 1990), [8]. (Page numbers provided in brackets indicate that there are no page numbers in the source, but this would be the correct page number.)

100. Irving Wardle, "*Godspell*, Round House," *Times*, 18 November 1971, 11.

101. Kurt Gänzl, *The Encyclopedia of Musical Theatre* (Oxford: Blackwell Publishers, 1994), 556.

102. Spencer, "Behold the Man," [8–9].

103. Andrew Lloyd Webber, "Saving Round House," letter to *The Times*, 16 August 1982, 9.

104. *Daily Telegraph*, 23 December 1971.

105. Rupert Brooke, "The Times Diary," *Times* (London), 5 January 1972, 10.

106. *Evening Standard* (London), 28 January 1972.

107. *Evening Standard* (London), 25 April 1973.

108. "BBC Will Film 'Godspell' in St Paul's," *Daily Telegraph* (London), 3 March 1972 and "No Protest at 'Godspell' in St Paul's," *Daily Telegraph* (London), 9 March 1972.

109. Gänzl, *Encyclopedia of Musical Theatre*, 556.

110. Wardle, "*Godspell*, Round House," 11.

111. Felix Barker, "First Night/Theatre: Godspell: Wyndham's Theatre," *Evening News*, 2 February 1972.

112. Harold Hobson, "Hot Gospel," *Sunday Times* (London), 27 February 1972.

113. The material in this paragraph summarizes research performed in July 2009 at the Theatre Collection of the Victoria and Albert Museum, at the time located at the Blythe House.

114. Telephone interview with Nina Faso, 3 June 2013.

115. PHS, "The Times Diary: McGovern It Is—by an Inch," *Times* (London), 12 July 1972, 14.

116. "Church Asks for Ban on Musical," *Times* (London), 16 December 1972, 3.

117. Andrew Gans, "Broadway Revival of *Godspell* Postponed," *Playbill.com*, 19 August 2008, http://www.playbill.com/news/article/120416-Broadway-Revival-of -Godspell-Postponed (accessed 31 May 2013).

118. http://ibdb.com/production.php?id=490436 (accessed 31 May 2013).

119. Charles Isherwood, "A Vision of Spirituality Returns to Broadway," *New York Times*, 7 November 2011, http://theater.nytimes.com/2011/11/08/theater/ reviews/godspell-at-the-circle-in-the-square-review.html?_r=0&pagewanted=1 (accessed 31 May 2013).

Chapter 3: Leonard Bernstein's *Mass*

1. An earlier version of this chapter appeared in Paul R. Laird, "Stephen Schwartz and Bernstein's *Mass*," in *On Bunker's Hill: Essays in Honor of J. Bunker Clark*, ed. William A. Everett and Paul R. Laird (Sterling Heights, MI: Harmonie Park Press, 2007), 263–70. I would like to thank Elaine Gorzelski, President of Harmonie Park Press, for the permission to republish the article here.

2. Humphrey Burton, *Leonard Bernstein* (New York: Doubleday, 1994), 403.

3. Burton, *Leonard Bernstein*, 386. A history of *Mass*'s creation appears in Burton on pp. 386–87 and 400–7.

4. Burton, *Leonard Bernstein*, 400.

5. For more on Schwartz's entry into the project, see Carol de Giere, *Defying Gravity: The Creative Career of Stephen Schwartz from* Godspell *to* Wicked (New York: Applause Theatre & Cinema Books, 2008), 70. See also Burton, *Leonard Bernstein*, 403.

6. De Giere, *Defying Gravity*, 70; Burton, *Leonard Bernstein*, 403.

7. Telephone interview with Stephen Schwartz, 23 July 2004. Another source where Schwartz has answered questions about *Mass* and his collaboration with Bernstein is http://www.stephenschwartz.com/wp-content/uploads/2010/08/mass1 .pdf (13 September 2012). This was prepared by Carol de Giere, webmaster of www .stephenschwartz.com.

8. Burton, *Leonard Bernstein*, 403.

9. Telephone interview with Stephen Schwartz, 23 July 2004.

10. As described in Burton (*Leonard Bernstein*, 403), Bernstein met Philip Berrigan in prison on 25 May 1971 and apparently discussed politics and matters having to do with *Mass*. For further consideration of politics and *Mass*, see Barry Seldes, *Leonard Bernstein: The Political Life of an American Musician* (Berkeley: University of California Press, 2009), 126–27.

11. My opportunity to meet Stephen Schwartz for the first time took place at a symposium on Bernstein's *Mass* hosted by the Columbus Pro Musica Chamber Orchestra in May 2004. These questions that Schwartz mentioned took place in the context of his address at that event on 5 May 2004.

12. Schwartz symposium address. The material in the following paragraph came from the same source.

13. Leonard Bernstein, *Mass: A Theater Piece for Singers, Players and Dancers. Text from the Liturgy of the Roman Mass. Additional Texts by Stephen Schwartz and Leonard Bernstein* (N.p.: Boosey & Hawkes/Jalni Publications, 1989), 112.

14. Telephone interview with Stephen Schwartz, 23 July 2004. Unless otherwise stated, all other quotations or specific information from Schwartz in this article derive from this interview.

15. Schwartz symposium address.

16. Schwartz symposium address.

17. http://www.leonardbernstein.com/works_mass.htm (accessed 10 September 2012).

18. Schwartz symposium address.

19. Schwartz symposium address.

20. Electronic message from Stephen Schwartz to the author, 19 December 2005.

21. See note 11.

22. Schwartz reported this in our interview. For an announcement of the performance at the Hollywood Bowl, see http://www.hollywoodbowl.com/tickets/bernstein039s-mass/2004-08-19 (accessed 18 February 2013).

23. Stephen Schwartz, *Mass—Libretto Revisions* (unpublished, July 2004). Electronic document shared by Schwartz's office.

24. http://www.boosey.com/cr/perusals/score.asp?id=10447 (accessed 11 September 2012).

25. *Leonard Bernstein's Mass: A Theatre Piece for Singers, Players and Dancers.* Conducted by the composer. Text from the liturgy of the Roman Mass. Additional texts by Stephen Schwartz and Leonard Bernstein. LP. Columbia Masterworks M2 31008, n.d. Reissued on CD: *Bernstein Century: Bernstein Mass.* Alan Titus, the Norman Scribner Choir, the Berkshire Boy Choir, Orchestra Conducted by Leonard Bernstein. Sony Classical SM2K 63089, 1977.

26. Leonard Bernstein, *Mass.* Jubilant Sykes, Asher Edward Wulfman, Morgan State University Choir, Peabody Children's Chorus, Baltimore Symphony Orchestra/Marin Alsop. Naxos 8.559622–23, 2009.

27. Stephen Schwartz, "Co-lyricist Stephen Schwartz on the Northwestern Production of *Mass*," Facebook, 29 November 2009, http://www.facebook.com/note.php?note_id=186881577367 (accessed 10 September 2012).

28. The collaboration between Bernstein and Sondheim on *West Side Story* has been considered by a number of writers. Mention of their mutual love for word games and crossword puzzles appears, for example, in the following: Meryle Secrest, *Stephen Sondheim* (New York: Alfred A. Knopf, 1998), 117.

29. Schwartz, *Mass—Libretto Revisions*, 4.

30. Meryle Secrest, *Leonard Bernstein: A Life* (New York: Vintage Books, 1994), 328–29.

31. An oft-quoted review on *Mass* appeared from Harold C. Schonberg: "Bernstein's New Work Reflects His Background on Broadway," *New York Times*, 9 September 1971, 58. Schonberg was frequently scathing concerning Bernstein's

conducting and music. A more positive review of Bernstein's music in *Mass* is the following: Speight Jenkins, "Reports: U.S., Washington," *Opera News* 36 (October 1971): 20–21.

32. Schwartz symposium address.

Chapter 4: *Pippin*

1. Carol de Giere, *Defying Gravity: The Creative Career of Stephen Schwartz from "Godspell" to "Wicked"* (New York: Applause Theatre & Cinema Books, 2008), 75–105. Another important look at the creation of *Pippin* appears in Martin Gottfried's *All His Jazz: The Life & Death of Bob Fosse* (New York: Bantam Books, 1990), 239–62.

2. De Giere, *Defying Gravity*,122. Howard Kissel confirms that Merrick took an option on *Pippin*, but he released Schwartz from the contract when it did not seem that the show was working. Later, Merrick informed Shirley Bernstein of his anger when it appeared that *Pippin* would be a success during the Washington tryout. Schwartz's agent told Merrick that her client would do his next show with him, which became *The Baker's Wife*. See Howard Kissel, *David Merrick: The Abominable Showman* (New York and London: Applause Books, 1993), 439.

3. Personal interview with Stephen Schwartz in New York City, 18 March 2008. Quotations from Schwartz in this chapter, unless otherwise noted, are from this source.

4. *Pippin: A Musical*. Book by Roger O. Hirson. Music and lyrics by Stephen Schwartz. Undated. Unpublished.

5. Stuart Ostrow, *A Producer's Broadway Journey* (Westport, CT, and London: Praeger, 1999), 115.

6. De Giere, *Defying Gravity*, 83.

7. Scott Miller, *From "Assassins" to "West Side Story"* (Portsmouth, NH: Heinemann, 1996), 189ff.

8. http://www.imdb.com/title/tt0068327/ (accessed 5 February 2013).

9. Stuart Ostrow, "How an Exciting, Tuneful, Contemporary, Joyous, Unique Broadway Musical Got Better," souvenir book of Washington production of *Pippin* [1972], inside front cover. (Brackets around the year indicate the source appeared in this year although the year itself did not appear on the document.) Consulted in New York Public Library for the Performing Arts, Billy Rose Theatre Collection. One should note that Ostrow had already chosen to produce *Pippin* before Fosse became involved, a different story than Mark Grant tells when he states that accepting Fosse's role as choreographer/director was the only way that Schwartz and Hirson could get their show produced. See Mark Grant, *The Rise and Fall of the Broadway Musical* (Boston: Northeastern University Press, 2004), 280.

10. Ostrow, *Producer's Broadway Journey*, 117.

11. Douglas Watt, "Bob Fosse Added a 'Leading Player' Made 'Pippin' Easy," *Sunday News*, 19 November 1972, Leisure, p. 3.

12. Miller, *"Assassins" to "West Side Story,"* 192–93. Miller appears to be no fan of the score to *Pippin*, and in his chapter (pp. 189–204) he does not deal with it in any detail.

13. Ostrow, *Producer's Broadway Journey*, 116.

14. Gottfried (*All His Jazz*, 252–53) reports on the moment that Fosse barred Schwartz from rehearsals in Washington, and notes that from that point he proceeded to change the show however he wanted (pp. 253–57). This included clashes with actor John Rubinstein concerning the portrayal of his role.

15. Ostrow, *Producer's Broadway Journey*, 116, and de Giere, *Defying Gravity*, 90.

16. For more on the creators' varying conceptions of what the show should have been, see Kevin Boyd Grubb, *Razzle Dazzle: The Life and Work of Bob Fosse* (New York: St. Martin's Press, 1989), 161–63. Another book that includes commentary on the show from Fosse's perspective is Ethan Mordden's *One More Kiss: The Broadway Musical in the 1970s* (New York: Palgrave Macmillan, 2004), 108–13.

17. Margery Beddow describes several of Fosse's dances and scenes in her *Bob Fosse's Broadway* (Portsmouth, NH: Heinemann, 1996), 46–52.

18. Gottfried (*All His Jazz*, 259) suggests that the sexual content of this number stemmed from Fosse's desire to comment, mostly to himself, upon the fact that he was at the time sleeping with more than one of the show's dancers. Robert Emmet Long suggested the same in his *Broadway, the Golden Years: Jerome Robbins and the Great Choreographer-Directors* (New York and London: Continuum, 2001), 167. Grubb (*Razzle Dazzle*, 165–67) also covers the show's sexuality.

19. Emory Lewis, "Fosse Can't Get Used to Success," *Sunday Record*, 8 July 1973, B14.

20. Miller, *"Assassins" to "West Side Story,"* 202.

21. Watt, "Bob Fosse," 3.

22. De Giere, *Defying Gravity*, 97.

23. Writing in the mid-1990s, Scott Miller, a theatrical director, suggested his discomfort with the entire sequence at Catherine's house because "It can easily be long and boring" (*"Assassins" to "West Side Story,"* 200). His suggestion is to eliminate Theo as a character, but notes that this cannot be done without permission of Music Theatre International.

24. *Pippin* script dated 1 April 1976, New York Public Library for the Performing Arts RM #543 in pocket folder from the American Arbitration Association along with *Pippin* script dated 23 October 1972, RM #7450.

25. Chris Chase reported in the *New York Times* that Ostrow might have spent $120,000 of his own money in the show. See Chris Chase, "Fosse: From Tony to Emmy?" *New York Times*, 29 April 1973, 125ff.

26. "Scale Down 'Pippin' Budget $200,000; Guarantee for D.C. Tryout Is Factor." *Variety*, 13 September 1972, 89. Grubb (*Razzle Dazzle*, 169) states that the Kennedy Center invested $100,000 in the show and guaranteed a weekly gross of $50,000 in Washington.

27. "'Pippin' Netting $30,000 a Week; Recoups Feb. 24," *Variety*, 24 January 1973, 57.

28. *Daily News*, 14 June 1977, 7.

29. Grubb, *Razzle Dazzle*, 171.

30. Stuart Ostrow, "Letters: Broadway's Long Runs: The Ad That Started It All," *New York Times*, 17 September 2006, A6.

31. Leonard Sloane, "Advertising" L'eggs Stepping Out," *New York Times*, 17 August 1973, 47. The article also states that Ostrow had been using television advertising for his Broadway shows for three seasons (probably meaning for *1776* before *Pippin*), confusing the notion that *Pippin* was the first show advertised on the small screen.

32. Hobe Morrison, "TV Spots Boosting 'Pippin' B.O.; Musical Has Paid $800G Profit," *Variety*, 23 January 1974, 59.

33. Beddow (*Bob Fosse's Broadway*, 48) explains this effect in some detail.

34. PJM, "Designing Costumes for Broadway and Hollywood: Patricia Zipprodt Talks about 'Pippin' and the Film of '1776.'" *Theatre Crafts* (January–February 1973), 7–10ff.

35. Steven Suskin, *The Sound of Broadway Music: A Book of Orchestrators & Orchestrations* (Oxford: Oxford University Press, 2009), 33–40.

36. Biography of Abe Jacob in souvenir book of Washington production of *Pippin*, [1972].

37. http://ibdb.com/production.php?id=493954 (accessed 2 April 2013).

38. De Giere, *Defying Gravity*, 90ff.

39. Larry Mickie, "Kennedy Center Angels 'Pippin': Nederlanders Claim Dirty Tactics," *Variety*, 2 August 1972, 1, 54.

40. "Musical Is Canceled by Kennedy Center," *New York Times*, 25 May 1972, 17; "Kennedy Center Has Union Deal, Regains 'Pippin,'" *Variety*, 6 September 1972, 57.

41. James Davis, "Washington Recaptures Tryout Date of 'Pippin,'" *Daily News*, 8 September 1972.

42. Richard L. Coe, "'Pippin': A Rare, Welcome Original," *Washington Post*, 21 September 1972, B1, B4.

43. Richard Lebherz, "Pippin Is a Brilliant Musical," *Frederick News Post*, 22 September 1972.

44. Mick, "Shows out of Town: *Pippin*," *Variety*, 27 September 1972, 60.

45. De Giere, *Defying Gravity*, 75–105, esp. 102–05.

46. The published score of *Pippin* consulted for this study was Stephen Schwartz, *Pippin, Book of Roger O. Hirson; Music & Lyrics by Stephen Schwartz; Complete Vocal Score* (Miami: CPP/Belwin, 1988).

47. De Giere, *Defying Gravity*, 77–78.

48. Grant, *Rise and Fall*, 155–56.

49. Gottfried (*All His Jazz*, 248) reports that Fosse choreographed the opening number to "Down by the Riverside," only changing the music to themes from Schwartz's score before he showed the dance to the composer/lyricist.

50. Ostrow, *Producer's Broadway Journey*, 117.

51. Lewis Funke, "News of the Rialto: 'Pippins' Pip," *New York Times*, 3 December 1972, D1.

52. "Miss Stickney Takes 'Pippin' Role," *New York Times*, 22 May 1973, p. 47.

53. In an article of appreciation on the influence of Stephen Sondheim on his lyrics, Schwartz spoke of Sondheim's influence, for example, on the lyrics of "No Time at All." See Stephen Schwartz, "Learning from Sondheim," *Sondheim Review* 17, no. 1 (Fall 2010): 33.

54. Schwartz, *Pippin; Complete Vocal Score*, 137.

55. Schwartz states that he has "never really gotten jazz." He likes Manhattan Transfer (as may be heard in the song "In Pursuit of Excellence" from *Children of Eden*), but most modern jazz has never interested him.

56. Several *Pippin* programs from the original Broadway production are available in the New York Public Library for the Performing Arts, Billy Rose Theatre Collection.

57. Beddow (*Bob Fosse's Broadway*, 49–50) describes how Fosse hilariously used a man and woman dancing to represent their two attempts at sex.

58. Leonard Bernstein, *Mass: A Theater Piece for Singers, Players and Dancers. Text from the Liturgy of the Roman Mass. Additional Texts by Stephen Schwartz and Leonard Bernstein.* (N.p.: Boosey & Hawkes/Jalni Publications, Inc., 1989), 116–19 ("I Go On"), 156–59 ("Hurry").

59. Miller, *"Assassins" to "West Side Story,"* 201.

60. Script for *Pippin*, 3 January 2005, 76–77, book by Roger O. Hirson, music and lyrics by Stephen Schwartz.

61. Clive Barnes, "Theater: Musical 'Pippin' at Imperial," *New York Times*, 24 October 1972, 37.

62. Douglass Watt, "'Pippin' Is a Splendid Musical, Magnificently Staged & Played," *Daily News*, 24 October 1972, 50.

63. Richard Watts, "Theater: The Son of Charlemagne," *New York Post*, 24 October 1972, 53.

64. Martin Bookspan, review on WPIX-TV, Channel 11, 23 October 1972, text consulted in review scrapbooks at the New York Public Library for the Performing Arts.

65. Edwin Wilson, "Charlemagne, Magic and Music," *Wall Street Journal*, 24 October 1972, 20.

66. Martin Gottfried, review of *Pippin*, *Women's Wear Daily*, 25 October 1972, 29.

67. Hobe Morrison, "Shows on Broadway: *Pippin*," *Variety*, 25 October 1972, 64.

68. Walter Kerr, "It's a Lovely Way to Do a Show," *New York Times*, 29 October 1972, 1, 37.

69. Helen Kruger, *"Pippin,"* *Chelsea Clinton News*, 2 November 1972, 17.

70. Julius Novick, "Sour Pippin," *Village Voice*, 2 November 1972, 73.

71. Brendan Gill, "Carolingian Razzle-Dazzle," *New Yorker*, 4 November 1972, 105.

72. Rex Reed, Review of *Pippin*, *Sunday News*, 5 November 1972, Section 3, 5.

73. T. E. Kalem, "Medieval Hippie," *Time*, 6 November 1972, 83.

74. Jack Kroll, "Charley's Kid," *Newsweek*, 6 November 1972, 134.

75. John Simon, Review of *Pippin*, *New York*, 6 November 1972, 84.

76. Harold Clurman, "Theatre," *Nation*, 13 November 1972.

77. Tom Prideaux, "Pippin," *Life*, 24 November 1972, 30.

78. Henry Hewes, Review of *Pippin*, *Saturday Review*, 2 December 1972, 92.

79. John Beaufort, "Musical 'Pippin' Conquers Broadway: Comedy, Morality Play, Pseudo-History Combined," *Christian Science Monitor*, 26 December 1972, 8.

80. "Jack Tinker at the Theatre: Oh, What a Lovely Bag of Tricks," *Daily Telegraph* (London), 31 October 1973.

81. The Victoria and Albert Theatre Collection, accessed at the Blythe House in July 2008, showed little evidence of *Pippin* performances in the United Kingdom, with the card file of productions showing mention of six (including the original run) from the 1970s to 1990s.

82. See http://www.milesago.com/industry/brodziak.htm and http://www.liveperformance.com.au/halloffame/kennbrodziak3.html (accessed 7 February 2013).

83. "'Pippin' Clicks in Melbourne; Snaps London Jinx Tradition," *Variety*, 13 March 1974, 75ff.

84. Clive Barnes, "Roles for Pop Stars," *New York Times*, 26 July 1974, 22.

85. *"Pippin" Based on Bob Fosse's Original Staging & Choreography of His Broadway Musical Hit*. DVD. VCI Entertainment #8245, 1981.

86. John J. O'Connor, "'Pippin' on Showtime," *New York Times*, 15 February 1984, C26.

87. Schwartz wrote these new lyrics for the Deaf West Theatre production in Los Angeles in 2009. He had always wanted to trim the song and improve it, and he made use of ironic language that one tends to hear from military officials concerning unfortunate civilians who get killed or injured in wars. This material was part of an e-mail message from Schwartz to the author from 13 June 2013.

88. Schwartz reported in an e-mail message to the author from 13 June 2013 that Diane Paulus, director of the 2013 production, wanted to change where the act ended from where Schwartz and Hirson had decided years before about a two-act version: after Pippin has failed as king. Schwartz suggested they place it after "Morning Glow," which necessitated an extra verse, some dialogue about the anticipated finale, and the Leading Player's contrapuntal reference to "Magic to Do." The original version of the show ran without an intermission. According to Grubb (*Razzle Dazzle*, 169–70), writer Paddy Chayefsky suggested this to his friend Bob Fosse.

Chapter 5: *The Magic Show*

1. Personal interview with Edgar Lansbury in New York City, 22 January 2008. Although magic was long a staple of vaudeville and other types of Broadway shows, there have been few Broadway book shows based around magic acts. One of the few was *Sim Sala Bim*, which starred the magician Dante and played fifty-four perfor-

mances in the fall of 1940. See Jim Robertson, "Doug Henning Stars in 'The Magic Show,'" *Genii: The International Conjurors' Magazine* 38, no. 2 (February 1974): 71 and www.ibdb.com (accessed 10 September 2011).

2. Marvin A. Krauss (1928–2002) had a long career as a general manager of shows in New York (www.ibdb.com [accessed 12 September 2011]). He served Lansbury and Beruh in that capacity for both *Godspell* and *The Magic Show*, and Carol de Giere reports that Krauss was in Toronto and saw Henning's show, *Spellbound* (see Carol de Giere, *Defying Gravity: The Creative Career of Stephen Schwartz from "Godspell" to "Wicked"* [New York: Applause Theatre & Cinema Books, 2008], 107). Carol de Giere's book is an important source on *The Magic Show*, as it is for all of Schwartz's activities. For further details on Krauss's role in bringing Doug Henning to Broadway, see John Harrison, *Spellbound: The Wonder-Filled Life of Doug Henning* (New York: BoxOffice Books, 2009), 66ff. Harrison's book includes lengthy consideration of the creation and run of *The Magic Show*, and his coverage is not limited to Henning's role.

3. Originally from Winnipeg, Henning settled on magic as a career from a young age and studied with several important magicians, some of it made possible by a grant from the Canadian government. Among his many performances before *Spellbound* was a four-week stint at The Magic Castle in Hollywood. He preferred to be called an "artist of illusion." See Harrison's book for a detailed consideration of Henning's career.

4. This is how de Giere reports the property's discovery. There is some confusion as to who flew to Toronto when and with whom. See de Giere, *Defying Gravity*, 107–8. For further coverage of their discovery of the show, and some conflicting information, see Harrison, *Spellbound*, 67–73.

5. De Giere, *Defying Gravity*, 108.

6. Personal interview with Stephen Schwartz in New York City, 18 March 2008. All quotations from Schwartz in this chapter and other material attributed to him concerning *The Magic Show*, unless otherwise documented, came from this interview.

7. See note 2.

8. Personal interview with Edgar Lansbury in New York City, 22 January 2008. All materials attributed to Lansbury, unless otherwise documented, are derived from this interview.

9. Laurie Johnston, "Strollers See Magic in Midtown Plaza," *New York Times*, 8 April 1974, 39. Another publicity stunt involved sawing Barbara Walters in half on the *Today Show*. See de Giere, *Defying Gravity*, 114. Harrison (*Spellbound*, 106–10) considers the publicity surrounding *The Magic Show* in some detail.

10. Grover Dale, "The Feeling of Magic," in *The Magic Show Souvenir Book* (New York: M.E.I. Industries, 1974), [3–5].

11. Dale, "Feeling of Magic," [4]. Harrison (*Spellbound*, 72–76) reports that Henning came to New York City in January 1974 to work with Dale, who evaluated whether or not the magician would be able to star in a Broadway show. He decided they could, if Henning "was playing himself and was surrounded by a strong cast." (p. 76)

12. Dale, "Feeling of Magic," [4].

13. Dale, "Feeling of Magic," [4].

14. Harrison reports that the show was budgeted at $310,000. He provides a number of details on how the producers cut costs (*Spellbound*, 80–81).

15. For consideration of some of Henning's illusions used in the show in a magic industry journal, see Robertson, "Doug Henning Stars," 71.

16. Dale, "Feeling of Magic," [5]. There is controversy in the existing accounts as to when Randall actually became involved in the show.

17. Harrison, *Spellbound*, 77–79.

18. Dale, "Feeling of Magic," [5].

19. Dale, "Feeling of Magic," [5]. Harrison considers moving the production into the theater and the rehearsal period in detail (*Spellbound*, 103–14). He also reports (p. 113) that few changes were made during the previews.

20. Undated press release from Gifford/Wallace, Inc, consulted in the New York Public Library for the Performing Arts, Billy Rose Theatre Collection. Harrison describes how Henning acquired the devices that produced the illusions (*Spellbound*, 82–85).

21. Nina Faso, Schwartz's friend and colleague, had known David Ogden Stiers when she had worked briefly in California and suggested him for this role. See de Giere, *Defying Gravity*, 111–12.

22. Harrison, *Spellbound*, 97.

23. Debbi Wasserman, "Overcoming Critical Disapproval: Adept Magician + Philosopher = New Star," *Show Business*, 4 July 1974, 1, 3.

24. See chapter 4, note 58.

25. Electronic communication from Stephen Reinhardt to the author, 9 March 2013.

26. Stephen Schwartz, *The Magic Show: Original Cast Recording*, LP, Bell Records, 1974. Stephen Schwartz, *Vocal Selection* [sic] *from the Hit Show "The Magic Show"* (Melville, NY: Belwin Mills Publishing, n.d.).

27. One of the many stage effects in *The Magic Show* involved the two halves of Charmin being moved around on the stage for a good part of the show, a suggestion made by Schwartz and Bob Randall and embraced by Henning. See de Giere, *Defying Gravity*, 116.

28. David Spangler's relationship with Schwartz as his longtime friend from their college days and his work as the dance arranger is explained further by de Giere, *Defying Gravity*, 108–9, 113. Spangler was working on a musical called *Houdini* when development of *The Magic Show* began. Schwartz knew this and called his friend, offering to back out of *The Magic Show* if Spangler so desired. Spangler told Schwartz to go ahead, and Schwartz made his friend the dance arranger for *The Magic Show*, meaning that Spangler worked closely with Dale on the music for choreographed moments and with Henning on underscoring for his illusions. Harrison states that Schwartz served as his own dance arranger for the

show (*Spellbound*, 89), but this appears to be incorrect. David Sheridan Spangler is listed as the dance arranger at http://ibdb.com/production.php?id=3468 (accessed 22 September 2011).

29. Carol de Giere, "*The Magic Show* Overview," http://www.musicalschwartz .com/magicshow.htm (accessed 6 September 2011).

30. Harrison (*Spellbound*, 250–58) covers this video project of *The Magic Show* in some detail.

31. *The Magic Show*, directed by Norman Campbell, Moviemagic Productions, Ltd., 1981; reissued Image Entertainment, 2001, DVD.

32. Harrison, *Spellbound*, 250.

33. Harrison, *Spellbound*, 254.

34. Harrison (*Spellbound*, 254) describes how Henning wished to update the illusions in the show to ones he was using at the time.

35. Harrison, *Spellbound*, 254.

36. Harrison, *Spellbound*, 380–81.

37. Gifford/Wallace, Inc., untitled press release, 30 November 1978, consulted in the New York Public Library for the Performing Arts, Billy Rose Theatre Collection.

38. Gifford/Wallace, Inc., untitled press release.

39. "'Magic Show' Flags, Shuberts to Rescue," *Variety*, 11 October 1978, 179. Harrison (*Spellbound*, 118) reports that the show grossed $15 million.

40. "'Magic Show' Flags," 179.

41. Ethan Mordden provides his appreciation of what helped make the show work in his *One More Kiss: The Broadway Musical in the 1970s* (New York: Palgrave Macmillan, 2004), 174–75.

42. Harrison, *Spellbound*, 115. Harrison (pp. 116–18) also considers newspaper reviews for *The Magic Show*.

43. Clive Barnes, "Stage: 'The Magic Show': Doug Henning Delights as Atypical Illusionist," *New York Times*, 29 May 1974, 49.

44. Douglas Watt, "'The Magic Show' Winds Up Season," *Daily News*, 29 May 1974, 64.

45. Richard Watts, "Evening with a Master of Magic," *New York Post*, 29 May 1974, 46.

46. Hobe Morrison, "*The Magic Show*," *Variety*, 29 May 1974, 56.

47. Martin Gottfried, "*The Magic Show*," *Women's Wear Daily*, 30 May 1974, 24.

48. John Beaufort, "The Magic Show—a Brand New Form—Ends the Season," *Christian Science Monitor*, 31 May 1974, F6.

49. Ross Wetzsteon, "Theatre: It's Magic," *Village Voice*, 6 June 1974, 83.

50. Lillian Africano, "'Magic Show' Is Sluggish," *Villager*, 6 June 1974, 6.

51. Edwin Wilson, "A Bright Bit of Legerdemain," *Wall Street Journal*, 8 June 1974, 14.

52. Walter Kerr, "The Theater Means Transformation," *New York Times*, 9 June 1974, Sec. 2, 1.

53. Brendan Gill, "That Half-There Feeling," *New Yorker*, 10 June 1974, 64.

54. T. E. Kalem, "Presto!" *Time*, 10 June 1974, 106.

55. Jack Kroll, "Ala Kazam!" *Newsweek*, 10 June 1974, 84.

56. John Simon, Review of *The Magic Show*, *New York*, 17 June 1974, 76.

57. Indeed, in a 1976 interview, producer Edgar Lansbury estimated that Henning's appeal to children had perhaps "doubled or tripled" the popularity of *The Magic Show*. See Richard Flaste, "A Magical Day for Children," *New York Times*, 6 August 1976, C3.

58. Robert Adels, "'Magic Show': Tuneful Prestidigitation," *Record World*, 22 June 1974, 20, 52.

59. Richard Philip, "Reviews: Theater On Broadway and Off," *After Dark* (July 1974), 72.

60. Debbi Wasserman, "Overcoming Critical Disapproval: Adept Magician + Philosopher = New Star," *Show Business*, 4 July 1974, 1, 3.

61. The programs of the productions consulted for this segment are in the Billy Rose Theatre Collection (*T – Programmes) at the New York Public Library Performing Arts Library at Lincoln Center. Harrison (*Spellbound*, 120) states that there was a single touring company for *The Magic Show*.

62. Harrison (*Spellbound*, 135) reports that Henning originally trained Peter De-Paula for an Australian tour cut short by poor local producers.

63. According to Pippa Pearthree's online biography, she starred in *The Magic Show* tour in 1974–1975, which would mean that producers mounted a tour starting in the same year that the show opened on Broadway. See http://www.filmreference.com/film/15/Pippa-Pearthree.html (accessed 10 September 2011).

64. Richard Seff and Isobel Robins, *This Is Broadway*, interview with Joseph Abaldo, 1978, available at http://ibdb.com/production.php?id=3468 (accessed 21 May 2013). All material in this paragraph is derived from this source. Harrison (*Spellbound*, 134–35) describes Henning training Abaldo and others for the role.

65. Harrison, *Spellbound*, 146.

66. Sarey Bernstein, Review of *The Magic Show*, *Westport News*, 6 July 1979.

67. Harrison, *Spellbound*, 120.

68. Harrison, *Spellbound*, 120–21.

Chapter 6: *The Baker's Wife*

1. Personal interview with Stephen Schwartz in Schroon Lake, NY, 20 July 2007.

2. Personal interview with Gordon Greenberg in New York City, 23 January 2008. All quotations from Greenberg in this chapter came from this interview.

3. Carol de Giere, *Defying Gravity: The Creative Career of Stephen Schwartz from "Godspell" to "Wicked"* (New York: Applause Theatre & Cinema Books, 2008), 120–43. A brief, appreciative look at the musical appears in Ethan Mordden's *One More Kiss: The Broadway Musical in the 1970s* (New York: Palgrave Macmillan, 2004), 210–12.

4. Unless otherwise stated, information on Schwartz's participation in and opinions on this show are derived from a personal interview with him in New York City on 16 January 2008.

5. Charles Wright, "Program Note" in "Musicals at Mufti" program, 2007, consulted at New York Public Library for the Performing Arts, Billy Rose Theatre Collection in the "T-clipping" files under *The Baker's Wife*. The story of Merrick convincing the reluctant Pagnol to give him the rights for *La femme du boulanger* appears briefly in Howard Kissel's *David Merrick: The Abominable Showman* (New York and London: Applause Books, 1993), 437–38.

6. Wright, "Program Note." Kissel (*David Merrick*, 438) reports that Neil Simon suggested the project to Joseph Stein.

7. Unless otherwise stated, material on Stein's work in *The Baker's Wife* is taken from a telephone interview with him on 18 December 2007.

8. Personal interview with Stephen Schwartz in Schroon Lake, NY, 20 July 2007.

9. Carol de Giere covers the tour (*Defying Gravity*, 128–38).

10. Joseph Stein and Stephen Schwartz, *The Baker's Wife*, unpublished script, [1976]. It was presented to the New York Public Library for the Performing Arts (RM #8001) by David Rounds, who played the priest on the tour.

11. Carol de Giere (*Defying Gravity*, 132) does not list Philadelphia as one of the tour's stops, suggesting that time for Berry's rehearsals came from cancelling the later Philadelphia run.

12. According to Kissel (*David Merrick*, 438), Mostel had tried to secure rights for *La femme du boulanger* from Pagnol at one point.

13. Wright, "Program Note."

14. De Giere, *Defying Gravity*, 135.

15. De Giere, *Defying Gravity*, 132.

16. Wright, "Program Note." On this recording Schwartz used orchestrations by both Thomas Pierson and Don Walker.

17. According to Kissel (*David Merrick*, 439–40), Merrick compared it to an opera set.

18. Kissel, *David Merrick*, 440.

19. According to de Giere (*Defying Gravity*, 137), Merrick had promised Motown Records, who had money in the show, that there would be a Broadway opening. Bernstein convinced Motown that a poor critical reception would doom the show. Kissel (*David Merrick*, 441–42) adds that Motown had provided all of the funding and its contract with Merrick specified that there would be a Broadway opening.

20. Wright, "Program Note."

21. The original LP: Stephen Schwartz, *The Baker's Wife*. Take Home Tunes 772, n.d. That recording was reissued in 1992 as Take Home Tunes CD 9216.

22. De Giere, *Defying Gravity*, 139. The songs "Meadowlark," "Where Is the Warmth?," and "If I Have to Live Alone" appeared in Stephen Schwartz, *Selections from "The Baker's Wife": A Musical* (N.p.: Grey Dog Music, 1990).

23. Elsewhere Schwartz has spoken about lyric writing being something he is "not consciously controlling," the idea being trying to "let the character speak through" him. See Stephen Schwartz, "Lyricists on Lyrics," *Dramatist* 7, no. 6 (July–August 2005): 14.

24. Stephen Holden, "Stage: 'Baker's Wife' in a Revised Version," *New York Times*, 31 March 1985, 52.

25. Holden, "Stage," 52.

26. Don Nelson, "'The Baker's' Stale Cakes," *Daily News*, 5 April 1985, 9.

27. Clive Barnes, "Alas Poor York, 'Baker' Bombs," *New York Post*, 4 April 1985, 30.

28. Howard Kissel, "Theater: 'The Baker's Wife,'" *Women's Wear Daily*, 26 March 1985, 28.

29. John Beaufort, "Theater: York Theatre Uncorks a Charming, Intimate Production of 'The Baker's Wife,'" *Christian Science Monitor*, 9 April 1985, 28.

30. Terry Miller, "Half-Baked," *New York Native*, 22 April 1985, 53.

31. Debbi Wasserman, "The Baker's Wife," *Stages*, July–August 1985, 11.

32. Pauline Peters, "The Cat That Got the Cream," *Telegraph Weekend Magazine*, 12 August 1989, 17.

33. Matt Wolf, "Needing the Dough? Matt Wolf Talks to Trevor Nunn," *City Lights*, 23–30 November 1989.

34. "Questions and Answers: Trevor Nunn on *The Baker's Wife*," in *The Baker's Wife: A Comedy Musical*, Phoenix Theatre, London, souvenir program book.

35. Peters, "Cat That Got the Cream," 17.

36. Electronic message from Stephen Schwartz to the author, 17 July 2011.

37. Electronic message from Stephen Schwartz to the author, 17 July 2011.

38. *The Baker's Wife: A Comedy Musical*, Phoenix Theatre, London souvenir program book.

39. Hilary Finch, "Well-Bred and Good Pedigree," *Times* (London), 16 November 1989.

40. Finch, "Well-Bred."

41. Elizabeth Grice, "Trevor Nunn Takes the Long Route Home," *Sunday Times* (London), 6 August 1989.

42. De Giere, *Defying Gravity*, 482.

43. The original cast London recording on CD: *The Baker's Wife: A Comedy Musical. Book by Joseph Stein. Music and Lyrics by Stephen Schwartz.* Jay CDJAY 2 1323, 1999.

44. De Giere, *Defying Gravity*, 482.

45. Michael Coveney, "Arts: *The Baker's Wife*—Phoenix Theatre," *Financial Times* (London), 28 November 1989.

46. Irving Wardle, "Pain Wafts from Provence—Theatre," *Times* (London), 28 November 1989.

47. John Peter, "Puppets with the Power to Persuade—Theatre," *Times* (London), 3 December 1989.

48. Matt Wolf, "Half a Loaf—'Baker's Wife' Continues to Rise in London," *Chicago Tribune*, 7 January 1990.

49. Sheridan Morley, "Diary," *Times*, 15 January 1990. An interesting appraisal of the show and its history to this point appeared in Ken Mandelbaum's *Not since Carrie: 40 Years of Broadway Musical Flops* (New York: St. Martin's Press, 1991), 173–76.

50. http://www.floormic.com/production/2898495 (accessed 11 July 2011). This site included information on the production with the song list.

51. http://www.floormic.com/production/2889872 (accessed 11 July 2011).

52. Naomi Siegel, "Theater Review; Heartbreak and Baguettes in Provence," *New York Times*, 24 April 2005, http://query.nytimes.com/gst/fullpage.html?res=9A06E5 D81731F937A15757C0A9639C8B63 (accessed 17 February 2013).

53. RM#8001; see note 10.

54. See de Giere, *Defying Gravity*, 124–25. Schwartz told de Giere only about his study of Debussy and Ravel and interest in the work of Piaf, Montand, and Aznavour. In a newspaper interview publicizing the London production, Schwartz offered the following when describing the orchestration: "the three types of music I've drawn from: Provençal folk music (recorder, shawm, harp); French music-hall, the Piaf sound (accordion and rinky-tink piano); and the impressionistic romance of a Debussy and a Ravel (harp, flute, clarinet, viola)." See Finch, "Well-Bred."

55. http://www.youtube.com/watch?v=Fw_H1kZ97Pg (accessed 17 February 2013).

56. De Giere, *Defying Gravity*, 125–26. Alice Ripley's performance of "Meadowlark" in the 2005 Paper Mill production is available on YouTube: http://www.youtube.com/watch?v=0K269vRf3aQ (accessed 17 February 2013).

57. Kissel (*David Merrick*, 440) confirms that Schwartz produced a shorter version of the song, but Merrick's general manager, Helen Nickerson, did not think that it worked.

58. Among the people who worked on *Snapshots* was David I. Stern, Schwartz's collaborator for *Geppetto*. For a bit more on the revue *Snapshots*, see chapter 11.

Chapter 7: *Working*

1. Carol de Giere, *Defying Gravity: The Creative Career of Stephen Schwartz from "Godspell" to "Wicked"* (New York: Applause Theatre & Cinema Books, 2008), 144–73.

2. Studs Terkel, *Working: People Talk about What They Do All Day and How They Feel about What They Do* (New York: Pantheon Books, 1972, 1974).

3. De Giere, *Defying Gravity*, 146.

4. Personal interview with Stephen Schwartz in New York City, 8 April 2008. Also, see Terkel's segment on telephone operator Heather Lamb (*Working*, 36–39). Lamb describes her desire to be asked about her day on p. 39.

5. De Giere, *Defying Gravity*, 147.

6. Telephone interview with Nina Faso, 3 June 2013.

7. Personal interview with Stephen Schwartz in New York City, 8 April 2008. All quotations and facts attributed to the composer/lyricist in this chapter, unless otherwise stated, came from this interview.

8. De Giere, *Defying Gravity*, 150, and she also covers the workshops in more detail on pp. 150–52.

9. Telephone interview with Nina Faso, 3 June 2013.

10. De Giere, *Defying Gravity*, 151.

11. Telephone interview with Nina Faso, 3 June 2013.

12. De Giere, *Defying Gravity*, 159–60, provides additional details on the Ringley family's brief presence in *Working*. Terkel's interview with Fred Ringley, who left his job as a print salesman in Chicago to live with his family in a rural area in Arkansas, appears on pp. 532–37 of *Working*.

13. De Giere, *Defying Gravity*, 159–60.

14. De Giere, *Defying Gravity*, 149.

15. De Giere, *Defying Gravity*, 149.

16. The steel worker Schwartz mentions from Terkel's book is Mike LeFevre, whose interview appears in the introduction on pp. xxxi–xxxviii.

17. De Giere, *Defying Gravity*, 151.

18. De Giere, *Defying Gravity*, 152–53. Terkel's parking lot attendant, who called himself a "car hiker," was Alfred Pommier (*Working*, 219–23).

19. The summaries of Broadway histories offered in this paragraph are based on information in the *Internet Broadway Database*, www.ibdb.com (accessed 29 July 2012).

20. The millworker was felter Grace Clements, who at that point had worked for a luggage company for twenty-one years. See Terkel, *Working*, 289–93.

21. De Giere, *Defying Gravity*, 161. The domestic worker that Terkel interviewed was Maggie Holmes (pp. 112–18), who had toiled in that capacity in various venues for twenty-five years.

22. De Giere, *Defying Gravity*, 154. Terkel interviewed Frank Decker (*Working*, 206–18), an independent trucker who regularly hauled steel out of Gary, Indiana, into Wisconsin.

23. Terkel interviewed Therese Carter, a mother of three in a blue collar family who lived west of Chicago (*Working*, 299–303), and Jesusita Novarro, a mother of five who was on welfare and worked part-time (pp. 303–06).

24. Stephen Schwartz, *Working: A New Musical*. Original cast recording. Sony Music Special Products 302 062 114 2, 1978; compact disc reissue, 2001.

25. The mason who appears in Terkel's book (*Working*, xlv–xlix) was Carl Murray Bates, who had been proudly plying his trade for forty years.

26. Terkel interviewed three newsboys in Newburgh, Indiana (*Working*, xxxix–xliii): Billy Carpenter, Cliff Pickens, and Terry Pickens.

27. Rose Hoffman had been a teacher for thirty-three years when Terkel interviewed her (*Working*, 483–88). She taught third grade in a changing neighborhood.

28. Taylor's song ("A Better Day Will Come" in English) involves the lives of migrant farm workers. Terkel spoke to Roberto Acuna (*Working*, 7–14), who two years before had left working in the fields to organize for the United Farm Workers of America, trying "to change the California feudal system." (p. 7). His mother would often express the sentiment that forms the title of this song.

29. This song is the finale of Act 1, expressing the notion that some workers feel they could have accomplished more in their lives if they had had a chance.

30. Joe Zmuda (Terkel, *Working*, 430–34) was a seventy-five-year-old widower and retiree who lived in a basement apartment on Chicago's West Side. During his working life he had been a shipping clerk, among other jobs.

31. Schwartz credits this number with teaching him how to write music that describes character. See Stephen Schwartz, "Composing," *Dramatist* 12, no. 1 (September–October 2009): 32.

32. The unforgettable waitress whom Terkel interviewed (*Working*, 293–98) was Dolores Dante, who had worked at the same restaurant for twenty-three years.

33. Terkel included a section called "Fathers and Sons" (*Working*, 545–89) where people describe their work as policemen, firemen, and other professions. The subjects tend to be related, but the focus is not on family relationships, the topic of Schwartz's song.

34. Terkel interviewed Hots Michaels (*Working*, 250–52), who had played piano in a downtown hotel bar since 1952.

35. Babe Secoli (Terkel, *Working*, 282–86) had been a supermarket checker for nearly thirty years when Terkel interviewed her.

36. See de Giere, *Defying Gravity*, 156, where she describes Schwartz's work with Daniele and her ability to fashion stage movement from movements associated with workplaces.

37. http://www.ibdb.com/person.php?id=12203 (accessed 27 August 2012).

38. Electronic communication from Stephen Reinhardt to the author, 9 March 2013.

39. Richard Eder, "Theater: 'Working' Opens at 46th Street," *New York Times*, 15 May 1978, C15.

40. The producers of *Working* were Irwin Meyer and Stephen R. Friedman, who had great success the previous year with *Annie*. Carol de Giere covers the producers of *Working* starting on p. 158 of *Defying Gravity*.

41. De Giere, *Defying Gravity*, 164–68, also considers the premature move to New York.

42. Personal interview with Stephen Schwartz, New York City, 1 April 2008.

43. Terkel, *Working*, xi.

44. The copyboy was Charlie Blossom (Terkel, *Working*, 437–46), who worked at a newspaper and alternately espoused flower child and pacifist principles while also dreaming of shooting up his office with a machine gun or killing the editor.

45. Eder, "Theater," C15.

46. Douglas Watt, "'Working': It's Exciting and Dull," *Daily News*, 15 May 1978, 27.

47. Clive Barnes, "'Working' Musical Falls Flat," *New York Post*, 15 May 1978, 22.

48. Howard Kissel, "'Working,'" *Women's Wear Daily*, 16 May 1978, 18.

49. Hobe Morrison, "Working," *Variety*, 17 May 1978, 45.

50. Rex Reed, Review of *Working*, *Daily News*, 17 May 1978, 73.

51. Gerald Rabkin, "Heavy Freight," *Soho Weekly News*, 18 May 1978, 42.

52. For a review of this production, see Richard Eder, "The Talking Band Presents 'Worksong' at the New City," *New York Times*, 25 February 1978, 16.

53. Leo Shull, "*Working*: A Musical," *Show Business*, 25 May 1978, 22.

54. Leah D. Frank, "Working Rut a Potpouri [sic] of Dissatisfaction," *East Side Express*, 25 May 1978, 10.

55. Marjorie Gunner, Review of *Working*, *Nassau Star*, 25 May 1978, 4.

56. Barbara Lewis, "Blacks, Biko, Workers Topics of New Offerings," *New York Amsterdam News*, 27 May 1978, D-5.

57. Walter Kerr, "Stageview: Documents Posing as Dramas," *New York Times*, 28 May 1978, D-3.

58. Erika Munk, "Sing Me a Song of Social Significance," *Village Voice*, 29 May 1978, 83–84.

59. T. E. Kalem, "Blue-Collared," *Time*, 29 May 1978, 83.

60. Brendan Gill, "Daily Bread," *New Yorker*, 29 May 1978, 84.

61. Martin Gottfried, Review of *Working*, *Saturday Review*, 8 July 1978, 24.

62. John Simon, Review of *Working*, *New York*, [1978], 78. Consulted in review scrapbooks at the New York Public Library for the Performing Arts, which included incomplete information.

63. John Bush Jones, for example, reports that Music Theatre International licensed *Working* for 351 separate productions between 1990 and 1 August 2000. See his *Our Musicals, Ourselves: A Social History of the American Musical Theatre* (Hanover and London: Brandeis University Press, 2003), 289.

64. The tie salesman appears to have been Ralph Werner (Terkel, *Working*, 452–57), a twenty-year-old who worked in a department store.

65. See de Giere, *Defying Gravity*, 174–81.

66. The production is available on DVD: *Studs Terkel's Working*. Broadway Theatre Archive. Directed by Stephen Schwartz and Kirk Browning. Produced by Phylis Geller and Lindsay Law. Image Entertainment 14381–0882–2, 1982.

67. Telephone interview with Nina Faso, 3 June 2013.

68. Schwartz wrote briefly about the 1999 revision in his liner notes for the 2001 reissue of the OCR of *Working*. He again worked with Studs Terkel and Nina Faso. Schwartz interviewed workers who represented updated versions of some segments from the original show. He also wrote "I'm Just Movin'" about a modern supermarket checker and enlisted the assistance of his fellow songwriters for the show in updating their lyrics. See "2001 Notes on *Working* from the Instigator Stephen Schwartz," CD booklet from *Working: A New Musical*.

69. http://artssarasota.com/2012–07–25/section/theater/asolo-reps-working
-scheduled-for-new-york-run/ (accessed 19 August 2012).

70. http://www.playbill.com/news/article/168298-Stephen-Schwartzs-Revised
-Working-With-New-Songs-by-Lin-Manuel-Miranda-Will-Be-Given-NYC-Pre
miere (accessed 19 August 2012).

71. Two published versions of the poem appear at the following website: http://
www.potw.org/archive/potw345.html (accessed 25 August 2012).

72. *Working*. From the Book by Studs Terkel. Adapted by Stephen Schwartz and
Nina Faso. Heelstone Parc Productions, 1978. Available from Music Theatre International, [1].

73. Terkel, *Working*, xxxix–xliii.

74. Terkel, *Working*, xl.

75. Terkel, *Working*, 293–98. Dante actually says "it's an art" concerning her profession (p. 297). Also see de Giere, *Defying Gravity*, 156–58, who considers this song
as well, covering some of the points that Schwartz also mentioned in my interview.

76. Dante actually compares herself to Carmen when she describes her feeling
about tips. See Terkel, *Working*, 295.

77. As noted earlier, Terkel has an entire section called "Fathers and Sons"
(*Working*, 545–89), but the subjects seldom cover the emotional ground that
Schwartz does in this song.

78. Telephone interview with Nina Faso, 3 June 2013.

79. Terkel's supermarket checker, Babe Secoli, provided Schwartz with the title
for his song: "I'm just movin'—the hips, the hand, and the register" (*Working*, 282).

80. De Giere, *Defying Gravity*, 147–48, describes Schwartz's inspiration from *A
Chorus Line*.

Chapter 8: *Rags*

1. Schwartz's comments about *Rags* are derived from a personal interview in
Schroon Lake, NY, on 20 July 2007. All direct quotations came from this interview.

2. Schwartz has very strong feelings about this topic, stating that "structure is everything in a musical," going on in the passage to compare the significance of structure in a show to its importance in architecture. See Stephen Schwartz, "Lyricists on
Lyrics," *Dramatist* 7, no. 6 (July–August 2005): 11.

3. Joseph Stein's account of the creation of *Rags* is derived from a telephone interview with him on 18 December 2007. All of his direct quotations came from this
interview.

4. Tim Boxer, "Traveling with the Stars: Welcome to America," *Jewish Week,
Inc.*, 15 August 1986, 22.

5. Guber reported that he also tried to pursue the project as a film with 20th
Century Fox. See Carol Lawton, "Broadway," *New York Times*, 23 March 1984, C2.

6. Personal interview with Charles Strouse in New York City, 23 January 2008.
All quotations from Strouse came from this interview.

7. The Triangle Shirtwaist Factory was located on the ninth floor of a building at 23–29 Washington Place in Lower Manhattan, where working and safety conditions were deplorable. A fire there on 25 March 1911 resulted in the deaths of 146 workers, mostly immigrant women. See, among other sources, Dave Von Drehle, *Triangle: The Fire That Changed America* (New York: Atlantic Monthly Press, 2003).

8. Don Nelson, "From 'Rags' to—Maybe—B'way Riches," *Daily News*, 7 September 1983, 41.

9. Carol Lawton, "Broadway: 'Rags,' a Sequel about the People in 'Fiddler' Story," *New York Times*, 14 January 1983, C2.

10. Nelson, "From 'Rags,'" 41.

11. Lawton, "Broadway," C2.

12. Stephen Holden, "How the Curtain Came Down on the Dream of 'Rags,'" *New York Times*, 21 September 1986, H5.

13. Telephone interview with Nina Faso, 3 June 2013.

14. Holden, "How the Curtain Came Down," H5.

15. "No Stock for 'Cage'; Silver Exits 'Rags,'" *Variety*, 18 June 1986, 92.

16. Announcement of show's run, *Rhode Island Herald*, 9 May 1986.

17. "No Stock," 92.

18. "Paul McMahon's Curtain Call," *New England Connection*, 7 July 1986.

19. "A Book Doctor, or Just a Friend," *Newsday*, 21 July 1986, 6. The same story mentioned that playwright and screenwriter Jay Presson Allen consulted informally on the book.

20. "'Rags' Finds Tailor to Sew Up Broadway," *Newsday*, 23 July 1986.

21. Holden, "How the Curtain Came Down," H35.

22. Holden, "How the Curtain Came Down," H35.

23. Holden, "How the Curtain Came Down," H35.

24. Bob Hilliard, "'Rags' a Super-Hit Musical in Every Way," *Manchester Union Leader*, 12 July 1986, 27.

25. Arthur Friedman, "'Rags' Is a Rich Production," *Boston Herald*, 10 July 1986, 34.

26. Arnold Howard, "*Rags* Not Too Shabby," *Boston Jewish Times*, 17 July 1986, 7.

27. Jon Lehman, "Stratas Gives the Theater a New Jewel in 'Rags,'" *Patriot Ledger*, 17 July 1986, 24.

28. Jay Carr, "Stratas Makes a World of Difference," *Boston Globe*, 17 July 1986.

29. Vito Russo, "Tailoring 'Rags' for Broadway," *Newsday*, 17 August 1986, II/3ff.

30. http://ibdb.com/production.php?id=4420 (accessed 22 February 2013).

31. Dena Kleiman, "Broadway Beats Summer Doldrums," *New York Times*, 5 June 1986, C21.

32. Holden, "How the Curtain Came Down," H35.

33. Such an effort was announced in Dena Kleiman, "Producers May Reopen 'Rags,'" *New York Times*, 26 August 1986, C15. The producers had issued a press release making this announcement on 25 August; a copy survives at the New York Public Library, Billy Rose Theatre Collection.

34. John Simon, "Sad Rags," *New York*, 1 September 1986, 46.

35. Douglas Watt, "These New 'Rags' Don't Wear Well," *Daily News*, 22 August 1986, B/5.

36. Michael Feingold, *"Rags," Village Voice*, 2 September 1986, 81–82.

37. Togi, "Rags," *Variety*, 27 August 1986, 100, 104.

38. Frank Rich, "Stage: Teresa Stratas as a Jewish Immigrant in 'Rags,' a Musical," *New York Times*, 22 August 1986, C3.

39. Clive Barnes, "A New Star Is Born: Diva Bows on B'way in 'Rags,'" *New York Post*, 22 August 1986, 41–42.

40. Julius Novick, *"Rags," Village Voice*, 2 September 1986, 81.

41. When writing both lyrics and music, Schwartz has found that "the lyric leads a bit more, because somewhere in the back of my head, I know what the music will be or at least the rhythm will be." When writing lyrics only, the music usually does come first, and Schwartz states, "I didn't know that would happen." See Schwartz, "Lyricists on Lyrics," 8.

42. *Rags: The New American Musical.* Book by Joseph Stein. Music by Charles Strouse. Lyrics by Stephen Schwartz. Sony Masterworks SK 42657, 1991.

43. Schwartz has noted that he often finds himself writing lyrics backward, stating, "I know where I'm trying to go—the end of the song or the end of the verse." The problem is making it to that point "without making it obvious you knew where you were going all along." See his "Lyricists on Lyrics," 9.

44. Russo, "Tailoring 'Rags,'" II/3ff.

45. See the following website for a PDF concerning details of changes in *Rags* scripts over the history of the show's development: http://www.music.ku.edu/paul-laird.

46. Nathan's willingness to turn his back on his Jewish heritage was an aspect of the show with which Stein and his collaborators wrestled. John Bush Jones reports on this and some other Jewish aspects of *Rags* in his *Our Musicals, Ourselves: A Social History of the American Musical Theatre* (Hanover and London: Brandeis University Press, 2003), 222–24. Jones also notes (p. 222) that the Rodgers and Hammerstein Organization licensed *Rags* for about 200 productions in the United States between 1992 and the end of 2000.

47. Electronic communication from Stephen Schwartz to Joseph Stein, 7 April 2005.

48. In an electronic communication that Schwartz sent to the author on 22 March 2013, he stated that he had recently been to a *Rags* reading where "Children of the Wind" was the Act 1 finale, and he now thinks he was wrong in the 2005 memo to suggest that it should be saved for closing Act 2. The quest for a final version of *Rags* continues!

49. Numbering of the scenes is off in the original, as shown here.

50. Another useful list of these strengths appears in Ethan Mordden's *The Happiest Corpse I've Ever Seen: The Last Twenty-five Years of the Broadway Musical* (New York: Palgrave Macmillan, 2004), 62–65. Ken Mandelbaum offers fairly strong apprecia-

tion for the show, while still speculating on what the problems might have been in the original production, in his *Not Since Carrie: 40 Years of Broadway Musical Flops* (New York: St. Martin's Press, 1991), 321–23.

Chapter 9: *Children of Eden*

1. Personal interview with Stephen Schwartz in New York City, 19 March 2008. All quotations from Schwartz and information that he provided, unless otherwise noted, came from this source.

2. "Youth Sing Praise" remains an annual event each summer. On 25 June 2011, for example, their production was *Godspell*, and on 23 June 2012 they presented *Children of Eden*. See http://youthsingpraise.com/about/previous-productions/2012–2/ show2012/ (accessed 10 February 2012).

3. Carol de Giere, *Defying Gravity: The Creative Career of Stephen Schwartz from "Godspell" to "Wicked"* (New York: Applause Theatre & Cinema Books, 2008). Her coverage of *Children of Eden* is on pp. 205–26, including material from an interview with Charles Lisanby. (Lisanby had previously worked on the Radio City Music Hall Easter and Christmas programs.) De Giere (p. 206) reports that the production at the Crystal Cathedral would not work because there was no way to make the unusual structure dark enough in the early evening to present a play.

4. De Giere, *Defying Gravity*, 209.

5. Telephone interview with John Caird, 4 January 2008. All quotations from Caird and information that he provided, unless otherwise noted, came from this source.

6. Among Caird's personal papers consulted in his home are references to the play *The Flowering Peach* by Clifford Odets, which includes conflict between Noah and his son Japheth. It is Odets's play that Richard Rodgers, Martin Charnin, and Peter Stone adapted for the musical *Two by Two* (1970). Notes that Caird wrote on a restaurant's placemat (an undated source) demonstrate his concern for telling Japheth's story. He suggests that Japheth's story needs more details, such as his departure for Damascus so that he could flee responsibility for helping to build the ark, and that his return was to reassure Anah, not to help his family.

7. John Caird said this on one of my visits to his house in London in July 2008.

8. Caird informed me during my visit that the spiral notebook included some of his earliest notes on *Children of Eden*.

9. A major departure that Caird and Schwartz made from the biblical account of Noah and the flood is Yonah, who carries the Mark of Cain. Japheth takes her on the ark, against God's will. In Lisanby's version, Act 2 lacked conflict; Schwartz and Caird made Yonah become a focal point in Japheth's battle with Noah. Her name, suggested by Topol's daughter when she participated in the Guildhall workshop, is the Hebrew word for "dove" and close to the name "Jonah," almost responsible for sinking another ship in Hebrew scriptures. Caird described this character's development in our interview.

10. Caird's notes on a restaurant placemat (see note 6) also demonstrate his concern that the audience sense parallels between the acts. He suggests that Adam should be identified with Noah, Eve with Mama Noah, Cain with Japheth, and Abel with Anah. The final comparison is a stretch; there is no direct comparison for Abel in Act 2. Given Caird's early recognition of these parallels, it is hardly surprising that a few years later they started to double cast the show. On the same side of the placemat, Caird suggested that Adam, Eve, Mama, Ham, Shelia, Shem, and Asai should be played by blacks, while Noah should be white.

11. Antony Thorncroft, "Art: Prospects—Guaranteed Criticism/As Terry Hands Plans His Final Season," *Financial Times*, 20 January 1990.

12. "Parting Is Such Sweet Sorrow—Theater," *Times* (London), 19 July 1990.

13. "British Equity Panel Accepts Page as God," *Variety*, 17 September 1990, 107.

14. Jim Hiley, "Faith in a Good Book—Musical Theatre," *Times* (London), 11 December 1990. Hiley states that there were twenty-three musicians, but the West End program lists twenty-two playing the following instruments: flute/piccolo/recorder, oboe/English horn/recorder, alto saxophone/flute/clarinet, bass clarinet/soprano saxophone/tenor saxophone, clarinet/tenor saxophone/baritone saxophone, bassoon/contrabassoon/shawm, trumpet/flugelhorn, horn, tenor trombone, bass trombone/euphonium, violin/viola/mandolin, viola/mandolin, two cellos, three keyboards, drums, two guitarists, bass guitar, and percussion.

15. Geordie Greig, "Pushing the Boat Out to Save a Lyrical Creation—Christmas Shows," *Sunday Times* (London), 23 December 1990.

16. Hiley, "Faith in a Good Book."

17. Hiley, "Faith in a Good Book." In a source consulted at Caird's house, the director received a letter dated 10 October 1996 from Carolyn Jennings concerning Japanese businessmen who lost money in the West End production. Now that the show was enjoying some popularity they wanted a financial cut, but the rights had reverted to the authors.

18. Greig, "Pushing the Boat."

19. Greig, "Pushing the Boat."

20. See Matthew Bourne, *Matthew Bourne and His Adventures in Dance: Conversations with Alastair Macauley*, rev. ed. (London: Faber and Faber, 2011), for material on Bourne and a few comments on his participation in *Children of Eden*. Caird and Schwartz first saw Bourne's choreographic work in *The Infernal Galop* (p. 59), and then Bourne choreographed Caird's version of Shakespeare's *As You Like It* at the RSC in 1989, and then *Children of Eden* (p. 15).

21. The weekly and overall grosses for the production of *Children of Eden* at the Prince Edward Theatre were found among Caird's papers.

22. "'Eden' May Find Paradise in U.S. Pix," *Variety*, 28 January 1991, 77.

23. Most of the West End reviews of *Children of Eden* were consulted in the compilation journal *Theatre Record* 11, no. 1 (1991): 24–30. Michael Covenay's review appeared in the *Observer*, 13 January 1991, in *Theatre Record*, 29–30.

24. Jack Tinker's review appeared in the *Daily Mail*, 9 January 1991, in *Theatre Record*, 27.

25. Paul Taylor's review appeared in the *Independent*, 10 January 1991, in *Theatre Record*, 29.

26. Charles Osborne's review appeared in the *Daily Telegraph*, 9 January 1991, in *Theatre Record*, 28.

27. Clive Hirschhorn's review appeared in the *Sunday Express*, 13 January 1991, in *Theatre Record*, 25.

28. Michael Church's review appeared in the *Independent on Sunday*, 13 January 1991, in *Theatre Record*, 26–27.

29. Michael Darvell's review appeared in *What's On*, 16 January 1991, in *Theatre Record*, 26.

30. Unfortunately this fax is undated, but surely it was sent shortly before Caird's response on 29 April 1991.

31. Fax from Stephen Schwartz to John Caird, 25 June 1991.

32. According to a letter that Schwartz sent on 27 August 1991, the song was on a tape that Schwartz had sent earlier in the month, but it was lost in the mail.

33. Fax from Stephen Schwartz to John Caird, 25 June 1991. Schwartz's fax was a letter followed by a four-page outline of the show. On p. 3 of the outline, "Act Two, Part One," begins parenthetical marks such as the following: "Noah is played by actor who played Adam." Over pp. 3–4, he also equates Japheth with Cain and Mama Noah with Eve in terms of who plays these roles.

34. Telephone interview with Ernie Zulia, 12 February 2008. Each quotation from Zulia in the text was derived from this interview.

35. Zulia amplified this quotation in an electronic communication sent to the author on 24 March 2013.

36. Linda Eisenstein, "An Interview with Stephen Schwartz, Composer & Lyricist, *Children of Eden*," *Cleveland Plain Dealer*, October 1997, consulted at http://my.en.com/~herone/Schwartz.html (accessed 19 April 2012).

37. Fax from Stephen Schwartz to John Caird, 10 March 1993.

38. Fax from Stephen Schwartz to John Caird, 13 November 1994.

39. De Giere, *Defying Gravity*, 222. For a list of the shows at the festival, see http://namt.org/festival-history.aspx#1996 (accessed 22 April 2012).

40. *Children of Eden: American Premiere Recording. Music & Lyrics by Stephen Schwartz. Book by John Caird*. RCA Victor 09026–63165–2, 1998.

41. Peter Filichia, "A Musical Paradise," *Newark Star-Ledger*, 18 November 1997.

42. Alvin Klein, "The Old Testament in Song and Dance," *New York Times*, 23 November 1997, 16.

43. Linda Armstrong, "The Bible, Told through 'Children of Eden,'" *New York Amsterdam News*, 20–26 November 1997, 28.

44. Clive Barnes, "A Little Bit of Paradise," *New York Post*, 24 November 1997, 44.

45. Robert J. Daniels, Review of *Children of Eden*, *Variety*, 24 November 1997, 73.

46. http://www.ibdb.com/production.php?id=4498 (accessed 26 July 2012).

47. Frank Rich, "A Musical of Sophocles and Pentecostalism," *New York Times*, 25 March 1988, C5.

48. Mark Steyn, "Beginners Please," *Independent*, 5 January 1991.

49. Fax from Stephen Schwartz to John Caird, 27 August 1991.

50. See Paul R. Laird, *"Wicked": A Musical Biography* (Lanham, MD: Scarecrow Press, 2011), 153, 209–10.

51. *Children of Eden: Original London Cast.* London 828 234 2, 1991.

52. In an article on composing for musical theater, Schwartz described the need to "button" a song, a place where the composer kicks the energy up to a new level to provide a swell of emotion. He cites "Lost in the Wilderness" as an example of where he tried to do this, and it probably is at this moment in the song. See his "Composing," *Dramatist* 12, no. 1 (September–October 2009): 33.

53. Stephen Schwartz, *Children of Eden: Vocal Selections* (Miami: Warner Bros. Publications, 1999), 35–41.

54. Schwartz, *Children of Eden: Vocal Selections*, 72–79.

55. http://www.playbill.com/news/article/152751-In-Pursuit-of-Excellence -55-Piece-Symphonic-Children-of-Eden-Begins-in-Kansas-City-July-15 (accessed 26 July 2012).

Chapter 10: Animated Features for Disney and DreamWorks

1. Carol de Giere, *Defying Gravity: The Creative Career of Stephen Schwartz from "Godspell" to "Wicked"* (New York: Applause Theatre & Cinema Books, 2008), 230–31.

2. De Giere, *Defying Gravity*, 229.

3. De Giere, *Defying Gravity*, 230.

4. "The Music of *Pocahontas*," bonus track in *Pocahontas 10th Anniversary Edition*, Walt Disney Pictures 22960, 2005, DVD.

5. De Giere, *Defying Gravity*, 232–33.

6. De Giere, *Defying Gravity*, 235.

7. De Giere, *Defying Gravity*, 238.

8. A summation of what is know about Pocahontas's life appears on the National Parks Service Jamestown website. See "Pocahontas: Her Life and Legend," http:// www.nps.gov/jame/historyculture/pocahontas-her-life-and-legend.htm (accessed 11 July 2013). The animated feature's plot has very little to do with history.

9. "The Making of *Pocahontas*," bonus track in *Pocahontas 10th Anniversary Edition*, Walt Disney Pictures 22960, 2005, DVD.

10. According to "Pocahontas: Her Life and Legend," at about the age of fourteen she did marry a man by this name.

11. http://www.imdb.com/title/tt0114148/ (accessed 19 November 2012).

12. Schwartz praises the way that Menken establishes the musical sound world in his score in an article on what one needs to think about when composing for musical

theater. Menken calls this quality a score's "palette." See Schwartz's "Composing," *Dramatist* 12, no. 1 (September–October 2009): 31.

13. Commentary track in *Pocahontas 10th Anniversary Edition*, Walt Disney Pictures 22960, 2005, DVD. Includes contributions from James Pentecost, producer; Eric Goldberg, director; and Mike Gabriel, director.

14. De Giere, *Defying Gravity*, 236.

15. De Giere, *Defying Gravity*, 236.

16. "The Making of *Pocahontas*."

17. Commentary track in *Pocahontas 10th Anniversary Edition*.

18. De Giere, *Defying Gravity*, 233–35, 239–41.

19. De Giere, *Defying Gravity*, 241.

20. Commentary track in *Pocahontas 10th Anniversary Edition*.

21. "The Making of 'If I Never Knew You,'" a bonus track in *Pocahontas 10th Anniversary Edition*. DVD. Walt Disney Pictures 22960, 2005.

22. De Giere, *Defying Gravity*, 242–47. Schwartz's biographer questions the wisdom of adapting Hugo's novel in her first sentence in the section and remains vaguely critical of the project.

23. "The Making of *The Hunchback of Notre Dame*" and commentary track to *The Hunchback of Notre Dame*. Walt Disney Pictures 023315, 2002, DVD. During the course of the commentary track, one hears that 600 people worked on this film.

24. http://www.imdb.com/title/tt0116583/ (accessed 23 September 2012).

25. Commentary track in *The Hunchback of Notre Dame*.

26. Commentary track in *The Hunchback of Notre Dame*.

27. De Giere, *Defying Gravity*, 244.

28. De Giere, *Defying Gravity*, 244.

29. Commentary track in *The Hunchback of Notre Dame*.

30. De Giere, *Defying Gravity*, 243.

31. Commentary track in *The Hunchback of Notre Dame*. De Giere also covers the two songs written for this song placement (*Defying Gravity*, 246).

32. De Giere, *Defying Gravity*, 245.

33. http://media.musicasacra.com/pdf/pbc-extract3.pdf (accessed 27 September 2012).

34. Commentary track in *The Hunchback of Notre Dame*.

35. Commentary track in *The Hunchback of Notre Dame*.

36. De Giere, *Defying Gravity*, 245.

37. De Giere, *Defying Gravity*, 243.

38. Commentary track in *The Hunchback of Notre Dame*.

39. Commentary track in *The Hunchback of Notre Dame*.

40. Disney's *Die Glöckner von Notre Dame*. Stella Music 547 836–2, 1999. CD.

41. De Giere, *Defying Gravity*, 249–50.

42. De Giere, *Defying Gravity*, 250–52.

43. De Giere, *Defying Gravity*, 252–53.

44. Commentary track on *The Prince of Egypt*. DreamWorks 84853, 2006. DVD.

45. http://www.imdb.com/title/tt0120794/ (accessed 2 October 2012).

46. De Giere, *Defying Gravity*, 253. On the commentary track of the DVD, the directors agreed that it was this song that solidified the film's overall themes.

47. Schwartz decided that the theme should be played first by solo trumpet. See de Giere, *Defying Gravity*, 255.

48. De Giere, *Defying Gravity*, 257.

49. Carol de Giere covers the story of Schwartz's friend who wrote these lines for him (*Defying Gravity*, 254).

50. De Giere, *Defying Gravity*, 256–57.

51. De Giere, *Defying Gravity*, 259–60.

52. De Giere, *Defying Gravity*, 266–67.

53. De Giere (*Defying Gravity*, 260), citing director Steve Hickner, also points out that Schwartz connected the poem's simple thoughts with the film's larger theme.

54. De Giere, *Defying Gravity*, 258.

55. Commentary track on *The Prince of Egypt*.

56. Commentary track on *The Prince of Egypt*.

57. Commentary track on *The Prince of Egypt*.

58. De Giere, *Defying Gravity*, 260–61.

59. De Giere, *Defying Gravity*, 261.

60. De Giere, *Defying Gravity*, 261–62.

61. De Giere, *Defying Gravity*, 262.

62. De Giere, *Defying Gravity*, 262.

63. An example of the film's generally positive critical reception may be seen in Todd McCarthy's review for *Variety*, available online at http://www.variety.com/review/VE1117935452?refcatid=31 (accessed 17 September 2012). For information on the film's gross revenue, see http://www.imdb.com/title/tt0461770/ (accessed 17 September 2012).

64. De Giere, *Defying Gravity*, 492.

65. De Giere, *Defying Gravity*, 492.

66. De Giere, *Defying Gravity*, 492.

67. *Enchanted*. DVD. Walt Disney Pictures 52391, 2008. The DVD includes a set of extra features entitled "Fantasy Comes to Life" with short documentaries on filming "Happy Working Song," "That's How You Know," and the climactic sequence in "A Blast at the Ball."

68. De Giere, *Defying Gravity*, 492.

69. De Giere, *Defying Gravity*, 492–93.

70. De Giere, *Defying Gravity*, 493–94.

Chapter 11: *Geppetto* Becomes
My Son Pinocchio: Geppetto's Musical Tale

1. Electronic communication from David I. Stern to author, 13 July 2006.

2. Personal interview with Stephen Schwartz, Kansas City, MO, 26 June 2006. All material attributed to Schwartz, unless otherwise noted, is derived from this interview.

3. Personal interview with Jeff Church, Kansas City, MO, 20 June 2006. All material attributed to Church, unless otherwise noted, is derived from this interview.

4. The Coterie has remained an important developer for new family musicals. At this point Church and his theater have participated in incubating the following shows between the 2003–2004 season and 2012–2013 (several of them family versions of larger shows): *Seussical*, *The Dinosaur Musical*, *Disney's Geppetto & Son*, *Twice Upon a Time: The Lorax & The Emperor's New Clothes by Dr. Seuss & Hans Christian Andersen*, *The Happy Elf*, *Once on This Island*, *U: Bug: ME*, *Life on the Mississippi*, *Lucky Duck*, *Once Upon a Mattress*, and *Shrek the Musical*. During the 2013–2014 season came a family version of *Chitty Chitty Bang Bang*. From *Coterie Theatre's Lab for New Family Musicals*, an unpublished PDF supplied by the Coterie Theatre.

5. Kenneth Jones, "Stephen Schwartz's Family-Friendly *Geppetto & Son* Tests Its Strings in Kansas City," *Playbill.com*, 27 June 2006, http://www.playbill.com/news/article/100532-Stephen-Schwartzs-Family-Friendly-Geppetto-Son-Tests-Its-Strings-in-Kansas-City (accessed 14 February 2013).

6. Robert Trussell, "A Real Hit? Stage Story of Pinocchio's Dad Shows Promise at the Coterie," *Kansas City Star*, 5 July 2006, http://infoweb.newsbank.com.www2.lib.ku.edu:2048/iw-search/we/InfoWeb?p_product=NewsBank&p_theme=aggregated5&p_action=doc&p_docid=112B426C84A312A0&p_docnum=3&p_queryname=1 (accessed 8 January 2014).

7. Alan Scherstuhl, "Puppet Love," *Pitch*, 6 July 2006, http://www.pitch.com/kansascity/puppet-love/Content?oid=2182468 (accessed 8 January 2014).

8. Steve Walker, "*Geppetto & Son*," Theatermania, 3 July 2006, http://www.theatermania.com/new-york-city-theater/reviews/07-2006/geppetto-and-son_8565.html (accessed 8 January 2014).

9. Electronic communication from Stephen Schwartz to author, 22 August 2012.

10. Electronic communication from David I. Stern to author, 26 March 2013.

11. Electronic communication from Stephen Schwartz to author, 22 August 2012.

12. http://www.mtishows.com/show_detail.asp?showid=000306 (accessed 22 August 2012).

13. Electronic communication from Stephen Schwartz to author, 22 August 2012.

Chapter 12: *Wicked*

1. Carol de Giere, *Defying Gravity: The Creative Career of Stephen Schwartz from "Godspell" to "Wicked"* (New York: Applause Theatre & Cinema Books, 2008), and David Cote, *"Wicked": The Grimmerie: A Behind-the-Scenes Look at the Hit Broadway Musical* (New York: Hyperion, 2005). De Giere made *Wicked* the major part of her book (pp. 268–426) and had access to Schwartz around the time of its opening, recording, and other major events. Cote's "coffee table book" includes useful interviews with a number of actors and creators involved with the production and many photographs.

2. Gregory Maguire, *Wicked: The Life and Times of the Wicked Witch of the West* (New York: ReganBooks, 1995).

3. See Paul R. Laird, *"Wicked": A Musical Biography* (Lanham, MD: Scarecrow Press, 2011), 1–17, for a detailed synopsis of Maguire's novel and brief comparisons of its plot with the show. How *Wicked* compares with other projects based on Baum's famous stories has been considered by Alissa Burger in her "From *The Wizard of Oz* to *Wicked*: Trajectory of an American Myth" (PhD dissertation, Bowling Green State University, 2009).

4. Laird, *"Wicked,"* 30–31.

5. Laird, *"Wicked,"* 31–46.

6. Laird, *"Wicked,"* 33.

7. Laird, *"Wicked,"* 35.

8. Laird, *"Wicked,"* 34–35.

9. Laird, *"Wicked,"* 38–40.

10. Cote, *"Wicked,"* 134.

11. *"Wicked*: The Road to Broadway," an extra feature on disc 3 of *B'Way/Broadway: The American Musical*, dir. Michael Kantor (Educational Broadcasting Corporation and the Broadway Film Project, 2004).

12. Laird, *"Wicked,"* 41.

13. Laird, *"Wicked,"* 41.

14. De Giere provides Schwartz's September 1998 synopsis (*Defying Gravity*, 503–9) and offers many useful comments on the show's development throughout her coverage of the show. A detailed consideration of development of the show's script appears in Laird, *"Wicked,"* 53–87. Each of the remaining points in this paragraph are covered in this chapter.

15. Laird, *"Wicked,"* 95–100.

16. Laird, *"Wicked,"* 89–211. All specific musical references to *Wicked* are addressed in more detail in this chapter.

17. In addition to frequent discussion of Schwartz's manipulation of musical motives in my chapter on music in *"Wicked": A Musical Biography* (pp. 89–211), Stephani Bee approached the issue in detail in her "Defying Conventional Broadway: A Post-Feminist Criticism of *Wicked*" (MA thesis, California State University, Fullerton, 2012).

18. Laird, *"Wicked,"* 164–67.

19. Laird, *"Wicked,"* 131, 167, 203–4.

20. Laird, *"Wicked,"* 142–43, 157.

21. For a report on Brohn's career, see Laird, *"Wicked,"* 216–18.

22. Laird, *"Wicked,"* 219.

23. Laird, *"Wicked,"* 219.

24. Laird, *"Wicked,"* 221. The chapter involving *Wicked*'s orchestration is on pp. 213–50.

25. Laird, *"Wicked,"* 221.

26. Laird, *"Wicked,"* 221–22, 249 notes 40, 43.

27. Laird, *"Wicked,"* 222.

28. Laird, *"Wicked,"* 251–59, is a detailed consideration of the critical reaction to the Broadway production..

29. See http://ibdb.com/production.php?id=13485 (accessed 29 September 2013), and for the show's latest attendance statistics, see http://www.playbill.com/features/section/7/Broadway-Grosses-News/.

30. For information on most productions listed in this paragraph, see Laird, "Wicked," 261–64.

31. The Netherlands website for the show is http://www.musicals.nl/wicked.asp (accessed 12 January 2013 [the day after the show closed]).

Chapter 13: *Séance on a Wet Afternoon*

1. Personal interview with Stephen Schwartz in New York City, 22 March 2005.

2. Stephen Schwartz, "Stephen Schwartz: How the Hit Broadway Musical Writer's Classical Beginnings Helped Shape His Theatrical Career," *Gramophone* 86 (November 2008): 146.

3. Paul R. Laird, *"Wicked": A Musical Biography* (Lanham, MD: Scarecrow Press, 2011), 220.

4. Personal interview with Stephen Schwartz in New York City, 22 November 2008.

5. Personal interview with Stephen Schwartz in New York City, 22 April 2011.

6. Telephone interview with Stephen Schwartz, 26 July 2009.

7. Michael Jackowitz, "Genesis of *Séance on a Wet Afternoon*," Séance on a Wet Afternoon, http://www.seancetheopera.com/about_us.html (accessed 11 November 2011).

8. Jackowitz reports that Schwartz heard the idea of *Séance on a Wet Afternoon* as a possible musical theater piece from agent Peter Franklin, but Schwartz thought it more of a possibility for an opera because of the dark story.

9. Personal interview with Stephen Schwartz in New York City, 22 November 2008.

10. Charity Wicks has suggested that the story's psychological bent might be another reason that Schwartz chose it, noting the composer's interest in psychology and his brief study in the field before his Hollywood career took off in the early 1990s. See Charity Wicks, "An Introduction to and Musico-Dramatic Analysis of *Séance on a Wet Afternoon*: An Opera by Stephen Schwartz" (DMA document, Manhattan School of Music, 2011), 4. Wicks (pp. 7–10) goes on to explain the opera's plot largely in terms of possible psychological profiles for the two main characters.

11. Mark McShane, *Séance on a Wet Afternoon* (New York: Carroll & Graf, 1961).

12. Frank J. Oteri, "Stephen Schwartz and Lauren Flanigan: Corners of the Sky," NewMusicBox, http://www.newmusicbox.org/articles/stephen-schwartz-and-lauren-flanigan-corners-of-the-sky/ (accessed 24 September 2011).

13. McShane, *Séance*, 50.

14. Telephone interview with Stephen Schwartz, 25 January 2012.

15. McShane, *Séance*, 51.

16. Wicks ("Introduction," 23) suggests it is this moment in Act 1 when Arthur states that Adriana should be killed.

17. Charity Wicks ("Introduction," 48–49) explains the opera's conclusion differently, stating that by the third séance, Myra has gone completely insane and she reveals the plot while believing that she is using her psychic abilities. The end could be interpreted several ways, but during the séance Adriana's ghost is above the table and she appears to speak through the medium.

18. Oteri, "Stephen Schwartz."

19. Telephone interview with Stephen Schwartz, 26 July 2009.

20. Telephone interview with Scott Schwartz, 15 October 2009.

21. Personal interview with Stephen Schwartz in Santa Barbara, CA, 2 October 2009.

22. Personal interview with Stephen Schwartz in Santa Barbara, CA, 2 October 2009.

23. Personal interview with Stephen Schwartz in New York City, 22 November 2008.

24. Personal interview with Stephen Schwartz in New York City, 22 November 2008.

25. Personal interview with Stephen Schwartz in Santa Barbara, CA, 2 October 2009.

26. Personal interview with Stephen Schwartz in New York City, 22 November 2008.

27. Personal interview with Stephen Schwartz in New York City, 22 November 2008.

28. Personal interview with Stephen Schwartz in New York City, 22 November 2008.

29. Personal interview with Stephen Schwartz in New York City, 22 November 2008.

30. Personal interview with Stephen Schwartz in New York City, 22 November 2008.

31. All quotations in this paragraph are from a personal interview with Stephen Schwartz in New York City, 22 November 2008.

32. Telephone interview with Stephen Schwartz, 26 July 2009. We discussed assembling the cast for the premiere in this telephone interview and in New York on 22 November 2008.

33. Oteri, "Stephen Schwartz."

34. Personal interview with Stephen Schwartz in New York City, 22 November 2008.

35. Personal interview with Stephen Schwartz in New York City, 22 November 2008.

36. Telephone interview with Stephen Schwartz, 26 July 2009.

37. Personal interview with Stephen Schwartz in New York City, 22 November 2008.

38. Adam Hetrick, "NYCO Presents a *Séance on a Wet Afternoon*, by Stephen Schwartz, May 1," *Playbill.com*, 1 May 2009, http://www.playbill.com/news/article/128796-NYCO-Presents-a-Sance-on-a-Wet-Afternoon-By-Stephen-Schwartz-May-1 (accessed 11 November 2011).

39. Personal interview with Stephen Schwartz in New York City, 22 November 2008. All quotes from Schwartz in this paragraph came from this interview.

40. Telephone interview with Stephen Schwartz, 26 July 2009.

41. Personal interview with Stephen Schwartz in New York City, 22 April 2011. All direct quotations in this paragraph came from this interview.

42. Wicks ("Introduction," 45–48) describes "Before You" in detail, noting that it gives Myra a chance to ruminate on what has occurred and reminisce about her time before Arthur.

43. See my chapter on orchestration in *"Wicked,"* 213–50.

44. Leonard Bernstein, *West Side Story Suite, Lonely Town,* and *New York New York* (arranged by William David Brohn, cadenza by Joshua Bell), *Make Our Garden Grow* (arranged by John Corigliano); Joshua Bell, violin; Philharmonia Orchestra; David Zinman, conductor. Sony SK 89358, 2001.

45. Joint personal interview with Stephen Schwartz and William David Brohn in New York City, 22 November 2011.

46. Personal interview with Stephen Schwartz in New York City, 22 November 2011.

47. Joint personal interview with Stephen Schwartz and William David Brohn in New York City, 22 November 2008.

48. Personal interview with Stephen Schwartz in Santa Barbara, CA, 2 October 2009.

49. Personal interview with Stephen Schwartz in Santa Barbara, CA, 2 October 2009.

50. Telephone interview with Stephen Schwartz, 26 July 2009.

51. Telephone interview with Stephen Schwartz, 26 July 2009.

52. For Schwartz, music should provide an emotional subtext when writing for the theater. See his "Composing," *Dramatist* 12, no. 1 (September–October 2009): 32.

53. Personal interview with Stephen Schwartz in New York City, 22 April 2011.

54. Personal interview with Stephen Schwartz in Santa Barbara, CA, 2 October 2009.

55. Personal interview with Stephen Schwartz in Santa Barbara, CA, 2 October 2009.

56. Personal interview with Stephen Schwartz in Santa Barbara, CA, 2 October 2009.

57. Personal interview with Stephen Schwartz in Santa Barbara, CA, 2 October 2009.

58. Wicks ("Introduction," 30–35) describes "You Didn't Know Her" in detail, placing the climax of the aria at the point where he admits he cannot stop loving Myra, the crux of their relationship and what makes the story possible.

59. Wicks ("Introduction," 35–45) describes this confrontation, the climax of the opera, in considerable detail concerning its musico-dramatic cohesion.

60. Personal interview with Stephen Schwartz in Santa Barbara, CA, 2 October 2009.

61. Josef Woodard, "Opera Review: 'Seance on a Wet Afternoon' at Opera Santa Barbara," *Los Angeles Times*, 27 September 2009, http://latimesblogs.latimes.com/culturemonster/2009/09/opera-review-seance-on-a-wet-afternoon-at-opera-santa-barbara.html (accessed 2 January 2012).

62. Bob Verini, "*Séance on a Wet Afternoon*," *Variety*, 28 September 2009, http://www.variety.com/review/VE1117941261 (accessed 2 January 2012).

63. Personal interview with Stephen Schwartz in Santa Barbara, CA, 2 October 2009.

64. Personal interview with Stephen Schwartz in Santa Barbara, CA, 2 October 2009.

65. Barry Singer covered much of the same ground as appears in this chapter in his interview with Schwartz before the New York premiere. See Barry Singer, "Composer's Medium," *Opera News* 75, no. 10 (April 2011): 16–17.

66. Personal interview with Stephen Schwartz in New York City, 22 April 2011.

67. Anthony Tommasini, "A Crime Lurks on the Dark Side of a Clairvoyant Realm," *New York Times*, 20 April 2011, http://www.nytimes.com/2011/04/21/arts/music/seance-on-a-wet-afternoon-at-city-opera-review.html?pagewanted=all (accessed 2 January 2012).

68. Judith Malafronte, writing for *Opera News*, was considerably less sanguine about *Séance*, finding it wanting in most every area. See her review in "New York City," *Opera News* 76, no. 1 (July 2011): 43–44.

69. Personal interview with Stephen Schwartz in New York City, 22 April 2011. Schwartz demonstrated his dislike for one contemporary musical technique when he indicated his satisfaction that modern opera composers have "broken out of the hideous 12-tone cage." See Stephen Schwartz, "Stephen Schwartz: How the Hit Broadway Musical Writer's Classical Beginnings Helped Shape His Theatrical Career," *Gramophone* 86 (November 2008): 146.

70. Personal interview with Stephen Schwartz in New York City, 22 April 2011.

71. http://www.boosey.com/cr/perusals/ (accessed 2 January 2012).

72. Personal interview with Stephen Schwartz in New York City, 22 April 2011.

73. This material on Josephson's role in the creation of *Séance on a Wet Afternoon*, except where otherwise noted, was based on a telephone interview with him on 3 November 2009.

74. Personal interview with Stephen Schwartz in New York City, 22 November 2008.

75. http://hilaplitmann.com/bio (accessed 10 January 2012).

76. All of the material in this paragraph, unless otherwise noted, is based upon my telephone interview with Hila Plitmann on 3 November 2009.

77. Personal interview with Stephen Schwartz in New York City, 22 November 2008.

78. For additional material on Ryvkin and the Opera Santa Barbara, see http://www.belcantoglobalarts.com/ryvkin/Valery%20Ryvkin%20Classical%20Singer%20June%202009.pdf (accessed 12 January 2012); Lois Barth, "Maestro Valéry Ryvkin: A 'Singer's Conductor' on Orchestrating the Key Elements of Opera," *Classical Singer* (June 2009): 20–29.

79. Most of the material in this section, except when otherwise noted, is from a personal interview with Valéry Ryvkin, Santa Barbara, CA, 2 October 2009.

80. Barth, "Maestro Valéry Ryvkin," 28, and http://www.operasb.org/event.php?event_id=20 (accessed 15 October 2011).

81. Personal interview with Stephen Schwartz in New York City, 22 November 2008.

82. Telephone interview with Kim Josephson, 3 November 2009.

83. The material concerning Scott Schwartz and his role in the design and direction of *Séance on a Wet Afternoon*, including all quotations, was taken from my telephone interview with him on 15 October 2009.

84. Telephone interview with Stephen Schwartz, 26 July 2009.

85. Telephone interview with Stephen Schwartz, 26 July 2009.

86. Personal interview with Stephen Schwartz in Santa Barbara, CA, 2 October 2009.

87. Personal interview with Stephen Schwartz in New York City, 22 April 2011.

88. http://www.mattwilliamschoreographer.com/bio.php (accessed 6 January 2012).

89. Telephone interview with Stephen Schwartz, 26 July 2009.

90. See the following website for a PDF providing this table of section lengths in the various sources for *Séance*: http://www.music.ku.edu/paul-laird.

91. Telephone interview with Scott Schwartz, 15 October 2009.

92. Wicks ("Introduction," 16–19) considers this aria in detail.

93. Personal interview with Stephen Schwartz in New York City, 22 November 2008.

94. Personal interview with Stephen Schwartz in New York City, 22 November 2008.

95. Telephone interview with Stephen Schwartz, 26 July 2009.

96. Wicks, "Introduction," 19–20, 28–29, 42–44.

97. Personal interview with Stephen Schwartz in New York City, 22 November 2008.

98. Personal interview with Stephen Schwartz in New York City, 22 November 2008.

99. Wicks, "Introduction," 14.

100. See Wicks, "Introduction," 13, 18, 23, 49, for discussion of the importance of the significance of pitch class c in the opera.

101. Wicks, "Introduction," 16, 18, 42.

102. Wicks, "Introduction," 22, 44. In the online orchestral score, compare Act 1, pp. 207ff with Act 2, pp. 197ff.

103. Wicks, "Introduction," 26.

104. Wicks, "Introduction," 46.

105. Laird, "Wicked," 209–10, note 61.

106. Personal interview with Stephen Schwartz in New York City, 22 November 2008.

107. Personal interview with Stephen Schwartz in Santa Barbara, CA, 2 October 2009.

108. Personal interview with Stephen Schwartz in New York City, 22 November 2008.

109. Personal interview with Stephen Schwartz in New York City, 22 November 2008.

110. Laird, "Wicked," 103.

111. Wicks, "Introduction," 49.

112. See, for example, Michael Portantiere's interviews with Schwartz and other contemporary musical theater composers such as Adam Guettel and Jason Robert Brown in "Over the Borderline," Opera News 73, no. 3 (September 2008): 48–51.

113. Personal interview with Stephen Schwartz in New York City, 22 April 2011. Quotes from Schwartz through the end of this chapter came from this interview.

Chapter 14: Stephen Schwartz's Works outside of Broadway and Hollywood

1. http://www.mtishows.com/show_detail.asp?showid=000287 (accessed 18 January 2013).

2. "Meridee Stein, Producer/Director," Silas, http://silasthemusical.com/Meridee_Stein.html (accessed 16 January 2013).

3. "Anthony Stein, Book Writer," Silas, http://silasthemusical.com/Anthony_Stein.html (accessed 16 January 2013).

4. Carol de Giere, Defying Gravity: The Creative Career of Stephen Schwartz from "Godspell" to "Wicked" (New York: Applause Theatre & Cinema Books, 2008), 483.

5. Captain Louie: World Premiere Recording. Music & Lyrics by Stephen Schwartz. Based on "The Trip" by Ezra Jack Keats. Book by Anthony Stein. PS Classics 530, 2005. Liner notes, [4].

6. De Giere, Defying Gravity, 483, and recording liner notes, [4].

7. De Giere, Defying Gravity, 483.

8. Recording liner notes, [4].

9. For reviews, see Miriam Horn, "Theater Review: A Halloween Tale for Children, No Great Pumpkin Required," New York Times, 8 November 2005. She was full of praise for the music and its performances, but was less interested in the book: "Fortunately, the show is mostly music, because when the music stops, the energy

drains away." Her appraisal of the earlier York Theatre production, published 11 May 2005, was similar. See Miriam Horn, "Theater Review: Halloween, Where Spirits Soar," *New York Times*, 8 November 2005, E4.

10. Synopsis based upon http://www.mtishows.com/show_detail.asp?showid= 000287 (accessed 16 January 2013).

11. For most of the music in a piano/vocal version, see: *Vocal Selections: "Captain Louie," Music & Lyrics by Stephen Schwartz, Based on "The Trip" by Ezra Jack Keats* (N.p.: Williamson Music, 2009.)

12. Leonard Bernstein, *Mass: A Theater Piece for Singers, Players and Dancers. Text from the Liturgy of the Roman Mass. Additional Texts by Stephen Schwartz and Leonard Bernstein* (N.p.: Boosey & Hawkes/Jalni Publications, 1989), 66–71. For example, Schwartz employs an augmented triad built on E-flat in eighth notes over a pedal C four times in the introduction's accompaniment, not unlike the augmented triad with added tones that Bernstein uses to set such text as "Mariae semper Virgini" in eighth notes over longer notes (p. 68) and recurs a number of times over the next several pages of the score. (Compare CD 1, track 9, 0'24"ff in Bernstein's *Mass* OCR with track 4, 0'06"ff in "Shadows." For the OCR of *Mass* see *Leonard Bernstein's Mass: A Theatre Piece for Singers, Players and Dancers*. Conducted by the composer. Text from the liturgy of the Roman Mass. Additional texts by Stephen Schwartz and Leonard Bernstein. LP. Columbia Masterworks M2 31008, n.d. Re-issued on CD: *Bernstein Century: Bernstein Mass*. Alan Titus, the Norman Scribner Choir, the Berkshire Boy Choir, orchestra conducted by Leonard Bernstein. Sony Classical SM2K 63089, 1997.) Also, Schwartz's arpeggiated, descending material in the opening vocal gesture of "Shadows" is reminiscent of Bernstein's setting of "Confiteor," but Schwartz uses an augmented arpeggio while Bernstein uses a combination of major and minor triads.

13. John Bush Jones, *Our Musicals, Ourselves: A Social History of the American Musical Theatre* (Hanover and London: Brandeis University Press, 2003), 300. Jones (pp. 299–301) provides a useful appreciation of the show.

14. Frank Rich, "Stage: 'Personals,' Musical Comedy," *New York Times*, 25 November 1985, C16.

15. A production of *Personals* opened in London's West End on 3 September 1998 and the company made an original cast recording: *Personals: The Comedy-Musical Revue/Original London Cast* (Jay Productions Ltd., CDJAY 1319, 1999). Schwartz's songs appear on this recording on tracks 1, 9, and 15.

16. Carol de Giere considers a "Stephen Schwartz and Friends" concert on p. 499 of *Defying Gravity*.

17. For de Giere's consideration of these albums, see *Defying Gravity*, 511.

18. A songwriter himself, Pitchford is one of Schwartz's good friends; de Giere considers him in a number of places in her book.

19. "Snapshots" is part of a revue of Schwartz songs by the same name that has played in various guises for a number of years. David I. Stern wrote the book. The score also includes "Code of Silence" from *Reluctant Pilgrim*. See "Snapshots: A Mu-

sical Scrapbook!" MusicalSchwarz.com, http://www.musicalschwartz.com/snapshots
.htm (accessed 2 February 2013).

20. Mary Fahl is a singer/songwriter. See http://maryfahl.com/ (accessed 2 February 2013).

21. Steven Lutvak is a singer/songwriter who has composed songs and scores for a number of musicals. See http://www.stevenlutvak.com/pages/about.html (accessed 2 February 2013).

22. *Life with Mikey* is a film with its score composed by Alan Menken. See http://www.imdb.com/title/tt0107413/ (accessed 2 February 2013).

23. Lindy Robbins is a successful songwriter in Los Angeles who has written songs for many well-known pop singers. For more information, see http://www.american songwriter.com/2013/01/la-songwriter-series-lindy-robbins/ (accessed 2 February 2013).

24. A close friend of Schwartz's, John Bucchino is a singer/songwriter who, according to de Giere, encouraged Schwartz to write the kind of personal songs that fill his two albums. For more on Bucchino, see de Giere, *Defying Gravity*, 199–200, and elsewhere.

25. For a look at original musicals in Europe, see Judith Sebesta's "'Something Borrowed, Something Blue': The Marriage of the Musical and Europe," in *The Cambridge Companion to the Musical*, 2nd ed., ed. William A. Everett and Paul R. Laird (Cambridge: Cambridge University Press, 2008), 270–83.

26. For biographical material on Flemming Enevold, see the press release from Pacific Conservatory for the Performing Arts on the production dated May 2011: http://www.pcpa.org/myfairytalepr.html (accessed 19 January 2013).

27. Pacific Conservatory for the Performing Arts, press release.

28. http://micechat.com/forums/theatre/158481-my-fairytale-new-musical-ste phen-schwartz-includes-my-interview-him.html (accessed 19 January 2013).

29. http://micechat.com/forums/theatre/158481-my-fairytale-new-musical-ste phen-schwartz-includes-my-interview-him.html.

30. Among the many biographies of Andersen, see, for example, Jack Zipes, *Hans Christian Andersen: The Misunderstood Storyteller* (New York: Routledge, 2005).

31. Schwartz offered this opinion in an interview that can be seen at http://www .youtube.com/watch?v=TrirzUjT0jY (accessed 19 January 2013).

32. The English translations of these titles is based upon a listing of the titles of the songs from the Pacific Conservatory of the Performing Arts production in 2011 found in the review by Bob Verini: "Review: 'My Fairytale,'" *Variety*, 30 August 2011, http://www.variety.com/review/VE1117945914/ (accessed 19 January 2013).

33. Stephen Schwartz, *My Fairytale Piano/Vocal Score*, Score, 6/9/2011, *Prepared by Andrew Fox*. Act 1, 35.

34. *g.t./gladsaxe teater præsenterer "Mit eventyr."* CD. Gladsaxe Teater, 2006.

35. Andersen on his swan may be seen along with other scenes from the show on the following video: http://www.youtube.com/watch?v=TrirzUjT0jY (accessed 21 January 2013). The swan appears at 2'11"ff.

36. http://micechat.com/forums/theatre/158481-my-fairytale-new-musical-stephen-schwartz-includes-my-interview-him.html.

37. Pacific Conservatory for the Performing Arts, press release.

38. http://www.youtube.com/watch?v=REMTR0Uxu4Y (accessed 19 January 2013). The song title has been taken from a list of songs for the production found in the press release by the Pacific Conservatory for the Performing Arts (see note 26).

39. See http://www.stagescenela.com/2011/09/my-fairytale/ (accessed 19 January 2013) and Verini, "Review." Sarah Linn reviewed *My Fairytale* in "Fairytales a Fit for 'Wicked' Composer Stephen Schwartz," *Tribune* (San Luis Obispo, CA), 20 August 2011, http://www.sanluisobispo.com/2011/08/20/1724622/fairytales-wicked-composer-schwartz.html (accessed 19 January 2013).

40. The background for Scott Schwartz's version of *My Antonia* in this paragraph was derived from the following source: Karen Lindell, "Scott Schwartz Brings Willa Cather's Novel to the Stage, with Her Voice Intact," *Ventura County Star*, 8 May 2008; http://www.vcstar.com/news/2008/may/08/adapting-antonia/?print=1 (accessed 13 January 2013).

41. Edward Guthmann, "A Stage Director Refuses to Respect Willa Cather's Wishes, but Does So Respectfully," *SFGate*, 29 March 2004, http://www.sfgate.com/bayarea/article/A-stage-director-refuses-to-respect-Willa-2801952.php (accessed 12 January 2013).

42. Guthmann, "Stage Director."

43. Guthmann, "Stage Director."

44. Andrew Gans, "Scott Schwartz's *My Antonia*, with Stephen Schwartz Underscoring, Begins CA Run May 8," *Playbill.com*, 8 May 2008, http://www.playbill.com/news/article/117520-Scott-Schwartzs-My-Antonia-with-Stephen-Schwartz-Underscoring-Begins-CA-Run-May-8 (accessed 12 January 2013).

45. Lindell, "Scott Schwartz."

46. Lindell, "Scott Schwartz."

47. Lindell, "Scott Schwartz."

48. Most of the information in this paragraph comes from an electronic message that Stephen Schwartz sent to the author on 23 January 2013.

49. This is the hymnal from which John Michael Tebelak took the texts for songs in *Godspell*: *The Hymnal of the Protestant Episcopal Church in the United States of America* (New York: The Church Hymnal Corporation, 1940).

50. See Michael Kilgarriff, *Sing Us One of the Old Songs* (New York: Oxford University Press, 1998), 101.

51. For the historical background of this opera, see Caryl Emerson, *Modest Musorgsky and Boris Godunov: Myths, Realities, Reconsideration* (Cambridge: Cambridge University Press, 1994).

52. Modest Mussorgsky, *Boris Godunov 1869/Boris Godunov 1872*, Valery Gergiev, Kirov Opera & Orchestra (Philips 462 230-2, 1998), program booklet, 1872 libretto, 274–280.

53. Vladimír Stepánek and Bohumil Karásek, *An Outline of Czech and Slovak Music, Part 1* (Prague: Orbis, 1964), 10–11. For additional information on this medieval chant, see Rosa Newmarch, *The Music of Czechoslovakia* (New York and Evanston: Harper and Row, 1969), 4.

54. Electronic message from Stephen Schwartz to the author, 23 January 2013.

Epilogue

1. The title and arrangers for this selection appear in this review: http://www .playbill.com/features/article/176943-The-Wizard-and-I-The-Musical-Journey-of -Stephen-Schwartz-Made-Magic-at-Carnegie-Hall (accessed 30 May 2013).

~

Bibliography

Some sources listed here from periodicals were consulted in scrapbooks or clippings files at the New York Public Library for the Performing Arts and elsewhere. In some cases, the scrapbooks did not include page numbers from the original sources, and it was not always possible to locate those page numbers.

Main Sources

Adels, Robert. "'Magic Show': Tuneful Prestidigitation." *Record World*, 22 June 1974, 20, 52.

Advertisement announcing the run of *Rags* in Boston. *Rhode Island Herald*, 9 May 1986.

Africano, Lillian. "'Magic Show' Is Sluggish." *Villager*, 6 June 1974, 6.

American Arbitration Association. Decision on ownership of various parts of *Children of Eden* creative property. Unpublished. 25 August 1989.

"Anthony Stein, Book Writer." Silas, http://silasthemusical.com/Anthony_Stein .html (accessed 16 January 2013).

Armstrong, Linda. "The Bible, Told through 'Children of Eden.'" *New York Amsterdam News*, 20–26 November 1997, 28.

Attinson, Sue. "'Pippin, Pippin' Called Best Collaborative Effort." *Tartan* [Carnegie Mellon University], 26 April 1967, 1ff.

The Baker's Wife: A Comedy Musical, Phoenix Theatre. London souvenir program book, [1990].

Barker, Felix. "First Night/Theatre: *Godspell*: Wyndham's Theatre." *Evening News*, 2 February 1972.

Barnes, Clive. "Alas Poor York, 'Baker' Bombs." *New York Post*, 4 April 1985, 30.

———. "A Little Bit of Paradise." *New York Post*, 24 November 1997, 44.

———. "A New Star Is Born: Diva Bows on B'way in 'Rags.'" *New York Post*, 22 August 1986, 41–42.

———. "Roles for Pop Stars." *New York Times*, 26 July 1974, 22.

———. "Stage: 'The Magic Show': Doug Henning Delights as Atypical Illusionist." *New York Times*, 29 May 1974, 49.

———. "The Theater: 'Godspell,' Musical about Jesus Is at Cherry Lane." *New York Times*, 18 May 1971, 45.

———. "Theater: Musical 'Pippin' at Imperial." *New York Times*, 24 October 1972, 37.

———. "'Working' Musical Falls Flat." *New York Post*, 15 May 1978, 22.

Barth, Lois. "Maestro Valéry Ryvkin: A 'Singer's Conductor' on Orchestrating the Key Elements of Opera." *Classical Singer* (June 2009): 20–29, http://www.belcanto globalarts.com/ryvkin/Valery%20Ryvkin%20Classical%20Singer%20June%20 2009.pdf (accessed 12 January 2012).

"BBC Will Film 'Godspell' in St Paul's." *Daily Telegraph* (London), 3 March 1972.

Beaufort, John. "The Magic Show—a Brand New Form—Ends the Season." *Christian Science Monitor*, 31 May 1974, F6.

———. "Musical 'Pippin' Conquers Broadway: Comedy, Morality Play, Pseudo-History Combined." *Christian Science Monitor*, 26 December 1972, 8.

———. Review of *Godspell*. *Christian Science Monitor*, 24 May 1971.

———. "Theater: York Theatre Uncorks a Charming, Intimate Production of 'The Baker's Wife.'" *Christian Science Monitor*, 9 April 1985, 28.

Beddow, Margery. *Bob Fosse's Broadway*. Portsmouth, NH: Heinemann, 1996.

Bee, Stephani. "Defying Conventional Broadway: A Post-Feminist Criticism of *Wicked*." MA thesis, California State University, Fullerton, 2012.

Bernstein, Sarey. Review of *The Magic Show*. *Westport News*, 6 July 1979.

"A Book Doctor, or Just a Friend." *Newsday*, 21 July 1986, 6.

Bookspan, Martin. Review of *Godspell* for WPIX-TV, New York, 17 May 1971. Text read on the air consulted in New York Library for the Performing Arts, Billy Rose Theatre Collection.

———. Review of *Pippin* for WPIX-TV, New York, 23 October 1972. Text read on air consulted in review scrapbooks in New York Public Library for the Performing Arts.

Bourne, Matthew. *Matthew Bourne and His Adventures in Dance: Conversations with Alastair Macauley*. Revised edition. London: Faber and Faber, 2011.

Boxer, Tim. "Traveling with the Stars: Welcome to America." *Jewish Week, Inc.*, 15 August 1986, 22.

Bradley, Ian. *You've Got to Have a Dream: The Message of the Musical*. Louisville, KY: Westminster John Knox Press, 2004.

Brief item concerning end of *Godspell*'s run at the Roundhouse in London. *Daily Telegraph*, 23 December 1971.

Brief item concerning *Pippin*'s profit. *Daily News*, 14 June 1977, 7.

"British Equity Panel Accepts Page as God." *Variety*, 17 September 1990, 107.

Brooke, Rupert. "The Times Diary." *Times* (London), 5 January 1972, 10.

Brukenfeld, Dick. "The Gospel Truth and a Few Fibs." *Village Voice*, 20 May 1971, 55.

Burger, Alissa. "From *The Wizard of Oz* to *Wicked*: Trajectory of an American Myth." PhD dissertation, Bowling Green State University, 2009.

Burton, Humphrey. *Leonard Bernstein*. New York: Doubleday, 1994.

Campbell, Mary. Review of *Godspell* for Associated Press, New York, 17 May 1971. Text read on the air consulted in New York Library for the Performing Arts, Billy Rose Theatre Collection.

Canby, Vincent. "The Gospel According to 'Godspell' Comes to Screen." *New York Times*, 22 March 1973, 52.

"Captain Louie." Music Theater International. http://www.mtishows.com/show_detail.asp?showid=000287 (18 January 2013).

"*Captain Louie*: Synopsis." Music Theater International. http://www.mtishows.com/show_detail.asp?showid=000287 (16 January 2013).

Carr, Jay. "Stratas Makes a World of Difference." *Boston Globe*, 17 July 1986.

Chase, Chris. "Fosse: From Tony to Emmy?" *New York Times*, 29 April 1973, 125ff.

"Church Asks for Ban on Musical." *Times* (London), 16 December 1972, 3.

Clurman, Harold. "Theatre." *Nation*, 13 November 1972.

Coe, Richard L. "'Pippin': A Rare, Welcome Original." *Washington Post*, 21 September 1972, B1, B4.

Commentary track. *The Hunchback of Notre Dame*. Walt Disney Pictures 023315, 2002. DVD.

Commentary track. *Pocahontas 10th Anniversary Edition*. Walt Disney Pictures 22960, 2005. DVD.

Commentary track. *The Prince of Egypt*. DreamWorks 84853, 2006. DVD.

Contract between Playwrights Horizons and John Caird for directing *Children of Eden* workshop. 1993.

Cote, David. *"Wicked": The Grimmerie: A Behind-the-Scenes Look at the Hit Broadway Musical*. New York: Hyperion, 2005.

Coterie Theatre's Lab for New Family Musicals. Unpublished PDF distributed by the Coterie Theatre, Kansas City, MO.

Coveney, Michael. "Arts: *The Baker's Wife*—Phoenix Theatre." *Financial Times* (London), 28 November 1989.

Cox, Harvey. *The Feast of Fools*. Cambridge, MA: Harvard University Press, 1969.

Crocker, David . "S'n'S First—Double Feature, Men of Letters Contrast." *Tartan*, 13 March 1968, 5ff.

Dale, Grover. "The Feeling of Magic." In *The Magic Show Souvenir Book*. New York: M.E.I. Industries, 1974, [3–5].

Daniels, Robert J. Review of *Children of Eden. Variety*, 24 November 1997, 73.

Davis, James. "Washington Recaptures Tryout Date of 'Pippin.'" *Daily News*, 8 September 1972.

De Giere, Carol. *Defying Gravity: The Creative Career of Stephen Schwartz from "Godspell" to "Wicked."* New York: Applause Theatre & Cinema Books, 2008.

———. "*The Magic Show* Overview." http://www.musicalschwartz.com/magicshow .htm (accessed 6 September 2011).

Duncan, Stuart. "Packet Online" (Princeton, NJ), http://www.zwire.com/site/nyz-wire.cfm?.newsid=11169165&BRD=1091&PAG=461&dept, printed from the Web on 25 March 2004. Consulted in *Godspell* clipping file, New York Public Library for the Performing Arts, Billy Rose Theatre Division.

"'Eden' May Find Paradise in U.S. Pix." *Variety*, 28 January 1991, 77.

Eder, Richard. "Stage: 'Godspell' Moves Up to Broadway." *New York Times*, 23 June 1976.

———. "The Talking Band Presents 'Worksong' at the New City." *New York Times*, 25 February 1978, 16.

———. "Theater: 'Working' Opens at 46th Street." *New York Times*, 15 May 1978, C15.

Eisenstein, Linda. "An Interview with Stephen Schwartz, Composer & Lyricist, *Children of Eden.*" *Cleveland Plain Dealer*, October 1997, http://my.en.com/~herone/ Schwartz.html (accessed 19 April 2012).

Emerson, Caryl. *Modest Musorgsky and Boris Godunov: Myths, Realities, Reconsideration.* Cambridge: Cambridge University Press, 1994.

Feingold, Michael. "*Rags.*" *Village Voice*, 2 September 1986, 81–82.

Filichia, Peter. "A Musical Paradise." *Newark Star-Ledger*, 18 November 1997.

Finch, Hilary. "Well-Bred and Good Pedigree." *Times* (London), 16 November 1989.

Flaste, Richard. "A Magical Day for Children." *New York Times*, 6 August 1976, C3.

Frank, Leah D. "Working Rut a Potpouri [sic] of Dissatisfaction." *East Side Express*, 25 May 1978, 10.

Friedman, Arthur. "'Rags' Is a Rich Production." *Boston Herald*, 10 July 1986, 34.

Funke, Lewis. "News of the Rialto: 'Pippins' Pip." *New York Times*, 3 December 1972, D1.

Gans, Andrew. "Broadway Revival of *Godspell* Postponed." *Playbill.com*, 19 August 2008, http://www.playbill.com/news/article/120416-Broadway-Revival-of-God spell-Postponed (accessed 31 May 2013).

———. "Scott Schwartz's *My Antonia*, with Stephen Schwartz Underscoring, Begins CA Run May 8," *Playbill.com*, 8 May 2008, http://www.playbill.com/news/ article/117520-Scott-Schwartzs-My-Antonia-with-Stephen-Schwartz-Underscor ing-Begins-CA-Run-May-8 (accessed 12 January 2013).

Gänzl, Kurt. *The Encyclopedia of Musical Theatre.* Oxford: Blackwell Publishers, 1994.

Gaver, Jack. Review of *Godspell* for UPI, New York, 17 May 1971. Text read on the air consulted in New York Library for the Performing Arts, Billy Rose Theatre Collection.

Gill, Brendan. "Carolingian Razzle-Dazzle." *New Yorker*, 4 November 1972, 105.

———. "Daily Bread." *New Yorker*, 29 May 1978, 84.

———. "That Half-There Feeling." *New Yorker*, 10 June 1974, 64.

Godspell advertisement. *Wall Street Journal*, 5 September 1974.

Goldman, David. Review of *Godspell* for CBS Radio, New York, 17 May 1971. Text read on the air consulted in New York Library for the Performing Arts, Billy Rose Theatre Collection.

Gottfried, Martin. *All His Jazz: The Life & Death of Bob Fosse*. New York: Bantam Books, 1990.

———. "The Magic Show." *Women's Wear Daily*, 30 May 1974, 24.

———. Review of *Pippin*. *Women's Wear Daily*, 25 October 1972, 29.

———. Review of *Working*. *Saturday Review*, 8 July 1978, 24.

———. "Will the 'Godspell' Work on Broadway?" *New York Post*, 23 June 1976, 48.

Grant, Mark. *The Rise and Fall of the Broadway Musical*. Boston: Northeastern University Press, 2004.

Greig, Geordie. "Pushing the Boat Out to Save a Lyrical Creation—Christmas Shows." *Sunday Times* (London), 23 December 1990.

Grice, Elizabeth. "Trevor Nunn Takes the Long Route Home." *Sunday Times* (London), 6 August 1989.

Grubb, Kevin Boyd. *Razzle Dazzle: The Life and Work of Bob Fosse* (New York: St. Martin's Press, 1989.

Gunner, Marjorie. Review of *Working*. *Nassau Star*, 25 May 1978, 4.

Guthmann, Edward. "A Stage Director Refuses to Respect Willa Cather's Wishes, but Does so Respectfully." *SFGate*, 29 March 2004, http://www.sfgate.com/bayarea/article/A-stage-director-refuses-to-respect-Willa-2801952.php (accessed 12 January 2013).

Harris, Leonard. Review of *Godspell* for CBS-TV, New York, 17 May 1971. Text read on the air consulted in New York Library for the Performing Arts, Billy Rose Theatre Collection.

Harrison, John. *Spellbound: The Wonder-Filled Life of Doug Henning*. New York: Box-Office Books, 2009.

Hetrick, Adam. "NYCO Presents a *Séance on a Wet Afternoon*, by Stephen Schwartz, May 1." *Playbill.com*, 1 May 2009, http://www.playbill.com/news/article/128796-NYCO-Presents-a-Sance-on-a-Wet-Afternoon-By-Stephen-Schwartz-May-1 (accessed 11 November 2011).

Hewes, Henry. Review of *Pippin*. *Saturday Review*, 2 December 1972, 92.

Hiley, Jim. "Faith in a Good Book—Musical Theatre." *Times* (London), 11 December 1990.

Hilliard, Bob. "'Rags' a Super-Hit Musical in Every Way." *Manchester Union Leader*, 12 July 1986, 27.

Hipp, Edward Sothern ."'Godspell,' and More." *Newark Evening News*, 18 May 1971.

Hischak, Thomas S. *Through the Screen Door: What Happened to the Broadway Musical When It Went to Hollywood*. Lanham, MD: Scarecrow Press, 2004.

Hobson, Harold. "Hot Gospel." *Sunday Times* (London), 27 February 1972.

Hodgson, Martha. "S'nS Comes of Age in 1965 Production." *Carnegie Tech Tartan*, 5 May 1965, 2.

Holden, Stephen. "How the Curtain Came Down on the Dream of 'Rags'." *New York Times*, 21 September 1986, H5.

———. "Stage: 'Baker's Wife' in a Revised Version." *New York Times*, 31 March 1985, 52.

Horn, Miriam. "Theater Review: A Halloween Tale for Children, No Great Pumpkin Required." *New York Times*, 11 May 2005, E8.

———. "Theater Review: Halloween, Where Spirits Soar." *New York Times*, 8 November 2005, E4.

Howard, Arnold. "*Rags* Not Too Shabby." *Boston Jewish Times*, 17 July 1986, 7.

Internet Broadway Database, www.ibdb.com (consulted multiple times).

Internet Movie Database, www.imdb.com (consulted multiple times).

Isherwood, Charles. "A Vision of Spirituality Returns to Broadway." *New York Times*, 7 November 2011, http://theater.nytimes.com/2011/11/08/theater/reviews/godspell-at-the-circle-in-the-square-review.html?_r=0&pagewanted=1 (accessed 31 May 2013).

"Jack Tinker at the Theatre: Oh, What a Lovely Bag of Tricks." *Daily Telegraph* (London), 31 October 1973.

Jackowitz, Michael. "Genesis of *Séance on a Wet Afternoon*." Séance on a Wet Afternoon, http://www.seancetheopera.com/about_us.html (accessed 11 November 2011).

Jenkins, Speight. "Reports: U.S., Washington." *Opera News* 36 (October 1971): 20–21.

Johnson, Tod, ed. *Thistle 1965*. Pittsburgh: Carnegie Institute of Technology, 1965.

Johnston, Laurie. "Strollers See Magic in Midtown Plaza." *New York Times*, 8 April 1974, 39.

Jones, John Bush. *Our Musicals, Ourselves: A Social History of the American Musical Theatre*. Hanover and London: Brandeis University Press, 2003.

Jones, Kenneth. "Stephen Schwartz's Family-Friendly *Geppetto & Son* Tests Its Strings in Kansas City." *Playbill.com*, 27 June 2006, http://www.playbill.com/news/article/100532-Stephen-Schwartzs-Family-Friendly-Geppetto-Son-Tests-Its-Strings-in-Kansas-City (accessed 14 February 2013).

Kalem, T. E. "Blue-Collared." *Time*, 29 May 1978, 83.

———. "Medieval Hippie." *Time*, 6 November 1972, 83.

———. "Presto!" *Time*, 10 June 1974, 106.

"Kennedy Center Has Union Deal, Regains 'Pippin.'" *Variety*, 6 September 1972, 57.

Kerr, Walter. "It's a Lovely Way to Do a Show." *New York Times*, 29 October 1972, 1, 37.

———. "Stageview: Documents Posing As Dramas." *New York Times*, 28 May 1978, D-3.

———. "The Theater Means Transformation." *New York Times*, 9 June 1974, Sec. 2, 1.

———. "Why Make St. Matthew Dance? For the Fun of It." *New York Times*, 30 May 1971, Sec. 2, 1 and 9.

Kilgarriff, Michael. *Sing Us One of the Old Songs*. New York: Oxford University Press, 1998.

Kissel, Howard. *David Merrick: The Abominable Showman*. New York and London: Applause Books, 1993.

———. "Theater: 'The Baker's Wife.'" *Women's Wear Daily*, 26 March 1985, 28.

———. "'Working.'" *Women's Wear Daily*, 16 May 1978, 18.

Kleiman, Dena. "Broadway Beats Summer Doldrums." *New York Times*, 5 June 1986, C21.

———. "Producers May Reopen 'Rags.'" *New York Times*, 26 August 1986, C15.

Klein, Alvin. "The Old Testament in Song and Dance." *New York Times*, 23 November 1997, 16.

———. Review of *Godspell* for WNYC, New York, 17 May 1971. Text read on the air consulted in New York Library for the Performing Arts, Billy Rose Theatre Collection.

Kroll, Jack. "Ala Kazam!" *Newsweek*, 10 June 1974, 84.

———. "Charley's Kid." *Newsweek*, 6 November 1972, 134.

Kruger, Helen. "*Pippin*." *Chelsea Clinton News*, 2 November 1972, 17.

Laird, Paul R. "The Creation of a Broadway Musical: Stephen Schwartz, Winnie Holzman, and *Wicked*." In *Cambridge Companion to the Musical*, 2nd ed., edited by William A. Everett and Paul R. Laird, 340–52. Cambridge: Cambridge University Press, 2008.

———. "'It Couldn't Happen Here in Oz': *Wicked* and the Creation of a 'Critic-Proof' Musical." *Studies in Musical Theatre* 5, no. 1 (2011). 35–47.

———. "Stephen Schwartz and Bernstein's *Mass*," in *On Bunker's Hill: Essays in Honor of J. Bunker Clark*, edited by William A. Everett and Paul R. Laird, 263–70. Sterling Heights, MI: Harmonie Park Press, 2007.

———. "*Wicked*": *A Musical Biography*. Lanham, MD: Scarecrow Press, 2011.

Lawton, Carol. "Broadway." *New York Times*, 23 March 1984, C2.

———. "Broadway: 'Rags,' a Sequel about the People in 'Fiddler' Story." *New York Times*, 14 January 1983, C2.

Lebherz, Richard. "Pippin Is a Brilliant Musical." *Frederick News Post*, 22 September 1972.

Lehman, Jon. "Stratas Gives the Theater a New Jewel in 'Rags.'" *Patriot Ledger*, 17 July 1986, 24.

Lewis, Barbara. "Blacks, Biko, Workers Topics of New Offerings." *New York Amsterdam News*, 27 May 1978, D-5.

Lewis, Emory. "Fosse Can't Get Used to Success." *Sunday Record*, 8 July 1973, B14.

———. "'Godspell' Sings of Jesus—a Jubilant Rock of Ages." *Record*, 18 May 1971.

Lindell, Karen. "Scott Schwartz Brings Willa Cather's Novel to the Stage, with Her Voice Intact," *Ventura County Star*, 8 May 2008, http://www.vcstar.com/news/2008/may/08/adapting-antonia/?print=1 (accessed 13 January 2013).

Linn, Sarah. "Fairytales a Fit for 'Wicked' Composer Stephen Schwartz." *Tribune* (San Luis Obispo, CA), 20 August 2011, http://www.sanluisobispo

.com/2011/08/20/1724622/fairytales-wicked-composer-schwartz.html (accessed 19 January 2013).

Lloyd Webber, Andrew. "Saving Round House." Letter to the *Times* (London), 16 August 1982, 9.

Long, Robert Emmet. *Broadway, the Golden Years: Jerome Robbins and the Great Choreographer-Directors.* New York and London: Continuum, 2001.

"'Magic Show' Flags, Shuberts to Rescue." *Variety*, 11 October 1978, 179.

The Magic Show programs from Broadway and tour productions. New York Public Library for the Performing Arts Billy Rose Theatre Collection.

Maguire, Gregory. *Wicked: The Life and Times of the Wicked Witch of the West.* New York: ReganBooks, 1995.

"The Making of 'If I Never Knew You.'" Bonus track in *Pocahontas 10th Anniversary Edition.* Walt Disney Pictures 22960, 2005. DVD.

"The Making of Pocahontas." Bonus track in *Pocahontas 10th Anniversary Edition.* Walt Disney Pictures 22960, 2005. DVD.

"The Making of *The Hunchback of Notre Dame.*" *The Hunchback of Notre Dame.* Walt Disney Pictures 023315, 2002. DVD.

Malafronte, Judith. "New York City." *Opera News* 76, no. 1 (July 2011): 43–44.

Mandelbaum, Ken. *Not since Carrie: 40 Years of Broadway Musical Flops.* New York: St. Martin's Press, 1991.

Mazo, Joseph H. Review of *Godspell. Women's Wear Daily*, 18 May 1971, 12.

McCarthy, Todd. Review of *Enchanted. Variety*, 18 November 2007, http://www.variety.com/review/VE1117935452?refcatid=31 (accessed 17 September 2012).

McShane, Mark. *Séance on a Wet Afternoon.* New York: Carroll & Graf, 1961.

"Meridee Stein, Producer/Director." Silas, http://silasthemusical.com/Meridee_Stein.html (accessed 16 January 2013).

Mick. "Shows out of Town: *Pippin.*" *Variety*, 27 September 1972, 60.

Mickie, Larry. "Kennedy Center Angels 'Pippin': Nederlanders Claim Dirty Tactics." *Variety*, 2 August 1972, 1, 54.

Miller, Scott. *From "Assassins" to "West Side Story."* Portsmouth, NH: Heinemann, 1996.

Miller, Terry. "Half-Baked." *New York Native*, 22 April 1985, 53.

Mishkin, Lee. "The 'Godspell' according to Schwartz." *Morningside Telegraph* (New York), 19 May 1971.

"Miss Stickney Takes 'Pippin' Role." *New York Times*, 22 May 1973, p. 47.

Mordden, Ethan. *The Happiest Corpse I've Ever Seen: The Last Twenty-five Years of the Broadway Musical.* New York: Palgrave Macmillan, 2004.

———. *One More Kiss: The Broadway Musical in the 1970s.* New York: Palgrave Macmillan, 2004.

Morley, Sheridan. "Diary." *Times* (London), 15 January 1990.

Morrison, Hobe. "Godspell." *Variety*, 30 June 1976.

———. "The Magic Show." *Variety*, 29 May 1974, 56.

———. "Shows on Broadway: *Pippin.*" *Variety*, 25 October 1972, 64.

———. "TV Spots Boosting 'Pippin' B.O.; Musical Has Paid $800G Profit." *Variety*, 23 January 1974, 59.

———. "Working." *Variety*, 17 May 1978, 45.

Munk, Erika. "Sing Me a Song of Social Significance." *Village Voice*, 29 May 1978, 83–84.

"The Music of *Pocahontas*." Bonus track in *Pocahontas 10th Anniversary Edition*. Walt Disney Pictures 22960, 2005. DVD.

"Musical Is Canceled by Kennedy Center." *New York Times*, 25 May 1972, 17.

Nelson, Don. "'The Baker's' Stale Cakes." *Daily News*, 5 April 1985, 9.

———. "From 'Rags' to—Maybe—B'way Riches." *Daily News*, 7 September 1983, 41.

Newmarch, Rosa. *The Music of Czechoslovakia*. New York and Evanston: Harper and Row, 1969.

"No Protest at 'Godspell' in St Paul's." *Daily Telegraph* (London), 9 March 1972.

"No Stock for 'Cage'; Silver Exits 'Rags.'" *Variety*, 18 June 1986, 92.

Novick, Julius. "*Rags*." *Village Voice*, 2 September 1986, 81.

———. "Sour Pippin." *Village Voice*, 2 November 1972, 73.

O'Connor, John J. "'Pippin' on Showtime." *New York Times*, 15 February 1984, C26.

Oja, Carol J. "*West Side Story* and *The Music Man*: Whiteness, Immigration, and Race in the US during the Late 1950s," *Studies in Musical Theatre* 3, no. 1 (2009): 13–30.

Oliver, Edith. Review of *Godspell*. *New Yorker*, 24 May 1971, 56.

Ostrow, Stuart. "How an Exciting, Tuneful, Contemporary, Joyous, Unique Broadway Musical Got Better." Souvenir book of Washington production of *Pippin* [1972], inside front cover. Consulted in New York Public Library for the Performing Arts, Billy Rose Theatre Collection.

———. "Letters: Broadway's Long Runs: The Ad That Started It All." *New York Times*, 17 September 2006, A6.

———. *A Producer's Broadway Journey*. Westport, CT, and London: Praeger, 1999.

Oteri, Frank J. "Stephen Schwartz and Lauren Flanigan: Corners of the Sky." *NewMusicBox*, 1 April 2011, http://www.newmusicbox.org/articles/stephen-schwartz-and-lauren-flanigan-corners-of-the-sky/ (accessed 24 September 2011).

"Parting Is Such Sweet Sorrow—Theater." *Times* (London), 19 July 1990.

"Paul McMahon's Curtain Call." *New England Connection*, 7 July 1986.

Peter, John. "Puppets with the Power to Persuade—Theatre." *Times* (London), 3 December 1989.

Peters, Pauline. "The Cat That Got the Cream," *Telegraph Weekend Magazine* (London), 12 August 1989, 17.

Philip, Richard. "Reviews: Theater On Broadway and Off." *After Dark* (July 1974), 72.

Photograph and caption concerning actress Gay Sopor greeting Prince Charles from the stage during *Godspell* performance in London. *Evening Standard* (London), 28 January 1972.

Photograph and caption concerning Princess Margaret and her family attending *Godspell* in London. *Evening Standard* (London), 25 April 1973.

PHS. "The Times Diary: McGovern It Is—by an Inch." *Times* (London), 12 July 1972, 14.

"'Pippin' Clicks in Melbourne; Snaps London Jinx Tradition." *Variety*, 13 March 1974, 75ff.

"'Pippin' Netting $30,000 A Week; Recoups Feb. 24." *Variety*, 24 January 1973, 57.

Pippin programs from the original Broadway production. New York Public Library for the Performing Arts, Billy Rose Theatre Collection.

PJM. "Designing Costumes for Broadway and Hollywood: Patricia Zipprodt Talks about 'Pippin' and the Film of '1776.'" *Theatre Crafts*, January–February 1973, 7–10ff.

Portantiere, Michael. "Over the Borderline." *Opera News* 73, no. 3 (September 2008): 48–51.

Prideaux, Tom. "Pippin." *Life*, 24 November 1972, 30.

Probst, Leonard. Review of *Godspell* for NBC-TV, New York, 17 May 1971. Text read on the air consulted in New York Library for the Performing Arts, Billy Rose Theatre Collection.

Productions in Great Britain card file at Victoria and Albert Theatre Collection, accessed at the Blythe House in July 2008.

"Questions and Answers: Trevor Nunn on *The Baker's Wife*." In *The Baker's Wife: A Comedy Musical*, Phoenix Theatre, London, souvenir program book.

Rabkin, Gerald. "Heavy Freight." *Soho Weekly News*, 18 May 1978, 42.

"'Rags' Finds Tailor to Sew Up Broadway." *Newsday*, 23 July 1986.

Raidy, William. "First Nighter: 'Godspell' Is a Blessing." *Long Island Press* and *Newark Star-Ledger*, 18 May 1971.

Reed, Rex. "Forget 'Godspell'; 'Sawyer' Family Treat." *Daily News*, 23 March 1973, 66.

———. Review of *Pippin*. *Sunday News*, 5 November 1972, Section 3, 5.

———. Review of *Working*. *Daily News*, 17 May 1978, 73.

Review of *Godspell*. *Time*, 24 May 1971, 48.

Reviews of the London production of *Children of Eden*. *Theatre Record* 11, no. 1 (1991): 24–30: Michael Church in *The Independent on Sunday*, 13 January 1991; Michael Covenay in *Observer*, 13 January 1991; Michael Darvell in *What's On*, 16 January 1991; Clive Hirschhorn in *Saturday Express*, 13 January 1991; Charles Osborne in *The Daily Telegraph*, 9 January 1991; Paul Taylor in *The Independent*, 10 January 1991; Jack Tinker in *Daily Mail*, 9 January 1991.

Rich, Alan. "Summer Reruns." *New York*, 12 July 1976, 64.

Rich, Frank. "A Musical of Sophocles and Pentecostalism." *New York Times*, 25 March 1988, C5.

———. "Stage: 'Personals,' Musical Comedy." *New York Times*, 25 November 1985, C16.

———. "Stage: Teresa Stratas as a Jewish Immigrant in 'Rags,' a Musical." *New York Times*, 22 August 1986, C3.

Robertson, Jim. "Doug Henning Stars in 'The Magic Show.'" *Genii: The International Conjurors' Magazine* 38, no. 2 (February 1974): 71.

Russo, Vito. "Tailoring 'Rags' for Broadway." *Newsday*, 17 August 1986, II/3ff.

"Scale Down 'Pippin' Budget $200,000; Guarantee for D.C. Tryout Is Factor." *Variety*, 13 September 1972, 89.

Scherstuhl, Alan. "Puppet Love." *Pitch*, 6 July 2006, http://www.pitch.com/kansas city/puppet-love/Content?oid=2182468 (accessed 8 January 2014).

Schonberg, Harold C. "Bernstein's New Work Reflects His Background on Broadway." *New York Times*, 9 September 1971, 58.

Schubeck, John. Review of *Godspell* for ABC-TV, New York, 17 May 1971. Text read on the air consulted in New York Library for the Performing Arts, Billy Rose Theatre Collection.

Schulern, Richard. Review of *Godspell* for WCTC AM-FM, WCBB-AM, and WGSM AM-FM, New York, 17 May 1971. Text read on the air consulted in New York Library for the Performing Arts, Billy Rose Theatre Collection.

Schwartz, Stephen. "2001 Notes on *Working* from the Instigator Stephen Schwartz." Booklet from *Working: A New Musical*. Original cast recording. Fynsworth Alley 302 062 1142, 1978. CD.

———. Address on his participation in the composition of Bernstein's *Mass* at symposium sponsored by Columbus (Ohio) Pro Musica Chamber Orchestra, 5 May 2004.

———. "Co-lyricist Stephen Schwartz on the Northwestern Production of *Mass*." Facebook, 29 November 2009, http://www.facebook.com/note.php?note _id=186881577367 (accessed 10 September 2012).

———. "Composing." *Dramatist* 12, no. 1 (September–October 2009): 31–33.

———. "Learning from Sondheim." *Sondheim Review* 17, no. 1 (Fall 2010): 33–34.

———. "Lyricists on Lyrics," *Dramatist* 7, no. 6 (July–August 2005): 6–15.

———. "Stephen Schwartz: How the Hit Broadway Musical Writer's Classical Beginnings Helped Shape His Theatrical Career." *Gramophone* 86 (November 2008): 146.

Sebesta, Judith. "'Something Borrowed, Something Blue': The Marriage of the Musical and Europe." In *The Cambridge Companion to the Musical*, 2nd ed., edited by William A. Everett and Paul R. Laird, 270–83. Cambridge: Cambridge University Press, 2008.

Secrest, Meryle. *Leonard Bernstein: A Life*. New York: Vintage Books, 1994.

———. *Stephen Sondheim*. New York: Alfred A. Knopf, 1998.

Seff, Richard, and Isobel Robins. "This Is Broadway." Interview with Joseph Abaldo, 1978, available at http://ibdb.com/production.php?id=3468 (accessed 21 May 2013).

Sege. "Godspell." *Variety*, 28 March 1973, 18.

———. "Off-Broadway Review: *Godspell*." *Variety*, 2 June 1971.

Seldes, Barry. *Leonard Bernstein: The Political Life of an American Musician*. Berkeley: University of California Press, 2009.

Shull, Leo. "*Working*: A Musical." *Show Business*, 25 May 1978, 22.

Siegel, Naomi. "Theater Review: Heartbreak and Baguettes in Provence." *New York Times*, 24 April 2005, NJ10.

Silver, Lee. "St. Matthew's Gospel Grooves in 'Godspell.'" *Daily News*, 18 May 1971.

Simon, John. Review of *The Magic Show*. *New York*, 17 June 1974, 76.

———. Review of *Pippin*. *New York*, 6 November 1972, 84.

———. Review of *Working*. *New York*, [1978], 78. (Consulted in review scrapbooks at the New York Public Library for the Performing Arts, which included incomplete information.)

———. "Sad Rags." *New York*, 1 September 1986, 46.

———. "Theater: *The Antigone* and *The Ecstasy*." *New York*, 31 May 1971, 50.

Singer, Barry. "Composer's Medium." *Opera News* 75, no. 10 (April 2011): 16–17.

Sloane, Leonard. "Advertising L'eggs Stepping Out." *New York Times*, 17 August 1973, 47.

"Snapshots: A Musical Scrapbook!" MusicalSchwarz.com, http://www.musicalschwarz.com/snapshots.htm (accessed 2 February 2013).

Spencer, H. L. "Behold the Man." Program for *Godspell* production at Manchester Opera House, 14–25 August 1990. Proscenium Publications, 1990.

Stasio, Marilyn. Review of *Godspell*. *Cue*, 22 May 1971, 14.

Stepánek, Vladimír, and Bohumil Karásek. *An Outline of Czech and Slovak Music, Part 1*. Prague: Orbis, 1964.

Steyn, Mark. "Beginners Please." *Independent*, 5 January 1991.

Stockton, Peggy. Review of *Godspell* for WMCA, New York, 17 May 1971. Text read on the air consulted in New York Library for the Performing Arts, Billy Rose Theatre Collection.

Suskin, Steven. *The Sound of Broadway Music: A Book of Orchestrators & Orchestrations*. Oxford: Oxford University Press, 2009.

Swain, Joseph P. *The Broadway Musical: A Critical and Musical Survey*. Revised and expanded ed. Lanham, MD: Scarecrow Press, 2002.

Tallmer, Jeffrey. "Off-Broadway: Surprise in Nazareth." *New York Post*, 18 May 1971.

Terkel, Studs. *Working: People Talk about What They Do All Day and How They Feel about What They Do*. New York: Pantheon Books, 1972, 1974.

Thorncroft, Antony. "Art: Prospects—Guaranteed Criticism/As Terry Hands Plans His Final Season." *Financial Times* (London), 20 January 1990.

Togi. "*Rags*." *Variety*, 27 August 1986, 100, 104.

Tommasini, Andrew. "A Crime Lurks on the Dark Side of a Clairvoyant Realm." *New York Times*, 20 April 2011, http://www.nytimes.com/2011/04/21/arts/music/seance-on-a-wet-afternoon-at-city-opera-review.html?pagewanted=all (accessed 2 January 2012).

Trussell, Robert. "A Real Hit? Stage Story of Pinocchio's Dad Shows Promise at the Coterie." *Kansas City Star*, 5 July 2006, http://infoweb.newsbank.com.www2.lib.ku.edu:2048/iw-search/we/InfoWeb?p_product=NewsBank&p_theme=aggregated5&p_action=doc&p_docid=112B426C84A312A0&p_docnum=3&p_queryname=1 (accessed 8 January 2014).

Verini, Bob. "Review: 'My Fairytale.'" *Variety*, 30 August 2011, http://www.variety.com/review/VE1117945914/ (accessed 19 January 2013).

———. "Review: 'Séance on a Wet Afternoon.'" *Variety*, 28 September 2009, http://www.variety.com/review/VE1117941261 (accessed 2 January 2012).

Von Drehle, Dave. *Triangle: The Fire That Changed America*. New York: Atlantic Monthly Press, 2003.

Walker, Steve. "*Geppetto & Son*." Theatermania, 3 July 2006, http://www.theatermania.com/new-york-city-theater/reviews/07-2006/geppetto-and-son_8565.html (accessed 8 January 2014).

Wallach, Allan. "In Review/Stage: Off-Broadway Gospel." *Newsday*, 18 May 1971.

Wansell, Geoffrey. "John-Michael Tebelak." *Times* (London), 2 February 1972.

Wardle, Irving. "*Godspell*, Round House." *Times* (London), 18 November 1971, 11.

———. "Pain Wafts from Provence—Theatre." *Times* (London), 28 November 1989.

Wasserman, Debbi. "*The Baker's Wife*." *Stages*, July–August 1985, 11.

———. "Overcoming Critical Disapproval: Adept Magician + Philosopher = New Star." *Show Business*, 4 July 1974, 1, 3.

Watt, Douglas. "Bob Fosse Added a 'Leading Player' Made 'Pippin' Easy." *Sunday News*, 19 November 1972, Leisure, p. 3.

———. "'The Magic Show' Winds Up Season." *Daily News*, 29 May 1974, 64.

———. "'Pippin' Is a Splendid Musical, Magnificently Staged & Played." *Daily News*, 24 October 1972, 50.

———. "These New 'Rags' Don't Wear Well." *Daily News*, 22 August 1986, B/5.

———. "'Working': It's Exciting and Dull." *Daily News*, 15 May 1978, 27.

Watts, Richard. "Evening with a Master of Magic." *New York Post*, 29 May 1974, 46.

———. "Theater: The Son of Charlemagne." *New York Post*, 24 October 1972, 53.

Wetzsteon, Ross. "Theatre: It's Magic." *Village Voice*, 6 June 1974, 83.

"*Wicked*: The Road to Broadway." *B'Way/Broadway: The American Musical*. Educational Broadcasting Corporation and the Broadway Film Project, 2004.

Wicks, Charity. "An Introduction to and Musico-Dramatic Analysis of *Séance on a Wet Afternoon*: An Opera by Stephen Schwartz." DMA document, Manhattan School of Music, 2011.

Wilson, Barbara. "In the Beginning, 'Godspell' Was Matter of Degree." *Philadelphia Inquirer*, 1 April 1973.

Wilson, Edwin. "A Bright Bit of Legerdemain." *Wall Street Journal*, 8 June 1974, 14.

———. "Charlemagne, Magic and Music." *Wall Street Journal*, 24 October 1972, 20.

Wolf, Matt. "Half a Loaf—'Baker's Wife' Continues to Rise in London." *Chicago Tribune*, 7 January 1990.

———. "Needing the Dough? Matt Wolf Talks to Trevor Nunn." *City Lights*, 23–30 November 1989.

Wollman, Elizabeth L. *The Theater Will Rock: A History of the Rock Musical, from "Hair" to "Hedwig."* Ann Arbor: University of Michigan Press, 2006.

Woodard, Josef. "Opera Review: 'Seance on a Wet Afternoon' at Opera Santa Barbara." *Los Angeles Times*, 27 September 2009, http://latimesblogs.latimes.com/culturemonster/2009/09/opera-review-seance-on-a-wet-afternoon-at-opera-santa-barbara.html (accessed 2 January 2012).

Wright, Charles. "Program Note." In "Musicals at Mufti" program, 2007. New York Public Library for the Performing Arts, Billy Rose Theatre Collection.

Zipes, Jack. *Hans Christian Andersen: The Misunderstood Storyteller.* New York: Routledge, 2005.

Other Websites

"Alice Ripley Sings 'Meadowlark' from *The Baker's Wife*," at http://www.youtube .com/watch?v=0K269vRf3aQ (accessed 17 February 2013).

http://artssarasota.com/2012–07–25/section/theater/asolo-reps-working-scheduled -for-new-york-run/ (accessed 19 August 2012).

http://hilaplitmann.com/bio (accessed 10 January 2012).

http://maryfahl.com/ (accessed 2 February 2013).

http://media.musicasacra.com/pdf/pbc-extract3.pdf (accessed 27 September 2012).

http://micechat.com/forums/theatre/158481-my-fairytale-new-musical-stephen -schwartz-includes-my-interview-him.html (accessed 19 January 2013).

http://namt.org/festival-history.aspx#1996 (accessed 22 April 2012).

http://www.americansongwriter.com/2013/01/la-songwriter-series-lindy-robbins/ (accessed 2 February 2013).

http://www.filmreference.com/film/15/Pippa-Pearthree.html (accessed 10 September 2011).

http://www.floormic.com/production/2889872 (accessed 11 July 2011).

http://www.floormic.com/production/2898495 (accessed 11 July 2011).

http://www.grammy.com/GRAMMY_Awards/Winners/Results.aspx?title=godspell& winner=&year=0&genreID=0&hp=1 (accessed 4 January 2009).

http://www.grammy.com/nominees/search?artist=%22stephen+schwartz%22&title= &year=All&genre=All (accessed 2 February 2013).

http://www.hollywoodbowl.com/tickets/bernstein039s-mass/2004–08–19 (accessed 18 February 2013).

http://www.lamama.org/archives/year_lists/1971page.htm (accessed 3 February 2013).

http://www.leonardbernstein.com/works_mass.htm (accessed 10 September 2012).

http://www.liveperformance.com.au/halloffame/kennbrodziak3.html (accessed 7 February 2013).

http://www.mattwilliamschoreographer.com/bio.php (accessed 6 January 2012).

http://www.mtishows.com/show_detail.asp?showid=000306 (accessed 22 August 2012).

http://www.milesago.com/industry/brodziak.htm (accessed 7 February 2013).

http://www.musicals.nl/wicked.asp (accessed 12 January 2013).

http://www.operasb.org/event.php?event_id=20 (accessed 15 October 2011).

http://www.playbill.com/features/article/176943-The-Wizard-and-I-The-Musical -Journey-of-Stephen-Schwartz-Made-Magic-at-Carnegie-Hall (accessed 30 May 2013).

http://www.playbill.com/news/article/152751-In-Pursuit-of-Excellence-55-Piece
-Symphonic-Children-of-Eden-Begins-in-Kansas-City-July-15 (accessed 26 July
2012).

http://www.playbill.com/news/article/168298-Stephen-Schwartzs-Revised-Working
-With-New-Songs-by-Lin-Manuel-Miranda-Will-Be-Given-NYC-Premiere (accessed 19 August 2012).

http://www.potw.org/archive/potw345.html (accessed 25 August 2012).

http://www.stagescenela.com/2011/09/my-fairytale/ (accessed 19 January 2013).

http://www.stephenschwartz.com, Webmaster: Carol de Giere (accessed multiple
times).

http://www.stephenschwartz.com/wp-content/uploads/2010/08/mass1.pdf (accessed
13 September 2012).

http://www.stevenlutvak.com/pages/about.html (accessed 2 February 2013).

http://www.variety.com/review/VE1117945914/ (accessed 19 January 2013).

http://youthsingpraise.com/about/previous-productions/2012–2/show2012/ (accessed
10 February 2012).

"Max von Essen sings 'Proud Lady' from *The Baker's Wife* at Paper Mill Playhouse."
http://www.youtube.com/watch?v=Fw_H1kZ97Pg (accessed 17 February 2013).

"My Fairytale." http://www.youtube.com/watch?v=TrirzUjT0jY (accessed 21 January
2013).

Pacific Conservatory for the Performing Arts. Press release, May 2011, http://www
.pcpa.org/myfairytalepr.html (accessed 19 January 2013).

"Stephen Schwartz Exclusive Interview." http://www.youtube.com/watch?v=
REMTR0Uxu4Y (accessed 19 January 2013).

Unpublished Scripts, Revisions, and Notes

The Baker's Wife. Book by Joseph Stein. Music and lyrics by Stephen Schwartz.
[1976]. New York Public Library for the Performing Arts, RM #8001.

Brand New World. Book by Joseph Stein. Music by Charles Strouse. Lyrics by Stephen Schwartz. January 2007. [Revision of *Rags*.]

Caird, John. Notes from performance of *Children of Eden* in Wichita, KS, December
1994.

———. Restaurant placemat. Includes notes on *Children of Eden*. Undated.

———. Undated notes concerning Charles Lisanby. *Family Tree*. Undated script of
Act 1.

———. Undated notes in spiral notebook concerning *Children of Eden*.

Caird, John, and Stephen Schwartz. *Children of Eden*. Current script. Undated.

———. *Children of Eden*/To Do. 30 November 1992.

———. Draft scripts of *Children of Eden*. Undated, 21 February 1989, 1 May 1989, 4
October 1989, 19 March 1990, 1 July 1990, 11 July 1990, 18 March 1991, 9 September 1991, and September 1996.

———. Folder of materials from meeting concerning *Children of Eden*. 9–19 September 1991.

Lisanby, Charles. *Family Tree*. Undated script of Act 1.

Outline—Rebecca Story, 14 July 1986. [Anonymous treatment of story for the main character in *Rags*.]

Pippin: A Musical. Book by Roger O. Hirson. Music and lyrics by Stephen Schwartz. Undated.

Pippin script, 23 October 1972. New York Public Library for the Performing Arts, RM #7450.

Pippin script, 1 April 1976. New York Public Library for the Performing Arts, RM #543.

Pippin script, 3 January 2005. Book by Roger O. Hirson. Music and lyrics by Stephen Schwartz.

Rags. Book by Joseph Stein. Music by Charles Strouse. Lyrics by Stephen Schwartz. Walnut Street Theatre. May 2000.

Rags. Book by Joseph Stein. Music by Charles Strouse. Lyrics by Stephen Schwartz. Rodgers and Hammerstein Theatre Library. Revision from November 2005.

Rags. Revisions for the Candlelight Dinner Playhouse, Summit, IL. 7 May 1987.

Rags. Revisions for possible, unrealized London production. 13 January 1988.

Rags. Script revisions. October 2006.

Rags: The New American Musical. Book by Joseph Stein. Music by Charles Strouse. Lyrics by Stephen Schwartz. 22 June 1986. [Marked: "Boston Script/Joe Stein."]

Rags: The New American Musical. Rodgers & Hammerstein. Paper Mill Theatre Version. April 1999.

Schwartz, Stephen. "*Godspell* Script Notes and Revisions," 1999. Consulted in electronic file of *Godspell* script made available by Schwartz's office.

———. *Mass-Libretto Revisions*. July 2004.

———. *Séance on a Wet Afternoon*. Drafts of libretto. September 2007, December 2008, and May 2009.

Stein, Joseph. *A New Musical*. 1981. Unpublished. [First draft of what became *Rags*.]

Musical Sources and Recordings

The Baker's Wife. Book by Joseph Stein. Music and Lyrics by Stephen Schwartz. Piano Conductor Score. Music Theatre International, 1977, 1988, 1990, 1993.

The Baker's Wife: A Comedy Musical. Book by Joseph Stein. Music and Lyrics by Stephen Schwartz. Original cast recording of London production. Jay CDJAY 2 1323, 1999. CD.

Bernstein, Leonard. *Mass*. Jubilant Sykes, Asher Edward Wulfman, Morgan State University Choir, Peabody Children's Chorus, Baltimore Symphony Orchestra/ Marin Alsop. Naxos 8.559622–23, 2009. CD.

———. *Mass* (full version). http://www.boosey.com/cr/perusals/score.asp?id=10447 (accessed 11 September 2012).

——. *Mass: A Theater Piece for Singers, Players and Dancers. Text from the Liturgy of the Roman Mass. Additional Texts by Stephen Schwartz and Leonard Bernstein.* N.p.: Boosey & Hawkes/Jalni Publications, 1989.

——. *West Side Story Suite, Lonely Town,* and *New York New York* (arranged by William David Brohn, cadenza by Joshua Bell), *Make Our Garden Grow* (arranged by John Corigliano); Joshua Bell, violin; Philharmonia Orchestra; David Zinman, conductor. Sony SK 89358, 2001. CD.

Captain Louie: World Premiere Recording. Music & Lyrics by Stephen Schwartz. Based on "The Trip" by Ezra Jack Keats. Book by Anthony Stein. PS Classics 530, 2005. CD.

Children of Eden: American Premiere Recording. Music & Lyrics by Stephen Schwartz. Book by John Caird. RCA Victor 09026–63165–2, 1998. CD.

Children of Eden. Book by John Caird. Music and lyrics by Stephen Schwartz. Based on a concept by Charles Lisanby. Piano Vocal Score. 2 volumes. Music Theater International, 1997.

Disney's *Die Glöckner von Notre Dame.* Stella Music 547 836–2, 1999. CD.

Enchanted. Walt Disney Pictures 52391, 2008. DVD.

The Godspell. John-Michael Tebelak, director. Music by Duane Bolick. Unpublished recording of excerpts from 14 December 1970 performance at Carnegie Mellon University. CD.

Godspell Piano Vocal Score. Conceived and Originally Directed by John-Michael Tebelak. Music and New Lyrics by Stephen Schwartz. New York: Music Theatre International, 1999.

g.t./gladsaxe teater præsenterer "Mit eventyr." Gladsaxe Teater, 2006. CD.

The Hunchback of Notre Dame. Walt Disney Pictures 023315, 2002. DVD.

The Hymnal of the Protestant Episcopal Church in the United States of America. New York: The Church Hymnal Corporation, 1940.

Leonard Bernstein's Mass: A Theatre Piece for Singers, Players and Dancers. Conducted by the composer. Text from the Liturgy of the Roman Mass. Additional texts by Stephen Schwartz and Leonard Bernstein. Columbia Masterworks M2 31008, n.d. LP. Reissued on CD: *Bernstein Century: Bernstein Mass.* Alan Titus, the Norman Scribner Choir, the Berkshire Boy Choir, orchestra conducted by Leonard Bernstein. Sony Classical SM2K 63089, 1997.

The Magic Show, directed by Norman Campbell. Moviemagic Productions Ltd., 1981. Reissued: Image Entertainment, 2001. DVD.

Mussorgsky, Modest. *Boris Godunov 1869/Boris Godunov 1872,* Valery Gergiev, Kirov Opera & Orchestra. Philips 462 230–2, 1998.

Nouveau. Written by Iris Rainer Dart and Stephen Schwartz. 1966. Carnegie-Mellon University Hunt Library Audio Collection. LP.

Personals: The Comedy-Musical Revue/Original London Cast. Jay Productions Ltd., CDJAY 1319, 1999. CD.

"Pippin" Based on Bob Fosse's Original Staging & Choreography of His Broadway Musical Hit. VCI Entertainment #8245, 1981. DVD.

Pippin, Book of Roger O. Hirson; Music & Lyrics by Stephen Schwartz; Complete Vocal Score. Miami: CPP/Belwin, 1988.

Pippin, Pippin. Written by Ron Strauss and Stephen Schwartz. 1967. Carnegie-Mellon University Hunt Library Audio Collection. LP.

Pocahontas 10th Anniversary Edition. Walt Disney Pictures 22960, 2005. DVD.

The Prince of Egypt. Cherry Lane Music Company, 1998.

The Prince of Egypt. DreamWorks 84853, 2006. DVD.

"Rags": The New American Musical. Book by Joseph Stein. Music by Charles Strouse. Lyrics by Stephen Schwartz. Sony Masterworks SK 42657, 1991. CD.

Schwartz, Stephen. *The Baker's Wife*. Take Home Tunes 772, n.d. LP. Reissued in 1992 as Take Home Tunes CD 9216. CD.

———. *Children of Eden: Original London Cast*. London 828 234 2, 1991. CD.

———. *Children of Eden: Vocal Selections*. Miami: Warner Bros. Publications, 1999.

———. *Godspell: A Musical Based upon the Gospel According to St. Matthew*. Arista ARCD-8304, 1974. CD.

———. *Godspell: The New Broadway Cast Recording*. Ghostlight Records 8–4456, 2011. CD.

———. *The Magic Show: Original Cast Recording*. Bell Records, 1974. LP.

———. *Mass-Libretto Revisions*. Unpublished. July 2004.

———. *My Antonia*. Incidental musical score to play by Scott Schwartz. Unpublished. Undated.

———. *My Fairytale Piano/Vocal Score, Score, 6/9/2011, Prepared by Andrew Fox*. Unpublished.

———. *Reluctant Pilgrim*. New York: Midder Music Special Projects. MMCD007, 1997. CD.

———. *Séance on a Wet Afternoon*. http://www.boosey.com/cr/perusals/ (accessed 2 January 2012).

———. *Séance on a Wet Afternoon*. Unpublished piano/vocal scores from various moments during the opera's creation. Act 1, December 2006 to August 2007; Act 1, 3 October 2007; Acts 1 and 2, September 2008; Acts 1 and 2, December 2008; Acts 1 and 2 for Opera Santa Barbara, late May 2009; and Acts 1 and 2 for New York City Opera, 28 October 2010.

———. *Selections from "The Baker's Wife": A Musical*. N.p.: Grey Dog Music, 1990.

———. *Uncharted Territory*. Fynsworth Alley 302 062 119 2, 2002. CD.

———. *Vocal Selection [sic] from the Hit Show "The Magic Show."* Melville, NY: Belwin Mills Publishing, n.d.

———. *Vocal Selections: "Captain Louie," Music & Lyrics by Stephen Schwartz, Based on "The Trip" by Ezra Jack Keats*. N.p.: Williamson Music, 2009.

———. *Working: A New Musical*. Original cast recording. Fynsworth Alley 302 062 1142, 1978. CD.

Studs Terkel's Working. Broadway Theatre Archive. Directed by Stephen Schwartz and Kirk Browning. Produced by Phylis Geller and Lindsay Law. Image Entertainment 14381–0882–2, 1982. DVD.

Twice Upon a Time. Written by David Sheridan Spangler and Stephen Schwartz. 1968. Carnegie-Mellon University Hunt Library Audio Collection. LP.

Walt Disney Pictures Presents "Enchanted." Wonderland Music Company and Walt Disney Music Company, 2007.

Walt Disney Pictures Presents "The Hunchback of Notre Dame." Wonderland Music Company and Walt Disney Music Company, 1995.

Walt Disney Pictures Presents "Pocahontas." Wonderland Music Company and Walt Disney Music Company, 1996.

Whatserface. Written by Iris Rainer Dart, Michelle Brourman, and Stephen Schwartz. 1965. Carnegie-Mellon University Hunt Library Audio Collection. LP.

Wicked: Piano/Vocal. Undated score of entire score with revisions dated between March 2004 and 21 January 2005.

Working. From the book by Studs Terkel. Adapted by Stephen Schwartz and Nina Faso. Heelstone Parc Productions, 1978. Available from Music Theatre International, [1].

Interviews

Herbert Braha, by telephone, 25 February 2008.

William David Brohn (jointly with Stephen Schwartz), personal, New York, 22 November 22, 2008.

John Caird, by telephone, 4 January 2008; personal, London, 11–13, 15 July 2008.

Jeff Church, personal, Kansas City, MO, 30 June 2006.

Nina Faso, by telephone, 6–7 February 2008 and 3 June 2013.

Peggy Gordon, personal, New York, 17 January 2008.

Gordon Greenberg, personal, New York, 23 January 2008.

Kim Josephson, by telephone, 3 November 2009.

Leon Katz, by telephone, 1 February 2008.

Robin Lamont, by telephone, 22 February 2008.

Edgar Lansbury, personal, New York, 22 January 2008.

Sonia Manzano, by telephone, 31 January 2008.

Stephen Nathan, by telephone, 6 February 2008.

Stephen Oremus, by telephone, 5 February 2008 and 28 September 2010.

Hila Plitmann, by telephone, 3 November 2009.

Stephen Reinhardt, by telephone, 8 January 2008.

Andrew Rohrer, by telephone, 30 March 2008.

Valéry Ryvkin, personal, Santa Barbara, CA, 2 October 2009.

Scott Schwartz, by telephone, 15 October 2009.

Stephen Schwartz, by telephone, 23 July 2004; personal, New York, 22 March 2005; by telephone, 23 July 2005; personal, Kansas City, MO, 26 June 2006; personal, Schroon Lake, NY, 20 July 2007; personal, New York, 14 January 2008; personal, New York, 16 January 2008; personal, New York, 18 March 2008; personal, New York, 19 March 2008; personal, New York, 1 April 2008; personal, New York, 22

November 2008 (part of it jointly with William David Brohn); by telephone, 26 July 2009; personal, Santa Barbara, CA, 2 October 2009; by telephone, 15 October 2009; personal, New York, 22 April 2011; by telephone, 25 January 2012; and personal, New York, 24 May 2012.

Joseph Stein, by telephone, 18 December 2007.

Jamie Stevens, by telephone, 4 February 2008.

Charles Strouse, personal, 23 January 2008.

Susan Tsu, by telephone, 3 February 2008.

Ernie Zulia, by telephone, 12 February 2008.

Unpublished Documents and Correspondence

Adler, Gerald, organizer. File of letters concerning retrospective of Carnegie Mellon University Scotch 'n' Soda shows, 26 October 1996. Carnegie Mellon University Archive.

Caird, John. Letter to Carolyn Jennings from 8 February 1989.

———. Letter to Stephen Schwartz from 9 November 1994.

———. Undated letter to Stephen Schwartz from about June 1988.

"Circus, Spirit, & Rock of Hit Musical to Weave 'Godspell' at Mark Taper/Nov. Opening Set For Sweet Rock Show." Press release. Center Theatre Group Mark Taper Forum, 25 August 1971. New York Public Library for the Performing Arts, Billy Rose Theatre Collection.

Drama—List of Productions—1914–1970, Carnegie Mellon University Department of Drama.

Finding Aids and Inventories for Official University Records. Carnegie-Mellon University Archives.

Gifford/Wallace, Inc. "High Sales and Musical Honors Afforded 'Godspell' Albums Reflect World-Wide Popularity of Musical." Press release, 5 June 1972. New York Public Library for the Performing Arts, Billy Rose Theatre Collection.

———. Untitled press release concerning Broadway closing of *The Magic Show*, 30 November 1978. New York Public Library for the Performing Arts, Billy Rose Theatre Collection.

———. Untitled press release concerning *The Magic Show*. n.d. New York Public Library for the Performing Arts, Billy Rose Theatre Collection.

———. Untitled press release concerning opening of *Godspell* on Broadway, 22 June 1976. New York Public Library for the Performing Arts, Billy Rose Theatre Collection.

Jennings, Carolyn. Letter to John Caird from 10 October 1996.

McCraty, Joanne Jonas. E-mail message to author from 16 February 2008.

Macnaughton, Patricia. Letter to John Caird from 26 February 1991.

Reinhardt, Stephen. E-mail message to author from 9 March 2013.

Royal Shakespeare Company. Letter to William McDonald of Upstart Productions from 13 July 1989.

Schwartz, Stephen. E-mail message to the author from 19 December 2005.
———. E-mail message to the author from 17 July 2011.
———. E-mail message to the author from 22 August 2012.
———. E-mail message to the author from 23 January 2013.
———. E-mail message to the author from 22 March 2013.
———. E-mail message to the author from 13 June 2013.
———. E-mail message to Joseph Stein from 7 April 2005.
———. Fax to John Caird from 20 April 1988.
———. Fax to John Caird from 21 March 1991.
———. Fax to John Caird, undated but from shortly before 29 April 1991.
———. Fax to John Caird from 25 June 1991.
———. Fax to John Caird from 27 August 1991.
———. Fax to John Caird from 28 February 1993.
———. Fax to John Caird from 10 March 1993.
———. Fax to John Caird from 13 November 1994.
———. Fax to John Caird from 17 October 1995.
———. Handwritten note to John Caird from 8 December 1987.
———. Letter and package to John Caird from 20 March 1988.
———. Letter to John Caird from 16 June 1988.
———. Letter to John Caird from 14 December 1988.
———. Letter to John Caird from 26 June 1989.
———. Letter to John Caird, undated.
———. Letter to Charles Lisanby from 29 November 1988.
Spiegel, Steve. Letter to John Caird from 16 March 1998.
Stern, David I. E-mail message to the author, 13 July 2006.
———. E-mail message to the author, 26 March 2013.
Wicks, Charity. E-mail message to author from 29 July 2013.
Zulia, Ernest. E-mail message to the author from 24 March 2013.

Index

~

About the Author

Paul R. Laird is professor of musicology at the University of Kansas, where he teaches courses on music of the Baroque and twentieth century, American music, and the history of the musical theater, and directs the Instrumental Collegium Musicum. He holds a PhD in music from the University of North Carolina at Chapel Hill. Laird's previous books have included *Towards a History of the Spanish Villancico* (1997), *Leonard Bernstein: A Guide to Research* (2002), *The Baroque Cello Revival: An Oral History* (Scarecrow Press, 2004), *Leonard Bernstein's Chichester Psalms* (2010), and *"Wicked": A Musical Biography* (Scarecrow Press, 2011). With William A. Everett, Laird is coeditor of both editions of *The Cambridge Companion to the Musical* (2002, 2008), the coauthor of *The Historical Dictionary of the Broadway Musical* (Scarecrow Press, 2008), and a co-contributing editor in the area of musical theater for *The Grove Dictionary of American Music*, second edition (2013). Laird's articles, chapters, and reviews have appeared in numerous journals, edited collections, and encyclopedias. He lives in Lawrence, Kansas, with his wife, Joy, and daughter, Caitlin.